Empires, Nations, and Families

Empires, Nations, and Families

A New History of the North American West, 1800–1860

Anne F. Hyde

An Imprint of HarperCollins*Publishers*

HarperCollins books may be purchased for
educational, business, or sales promotional use.
For information please write: Special Markets
Department, HarperCollins Publishers, 10 East
53rd Street, New York, NY 10022.

A hardcover edition of this book was published
in 2011 by the University of Nebraska Press.

FIRST ECCO PAPERBACK EDITION PUBLISHED 2012

Designed by Bob Reitz

Library of Congress Cataloging-in-Publication
Data is available upon request.

ISBN 978-0-06-222515-3

12 13 14 15 16 OV/RRD 10 9 8 7 6 5 4 3 2 1

Contents

Illustrations

Maps

Acknowledgments

Adventures in the Land of the Dead

This book has its own story, which continues to surprise me. I'm amazed by and grateful to the Bancroft Prize committee that included Alice Kessler-Harris, Eric Foner, and Timothy Breen, and to the Pulitzer Prize jury of Laurel Thatcher Ulrich, Ned Blackhawk, and Walter McDougall, who pulled the book out of a sea of wonderful scholarship.

Life often interfered as I wrote, so it took a while. My perspectives are partly training, partly experience, and partly personal. I've been a historian, a teacher, a parent, a wife, a daughter, a friend, and have been embedded in various communities for a long time. These relationships form my relationship with the past. I can, I think, empathize with Marguerite McLoughlin as she watched her young children head off for school knowing she might not see them for years at a time, or the worry Island Bent felt about what might happen to her children if she were not there to protect them. I teach at a small liberal arts college where research is important, but the intellectual and personal relationships I build with students matter more. We spend a lot of time talking about what history is and why it might matter—daily practice in perspective taking and in endless revision. These conversations have certainly influenced how I chose to tell this story.

The progressive historian Charles Beard gave us good advice in his presidential address to the American Historical Association in 1933. He insisted that despite the best efforts to make history into a science, writing history remained "an act of faith." He recognized that we take our flawed, biased contemporary selves to face the "wreck of matter and crush of worlds" that is the past. From that mess and from a position in the present, historians must make decisions about the stories to tell and the details to include, and "face them boldly, aware of the intellectual and moral perils inherent in any decision." I read that essay almost every year with my students and it still resonates deeply about the responsibility we have to the past to retell it with faith in the present.

The nexus of families and relationships that undergirds this book has its own structural support—a dense web of scholarship that has emerged over the past twenty-five years. How we have thought about power, nations, and families has shifted seismically and I have benefited from my opportunity to read and think broadly. I have a long list of what I call "just-in-time" books that I read just at the right moment to understand what I was seeing in the record and what I was trying to describe. I'm indebted to those historians who worked so hard to make the trans-Mississippi West such an untidy place and to those scholars who had no idea that their work on Australia, Morocco, France, China, Chile, or England would make the North American West look so different. And, my debt to those western university presses that continue to publish the books and documents that make this research possible and exciting is vast indeed.

I got much support from Colorado College. The Social Science Division funded much of this research, as did the Hulbert Center for Southwest Studies, and Cosgrove Funds in the History Department. Dean Susan Ashley helped me figure out time to write and resources to hire two fabulous research assistants who checked footnotes, typed bibliographies, and organized me: Tessa Cheek and Kelsey Speaks.

More specifically, I need to thank the people who helped me imagine, research, and write and rewrite this book. Librarians at Colorado College have always made my life easier and better. Librarian Carol Dickerson made the library a perfect place to work and LaDreka Davis and Mike McEvers found books and space with grace and humor. Beyond this home turf I worked at several wonderful institutions and, with the help of their talented and knowledgeable staffs, found incredibly rich materials. Close to home the Denver Public Library and the Colorado Historical Society provided many resources. George Miles and the Beinecke Library at Yale offered a great place to begin my research and the Missouri Historical Society in St. Louis yielded innumerable treasures about the fur trade and its cast of characters. In California, I worked mostly at the Huntington Library, making three different research trips there. Finally I had the gift of a two-month fellowship at the Huntington as a Caughey Western History Fellow that allowed me to finish a full draft.

I had many patient readers along the way. The Hulbert Center for

Southwest Studies hosted a "draft seminar" that brought western historians Thomas Andrews, Barbara Berglund, and Monica Rico to our campus to read an early draft. They have no idea how much their comments and conversations helped. The History Department at Colorado College read several chapters as part of our monthly "work in progress" seminars and their counsel shaped the text in important ways. A set of expert, careful (and a little scary) readers—Bill Deverell, Johnny Faragher, Sally Deutsch, and Dick Etulain—read the whole manuscript and gave me timely, sometimes hard, but always right advice.

I worked with three editors, Clark Whitehorn, Heather Lundine, and Bridget Barry, at the University of Nebraska Press who encouraged me and gave me deadlines. Project editor Joeth Zucco, copy editor Jane Curran, and indexer Chris Dodge were meticulous, patient, and kept their senses of humor while helping me finish a big book. Hilary Redmon at Ecco/HarperCollins took this book under her wing and helped me think about a broader audience.

My friends and family, categories I can no longer separate, have helped in many ways over many years. Deep friendship, intellectual support, advice about life, childcare, and writing weave the web that holds me up. Liz Feder, Sarah Hautzinger, Jane Hilberry, Mark Johnson, Doug Monroy, Carol Neel, Suzi Nishida, Sandy Papuga, Eric Perramond, Mary Pulvermacher, Tomi-Ann Roberts, Tip Ragan, Maria Varela, Tricia Waters, and Deanna Zobel-Grey all know how much I count on them for their brains, humor, and sense. Thanks. Colin, Tim, and Grace McCall and their dad, Jim McCall, are my center and everything depends on that core.

Manitou Springs, Colorado
June, 2012

Empires, Nations, and Families

Introduction

The Geography of Empire in 1804

Wearing a fur-trimmed cloak imported from Paris, Thérèse Cerré Chouteau watched as Lieutenant Amos Stoddard and Colonel Carlos Delassus exchanged control of Louisiana Territory. She looked considerably more elegant than either Stoddard, who had scrounged up a poorly fitting uniform, or Delassus, who was suitably dressed but so short and pudgy that his sword dragged on the ground. Along with nearly everyone living in St. Louis, Madame Chouteau cheered as the French *tricolore* went up first. More reserved as the U.S. Stars and Stripes replaced it, she clapped politely on that cold March afternoon in 1804.

Having lived in St. Louis for her entire adult life and having married one of the leading men in the region, Auguste Chouteau, Thérèse knew far more about the world into which the United States was stepping than did Amos Stoddard, the young lieutenant who suddenly found himself governor of five hundred million acres. She knew, for example, who was important in the crowd. Her own husband and his brother, Pierre Chouteau, had wealth because they shared power and kinship with Osage people. The Osage headman Pawhuska watched the ceremony as well, along with Auguste Chouteau's own Osage son, Antoine Chouteau. How much Madame Chouteau admitted knowing about her husband's other families we don't know, but she had much wisdom about how life worked on the Missouri River. Broad family networks underlay the trade relationships that allowed St. Louis to prosper as a French, then Spanish, then U.S. city, but always as part of the mosaic of Native communities.[1]

Euro-American contemporaries often ignored the human complexity of these communities. Even though this pattern of settlement was common, it represented an intermingled racial past that many Americans found uncomfortable. At least three worlds had come together here, sometimes clashing but often building new ways of co-existing. George Caleb Bingham,

1. George Caleb Bingham, American (1811–79), *Daniel Boone Escorting Settlers through the Cumberland Gap*, 1851–52. Oil on canvas, 36 1/2 x 50 1/4 in. Mildred Lane Kemper Art Museum, Washington University in St. Louis. Gift of Nathaniel Phillips, 1890.

Boone and the settlers, aglow in light, recall the passage of Christian pilgrims into the desert. Such notions of Boone and Anglo-American immigrants bringing light into a dark and uninhabited West have informed popular notions of western settlement for more than two centuries.

the mid-nineteenth-century Missouri artist registered the reality of this blended world and his discomfort with it in a series of history paintings. The epic *Daniel Boone Escorting Settlers through the Cumberland Gap* crowned the series. The 1851 painting depicted a foundational moment of American nationhood that had occurred nearly a century earlier: American pioneers breached the line between civilization and savagery that lay at the crest of the Appalachian Mountains.

The painting offers a common and still popular vision of how settlement occurred, a view that stripped the region of its human complexity but anointed it with Christian symbolism. It moved from east to west, conducted by virtuous Anglo-American settlers who dared enter a vast wilderness lightly inhabited by a few very scary Indian people. However, even Bingham recognized the story as mostly wishful thinking. The saintly women in Bingham's painting are escorted by men wearing Indian leggings

2. George Caleb Bingham, American (1811–79), *The Squatters*, 1850. Oil on canvas, 23 1/8 x 28 1/4 in. (58.74 x 71.75 cm). Museum of Fine Arts, Boston. Bequest of Henry Lee Shattuck in memory of the late Ralph W. Gray. 1971.154. Photograph © 2010 Museum of Fine Arts, Boston.

In this far less heroic painting, shiftless Anglo-American men lounge on logs and rest on sticks while women do all the work in the background. They peer out suspiciously at the viewer, challenging anyone to question their right to the land they've taken.

and leading lives far more like Cherokee, Shawnee, and Delaware hunters than Anglo-American farmers. He began the series with a group of smaller paintings that included *Fur Traders Descending the Missouri* (1845), *Captured By Indians* (1848), and *The Squatters* (1850).

These images depicted three streams of people who would leave deep marks on the North American West in the nineteenth century. These earlier paintings hint at the potential complications between Native nations, long-time French, Spanish, and English residents, and a group of aggressive Anglo-American squatters who would be the newcomers in the early nineteenth-century West. We see vying empires, Native and sometimes hostile residents, and shiftless and profligate immigrants, not the virgin wilderness and virtuous Anglo entrepreneurs many people have hoped and imagined as part of this scene.[2]

3. George Caleb Bingham, American (1811–79), *Fur Traders Descending the Missouri*, 1845. Oil on canvas, 29 x 36 1/2 in. (73.7 x 92.7 cm). Morris K. Jesup Fund, 1933 (33.61). The Metropolitan Museum of Art, New York City.

Bingham named this painting "French Trader—Half Breed Son," emphasizing its racial exoticism. His depiction makes the pair foreign, but alluring. They smile as they pass the viewer, confident in their place in the region.

Even Bingham's more messily human paintings, however, left out many important people from the cast that humanized this show. The only women in his paintings were Anglo-Americans, either being held hostage by Indians or working hard while their shiftless male family members watched. The only Native people in Bingham's vision were violent savages who threatened the brave settlers daring to enter this wilderness.

As both Thérèse Cerré Chouteau and Pawhuska understood, Daniel Boone and the Anglo-Americans were newcomers in a world that was anything but wilderness. It turns out George Caleb Bingham understood this too, as he demonstrated in the painting *Fur Trappers Descending the Missouri*, which depicts people of mixed race and mysterious animals drifting on a quiet river. These river systems of the trans-Mississippi West served as the basis of a globally significant trade in furs that had operated for hundreds of years in various forms before the United States existed. Rivers linked the

Atlantic and the Pacific, the Gulf of Mexico and the Great Lakes, Hudson's Bay and Monterey Bay. They also carried families, trade goods, diseases, and ideas into a region where the residents had built a distinctive set of communities in the West long before the Louisiana Purchase made the region part of the United States. Communities like Green Bay, Santa Fe, Michilimackinac, San Antonio, Cape Girardeau, Nacogdoches, Monterey, Prairie du Chien, Nootka Sound, and St. Louis had populations that spoke many languages and that were more than 80 percent mixed race.[3] Family connections across national and ethnic lines allowed business and diplomacy to flourish in these places, but in ways that surprise us now and that shocked people in the late nineteenth century. These linkages, however, were business—and family—as usual in the century before 1850.[4]

A story has to begin somewhere and sometime. I've chosen four western sites to examine in the year 1804 as a beginning, but they function as a proper epic beginning *in media res*. St. Louis, the Great Lakes, Santa Fe and the Arkansas River, and the Pacific Coast had variously developed trade complexes and ways of relating—or at their peril not relating—to local Native nations. At the moment the United States began its official relationship with the region, much had already transpired. On March 10, 1804, French, Spanish, and U.S. officials conducted a formal ceremony in St. Louis to transfer ownership of what would be known as the Louisiana Purchase from France to the United States. The news spread out through the river systems that underlay the economy and society of the fur trade. The cast of characters that inhabit the stories in this book responded to the news of the Louisiana Purchase depending on location and family situation.

To most people living in the region in question, such news made no difference at all. The United States represented just another imperial landlord to be assessed and manipulated. Similarly, to most people living in the United States, a small nation of about five million people, the announcement of the Louisiana Purchase merited no more than a shrug. For the half-million Euro-Americans and the perhaps two million Native Americans living west of the Appalachians, the Mississippi River was essential, but the lands west of it remained mysterious. Even diplomats, scientists, and entrepreneurs had little notion of what this piece of land included and had little interest in finding out. Only the significant numbers of people directly involved in the world of the fur trade or the small group involved in Louisiana land speculation had any sense of its potential value or how it worked. The world of river and maritime trade effectively decentered traditional political power, locating knowledge outside of traditional military and diplomatic circles and firmly in the hands of local people, both Native and newer residents.

This time and these places are mostly unfamiliar to us, and so is the cultural world in which they operated. Most of us continue to imagine the space west of the Mississippi as blank space, with little action that mattered before the go-go years of the 1840s. My task here is threefold: to depict these unfamiliar times and places, to demonstrate their importance in the trans-Mississippi West, and to describe how and why they have disappeared from our view. My argument about the significance and longevity of this world and the families who inhabited it is quite simple, but the stories that undergird it are not. They unfold in many places at the same time, making our map an interlinking set of points that creates a rather abstract shape. Each of these sites demonstrate the ways in which trade and family were intermingled and how much local knowledge mattered in conducting business and life. Exploring what nations meant, how much they mattered, and when the national and personal come together lies underneath. Neither "nations" nor "empires" are fixed categories, and nobody agrees where the line between them lies, but the ambitions and behaviors around creating them are in constant flux, which makes them important to track as ideas.[5]

St. Louis

In the summer of 1804 young Auguste Pierre (A.P.) Chouteau spent only a short time in St. Louis, the city of his birth. In 1804 St. Louis stood at the center of a vast and cosmopolitan trade network, not at the edge of a virgin wilderness. The Chouteau family had built and would continue to control a city that centered the continent, no matter which nation housed it. A.P.'s ambitious father had sent him to West Point to receive an education suitable for an American gentleman, and he had just arrived home for a visit. The city's business operated on the docks along the Mississippi River, where A.P. could see the Chouteau family counting house, warehouses, flour mills, and wharves that supported the family's commercial wealth.

Their dominance in the region came from their partnership with the Osages in the fur trade, the central economic driver of the region. Their business penetrated deep into the Arkansas and Missouri river country, and their counting house in St. Louis outfitted independent trappers and expeditions of every size. The Chouteaus were the primary suppliers of furs from the Mississippi Valley to European markets, and the family's commerce ranged from Le Havre, France, to Montreal and New Orleans. The Chouteaus had diversified into transportation and supply, grain milling, lead mining, and banking, and their extensive holdings of land would give their commercial success an unusual permanence.

St. Louis was now part of Upper Louisiana, a huge territory governed by a few American administrators, but it looked very different from other American cities. Most people, powerful and common, had families of mixed race. This included the Chouteaus, who had many relatives among the Osage people. St. Louisans had become accustomed to adapting to the whims of shifting imperial rule. Founded in 1763 by French traders, the outpost had almost instantly become part of the Spanish Empire in that unlucky year of 1764 when the French lost control of their land claims in North America. This did not mean, however, that French people no longer had land, businesses, relationships, and communities in North America. St. Louis lay at the heart of this French and Indian world.[6]

Walking through the town to his family compound west of the river, A.P. could see delegations of Osage, Sauk, Shawnee, Fox, Omaha, Kansa, and Pawnee people. St. Louis had developed as a peaceful free trade zone where groups of Native people came to trade, visit, and see their relatives. Having been gone for almost a year, A.P. recognized that the city had grown and changed. Though most of the signs continued to be in French, many more stores welcomed their customers in English, hoping to serve the growing numbers of Anglo-American immigrants who had poured over the river from the unsettled and unsafe Ohio and Mississippi river valleys. Drawn by promises of rich land and lack of government meddling in this mixed world, people like Daniel Boone of Kentucky fame and Moses Austin, soon to be from Texas, along with their extended families, had settled to the south and west of St. Louis. No change in imperial governance or even in the ethnicity of its inhabitants could shift the centrality of the fur trade, which dominated all business in the city. For A. P. Chouteau, a son of the founding family of St. Louis and speaker of many languages, the Missouri River and its peoples seemed far less intimidating than the customs of West Point.

A.P. would not get to see his father, Pierre Chouteau, now family co-patriarch, on this trip home, because Pierre had headed to Washington DC. As the newly appointed U.S. agent to the Osages, the most important trading tribe in the middle Missouri region, the elder Chouteau had accompanied a delegation of Osages to meet with the new president, Thomas Jefferson.[7] Representatives of various Native nations visited St. Louis that summer, expecting to receive gifts and recognition from the new government. Members of various Osage clans, calling on their relatives in the city, threatened to clash with their rivals, the Pawnees, Otoes, Sacs, and Foxes, who all wanted to make sure the United States would grant them advantageous trading relationships, as the French and Spanish had for many generations.[8]

St. Louis functioned as an exchange point in the fur trade. Trappers and traders brought furs to the city on small boats, where a smaller industry developed around packing, weighing, and pressing the furs so that they could be loaded onto much larger ships bound for New Orleans, New York, London, and Canton. Goods destined for trade with Native people—guns, cloth, blankets, lead, beads, bridles, needles and thread, gunpowder, jewelry, kettles, axes, and more—were stored in the Chouteau family warehouses and then shipped up river at the end of the summer for the winter trading season. A small battalion of clerks kept careful records of each trader, the number of furs he brought in, and the amount of credit he used to buy trade goods. The fur trade and its ancillary businesses were among the largest and most profitable in the world, involving thousands of traders, merchants, bankers, and politicians. In St. Louis alone, traders made profits of $200,000 a year by 1804.[9] Anglo-Americans came late to this business, but in the context of Jeffersonian America St. Louis and the fur-trading world suddenly looked appealing. In just a few years Phillip and Isabella Sublette from Kentucky would bring their eight children to St. Louis, the Bent family and their restless children would arrive from Virginia, and the ambitious young George Sibley would emigrate from North Carolina. They would all spend their lives in the fur trade. This business and its need for Native American partners would continue to dominate the region until the 1860s, though its personnel, range, and systems would certainly shift.

Signs of other changes, however, rippled the surface of this mostly French and Indian fur-trading community. Just up the river near what is now Kansas City, the newly formed Corps of Discovery led by William Clark and Meriwether Lewis, celebrated July 4 with fifty men. Each man got an extra dram of whiskey and they named a stream "Independance [*sic*] Creek" in honor of the day, an indication of the vast naming project to come. Their small expedition, in the guise of a mission of peace and diplomacy, represented the first official demonstration of U.S. presence in Upper Louisiana.[10] The company caused hardly a ripple among the Native nations of the Missouri River because of the long history of the fur trade and the careful work of building relationships with those tribes undertaken by people like the Chouteaus.[11]

MICHILIMACKINAC

Many of the goods exchanged in St. Louis trade came from the Great Lakes, and the Chouteau family had direct connections with traders in the great Canadian firms of the Hudson's Bay Company and the North West Company. Most people at the numerous fur-trading forts in this region ignored imperial intrigue and political wrangling among nations and went on with life as they had created it over the last century. In July of 1804 at least twelve couples had their marriages formally recognized by the Catholic Church in a ceremony at Fort Michilimackinac, located on an island between Lakes Michigan and Huron. Cree and Ojibwe traditions blended smoothly with French and English ones as these new families joined the community there. They toasted with West Indian rum, French brandy, and local wine, beer, and cider.[12] The Great Lakes, the largest inland lake system in the world, had become a center of business and social interaction for a surprising variety of people by the beginning of the nineteenth century. Europeans who worked and lived in the Great Lakes area existed in a world dominated by Native ways of doing things. A century of intermarriage created a social system that paralleled and supplemented that of indigenous societies. French and British participation in the region's major industry occurred with indigenous support and the development of intimate relationships, including marriage and parenthood.

Because of Fort Michilimackinac's location and its long significance in the fur trade, families traveled there each summer to marry, baptize children, and conduct business of all kinds. Known as the "grand emporium of the West" Michilimackinac remained entirely controlled by fur-trading families of mixed race. Originally founded by French priests in 1671 and fortified as a trading fort in 1715, it had become British property in 1761 though most of its residents continued to be Native people, French traders, and their families of mixed race. The fur trade, much to the dismay of the British, remained in the hands of these fur-trading families with deep roots in local Native communities.

This business was run by families and communities, not individuals. This cultural fact remained evident in 1804 as the summer burst of marriages and baptisms took precedence over trading, and the population swelled to more than four thousand people. By 1804 the community confused Anglo-American observers because of how business got done. Its combination of elite British traders and detailed record keeping, French and Indian residents and workers, and varieties of labor systems defied notions of how life and business should be conducted. Native people, women, and illiterate immigrants played important roles in all parts of the operation, and some amassed power and fortune as a result. When other people interfered with common practice too much, they could expect protest and rebellion. As of this writing the fort still hosts the annual Fort Michilimackinac Pageant, the oldest organized event in Michigan, to celebrate the 1763 victory of Native people taking the fort.[13]

One of the couples having their marriage recognized in a Catholic ceremony was Thérèse La Framboise, an Ottawa (or Odawa) woman long involved in the fur trade, and George Schindler, a British trader operating among the Odawas for several years. Her sister Magdaleine would marry the British commandant of the fort, Benjamin Pierce, several years later. Both women retained Native dress and habits, including their professions as traders, though they changed names easily. Schindler, as aspiring schoolteacher, and Pierce, a military man, both recognized the value and appeal of building intimate connections with Native women. Newlyweds La Framboise and Schindler would have few concerns about the news of the United States and the new land acquired in the Louisiana Purchase. The Great Lakes had offered very permeable borders, and Native people had figured out how to mediate between European powers. La Framboise knew that her network of kin, built through Native practices and godparenting in the Catholic tradition, would matter far more in the long run than which flag flew over the fort.[14]

Only a hundred miles north and west, a young Canadian fur trader named John McLoughlin began his second year in the fur trade, spending his summer at Fort Kaminisitiquia—later named Fort William—located on the northern shore of Lake Superior. In the summer of 1804 the docks overflowed with all sizes of boats filled with packs of fur, trade goods, and people. Kaminisitiquia had become a major Great Lakes trading post because of concerns over where the U.S.-Canada border would be located. The northern edge of Lake Superior was clearly Canada, but Michilimackinac was far enough south to be questionable. McLoughlin, who would end his life embroiled in border questions in the Pacific Northwest, was hardly concerned about them now. He watched as streams of people set up camp outside the fort and as trading occupied people during the day and drinking, singing, and boasting occupied them at night. Because men received their yearly wages in the summer at Kaminisitiquia, all kinds of traders also gathered there, along with extended family groups.

McLoughlin, a Canadian native of Scottish and French descent, would marry two Native women and have children of mixed race as part of his impressive career as an officer in the fur trade. In 1804, at the tender age of nineteen, he served as the fort's physician, in charge of the health of thousands of men, women, and children who lived in and near the fort. McLoughlin married his first wife, an Ojibwe woman, in 1808, and after her death he spent the rest of his life with Marguerite Wadin McKay, of Cree and French Canadian heritage. The lives of their children would etch a fine set of stories, embedded in the fur trade, across the entire North American West. Families like the McLoughlins provide a window into how personal relationships and intercultural connections underlay trade, business, and politics in the early American West.[15]

SANTA FE

Another community based on trading relationships between nations and empires radiated out from what is now northern New Mexico. As Thérèse Chouteau surveyed her world in St. Louis, so too did Don Antonio Jose Ortiz and his wife, Rosa Bustamante, the largest merchants and sheep ranchers in Santa Fe. As they walked through the plaza on a cool early summer evening in 1804, they wore beautiful light wool sarapes from their weaving workshop. The sheep industry had succeeded in New Mexico because of its significance to Native and Hispanic people alike. A relative peace with the Comanches and Apaches allowed people to graze sheep outside the confines of pueblos. This generation of peace and intermarriage with the region's Natives and a relaxation of New Mexico's colonial tax burden brought new wealth streaming into the region. Santa Fe's buildings and inhabitants reflected this well-being. The large central cathedral had been renovated and expanded, largely with Ortiz family money. As Don Antonio and Doña Rosa strolled through the streets they saw small shops producing fine woolen clothing, saddles, boots and shoes, pottery, carved wooden statues, furniture, and jewelry.[16]

By 1804 Santa Fe had been the capital of the northernmost province of New Spain for nearly two centuries. Similar in size and significance to St. Louis, but essential in another important set of trade relationships, Santa Fe served as the fulcrum between a global trade that linked New Spain, New France, the United States, Britain, and, increasingly, Comanches. Its several thousand residents, an intermingled population of Spaniards, Mexicans, Pueblo Indians, Apaches, Navajos, and, more recently, Utes and Comanches, had lived and worked together under loose Spanish control for several generations. Officials in Mexico City assumed New Mexicans looked south for their wants and needs, along the Camino Real, or Royal Road, that linked New Spain's trade centers, but most people sought their livelihoods and relationships elsewhere. Wealth, status, and safety came from trade with Native nations who lived all around them. The Louisiana Purchase made little immediate difference in their lives, aside from bringing the border between the United States and New Spain closer, a fact that concerned diplomats in Mexico City but intrigued local people. In the long run the presence of the United States would encourage new trading relationships with Native people to the north and would eventually lead much of New Mexico to rebel against both New Spain and Mexico.

In fact, in that July of 1804 many Santa Fe residents had traveled north to Taos to attend the annual Native trade fair. Comanches and Utes arrived, creating summer camps that attracted French, British, and New Mexican traders along with many northern New Mexico residents. The trade in horses, buffalo hides, furs, weapons, cloth, agricultural products, and slaves provided for most of the regional economy. To begin and end bartering sessions, people drank *pulque,* a local fermented beverage made from yucca leaves. Officially, such trade was illegal since authorities in New Spain intended New Mexico to be part of a mercantile colonial exchange, with New Spain as the only market for resources and the only supplier of goods. In spite of these legal restrictions, Governor Fernando de Chacón sent official emissaries with official greetings and gifts for important Comanche leaders who came to these fairs, part of his charge to keep the peace.

Canaguaipe, head man of the Western Comanches, accepted the gifts but understood that Comanche politics depended entirely on consensus among a much wider group of leaders. The discussion among Comanche leaders that summer concerned new groups of American traders and how to build relationships with them far to the east along the Arkansas River, which would make the Comanches independent of the Spanish. This conversation was not welcomed by Spanish authorities, who feared such contact would bring another round of raiding in New Mexico. Governor Chacón had encouraged Spanish New Mexicans to settle beyond their garrisoned pueblos, and some had, often settling in Comanche and Ute lands. This worked when the Comanches were raiding far to the south or making war against the Navajos, but it looked as if a new period of warfare and its accompanying dangers was about to begin as this set of new trade relationships would have to be worked out.[17]

The Arkansas River connected the Mississippi and Missouri river worlds to the centers of colonial Spain, but it also gave Native traders easy access to all of these places. As along the Mississippi River, however, some changes became evident in the years just before the Louisiana Purchase. As Native nations in the border regions on the Arkansas River found themselves increasingly pressured by Euro-American and Native immigrants, they also became empowered and enriched by horses, guns, and trade goods. The Native world blossomed in this borderland region where Native nations determined trade, diplomacy, and personal safety. No middle ground existed here; this was Native ground, and it was expanding.

As trade had developed on the river borders with the French and Spanish and onto the plains, the Osages and the Pawnees stepped in to dominate it, so that other Native groups looked further west to improve their circumstances or to protect their children. The Comanches built a trade network that spread over the forbidden borders from central Mexico up to the southern plains. New groups, including the Cheyennes, Arapahos, and Kiowas, began looking west to opportunities on the central plains where the Arkansas River originated. Euro-American traders would follow these shifts of people and trade, and like John McLoughlin and Thérèse Chouteau, they would find themselves intimately linked with Native people.

THE PACIFIC COAST

Compared to New Mexico and the southern plains, the Pacific Coast, our final site for western stories, was crowded with the highest population density of any region in North America. Most of these people, of course, were members of the thousands of groups of Native people that populated the temperate coast and interior valleys. Only a very small population of Europeans had entered this world, and they clung tenuously to a long strip of the coast in California. Monterey, the capital and major port of Alta California, was a small village in 1804. That summer Maria Lugo y Vallejo watched as her six young children played in the plaza while old Native women wove baskets and shawls. The oldest boy, Salvador, always wanted to watch the soldiers drill, and he often escaped the careful watch of his mother to observe the action. Located along the central coast of California, the town housed most of California's military presence and its thin administrative fringe, but it also had the daily rhythms of family life. Like other Spanish settlements, the town focused on a central square or plaza surrounded by walls and low buildings, but in Monterey the large structure of the presidio or fort dominated the view from the harbor. The presidio soldiers and their families, including Lt. Ignacio Vicente Ferrer Vallejo and his spouse, Maria Antonía Lugo, busily produced a first generation of *Californios* who would become landowners, merchants, and soldiers in this new community. They raised their children to ride horses, appreciate wine and olives, and make a living from the California landscape and its human residents.

Just outside the village and the presidio lay the mission and its Native village, which housed the workforce that enabled New Spain to exist. In 1804 most labor came from Native people forced into the system of missions, and a whole generation of Native Californians had been born and died in these religious institutions. Much to the frustration of the mission fathers and the Spanish Californian population, a considerable number of Native people lived well outside the missions and increased their standard of living by raiding the missions and ranchos surrounding them. Most of the work of the presidio soldiers was not protecting California from foreign invasion, but protecting mission herds from Native thieves and searching for mission runaways.[18]

Nearly as much as a colonial afterthought as Santa Fe, and much more recently settled, Monterey was still part of a broad system of trade that included Russian, American, French, and British ships that traveled all over the Pacific. Much of this trade, as in the worlds of the Great Lakes and Missouri River, revolved around furs, with the California addition of hides and tallow produced by its growing cattle industry. The human flotsam of a global trade that began with furs, but ended up with silk, furniture, and silver, sailed, rode, and walked up and down the Pacific Coast as Hawaiian, Iroquois, Mexican, Tlingit, French Canadian, and British workers. The significance of this Pacific trade was underscored in 1789 with a diplomatic snafu that became known as the Nootka Sound Controversy in which various sailors of various nations threatened to begin war in a harbor on what is now Vancouver Island. The events and the ensuing diplomatic debate attracted enough attention to divert both English and Spanish attention from the worrisome French Revolution.

The potential of this Pacific trade attracted enthusiastic entrepreneurs of many stripes, but it would take time to develop. Only a few years later a multinational venture including Russians, Americans, Native Aleuts, and Spanish Californians had founded a colony at Sitka in what is now Alaska that aimed to bring Pacific Coast furs to China, New England trade goods to California, and fruit, vegetables, and meat to the bleak Alaska colonies. Success in this venture required more than enthusiasm; it required local knowledge. Either Thérèse Chouteau or the Comanche leader Canaguaipe could have offered some suggestions about how to build local trade networks.[19]

Because of their lack of preparation and connections, the situation in 1804 did not resemble the orderly and profitable venture that the Russian-American Company investors or participants had imagined. Two hundred starving Russians and Hawaiians had subsisted for a year without any supply ships arriving. They had long since used up their imported goods and now ate all the crows, eagles, and manta rays they could find, but they still suffered from scurvy and other diseases. And no ship would come that summer of 1804, no matter how much time they spent staring out at the sea through the cold rain. Local Aleuts and Tlingit people had brought furs early on, but the Russians had nothing to trade, and when they tried to kill the Natives and steal their food, the Tlingits simply left them to starve. Most had died or wandered off to join Native groups who would feed them until the ships came back in 1806. It would take another generation before the northern edge of the Pacific Coast would be well incorporated into the fur trade system, and the Vallejo family of California would be significant in this process.[20]

As much as the world of the Tlingits differed from the Chouteaus' St. Louis world or the Ortiz family's Santa Fe world, these sites share important linkages in terms of the resources they produced and traded and the human relationships that developed in each. Each place and the people who lived there had ever widening networks because of how trade worked, so that by the 1820s and 1830s these circles overlapped. A child born near Fort Michilimackinac might find herself tending crops on the Columbia River, while a sheep trader from New Mexico had business in St. Louis and in southern California.

FAMILY STORIES

The task of this book is to impose narrative and analytical order over such disparate stories and geographic space to build a larger story about the trans-Mississippi West between 1804 and about 1860. No problem. "The West"—whatever that includes—has a number of foundational Ur-stories told about it. It could be a mythic place where people—well, at least some people—tested and remade themselves into powerful individuals independent of social pressures. A second story is the West as place of Colossus bashing where great empires and great fighters fought over great resources

4. Aaron Arrowsmith, *A Map Exhibiting All the New Discoveries in the Interior Parts of North America, additions to 1811*. Library of Congress, Geography and Map Division.

in which the winner took all, leaving trails of post-Conquest wreckage everywhere. This eternally violent frontier/borderlands world gobbled up cultures and left environmental havoc in its wake. Neither of these stories works particularly well for the early nineteenth century or for the kinds of interests I have in writing history.

A third story, the one I heard and told most often, presented the early nineteenth-century West as blank slate whose geographic features flattened and became imaginary at the Mississippi River. I carry Aaron Arrowsmith's 1811 map firmly in my head, along with other versions with geographic features like "Terra Incognita" or "Great River of the West" or that hopeful single line of mountains. Few people or place-names break up the silent and empty region. The West became just space to be filled up, an empty stage waiting for dynamic action. This vision of the past is plagued by the problem of inevitability; how it played out was preordained by hindsight about who would provide that energy in the end. We end up, despite ourselves, looking for tracers of those dynamos in the past to provide a logical explanation for our present. Such a view leads to several problems. Native peoples get erased as part of that blank slate that warps the story considerably. In this version of the story we have no sense of how actual people experienced their lives in the region. Given the twenty-year boom in western American history that has given us a wholly changed view of who lived in the West and how they understood the region, I should have known better. But those old stories are seductive and powerful.

When the University of Nebraska Press decided to publish a new six-volume history of the trans-Mississippi West and invited me to write a volume, I had to consider how to recast those stories. The series had the usual dividing lines that make up official American history, but this history fits poorly within those lines. I decided that mostly I wanted to build a narrative that fills this space with human action and gives credit to the complex lives people carved out in this period in spite of how it might turn out in the end. As I read about these people, I found the outlines of a different story. It privileges stability and lack of change (not entirely promising for historians who crave novelty like a drug) by looking at the way people make families and do business in a region where no one knew who would win.

I wanted to naturalize a certain kind of accommodation that lasted at least until the middle of the nineteenth century. It's very important to remember that this huge swath of land did NOT belong to the United States until the very end of our period. Even when it did, *belong* turns out to be a very capacious term. Throughout this period, any group could emerge as the one in control: it could be Native nations, it could be European invaders, it could be imperial Anglo-America, or it could be personally motivated pirates. People living there had to accommodate to a lack of political certainty, and their choices about how to navigate it shaped the communities they built. Such accommodation required the efforts of men and women and revealed a set of deeply gendered and always contested definitions of who mattered.

This story had other advantages. I could make my way through the period, using the experiences of specific families to carry the narrative. It allows me to keep the story at an intimate scale that reflects how people actually experience life as it unfolds. I could listen for lost voices—Native people, women, and children—who are essential to the story. They included very famous people and very ordinary people: Chouteaus, McLoughlins, Jollys, Sublettes, Vallejos, Herefords, Austins, Wilsons, networks of tribal leaders, merchants, government officials, and their families. These people—Native, Euro-American, Californio, Mexican—have incredibly broad sets of connections because of the groundwork laid by the fur trade, which was, of course, the biggest business of the early nineteenth-century North American West. As I traced these connections by mapping names of people and seeing how they traversed the continent, the analogy became obvious: a web. The web that holds the West together gets built by individual men and women using similar techniques in different settings. And how they deploy these connections is the story of the early American West.

"Died Single"

As I began the research to find families and people to help me tell this story, I found some wonderful help, some mysteries, and some deliberate erasures. I located a few fabulous collections of family papers that included personal letters, diaries, and account books that allowed me to see the decisions families and individuals faced and the choices they made. But mostly people leave only a few traces or record only one aspect of their lives: one exciting moment, a series of business deals, a journey, solitary entries of births, marriages, and deaths. Because I sought linkages and liaisons I soon discovered that the official written history often portrayed a denuded version of these intimate connections that the family papers had laid out. When I read accounts of famous personalities in the region I kept finding two phrases: "Died single" and "no children." What did it mean to leave out peoples' most intimate connections?

For example, the *Annals of St. Louis*, a typical nineteenth-century "accounts of the pioneers" text, describes the Bent family. One listing reads: "Charles Bent, born in 1799, died single, Governor of Taos, New Mexico, murdered."[21] This entry has us picturing a lonely death, but, in fact, Charles Bent died in the arms of his wife, Ignacia Jaramillo Bent, and three of his children, Teresina, Alfredo, and Rumalda. Why is this left out—in a story so famous that even *annalistes* in St. Louis would have known it? Was it so distasteful or unthinkable to write about a scion of a St. Louis family with a Mexican wife that Ignacia is effectively disappeared? Charles's brothers, William, George, and Robert, were all listed as "unmarried"; in fact, all had wives, but they were Mexican or Native women. William even named his children from these marriages after his Bent family siblings: Mary, Julia, Robert, and George. The story changes when we excise these relationships, and it becomes a tale of a few powerful men and the way they wanted to construct the narrative later. Does knowing that these family members existed and that they shifted the outcome of the story matter?[22]

Another phrase, equally cold—"no children"—comes from the same book. We read, "Mary Easton, born in Rome, New York, married Geo. C. Sibley, Sept. 1815, no children."[23] In fact, Mary and George adopted three children, the orphans of their long-time Osage friend Sans Oreille, gave them their first and last names, and enrolled them in the mission schools. This erasure of intimate relationships happens everywhere: in accounts of founding families in Alta California, New Mexico, Oregon, and Missouri we find unmarried men and childless women. What a sad and barren past, if it were true. The work of many historians in the past twenty years reveals a far messier and connected past of marriages, casual liaisons, and children among many groups of people that, to later observers, mixed people and nations in dangerously promiscuous ways. As Charles Bent and many others found out, their success depended on family and community relationships, the work and status of women, and not on their own individual efforts.

Why Fur and Why Families?

These people—Tlingit and Miwok Natives on Nootka Sound, Vallejos and Lugos in Monterey, Ortiz and Canaguaipe in New Mexico, McLoughlin and McKay at Fort William, and Chouteau, Pawhuska, and Lewis in St. Louis—lived in very different places, but places that were surprisingly interconnected even at the opening of the nineteenth century. And it was fur that linked them. Furs seem like a sort of silly luxury product—mink coats, fox stoles, and ermine robes adorning wealthy aristocrats who could afford them. Two things make such items into an industry that dominated commerce in North America and provided the underpinning for its first capitalist boom. First, fur encompasses a much broader category of things. Animal skins include fur, pelts, and hide. And hide becomes leather, so that animals like deer, cattle, and buffalo can be made into shoes, belts, clothing, bags, book covers, housing, straps, fasteners, and floor coverings, so that the market is wide and broad. Second, some furs and pelts are a scarce luxury product that come from a small number of fur-bearing animals that live only in certain habitats, which gives them great value—worth transporting around the world.

Because the great transformations of capitalism and western ideological revolutions increased wealth and spread it far down the social scale, markers of status became ever more valued. Fur, particularly in the form of hats, became an important marker, like tea, coffee, chocolate, and sugar, which created their own global networks at the same time. The fur hat did not mean the Davy Crockett version of a raccoon hat with a tail jauntily hanging down, but a dignified and expensive hat made from the fine soft under-pelt of beavers that could be shaped into stovepipes, tricorners, cloches, and other fashionable forms. Because the number of people who wanted hats to wear in coffee houses or while sipping tea increased dramatically between the seventeenth and nineteenth centuries, and the number of animals available to provide these pelts decreased, the trade continued to be enormous and profitable. The great early fortunes in North America—the Dutch poltroons of New York, New England Puritans, Russian czars, British lords, and French *negociants* in Canada—began with fur, though the smartest capitalists diversified quickly into slaves and land. When we start thinking about the huge numbers of tasks and systems needed to get a dead beaver from the streams of Wisconsin or British Columbia onto the head of a British accountant, we begin to get a sense of the numbers of people involved.

The North American West and its residents provided the basic resource and the labor on the production end, and this required a mixing of world-views and ideologies in an often uneasy "middle ground" that lasted far longer and with different outcomes than we have imagined. The people of the fur trade shared the making of the world that would develop in this region in the early nineteenth century. Their children, friends, spouses, and partners would link them into a web of families that shaped dominant social and economic networks in the North American West until about 1860.

Families provide the central core of this story. As the most common human way to be interconnected, families determine much about how gender is understood, how children are acculturated into their worlds, and how economies operate. Because people living in the nineteenth century experienced radical redefinitions of family, gender roles, childhood, and business, these categories serve as a useful way to look at our region. This personal terrain—what it meant to be a woman, a man, or a child—seemed even more unsettled in places where cultures met and accommodated, where frontiers became new borders. Where cultures and communities struggled to metabolize the vast changes brought by conquest and migra-tion, people used families to protect themselves and to practice important new ways of being in the world.[24] Few people died single and childless; they left behind a very human trace that we can use to understand this period in what would become the American West. Shifting definitions of basic social building blocks like marriage and kinship worried and surprised observers of the region, particularly because those definitions were under stress everywhere in North America. Fault lines threatened much of what residents of North America considered bedrock.

SOURCES AND DEFINITIONS

Much of what I describe is really an updated version of "great man" history. These families are important, and their papers and letters get saved because the men in them did great things by somebody's definition. We have to broaden the circle of the great man in two directions: to look at the set of relationships that allowed for success but also to include powerful Native men who participated as great men in the early nineteenth century. Including Native people doesn't make this history from the bottom up, but it increases the range of actors at the top, and that alone shifts the story in surprising ways.

What these families have left us to understand them are business records, letters, and reports written in the form of letters. Men and women in the nineteenth century spend a huge amount of time writing letters, and they write them for all kinds of reasons. What do they intend for us to see in them? Words on a page don't mean that letters are transparent windows into character or place; they are constructed for complicated reasons, and there are epistolary styles and conventions. The novelist Joyce Carol Oates suggested letter writing as a cure for alienation because "should you doubt you exist, you have only to write a letter—a personality will immediately define itself in the act of writing."[25] What writers decide to put into ink and to send to their most intimate friends or creditors is very personal. Letter writing is a self-conscious art, and one that is profoundly social, linking people to family, friends, and associates across wide distances. In the context of the West and the special isolation of running a family or business without a net—on a frontier, without reliable sources of credit or supplies—people needed these social networks built with letters. Letters became investments in relationships.

We can track men's relationships and social and business circles with letters that are themselves mixtures of personal and business documents. Cultural historian Toby Ditz reminds us that commercial letters are texts rather than documents and explains how much we can read if we are careful. She sees in such business documents a "world-making" genre in which we see how people build markets and create norms of merchant and customer behavior and how negotiated and imperfect all of these systems were.[26] When people wrote letters connecting themselves and their businesses and their families across the entire North American West, they were, indeed, making new worlds.

The people living and writing in these new worlds sometimes defined themselves in ways that are puzzling to us now. What does it mean to be a man or a woman, a child or an adult, European, Native, or mixed race? How do these categories matter, and how do they shift in the nineteenth century? We can learn a lot about the malleability of both gender and race from looking at the relationships people constructed together. We can ask questions about what it meant to be a Euro-American, Native American, or person of mixed race in the nineteenth century. How do ideas about gender affect men's intimate choices about relationships with women, about being good fathers, effective leaders, or successful merchants? How do these shifting definitions change women's options or the kinds of relationships they have with men inside and outside their communities? What options do children have in such shifting circumstances?

Maps and Signposts

As it considers these questions about human relationships, my narrative moves both chronologically and spatially to fill up that large blank space on the map: the terra incognita of 1804. Using numerous families as they moved across the region as informants and organizing devices, we build a view of relationships that vary from intimate connections to global economic and diplomatic maneuvers. I have made choices, some driven by the people in the record and some entirely my own, about themes to emphasize, events to describe, and people to introduce. I began with the materials people left behind, but much of the text rests on the work of other historians and observers. The result is neither encyclopedia nor monograph, but one way of exhuming and retelling a past we have lost. I'm still surprised by what I found and how it turned out. The book has three parts: the first focuses on describing and understanding the web of families, businesses, and personal empires that organized the region before conquest; the second looks particularly at Native nations and the economies and societies they built, under duress, at this time and place; and the third assays the long slow process of U.S. conquest and how it undermined this western world of trade, intimate relationships, and uneasily shared power.

Part 1 has three chapters and works from the perspective of individuals and families, but with enough context to connect them to larger stories. Chapter 1 introduces us to two large and important families, the Chouteaus and the Sublettes/Wilsons, who operate in the world of the trans-Mississippi West from the 1790s to the 1860s. As they trace and retrace paths across the region from St. Louis to Los Angeles, from Montreal to Santa Fe, they marry and make career and business decisions allowing us to see how interconnected this vast space becomes. The second chapter tells the story of the North American fur trade from the perspective of one family—the McLoughlins of Montreal, Vancouver, San Francisco, Paris, and Porthill, Idaho. Here we see the incredible spread of the fur trade and the particular kinds of family arrangements it fostered, and then abandoned, in the middle of the nineteenth century. We can examine the fur trade as big business, intensive labor, and personal drama. The third chapter looks at three places that trade and colonization schemes spawned, but that families developed and built into distinctive communities with surprising staying power. The Arkansas River valley, northern California, and eastern Texas and the personalities that gathered in those particular places in the 1830s and 1840s provide the settings.

With the blank space largely filled, part 2 circles back to the long history of Indian Country and what that meant, considering how Native nations controlled and recontoured the West in these years. The chapters have a different tone and structure, driven less by stories of individuals because Native people have fewer collections of family documents in the archives and more by a traditional narrative. This isn't the happy history of some recent revisionism, but it looks at the hard choices people made and the successes and failures of their efforts to make sense of new situations. The business of the fur trade met with a variety of responses from Indian people as did British, Spanish, Mexican, and U.S. policies. Chapter 4 looks primarily at the Missouri, Mississippi, and Arkansas river nations and their experiences with the fur trade, removal, and Indian War in the early part of the century. The chapter also details the complicated world of fur trade families and people of mixed race who faced difficult personal choices. Chapter 5 begins with the experiences of the Comanches on the southern plains and contrasts it with Native people in the interior of California, assessing the power some nations held and lost in midcentury. It also describes how Anglo-American immigrants responded to this power, and how the racial and ethnic reshaping of the region altered people's fates in the face of violence and waves of epidemic disease.

The final section of the book focuses on the tangled process of conquest and how it eroded the web of relationships and families laid out in earlier parts of the book. New racial ideologies and economic imperatives had grave consequences for everyone concerned. Chapter 6 takes a long view of the U.S. War with Mexico and how our far-flung families experience it. New groups of people begin to move into the West, but they do not repopulate it. War does much work to shift populations and ideologies, but the task of clarifying who won and what this might mean took decades. Chapter 7 examines the aftermath of war in several of our places, making the argument that the region experienced utter chaos in a vacuum of power. The 1850s, a sort of limbo between the easy military victories of the 1846 war and the great nationalizing project of the Civil War, emerge as a particularly mean and disorderly moment in American history. Chapter 8 concludes with a careful look at a sputtering state and its uneven imposition of power on unruly or unwelcome westerners: Mormons, Mexicans, and Native nations. And when we look at it through the eyes of western parents and children, it seems especially vicious. However, life did and does go on, and remnants of the world I describe here endured. People made families, gambled on how best to raise their children in a new version of the West, a place that called itself one nation but that seemed poorer for the loss of those many nations.

Part 1

Replacing a State

The Continental Web of Family Trade

Chapter 1

Families and Fur

The Personal World of the Early American West

Edward Sublette Hereford wrote tear-stained letters in 1857 to his parents from his Catholic boarding school in Santa Clara, California, claiming piteously, "I believe I will die as I feel I have no friends on earth."[1] His lament sounded much like another homesick child, Auguste Chouteau Jr., who wrote two generations earlier in 1802 to his father in St. Louis. With cousins and half-siblings among the Osages, the Illinois, and the Otoes, Auguste pleaded with his father to send him some moccasins to help him feel more at home at his school in Montreal.[2] Both boys came from powerful families who would successfully negotiate the changeable politics and economies of the trans-Mississippi West between 1800 and 1860. And both children reflected the complexity of the world the fur trade had created. Auguste, the son and nephew of the most important traders in St. Louis, had grown up in a world where family and cultural accommodation were paramount. Eddy, the son of Margaret Hereford and Benjamin Davis Wilson, came from a long line of fur traders who had linked old Mexican merchant elites with St. Louis and Taos traders, but he struggled to learn the Spanish he needed to live in Los Angeles. Auguste would return from his school experience, fluent in French and English in addition to the Pawnee, Spanish, and Osage he spoke already, ready to join his family's business empire.

Auguste's father had confidence in 1802 that French and Native connections and a broad knowledge of Indian languages would serve his son well on the Missouri River frontier, where this chapter and this book begin. By 1857 in California, Benjamin Davis Wilson had no idea how best to educate his adopted son for a world without a center. These dates and places are very traditional borders and watersheds for the history of the trans-Mississippi West. Most histories emphasize change through a nationalist lens, describing the steady pressure of the new American nation

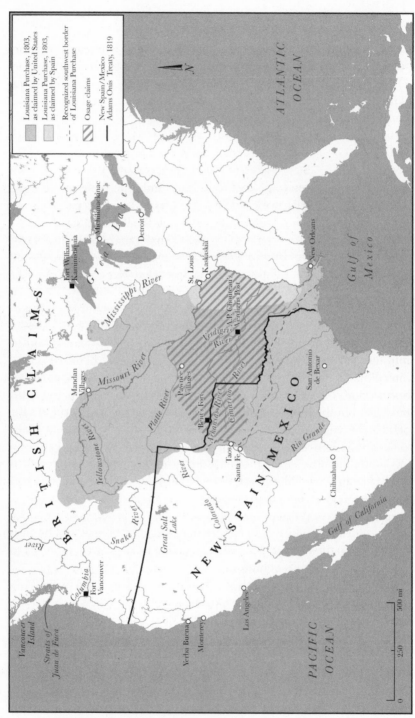

1. The Early North American West and Its Shifting Imperial Claims

as its people spread themselves across the western landscape. My story, however, emphasizes stability over time. Stability for tribal people and for Euro-Americans who traded with them meant confidence that you had the skills and networks to find furs, process and sell them, and support your family adequately while doing so. Stability meant knowing how to conduct business and form relationships with people who lived in other places and who spoke other languages because you understood the etiquette of gifts, favors, and trade. Stability meant, sometimes, going to war or kidnapping women and children to protect your place and rejuvenate your people. This stability enabled a worldwide trade in furs and evolved, paradoxically, out of accommodation and adaptability. This flexible and stable system, based in families who had the ability and desire to make powerful kinship links to other families, solidified over the entire period, protecting people against change and insulating them for a very long time against the rigid demands of American conquest.

The Sublettes, Wilsons, and Chouteaus illustrate the personally con-nected world of the early American West at the most elite level, but their experiences resonate much deeper. Fur and Indians, which have moved into the realm of quaint now, were at the center of local, national, and international concern between 1800 and 1860. And family enterprises operated at the trade's core. In a world of political revolution, nation building, and international rivalry, business and family life thrived in spite of these potentially destabilizing distractions. The stories of families whose businesses operated in the years between 1800 and 1860 reveal what was important and what mattered to the people who lived in the West. The Chouteau and the Sublette/Hereford/Wilson clans all began in St. Louis but used family connections to move through what would become the American West over several generations and through numerous changes in nationality. We also see very different versions of how the business of the fur trade worked: the Chouteaus always had a large, hierarchically or-ganized operation with its posts operating sort of like franchises, while the Sublettes tended toward small individual efforts. Both systems worked, but the Chouteaus certainly outlasted everyone else in this very risky business.[3]

Consider how much the region changed in political and demographic terms between 1800 and 1860. When Pierre Chouteau Jr. and his brother Auguste Pierre were born in St. Louis in the 1780s, the settlement resided clearly and legally in New Spain, but nearly everyone in St. Louis was French, Native American, or some combination of the two. When these two men, who would become essential to the fur trade and other businesses that drove the economic engines of the West, were adolescents, St. Louis became an American city that bordered on Indian Country and New Spain. By the time they were adults, the immigration of Anglo-Americans, black slaves, and new Indian nations had altered these demographics considerably. Represented by families like the Anglo Sublettes, who moved from Kentucky to Missouri in 1817, or the Cherokee Jollys, who moved to the Arkansas frontier in 1818, these immigrants fundamentally reshaped the world into which the Chouteaus had been born. Their strategies to survive and prosper, however, endured. Even as late as 1840, when young Margaret Sale, a Sublette cousin who would marry into several of our families, moved from Alabama to Missouri, her fortunes depended on her family connections and her abilities to understand the contingent qualities of the still Creole world of the Missouri border.

The great project of turning the West into part of the United States, initiated in 1803 and begun in earnest in the 1840s, had made little progress in many places. Much remained flexible and contingent about life on this complex border into the second half of the nineteenth century. Residents of the West seemed quite ambivalent about nationality, easily claiming new citizenship when it served personal or business needs. During a time when no one knew which nation or empire would finally impose control, effective trade was the sole source of power. And it continued to be a world defined by personal connections. The Chouteaus, the Sublettes, the Jollys, the Herefords, and the Wilsons all knew each other. They operated businesses that competed against one another, and they married into each other's families to build powerful family networks. Whether they lived in St. Louis, along the Arkansas River, in Santa Fe, Chihuahua, or southern California, these westerners depended on these webs to ensure safety in a very unstable world.

THE CHOUTEAU FAMILY AND THE MISSOURI RIVER WORLD

In 1831 newspapers reported on an occasion at Fort Smith, Arkansas, hosted by the Chouteau family. A group of men in the employ of the Chouteaus, who had been imprisoned by the Mexican government for ten years for illegally trapping in Mexican territory, had returned to the United States accompanied by their Mexican and Indian families. Delighted with this news, Pierre Chouteau Jr. funded a celebration of their return in order to re-cement relationships and to practice some diplomacy.[4] Fort Smith, which included soldiers, Indian agents, and traders of many nationalities among its inhabitants, served as military post and as gathering point for Caddo, Osage, and Pawnee people. For Chouteau, as for many in the fur trade, this would be a family event. As a member of St. Louis's founding family and a baron of the Missouri River fur trade, and with wives from the highest circles of the Osage nation and from French St. Louis, Chouteau had used his personal connections to build an empire. This was common practice in the merchant world of early St. Louis. Pierre René, the family patriarch, his sons Auguste Pierre (A.P.) and Pierre (Cadet), and several of their sons married into Indian families.[5] A.P. and Cadet made different choices about how to live in the two worlds, with A.P. abandoning St. Louis to live with his Osage family and with Cadet leaving his Osage family to live with his French wife, although several of his children chose to join Indian families.

At Fort Smith several Chouteau brothers and cousins welcomed back the traders, a mix of métis French Canadians and Anglo-Americans who had certainly been guilty of illegal trading with Spain and Mexico. A.P., who spoke Osage and Pawnee, as well as French, Spanish, and English, toasted his numerous guests and offered them whiskey and wines, sumptuous meats, and lavish gifts in the Osage tradition. This gathering represented the complex mix of peoples that negotiated trade and politics along the major river networks that formed the borders of the American West.[6]

The Chouteau family had been involved in the Indian trade and St. Louis since the city's founding. Figuring out exactly who did what is made challenging by the fact that nearly all the males in the family had some version of Auguste or Pierre in their first names.[7] The family emigrated from France in the early eighteenth century, settling in the Francophone world of New Orleans. As a result of business setbacks during the French and Indian War, the first Auguste Chouteau and his stepfather, Pierre LaClede, got involved in the fur trade, which offered quick profits that could make the company solvent in this moment of national uncertainty. After the 1763 Treaty of Paris made it clear that the French would no longer control much of the politics and economy in North America, the LaClede-Chouteau family decided that a move upriver to specialize in the fur trade and to get away from the British made sense.[8] They were not, however, moving to an unpeopled frontier. The central Mississippi River valley in what is now Arkansas, Missouri, Kentucky, and Illinois already had active communities of French *habitants*, Siouan- and Algonquian-speaking Indians, and a few Spanish and English traders. Kaskaskia, for example, had several thousand residents "as cheerful and as happy as any people in existence" who remained very attached, according to a puzzled observer, "to their ancient customs," which included open-field communal agriculture.[9] Despite the fact that French political control disappeared from the map of the region, French social and cultural influences continued for generations.[10]

In 1764 LaClede and Chouteau searched for the site that would become St. Louis, choosing it both for topography and because most of the good locations to the south had already been settled. They hoped a community at this spot would attract settlers who would then buy land and do business or work for the Chouteau family enterprises. Across the river in Illinois, villages of former French Canadians had prospered for more than fifty years. These villages looked surprisingly French in architecture, but their inhabitants were extremely "new world," wearing animal skins, often married to Native women or owning Native slaves, and supporting themselves with hunting and farming. A few villages had also developed west of the river; St. Genevieve in particular was founded in the 1750s.[11]

Choosing a site well to the north of St. Genevieve, LaClede hoped to avoid competition with those settlers and to develop trading partnerships with the Osages in particular. After surveying the site, and noting that it had little good bottomland, LaClede designed a city according to a grid plan that stretched west from the Mississippi and south from the Missouri. They named it St. Louis after the French king. The LaClede/Chouteaus built their own house and then began organizing the new community. Auguste Chouteau, only fifteen, served as Pierre LaClede's major assistant. While LaClede attended to the business of trade, young Auguste supervised the building of houses for new residents and negotiated with groups of Indians to develop trade relationships. Native and French responses to this moment were instructive. As an old man, Auguste remembered his first nerve-wracking meeting with the local Missouri Indians, as they crowded around him explaining that they "wished to build a village around the house we intended building"—in other words, to surround and effectively metabolize the intruders. Auguste noted quickly that they had 135 warriors while "we were only thirty," so he and LaClede explained that they wanted many groups to come to the settlement. They dissuaded the Missouris with a vague threat that in the open valley of St. Louis, the Missouris might be "eaten by eagles," referring to English soldiers making war to the north at Fort Chartres.[12]

Despite the tense tone of this first meeting, St. Louis provided an ideal setting for trade because it stood in a free-trade zone recognized by the

Osage, Missouri, and Sac-Fox nations, an advantage LaClede understood when he planned the whole enterprise. These Native nations had been engaged in a generation-long war over access to furs, land, slaves, and British and French traders, but this spot on the Mississippi and Missouri rivers had evolved into a site where all tribes visited traders, but no particular tribe claimed absolute control. The Osages, larger in number than the other groups and more centralized in large villages, served as important go-betweens for the tribes west of the river and those to the east. They also prevented French traders from venturing west and required that the traders deal exclusively with them.[13] French Creole traders settling in St. Louis had less complex political entanglements with European nations. The fact that neither the French, the English, nor the Spanish enforced any regulations around the Indian trade in a very remote region made it even easier. This isolation, however, would not last.

When French and Creole residents in frontier areas, including the tiny settlement of St. Louis, learned that France had secretly agreed to surrender New Orleans and all the territories west of the Mississippi to Spain in the Treaty of Fontainebleau, no one was pleased. The news certainly dismayed LaClede and the rest of the mostly French-speaking inhabitants of St. Louis, who suddenly found themselves about to be Spanish subjects. St. Louis, safely west of the Mississippi, soon became a haven for refugees from formerly French areas that had suddenly become English as the final result of the French and Indian War. French *habitants* knew that they hated the English because of the war they had brought. On the other hand, no one knew what Spanish "ownership" would mean west of the river, so streams of French Creoles moved west, nearly deserting places like Kaskaskia and Cahokia. LaClede and Chouteau, resourceful businessmen, simply continued to develop their community. Spanish officials, in fact, did not arrive for several years. By that time LaClede and Chouteau had firmly established themselves as the major Indian traders in the region, and they made St. Louis central to the fur trade.[14]

As the generation of the family who had to deal with national border issues and with the fierce rivalry between fur traders of various nations, Auguste and his younger half-brother Pierre, born in 1758, developed diplomatic skills. They successfully negotiated distant political upheavals by developing strong relationships with the Indian nations that surrounded them. Political disarray presented opportunities for traders who could outlast it and who could offer new trading partnerships as the international wrangling interrupted others. As the English and the Spanish battled over the assets of the Mississippi River valley, supplies dried up, especially trade goods and presents for the Indians. In the midst of international war, the Chouteau brothers managed to develop excellent trading relationships with British traders on the Great Lakes while demanding protection from the Spanish. In the years between the Treaty of Paris in 1763, the end of the American Revolution in 1781, which made land east of St. Louis American but St. Louis and Missouri Spanish, and the Louisiana Purchase in 1803, which made the Missouri River basin clearly part of the United States, the Chouteau family enjoyed remarkable success. Madame Chouteau, a poor unmarried mother when she arrived at the site of St. Louis, died with a hundred living descendents and considerable wealth, a sign of a life well lived.[15]

Meanwhile, another generation of Chouteaus rose up in St. Louis society—a closely linked set of French cousins, kissing and otherwise—by the beginning of the nineteenth century. Pierre had married Pélagie Kiersereau in 1783, and Brigitte Saucier, another cousin, in 1794 after Pélagie's death, and had nine children. These marriages represented careful alliances within the close-knit Mississippi River Creole community. Auguste married Thérèse Cerré, the daughter of a prosperous Kaskaskia merchant in 1783. They remained together for nearly forty years and had seven children live to adulthood. Both Auguste and Pierre, with their own wealth and the considerable dowries of their wives, built impressive mansions in central St. Louis. They educated their children in Montreal and Paris, though they also recognized the distinctive skills required for life as a frontier trader. Auguste's son, Auguste, sent to Montreal in 1802, wrote to his father requesting "a bow and quiver of arrows . . . the deer Horns I forgot in the garret . . . and shoes ornamented with porcupine quills," demonstrating the young St. Louisan's connection to the Native qualities of his home.[16]

Appreciating Native skills would lead to excellent relations with Indian nations, a trademark of the Chouteau family. They did most of their business with the Osages and other lower Missouri Central Siouan peoples who cultivated corn and hunted: Poncas, Omahas, Kansas, Otoes, and Iowas. These nations also served as important intermediaries in the interband trade network and had come to embrace customs and cultures that blended aspects of eastern and western Native peoples. The lower river tribespeople developed customary practices for engaging various groups as economic partners, military allies, and kin. They were a powerful match for the French and taught the Chouteaus much about how to participate in the fur trade.[17] Both brothers spent a great deal of their lives among these people. Though they had wives and children in St. Louis, Chouteau men also had wives and children among the Osages.

"MIDDLE GROUND" OR "NATIVE GROUND"?

From its founding, St. Louis had a cosmopolitan outlook. Many of the French-speaking people in the vicinity of the city in the late eighteenth century were biracial and bicultural.[18] The French-speaking people of the Mississippi Valley had no country after the Treaty of Paris in 1763. They operated as a people "in between," whose national identities were fluid. The Chouteau family made the most of this situation. The Spanish government turned out to be an easy obstacle. No Spanish governor ever lived in St. Louis, and few even visited what they considered to be a raw frontier outpost. More than thirty years of Spanish occupation had little impact on the community's architecture, customs, or language. Most official business was conducted in French, because French-speaking clerks from St. Louis and New Orleans ran the "Spanish" government.[19] And underneath the official but ephemeral world of imperial politics lay a deep core of tradition around trade and cooperation with Native people built on the basis of personal relationships.

Such relationships, which included adoption, marriage, and concubinage,[20] cemented the cultural practices of calumet pipe ceremonialism, a set of behaviors and vision that created a rule of law and a peace ethic that fostered trade among the tribes of the lower Missouri River. These groups had been deeply affected by decades of warfare between Native peoples in the Ohio Valley and the Great Lakes region, so fully described by Richard White and Alan Taylor.[21] In order to survive the "middle" and "divided" grounds, Central Siouan and other horticultural people developed ceremonial practices that enabled them to become active as middlemen. Pipe ceremonialism developed as part of revitalization movements that occurred among these Native groups after the terrible epidemics and forced migrations of the eighteenth century, the result of contact with European traders, missionaries, and settlers. Making, sharing, and smoking the ornate pipes served groups who gathered together into new villages and bands, and created new forms of authority for chiefs of these newly created peoples. The new traditions included the Sun Dance and Midéwiwin, as well as calumet pipe ceremonies. Ceremonies taught people proper manners and provided ways of linking nonrelated individuals and clans in ways that could be closer than blood. These newly reconstituted groups encouraged marriages and reciprocity among peoples of differing kin groups and ethnicities—as long as they had pipes and corn. Calumet pipe production and its associated symbolism also provided a medium for dealing with incoming Europeans, integrating them as trading partners and kin.[22]

Ethnohistorian Kathleen DuVal has complicated this picture by demonstrating that the Indians of the Arkansas River valley—in particular, the large, well-organized groups like the Osages, Pawnees, and Quapaws—had a very different relationship with Europeans. Rather than a "middle ground" or a "divided ground" DuVal describes this part of the continent as a "Native ground" where Indian nations determined the arrangements, incorporating Europeans, rather than accommodating them. Indian people retained sovereignty over land and trade policy up until the early nineteenth century, and Europeans recognized their power and savvy. The Osages, in particular, gained increased regional power as a result of their early acquisition of guns and trade goods from French traders that gave them absolute domination over other Native peoples.[23]

The Chouteaus had decided to build their trade in St. Louis because they understood how relationships with the Osages would provide them with links to other Native groups. In contrast to Spanish authorities who had spent years and fortunes trying entirely unsuccessfully to subjugate and control the Osages, the Chouteaus joined them. In the 1780s and 1790s, while the Spanish government was officially at war with the Osages and Spanish trading parties were regularly attacked, Pierre and Auguste Chouteau traded with them, bought land, and spent time in their villages, recognizing the fact that Indian nations really controlled the middle of the continent. The Osages in particular understood the utility of a central trading center like St. Louis and used it as place to do business and to develop useful diplomatic relationships with a variety of peoples. So many Indian delegations visited St. Louis in its early years that French agricultural families settled around the city because of the profitability of selling grain, vegetables, and meat to the constant visitors.[24]

Most basically, the Chouteaus and other successful traders recognized the importance of presents. Gift giving and exchange operated as a crucial way to reduce tension between the fragmented groups of Native people trying to reorganize themselves in the Ohio and Missouri river valleys. Feuds, botched marriages, raids, and even deaths could be compensated for with proper gift giving. Often gift giving involved the exchange of human beings, a common practice everywhere on the American continent.

Many of these slaves, mostly women and children, had been captured as part of intertribal warfare that became big business once European traders got involved. The trade in human beings evolved on British colonial frontiers, Spanish colonial frontiers, and on the Mississippi River frontier, but it remained as much a practice of undoing harm and building kin connections as it was an exchange of property. No matter what actually got exchanged, children or beads, any trade relationship had to be cemented with gifts, which French traders and smart British officials had long recognized. Spanish governors and most Americans politicians or traders never understood the practice and simply saw gift giving as bribery and a business expense that should be curtailed.[25]

As a result, both the Spanish and the Americans had much poorer relationships with the tribes, which the Chouteaus used to their advantage. In 1794, as yet another wave of warfare built between the Spanish and their Indian allies against the Osages, Auguste Chouteau proposed building a trading fort in the heart of the Osage villages as an alternative to expensive and wasteful warfare. In return for a six-year trading monopoly, the Chouteaus would build a fort and underwrite the costs of the soldiers stationed there. Such an arrangement served the commercial desires of the Chouteaus, the mercantile and military needs of the Spanish, and the growing market in trade with the Indians. In those years the Chouteaus sold literally tons of goods to the Osages: guns, blankets, mirrors, bridles, kettles, and hatchets by the thousands, more than a ton of lead for bullets, hats, feathers, thousands of scarlet ribbons, bolts of cloth, ten thousand gun flints, and hundreds of thousands of trade beads. They received in return hundreds of thousands of pelts and hides. The Osages, pleased with this profitable relationship and the control this fort and the goods it brought gave them, in 1798 granted both Pierre and Auguste honorary membership in a tribal clan as recognition of their diplomatic importance to the group. Both men also married within those tribes and had children whom they recognized but did not encourage to live as part of their St. Louis families.[26]

St. Louis and other Missouri River towns flourished in settings that involved numerous legal gray areas. Traders obtained English, French, and Spanish goods but concealed some of their trading activities to avoid angering the Spanish, who were, technically, in charge. Much of this illicit trade was protected by the close and familial relationships developed with local Indian groups. Many men in St. Louis had Sac, Fox, and Osage wives because members of these tribes had always been permitted to trade with the English, which gave these traders married to women of these nations

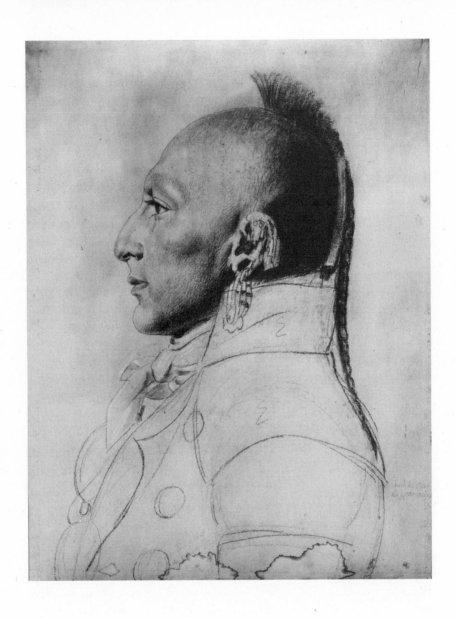

5. Charles Balthazar Julien Févret de Saint-Mémim, *Chief of the Little Osages*, 1807. Library of Congress, Prints and Photographs Division.

A famous French portraitist, Saint-Mémim made this ink drawing of Little Osage leader Pawhuska, also known as White Hair, when Pawhuska visited Washington DC in 1806–7. Indian superintendent William Clark wanted to cement relationships with the powerful Osages and escorted a group of Osage leaders to meet with the president and members of Congress.

particular advantages. Nearly half of all St. Louis households had Native slaves—not legal either but tolerated at every level—living in them. The St. Louis Chouteaus had numerous Indian or métis slaves listed in the census records, most with French names, which makes untangling the relationships challenging.[27]

During this period, biracial families with bicultural skills enjoyed status and prosperity, even though a legal debate had raged around the mixing of races or *métissage* as long as Europeans had been on the continent. However, while clerics and politicians in New Orleans and in Paris argued about the dangers to the purity of the French race, people in New France, Louisiana, and St. Louis acted with their hearts, minds, and bodies and created a métis world. Having kinship ties to many different Indian nations became a business advantage.[28]

In addition to the complexity of relationships with Native people, other groups of newcomers had to be metabolized. Decades of war in the Ohio River valley and new taxes to support these wars had disaffected and frightened Anglo-Americans as well. Spanish officials, eager to increase the population on the Spanish side of the river, actively played on these fears to recruit settlers. They advertised Missouri as having rich land, peaceful Indian relations, and freedom from "chicanery and lawyers," a combination that attracted a large number of migrants in the 1780s and 1790s. The newest arrivals included people like Moses Austin and his son Stephen, who would eventually become famous in Texas, and Daniel Boone and several of his sons. By 1800 these migrants outnumbered the early French settlers, and their different farming and settlement styles caused real tension between the groups living there. Spanish authorities found the new friction especially irksome because the promise of peaceful Indian relations became an outright lie as American ideas about inviolate private property clashed with Indian and French ideas about fair use. As a second generation of Chouteaus came of age, they considered the best way to use these newcomers and even joined in a lead-mining venture with Moses Austin and several trade operations with the Boones.[29]

"Tough Love" and Family Loyalty

The news of the Louisiana Purchase, made in secret in 1803, came as a complete surprise when it reached St. Louis in 1804. The fact that St. Louis and all of the Missouri River drainage now stood in the "territories" of the United States would certainly matter, but no one knew how. When the Chouteaus sent the news to the Osages in 1804 the Indians simply refused to believe such a ridiculous story. American diplomats and politicians found the sudden change perplexing as well. Certainly they didn't recognize the cultural complexity of this world. In 1800 perhaps 80 percent of people born in St. Louis had at least one parent with a significant quantum of Native blood, the result of generations of marriage between French Creoles, French Canadians, and Indian people. The first American governor of Louisiana, Amos Stoddard, found the variety of people he saw in St. Louis bewildering, and he identified at least seven different "castes" of mixed-bloods in his effort to make sense of the situation. He was careful to have good relationships with the Chouteau family and valued their knowledge about trade and local politics.[30]

Pierre's older sons, Auguste Pierre (A.P.), born in 1786, and Pierre Jr., who was often known as Cadet, a nickname that signified the second son, and born three years later in 1789, would take on the family business in this complex cultural and political setting. The messiness of this world and the accommodations people made to thrive within it could be demonstrated by nearly anyone in the Chouteau family. However, for our purposes, we'll focus on Auguste Pierre, the eldest son of the grand old man Pierre. The family's aspirations to profit from the new American nation that had imposed itself upon them were demonstrated when Captain Meriwether Lewis nominated young A.P. for an appointment at West Point. He graduated from the military academy in 1806, and his first position was serving in Natchitoches as aide-de-camp to General James Wilkinson, perhaps the most influential man in the lower Mississippi River valley. Young A.P. showed his independent streak, however, when he resigned his commission and headed off to join a fur-trapping expedition less than a year later.[31]

A.P. would always be torn between the demands of his powerful St. Louis family and the independence that life on the trading frontier seemed to offer. He bowed to family wishes in 1809 when he married his first cousin, Marie Anne Sophie Labbadie. Sophie was the daughter of the St. Louis merchant Silvestre Labbadie and Pelagie Chouteau, A.P.'s aunt. The same year as his marriage, A.P. and his father organized the Missouri Fur Company along with Manuel Lisa, their old business competitor. Because Pierre Sr. still served as the Indian agent for the Osages and had to avoid the too obvious conflicts of interest of being in business with the Osages and representing them for the U.S. government., A.P. represented the family interests in the new company. Despite the fact that Pierre, as agent,

1. Marie Thérèse Bourgeois (1733–1814) m. René Auguste Chouteau (1723–1776)
- 1. Auguste Sr. (1749–1829) m. Thérèse Cerré [Chouteau]
  - 9 children total
- 2. Auguste Sr. (1749–1829) **m. Osage woman**
  - Antoine Chouteau (1769–1842)

2. Marie Thérèse Bourgeois (1733–1814) m. Pierre La Clède (1729–1778)
- Marie Pelagie Chouteau (1760–1812) m. Silvestre Labbadie
  - 9 children total
- Victoire Chouteau (1764–1825) m. Charles Gratiot (1752–1817)
- 1. Pierre Chouteau (Sr.) (1758–1849) m. Pélagie Kiersereau
  - 1. Paul Liguest (1792–1851) m. Constance Dubreul
  - 2. Paul Liguest (1792–1851) m. Aurora Hay
    - 6 boys from first two marriages, all died
  - 3. Paul Liguest (1792–1851) **m. Osage woman**
    - Alexander Chouteau
    - Edward Liguest
    - Pélagie
  - Pierre Jr. (Cadet) 1789–1865) m. Emilie Anne Gratiot (*1793–1862*)
  - 1. Auguste Pierre (A.P.) m. Sophie Labbadie
    - 11 children
  - 2. Auguste Pierre (A.P.) **m. Mihanga (Osage)**
    - Amelia
  - 3. Auguste Pierre (A.P.) m. Rosalie and **m. Masina (Osage)**
    - Amelia
    - James Liquest
    - Augustus Clermont
    - Henry
    - Anthony
- 2. Pierre Chouteau (Sr.) (1758–1849) **m. Osage woman**
  - James Chouteau
  - Paul Loise (1775–1832)
    - Pélagie
- 3. Pierre Chouteau (Sr.) (1758–1849) m. Brigitte Saucier
  - 1. François (1797–1838) m. Berenice Menard
    - 9 children
  - 2. François (1797–1838) **m. Osage woman**
    - James Gesso
  - Charles
  - Cyprien (1802–1879) m. Mary Francis (Shawnee)
    - Frederick Lewis
    - Francis Edmond
    - Mary Francis
  - Pharamond
  - 1. Frederick (1809–1891) m. Elizabeth Tooley
  - 2. Frederick (1809–1891) m. Mathilda White
  - 3. Frederick (1809–1891) m. Elizabeth Carpenter
- Marie Louise Chouteau (1762–1817)

6. The Chouteau family and their Osage relations. Compiled by Leá Norcross. This truncated chart shows only the small segment of the numerous branches of the Chouteau family tree of concern in this book. Important to note would be the several generations of the family that married into Osage and Shawnee families and the naming practices that used family names for all children.

was prohibited from engaging in trade, he brokered most of the deals with Indians on the lower part of the river, with his son building alliances and making arrangements with tribes far up the river, past the Mandan villages, into Blackfoot and Arikara territory. A.P. worked as a full partner of the Missouri Fur Company until 1813, when the company dissolved.[32]

Though he and Sophie had eleven children together, A.P. spent little time in St. Louis with this family. Whether or not he explained his decision to his French Creole wife, by 1815 he had several children with Osage women, including a namesake, Augustus Clermont Chouteau. The name of this child demonstrates A.P.'s intent to deepen his connection to the important Clermont band of Osage. Washington Irving, when he described life in St. Louis in 1810 in his best seller *Astoria,* wrote, with evident disgust, that "the old French houses engaged in the Indian trade had gathered round them a train of dependents, mongrel Indians and mongrel Frenchmen, who had intermarried with Indians."[33] A.P., of course, was not the only Chouteau to engage in this practice. His father, uncles, and brothers certainly had Indian families as well, but they remained in the background in their officially presented lives. St. Louis baptismal records show Chouteau children with Native and *métisse* mothers who had Chouteau family members and other important St. Louisans as their godparents but never became part of their fathers' households. A.P. broke with these family practices. He chose to foreground his Native family by becoming a trader with the Osages and living his life among them. He abandoned his St. Louis family entirely in 1822, when some of these children were still very young, which angered his extended family.[34]

His decision to leave St. Louis had other factors. A.P. believed he had failed to meet the expectations of his family in numerous ways. Before he made the decision to move to the Osage village, he had convinced his brother Pierre Chouteau Jr. and Sophie's brother, Bartholomew Berthold, to back him in one more one fur-trading trip, dabbling in the illegal Santa Fe trade. A.P.'s 1815 trip to the headwaters of the Arkansas demonstrates the real gamble that investing in the fur trade really was, especially in territory that the Spanish had clearly marked as their own. He and his men reached the mountains with little trouble and had a successful hunt, but on their return trip to St. Louis disaster struck. In what is now western Kansas, a group of Pawnees attacked Chouteau and his men, forcing them to cache their belongings on an island in the Arkansas, known ever after as Chouteau's Island. While trying to hide from the Indians, they escaped to the south, where they were arrested by Spanish officials, taken to Santa Fe, and held in prison. The Spanish government confiscated all of their furs and trade goods, which A.P. estimated were worth $30,000. They returned safely, but A.P. had lost his brother's and brother-in-law's money. He never repaid them, and they never forgave him.[35]

This setback was only one of a lifetime of financial mistakes, but because of this embarrassing loss A. P. Chouteau never took another trapping expedition to the mountains. In 1831 he wrote to the Secretary of War Lewis Cass, still trying to get some compensation for his loss, that "I was arrested, thrown into prison, charged with revolutionary designs, my property confiscated. . . . I was discharged, without any compensation for my property which had been taken by violence. Upon my return home, I was determined to abandon a trade that was attended with so much risk."[36] A.P. could never forget this loss of his early fortune and blamed it for much of his later financial difficulty. The next year he took another big loan from his brother Pierre Jr. to go into the mercantile business, but that year, 1819, was marked by a worldwide financial depression. A.P. lost every penny, ending up owing Pierre $66,000, an amount that so large that he surely knew he could never pay it back. Compared to his brothers and cousins, A.P. could only see himself as a colossal failure. Those family pressures helped push him out of St. Louis, but surely imagining a completely different kind of life with his Osage family offered a powerful pull as well. By 1822 he had several children with several women, but he had begun a much longer relationship with an Osage woman named Rosalie Lambert, the daughter of a Big Osage leader, and he may have been getting pressure from her to be a more permanent husband.[37]

Though he had failed at St. Louis merchandising, A.P. began a successful life as an Osage trader. His personal, legal, and business decisions offer us a window into the complicated world that was evolving along the Arkansas River and how intermingled its people really were. A.P. followed a long-standing French settlement pattern in which French settlers established outposts along rivers next to Native agricultural villages. These tiny settlements succeeded only because of close relationships with local Indian bands that provided food, military protection, furs, and sources for trade. In turn, Indians appreciated these French settlements for their convenient access to trade goods and markets for furs and hides. Once the United States supervised this region, it required that traders be licensed, and the Chouteau family used its influence to control nearly all of these licenses. A.P. and his brother Liguest took out a license to trade with the Osages and the Kickapoos on the Arkansas River in 1822. But the real permission

2. Native Nations and the Chouteau Family Trade Network

they needed had to come from the Osages. They wanted Chief Pawhuska's Osage band, who lived south of the Missouri River and were feeling pressures from Anglo-American settlers, to move south to the junction of the Verdigris, Neosho, and Arkansas rivers, a still unsettled country where the Osages could hunt, raise crops, and avoid too much contact with settlers.[38]

Chouteau knew he had chosen a dangerous but potentially profitable site. At La Saline, a big salt spring thirty-five miles up the Neosho River from its mouth, A. P. Chouteau settled down in a house with a somewhat bloody history. It had been built by a half Osage trader named Joseph Rivar just before he was killed by the Cherokees, but its location was far enough from the roads taken by the Cherokees, forced from their own territory and searching for new homes, to seem safe. For nearly a year, Pawhuska (the younger White Hair) and his Osage Indians lived at La Saline, accepting Chouteau's hospitality and making up their minds about moving there. They finally decided on a spot about fifty miles further up the Neosho from La Saline. Despite this setback, Chouteau and his Osage family lived at La Saline and considered it their home, though A.P.'s business was centered on the river at Verdigris. At this site, a few hours travel from his home, he had an office, warehouse, boat landing, and fields producing corn and wheat. Here he could trade with anyone who needed his merchandise—immigrating Creeks, Cherokees, and Choctaws, Euro-Americans moving into the Mississippi Valley, and French Catholic Anglos headed for Texas—without endangering or insulting his Osage kin.[39]

Chouteau had not regressed into a trapper hermit; the West Point–educated man still traveled in the highest circles of Osage, St. Louis, New Orleans, and New York society and business. The complexity of peoples along the river required diplomatic finesse. His trading operation was a big one, and despite leaving his St. Louis wife and the Creole world, he remained entangled in the Chouteau trading empire. A.P. bought his goods from and sold his furs to Bernard Pratte and Company of St. Louis, his brother Cadet's company, and he kept up a regular correspondence with his brothers, cousins, and uncles. He reported on successes and failures, arrivals and departures, expenses and deliveries, clearly a midlevel manager in a large commercial enterprise. He never discussed personal matters in these letters, aside from asking about the health of various St. Louis relatives or the condition of their businesses. A.P's territory, the Osage Outfit, included four trading posts that in 1825 handled about $30,000 worth of goods brought by keelboats from St. Louis. In late spring and late fall, after the Indians made their hunts, the peltry was floated down to New

Orleans on barges and then shipped to New York and beyond. A.P. often accompanied his shipments to New Orleans in the spring, and after 1830 he often went to New York to oversee the sale of his furs, taking along his half-Osage son Augustus Clermont on several occasions.[40]

Chouteau's operation grew and solidified in the summer of 1824, when soldiers from Fort Smith came to establish Fort Gibson on the east side of the Neosho about three miles from its mouth, and Chouteau traded with them for provisions and building materials. He sent 4,445 pelts to St. Louis in the spring of 1824, but the following summer sent none, reporting to his cousin that "no hunting this summer because the men have been ill" and the "Osages sensitive to their new situation."[41] The "new situation" referred to two things: a new treaty signed with the federal government and what the Osages perceived to be an invasion of Cherokee migrants. A treaty with Osages made at St. Louis in June 1825 required them to give up all of their land in Missouri and settle on land between the Arkansas River and the Kansas border, with a specific clause allowing Osages to hunt freely to the west. The move improved prospects for A.P. He wrote to his cousin that his business had shifted from hunting to selling goods to Osages who had annuity payments, and that "I hope to do better with the Creeks, who are beginning to surround me."[42] The treaty made A.P.'s family "half-breeds" in the official record, but it also gave them valuable land claims. The treaty specifically set aside eight sections of the new Osage reserve including the big salt spring and the La Saline house for Chouteau's children, his Osage wife Rosalie Lambert, and her brother Anthony.[43]

Despite his efforts to make a new business and to protect his family with land, A.P. could not protect anyone from the inherently violent situation on the Arkansas as various expelled Native nations moved in on top of each other. The Osage move to the Arkansas increased tensions between the Osages and Cherokees, which would eventually cost A.P. a lot. In the early 1820s some five thousand Cherokee farmers migrated west looking for new lands to settle and chose this Osage trading and hunting territory. Grudgingly, the Osages agreed to share it, but on Osage terms: requiring the Cherokee to declare allegiance to the Osages and allowing the Osages to hunt first. The Cherokees, among one of several Indian nations who had been "removed" as a result of federal legislation, reacted violently to Osage demands. A devastating war developed between the two peoples, complete with raiding, burning villages, and kidnapping and enslaving hostages. The Cherokees, more numerous and having the support of the U.S. government, officially prevailed, but the Osages remained in the area and never gave up their claims to it.[44]

7. Charles Bird King, "Mo-hon-go," 1830. Lithograph in *History of the Indian Tribes of North America*, edited by Thomas L. McKenney and James Hall, 3 vols. (Philadelphia: J. T. Bowen, 1848–50). Courtesy of Smithsonian Institution Libraries, Washington DC.

A. P. Chouteau's first Osage wife and the mother of his son, Mihanga was the daughter of an important Osage leader, Clermont, who did business with several generations of the Chouteaus. She posed for King with her child (not A.P.'s son) as part of a delegation of Osages who visited Washington DC, via Paris, in 1830.

To our eyes, A.P.'s family is hard to decipher, if only because of the plethora of Augustes. Only two of Chouteau's children, Auguste James and Henry, were borne by Rosalie; three other sons, Augustus Clermont, Paul Auguste, and Auguste Gesseau, came from Rosalie's sister Masina, who formed part of the household. In addition, Chouteau had two daughters, both named Amelia, whose mothers were other Osage women. This wasn't wanton procreation, but part of a recognized Osage and other Central Siouan groups' patterns of family creation. Both wealthy traders and leading men had multiple wives as a sign of status and a social obligation to create connections between groups. Building relations helped Native, Anglo, and mixed-blood people to protect their interests in a changing world. In scores of federal treaties between 1830 and the 1840s, Chouteau family mixed-bloods from various tribes were recognized by name as being protected by federal law and being deserving of land set-asides. Various Chouteaus, in particular Pierre Sr., Auguste, A.P. and Cadet, personally negotiated these treaties to ensure that their wives, children, nieces, and nephews would receive land.[45]

It would be easy to romanticize the world of traders and trading posts as one of biracial harmony, but it often involved a lot of human pain. The range of relationships went from slavery and concubinage or serial and casual sexual encounters that left women and their children of mixed race abandoned and alone to monogamous and harmonious relationships in which parents shared the burden of raising children. Many children of French and Indian background were raised by Native nations, others by their Creole relatives. We can also look at life in the fur trade and see the breakdown of both Central Siouan and French Catholic moral codes. Observers at the time certainly did, seeing French fur traders as "grossly licentious and profligate," with wives in every Indian village.[46]

It would also be easy to see these relationships as entirely exploitative for the women involved, and for some women it surely was. But our assumptions either that monogamy is the highest choice or that European men always took advantage of Native women need to be examined as well. The rigid ideas we carry with us about marriage being lifelong and monogamous came only from the late nineteenth century and took a lot of effort to impose. Native and French customs allowed for various informal mechanisms of marriage, divorce, and remarriage that challenged these more recent practices. In both European and Native traditions, both women and men could leave a marriage if either party was dissatisfied because a spouse was cruel, lazy, or had committed some breach of behavior.[47]

The mobility and ambitions of fur trade men combined with Native traditions that encouraged multiple wives and remarriage mitigated against long and stable relationships. Many Native and mixed-blood women frequently had more than one spouse, because they had been abandoned by their fur trade husbands but also because of their own needs and ambitions. Some women disliked living among strangers or found traveling too difficult after they had children, so they severed their ties with fur traders and went back to their own communities. Some relationships, however, endured with various levels of formal recognition. A. P. Chouteau's long connection with Rosalie Lambert and Manuel Lisa's with Mitain were recognized in wills and deed of property, though neither man was married to these women in the view of civil authorities. These women represented important connections for their husbands and were accorded a great deal of respect within the fur-trading world. Many Euro-American observers found such relationships confusing. Washington Irving observed the deferential treatment that Rosalie Lambert and other Indian women received and the proud way they conducted themselves with evident disorientation. He remarked with dismay that at Chouteau's post "the world is turned upside down: the slave is the master and the master the slave" because Indian women did not behave in the servile manner he expected.[48]

Raising children in this complex world challenged even the most dedicated parents. As recent fur trade scholars have elucidated, the records indicate that these children truly moved between both worlds, living alternately with French and Indian relatives. French Creoles, Central Siouans, and métis people shared flexible and broad definitions of family and ideas about corporate responsibility for child rearing. For the families we can trace in the records, we see individual children living with Native groups, then attending school in St. Louis or Kaskaskia, later apprenticing to tradesmen or serving as household servants, combined with stints at mission schools and with St. Louis or St. Genevieve family members. We see that A.P.'s children would find the deeply bicultural society that he had helped to define compelling and personally enriching. He sent his children to the mission school near La Saline, but also saw that they spent time in St. Louis among his extended family. However, all of his assumptions were based on the ideas about race and identity forged in Creole St. Louis, not those that would evolve in American St. Louis or that would be necessary along the Arkansas in the stressful years of the 1830s and 1840s.[49]

However skillfully managed, family connections in the French or Native world did not always guarantee financial success. Much of A. P. Chouteau's business depended on the wealth of Indians, especially the Osages and the Creeks, several thousand of whom had gathered along the banks of the Verdigris and Arkansas rivers. The Creeks had moved to the region as part of the removal process and had expected to receive food, money, and clothing from the U.S. government. They received nothing and simply went into debt at Chouteau's establishment. Chouteau fed and clothed them, and charged the government $5201.93 to their annuities, for which the government never reimbursed him. Similarly, when the government arbitrarily cut back on Osage annuities and gave another chunk of their land to the Cherokees, A.P. covered their expenses. When the agent for the Osages, who had probably stolen much of the missing money himself, refused to intervene, A.P. wrote to his uncle Auguste for help, complaining that "business is so bad we may have to move again."[50]

His situation illustrates how poorly conceived and managed Indian affairs were in this period. In the federal government's view, two kinds of Native people existed: those who had been removed and had given up, or "extinguished," title to their lands and those who had not. All Indians that the government had contacted, traded with, or been to war against—most large tribes at this point—had an agent assigned to them by the government. These agents ranged from complete political hacks who had never seen Indian people but were eager for a government position to people who had deep connections and knowledge about Native needs. The agent's task involved either convincing Native people to make treaties and give up land or managing the annuities, goods, stock, and lands they received in return for making a treaty with the United States. Either task involved numerous opportunities for graft and personal enrichment by the agent. Thomas Forsyth, a long-time trader with the upper Mississippi tribes, commented with evident frustration in 1831 that the Indian Service was run by "men who have never seen more than three or four Indians in the course of their lives" and keep the Indians in "continual broils and quarrels purely for their own pleasure and profit."[51] The other essential, and flawed, piece in the whole system was the treaty commission. These appointed bodies, generally combinations of missionaries, Indian Office officials, and regional politicians, decided how much land a particular Native nation needed, where the new reserve should be, and how much they should be paid for the land they gave up. The commissioners met with the Native men they perceived as leaders, made the government's offer, and got some members of the tribe to sign the treaty. What each side understood about the process, of course, differed with every group of commissioners and every Native nation.

An episode in the story of Sam Houston, the big ex–Indian fighter and ex-governor of Tennessee who would become a hero at the Alamo, illustrates the playing out of the treaty process and how it undermined relationships along the Arkansas. Houston's first marriage was notoriously shattered when his young wife discovered on their wedding night that Houston had suffered a "dreadful injury" in the Creek War of 1814. She publicly proclaimed he had been emasculated, which caused him to resign as governor of Tennessee.[52] Bitter and humiliated, Sam fled Tennessee to live with his old friends the Cherokees on the Arkansas in the spring of 1829. He had spent much of his childhood living with the Cherokees, but he hadn't seen them following their removal. After recovering a bit of his self-esteem, Houston found renewed interest in Indian affairs. John Jolly, a wealthy Cherokee leader, alerted him to the fact that graft on the part of Indian agents had robbed his friends of their land and annuities. Looking around, he discovered how widespread the graft was, particularly for the Osages, saddled with a terrible agent, John Hamtramack—a man about whom A. P. Chouteau had complained for years. Furious at this injustice to the Indians and eager to be effectively angry at someone other than himself, Houston embarked on a six-hundred-mile trip through Indian Country gathering evidence against corrupt Indian agents, which he presented in person to President Jackson in the spring of 1830.[53]

Jackson, shocked by the quality and quantity of Houston's evidence that reportedly measured a stack nearly six feet high on the floor of the Oval Office, fired many of the worst agents and personally ensured that full annuities would reach the tribes. Houston's efforts benefited the Chouteau family enormously. As a result Liguest Chouteau (A.P.'s brother) was made Osage agent and A. P. Chouteau received the money he had advanced to Clermont's band the summer before. Despite the fact that Houston had championed the Cherokees and Chouteau was firmly linked to the Osages, the two became fast friends. Houston settled down on Cherokee lands near Chouteau's Verdigris post in a log trading post he called Wigwam Neosho with a Cherokee widow of means, Diana Gentry; here he did business as a trader without a U.S. license, insisting that his Cherokee wife and his adoption into the tribe many years earlier exempted him from U.S. law. He also began to drink heavily—the Osage name for him was "Big Drunk." When he lost an election for a seat on the Cherokee council in spring of 1831, he again took his frustrations to Washington DC, where he assaulted a congressman and then fled to Mexican Texas. He stopped at his trading post on the Verdigris long enough to deed his business and land to his wife Diana, following Cherokee rules about spousal separation, something that would not have been possible for Anglo-American women at the same time.[54]

A. P. Chouteau learned some lessons from Houston's performance, but he had neither Houston's political connections nor hero status. When he set out for Washington that spring of 1832 he wanted to get the money owed to himself and to the Creeks and Osages. The government, obviously reluctant to pay the large sums that included six years' worth of supplies and annuities, balked. Even armed with a power of attorney from the Creeks and a stack of paperwork from officials, Chouteau failed because he was viewed as a mere Indian trader. He did get the "privilege" of being asked by the secretary of war to help a commission examining suitable land for Indians emigrating from the East. Wanting to protect his own land claims and hopeful that the secretary would find favor with his efforts, Chouteau agreed. He escorted the commissioners, along with three distinguished gentleman—Washington Irving, Charles Joseph Latrobe, and the young Count de Pourtalès—to his trading house and home at La Saline.[55]

Despite Chouteau's hospitality, Washington Irving wrote about his stay in Chouteau's establishment with vicious humor. His account described a world that was partly Edenic paradise: "Came in sight of Cols house—white log house with Piazza, surrounded by trees. Come to beautiful, clear river, group of Indian nymphs half naked on banks—with horses near. . . . Group of Indians round tree in courtyard—roasting venison." The other part Irving saw was, in his view, a racial hell: "Half breeds, squaws, negro girls running and giggling—dogs of all kinds—hens flying and cackling—wild turkeys, tamed geese—Piazza with buffalo skin thrown over railing—room with guns—rifles." He commented particularly on Chouteau's family when the "half-breed-sister of Mr. Choteau's concubine" served them. The sight of Osage people living in the house made him uncomfortable. Irving described the foreignness of it all, "a hall in which Indians are seated on the floor—another Indian glares in at the window. . . . Half-breeds loitering about the house—dogs and cats of all kinds strolling about the hall or sleeping among harness at one end of the piazza."[56] Irving's vision, littered with descriptors like "squaw," "half-breed," "negroes," and "blacks," has the feel of a world gone culturally mad, with Indians inside, people and animals sleeping in inappropriate places, a sign of what happens when whites mix. The disorder of this place and time, in Irving's view, obviously needed re-ordering, indicating what might happen to A.P.'s racially complex family once the commissioners did their work.

A.P. knew his position was precarious. His personal and economic relationships with the Osages made him want to protect their interests, but he could not afford to alienate the U.S. government. When the commissioners met with the Osages at Fort Gibson in March 1833, eight hundred Osages and three Chouteaus discussed the options that the commissioners presented. Liguest Chouteau (A.P.'s brother) represented the Osages as their agent, August A. Chouteau (A.P.'s son) worked as interpreter for the meeting, and A. P. Chouteau furnished rations and served as negotiator. The commission, having surveyed the land, wanted Clermont's Osages to give up a large tract of land along the river and to trade it for a smaller and more remote piece. A.P. insisted that the Osages demand more land and bigger annuities. The commissioners blamed Chouteau for this uncooperative behavior and retaliated by refusing to help Chouteau's case to get payment for his claims against the government. This turn of events must have soured Chouteau's loyalty to the Osages, especially after a flood washed away all of his buildings along the Verdigris, along with the Creek agency and much of the Osage settlement, turning his paying customers into paupers.[57]

Not one to simply wait and hope, and having lost some faith in the government as a source of peace or income, Chouteau decided that he could no longer run a business among the removed and resettled Native nations and that he might find better prospects among the supposedly wild Indians of the southern plains. He left Rosalie and his younger children among their Osage family on land that had been granted to them legally, and with his two oldest sons headed west to build a new trading post. This choice had risks. The Kiowas and Pawnees were longtime enemies and rivals of the Osages. However, in August 1835, a "treaty of perpetual peace and friendship" was made between the newly removed "civilized tribes" that included the Osage, Cherokee, and Creek tribes on the Arkansas and the "wild Indians on the plains," primarily meaning the Pawnees and Wichitas. Though A.P. had lived in the Arkansas country long enough to know that perpetual peace was unlikely, he hoped that a temporary and merely tense detente might occur. His decision looked especially promising when Liguest Chouteau resigned as Osage agent, partnered with A.P., and brought several large bands of Osages to live near Chouteau's new fort.[58]

No decision is without its unintended consequences. A.P. became a marked man. First, the Comanches, the true lords of the southern plains who controlled all commerce and trade relationships south of the Arkansas and into Mexico, had noted his presence. They sent emissaries to explain their position, and A.P. decided to establish a different fort, further north and west, for the Kiowas who served as Comanche agents in the north. Second, the government and particularly the secretaries of war, had noted A.P.'s skills and reliable knowledge about Native people. Chouteau again became the "go-to" man for the U.S. government, this time serving as a treaty commissioner with the specific charge of getting the Comanches to come to the table. Another round of negotiations resulted in another treaty signed at Fort Gibson on May 26, 1837, by the Kiowa, Kiowa Apache, Comanche, Wichita, Cherokee, Creek, Choctaw, Osage, Seneca, and Quapaw nations. However, in spite of the recent treaties that all spoke of "perpetual peace," the treaty-making process had only served to bring old enemies into closer contact and to remind people of old grievances. That general bad mood, combined with the disruptions caused by the Texas Revolution, created a threat of general Indian warfare.[59]

In this emergency A. P. Chouteau was commissioned as special agent to the Comanches and Kiowas to prevent such hostilities. His charge involved traveling among these very hostile and very powerful Indians "to make peace" and to invite the Comanches and Kiowas to send a delegation to Washington in the spring of 1838. He and his son and two other interpreters traveled all winter, and by May Chouteau had visited twenty-two principal chiefs in eight different plains tribes. He reported to the commissioner of Indian Affairs that he gave the Indians presents, urged them to keep the peace, and told them he would meet them again at Camp Holmes in October.[60]

Exhausted and troubled by a wound in his thigh, A.P. returned to his Camp Holmes post only to find a new set of personal disasters. While he had acted as government agent, tour guide, and diplomat, his business had effectively ground to a halt. His debts, however, had continued to mount, and now a rain of trouble came down on A.P. from his family in St. Louis. In January 1838, because he was being sued for debts, Pierre Chouteau sued A.P. for $500,000, an unimaginable sum for the time. The courts reduced the sum to $66,000, an amount equally impossible for A.P. to manage. A.P. was summoned back to St. Louis to meet his creditors, but he refused to go. His St. Louis house and all its property, furnishings, and slaves were sold at public auction for $26,844.40 to satisfy the debt. Chouteau's St. Louis wife Sophie and their children had to move in with other family members. A.P. seemed surprisingly unconcerned about this last humiliation, but we have no record of how Sophie felt. He could see no other way to solve his financial problems, and he had turned his back on St. Louis long ago.[61]

His actions demonstrated his commitment to the Native people with whom he had spent his adult life. He had worked very hard to negotiate a treaty meeting with the Comanches and Kiowas and had promised to meet them at Camp Holmes. But A.P. never made it to Camp Holmes. Sick and tired, he went back to Rosalie and his family at La Saline, where he died on Christmas Day, 1838. He died as he lived, in debt, and his Osage family inherited nothing. He was honored with a full military funeral at Fort Gibson and was buried there, next to two other Chouteaus, his uncle Auguste and his cousin Pharamond.[62]

A.P. thought he had protected his family by getting them land in 1825, but that had been taken away in the treaty of 1835 with the Cherokees when the Osages gave up that territory. Rosalie Lambert and all of A.P.'s children had been awarded $15,000 for their eight sections of land. Seeing how risky owning land had become, Chouteau had decided to invest that money in the other sure thing in the early nineteenth century: he bought thirty-two valuable slaves from the Creeks who lived around La Saline. After A.P.'s death, most of the slaves disappeared into the small communities of their former masters, leaving Rosalie and the children living penniless at La Saline, land now belonging to the Cherokee nation. Chouteau's old friend Montfort Stokes, now the Cherokee agent, interceded on their behalf. He wrote to the commissioner of Indian Affairs about the injustice being done to this family. He noted that this was a "delicate subject" but then stated bluntly that no matter that it might be a "reproach on his character, almost all Traders who continue long in an Indian country have Indian wives." He went on to explain the entire tragic mess of their property and concluded that he "would not consent that these Half-Breed Reservees shall be wronged."[63] No one stepped up to right this wrong until 1843, when Rosalie and her three sons each got small payments, most of which went immediately to A.P.'s St. Louis creditors. Rosalie, however, took matters into her own hands. She and several of her children joined the Cherokee Nation that had title to the land surrounding La Saline. To make this safety net more secure, Rosalie married a Cherokee man, and then she disappears from our view. A.P.'s other wives, Rosalie's sisters, and their children stayed among the Osages as they made the long transition to settled reserve Indians.[64]

When A.P. died in 1838, the Creole-Native world had retreated in important ways. Several more generations of Chouteau family people would continue living in this culturally mixed world, but increasingly race mattered and was defined in ways unfamiliar to old St. Louisans. Fewer men, even those in the fur trade, married Indian women, and people of mixed race became marked with their race and began marrying each other because, though they were labeled as Indian, many tribal people did not recognize them as such. A series of new connections, loyalties, and ways of doing business would challenge the Chouteau empire, but Pierre (Cadet) Chouteau Jr. would manage those changes far better than his older brother A.P.

Pierre Chouteau Jr. created a fur-trading empire in the trans-Mississippi West from 1813 to 1865 as part of a very volatile trade. When his brother decided to leave St. Louis in 1822, Cadet began building a business that would outlast nearly everyone and make money in places where no one else could. These two brothers and their extended connections into Native nations demonstrate the significance of kinship in diplomacy and capital formation. Were they both anachronisms of an old trade that no longer mattered once the Euro-American residents of the United States migrated west? No, but the scope of the fur trade and the fact that the Chouteaus represented only one particular path through it suggests we need to look further at how the trade actually worked and how people found ways to live within it.

On the Trail of Wealth and Opportunity

The story of Margaret and Thomas Hereford, whose families linked St. Louis, Santa Fe, Chihuahua, New York, and Los Angeles, illustrates how an Anglo-American family worked in trade. It is no coincidence that they found family members and people they trusted everywhere. Anglo-Americans, just like Native Americans or French Creoles, recognized the utility of this system and accommodated to it. Trade depended on a tightly bound set of personal relationships. People living and trading in the region could not rely on armies or nations to protect their interests, so they built a world of linkages as business practice and safety net. These relationships—marriage, adoption, bondage, partnership, apprenticeship, and friendship—provided the glue that held this world together against the centrifugal forces of imperial rivalry and warfare.

The story of the Hereford/Sublette/Wilson clan describes a very different group of people from the fierce French traders of the Chouteau family. However, these Americans of a different generation used similar strategies to make and lose fortunes in the American West. When the widow Margaret Hereford agreed to marry Benjamin Davis Wilson in 1853, she joined together two families with deep connections to the world of trade, fur, and commerce that linked St. Louis to Los Angeles, via Santa

Fe and Chihuahua. These commercial empires competed directly with the Chouteaus. Her story, and that of her children, who became the last generation of Californios, began much earlier when the Sublettes moved to Missouri in 1817.

THE SUBLETTE BROTHERS AND THEIR FAMILY BUSINESS

The Sublettes could be the poster children for the opportunities and dangers of the fur trade. Echoing the restless patterns of a generation of Americans, Phillip Allen Sublette and Isabella Whitley Sublette took their eight children from Lincoln County, Kentucky, to St. Charles, Missouri, just north of St. Louis. Emblematic of a sector of American society that moved west every generation or so, their transiency reflected the desire to find more and better land and, especially in the 1810s, to escape financial disaster. The tide of movement crested in 1819 with a worldwide financial panic that ruined businesses, foreclosed farms, and sent people searching for fresh starts. The Sublettes, however, did not find instant success or happiness in Missouri. Phillip died in 1820 and Isabella barely a year later, leaving their eldest son, William, as head of the family. When William entered the fur trade in 1823, his siblings were scattered among various relatives. Most of the boys followed him into the fur trade, and their successes and failures illustrate the risks of that business. None of them survived into old age, but the five Sublette brothers touched every aspect of the fur and hide trades and participated in the most important cultural and political revolutions of the Far West before the Civil War as we see them marry, run for office, speculate in land, and head west.[65]

William Sublette, born in Kentucky in 1799, arrived in Missouri with his family in 1817, bought land with his father's help, and at the age of twenty became a town constable. His coming of age and a change in business practices and federal policy concerning the fur trade coincided handily. By the mid-1820s, the fur trade in the American West had stabilized into two major systems: the Rocky Mountain fur trade based on beaver pelts, Euro-American trappers, and overland systems of transportation, and the upper Missouri system that focused on bison hides hunted and processed by Native people and on the river networks of the upper Missouri for transportation. Both systems depended on Native labor and skill for their success, and they joined in St. Louis, which served as an international entrepôt for everyone in the trade.[66] The Sublette family specialized in the Rocky Mountain trade and the Chouteaus in the upper Missouri outfits, but they both experimented in the Santa Fe business as did all of their competitors.

The two major companies operating on the Missouri River in the first decades of the nineteenth century were the French Fur Company and the Missouri Fur Company. In 1802 Manuel Lisa had managed to wrest the coveted Osage contract away from the Chouteaus by promising the Spanish government he would build a flour mill and support the troops at the fort. Lisa didn't gain much advantage from his license because most Osages refused to deal with Lisa, but his action ignited a feud between Lisa and the Chouteaus, one that would shape the fur trade through the first decades of the nineteenth century. Partly it was personal, but partly it was a different vision of how trade should operate.[67]

Lisa's vision meshed with the new official presence of the United States, which began in 1804. The Americans had no intention of granting anyone any monopolies and clearly meant to continue with their system of government-run trading "factories." The War of 1812 destabilized the fur trade considerably and gave Americans (including, in this case, the Chouteaus) the opportunity to get into the trade as British traders were forced out of territory that was clearly on American soil. It had also ruined the tenuous partnership between the Chouteaus and Manuel Lisa, who had formed the Missouri Fur Company in 1808 and dissolved it in 1813. Out of the ashes of this business setback came two new companies: the French Fur Company and the Missouri Fur Company. The French Fur Company, managed by Bartholomew Berthold, Bernard Pratte, and Pierre Chouteau, had various names, but these cousins and brothers-in-law remained fully in control. This company relied on a network of Native people to trap animals, process their furs, and bring the packs of fur to a series of trading posts built near important Indian settlements and run by family members solidly intermarried with local tribes. The Missouri Fur Company, run by Manuel Lisa and then by Thomas Hempstead and Joshua Pilcher after Lisa's death in 1820, hoped to cash in on the rich areas inhabited by the Blackfoot by sending hunters beyond the reach of the Chouteau forts.[68]

These companies operated in the context of a highly regulated trade—at least by the standards of the early nineteenth century. The U.S. government paid a great deal of attention to the fur trade because of its commercial importance and political delicacy. No one wanted blundering Anglo-American migrants and hunters to touch off a war with Native nations or with the British. In 1806 Congress established the Office of Superintendent of Indian Trade within the War Department, which says something about the range of issues that worried government officials. This office replicated the old

British system that operated out of trading posts. Congress (and British Parliament before that) intended to take the task of dealing with Indian trade and land out of the hands of individual citizens. The goals were peace, safety, and unimpeded commerce. All traders wanting to participate in the fur trade needed a license from the superintendent of each district and had to work out of an official "factory." Anyone caught in Indian Country without a license was subject to the forfeiture of his goods, one half to go to the person prosecuting, one half to the U.S. government. Obviously such laws made little impression on the sea of illegal trading. Much to the frustration of businessmen like the Chouteaus or Manuel Lisa, British traders operated all over the Old Northwest and on the upper Missouri, and if challenged by American traders or officials, they just disappeared into Canada. Another huge problem was that these rules applied only to Indian Country, the region where the Indians still controlled their land, an often vague and indistinct line. Traders had little incentive to follow the rules. Too much money could be made in clandestine trade.[69]

The long-established venture run by the Chouteau family continued to do business as usual, but the family made sure that people who worked in the government factories had personal ties and obligations to the Chouteaus and their relatives. Their operatives became masters at apprehending illegal traders and confiscating their goods, thus providing a policing arm for the U.S. government, a service much appreciated when it was time to appoint agents and hand out licenses. Into this complicated, but potentially lucrative, situation came John Jacob Astor's American Fur Company. Astor had failed at his scheme to control the entire continent, including the Pacific Northwest, the Rocky Mountains, and the upper Missouri, because of the War of 1812 and its aftermath. However, Astor's St. Louis connection and right-hand man, Ramsey Crooks, had convinced him that controlling the Missouri River was essential to recovering from that loss and that marriage would provide the commercial link he needed. Ramsey Crooks married Bernard Pratte's daughter Emilie, sixteen years his junior, in 1823, just before he merged John Jacob Astor's American Fur Company with the French Fur Company. In 1826 what was now called Bernard Pratte and Company became an independent outfit of the American Fur Company and the sole supplier of all trade goods to the region reifying the Chouteaus near monopoly on the upper Missouri trade.[70]

Three events changed the fur trade in the early 1820s and opened it up for young men like the Sublettes. The conclusion of the Mexican Revolution and the creation of a new government in Mexico loosened

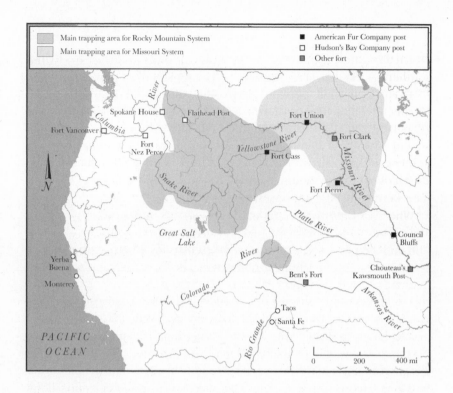

3. Missouri and Rocky Mountain Fur Trade, 1820–40

restrictions on trade and made the Santa Fe trade and trapping in the southern Rockies legal for Americans. The terrible doldrums of the Panic of 1819 began to let up, encouraging banks to give credit once again. Finally, similar to the moment of airline deregulation more than 150 years later, Congress decided to end the decades-old government-run system of Indian trading factories and to open the fur trade to private enterprise. Not everyone would have the capital or expertise to take up the challenge, though the Missouri papers reported at least "a thousand men were employed on the waters of the Missouri."[71]

When William Ashley, lieutenant governor of Missouri and a respected and wealthy trader, advertised for a hundred enterprising men to enter with him into this new phase of the fur trade, William and Milton Sublette, the two eldest brothers who had ambition but no cash, were eager to sign up. Because of the sudden new opportunities in the Santa Fe and Mexico trade and in the Missouri fur trade, young men all over the Missouri River valley could grab for the more real than usual brass rings. At the same moment that A. P. Chouteau abandoned life in St. Louis and took up trading with the Osages, William and Milton Sublette left their siblings and headed up the Missouri River.[72]

When William Sublette joined William Ashley's party on a hunting and trading expedition to the Yellowstone River in 1823, no one in St. Louis knew exactly what Ashley had planned. An old fur trade hand, Thomas Hempstead, expressed his concerns about this new way of doing business in a letter to his partner Joshua Pilcher. "Genl. Ashley's company starts this day with one boat and one hundred & fifty men by land and water they ascend the Missouri River to the Yellow Stone where they build a fort," he reported. With some distaste he noted that Ashley's employees were "all generally speaking untried and of evry description and nationality." He described the way that Ashley was running the business: "My opinions as regards the matter that those men are employed they are engaged in three different ways I am told the hunters and trappers are to have one half of the furs and they make the Company furnish them with Gun Powder, Lead etc., . . . the boat hands are engaged as we engage ours." He warned rather darkly that "this kind of business of making hunters will take some time and much trouble."[73] Hempstead was clearly worrying about Ashley's method of making hunters independent businessmen rather than employees. The notion of hiring the young men to hunt on their own, without relying on Native hunters or guides, struck Hempstead as dangerous.

Hempstead was right; the fur-trading season was a bloody one that year.

Joshua Pilcher's party from the Missouri Fur Company ran into trouble with the Blackfoot as soon as they got north of the Missouri. In May 1823, five trappers were killed, all of their horses and pelts were lost, and so too were the hopes of the Missouri Fur Company on the upper river. Joshua Pilcher wrote later: "This our second adventure to the mountains had surpassed my most sanguine expectations; success was complete, and my views were fulfilled in every respect . . . but now the flower of my business is gone; my mountaineers have been defeated, and the chiefs of both parties slain."[74] Pilcher blamed the British for the killing. Furious over the situation, Indian agent Benjamin O'Fallon wrote to his uncle, William Clark, comparing the British traders to wolves: "They ravage our fields and are unwilling that we glean them. . . . Alarmed at the individual interprise of our people, they are exciting the Indians against them. They furnish them with the instruments of death and a passport to our bosoms . . . and the scalps of our men are now bleeding on their way to the British trading establishments."[75]

Whether or not the British had incited them, the Native nations on the Missouri clearly had little patience with the fur traders that year. Ashley's expedition followed a similar pattern. The trip went well until the group passed Fort Atkinson, where the relationship with the Indians deteriorated rapidly. The Indians didn't like the new free enterprise system and the wave of trappers and traders who would displace them as hunters. Ashley's expedition was the biggest one to arrive that season, and they were immediately attacked by the Arikaras. However, with the support of six companies of the U.S. Army, Ashley's traders retaliated two months later and defeated the Indians in a very controversial battle. This victory, however, could only be described as a Pyrrhic one, as it engendered at least two decades of warfare with the tribes on the Missouri. William Sublette served as brevet sergeant major in the altercation and learned a great deal about fur trade diplomacy.[76]

Because the Missouri River nations made it impossible for traders to venture up the river, the entire focus of the trade shifted south and west. Sublette spent the next two years trapping in the northern Rockies, ending up at the 1825 rendezvous on the Green River, where he once again met up with Ashley. This gathering in the central Rocky Mountains provided the model for the next several decades as the trade experimented with an entirely transient system. Companies of various sizes would contract with individual trappers, buying furs from them in the summer and providing them with supplies to hunt through the winter. This meant no one had to go to the expense of building and maintaining trading posts, but big operators had to figure out ways to get huge amounts of supplies into the Rocky Mountains and furs back to St. Louis without any rivers to assist them.

Solving these logistical problems and assessing how many goods and how much to charge for them turned out to be William Sublette's gift. He impressed Ashley with his ideas about how to organize the business and how to solve the problem of supplies for trappers in the field so much that Ashley put him in charge of planning the entire expedition in 1825. In 1826 Ashley transferred his entire business to Jedediah Smith, David E. Jackson, and William Sublette. Sublette spent the next three years organizing supply trains and rendezvous and then supervised the dangerous task of getting the furs, horses, and wagons back to St. Louis. Sublette did introduce some efficient practices into the trade, but it remained extraordinarily dangerous. In 1829, as part of a petition for an increased military presence, Sublette made a tally of the human, animal, and material costs of the trade between 1823 and 1829 and noted that from his company alone 95 men, 480 horses, and $43,500 worth of goods had been lost to Indian raids.[77]

We don't know much about Sublette's relationships with Native people. As one of the elite administrators of the enterprise, William accompanied the supply trains to each year's rendezvous site, but he didn't usually spend his winters in the field. Sublette never wrote about his activities at those month-long gatherings of mountain men and Native people that still fire the imaginations of re-enactors in the present, but other people certainly described theirs. Sublette did claim to have honorary tribal membership with the Omahas and Crows, he allowed Native people to camp at his farm, and he is reported to have buried Native people there. Even in this more transient version of the trade, Native people still played important roles. Several analyses of marriage patterns demonstrate that a majority of trappers did marry Indian women or women of mixed race because of the enormous advantages it gave them in terms of finding fur and in domestic comforts. This pattern extended to the upper echelon of the trade as well; William Ashley had at least three Native partners and didn't marry an Anglo-American woman until he had political ambitions and had left the fur trade world. William Sublette may well have had fleeting or much longer relationships, but we may never know.[78]

While William spent his time organizing the trade in the central Rockies, his brother Milton headed further south where he became one of the most renowned of the early Anglos trapping in the Southwest. Milton achieved his first notoriety in 1826–27 when his trapping party fought off a group of Mojave Indians near the Gila River, continued along the San Juan River into what is now Colorado, and then followed the Colorado and Platte rivers to the site of present-day Denver, fighting off an attack of Blackfoot warriors. Eventually, they returned to Santa Fe with a huge cache of furs, which aroused the attention of the officials in Santa Fe. Every member of the party had his furs confiscated, except for Milton, who walked away with a handsome profit—and the clear understanding that he had best stay away from hunting in Mexican territory. He, of course, ignored this imposition of Mexican law and joined an expedition headed up by Ceran St. Vrain, which began in Taos but moved to the Platte River.[79]

Here the party ran into trouble with an Arapaho hunting party, and one of the Anglo-American trappers, soon to be known as "Peg-Leg" Smith, was shot through the ankle. Milton Sublette got the unenviable job of amputating the foot. After this unfortunate event, Milton decided that he had done enough trapping, and he managed to round up a herd of twelve hundred horses (which meant stealing them from someone else), hoping to sell them in St. Louis. He lost half the herd when they were driven off by a Comanche party and finally arrived in St. Louis in late 1829, where he went to work for his brother William. Milton would eventually become a partner in the Rocky Mountain Fur Company. They had several near disasters, lost a lot of men—including their younger brother Pinckney—to Indian attacks and to disease but made enough money to make it worthwhile. The company competed directly with Pierre Chouteau Jr., and indirectly with John Jacob Astor, for supplies, men, and funding.[80]

William Sublette, however, recognized that the increased competition in the fur trade industry could destroy his profits in a heartbeat. He made a foray into the Santa Fe trade in 1831 and decided that it was too personally and financially risky. He wrote to William Ashley upon his return that he was "not pleased with the country or the business."[81] In 1832 he agreed to prepare the supply train for his brother Milton's company and to lead it to their rendezvous that summer. We have a description of William that year, from his application for a passport to travel in Mexican territory. With blue eyes, Roman nose, straight forehead, conventional chin, and brown hair and standing at six feet two inches, William seemed to be a man in his prime, but after several serious skirmishes with the Blackfoot on his return trip, which included an arrow in his own arm, he felt battered. William decided that the way to survive in the fur trade was to operate out of permanent forts, but to do that he would have to compete directly with the Chouteaus.[82]

Sublette

Isabella Whitley (1774–1827) m. Phillip Allen Sublette (1774–1820)
____William Lewis Sublette (1799–1845) m. Frances Hereford (1821–1857) – – – – – – ┐
____Milton Sublette (1801–1837)
____Polly Sublette (1807–1845)
____Sophronia Sublette (1808–1843)
____Sally Sublette (1810–1821)
____Pinckney Sublette (1812–1828)
____Andrew Sublette (1814–1853)
____Solomon Sublette (1816–1857) m. Frances Hereford (1821–1857) – – – – – – – – ┐ ┊
        └___ Fanny Sublette (1851–1860)   ┊ ┊

Hereford

Esther Sale Hereford (1804–1873) m. (1819) Dr. Thomas S. Hereford (1797–1844)   ┊ ┊
____1. Margaret Sale Hereford (1820–1898) m. (1842) Dr. Thomas A. Hereford   ┊ ┊
   │ (1818–1852) (Margaret's first cousin)   ┊ ┊
   └__ Edward Sublette Hereford (1843–1913)   ┊ ┊
   ___ Mary Catherine Hereford (b. 1828)   ┊ ┊
   ___ 1. Frances Hereford (1821–1851) m. (1844) William Lewis Sublette (1799–1845)
   ___ 2. Frances Hereford (1821–1851) m. (1849) Solomon Sublette (1816–1857)┘
        └___Fanny Sublette (1851–1860)
   ___ Esther Medora Hereford (1840–1862)
   └___ Thomas S. Hereford (1838–1859)

 2. Margaret Sale Hereford (1820–1873) m. (1853) Benjamin Davis Wilson (1811–1878)
____Margaret (Maggie) Wilson (1854–1857)   ┊
____Annie Wilson (b. 1858)   ┊
└___Ruth Wilson (b. 1861)   ┊

Wilson and Yorba

Bernardo Yorba (1801–1858) m. Maria Jesús Alvaro (b. 1809)   ┊
└___Ramona Yorba (1829–1849) m. (1843) Benjamin Davis Wilson (1811–1878)   ┊
   ___ María Jesús Yorba Wilson (1844–1917)   ┊
   └___Juan Bernardo Wilson (1846–1870)   ┊

Benjamin Davis Wilson (1811–1878) m. (1853) Margaret Sale Hereford (1820–1898)___┘
____Margaret (Maggie) Wilson (1854–1857)
____Annie Wilson (b. 1858)
└___Ruth Wilson (b. 1861)

8. Sublette and Hereford/Wilson/Yorba family trees.
Compiled by Leá Norcross.

Having once again dodged a literal arrow, Sublette decided to get a license to enter the Indian trade from the federal government, and he built Fort William at the junction of the Missouri and Yellowstone rivers. He could make a profit and protect his men only by approaching two different kinds of powers, eastern capitalists and the powerful Blackfoot. In doing so, he knew he had thrown down the gauntlet to direct competition with John Jacob Astor's American Fur Company, which had just joined forces with the Chouteaus. Sublette was apparently seen as a worthy foe, and the two companies negotiated a division of the fur trade territory in meetings in New York in the winter of 1834. Sublette would cede the upper Missouri to Astor's (about to become Chouteau's) American Fur Company and in return would have a free hand to operate south of the Missouri River.[83]

Selling out while ahead is always a good move. With his profits, William bought eight hundred acres of land just west of St. Louis and intended to settle down and become a gentleman farmer on the farm he called Sulphur Springs. He ordered up exotic flower bulbs, built a large stone house, began several courtships, and corresponded with his friends about the joys of the settled life. He followed the pattern that most men in the fur trade did: after a decade or so in the trade and the constant movement it required, trappers and traders settled on land with their families or opened small stores or trading posts in the regions they had worked. William Sublette just did the same thing on a larger scale, and his scattered brothers often joined him there. In the fall of 1833 Milton stayed on William's St. Louis farm to be treated by Dr. Bernard Farrar for an inflammation in his foot. He still suffered from the effects of the arrow wound he received during the 1826 Gila River trapping trip with Peg-Leg Smith. Despite his best efforts to save it, Dr. Farrar had to amputate Milton's foot in February 1835.[84]

Even an amputation didn't stop Milton from venturing into the field. The scarcity of furs had convinced many of the big operators to get out of the business. In 1836, seeing that trading might not be profitable but not wanting to sit around the farm with William, Milton switched gears and agreed to lead the first major Oregon-bound emigrant train—the Whitman-Spaulding Party. He didn't make it all the way to Oregon but eventually succumbed to the infection in his leg while resting at Fort William. The *Missouri Republican* announced Milton's death in 1837, describing him as the "Thunderbolt of the Rocky Mountains."[85]

At this point, William understood that the fur trade had changed forever, and so he invested in St. Louis real estate, built a store selling "Indian goods" with Nathaniel Wyeth in St. Louis, and set up his younger brother

Solomon in a store in western Missouri. William, now spending most of his time at Sulphur Springs, got involved in politics. A protégé of Senator Thomas Hart Benton, he was appointed to the board of the new Bank of the State of Missouri. He ran for the state senate in 1838 but lost. He continued to be very interested in farming and experimented with seeds and hybrids, à la Thomas Jefferson. William imported pedigreed short-horned cattle from England and won prizes at local agricultural shows. He developed a menagerie of buffalo, deer, antelope, bear, and wild birds that Solomon had brought back from his trips along the Arkansas. He had a full complement of slaves and hired hands to work the fields, and his sister, Sophronia, served as his housekeeper.[86]

William never seemed satisfied. He continued to develop the farm, building cottages and a hotel for visitors who might benefit from the therapeutic waters. He also added a racetrack and a bowling alley, both illegal in St. Louis but permitted in the county, as other attractions. In the midst of all this activity he continued to correspond with old fur trade friends planning the perfect final expedition. In 1842 he wrote to Sir William Drummond Stewart, a Scottish lord who had made several trips west with William as guide, that he had just seen "the prettiest opening in the Indian trade that a man could wish and if I had of had the wherewith you would have seen me on the headwaters of the Platte this winter."[87] But he just didn't seem willing to risk the stability he had built, and he enjoyed having a place for his large extended family to gather. The farm seemed to cost him more money than it made until William leased the springs to a Dr. Thomas A. Hereford, an Alabama physician, to run it.[88]

Hereford arrived with his extended family in 1842. Hereford's second wife, Ester Sale, was a Sublette cousin, which gave the arrangement a family connection. In addition to the relief of having someone else deal with the details of the large farm, spa, and resort, William found the eldest daughter, Frances S. Hereford, very attractive, and the two married in 1844. He barely beat out his brother Andrew for Miss Hereford's hand and only proposed when Andrew threatened to "take up the cause if you don't speak up soon." He told his older brother bluntly to "either strike or give up the hammer." So, William finally struck.[89]

Before settling down with Frances, however, William took one more trip west, a pleasure trip with Sir William Drummond Stewart, planned as a sort of farewell tour of the fur trade. His old friend Albert Boone warned him against taking the trip, writing that William should "prefer marrying her to all the Sir Wm stewarts and Mountaineers and Buffalows this world ever produced," but Sublette couldn't disappoint Stewart.[90] The group attended the rendezvous on the Green River after spending most of the summer in Wyoming, but the annual gathering was disappointingly small. The trip, though leisurely and pleasant, seemed to have broken William's health. He may have had tuberculosis and complained about his symptoms quite regularly to his family at home. He was worried enough about his business and his health that on New Year's Day in 1844 he wrote a will that left his property to his remaining brothers, Solomon and Andrew, but also to Frances S. Hereford, his "estimed female friend and future wife."[91] He died only eighteen months later, while he and Frances were traveling to Cape May, New Jersey, in an effort to improve his health. He left his wife Frances and a lot of property in the care of Solomon and Andrew.[92]

These two younger Sublette brothers entered the trade in its waning years, as beaver were increasingly trapped out, and as even buffalo hides grew scarce. Their career paths took them all over the trans-Mississippi West in a pattern very typical for the time. Andrew Sublette began his fur trade career in 1830 as part of his brother William's trade caravan to the Wind River Mountains. He worked for several of his brother Milton's enterprises in Santa Fe and operated keelboats on the upper Missouri. In 1835 he started his own firm, Sublette and Vasquez, which specialized more in buffalo hides, but he entered the trade too late, and competition from other enterprises soon had the business deeply in debt. In 1840 he retreated to William's farm and took on its management, though he was hardly suited to be a business manager. Finally, in 1844, after falling in love with the woman his brother would marry, Andrew escaped the farm. He agreed to guide a group of Catholic missionaries to Fort Laramie in what is now Wyoming. After getting his charges to Fort Laramie, he went south to Bent's Fort, hoping to meet up with Solomon, his youngest brother, and to re-enter the Santa Fe trade.[93]

This constant movement was not unusual for young men in that age and place, but after William's death Andrew felt rudderless. He returned home to help Frances settle up the estate but quickly grew restless. As it did for so many young men in the spring of 1847, the Mexican War gave him some direction. Andrew eagerly volunteered with a group of friends who called themselves the Sublette Rangers. They only went as far as Fort Kearny, where they spent the war repairing the old fort, and Andrew left the army when the war ended in 1848 without seeing any battle duty.[94]

Solomon, the youngest Sublette son, born in 1816, got a better education than his brothers, and in 1836 his brother William offered to set him up in business in a clothing store in Independence, Missouri. He clerked for a relative in a St. Louis store for a while and then headed west to choose a location and to stock his own store. However, the Panic of 1837 and his own bad management gutted his business and made it impossible to repay William, so he simply left, becoming an itinerant mule trader. William bailed him out again, this time setting him up to operate in the Santa Fe trade in 1839. William could have taken some lessons from the tough-love school in the Chouteau family as he spent huge sums on both of his younger brothers and supported his sisters and their families at his farm for years. Solomon spent three years crisscrossing the trail, trading and trapping with his brother Andrew between 1840 and 1843. Once again, he and Andrew found themselves in debt. He wrote to William to "get some assistance," but we hear some testiness between the brothers in his words: "You requested to know the reason of my remaining here so long while so many had been down. To acknowledge the truth I had no means."[95]

Solomon wandered as far west as Fort Laramie in 1843 and decided to take up trading on the upper Arkansas in 1844. Instead of heading to Santa Fe (and selling his furs so that he might repay his debts to William) after a season of trapping and trading on the Arkansas, Solomon went into the Colorado Rockies to gather and capture sheep and antelope to send to William's farm in Missouri. In the fall of 1844 he met up with Andrew at Bent's Fort. The two brothers, recognizing how far in debt they both were to William, headed in different directions in 1845 in an attempt to make some money. Solomon went to California, reaching Sutter's Fort in November of 1845. He spent seven months in California surveying possibilities in land and livestock but concluded that he couldn't get into a trade there without any capital, and as he wrote to William, he "missed his family friends."[96]

That winter Solomon received word that William had died in July of 1845, and he headed home to help with family affairs—and to make sure he received what he deserved from William's estate. He arrived in Missouri in September of 1846 to learn that he had been freed of all debts in William's will. Both he and Andrew were now the proud owners of sizeable pieces of land along the Missouri River, St. Louis town lots, a herd of prize cattle, and William's favorite gun. Andrew, still mourning over his love for Frances, never returned to Missouri after the Mexican War, and late in 1848, ahead of most of the gold rushers, he went to California, where he worked in the southern California placer mines and was appointed sheriff of the District of San Francisco. He died in 1853.[97]

Solomon, however, stayed in Missouri for a while but managed to blow through most of his inheritance. In early 1847 he announced his intention to travel to Santa Fe. He also began courting his brother William's widow, Frances. He returned to Missouri when he was appointed the Indian agent to the Sac and Fox Indians on the upper Mississippi. Solomon had been angling for such an appointment for several years from his brother's old friend Thomas Hart Benton, but he wanted to deal with a more familiar Missouri River tribe. Solomon did marry Frances in May of 1848, but he resigned his commission to make another go at the Santa Fe trade with his new brother-in-law, Thomas Hereford. Solomon and Thomas made several trips to Santa Fe and one to Chihuahua before they concluded that the travel was too taxing and the profits too low to continue in that business. Both men had small children and family demands. Solomon retired to his family farm at Sulphur Springs, where his son died an early death and Frances continued to be in poor health after the birth of two more children. They both died in 1857, with only a small estate to pass on to their children, despite the fortunes that Solomon and his brothers had made and lost.[98]

Chasing Fortune and Family

The Sublette family illustrated the scope of the fur trade in the American West and the kinds of risks and opportunities it offered during its heyday between 1810 and 1840. The trade linked all kinds of people and introduced them to huge areas of the western landscape. The story of Margaret Sale Hereford Wilson follows the last phase of the fur trade, as it evolved from resource extraction to a more complex and varied business. It also demonstrates the continuing significance of political instability and the strategies families used to protect themselves against national growing pains. Margaret Sale Hereford Wilson and her two husbands, Thomas Hereford and Benjamin Wilson, would follow a trajectory that would take them all over what would become the United States and Mexico, but they would rarely be separated from their economically ambitious and interconnected families. Margaret, Thomas, and Benjamin (often known as B.D.) wrote letters to each other and to other family members throughout their lives, giving us a view into their experiences of the region's transition from Indian Country, Spain, Mexico, and finally the United States. Like the Chouteaus, this family also prospered as they maneuvered around business cycles, wars, gold rushes, rebellions, and changes in national control. Racial and ethnic identity came to be vexed questions for them as well.

9. Margaret Sale Hereford Wilson. Photograph, 1874. This item is reproduced by permission of *The Huntington Library, San Marino, California.*
(photCL 283 (12)).

This photograph, taken when Margaret was in her mid-fifties, shows a beautifully dressed but careworn woman who crossed the continent several times, married twice, and bore, raised, and lost children. Margaret's choices and actions linked families across cultural lines and national borders.

Born in 1820 and raised in Alabama, Margaret moved to St. Louis with her family in 1840. Her mother, Esther Sale, a Sublette family cousin, had married the widower Dr. Thomas Hereford in Alabama, and the whole blended family moved to Missouri. The Hereford family had leased the resort facilities at Sulphur Springs, the large Sublette family farm in St. Louis, in 1842. Keeping things in the family, Margaret married her first cousin, also Dr. Thomas A. Hereford, who had accompanied the extended family in their move to Missouri.[99] Arriving in St. Louis about the time A.P Chouteau died at La Saline, Dr. Thomas Hereford Jr. represented a new wave of American entrepreneurs, hoping to get in on the booming growth in the Mississippi River valley. In many ways, his story is far more typical—and far less successful—than any of the Sublette brothers. Trained as a medical doctor like his father, but deciding to become a merchant in these booming times, Hereford hitched his fortune to the Sublettes, one of the important trading families of St. Louis. The Herefords and the Sublettes would be connected by various marriages. Margaret's sister Frances was married to William Sublette in 1844 and then to Solomon Sublette in 1848. Margaret and Thomas had a son, Edward Sublette Hereford, in October of 1843.[100]

Now working for the Sublette family, Thomas made the first of his many moves, ever hopeful of cashing in on the western flow of people and goods. The young Hereford family moved first to Wisconsin in 1844, but the lumber business proved to be dull and the climate hard on Thomas's health.[101] After William Sublette's death in 1845, the Herefords decided to move their family to Independence, Missouri, now an important outfitting point for the trail to California, Oregon, and Santa Fe. Trade in the 1840s looked very different because of its variety. Fur still mattered, but trade goods, farming implements, cloth, and cash mattered more. Uncertainty and optimism characterized many men of Thomas's generation and class in the mid-nineteenth century, and the most uncertain of those seemed to be gathering in Missouri.

By late 1846 preparations for the Mexican War brought commercial possibilities to places like Independence as soldiers and volunteers amassed in Missouri River frontier towns, eager for war. Thomas reported to Margaret about his purchases in St. Louis: "I have been actively engaged in making my purchases for the upper country. I have bought five wagons, five head of horses and harnesses, a lot of oysters sardines, etc." He added with a touch of pride, "I have bought myself a handsome coat and I think after my return we will be able to shine with the elite of Independence."[102]

Thomas, ever optimistic that fortune lay just around corner, never actually found it, which made him like many men in the trans-Mississippi West, a hopeful failure. However, unlike most men, he had access to the capital, connections, and experience of the Sublette family.

Business in Independence did not go as well as Thomas or his employer, Solomon Sublette, had hoped. Seemingly unworried about the war, or perhaps hoping to take advantage of it, Thomas decided to go into business in the soon-to-be "American" Santa Fe. Suffering from some stomach ailment, he decided to go alone first, in the spring of 1847, in hopes of improving his health. His letters describe fear of Indian attacks and a very unsettled situation in Santa Fe. Margaret, stuck at her parent's house in St. Louis with little Eddy, reported that she was reading Josiah Gregg's *Commerce of the Prairies* so that she would understand what Thomas was experiencing. She also reminded him that he had promised "to bring little Sonny a Spanish pony." Meanwhile, Thomas set up shop in Santa Fe, selling everything he brought with him from St. Louis. He reported that selling liquor by the dram was extremely profitable because of all the soldiers in Santa Fe that summer of 1847, but that the cattle he had brought were a complete loss because they had either died or become emaciated and unsalable during the last part of the trip.[103]

Like many other Americans who hoped to find new opportunities in Santa Fe, Thomas was surprised at the disorder, and lack of hard cash, in the newly conquered city. He also reported, with shock and disgust, that many of the other American merchants and even Army officers were taking up with Mexican women. "To me it is perfectly disgusting," he wrote, assuring his wife that he could never consider such depraved activities and that "your virtues are only brightened by the distance and a separation like this could not be made by any other motives than those which drove me from the bosom of my family and relations, the pursuit of health and fortune."[104] Santa Fe did offer business opportunities, as it had been an important trading point linking Mexico with the United States. War and conquest gave American citizens with capital instant access to the rich trade in goods and silver coming out of northern Mexico. And it was a vibrant place in a foreign country, where a man like Thomas saw women gambling, setting themselves up with American soldiers, and hosting dances.

Perhaps worried about such temptations, or perhaps because business had been good, Thomas returned to Missouri in early 1848, gathered up his wife and son, and moved the whole family to Santa Fe. Always surrounded by family, the Herefords were accompanied by Thomas's sister Frances

Hereford Sublette, the widow of William Sublette, and by Solomon Sublette, who was now courting the available widow. Solomon and Thomas had made several trips to Santa Fe, but now decided to take their families with them. Ever impatient and hoping for a better "situation," Thomas began trading in Chihuahua, Mexico, where lots of Americans seemed to be making their fortunes. After several visits, he convinced Margaret that he would really settle in Chihuahua and take up medical practice, and she agreed to pack up and to head south. This included the now four-year-old Edward, who, Margaret reported to her mother, was "quite well and is growing fatter every day."[105] At this point, Solomon and Frances, now married and with one young child, had decided that Santa Fe and its opportunities did not offer enough enticement to move away from their families, and they headed back to Missouri, where they settled at the farm in Sulphur Springs.

Predictably, given Thomas's track record, Chihuahua did not seem to need more doctors or more merchants, and Thomas found its climate challenging for his own health. Like many people in Mexico, Santa Fe, and the West, the Herefords now decided to try their luck in California. Margaret, clearly testy over Thomas's constant moving, wrote to her mother in St. Louis: "I expected when I last wrote you to have been on my way home by this time, but I am again disappointed." She explained further: "Dr. Hereford has determined to go to California and I am going with him as there is no alternative." Margaret obviously hoped that, finally, the easy wealth in California might give them a chance to make some money and settle down. As Margaret noted rather acidly, given their recent adventures and failures, "The Doctor is too poor not to avail himself of the opportunity."[106] So, like many other people that year, the Herefords headed to California. Thomas sold all of his medical equipment and his other goods and invested in mules.

Though no one mentions the gold rush in these letters, surely this was the lure of California in March of 1850. Of course, several of the Sublette clan had been among the first American arrivals in California after the gold rush so they had already established a family network there. Dutiful wife that she was, Margaret, along with Eddy, traveled with Thomas's mule train loaded with goods as far as Mazatlan, and then she and Eddy took a ship to San Francisco. Thomas followed, hoping to sell the mules and the goods they carried to eager miners in California. In June of 1850 Margaret and Eddy were met by Andrew Sublette, now the sheriff of San Francisco County, who helped them find a place to live. Though she had cousins in Sacramento and a sister-in-law in Los Angeles, Margaret didn't feel at all safe until Thomas arrived, but that took him nearly six months. His trip, like that of so many others hoping to get rich quick, did not go smoothly at all. The mules got sick, the weather was bad, the cousin who accompanied him left. He wrote to Margaret in June of 1850, "If I can only reach California safely with the mules and make a few thousand dollars by the operation I will feel satisfied with my fortune. But if I had money I would not undergo this trip again for $20,000."[107]

Thomas did arrive and did make a little money from the mules, but unable to settle any place for very long, he decided to bring the family to Los Angeles. Again, he relied on the family network. Margaret's cousin, Andrew Sublette, had connected with an old friend from his Santa Fe trading days who owned a lot of property and needed help running a big merchandising enterprise. We next hear from the family in San Pedro, California, where Thomas now managed a freighting business along with Margaret's brother, in the spring of 1851. He notified his new employer, Mr. B. D. Wilson, that he and his family had arrived. He reported with some pride that "Margaret is well satisfied and has never spoken of wanting to return." Margaret showed less enthusiasm when she told her mother that their rented rooms in San Pedro were "in such filth and confusion that I cannot say when I will be prepared to live in any comfort."[108]

Typically for Hereford and for so many men like him in California during those years, none of his endeavors ever achieved much financial success. However, he chose an excellent local business partner, Benjamin Davis Wilson, who owned property all over Los Angeles and who served, in 1851, as mayor of Los Angeles. Thomas's peripatetic movement and poor health finally caught up with him, and he died on January 7, 1852, in San Pedro. His new business partner, B. D. Wilson, witnessed Thomas's will and found a place for his widow and young son, noting for the record that "Hereford resided, at and immediately before his death, at the house of B. D. Wilson, a merchant, aged 40."[109]

AMERICANS IN MEXICO, CALIFORNIOS IN AMERICA

The very same B. D. Wilson had quite a history in the region, and meeting him would change the fortunes of Margaret Sale Hereford, now a widow with a young child. Davis was a man much in the mold of William Sublette and René Auguste Chouteau, having made the transition from fur trapper and diplomat with Indian tribes to landowner and businessman. Unlike Thomas Hereford, who was a much more typical failure at busi-

10. Benjamin Davis Wilson. Photograph, 1855. This item is reproduced by permission of *The Huntington Library, San Marino, California.* (photCL Pierce 08212).

Wilson, born in Tennessee to a struggling but literate family, became a sort of western Horatio Alger. With luck and pluck, Wilson made fortunes in fur, freight, land, and wine, largely because of his choices in marriage. This photograph captures him as he entered politics as a state senator.

ness, Benjamin Davis Wilson was a stunning success, though it took him a long time. He had several careers, setbacks, and families that reflect the experience of a generation of men who played on the edge of frontiers amid imperial intrigue.

Like Margaret and Thomas Hereford, Benjamin Davis Wilson was also an educated southerner. He was born in Tennessee in 1811 and began his business life as an Indian trader with the Choctaws and Chickasaws. He gradually moved west and followed the peripatetic path of so many young men in the 1830s living in Missouri. Just like the Sublettes, B.D. joined a trapping party and found himself in Santa Fe in 1833. Part of the large and roving group of trappers who trapped furs illegally in Mexican territory, Wilson spent a lot of time around the Gila River and learned to speak Spanish, Apache, and other Native languages.[110]

He found life as a trapper dangerous and unprofitable and joined the growing number of American entrepreneurs who were becoming merchants in Santa Fe. He worked as a clerk for Josiah Gregg, famous as the author of *Commerce of the Prairies,* selling the items brought with such difficulty from St. Louis, but eventually went into business for himself. Though Santa Fe became more open to Euro-American traders and merchants after 1821, Americans in particular who had capital and connections to succeed where Native New Mexicans couldn't were treated with a certain distrust. The Texas Revolution and the loss of Texas made Mexican officials justifiably suspicious after 1836. After a completely failed effort on the part of a group of Texans to stage a coup in New Mexico, American merchants in Santa Fe became targets of suspicion and, finally, Wilson recalled, real anger. He and many other Anglo traders chose to leave New Mexico in a group in the fall of 1841 and ended up in southern California.[111]

His timing was perfect: the fur business soon came to end because the beaver had been entirely trapped out by the end of the 1830s. The trickle of trappers coming to California seeking a new livelihood became an important source of commerce as trappers evolved into mule traders, wagon train leaders, and Indian traders. Eventually, under Mexican law, some of these foreigners became naturalized citizens, obtained land, established businesses, and married into prominent California families.[112]

Wilson followed that pattern exactly: he first set himself up as a mule trader, next opened a store in Los Angeles, and then became a *ranchero,* or cattle rancher, by buying the Jurupa ranch in 1843. He completed the cycle by marrying Ramona Yorba, the daughter of the very wealthy Don Bernardo Yorba, one of the owners of the vast Santa Ana Ranch. This marriage gave him new legal rights around land ownership and the ability to participate in politics. And, just as Thomas Hereford's marriage gave him access to the Sublette family network, B.D. had now become allied with one of the most important families in southern California. Wilson, now known as Don Benito, became a Californio—that group of Mexicans and Anglos who thought of themselves as Californians rather than Mexicans or Americans.[113]

Though he insisted later in life that he had never become a Mexican citizen, Wilson certainly behaved as if he were. He raised cattle and sheep, he served with the Mexican military, and he held the office of *alcalde*, or justice of the peace. Now part of the Yorba family, he had power and economic clout in Los Angeles and gained the respect of his neighbors. B.D. and Ramona's children, Maria Jesús and Juanito, spoke Spanish and participated in the Catholic traditions of their Yorba relatives. Looking back nearly forty years later, Wilson remembered an idyllic world in which "there were no courts, no juries, no lawyers, nor any need for them . . . people were honest and hospitable, and their word was as good as their bond."[114] Given that he would spend the last decades of his life in government positions and in fighting the state of California to hold onto his land, a world without lawyers and courts would be glorious indeed.

When the news of American conquest came, no one in Los Angeles knew what that might mean. For Wilson and his family, adjusting to the new order had some bumpy spots as new categories like Mexican and American had to be worked out. We can only imagine how Ramona Yorba Wilson now worried about her children, their future, and the coming new order. She gave birth to their second child, Juanito, while Don Benito was in prison. Wilson declared himself an American early on but attempted to lessen the tension between the two groups. He remembered tension beginning when "the so-called 'Bear Party' seized Sonoma, making prisoners of some of the officers residing there. The news of these events caused general uneasiness in this part of the country."[115] Uneasiness devolved into distrust and fear, as diplomatic jockeying became military occupation and war.[116]

With the actual conquest in 1848, Don Benito Wilson had to make some choices that made him uncomfortable. He explained, "I was still discharging the duties of Alcalde, or Justice of the Peace, in my district, when I received a communication from the governor, asking my most active cooperation to raise forces wherewith to repel the invaders. I replied that I most respectfully declined, being an American citizen and not a military man. I was menaced with arrest." Feeling threatened, he sent word to the governor that though he would not serve in the Mexican militia, he would resist arrest, and he promised that if the governor would not arrest him, he would "remain quietly on my ranch. . . . I would pledge my word to be peaceable and do no act hostile to the country." He noted that this position of neutrality seemed to have been satisfactory, as he heard nothing more from Mexican officials and Los Angeles politicians "until Commodore Stockton arrived, with his squadron in San Pedro Bay, when I received a private friendly note from Governor Pico requesting me to come and see him." Pico asked Wilson to deliver a message to Stockton saying that Pico had left for Sonora, Mexico, and further that Pico earnestly hoped that Stockton and the Americans "would not ill-treat my people."[117]

Wilson continued to play a go-between role as Los Angeleños adjusted to their new status as Americans. Naturally, this adjustment was far easier for an American citizen who spoke English, and who was immediately made a captain in the U.S. Army. Despite his new status, Wilson remained loyal to his Californio friends and family. The first military commander in Los Angeles, Lieutenant Archibald Gillespie, turned out to be, in Wilson's words, "despotic and in every way unjustifiable." In fact, local people in Los Angeles routed, deposed, and imprisoned Gillespie almost immediately after he took command, an episode the U.S. officials found intensely embarrassing. Wilson made it clear that he would not tolerate poor behavior on the part of Americans and that he would not bear arms against his neighbors. In his view there were Americans who were bad and there were Mexicans who were bad, but those people who behaved civilly he described as "Californians"—no matter what their ethnicity.[118]

B.D's personal and business life was in considerable disarray as he tried to make sense of and participate in the new American order. As the gold rush brought huge numbers of people into the state, B.D. moved from being a rancher and landowner to being a supplier and middleman. Recognizing that fortunes could be made in transporting the goods that miners needed to the gold fields, B.D. partnered with two old friends from his trapping days, Albert Packer and Andrew Sublette, to build a business around freighting. He made a fortune on paper, but had a very hard time converting promissory notes and bills into actual cash. After the state of California was organized, Wilson was elected the first clerk of the county of Los Angeles. He also served as one of the first mayors of the town of Los Angeles when it was incorporated as an American city. But he served only a few months and then resigned. His wife, Ramona Yorba Wilson, died on March 21, 1849, leaving him with two young children, a rancho whose

11. Hereford-Wilson wedding photograph, 1853. This item is reproduced by permission of *The Huntington Library, San Marino, California.* (photCL 283 (3))

In a photograph taken at the time of their wedding, Margaret and B.D. pose with Margaret's younger brother Thomas (to the right of B.D.) and her son, Edward Sublette Hereford, 9, whom B. D. Wilson would adopt.

ownership was contested, and deep ties to the Mexican community.[119]

It was in this confusing moment of changing identity that the recent widower Don Benito Wilson met the dying Thomas Hereford and his wife Margaret. The two men met initially because of their connection to the fur trade and to the Sublette family, and now B.D.'s freighting business. As an American, he was in the midst of refashioning his national identity and business connections. His Californio Spanish-speaking children he now called Sue rather than Maria Jesús and Johnny rather than Juanito, and he held a commission from the U.S. Army. Who knows at what point Don Benito became B.D. or how much Margaret Hereford had to do with this, but by marrying Margaret in 1853, Benjamin Davis Wilson went far down the path of claiming his American identity.[120]

Margaret and Benjamin went into their marriage with many advantages and many similar experiences. Both had traveled widely and valued family connections enormously. Margaret moved into the world of Californio women in the Yorba family and quickly learned Spanish so she could communicate with her new family. B.D. made a new will almost immediately after the marriage, adopting Eddy Hereford and making him an equal heir with his own children. In 1852 he was appointed by President Fillmore as Indian agent for the southern district of California, which gave him a salary and allowed him to use the connections he had built between Anglos, Mexicans, and Indians. In a classic conflict of interest, Wilson was also heavily involved in this same trade, particularly with his new connections to the Sublette family, who were still bringing in mules from Mexico to sell to miners in the gold fields, a trade that required large numbers of Indians as mule tenders. Margaret described the business when she wrote to B.D. in September of 1853, "The Indians arrived here this afternoon, bringing your welcome letter. . . . Andrew [Sublette] came in last night, the mules are all here and the Indians will be ready to start back by two o'clock this afternoon."[121] B.D. hired Margaret's younger brother to serve as a sub-agent, working for the Tejon and Cahuilla Indians, and he hired Andrew Sublette, temporarily in need of work, to hunt for meat to supply the Tejon reserve with food. Ironically, or perhaps appropriately for someone who had been a true mountain man, Sublette was killed by a grizzly bear while hunting in the San Bernardino Mountains in 1853.[122]

Even though the Mexican War changed the government under which southern Californians operated, in many ways, daily life changed little after this initial period of readjustment. It would take a drought, a financial crash, and an earthquake to change the culture that had emerged there around the cattle trade, life on ranchos, use of Indian labor, and connections to the Pacific trade. The gold rush, which focused national attention and which brought huge new populations to parts of California, at first had far less impact on the region south of the Tehatchapi Mountains. As they waited for events to unfold, and as he and Margaret worked to create a new family and a new set of business connections, life on B. D. Wilson's ranch reflected the stability of the world that trade and family had created there. We get a more personal window into their marriage when Margaret lets B.D. have it for demanding that she be more cheerful. She explains the care and worry about the children and her health simply make it too hard to be artificially cheerful. We also find out later on that she has a baby in February 1854, so in September 1853 she is hot, pregnant, and left with three children—ample reason to be crabby.[123]

The Hereford-Wilsons now had to make many decisions about their growing family that demonstrated the tensions developing in southern California. The region remained mostly Spanish speaking, and the old-line

Californios controlled politics until the 1870s. The cattle trade, booming because of demand from the gold fields for meat, leather, and tallow, made Mexican and American Californios wealthy. In 1850, according to the census, B.D. numbered among the four wealthiest men in southern California, so his financial gambles had paid off well. But Los Angeles in particular had become a violent place as new migrants from Mexico, disappointed gold miners, and displaced Indians battled each other in the saloons and plazas.[124]

B.D. and Margaret watched the increasing violence with concern. The question of where to educate the children was first raised when Edward Beale, now leaving his post as superintendent of Indian Affairs, offered to take Sue Wilson, now nine, back to Washington DC to attend school there.[125] How should the children be educated? Did California offer enough educational and cultural opportunities for them? B.D. thought yes, Margaret no. Some of their disagreement came out of B.D.'s recognition that some eastern or midwestern people might see his children as "Mexicans," but in California, he believed, their upbringing, skills, and family connections would always be an advantage.

B.D.'s career continued to spiral upward. After he was elected as a state senator from the Los Angeles district in 1855, he and Margaret relocated the entire family to Sacramento, where the state legislature sat. It was a hard decision, but they sold the vineyard house near central Los Angeles to the Sisters of Mercy and kept the ranch, which B.D. continued to manage personally. The boys, Eddy and Johnny, were sent to a Jesuit boarding school in Santa Clara, where they were taught in Spanish and Latin, but not English. Sue attended a San Francisco "Female Institute" run by an Episcopal minister and his wife, where she had special tutoring in English and drawing. Eddy, not a native Spanish speaker, seemed particularly miserable and homesick, but no one in the family seemed to enjoy life in northern California. After a long year in Sacramento, Margaret, not having seen her own mother in St. Louis for more than eight years, took Eddy, Sue, and baby Maggie east via steamer through Panama and then up the Mississippi to St. Louis.[126]

B.D. stayed at home that summer and fall. He and young Johnny, now ten, happily managed the ranches and vineyards again after the stint in state government. They missed the rest of the family and worried about their safety. B.D. began his weekly letter to Margaret with a grimly charming nineteenth-century sentence: "I have been occupied this morning in going around the vineyard and orchard poisoning squirrels and passed by the apricot trees and picked up some fine ripe apricots and the first thing that occurred to me was the natural sad thought perhaps some of you are in the world of spirits." He admitted that he was "loansome" but that Johnny was "sitting near me and anxiously inquiring what I am writing to Ma and the children."[127] But living in Los Angeles that summer was not all the rural delights of poisoning squirrels; B.D. and Johnny went into town during much of the uprising and vigilantism that erupted in the summer of 1856, which B.D. reported to Margaret in great detail. The situation that he described exhibited all of the qualities of a place in which the Wilsons might not want to raise a family: chaotic, dangerous, and racially charged.

DANGEROUS PLACES

California in the 1850s greatly resembled the Missouri River region in the 1820s in its attempts to metabolize varieties of people, economic systems, family networks, and political change. The new political presence of the United States announced itself in both places; the waxing and waning power of the Mexican government influenced both places; Indian nations wielded considerable economic and political power; and a wide variety of people attempted to stake a claim in these very contingent moments. The land rush and boom and bust cycle that characterized the 1820s in the Mississippi River valley and the gold rush that catalyzed change in California both created chaotic but potentially profitable situations for people who could embrace change. Auguste Chouteau, William Sublette, and Benjamin Wilson all stood on true political and economic frontiers, and their families allowed them to capitalize on these moments. But their wives, Sophie Chouteau, Rosalie Lambert, Frances Hereford, Ramona Yorba, and Margaret Hereford, and their children represented a real cultural border. People made choices about whom they married and the identities they created within a certain context—but in these places that context was especially flexible.

The situation in southern California in the 1850s that Benjamin Wilson and his family witnessed feels remarkably similar to the complicated position A. P. Chouteau faced in the 1820s. California had changed dramatically since 1848 when gold was discovered and when it changed from a Mexican province to an American territory and then state. Most of the changes, however, occurred most drastically in central and northern California, where the Wilson family had just spent a miserable year. Part of their discomfort came from culture shock for a family that spoke a mix of

English and Spanish and were accustomed to the rural patterns of life in southern California. Northern California was aggressively Anglo, urban, and unfamiliar to the Wilson family, even though B.D. served as a senator and had carefully negotiated becoming part of the Anglo business community. When they arrived home in the summer of 1856, B.D. and his son felt some relief, but they recognized that even this familiar place was undergoing rapid change.

In 1856 Los Angeles was not an American community, though newer settlements outside the pueblo like El Monte and Wilmington had become Anglo enclaves. Families like Wilson's, some Mexican and some American, but all Californios, still held considerable social and political power and owned most of the good land in southern California. Los Angeles still operated around its central plaza, where elaborate religious processions, markets, and horse races provided social connections for everyone. In an 1853 census Los Angeles had a population of fewer than 4,000, including about 400 people labeled "Americanos," but also 3,700 Indians who lived just outside the pueblo.[128] These newer Anglo residents ranged from opportunistic carpetbaggers to families earnestly seeking a little land, but they all shared the assumption that California was theirs for the taking and that American government and culture would shortly prevail. The resulting mix of cultural style, economic competition, and political turmoil was potent, making southern California a particularly violent place as the system of family connections and intercultural diplomacy eroded.[129]

The consequence was a real crime wave, but one that became exaggerated and racialized in the context of the local situation in Los Angeles. Both Anglos and Mexicans, under economic pressure and fear of crime, but without a strong governmental presence, began to demonize each other. All Mexicans, whether citizens, recent immigrants, wealthy rancheros, or wandering bandits, became dark-skinned, threatening criminals in the eyes of Americans. Similarly, all Americans, whether long-present California residents, riff-raff from the gold diggings, or military officials, were all suspect collaborators. Mexican bandits, Anglo squatters, and thieves and murderers of all ethnicities terrorized Los Angeleños in the 1850s, but the only criminals brought to trial were Mexicans or Californios.[130]

Because of this real and perceived injustice, local citizens, American and Mexican, responded to the criminal mayhem that had rendered government powerless by forming extra-legal organizations. Labeling themselves as the "respectables," wealthy Californians of various ethnic backgrounds joined committees of safety and became citizen "rangers." Benjamin Davis Wilson, clearly one of the old-line respectables, was now well aware of the challenges that faced his community, but he hesitated to ally against his neighbors. In the summer of 1856, while living on his ranch with Johnny, he watched events unfold with a dreadful sense of foreboding. Reports of shootings, stabbings, and drunken brawls between recent Mexican immigrants in the rowdier parts of Los Angeles began to convince the Anglo population that all "Mexicans" were plotting violent revenge. As he explained in his letters to Margaret, "The country here is almost in a revolution. . . . I fear there will result violence among the people out of it."[131]

His worries turned out to be predictions as the tensions in Los Angeles devolved into what Leonard Pitt called a "race war." Early on the morning of Saturday, July 19, 1856, a young deputy tried to seize the property of one Antonio Ruiz for lack of payment. The property in question, a guitar, had a letter from Ruiz's mistress hidden in it. Ruiz wanted the letter, but the young deputy refused to let him touch the guitar, and so Ruiz grabbed it. Inexperience and the inability to speak Spanish made the deputy, William Jenkins, grab for his pistol. When Ruiz tried to knock the pistol, which according to some sources was aimed at Ruiz's mistress, a Señora Pollarena, out of Jenkins's hand, the panicked deputy shot Ruiz and wounded him mortally. Jenkins turned himself in but was quickly released. This news incensed the Spanish-speaking population who came out into the streets. The judge in charge, seeing his political error, immediately put Jenkins back in jail until a trial could be held. The "Spanish population" met after Ruiz's funeral to decide what to do. According to the *Los Angeles Star*, "the malign influences of several firebrands" suggested a lynching, but with the "exertions of several gentlemen, Mexican and Californian," the crowd was appeased with the creation of a "committee" to guard the jail and to make sure that Jenkins did not escape or disappear.[132]

As rumors circulated about gangs of "Mexicans" massing to attack the jail or to attack the "citizens," in the language used by the *Star* to indicate the players, Los Angeles became a racially divided community. Anglo-Americans imagined a broad popular revolution was afoot and began to gather in the plaza, where "every man who could procure a gun or a pistol" massed in front of the jail. As the night passed, various groups of "citizens" and "Mexicans" investigated each other's actions and galloped up and down the street, which, as the *Star* surmised, "tended to keep up the excitement." Finally, in the second tragedy of that July, the "mob" of the "lowest and most abandoned Mexicans and Sonorans" moved toward the citizens group and, in an exchange of fire, the local marshal was shot.

The "Mexicans" fled, and Los Angeles was put under military protection. Anglo citizens moved their families from isolated ranchos, demanding security, while the Mexican American population demanded justice from a local government that could provide neither safety nor legal protection.[133]

B. D. Wilson got involved as one of the supposed "cooler heads" when the local presiding judge, Benjamin Hayes, asked him to come into Los Angeles to speak to the "citizens" gathered on the plaza in hopes of talking them out of forming a vigilance committee. Unlike the *Star*, when B.D. used the word *citizen* he meant the Mexican and Californio population. At this moment B.D. supported the vigilante cause and thought those citizens were entirely correct in believing local officials inadequate. In a letter to Margaret, he affirmed stoutly that "nothing but the strong arm of the people united against the corrupt officials can remedy the abuses," but he worried that "before the work is completed . . . many misfortunes will happen and much hard feeling between neighbors."[134]

Anglo-American militia companies patrolled the streets, while groups of young Mexicans taunted them. A group of "respectable" citizens, both Anglo and Californio, worked hard to quiet both groups until a trial could be held. B.D. and Johnny watched as Don Andres Pico, a respected Californio and "citizen" brought in some of the "bandits" who had shot Marshal Getman. And as all of Los Angeles watched, Jenkins went before an all-Anglo jury and was acquitted. To prevent another outburst of violence, Judge Hayes also released all of the Mexican prisoners. Though B.D. refused to speak out against his neighbors for forming vigilante groups, he did support local American authorities during the actual trial and testified about the "bad character" of one of the witnesses. Margaret told him later that he and Johnny had been "reckless" and "impolitic" to spend time in the city that summer, but B.D., the former Don Benito, still felt powerfully connected to his fellow Californios.[135] In his memoirs, written in the 1870s, it is hard to tell if B.D. or Don Benito is writing. Both B.D. and Don Benito now romanticized an older southern California style in which business practice and personal happiness depended on neighborly intercultural connections, which by 1870 had nearly disappeared.

Like St. Louis in the years after the Louisiana Purchase, in 1856 Los Angeles retained much of its Mexican population and style. American presence mattered but could be accommodated in the way new governments always had. The French-speaking Chouteaus maintained control of their business and family fortune by linking their families firmly to the local Native people and to the new American immigrants. The skills they had learned over generations of trade on the Mississippi and Missouri river systems served them well and gave the city of St. Louis a distinctive complexion that continued well into the middle of the nineteenth century. The world that emerged along the Missouri and Arkansas rivers blended business, cultural, and diplomatic practices from an array of people and nations. Traders, soldiers, and politicians used their families to build networks, whether in St. Louis, Kaskaskia, Santa Fe, or Los Angeles, to create a system that worked in the midst of or in spite of successive conquests. Eventually this system would bump up against a newly aggressive American nation, but even then it took a surprisingly long time to erode.

John and Marguerite McLoughlin, part of another influential fur trade family, would have recognized the pressures faced by the Wilsons in southern California and Chouteaus in St. Louis as they watched strangers take over their communities. The McLoughlins dealt with American conquest in what would become Oregon in the 1840s, but their choices emerged out of a much different context. The world of mixed cultures and accommodation that characterized communities developing out of the Canadian and Great Lakes fur trade had an older history that forms the story of the next chapter.

Chapter 2

Fort Vancouver's Families

The Custom of the Country

In the fall of 1820, eight-year-old John McLoughlin got in a boat with his father and his younger sister, Eliza. As they pushed away from the dock at Fort William on the shores of Lake Superior, John watched as his mother got smaller and smaller. He was headed to school in Montreal, where he would be cared for by his aunts and uncles, grandparents, and cousins, family in name but all people he had never seen. John had his mother's dark eyes and hair, and his father's height and temper, but he also had a particular past all his own. Not British, not Canadian, not Indian, John was "a Native of Hudson's Bay." His parents, John McLoughlin and Marguerite Wadin McKay McLoughlin, knew that John and his siblings needed to be educated outside of the backcountry if they wanted choices about careers and families. As the son of an upper-level manager in the Hudson's Bay Company and a half-Cree woman, he would grow up with a rich trove of skills and some challenges as well. As the boat sailed toward "the civilized world," as his father called it, John had no idea that he would be away from his parents for sixteen years. As the mist on the lake obscured his mother, John curled up next to his sister and slept.

COGS IN THE FUR TRADE

To understand young John McLoughlin's world—what we now call the North American West in the first half of the nineteenth century—we have to understand the significance of fur and the insignificance of nation. The last chapter gave us an overview of the families and places that made up the West in the period from 1800 to 1860, but to understand who and what made the world of St. Louis, the Arkansas River, and southern California, we need to understand the fur trade in more detail. Fur and hides drove the largest commercial enterprises in the region. Fort Vancouver, along

4. Canadian Fur Trade World, 1780–1840

the Columbia River in what is now Washington, presented the rigidly hier-archical structure of a classic post of the fur trade behemoth, the Hudson's Bay Company. Company orders from London and Winnipeg, carried by company ships from Glasgow, York, Canton, and Montreal, were read and received by the "chief factor." This was Dr. John McLoughlin, who ran the fort with equal parts despotism and grace for more than twenty years between 1824 and 1846, producing millions of pounds of furs for the Company. By the 1840s McLoughlin's empire spread thousands of miles beyond Fort Vancouver and included hundreds of employees and thousands of their dependents. And McLoughlin's fort was only one of hundreds.

Imagine the fur trade as a set of wheels, connected by cogs, linking very separate parts of the trade. Spatially, the most significant cogs were forts, but operationally, the most crucial links in the system were families. We need to understand the global spread of the system as well as the in-timate patterns of gift giving, choosing spouses, and building families, as well as the rhythms of daily work in these forts and the communities that surrounded them. Fort Vancouver served as a microcosm of the social, familial, and economic systems that characterized the fur trade in the first half of the nineteenth century. The most successful practitioners of this trade operated out of forts, constructing communities that were far from the flimsy and transient entities the term often implies. A symbol of economic power, the fur-trading fort represented a set of imperial dreams and the new cultural arrangements necessary to make these a reality. The fort stood in a region whose ownership had been contested by European empires for more than two centuries and whose Native people maintained influence through all of those changes.

To understand John and Marguerite McLoughlin, we have to examine the contexts that created them: the corporate culture of the Hudson's Bay Company, the Native cultures of the Great Lakes and of the Pacific North-west, and the syncretic culture of forts and trade that linked all of these. Operating underneath all of these was a set of new cultural arrangements centered on relationships with Native women that anthropologists and historians have unraveled for us.[1] Our view of how the trade operated is not so much incorrect, but incomplete. We think of the fur trade as primally male, an enterprise with swashbuckling characters, with business being conducted in London board rooms, smoky trader's halls, or coffee houses in Montreal, St. Louis, or Santa Fe. Investors were men, fur company of-ficers were men, and trappers and traders were the manliest men of all. However, from the start, to get furs these men needed women—specifically women from Native nations. European men had no idea how to hunt, gather, process, or trade for the furs that had such value or how to feed themselves while doing it. McLoughlin and his work at Fort Vancouver was no exception; his dependence on Native people came out of 150 years of fur trade experience. Native women had the cultural knowledge and social skills to link the talents and resources of Native peoples with the needs of Europeans. Did European men see this dependence? How did they respond to it? Did their relationships with Native people shift their ideas about what good women and good men did? Maybe.[2]

This linkage of Native and European needs and the world it created can be illuminated by looking carefully at one family and how they negotiated this linkage over several generations. Because the McLoughlins had the record-keeping mania of the Hudson's Bay Company behind them, and because they lived in places visited by hundreds of people each year, we can see their paths through this world quite clearly. John is more clearly etched than Marguerite or their children because of his position as chief factor, but McLoughlin and his family provide us a view of how the industry worked, from boardrooms in London to daily life in a fort to the workings of fur-trapping brigades. This family illustrates the choices people made or that were imposed on them as we follow them from the Great Lakes to the Pacific Northwest over the course of a century.

THE LOCAL AND GLOBAL COMMUNITIES OF THE COLUMBIA

Fort Vancouver, which first opened in 1821, claimed the heart of the rich hunting grounds of the Pacific Northwest, grounds that included both sea and land animal pelts. Built on the failure of American, Russian, and Spanish efforts to settle the area, the fort's population reflected this history. Though the Hudson's Bay Company operated Fort Vancouver, it was unlike their other corporate enterprises. Because of the powerful tribes that surrounded it and the complex international situation that had created it, this fort depended on a very delicate diplomatic balance. The Scots Canadian chief trader and his corps of French Canadian, British, and Native clerks, traders, and trappers lived in a community that depended on cultural flexibility and global economy. The price of fur in Montreal or London dictated as much about the details of daily life in what is now the border between Oregon and Washington as did skill and ceremony around tea, tobacco smoking, or flag raising. No single people, nation, or corporate enterprise had uncontested control of the Pacific Northwest.

The distinctive community that lived in and outside of the fort acquired a cosmopolitan attitude demanded by a shifting situation.[3]

None of the European powers or the United States had a strong interest in that part of the continent while the wars of empire raged over the eastern half of North America. The English had a weak claim because of the Hudson's Bay Company, which basically said it owned everything anywhere near Canada. The Spanish saw it as an extension of Alta California. The Russians claimed it as part of their interests in Siberia after Vitus Bering sailed south to Alaska in 1741 and began trading for furs. The English got interested in the fur trade potential of the region when Captain James Cook sailed up the West Coast in search of the Northwest Passage in 1778. By the 1780s, English and American ships regularly stopped and traded along the coast of what is now Washington, Oregon, and British Columbia, where the local Indians offered Russian and Spanish goods as part of their trade repertoire. However, everyone aspired to trade Northwest Coast furs in the rapidly developing market in Canton, China, where perhaps 2.5 million fine furs were sold in the 1780s and 1790s.[4]

Native people were essential to this growing trade, and both coastal and interior tribes participated. The aboriginal peoples of the Northwest Coast shared cultural practices that encouraged trade. In most groups, status came from inherited wealth created by the buying and selling of slaves. In nearly every group, woodworking was a highly valued skill, primarily demonstrated with canoes, plank houses, and elaborate heraldry. Fishing and water travel linked these people, as did complex ceremonies that involved trade goods and carved and woven items. The Northwest Coast's rugged terrain and thin soil made agriculture less important, which meant people lived on fish, shellfish, sea animals, and water birds. Hunting skills allowed them to settle in relatively large villages and to evolve complex social, cultural, and artistic practices that celebrated their material comfort.[5]

Chinooks and Clatsops on the Columbia, Nootkas on Vancouver Island, and, moving north, Haidas, Tlingits, and Aleuts had long experience in commerce with tribes from the interior, trading shells, fish, and carved wooden items for elk and deer hides and slaves. These groups welcomed Europeans who behaved properly into their trade networks. Coastal peoples did the actual bartering (or hunting in the case of sea otters) with European sailors but then carried trade goods to the interior and traded with tribes there to obtain the lucrative furs. Russian traders boasted that "not one Russian knows how to hunt the animals," which, of course, made them entirely dependent on the Aleuts. In fact, they exploited the Aleuts rather mercilessly, employing more than half of the male population while holding their families hostage as pelt processors. A good 50 percent of the entire population died from disease and overwork in a thirty-year period, which worried Russian employers, fearful of losing their local labor source.[6]

Knowledge of hunting and of local trade networks gave coastal peoples a great deal of power and access to new material goods, but it also introduced them to epidemic disease and other destructive aspects of "contact." Coastal tribes fought fiercely on occasion to protect their trade system and to prevent Europeans from venturing too far inland. Sailors from various nations described attacks on ships and on landing parties from Haida, Chilkat, and Tlingit people, probably because Indians recognized ships as the "spirits of the Pestilence" that had reduced their numbers by as much as 75 percent in the first waves of disease. Despite the obvious costs to Indian people and despite the challenges of trading and fighting with well-equipped local tribes, an enormous trade developed by the 1780s.[7]

Occasional imperial spats interrupted this profitable Pacific trade. The Spanish, who had claimed Nootka Sound in 1774 as a way to prevent Russian incursions into their territory, cared little about otter or beaver pelts but cared a great deal about protecting their claim to the Pacific Northwest and Alta California. By the 1780s thirty to forty ships a year visited the Northwest Coast, a number the Spanish found worrisome. In 1789 a Spanish officer seized four British ships and sent their crews to prisons in Mexico, an incident that almost caused international war. The British, angry over Spain's action and its efforts to monopolize trade in the region, demanded the creation of a new international treaty. With not much diplomatic or military strength to support its territorial claims, Spain had to agree to the Nootka Treaty, which gave other nations the right to hunt, trade, and settle along the Northwest Coast but protected fishing and hunting near areas actually occupied by Spain. Clearly, the message to nations and their traders was that only occupation and settlement could guarantee control of the region. The big winners in this arrangement were the British and, eventually, the Hudson's Bay Company, which was inexorably extending its influence south and west from its Canadian stronghold.[8]

Secure in its supremacy in the Canadian fur trade and in its factory system of gathering, processing, and selling furs, the Hudson's Bay Company watched as new and not very expert nations and entities vied over the Pacific Northwest in the early years of the nineteenth century. Much of what was labeled "exploration" merely served as a cover for conducting illegal trade in furs and for finding ways to corner the China trade. Both the United States and Britain recognized the stakes involved in Lewis and Clark's expedition. Before leaving for the Great West, Meriwether Lewis insisted that the "signal Advantage" of the entire expedition "would be the establishment of a trading post at the mouth of the Columbia River, for expediting the commerce in furs to China."[9]

The post that Lewis envisioned, Fort Astoria, was established in 1810 as an American post when John Jacob Astor briefly made his mark on the Pacific Coast, but it became Fort George when the British claimed it after the War of 1812. The Adams-Onís Treaty of 1819 settled the northern border of New Spain at the 42nd parallel, making it clear where Alta California began and ended, but the area to the north remained a dispute between the United States and Great Britain. Not wanting war over such a distant, insignificant land, in 1818 those two nations had agreed to a "joint occupancy" of the land between the 42nd and 54th parallels, a huge swath of territory rich in furs, fish, and land but locked in by the Rocky Mountains on the east and the Pacific Ocean to the West. "Joint occupancy" meant that neither nation would have a government presence there, but that "the vessels, citizens, and subjects" from both nations could do business or settle in the region, but with the understanding that a border could be drawn at any moment, placing these claims in a foreign nation.[10]

The British took the first gamble in occupying this region with no government and no rules. Fort George now became Fort Vancouver, and Governor George Simpson of the Hudson's Bay Company gave the fort a new purpose and new location. Because Simpson knew that his nation's claim on the region was ephemeral, he moved the fort to the north side of the river. From here he intended to bolster England's argument that the Columbia should be the border between the United States and Canada. Not being entirely confident of that result, Simpson, the good capitalist, also decided to strip the region of furs as quickly as possible.[11]

To guide the Hudson's Bay Company in these economic and nationalistic purposes, Simpson brought in Dr. John McLoughlin to serve as chief factor of the Columbia District. He stayed in the post until the border issue was settled in 1846. In that twenty-year period McLoughlin built a community that reached far beyond the walls of the fort itself and that became legendary in the trade. The fort's thorny diplomatic history, its efficient—even ruthless—operation, and the ethnic and racial complexity of its personnel made an indelible mark on the region's development. McLoughlin's Fort Vancouver, with its grand dining hall and thousands of acres of farms, presided over a community with a distinctive blend of modern capitalism and Old World patronage in a place with an improbably diverse group of people.

Dinner at Fort Vancouver, along the Columbia River, would have looked familiar, except for the salmon, to the inhabitants of any large fur-trading fort. Thomas Farnham, an American missionary, described dinner at Fort Vancouver in 1839 as "an oasis in the vast social desert of Oregon." He observed that "at the end of a table twenty feet in length stands Governor McLoughlin, directing guests and gentlemen from neighboring posts to their places; and chief traders, traders, the physician, clerks, and the farmer slide respectfully into their places." He finished his account by noting that "everyone enjoys the food, even the velvet bedecked Indian wives of even the highest in command," probably referring to McLoughlin's wife Marguerite.[12] From his seat at the end of a great table, McLoughlin could see Scottish businessmen, French Canadian trappers, local Chinook dignitaries, American missionaries, Russian or English ship captains, Hawaiian laborers, and Iroquois and Shoshone hunters. Many of the men, including McLoughlin and his Scottish and Canadian associates, were married to Native or métis women, who sometimes sat at the great table.[13] The splendor of the meal, the symbolism of the seating, and the guests invited all reflected the importance of intercultural diplomacy in the operation of the business.

Everything about the place operated on a massive scale. Built from the tremendous Douglas firs of the Pacific Northwest, the fort that soon dominated the bluffs overlooking the river covered nearly an acre, enclosing enough space to house several hundred people and hundreds of horses and other livestock. The physically impressive nature of the fort signaled imperial and national power as the fort performed the role of border sentry. The fact that private enterprise, rather than the government itself, policed the border indicates something about the realities of nations and their weakness in the region. John McLoughlin did not work for the government and in truth generally ignored the niceties of federal law, borders, and military procedure. He operated more like a medieval lord, with intricate systems of duty and reciprocity, but immersed in a global system of markets and capital. Managing a far-flung business that depended on the whims of many nations and the skills of a huge variety of cultures and peoples in a setting isolated from commercial and urban entrepôts required intelligence, tact, flexibility, and diplomacy.[14]

However large and global the fur trade became, it functioned as a highly personal and familial enterprise. At both Fort Vancouver and at Bent's

Fort, family and marriage provided essential protections and entrée into crucial sets of information and skill. This required forming relationships across cultural lines in ways that would have been inconceivable or illegal in other places and times. Trade itself depended on personal relationships. We think of the barons of the fur trade as the nineteenth-century equivalents of modern corporate raiders—steely-eyed individuals, unfettered by personal ties, who cornered markets and lusted after conquest. This is an inaccurate view of a setting in which no one could operate alone. As was true for the Chouteaus in Missouri or the Wilsons in California, the people in this world needed relationships—marriage, adoption, bondage, partnership, apprenticeship, and friendship—to make business and life possible in the face of imperial rivalry and warfare. The big men in the trade, their employees, and the people dependent on the communities they created often married into Indian families who had essential local knowledge and trade networks. Anglo-American and British observers, travelers, and merchants found these cultural choices shocking and commented on the presence of people of mixed race at the highest levels of leadership at nearly every fort, demonstrating the ubiquity of this métis world.

THE MÉTIS WORLD OF JOHN MCLOUGHLIN

John McLoughlin, the powerful chief factor of Fort Vancouver, and his family illustrated the intricacy of these linkages. Biographers have tried to quantify the amount of Indian blood that the McLoughlin family had, but such calculations are inaccurate and reflect a world where a drop of blood matters. We don't know how much racial mixing a word like *métis* means—it was a cultural shorthand. Our own deep cultural worries about race have little to do with how these families thought about themselves.

John McLoughlin, born in Quebec in 1784, had ideal lineage for success in the fur trade. His parents baptized him Jean-Baptiste in honor of his French Canadian mother and grandmother but always called him John. McLoughlin's grandfather, Malcolm Fraser, was a Scotsman who came to Canada in 1759 to fight in the French and Indian War. Fraser was wounded in the battle of Quebec but received a large landholding north of Quebec as reward. Settling quickly into rural life, he married a French Canadian named Marie Allaire, and their first child, Angelique, was John's mother. Angelique married an Irish Canadian farmer named John McLoughlin in 1778, much to her parents' dismay since he was neither wealthy nor high-born. John and Angelique were Catholic—as Angelique's mother had been.[15] The McLoughlins had seven children, five girls and two boys. John spent much of his childhood living with his grandfather and his two uncles, Simon and Alexander Fraser. One made his living as a medical doctor and the other as an important fur trader, and John had lifelong relationships with both them. Though the McLoughlins were fairly modest farmers, they had high hopes for both of their sons, John and David, and paid for an education and for medical training. John apprenticed with Dr. James Fisher in Montreal and received his license to practice medicine in 1803 at the age of eighteen.[16]

However, instead of setting up a medical practice, McLoughlin signed on with a North West Company fur brigade. In one of those moments that is as much fate as poor judgment, the story goes that McLoughlin pushed a British soldier into the mud, making it ill-advised for him to stay in Montreal. He alluded to the incident in 1808 to his uncle Simon Fraser: "I cannot accuse no one but myself of my bad fortune as it was entirely by my own want of conduct that I came up to this country."[17] He signed on as a surgeon and apprentice clerk for a five-year stint and promised that he would "Obey the Company officers and go wherever whereunto required and into any part of the Indian or Interior Countries."[18]

Given McLoughlin's background and his location in Montreal, his choice of the North West Company as his employer in the fur trade, rather than the Hudson's Bay Company, was logical. The two companies had been in deadly competition for the last decade, and it appeared that the upstart North West Company, founded in Montreal in 1779, was winning in 1803. The Nor'Westers had more men, more forts, and far more profit than the Hudson's Bay Company. The venerable Hudson's Bay Company (HBC), founded as a royal monopoly in 1670, was vastly profitable and expanding rapidly in the eighteenth century but suddenly faltered at the start of the nineteenth. In 1800 the annual dividend dropped to 4 percent, in 1806 the HBC had to get a loan from the Bank of England, and from 1809 through 1814 it paid no dividends at all. The HBC's top-heavy and London-based system and expensive reliance on large forts that required Native hunters and Canadian traders to come to them proved unwieldy in an era of increased competition. The more versatile system adopted by the North West Company of building many satellite outposts, making it easier for the Native hunters to get furs to them or for traders to go to Indian villages directly, proved more effective. By 1795 they controlled 77 percent of Canada's fur trade compared to 14 percent held by the Hudson's Bay Company. The problem for the Nor'Westers was the trip from London to Montreal, followed by the expensive, long, and dangerous canoe trip from Quebec to the interior in comparison to the direct connection that HBC men had from York Factory to London. Despite the fierce competition at the highest levels, Nor'Westers began to set up posts in Rupert's Land, the great sweep of what is now northern Canada that drained into Hudson's Bay, and HBC men began building forts on the frontier beyond York Factory, so that rival establishments were often very close—a wasteful duplication that cost everyone money.[19]

The rivalry between the smaller trading enterprises occasionally led to violence and tragedy, along with a glut on the market for furs. The traders were after a fortune in furs, and the North Country was essentially ungoverned, with neither courts nor police nor military protection. One of the more infamous crimes was Peter Pond's 1782 murder of Jean Etienne Wadin, the father of Marguerite Wadin, John McLoughlin's future wife. Like other orphaned métis children, young Marguerite remained in the care of her Native mother, but without the financial resources of a fur trade income. Peter Pond went on to murder another trader, John Ross, in 1787 and then disappeared into the United States and became a legendary explorer. Another of Pond's traders killed a man named Joseph King in 1802 as part of this increasingly nasty rivalry.[20]

While conservative Londoners controlled the Hudson's Bay Company, the North West Company was run out of Montreal by Canadians of Scottish or French origin, much like John McLoughlin himself. His first posting took McLoughlin to Kaministiquia, which became Fort William in 1807, on the northern shore of Lake Superior and one of the largest and most central of the North West Company posts. A later observer described it as "the great emporium of the interior." After the Jay Treaty of 1794 moved the U.S.-Canada border and allowed both British and Americans to trade on either side of it, Kaministiquia became even more significant. It had a bakery, blacksmith, tinsmith, jail, cooperage for making kegs, yards for building and repairing canoes, a shipyard for larger ships capable of sailing on Lake Superior, fur sheds, farms, storehouses, counting house, great hall, and a hospital.[21]

Just as the United States secretly bought up the land to the west of the Great Lakes as part of the Louisiana Purchase, young Doctor McLoughlin took on the duties of fort physician and clerk, the starting point for most young gentlemen in the fur trade. McLoughlin arrived at the summer rendezvous, so that more than a thousand people filled the fort and its environs. At the age of eighteen he was the only physician in the vast complex. Laborers, both Indians and French Canadians, were housed in camps outside the palisade, but everyone feasted together inside the great halls. Distinctions were made between officers and regular employees, and only officers could be seated. A hundred officers gathered each night around long tables, where McLoughlin in his status as the lowest rank of officer, would join them enjoying fish, beef, venison, milk, butter, white bread, corn, peas, potatoes, wine, spirits, and cakes. As one trader remembered, summer was the "fashionable season" at Lake Superior, when "good living and festivities predominate; and the luxuries of the dinner-table compensate in some degree for the long fasts of winter quarters."[22]

Like most young officers in the North West Company, McLoughlin settled into a yearly pattern punctuated by movements from interior forts to the larger entrepôts. He practiced medicine at Kaministiquia in the summers, and in the fall he moved to a frontier post, where he supervised Indian and French Canadian *engagés* as they hunted, fished, built cabins, chopped wood, and traded for furs with the Indians. He learned a great deal about the business of the fur trade. Part of the business, and of human nature, was in developing personal relationships with local Native people. In 1808 John carefully considered what to do after his apprenticeship in the company ended. With much hesitation, he signed on as a partner. He wanted to make sure he had a steady income to support his brother David through medical school. He had also married an Ojibwe woman in 1808, and they had a son, named Joseph McLoughlin, in 1809.[23]

Scholars have long debated what marriage in the fur trade meant. Part of the romance of the trade was its supposed rough independence, which included men having lots of Indian women as partners, consorts, and simply sexual encounters, but not ever being "tied down." However, this independence and free sexual behavior was more a fantasy of later generations than actual practice in the fur trade. We haven't thought much about what it meant to be a man in these circumstances and the way gender definitions affected Euro-American men. Certainly men and women had fewer legally and religiously recognized relationships in isolated frontier areas, and it took a long time for customs and practices around marriage to solidify, but they did. The kinds of unions that were "the custom of the country" or "country marriages" were, in the words of the most careful scholars on the subject, "not casual, promiscuous encounters but the development of marital unions which gave rise to distinct family units."[24] Fur trade marriages rarely had state or church recognition, and it didn't mean they were life-long or monogamous, but they had significant personal and economic impact. Both the Hudson's Bay Company and the North West Company encouraged long-term relationships, had special forms to record them, and provided housing for families, education for children, and stipends for widows and orphans. Anxious investors in London worried about the expense of supporting all of these dependents but recognized the value (and inevitability) of these families.[25] By the time McLoughlin entered the fur trade, the world of the North American frontier was a complex of several generations of people of mixed race. This cultural setting had been created in the interests of the fur trade and the men who needed access to women to negotiate this trade. *Métis* is not yet the right word, and neither is *Creole*, in this place where English and French men had married Native women.

These "fur trade marriages" presented a range of possibilities that we can never fully assess because there are so few records. The clearest traces are for the officers in both companies who tended to be literate and to leave wills and other paper trails. However, these men may have been the least monogamous, especially those who went back to London or Glasgow or even Montreal after their terms of service with the Hudson's Bay Company or with the North West Company. Company servants (the term for workers who weren't officers) often settled in frontier areas with their Native families if they retired from the company and simply kept their families with them. After 1811, HBC employees had the option of retiring to the Red River Colony, an experimental land grant funded initially by Lord Selkirk. According to one of the colony's residents, Alexander Ross, Selkirk intended to "form a society of the Natives and the Company's old servants, together with their half-breed descendents."[26] Red River did provide a haven for servants with the desire and skill to become prairie farmers, which, frankly, few had. However, the London Committee of the Hudson's Bay Company supported it enthusiastically, paying for the passage of retiring servants and their families, as well as funds for seeds, tools, and supplies. Many fur trade parents in isolated forts chose to send their children to the Red River school to complete their early education.[27]

Unlike the laborers, voyageurs, and *engagés*, many officers and clerks only served for a five-year term and came from England or Scotland, fully intending to return home after their service ended. Many of them did marry Native women, but only a few took these women to England or even to Montreal, which Canadian fur traders called "taking down." Chief trader John Work, manager of the Hudson's Bay coasting trade, expressed a common view when he wrote to a colleague, "I understand he [John Warren Dease] has taken down his wife and several little ones to Canada, a step I fear he will repent. Among civilized people neither himself nor her can be happy, to join in anything like civilized society with her is out of the question." John McLoughlin's uncle, Alexander Fraser, apparently agreed with Work. He left a Native wife and several children when he left the fur trade and married an Anglo-Canadian woman, but when he died his mixed race family sued successfully for an equal share in his estate.[28]

If "taking down" was not a possibility, then fur trade wives were often "placed"—either with their Native families or with other traders in arranged marriages of sorts. This worked at several levels; the trader who left was assured that his wife and children were taken care of, and often the trader or clerk who married the wife being left behind was doing a favor for a more senior officer, helping his own career. The ubiquity of these relationships, given that so few Anglo-Canadian women lived in fur trade country and that marriage with Native women offered so many material advantages, resulted in a growing population of métis people. After several generations, the North West Company recognized this change and tried to shift their employees' behavior, making it against company policy to marry Indian women but encouraging fur trade men to marry women of mixed race.[29]

John McLoughlin's family life reflects these patterns. Like many officers who served in a frontier post, McLoughlin married a Native Ojibwe woman who could help him trade with local Indians and provide companionship and support during the long Canadian winters. He wasn't faced with the choice of "taking down" or "placing" her later in his career because she died soon after giving birth to their son Joseph in 1809. Though this woman remains nameless in the McLoughlin family record, everyone in the family knew of the marriage, and Joseph, who remained permanently with his father, was considered as legitimate as any of McLoughlin's other children. Left with a toddler after his first wife's death and promoted to a permanent position at Fort William, McLoughlin may have been anxious to marry again.

The woman who would become his second wife, Marguerite Wadin McKay, was in need of placing. Marguerite, the daughter of Swiss émigré and trader Jean Etienne Wadin and a Cree woman, had married prominent Nor'Wester Alexander McKay in 1793. They had four children, three daughters and a son. When McKay retired from the North West Company in 1808, he left dowries for his daughters but took his son Thomas, aged eleven, with him. Marguerite remained in the Rainy Lake District where John wintered, and the two apparently met in 1810. The problem with the language of "taking down" or "placing" is that it gives male fur traders all

12. Marguerite Wadin McKay McLoughlin (ca. 1780–1860) Photograph, 1857. Oregon Historical Society. (OrHi 260).

The photograph shows Marguerite in her seventies, grown heavy with age, poor health, and the stress of change. Born to a Cree mother and a French Canadian father, she became an aristocrat in the fur trade world of the Hudson's Bay Company. However, Marguerite's mixed race visage made her an object of derision in 1850s Oregon.

of the agency and makes it sound as if Euro-American men made all of the decisions. We don't know what Marguerite's options included or even who began and ended these relationships. We don't know the emotional content of the courtship between John and Marguerite or whether McLoughlin improved his standing in the North West Company by taking on McKay's wife, but we do know that they married in 1811. John McLoughlin was twenty-seven and a rising officer in the trade. Marguerite Wadin McKay was thirty-six and had three daughters whom she needed to support, ranging in age from two to sixteen.[30]

THE TENTACLES OF INTERNATIONAL TRADE

Alexander McKay resigned from the North West Company and left behind his wife Marguerite to go to work for John Jacob Astor's Pacific Fur Company, the fur trade pioneers at the site that would become Fort Vancouver. In 1808, just as Lewis and Clark returned from their epic adventure and as John McLoughlin settled into life at Fort William, the United States made its first foray into the international fur trade. An ambitious German immigrant, John Jacob Astor had already imagined a trade network that would link Europe, the American Great Lakes, the Pacific Northwest, Russian America, and China. To President Thomas Jefferson he proposed a combination of federal support, a set of trading posts, and Astor's own entrepreneurial imagination to assure American sovereignty in the fur trade. Jefferson turned him down, but Astor went ahead and created the Pacific Fur Company, which he intended to build into a competitor for the two great Canadian fur empires, the Hudson's Bay Company and the North West Company. The Canadian companies were well aware of Astor's aspirations but had little concern that he presented a real threat. Astor chose to launch the enterprise at a moment when the two giants were locked into mortal combat with each other and the United States and Great Britain were embarking on war over trade issues.[31]

None of international uproar seemed to worry Astor. He arranged for two expeditions to the mouth of the Columbia, one following the overland route taken by Lewis and Clark and the other by ship around Cape Horn. The ship *Tonquin* arrived first, in March of 1811, and its crew selected a site on the south side of the Columbia River for the new fort and named it Astoria. In the amazing small world of the fur trade, Alexander McKay and his son Thomas were part of this expedition. However, McKay was killed when the *Tonquin* was destroyed and its crew murdered by suspicious

Native people in Nootka Sound, and Thomas, then fourteen, was left with some North West Company trappers. He and his mother, now Marguerite McLoughlin, would be reunited a decade later at Fort Vancouver.[32]

Despite the loss of the *Tonquin*, by the time the overland group arrived in the late winter of 1812, they found an impressive structure. Surrounded by a palisade of Douglas firs, the store, dwelling houses, blacksmith shops, and fur sheds presaged the great commercial center that the fort would become. The varied group of people who built the fort, tended its gardens, worked to build relationships with local tribes, and hunted and processed furs modeled the kind of community that the trade in the West required. French Canadians and Mohawk Iroquois, long experienced in the fur trade, offered hunting and diplomatic skills in dealing with the Indians. Iroquois, Chinook, and Salish (Flathead) Indians did much of the labor, joined by a contingent of Hawaiians, who had been picked up for a three-year term of service on the trip out. Scotsmen and Anglo-Americans, including Wilson Price Hunt, David and Robert Stuart, and Duncan McDougall, provided much of the leadership.[33]

By 1813 Astoria appeared to be successful, though its establishment had been far more work and danger and less profit than the original partners had hoped. Two issues, however, combined to wreck Astor's dream. First, the North West Company, focused on beating the Hudson's Bay Company to the riches of the Rocky Mountain fur trade, sent famed trapper and explorer David Thompson to pioneer a route from Canada into the Columbia River Basin. He arrived at Astoria with a wealth of peltry, indicating that Astor would no longer have this region to himself. At nearly the same moment, the War of 1812 came to an end, and England asserted control over its claim to the Pacific Northwest as part of treaty negotiations. Astor lost his gamble. The traders at Astoria found out about their new national status when a group of North West Company trappers appeared at the fort in June of 1813 and demanded that the fort be turned over to them. After months of waiting for official word from New York and expecting British war ships to arrive at any moment, the partners on site decided to sell the fort to the North West Company for $80,000. On November 12, 1813, the North West Company took formal possession of Astoria. In December, to mark its new British status, Fort Astoria became Fort George.[34]

The coup of the North West Company in seizing control of this piece of the Rocky Mountain fur trade was, however, short-lived. The Hudson's Bay Company, lying in wait, initiated a destructive campaign to destroy its rival. Both companies raised the prices they paid for furs to levels that could not be sustained, and they encouraged their trappers to waste game and to trap out of season, which threatened the viability of animals in the region and angered Native groups considerably. John McLoughlin, made partner in the North West Company in 1814, was in the thick of this vicious competition and couldn't avoid some of uglier consequences. As the wintering partner at Fort William (formerly Kaministiquia), McLoughlin found himself involved in the dreadful massacre of British colonists at the Battle of Seven Oaks in 1816.[35]

The murder of twenty-one people came out of a philanthropic effort gone wrong. Lord Thomas Selkirk, new to the governing board of the Hudson's Bay Company, decided that he could solve two problems with one giant land grant in Canada. He could find homes for the most egregiously evicted Highlanders in Scotland and get a more diversified portfolio for the Hudson's Bay Company by funding and supervising a grand colonization experiment in the Red River valley. Highland Scots, Irish crofters, and retired fur traders and their families could learn to raise crops on the Great Plains of Canada. Selkirk didn't think much about the site being in the center of the North West Company's trapping and trading range, but HBC officials did. No one in the fur trade thought it made sense to turn the Red River region, the richest fur-producing site near the Great Lakes, into poor farmland, but if such a project helped drive the North West Company out of business the HBC would back it. In the end groups of colonists arrived in 1814 to begin their new lives but found enormous opposition everywhere. Native and métis people, determined to drive out the strangers who had arrived on their land, united with trappers and traders of the North West Company. McLoughlin supported what he called "the dispersal" of the colony and sent in food, supplies, and arms to assist. Most of the colonists fled before the invading force, but a few stayed to protect the land that had been given to them. On June 19, a force of angry men attacked the remaining colonists and killed twenty-one people. After a series of trials, including one for John McLoughlin for his material support of the massacre, the reputation of the North West Company hung in tatters.[36]

In 1820, when both companies were on the verge of bankruptcy, McLoughlin joined a number of North West Company partners at a negotiation between the HBC and the Nor'Westers held in Montreal. At the same time he and Marguerite made the hard decision to send their oldest children away to school. McLoughlin took the opportunity of the companies' meeting to take them to Montreal and to find suitable schools. They would board at school but be supervised by their great uncle, Dr. Simon

Fraser. Joseph was twelve, John eight, and Elisabeth six. Only Eloisa, three, stayed home with Marguerite, who was pregnant with David.[37] After settling his children and meeting with the partners of the North West Company, McLoughlin went on to London to meet with HBC officers in early 1821. Both companies recognized that the competition between them had to stop, and the British government gave them powerful economic incentives to merge, including a guarantee of exclusive trading rights to the entire area, including what would become the Oregon Country. McLoughlin, as leader of the "winterer's revolt," had much to do with the dissolving of the North West Company, though it pained him to do so. On March 26, 1821, representatives of both companies signed papers, uniting the old enemies under the name of the Hudson's Bay Company. McLoughlin was literally made so ill by this turn of affairs that he spent nearly six months in France under the care of his brother.[38]

Under the new twelve-thousand-word contract, the "Deed Poll of 1821," the officers of both companies would be chief factors and chief traders instead of wintering partners. Fifteen of the twenty-five chief factors—who ran whole divisions of forts—and seventeen of the twenty-eight chief traders—who ran individual forts—were former Nor'Westers, a lopsided division that acknowledged their superior administrative skills and field organization. The governors who oversaw the whole operation came from the Hudson's Bay Company with its deep resources in London. Blending these two groups would be challenging. John McLoughlin, appointed a chief factor, would run the Rainy Lake District that included his former post at Fort William.[39]

The McLoughlin family did not stay at Rainy Lake long. In July of 1824 the Council of the Northern Department convened at York Factory and offered McLoughlin the charge of the Columbia District, the largest, most distant, and potentially most profitable region. When McLoughlin took it over, four European nations aimed to control the Pacific Northwest. He would have to learn about international diplomacy as well as dealing with the powerful Native groups who maintained strict controls over the trade. The Hudson's Bay Company had been disappointed with their lack of profit from the Columbia District and had seriously considered pulling out of the region entirely in 1822. The newly appointed governor of the Northern Department, George Simpson, talked them out of such a rash move by promising new organization and clear profits.[40]

Simpson dropped these expectations, along with the murky legal situation of the entire Oregon Country, squarely in McLoughlin's lap. Only the legal title to Fort George, which would be McLoughlin's headquarters, though deeply circuitous, was clear. Because it lay on the south side of the Columbia River, the fort obviously stood on U.S ground under the joint occupancy agreement made in 1818. But when the American traders sold the fort to the North West Company in 1813, that put it in British hands. Finally, since the Hudson's Bay Company had swallowed the North West Company, the HBC now owned Fort George. However, Britain and the United States were still vying over the region, and part of Simpson's charge to McLoughlin was to strengthen British claims in the region.

On July 27, 1824, McLoughlin and his family set off for the Pacific Coast. The three-month journey through the Athabasca, the windy tundra of north-western Canada, over the Rocky Mountains on horseback or snowshoe, and then in boats down the Columbia, was not to be taken lightly. Because the McLoughlins took the exact route that Governor George Simpson would take a mere three weeks later, and because Simpson recorded every step of every trip he took, we know a lot about the McLoughlins' journey. The new chief factor headed for the Columbia District with his wife and their two youngest children, Eloisa and David. The other children remained in Canada. Elisabeth, then ten, was in school in the Ursuline Convent in Quebec, where John's sister was a nun. Sixteen-year-old Joseph was left at Sault Sainte Marie as an apprentice hunter. John Jr., then twelve, remained in school at Terrebonne, under the supervision of his great uncle Simon Fraser. Marguerite's other children were young adults, the daughters already married to traders and sea captains who worked for the Hudson's Bay Company.[41]

For John McLoughlin, wives who spoke Indian languages and who had family connections all over Canada enabled him to amass power and status. He saw this cultural mixing as a useful heritage for his children, who grew up at company forts, and who then went on to school in Montreal and Paris. The power of the Hudson's Bay Company and the cultural and social practices that had developed to support its core business of fur trading had created a family system that worked to protect "the daughters of the country," but that left the "sons of the country" with fewer options. Native and mixed-blood women were the norm for men in the fur trade to choose as wives. The complex kinship network that emerged by the early nineteenth century gave unique cohesion to this society that developed all over the North American West. It would serve John McLoughlin well when he arrived at Fort Vancouver, which was already part of a Native and European trading system.[42]

When John McLoughlin took his family to Fort Vancouver in the fall of 1824, he assumed the world of the fur trade would last forever. He knew that competition with the Americans and boundary disputes might change some details about national borders, but he could not imagine it would affect his family. But in the twenty years that he ran Fort Vancouver, the system that protected his loved ones and the business that made the fur trade profitable would erode in ways no one could have predicted.

THE MCLOUGHLINS AND THE COMPANY

Fort Vancouver was never a "frontier." It was a fully formed system of Canadian trade and culture dropped into another fully formed system of Chinook or Salish trade and culture. From the moment McLoughlin arrived, he operated with a strict set of instructions, based on 150 years of experience. Northwest Coast Indians had been dealing with Europeans and traders for several generations and had assimilated much of the material culture they brought. Indians appreciated metal goods and clothing, guns and glass, and quickly distained "trade beads and other Bawbles."[43] They had also become excellent traders, and many ships' captains complained about their prices and their skillful negotiation. By 1824 there was nothing raw or primitive about either Native people or the Hudson's Bay Company; Indians and HBC men already knew a considerable amount about each other. Neither side wanted to convert the other; rather, they wanted to do business. How this would be conducted took some compromise.

When McLoughlin arrived at the old Fort George in November of 1824, he knew he had a big job to make the Columbia Department of the Hudson's Bay Company into the jewel that George Simpson and the Company and its directors envisioned. Chief factor John McLoughlin oversaw this complex of business, family, and imperial outpost. His charge of making the Honorable Company a profit and of expanding the influence of the British Empire, while keeping his hundreds of employees satisfied and safe, was a tremendous responsibility. However, while McLoughlin performed his daily work far removed from London or from York Factory, he was far from unsupervised. In addition to almost yearly tours of inspection from Governor Simpson, the London Committee expected to hear from him regularly, and they did. From Fort Vancouver McLoughlin had two ways of communicating with his superiors in London or at York Factory: the express canoes from York Factory that came every fall and spring, carrying only mail and orders so that they could make the trip in only a few weeks, and sailing ships from England, which brought food, trade goods, and equipment and took back furs, people, and mail, but which took months to reach London.[44]

McLoughlin wrote detailed reports of his activities, goods produced at the fort, the comings and goings of visitors and employees, future plans, concerns, and news in general. This was a real correspondence with the London Committee providing numbered questions and concerns to which McLoughlin responded in detail. The committee sent an official letter twice a year that arrived with express canoes, but McLoughlin wrote to them much more often, taking the opportunity to send reports with nearly every ship that left the Columbia. Some years, he sent as many as ten official reports, supplemented with letters about events he thought they should know about more immediately.[45]

He also wrote regularly to Governor Simpson, who also received copies of the letters to the London Committee, and he sent copies of all of his official correspondence with other forts and with any Indian nation, foreign nation, or business enterprise to London as well. The detail in all of these reports indicates how carefully the Company ran its business and how seriously they took their supervisory role. McLoughlin asked for, and got, advice about numbers of men to hire, where to hunt, what to pay for furs, which Indian tribes to contact, what kinds of crops to plant, how to brew beer, what kind of furniture to buy or build, and how and when to say prayers in the fort. One quite typical letter, written in 1827, from McLoughlin to Governor Simpson, ran at least twenty manuscript pages in length and answered forty-one separate queries about various items. They ran the gamut from business details, such as prices paid for furs, trade goods, and food at various forts, to international affairs, such as debates over the use of joint occupancy territories, to farm reports about failed potato crops and healthy pigs.[46]

This was not the only letter writing McLoughlin did. He kept up a regular correspondence with the other chief factors and traders in the Columbia Division, exchanging orders, reports on movements of people and goods, commentary about politics, and personal news. Though he had several clerks to assist him with his correspondence, he did most of the original letter writing himself and spent a great deal of time on these letters each day. He also wrote regularly to numerous members of his family in Canada, to his brother in Paris, and to his children in school in Montreal and Quebec. Family letters allowed him to express emotional content, especially around his concern at being so distant from his loved ones. Even his reports to the Company had much personal detail about his own decisions, the work and productivity of his employees, and the health of the entire fort. For a man in an isolated setting with few peers to provide companionship and support, letter writing enabled McLoughlin to maintain a dense network of diplomatic and business relationships, friendships, and family ties that were essential to his life in the Northwest and to the conduct of his business. But letters that traveled by canoe and through company mail networks were not private, and McLoughlin wrote about personal matters with caution.[47]

Several major problems required his immediate attention: the poor location of the fort, the relationship among local Native groups, and competition with other traders in the "joint occupation" area—primarily Americans and Russians, but others as well. He took on the issue of location first. Fort George stood on a damp, windy spit of land, too far down the river to be convenient for trading brigades and on the south side of the river, which McLoughlin believed would eventually end up in American hands. With Simpson present, it made sense to get his advice and approval for this expensive and important move. Simpson and McLoughlin surveyed areas further inland, where farming would be easier and where contact and trade with more interior tribes could be facilitated.[48]

Quickly, Simpson and McLoughlin chose a site on the north side of the river, near where the Willamette River meets the Columbia. Simpson reported with satisfaction: "The place we have selected is beautiful as may be inferred from its name (Belle Vue) and the Country so open that from the Establishment there is good travelling on Horseback to any part of the interior." Always mindful of the bottom line, he continued hopefully, "the pasture is good and innumerable herds of swine can fatten so as to be fit for the Knife merely on nutricious Roots."[49] Though McLoughlin thought the new site was too far from the river, he acknowledged it would be easy to defend, if not to unload ships. Work on the new fort began immediately, and laborers spent the winter taking parts of the old Fort George down the river and sawing new timber for the twelve-foot stockade. They used large canoes to transport the fort's livestock—a few goats, milk cows, and oxen from California, and five good Indian ponies from Walla Walla—along with the trade goods and fur packets. On March 16, 1825, just as Governor Simpson prepared to leave, McLoughlin and his family moved into their house in the new fort.[50]

Next McLoughlin took on the challenge of building a relationship with the local Indians. The tribes in the immediate area, mostly Chinooks and Salishes, seemed very willing to trade. He invited the Chinook leader, Concomely, to visit Fort George and asked his advice about relocating the fort. Concomely was a powerful man who dominated the confederacy of the Columbia River. Two of Concomely's daughters had married Duncan McDougal and Alexander McKenzie, fur traders in the Columbia District, and he had done business with the North West Company long before the merger. Concomely's people were famous for a trading network that extended far up the Columbia and for Chinook jargon, a simplified tongue based on Chinook, other Indian languages, French, and English—a patois that worked over a huge region.[51]

However, as George Simpson had noted, these people were "wretched hunters, unaccustomed to the Chase," having little interest in fur and deriving most of their sustenance from salmon.[52] Salmon and its life cycle did organize the lives of these people. Important ceremonies marked the first salmon run and the first salmon caught. The salmon's mouth was filled with clean sand and its body brushed with moss to ensure that its kin would continue to come to the river. And, of course, debates about how to cook and eat salmon interested people deeply. Whether its heart should be burned or its eyes eaten were crucial cultural markers. Earlier settlers in the region, the Astorians and the Nor'Westers, had complained bitterly about having to eat so much salmon, but McLoughlin was determined to find a way to cure and ship salmon to make it a trade item. He also recognized the significance and ceremony involved in fishing for and eating salmon, and incorporated this into the feasts held at the fort.[53]

McLoughlin also knew that although the Chinooks and Clatsops might not be hunters, they were masterful traders, and he would have to use their networks to succeed in any relationships with local peoples. The Chinooks had a very rigid social hierarchy that arranged people from those born into high-status families down to slaves, generally taken in warfare or in exchange for highly coveted Chinook canoes. They determined status by wealth in slaves and displayed this status with insignia and crests painted on headdresses, clothing, and weapons. By the time McLoughlin arrived at Fort Vancouver, the Chinooks, and in particular Concomely, had complete control over all trade below the Dalles.[54]

McLoughlin demonstrated his respect for the Chinooks by infusing some of their ceremonial practices into activities at the fort and by recognizing marriages between his employees and local Native women. His stepson Thomas McKay married one of Concomely's daughters, Timmee, and they raised their son Donald at the fort with his McLoughlin cousins.

Such attention ensured that Concomely profited from the presence of the fort and increased his status as a result. These efforts allowed McLoughlin to develop strong working relationships with Native groups near the river and near his forts. He based these relationships on the Company's dual practices: to respect the Natives, treat them fairly, and make no effort to change their beliefs of way of life; but to respond with vigor if they harmed property or personnel. His daughter Eloisa remembered: "The whites themselves sometimes troubled Indians and then they complained to my father. He put men in chains who treated Indians badly. That is the way they kept peace with the Indians."[55] John McLoughlin insisted that every man in the Company show respect for the Indians, which included living up to promises of marriage and supporting children.

His attitude was pragmatic, not utopian. In 1843 he reflected back on his policy: "We are traders, and apart from more exalted motives, all traders are desirous of gain. Is it not self evident we will manage our business with more economy by being on good terms with Indian than if at variance. We trade furs, none can hunt fur bearing animals or afford to sell them cheaper, than Indians." Always a practical man, he concluded: "It is therefore in our interest, as it is unquestionably our duty to be on good terms with them and the Indians of the Columbia are not such poltroons as to suffer themselves to be ill-treated, particularly when the disparity of number is so great as to show but one white man to 200 Indians."[56]

In spite of the wisdom McLoughlin achieved in dealing with local Native people, during his early years he had several violent encounters, and some distant tribes remained permanently hostile. Part of McLoughlin's success came from the support he got from the London Committee of the Hudson's Bay Company around retaliating quickly against Indian attack. Company officers in London and in the field understood how outnumbered their men were in Indian Country and believed that Indians would respect them more if they demonstrated strength. McLoughlin retaliated when he thought the conditions warranted it. Several episodes that developed in 1828 and 1829 demonstrate the range of the situations he faced.

In June 1828 the Klallam tribe of Hood Canal attacked a Hudson's Bay Company hunting party. Four men were killed, and a woman accompanying them was kidnapped. McLoughlin believed that in such situations "to pass over such an outrage would lower us in the opinion of the Indians, induce them to act in the same way, and when an opportunity offered kill any of our people, and when it is considered that the Natives are at least an hundred Men to one of us it will be conceived how absolutely necessary it is for our personal security that we should be respected by them."[57] McLoughlin arranged for a retaliatory attack, led by Chief Trader Alexander McLeod, which resulted in the burning of the village and at least twenty Indians dead—and they did get the kidnapped woman back. This may have been more destruction than McLoughlin had intended; he defended it piously in his report: "it is certainly most unfortunate that we have to resort to hostile measures against our fellow beings."[58] Some of the men who had accompanied McLeod, like young Frances Ermatinger, who would later marry McLoughlin's granddaughter, thought the expedition had failed because so few Indians had been killed and because so much effort and money had been spent on a campaign aimed at damaging Native property more than taking lives.[59]

This situation had barely been controlled when news of another Native attack reached Fort Vancouver. This time it involved American trappers—in particular, the infamous Jedediah Smith. On August 8, 1828, a group of Tillamook Indians brought what they believed to be the lone survivor of Smith's brigade to the fort. Arthur Black, the survivor, was part of Smith's group that had come north from California working for the firm of Smith, Sublette, and Jackson. They had violent altercations with Indians all the way north and killed nine people, creating a dangerous situation for themselves and for everyone else in the region. When they reached southern Oregon, a group of Indians, possibly the Umpquas or their neighbors, the Kelawatsets, retaliated, killing nineteen of Smith's party.

McLoughlin recognized the trickiness of the situation. American trappers, especially groups of free trappers operating outside the restrictions of a large business enterprise, had deservedly bad reputations for violence during these early years in the Pacific Northwest.[60] McLoughlin's own brigades, in their effort to trap the region south of the Columbia "dry," had created some hostility as well. McLoughlin understood this but decided that, at the very least, he should recover the stolen property of the brigade—228 horses and mules, 780 beaver, 60 otters, and a large stock of beads, goods, and tobacco. As he explained to the governor and the London Committee of the Hudson's Bay Company, "This unfortunate affair is extremely injurious to us as the success and facility with which the Natives have accomplished their object lowers Europeans in their estimation and consequently very much diminishes our security."[61]

As McLoughlin mulled this over, Smith himself, accompanied by two of his men, stumbled into the fort. He confirmed the attack and the deaths of his men. At this point, none of McLoughlin's traders had much experience with the Native groups far south of the Columbia, and company policy directed them to act cautiously in matters with Indians. He decided to send out Chief Trader Alexander McLeod to reconnoiter the situation with written but deliberately vague instructions that said: "You know those Indians you know our means, and as a failure in undertaking too much, would make this unfortunate affair worse—& as you are on the spot—you will therefore decide on what is best to be done and depend that whatever decision may be least as far as I am concerned every allowance will be made for the situation you are placed in." Because he urged caution and emphasized recovering stolen property rather than revenge, McLoughlin's plan was very unpopular with the American trappers, who wanted war.[62]

McLeod had worked with the Umpquas so he went to them first, and they helped him contact the Kelawatsets. They explained that rumors of Smith's ruthlessness in northern California had filtered north, convincing the Kelawatsets that all Americans were dangerous enemies who intended to destroy any Natives who came within their reach. They also resented the Americans' slaughter of beaver, a major source of food. With this information, McLeod concluded that Smith's party had at least in part brought on its own trouble, so he did not punish the tribe. Instead he traveled with his Umpqua guides from village to village, listening to the Indians, assuring them that the British wanted peace but that they had to recover Smith's property in return for gifts and items of trade. He did get seven hundred beaver skins and thirty-six horses back, but the recovery effort cost the Company at least a thousand pounds, which irritated McLoughlin and, eventually, Simpson. They ordered Smith to sell his skins at Fort Vancouver and to stay east of the Rocky Mountains and out of Hudson's Bay Company territory.[63]

The final serious challenge from the Indians in the early years of Fort Vancouver came in March 1829 when the company ship *William and Ann* foundered on a bar in the mouth of the Columbia, and her crew disappeared. Obviously, they could have drowned, but a local Chinook Indian appeared at the fort claiming that the Clatsops had murdered them and stolen all of their cargo. The way the rumor arrived made McLoughlin suspicious: "our informant not being clear in his Statement caused us to apprehend his object was to endeavor to induce us to make war with the Clatsops with whom he was at variance."[64] Under pressure, the Clatsops admitted they had taken the goods, which were always in short supply at Fort Vancouver, but insisted they had not killed any of the crew. They refused to return the sizeable store of property and taunted McLoughlin's messenger by handing him an old brush and sending him back to McLoughlin with instructions to "tell him this is all he will get of his property."[65] Annoyed and feeling challenged, McLoughlin sent a force to take the goods back, but the men found only a few piddling items and no large store. They also found the sailors' bodies, but the crew appeared to have drowned, though some of McLoughlin's men insisted the bodies "had marks of Violence." In response to the refusal to return stolen goods, McLoughlin ordered the village burned, but he did not retaliate for the deaths of the sailors. This appeared to be the right decision because local Indians never again touched fort goods.[66]

These three difficult moments of 1828–29—at Puget Sound, the Umpqua River, and the Northwest Coast—were followed by years of peace and good business with the Columbia tribes. Indians served as interpreters, messengers, laborers, hunters, and even store clerks. In the usual Hudson's Bay tradition many servants of the Company married local Indian women and retired nearby with their families, creating a network of support. In the 1830s, when a fever epidemic decimated the tribes, hundreds of Indians came to Vancouver for medical care, and "giving as a reason that if they died, they Knew we would Bury them," at least according to McLoughlin as he explained the expense of caring for his Native neighbors.[67] The more remote areas, however, remained hostile. Peter Skene Ogden and John Work lost men in the Blackfoot region, and in 1832 the Tillamooks on the coast murdered two Fort Vancouver men. In the case of the local attack, McLoughlin sent out an expedition to get revenge. Fur brigades faced almost constant challenges with Native groups in the Rogue River area, and McLoughlin built Fort Umpqua on the mouth of the Umpqua where a few cooperative groups were willing to trade, but he never achieved more than an uneasy truce in that region.[68]

LIFE AND WORK ON THE COLUMBIA

With the fort situated in the right place and with his relationships with local Native nations clear, McLoughlin could now turn to the question of expanding trade. His larger goals, as directed by Governor Simpson and the London Committee of the HBC, were to discourage American business and potential settlement of the Columbia and to develop trade with China and Russia. In other words, McLoughlin was to use the power of the Hudson's Bay Company to create a profitable fiefdom in the Pacific Northwest. To do this, he needed to protect the core business of furs and expand

13. *Fort Vancouver.* J. S. Warre. Drawing, 1845.
Oregon Historical Society (OrHi 803).

No photographs remain of Fort Vancouver in its heyday under Chief Factor
John McLoughlin. This image, drawn by a visiting British navy officer, shows
the large central portion of the fort with the Hudson's Bay Company flag
flying over it. Native people, improbably garbed in feather headdresses,
gather in groups on the large parade ground.

beyond it. McLoughlin, Governor Simpson, and the London Committee
had a continual debate about exactly how to do this. McLoughlin, not terribly experienced with ships, sailors, and coastal trade, wanted to expand
Hudson's Bay Company influence by building forts, but the governor and
the committee saw this as too expensive. McLoughlin compromised and
developed a small coastal trade to bring goods to the Russian colonies,
California, and the Sandwich Islands (Hawaii), and he experimented with
lumber and salmon sales to Hawaii. He also began planning a system of
forts that would gird the coast north to Alaska.[69]

To support these enterprises, McLoughlin turned Fort Vancouver into a
factory. The fort now covered more than seven acres and was surrounded
by a stockade of twenty-foot poles, with a massive gate toward the river and
another in back. By 1834 the visiting naturalist and physician John Kirk
reported that the walls enclosed ten to twelve major structures—which
did not included sheds and "necessaries." The larger buildings included

dwellings, storehouses, bakeries, shops for blacksmiths, carpenters, and joiners, a brick-making building, and a powder magazine. The waterfront consisted of ship-building facilities and loading equipment. The "Big House," the McLoughlin family's home, was elevated several feet with storage underneath. A large porch stretched across the front, from which a double curved stairway led down to the courtyard, and four cannon stood at the foot of the stairs. The kitchen was a separate building, with a passageway to the house.[70]

Outside the palisade, company laborers built a village consisting of laborers' huts, company storehouses, stables, barns, and orchards. A hospital, dairy, and piggery stood on the plain near the river, and five miles to the east the fort had a gristmill and sawmill. Young George Emmons, a midshipman who arrived on the Columbia in 1841 aboard the American exploring vessel the USS *Peacock*, was especially impressed with McLoughlin's mills. He noted that "both the flour mill and the saw mill are carried by overshot wheels—the former has one set of stones which more than answers the present needs of the Co. The latter has 9 saws and I think Dr. McL told me it turned out 2500 feet of lumber daily." Emmons saw the business wisdom of this as well, stating, "thus the Co. are selecting the choice timber from our forests and supplying the Sandwich Island and California market—their vessels coming up the river and loading at the mills."[71]

Spreading beyond the fort were farms, eventually three thousand acres of pasture, orchard, and farm, designed to feed all of Fort Vancouver and to supply the sixteen other posts in the Columbia District as well. McLoughlin reported that in 1836 the fort's lands produced 8,000 bushels of wheat, 5,500 of barley, 6,000 of oats, 9,000 of peas, and 14,000 bushels of potatoes. Few Hudson's Bay Company facilities had the climate, land, or human power to have such extensive farms. Partly the unusual success came from McLoughlin's intense interest in farming. Like William Sublette in Missouri, he read journals and ordered expensive threshing machines to improve production, but agriculture was also part of Governor Simpson's grand plan.[72]

A well-organized human system underlay this factory-like structure, designed by the Hudson's Bay Company but orchestrated by McLoughlin. After the merger, and under the direction of George Simpson, the Company had regularized its employment system. It operated as a strict hierarchy, drawing an especially sharp line between gentlemen and servants as the two major categories of employees. At Fort Vancouver, like other large forts, the chief factor was assisted by several chief traders, who ran the fur-trading part of the business. Both factors and traders were full partners in the Hudson's Bay Company and received shares of the company profits. They also attended yearly council meetings at York Factory or Norway House, where they voted on profit sharing and how the operations at each fort would be conducted. McLoughlin didn't attend every meeting, but at least one representative from the Columbia District made the grueling trip to Hudson Bay each year.[73]

Beneath the rank of the field officers, factors, and traders who made up the council were employees known as clerks and apprenticed clerks. These young men, almost exclusively Scots, Scots Canadian, or English, were well educated and undertook a rigorous apprenticeship with the Company. The Company expected to develop its field officers from this corps of clerks. Apprenticed clerks did all of the writing and the accounting at the forts, houses, and York Factory, and after five years they could become clerks, who often ran small posts or expeditions. At Vancouver, around forty clerks kept ledgers, marked packs of fur, and copied papers and letters. Some accompanied fur brigades and conducted trading sessions. Though they worked long hours for relatively little pay, clerks did not engage in manual labor. They were, after all, gentlemen of the Company. After fourteen years of acceptable service, clerks (not unlike assistant professors) could be promoted to chief traders, which happened in the case of James Douglas, who arrived at Vancouver in 1830 as a clerk, eventually became McLoughlin's right-hand man, and finally the chief factor himself.[74]

Beneath the rank of clerks and apprentices were the ordinary employees, often called *engagés* or servants. These men were Native or French Canadian, often of mixed race and illiterate, so they had no hope of being assigned to the officer category. This group of employees had grades and classes as well: the highest being postmaster, followed by interpreters, mechanics, guides, steersmen, bowmen, hunters, voyageurs, and laborers, with apprenticed laborers at the bottom. Especially valued were blacksmiths, carpenters, and coopers. Many of these people had worked all over North America as part of the fur trade. The blacksmith at Fort Vancouver, William Cannon, had defected from William Sublette's operations in 1830. He designed and built the fort's hand-operated gristmill and other ingenious devices. Postmasters, at the top of the scale, were paid as much as forty pounds a year. Hunters came next, and typically they were French Canadians or Mohawk Iroquois from the Caughnawaga, Oka, and Saint Regis reserves in eastern and central Canada. The Company recruited its voyageurs and laborers from all over the world to do the hardest work in the fort: clearing land, hauling timber, unloading ships, cutting firewood. Charcoal pits needed constant tending, as did gardens and orchards. The great herds of sheep, pigs, goats, and cattle needed feeding, herding, and slaughtering. Thousands of salmon required drying and salting. The fur press demanded strong backs. Some local Indians were hired to be laborers, as well as Orkneymen, Hawaiians, and West Indians. Because of its location and function as a port, Fort Vancouver also employed ship captains, carpenters, and seamen, who served underneath Chief Factor McLoughlin as part of the vast hierarchy of the Honorable Company.[75]

This hierarchy appeared in the social system in the fort as well. Alexander Ross wrote that in the physical arrangement of the fort, "each class is provided with separate abodes. The apartments are appropriately divided into a bedrooms, antechambers, and closets. Here is seen the counting room, the mess room, the kitchen and pantry, the cellars, and Indian hall." He also noted, a bit bitterly, that at breakfast three grades of teas were served, along with three types of sugar, "the refined loaf, the common crushed, and the inferior brown."[76] Officers, *engagés*, and Indians all had their separate roles and their separate places. Hunters, trappers, mechanics, and laborers did not eat in the hall. The London Committee had made separate eating arrangements company policy in 1824. Only those who had been "mistered," entitled to be addressed as Mr. as a result of their company status as gentlemen, or who were special guests of some sort sat at the great table.[77]

Another group of people was absent from the dining table. At Fort Vancouver, as in most Hudson's Bay posts, men and women rarely ate together, as had been customary in eighteenth-century Scotland. Even at formal occasions, men were served by women, who then withdrew. Sometimes the women ate later in the same hall or they simply took their meals in a separate room. When McLoughlin honored Charles Wilkes, captain of an American exploring ship, with an official banquet in 1842, Wilkes noted with some surprise that not even the wives of the chief officers were present. Wilkes remarked in his journal about this insult to the women and that their exclusion could only "prevent improvement and retard the advancement of civilization."[78]

Again, women seem to have disappeared from the picture of life at fur-trading forts; few women's names appear on the HBC payrolls, and certainly none were "mistered." However, women did a huge amount of labor, both paid and unpaid. Because so many Hudson's Bay men, including officers, *engagés*, and servants, had their families with them at remote outposts like

Fort Vancouver, we hear about them between the business operations: when families traveled, built houses, or needed extra supplies; when children needed schooling or medical attention; when men got married or when women had babies. Chief Factor McLoughlin defended a flogging he ordered in 1837 for William Brown, a company servant, because Brown left an infant child at Fort Langley when he tried to leave the company service. Brown had complained publicly about this treatment, but company rules were clear about leaving young children and about obeying orders, though according to company lawyers, "corporal punishment was decidedly illegal." We see something here about McLoughlin's temper, conditions of work, and the challenges of managing human behavior in isolated spots.[79]

Governor Simpson, the man whom historian Frederick Merk rightly coronated as "the never wearying apostle of economy," complained mightily about families because they used so many supplies and ate so much food. He emphasized in his report to the London Committee about the Columbia Department that "it is highly necessary to reduce the number of Families at this place." However, saying and doing were two different things. When he tried to reduce food and clothing allowances he immediately received a petition from a long list of officers that explained they could not possibly keep their families on such a pittance. He relented, but he and the London Committee continued to complain about supporting families, though, of course, it was families who produced most of the food at the Fort's farms and who built a regional economy around the fort so that it could diversify.[80]

American and British travelers, trappers, and soldiers, in particular, commented on the presence of women and children because they saw this as unusual. Fur trader Alexander Ross, who spent a lot of time in and around Fort Vancouver, explained with pleasure that "even in this barbarous country, woman claims and enjoys her due share of attention and regard. Her presence brightens the gloom of the solitary post, her smiles add a new charm to the pleasures of the wilderness." He went on even more enthusiastically: "Nor are the ladies deficient in the accomplishments that procure admiration. . . . On holidays the dresses are as gay as in polished countries and on these occasions the gentleman puts on the beaver hat and the ladies make a fine show of silks and satins, and even jewelry is not wanting." However, Ross had to tell his readers that all was not as it seemed because these women were "descended from aboriginal mothers." It amazed him to find that "many of the females at the various establishments throughout Indian country are as fair as the generality of

European ladies." He explained this mystery by noting that in these women "the mixture of blood being so many degrees removed from the savage as hardly to leave any trace."[81] Now, of course, this blood had left a trace, or he wouldn't have needed to point it out.

Americans and Europeans did notice women of mixed race and Indian women because they were ubiquitous at the posts, processing furs, caring for children, and cleaning. One chief factor discovered this ubiquity when the he tried to cut food allowances, and the women in the fort went on strike, refusing to take on their regular Saturday duty of cleaning the fort.[82] At Fort Vancouver women grew, gathered, cooked, and prepared food, and did much of the work of turning animal skins and salmon into products that could be stored and shipped. Marguerite McLoughlin did not clean furs or the fort, but she did important work. Because she did not speak English, but rather French and Cree, and because she was illiterate, she left few records. Visitors to the fort and her own family noted the range of tasks she carried out in hosting important guests, taking care of orphaned children, making and repairing all of the clothing for her family and the officers at the fort, and advising her husband.[83]

The major function of any Hudson's Bay Company fort, including Fort Vancouver, was to obtain furs, process them for shipment, and send them either to York Factory or on company ships that docked at the fort. Most of this work was done by brigades, groups of between fifty and a hundred men, who headed out to hunt furs and to trade with the Indians. Officers led the brigades, but they consisted mostly of hunters, trappers, and packers, generally French Canadians, Hawaiians, Iroquois from the St. Lawrence, Ojibwes from Lake Superior, and Crees from Assiniboine. Many hunters were *engagés* of the Company, but others were "free trappers" who contracted individually with the chief traders at forts. Depending on the territory they covered, they could be gone for months at a time. In the Columbia District, where one of the concerns was competition with the Americans, brigades had a special responsibility to protect Hudson's Bay Company interests.

When Alexander Ross led the Snake River brigade in 1823, his group had fifty-five men, twenty of whom he felt he could trust as trappers; the rest were consigned to be laborers who processed the furs, took care of horses, and sometimes hunted for meat. He pointed out, too, that "we must not forget that twenty-five of the party [including himself] were married so that in our camp there were twenty-five women and sixty-four children." This human team required 392 horses, 75 guns, 212 beaver traps, one brass three-pounder cannon, and a vast store of provisions carried by the horses. Ross's greatest challenge was managing his varied work crew. He complained especially about the Iroquois, mostly free trappers, who continually threatened to defect to the Americans, who paid more for furs. Ross explained, and he was probably right, that they were welcome to go to the Americans if they felt safe traveling in groups of three or four people, as opposed to the group of more than a hundred that the Hudson's Bay Company used in the land of Nez Perce and Blackfoot Indians. Faced with that choice, few Iroquois left the Hudson's Bay brigades.[84]

Women played essential roles in these working groups. One of his clerks later explained: "It was the policy of McL to send, with the brigades, wives and children who acted as a restraint on the wilder spirits. The women, cooked, dressed skins and performed other duties in camp." Another less seasoned writer, emoting over the romance of the fur trade, noted the colorful qualities women added to the brigade. "When it left the river to travel overland, the dusky wife of the leader, the 'grande dame' was placed upon a horse whose trappings were adorned with colored quills, beads, fringes and tiny bells which tinkled with every movement of the horse. The grand dame herself was dressed in a crimson shawl and a petticoat of the finest blue broadcloth."[85] The writer, Mr. Johnson, may not have known this, but all of this sound and color served to warn everyone in the area that a trading party was coming and that it was friendly because of the women and children. Women also did more than tame their men, cook, and serve as human warning signals; they acted as cultural contacts and interpreters.

Governor Simpson believed "the family affair" of the brigade brought the Company "much expense and Inconvenience" because "business itself must give way to domestick considerations." But he complained about this practice largely in vain, because as even he had to admit, "almost every Man in the District has a family."[86] Even as Simpson wished that these women and children could be sent back to Canada or to their Indian families, he himself recommended that brigades from Fort Vancouver should make connections with the Indians in the Snake River area, including marrying their women and using them as interpreters to improve trade. The significance of women could be seen in the ceremonial practices of fur traders as well. When the brigades headed out, a kissing ritual "à la mode du pays" was held, which involved each member of the brigade kissing each woman at the post, "in the manner of a courtier," including the wives of the officers and company servants. They toasted, said prayers, and asked women to bless various objects important to the trip—guns, canoes, and trapping equipment. Many observers commented on these ceremonies; some saw it as charming, others found it distasteful or even shocking because of the contact between races. McLoughlin knew from long experience that these rituals helped his employees take on the very dangerous task of fur trading and bound them to each other as part of a culture that saw itself as distinctive.[87]

GLOBAL AMBITIONS

With the support and encouragement of the London Committee and Governor Simpson, John McLoughlin set out to build an empire from Fort Vancouver. His ambition wasn't exactly on behalf of Great Britain, but national interests meshed with his own. He imagined an empire based on fur that connected the entire Pacific basin to the river system that eventually led to York Factory, with forts up and down the Pacific Coast from Alta California to Alaska, a vigorous coasting trade, and strategic arrangements with Americans, Mexicans, and Russians. The success of such an ambitious plan depended on keeping interlopers like the Americans out and on cooperating and doing business with Mexico and Russia. McLoughlin succeeded in the first aim for nearly fifteen years by simply crushing his American fur trade rivals. He adopted pricing strategies that only a monopoly like the Hudson's Bay Company could afford. With Simpson's encouragement, he created a "fur desert" in the Rocky Mountains by deliberately and wastefully overhunting so that even if any Americans came west of the Rockies, they would find no fortune in furs.[88]

Before a single seed had been planted in the ground at Fort Vancouver, Governor George Simpson had imagined it as the great bread basket of the Northwest that could provide flour, beef, fruit, and vegetables to all of the posts of the Columbia division, as well as to the ever hungry Russian colonies to the north and even to the Sandwich Islands. He encouraged McLoughlin to reach out to the Russian outposts almost immediately. Russia had grand imperial visions about its Northwest Coast holdings as well, and they had a solid imperial claim, having hunted, traded with Native people, and built shipping facilities and posts beginning in the 1780s. The most energetic of those promoters was Gregorii Shelikhov. Beginning in 1783, Shelikhov and his partner, Ivan Golikov, mounted extensive fur voyages to Alaska. Unlike previous Russian efforts, these aimed at founding permanent settlements on the American mainland. In a 1788 report to Empress Catherine the Great, Shelikhov and Golikov detailed the rapid

14. Dr. John McLoughlin, chief factor, Fort Vancouver (1784–1857).
Photograph, unknown artist, ca. 1848. Oregon Historical Society
(OrHi 67763).

McLoughlin, known to the local Chinooks (and probably behind his back to his
employees) as "White-Headed Eagle," is shown in this photograph soon after
his forced retirement from the Hudson's Bay Company.

expansion of Russian trade along the Northwest Coast. The partners claimed
to have placed more than fifty thousand Native people under imperial rule.
Explorers stood ready, they insisted, to extend Russian America from the
Kurile Islands down the coast to Spanish America. All they needed was
the financial support of the empress (and a government monopoly), and
Russia could join the club of great imperial nations.[89]

Catherine, not entirely convinced of the profitability of Siberian schemes,
and not wanting to grant royal favor to one company when at least seven
others did business in the Pacific, stalled for nearly a decade. By 1797 two
of the largest firms had combined to form the United American Company.
The largest traders, including Shelikhov's heirs, urged the government
to create a semi-official monopoly company, the Russian-American Company, an entity that held an initial monopoly for twenty years. From 1799

to 1818, led by its keen and active field manager, Alexander Baranov, the Russian-American Company began to fashion a genuine trade empire that included posts at Sitka and at Fort Ross in northern California.

This organized, legal, and successful venture represented a true competitor for McLoughlin's ambitions, but also a business opportunity. Neither the Russians nor the Hudson's Bay Company wanted the Americans around, and the Russians genuinely needed a stable source of food and trade goods to keep their posts operating. Fort Vancouver ships and ship captains made lots of contacts with the Russians, but in 1829 McLoughlin decided to take a personal approach. As he politely explained in a formal letter, the Hudson's Bay Company now wanted to extend its business to "the Trade of the Coast, and to connect therewith the discovery and settlement of the Interior Country up to our most Northern limits." In other words, he wanted to build a post at Sitka. Of course, he added, "this will place us so near each other as to afford frequent and facile opportunities of communication." He concluded hopefully that such communication would "cultivate to Friendship, an acquaintance which we have long been desirous of forming." Delicately, McLoughlin pointed out the potential challenge if the "proximity" of the Hudson's Bay Company caused "any feelings of Rivalship or Competition in trade which could not fail of being highly injurious to the interests of both parties."[90] He then cut to the heart of his proposal: four to five thousand bushels of grain and eight to ten thousand pounds of salted beef per year, at "moderate Prices."[91]

He sent the letter north to be delivered in person by one of his ships' captains, who was also supposed to reconnoiter a spot for a fort that would be in British Territory but outside of the coastal strip claimed by the Russians. The Russians turned him down flat for the supply contract, and McLoughlin decided that the plan had been premature since his confidence in his coasting vessels to deliver the promised supplies was low. He did find a site for a fort, on the Nass River, and had his men build a small post, which he named Fort Simpson. Two years later he built two more forts: Fort Nisqually on the southern end of Puget Sound and Fort McLoughlin located between Puget Sound and Sitka.[92]

The legal status of these forts was not clarified until 1838 when the London Committee called McLoughlin for a meeting in London to assist them in direct negotiations with the Russian-American Company. He left Fort Vancouver in March of 1838, accompanied by his son John, and reached London by mid-November. The negotiations were successful, and the two companies signed trade agreements in February of 1839 to cooperate in the Northwest. The Russians got a stable source of supplies and payment for crossing their lands, and the Hudson's Bay Company got access to their lands in the North and a lucrative trade contract. Best of all, the Americans had been almost shut out entirely. Fulfilling the contract would require McLoughlin to step up farm production considerably at Vancouver and at Nisqually, which would serve the added purpose of cementing British claims to the region north of the Columbia with agricultural settlement.[93]

When McLoughlin returned home to Fort Vancouver in October of 1839, he began increasing the production of his farms to meet the demands of new Russian contracts. He built three dairies and hired three English families to run them, and then he sent men to start working on the new fort at Stikine. McLoughlin sent his daughter Eloisa and her new husband, William Glen Rae, to serve as the fort's leaders. His son John would be Rae's assistant. With this family phalanx, McLoughlin believed the new fort would have the strong leadership that it would need because of the fort's extreme isolation and the "rude and turbulent" Native people who lived there. Eloisa hated her exile at Stikine, describing the site "as a miserable place" with "only flat rocks and not trees around close," but she stayed there with her husband for nearly a year.[94]

With the northern part of his empire taking shape, McLoughlin then turned to California. The HBC needed a base to increase trapping and to develop a trade, and with the Russians out of northern California because of the deal with the Hudson's Bay Company, McLoughlin believed that officials in California would look favorably upon such an endeavor. The Russians, despised by the Californians, including the powerful Mariano Vallejo, had abandoned Fort Ross at Bodega Bay when they signed the new agreement with the Hudson's Bay Company. With the Russians out of the way in northern California, and worrying about the increasing American interest in the region, McLoughlin set his sights on building a post in Yerba Buena, the small settlement that would become San Francisco. He hoped he could sell lumber, salmon, and flour produced on the Columbia. The governor and London Committee agreed, notifying George Simpson in 1839: "At San Francisco or Monterrey we think a store for the sale of British manufactured goods and other articles might be in demand at the missions and by the Settlers or other residents . . . might be opened with advantage." The fort had purchased cattle and sheep over the years in California but had been frustrated with the rules, taxes, and the uncooperative attitude of Mexican officials.[95]

California, of course, was a territory of the Republic of Mexico, and any

post would require a license from the Mexican government and the support of the governor, Juan Bautista Alvarado, and the military commander,
Mariano Vallejo. McLoughlin sent his second in command, James Douglas,
to negotiate with Alvarado and Vallejo, who had both been annoyed with
the fact that Fort Vancouver brigades had been taking furs in northern
California for years without a license. Now, in return for the HBC paying
duties on the furs its men gathered, the Mexican government would grant
them licenses and would give them a free grant of land to build stores
and warehouses in Yerba Buena. In April of 1841, eager to get started,
McLoughlin transferred his son-in-law, William Glen Rae, along with his
daughter Eloisa and their new baby girl, Margaret, from the Stikine Post
to the new site at Yerba Buena.[96]

This may have been John McLoughlin's proudest moment. He had
built Fort Vancouver into a shining example of a Hudson's Bay Company
enterprise and had been lauded by his superiors. He had fulfilled a dream
of building a series of northern posts that would extend his reach considerably. Now, he had made the first move in pushing the HBC's influence
south. And while serving the Company and the British Empire, he and
Marguerite had created a family empire. Two of their sons held responsible
positions in the Columbia Department; their daughter Eloisa was married
to a competent post leader; two other daughters were married to Hudson
Bay traders, and their granddaughter Catherine had just married Frances
Ermatinger, who ran the farms at Cowlitz. John and Marguerite had stood
by proudly in 1838 as they witnessed a double wedding—that of their
daughter Eloisa to William Glenn Rae and that of James and Amelia Douglas
as they renewed their vows and made their "fur trade marriage" clerically
acceptable. Another generation seemed secure. They had achieved this
stability in the midst of the quicksand of international business and imperial competition. Who was white or Anglo or British or American and who
was Indian or Native and who was mixed race or métis or half-breed didn't
seem to matter. However, the system that had enabled the McLoughlin
family to reach this moment was about to be torn apart. Forces of cultural,
economic, and political change would sweep this web of connection away.

THE FINE MESH OF THE FAMILY NETWORK

Much of the pleasure McLoughlin took in observing his dominion came
from the way it involved his family. Like the Chouteaus and the Sublettes,
he could not have achieved his status without the assistance of brothers,

uncles, sons, sons-in-law, daughters, and grandchildren. He trusted family members in ways he could trust no one else. They also caused him immeasurable pain. The story of John McLoughlin Jr. tells us a lot about the changing context in which the McLoughlin family lived their lives. The Northwest, and the Far West in general, would be changed by the increasing presence of the United States, but the McLoughlin family would also be affected. John McLoughlin's mixed race family suffered. These children and grandchildren, who matured into a world that saw racial classification as a central dividing line, had very different experiences than had the children of an earlier generation of fur trade families.

John McLoughlin Jr.—let's call him "young John" to reduce confusion—went to school in Montreal at the age of eight. He was twelve when his family moved to Fort Vancouver, leaving young John and his sister Elisabeth, then ten, under the supervision of their great-uncle, Simon Fraser. Joseph, McLoughlin's oldest son from an earlier marriage to an Ojibwe, was apprenticed to some Hudson's Bay Company hunters in Sault Saint Marie. The McLoughlin family made this decision at great expense and emotional cost. Despite his success as a manager and his long tenure in the fur trade, McLoughlin had not amassed much personal fortune. When he arrived at Fort Vancouver, he was in debt, largely because of the great expense of educating his children away from home.

The McLoughlins, like many fur trade parents in this era, considered the expense and the education essential. Several generations of fur trade families now had children—creating a significant demographic presence in North America—flesh and blood proof of the culture and economy of the fur trade. A new set of challenges accompanied the mixed race offspring. Alexander Ross, long-time fur trader in the Columbia region, worried that without proper supervision these children would "form a composition of all the bad qualities of both races." He hoped, clearly including his own children in this category, that "half-breed children, instructed in the principles of religion and morality, would doubtless prove an ornament to society."[97] Increasing parental concern and attention to their children's futures reflected the changes in the way the fur trade operated in the era of the consolidated Hudson's Bay Company. Families could no longer count on the Company to provide employment or spouses. As a result, among the elite many sons were sent to Montreal or England for education and training, while daughters were more often kept at home.[98]

Not everyone agreed with this practice. British Canadians, especially more recently minted officers of the HBC, found the parental concern over these "half-breed" children excessive. Letitia Hargrave, the English wife of a chief trader at York Factory, wrote in her letters home to England in 1840 that "the state of society seems shocking." As proof of this sorry condition she described the McLoughlin family: "Dr. McLoughlin one of our grandees at a great expense gave two of his sons a regular education in England and keeps a third a common Indian. . . . I daresay the heathen is the happiest of them as the father is constantly upbraiding the others with the ransom they have cost him."[99] The nasty Mrs. Hargrave got some of the details wrong; John was educated in Paris, David in London, while Joseph, the "common Indian," received apprentice training. However, she was right in the fact that the expensive education did not buy happiness.

Young John's unhappiness at being away from his family and his anger at his situation appeared almost immediately. Elisabeth appeared to do fine, but John was bounced from school to school for problems like "soiling his breeches" and for "corrupting the morals of the other boys," according to his great-uncle Simon Fraser.[100] By 1827, when John was fifteen, Fraser warned McLoughlin that he was finding it difficult to find a school that would have young John, and also that at age seventy Fraser had tired of the responsibility. In 1828 young John beat another student in a very public fit of rage, which everyone in the fur trade seemed to hear about, including Governor Simpson, who wrote about it to McLoughlin. As a result of this episode, no one in Montreal would accept him as a student or an employee.[101]

McLoughlin, deeply concerned about his son's future, implored his uncle for advice. "I do not [know] what to do with my Son—what do you think he is fit for—I will be obliged to you for your Opinion." Fraser answered that "the best thing that can be done for the young man is to make him an Indian trader." However, he warned, "Governor Simpson tells me the Company have determined to take none of the Young Men into their service (for reasons which he explained to me & which you must know.)"[102] Fraser recognized what the combination of increasing prejudice against people of mixed race and the Hudson's Bay Company plan to curtail the long tradition of nepotism in the fur trade would mean for young John. Fraser recommended that McLoughlin buy his son an office in the army or an apprenticeship in a counting house, but McLoughlin insisted his son would have a career with the Hudson's Bay Company. With great pressure from McLoughlin, Simpson offered young John a post as a servant in Lachine. McLoughlin, terribly insulted that Simpson would not offer his son a position as a clerk and gentleman, refused to allow young John to take the job.[103]

Probably frustrated with the slowness of mail between Vancouver and Montreal and also angry at his father, John Jr. took matters into his own hands. In October of 1829 young John headed off to Paris to live with his uncle David, a successful medical doctor. With his father's approval and financial support, John began training for the medical profession in 1830 in Paris. John seemed to flourish away from Canada and under his uncle David's supervision. He described the exciting political situation in France to his friends in Canada and boasted about his near duels with several of his classmates. He reported proudly that he had passed his examinations with flying colors in 1833.[104]

Then, in 1834, at the age of twenty-two, John did something so serious that his uncle David sent him back to Canada with no explanation. The entire family expressed frustration at not knowing what "It" was. His father seemed both hurt and confused by the turn of events. Young John apparently tried to apologize, but as McLoughlin wrote to his cousin, "He writes me an Apology for his Misconduct but he does not write me what it was he did." Whatever "It" was, it occurred early in 1834 soon after David was married, and Roderick Finlayson, a family friend who knew the situation, said the marriage "was the cause of John's coming to Canada." Perhaps he approached David's new wife inappropriately or perhaps he displayed some of the anger he had shown as a child. We just don't know what "It" was.[105]

Back in Canada, young John found himself under a considerable cloud. He first attempted to finish his medical studies at McGill University. However, his angry uncle David would not arrange to have his transcripts sent from Paris, so he could not enroll. He applied to join the Hudson's Bay Company, but George Simpson, knowing his background, refused to hire him. So young John, now twenty-three and not really so young, drifted, ran up debts, and aggravated his relatives and supporters. McLoughlin, upon hearing of his son's behavior, wrote to everyone that John should be cut off from any extra money, "not one farthing more than you consider absolutely necessary."[106] Finally, John had exhausted even his great-uncle Simon Fraser's patience. When John asked for yet another loan, Fraser wrote, rather savagely, "I am convinced that you are depraved beyond any hopes of reform," and advised him to "retire to some distant far country that you may never be more be heard of."[107]

John took him at his word and made a decision that created another "It" in terms of family drama. Early in 1836 he joined up with a man named James Dickson, who had formed something called the "Indian Liberating Army." Dickson planned a sort of filibuster that involved gathering up disgruntled Indian and mixed-blood people, marching to Texas, New Mexico, and California, and founding a new Indian nation there. In Montreal, he recruited several supporters from the mixed-blood sons of fur traders, a group who had begun to see an identity in their mixed race status. Many of them, like young John McLoughlin, had been refused employment by the Hudson's Bay Company and were frustrated by their prospects in Canada. Dickson's message and promise of action appealed to these young men, who became "captains" and "majors" in "General" Dickson's army. John, a "major," got a loan from a cousin to have a suitable uniform made up with "a red coat, worked with silver lace on the chest and collar with large silver epaulettes."[108] In July of 1836 the army of sixty chartered a boat and made for Sault Sainte Marie. Without funds or food, they stole and slaughtered some cattle and then were arrested by a sheriff's posse just west of Detroit. They paid a fine, and the army, completely without funds and considerably reduced in number, headed toward the Red River settlements where they hoped they would find more young men willing to join the army.[109]

At this point the newspapers began to report about the "pirates on the lake," which got Governor Simpson's attention. Alarmed at the potential for "an infinity of trouble" if these "wild thoughtless young men of good education and daring character, half-breed sons of gentlemen in the fur trade," arrived at Red Lake, Simpson decided to break up the leadership of Dickson's "Army."[110] When the army, now numbering eleven, arrived at Red Lake in December, Simpson offered young John McLoughlin and Alexander McLeod clerkships in the Hudson's Bay Company. McLoughlin's family urged him to take the position, to "desist from these foolish expectations" as his aunt, Sister St. Henry, put it. He desisted and took the job, and Simpson sent him by the company express canoes to Fort Vancouver, where he was now officially stationed for a five-year term as clerk and surgeon.[111] We don't know whether his position with the Company felt like a victory or a failure to young John McLoughlin, but after sixteen years he was home with his family and seemed, finally, to have settled into a career path.

When young John arrived back home in August of 1837, he stepped into a complex set of expectations and a system that his parents had created at Fort Vancouver. And he was in a place that accepted and even celebrated his mixed race credentials. The situation should have been ideal, but because of a dreadful combination of personal failings and international events, John would fall through the safety net his family had built for him. The McLoughlin family empire was about to fall.

IMMIGRANTS, NATIONS, AND THE LOSS OF A FAMILY EMPIRE

The McLoughlin family's ambitions and plans depended on the stability of the Hudson's Bay Company and, on a larger plane, on the strength of the British position in North America, especially in that small corner of the Pacific Northwest. In 1837, when John Jr. arrived at Fort Vancouver, the British position in the region looked impenetrable. The Hudson's Bay Company and John McLoughlin Sr. had created a vast monopoly that had successfully kept out all competitors. McLoughlin was "much Gratified" to have his two sons working for him, and he reported to a cousin that "they are as attentive and smart at their work as most young men."[112] They had good relationships with local Indian nations and formal diplomatic ties with the Russians and the Mexicans. The Americans seemed to be a distant worry—a few trappers and a few ships and a few missionaries. The only settlements were in the Willamette valley, to the south of Fort Vancouver, which, according to a survey done by the Methodists in 1838, had a population of 57 adult males: 23 French Canadians, 18 Americans, and 16 clergy (apparently men of the cloth were nationless, and women and children didn't count at all).[113] To counter this American settlement, a number of retired Hudson's Bay Company servants, mostly French Canadians and métis, had with McLoughlin's blessing and financial support settled at a community called French Prairie down the Willamette River.

The Boundary Question, which McLoughlin always capitalized in his correspondence, floated in the back of every business and personal decision. The outcome of the constant diplomatic wrangling over establishing the border between Canada and the United States remained an open question for everyone. Both American settlers and the leadership and employees of the Hudson's Bay Company at Fort Vancouver had good reason both to fear and to hope. In spite of the attention Oregon Country got, relatively few American settlers had arrived even into the 1840s. By far the most significant Euro-American entity in the region was Fort Vancouver. McLoughlin didn't discuss the boundary much in his letters because it had been so well rehearsed other places and, frankly, there wasn't much he could do about it. It wasn't, really, a company matter. He later explained, "I considered it Expedient to avoid as much as possible speaking on the Boundary Question—merely telling those who spoke to us on the subject that I did not understand the merits of the case But as it was an affair that would be settled without asking my opinion and still less my consent I did not trouble my head about it—as I must take it as it was made for us."[114]

However, any astute observer could see that the delay in settling the boundary was strengthening the American position. American missionaries, settlers, and speculators continued to trickle in each year. As early as 1841, when American settlers were still relatively few in number, Simpson had practically abandoned hope that the Columbia River would become the boundary line. When reporting to the London Committee in March 1842 after his visit to the Columbia, he made the following prophetic comment: "In the final adjustment of the Boundary Question, it is more than probable a line drawn through the Straits of de Fuca . . . will become the Coast Boundary . . . because I am of the opinion the Government of the United States will insist on having a port on the North West Coast, and that Gt. Britain will, for the sake of peace, accept the Straits of de Fuca as a boundary on the Coast, and thereby give up Puget Sound & Hood's Canal, together with the country inbetween."[115] Despite his pessimism, Governor Simpson and the London Committee encouraged McLoughlin to continue developing commercial enterprises that would protect the Company's interests and the British claim to region.

The missionaries brought changes larger than their mere presence. A man named Jason Lee, sent by the Methodist Church in 1834, arrived in the region as part of a new national obsession with Christianizing the Indians of the American West. This interest in saving Indians evolved out of the Second Great Awakening that swept across the United States in the 1820s and 1830s. When Lee arrived in 1834, McLoughlin welcomed him warmly and offered him all the assistance that the fort could muster, including advice not to take on the Flatheads and Nez Perce Indians, who did not appreciate this interference in their affairs. Instead, McLoughlin recommended that the missionaries take on the more settled peoples in the Willamette Valley. He gave Lee and his followers seeds, lent them farm implements and oxen, and sent them on their way. The next missionaries to arrive came from the Congregational and Presbyterian churches, and in 1836 the immigrants included the soon-to-be infamous Marcus and Narcissa Whitman and their partners Henry and Eliza Spaulding.[116]

Even at their greatest influence, there were never more than nine missions, and these had less than a hundred people living in them. This small American presence, however, did encourage a group of zealous, vocal, and skilled patriots or troublemakers (depending on one's perspective) who began to give Oregon and its boundaries national attention. The most significant of these was Hall Jackson Kelley, a Boston schoolmaster who spent five months at Fort Vancouver in the winter of 1834–35. Kelley had first learned about Oregon from reading descriptions in Lewis and Clark's narratives and got obsessed with obtaining this region for the United States. He published his first pamphlet in 1830, long before he actually saw the Columbia region, and continued producing them by the ream until he died in 1868. He wrote, personally, to many members of Congress and to other organizations that had an interest in Oregon, keeping what became known as the "Oregon question" in the spotlight. In 1838 Senator Lewis F. Linn of Missouri introduced a bill to create a territorial government in Oregon, which, of course, was impossible as long as joint occupation continued, but it had great value as a piece of propaganda. Next Linn presented a petition in Congress in 1839, signed by thirty-five residents of Oregon, demanding American sovereignty. After the failure of this legislation, he and a group of fellow Oregon enthusiasts in Congress conducted a persistent campaign for the extension of American laws and sovereignty to Oregon.[117]

Central to their campaign was a vilification of the Hudson's Bay Company as a great, ruthless, unfair, foreign corporate giant. Many of these petitions, speeches, and pamphlets claimed that the Company starved immigrants, refused to sell supplies to them, and deliberately sent Indians to attack them, charges that McLoughlin took very seriously and personally. Much criticism he could let roll off his shoulders, but because he made so much of an effort to be hospitable to visitors and immigrants and had hosted many for a long time at the fort, he protested especially fiercely the assertion that the Company mistreated settlers. The other often repeated charge that Hudson's Bay Company servants slaughtered Indians by the hundred and incited the surviving Natives to massacre American settlers and immigrants was equally false and equally hard to counter.[118]

Despite the supposed cruelty of the Hudson's Bay Company, the imagined danger from angry Indians, and the very real issue of unclear national control, American immigrants did begin settling in the joint occupancy area, especially in the Willamette River valley. At first they came in very small numbers, less than fifty in the 1830s, just over a hundred in the first significant year of migration in 1842, but finally the "Great Migration" of 1843 brought between seven hundred and a thousand people to the valley.[119] To meet this challenge, McLoughlin made several business decisions that he regretted later. First, he stepped up food production at the fort both because he saw a new market developing and also because he thought cleared lands and agricultural products would improve the Company's position north of the Columbia. Second, he claimed land in his own name at the falls of the Willamette and built some sawmills and gristmills there to serve the settlers and to increase the Company's claims on that river. Third, he sold, but often on credit, supplies and agricultural implements to many of the immigrants, who arrived destitute and unprepared for farming. He made these decisions while attempting to increase his core business in the new northern posts and the trading establishment at Yerba Buena. Given the unstable situation, McLoughlin may have been badly overextended, but these decisions had solid thinking and long experience behind them.[120]

The Puget's Sound Agricultural Company had been created by the London Committee to meet the challenge of furnishing the wheat, flour, beef, and vegetables that the HBC had agreed to deliver to the Russian-American Company. The governor and London Committee decided that the expansion of farming should be entrusted to a new corporation. Legally, it was entirely independent of the Hudson's Bay Company, but for all practical purposes it was a subsidiary. McLoughlin supervised its operation though it had a resident manager. However, the Pugets Sound Agricultural Company was never a success, mostly because of the shipping problems that plagued McLoughlin. The hazards of landing at Fort Vancouver, or any spot on the Columbia, challenged even the most skilled seamen. The number of ship captains he sent home for drunkenness, disorderly behavior, or incompetence testifies to the difficulty of finding reliable employees. The expense and vexation of running this business added materially to McLoughlin's troubles.[121]

When Governor George Simpson arrived for a tour of inspection in 1841, he was well aware of the uncertainties facing the Columbia District, but over the years he had agreed with most of McLoughlin's decisions. This time he seemed shocked by what McLoughlin had done, especially in California, and sincerely believed the chief factor had gone way beyond his authority. McLoughlin knew Simpson was coming, and it is difficult to understand why he plunged into the California venture without waiting to consult his superior. True, he had reported fully to Simpson at every stage, but the fact remains that he acted without specific authorization. In any event, Simpson's opposition, when it developed, came as a great surprise to McLoughlin. The trouble started when Simpson and McLoughlin made an inspection trip to San Francisco and the Sandwich Islands in January 1842. Simpson suddenly became intractably hostile to the whole project. The change in his attitude may well have begun at Monterey when, according to Simpson. "a dozen rapacious customs collectors" had descended upon them, "like vultures to their prey."[122]

Whether it was being compelled by California shipping laws to pay duties several times over or having just received a very pessimistic report on the prospects of the interior fur trade from Frances Ermatinger, Simpson wanted to wash his hands of business in California. Whatever happened, Simpson decided that the business would never pay and that "the sooner we break off all communications, either directly or indirectly with California, the better."[123] He also decided that the Company was badly overextended in the northern posts as well and directed McLoughlin to curtail operations there. Given the iffiness of the Boundary Question and the fact that all of McLoughlin's businesses that involved dealing with ships had failed, none of this should have been a surprise. McLoughlin, however, simply refused to obey these directives from Simpson, even when they were repeated by the London Committee. Their dispute over business tactics became personal between the two men, especially after two personal tragedies would rock McLoughlin's whole world.[124]

MURDER AT FORT STIKINE AND SUICIDE IN CALIFORNIA

When Governor Simpson left McLoughlin with his unwelcome set of instructions, the governor was en route to Russia. He stopped in to visit the northern posts while waiting for a ship and discovered a dreadful situation at Fort Stikine. As Simpson put it in his official dispatch, "On arrival . . . my mind was filled with the apprehension that all was not right." He saw that the flags were at half-mast and that the clerk in charge of the post did not come to greet him. He approached the post with some foreboding and was "more shocked than words can describe to learn that Mr. McLoughlin was no more . . . having fallen by the hand of one of his own men." Young John McLoughlin, the officer in charge, had been murdered by Urbain Heroux, a servant of the Company, on April 20, 1842. This was bad news indeed, when McLoughlin and his family received it in June of 1842, but Simpson's harsh statement that the younger McLoughlin had brought it on himself by poor management and drunkenness made it even worse. He concluded that "any Tribunal by which the case could be tried, would find a verdict of 'Justifiable Homicide.'"[125]

The whole episode tells us a lot about fur trade life at a remote post, relationships with local Native people, and young John McLoughlin. A rash and impulsive young man, with a series of "Its" in his past so serious that the family never spoke of them, he carried his past into a very dangerous situation. Leading a post required maturity, a steady head, and excellent diplomatic skills. John may have settled down a bit, but he hardly met those requirements, and it was very hard for a father to see his son's limitations.

McLoughlin would never recover from this judgment of his son, and he spent years trying to clear John's name. Exactly what happened that night at Fort Stikine became another unknowable family "It." Simpson based his judgment of the situation on a very quick and incomplete investigation. He interviewed only a few of the workers at the post and seemed to take the word of the murderer that he had been mistreated and that John McLoughlin had threatened to kill him. Simpson's refusal to bring the accused man or any of the witnesses to Canada for trial or further investigation seems incredibly high-handed and even cruel. Perhaps Simpson had harbored an active dislike for the young man he called a "half breed." The two did have an unpleasant history in that Simpson had refused to employ young McLoughlin, had bailed him out of trouble several times, and had finally hired him only to end the possibility of a métis rebellion in 1836. That history, plus Simpson's anger at the senior McLoughlin, might explain Simpson's refusal to investigate the crime and his easy assumption of the younger McLoughlin's guilt. Whatever Simpson's animus, John McLoughlin never forgave him, and the two men never met again.[126]

As part of the downward spiral that eventually led to his being forcibly retired, McLoughlin Sr. did spend the better part of his energies for the next two years seeking vindication for his son. In the midst of this personal turmoil, McLoughlin renewed his Catholic faith and, after more than thirty years of partnership, he and Marguerite married in the Catholic rite in November of 1842. Perhaps this gave him the strength to battle Simpson, to whom McLoughlin attached blame for the entire event. Still stunned a year later, he wrote to an old friend in 1843 that he had concluded "the fact is that from the first moment Sir George Simpson heard of the Murder of my late Son John he Resolved on Smothering Investigation."[127] McLoughlin was probably right about Simpson's poor handling of the situation, but he probably felt guilty himself.

The post at Stikine had been trouble from the beginning. Local Tlingits had attacked the small fort twice because of disagreements over trade, and the men who staffed this post were a very rough lot. Putting an inexperienced leader in charge, especially one like young John McLoughlin who had always had difficulty controlling his anger, was probably a poor decision on McLoughlin Sr.'s part. Though young John told his brother David that he was "well satisfied with his situation being far away from the Old Gentleman," no doubt referring to McLoughlin Sr., John had also reported how much trouble he had getting the men to work and the fact that he disciplined some of the more incorrigible men.[128] One of the troublemakers had threatened to kill him earlier in the year when John had put him in the fort's prison for stealing alcohol.

Part of the tension came from what the Iroquois and Canadian servants perceived as unfair rules about sex with local women. Company policy and practice allowed and even encouraged long-term commitments to Native women on the part of officers but prohibited servants from having brief sexual encounters. At Fort Stikine this meant in practice that young John McLoughlin had a "country wife" and had sex with several other Native women, but his men were prohibited from bringing women to the fort. This infuriated the already testy fort workers—they vowed to kill Young John if he didn't step down—and one night, after they had been drinking, they murdered him, which was hardly the "justifiable homicide" that Sir George characterized.[129]

The subject of John's murder or the evil intentions of Sir George Simpson took up most of the space in McLoughlin's reports to the London Committee in that period. In November 1844 he wrote a final "thundering epistle to their Honours," as another fur trader put it, that covered eighty-five manuscript pages and answered every charge in great detail. McLoughlin got no response as "their Honours" had decided to support Simpson and believed that McLoughlin was behaving inappropriately.[130] However, after two years of single-minded effort McLoughlin had amassed so much evidence in support of his son that even though the Company never responded officially, several members of the London Committee wrote to him privately and admitted that Simpson may have made some mistakes. Nothing would satisfy McLoughlin, and he wore out even his closest associates with long letters and diatribes about the case. Like many nineteenth-century men of his status, McLoughlin was his own most important business and personal asset, and Simpson's accusations had tarnished both his and his son's names. McLoughlin's concern with reputation and clearing his son's name edged into an obsession, though not an uncommon one. Finally, as McLoughlin's claims began to sully Simpson's status with other chief factors and the debate began to be discussed in wider circles, Sir John Pelly, the governor of the Hudson's Bay Company, stepped in. He told McLoughlin he would have to resolve his feud with Simpson or retire.[131]

This message, and another dire piece of personal news, refocused McLoughlin's attention. His son-in-law, William Glenn Rae, who had left young John McLoughlin alone at Fort Stikine when McLoughlin had appointed him to run the post at Yerba Buena, committed suicide in January of 1845. Because of the lack of available ships, many months and even years had passed without any direct communication between Rae and McLoughlin. The isolation and lack of communication with McLoughlin or with London had contributed to Rae's sense of futility, a silence over which McLoughlin must have felt a great deal of guilt. But other issues added to the weight Rae felt as well. He had been forced to discharge three clerks and then had no one to assist him, plus he had a wife and three small children to support. On top of these difficulties, Rae became involved in Mexican politics. Governor Alvarado, who had been replaced by a new governor in December of 1842, was soon plotting against his successor. Rae yielded to Alvarado's pressure and supplied ammunition and a number of lances to the rebels. When the rebels failed in their coup against the sitting governor in January of 1845, Rae became convinced he would be arrested and executed and that the Company's property, which he valued at about $48,000, would be confiscated. His wife Eloisa, McLoughlin's daughter, later told her family that in his last few days Rae had gotten so paranoid about arrest by the Mexicans that he hadn't slept at all and just sat by the door with a loaded pistol. Finally one night, he began threatening to take his own life. Eloisa, who had given birth two days earlier, wrestled with him, but finally, "he put the pistol to his head, fired, and fell instantly dead."[132] Upon hearing this news, McLoughlin sent a ship and his son David, home from school in Paris, to pack up the store in Yerba Buena and to escort his grieving sister and her three children home to Fort Vancouver. The Hudson's Bay Company experiment in Mexican California had come to a miserable end.

In the midst of these two personal crises, Fort Vancouver continued to be besieged by American immigrants, and McLoughlin had to contend with a very unstable situation. During the first years of American immigration Fort Vancouver had been the only source of supplies in Oregon Country. Many of the earliest immigrant parties arrived without provisions, completely destitute after their long journeys, and they turned to Fort Vancouver for help. McLoughlin provided them with food, clothing, and building supplies, all on credit, as few immigrants had any cash or even goods to barter. He had also lent them company tools and farming implements and provided them with seed to plant. In the face of grave warnings from Simpson against extending credit, McLoughlin justified his policy by saying that it moved the settlers toward real independence and protected the whole country against a food shortage the next season. However, in the Company's view, this policy had gotten entirely out of hand when they discovered that by the spring of 1844 McLoughlin had made advances totaling £6,606 to between three and four hundred persons. Simpson and the London Committee reminded him sharply that the Hudson's Bay Company did not extend credit—only prompt payment in cash or goods was acceptable.[133]

McLoughlin certainly knew company policy. He advised Peter Skene Ogden, the trader in charge of Fort Nisqually on Puget Sound and very close to a number of new settlements, "that we see no objection, to your supplying the American settlers in your neighborhood with such articles as can be spared, without inconvenience to the business, from the Company's stores, either for cash or for such productions of the Country as we are in the habit of purchasing, in this quarter, such as wheat and shingles." That was policy, but then his instructions recognized the reality of local conditions: "In the present destitute circumstances of the few people at Nisqually, we shall dispense with the established regulations so far as to permit you to advance such of those now there as require assistance but no others to the amount of 20 or 25 dollars, in molasses, coffee or other articles of the sort; but their outstanding accounts ought never to exceed that amount."[134]

This policy, overly generous as it was from the perspective of the Hudson's Bay Company, still created resentment among the immigrants. Many of the arrivals had been saved from starvation by free supplies given to them by the U.S. Army at various forts along the Oregon Trail, and now they couldn't understand why the Hudson's Bay Company posts, which were, of course, British and private, would ask them to pay money for food in their time of need. Even the policy of extending credit led to the reputation of the Hudson's Bay Company as being anti-American and tight-fisted, although the Company wasn't doing anything that American merchants wouldn't have done and did do to their own countrymen in Oregon. McLoughlin knew that most of the immigrants had no intention of letting their families starve in the shadow of a well-stocked fort belonging to a British enterprise. If supplies had not been made available on credit, Fort Vancouver or other posts might well have been burned to the ground.

As it was, McLoughlin had to deal with a serious public relations challenge. Two episodes serve as examples. In 1843 a group of settlers circulated a petition to the U.S. Congress claiming that the Hudson's Bay Company, and McLoughlin in particular, were mistreating them by their rapacious behavior: refusing to sell them cattle, cheating them when buying and selling wheat, and overcharging for lumber. Furious at these charges, which even other settlers agreed were false, McLoughlin could do little to defend himself and had to swallow the insult. In February 1845, a young immigrant named Henry Williamson built a rough house just outside the doors of Fort Vancouver, clearly on company property. When McLoughlin sent a party to tear the house down, Williamson threatened loudly and publicly to "burn the finest building in Oregon," meaning the fort. Such incidents concerned McLoughlin enough that he made a request to the British consul general in Hawaii to have a warship stationed on the Columbia. The presence of a ship would demonstrate the company ties to the nation that, in theory, controlled the Columbia. None was stationed there, but the HMS *America* arrived in August of 1845 and stayed about a month.[135]

From the perspective of the governor and the London Committee things looked very bad in the Columbia District as diplomats debated the Boundary Question. Consider the news that reached London in the fall of 1844: McLoughlin had advanced alarming sums of credit to American immigrants; he had ignored specific instructions to close the post in California; the Hudson's Bay Company was being labeled anti-American and greedy in the halls of the U.S. Congress; the Puget Sound Agricultural Company was losing money; HBC property was being threatened. Further, McLoughlin's reports were still filled with angry discussions of his son's murder rather than careful reporting of business matters. The governor and London Committee decided that the Columbia District would be broken up, that John McLoughlin would no longer be the superintendant of the whole, and that he would go on furlough in 1846 and then either retire or be posted somewhere else.[136]

When McLoughlin received this announcement in June of 1845, he was stunned, though maybe he shouldn't have been. The world that surrounded the Columbia had changed, and the business of the Hudson's Bay Company that had flourished in that world would have to change as well. Fort Vancouver would be essentially abandoned as a result of the boundary decision in 1846, and the Company would operate out of a lone post on the Pacific, Fort Victoria, on the tip of Vancouver Island, safely in British territory. James Douglas and his wife Amelia would continue to preside there until 1861.

You could tell the end of this story in two ways: the first being the Oregon booster story of McLoughlin as the first white pioneer, the second being a narrative of denouement and destruction. Both would be right. The world of John McLoughlin and the fur trade, which had sustained him for a lifetime, had come to end. He would eventually be re-interpreted as a "pioneer," and streets and bridges would be named after him all over the state. In 1957 he would be named the "Father of Oregon," and statues of the old man with the flowing white hair would appear in public buildings everywhere. But Marguerite, with her clearly Native features and coloring, could never be the "Mother of Oregon." Her face and her family could be celebrated only in the world of the fur trade, and even there it challenged understanding. By the early twentieth century, John McLoughlin's mixed race heritage had been wiped entirely "clean" so that his granddaughter, Angeline McLoughlin, who lived on the Kootenay reservation and labeled herself as "Indian," was refused admittance to his house, now a museum, during a "Pioneer Day" celebration.[137]

On the denouement and disaster side, we can tell the very sad story of John McLoughlin's efforts to join the new American empire that arrived on his doorstep. Forcibly retired in 1846, the McLoughlins chose to stay in Oregon. After the border decision in 1846 was affirmed, McLoughlin believed that his personal land claims would be protected by the official language of the treaty. The family built a large house in Oregon City, near what would become Portland, on the land where McLoughlin had erected mills years earlier. It wouldn't be as busy as Fort Vancouver, but the new household included the McLoughlins' widowed daughter, Eloisa, and her three children, their youngest son David, their granddaughter Catherine Ermatinger and her little girl, another grandson, William McKay, and several Indian servants to help with the young children.

In his retirement McLoughlin had one basic goal: to provide for his family in the present and future. Given his struggles with the Hudson's Bay Company over ownership of the land claim and mills along with the generalized hostility that many American settlers in Oregon still felt for the Company, McLoughlin worried a great deal about protecting his property in the unfamiliar territory of U.S. land law. He made several efforts to become an American citizen but was rebuffed several times, first in 1847 because no territorial judges could administer the oath, and again in 1849 when he was told he would have to wait two years before he could claim the "rights of citizenship." As a result, in a series of shady deals worthy of Samuel Clemens's dourest imaginings, some Oregon landowners, including the provisional governor of the territory, managed to get a bill passed in the U.S. Congress that specifically denied John McLoughlin's land claims, because he was not a citizen.[138] In the end, McLoughlin lost his land but did become a citizen. He retained his mills and his store in Oregon City. When he died in 1857, he left all of his household goods to Marguerite and divided up the rest of his considerable estate among his living children. It consisted mostly of the mills and some real estate in Oregon City, which would continue to increase in value. In a monetary sense he had provided for his family.

McLoughlin could not protect his family from new social and cultural ideals. As the terrible land situation unfolded behind his back, McLoughlin acted as a citizen. He donated land for a jail, funded a new church, and invested in the local newspaper. He worried particularly about the increasingly tense relations between Indians, migrants, and new settlers. As chief factor of the Hudson's Bay Company, he took pride in the knowledge and relationships he had developed with Indian people and with people of mixed race whom he had brought to the region. McLoughlin felt enough concern about tensions in eastern Oregon and about "Reports that Half-Breeds will not have claims of land" appearing in the local papers that he wrote to the secretary of war about the issues. He explained that such as policy would "Blast the Prospects of these people" and force them to retire among their already stressed Indian relatives, when the "half-breeds" were "as peaceable, orderly and Industrious as any settlers in the Country."[139] He gave the secretary specific advice about how to keep the immigrants from creating trouble with the Indians, but it was perhaps too late. Only a month after McLoughlin wrote this letter, a group of Cayuses, pushed beyond their limits by the streams of immigrants and a measles epidemic, attacked the mission where Marcus and Narcissa Whitman lived. Eleven people were killed and another forty-seven taken captive. The result was the Cayuse War that would inflame Oregon in 1848. Another burst of Indian-settler frustration would nearly destroy Washington Territory ten years later.

McLoughlin never commented on his fears for his own "half-breed" children in this setting, but his actions demonstrate his concern. His daughters married men in the HBC, which gave them some security. Elisabeth remained in Quebec, and Eloisa stayed in Portland, marrying another former Hudson's Bay man, David Harvey, in 1850. As parents, Marguerite and John worried more about their sons, who did have a harder time finding a place in this world. Joseph, their eldest son, worked variously as a storekeeper at Fort Vancouver and then as a hunter in a brigade led by his half-brother, Thomas McKay, Marguerite's eldest son from her first marriage. Joseph was killed in 1848 in an accident while hunting in the Sacramento Valley.

McLoughlin struggled to find safe and steady employment for his youngest son, David. Like young John, David had been educated in France and had trained in England for service in the East India Company before returning to work for McLoughlin at Fort Vancouver in 1839. In 1846, after he left the Company, McLoughlin asked the new chief factors at Fort Vancouver to take David on, but on the London Committee's order, they refused. Hurt and frustrated by this snub, McLoughlin bought a partnership in a shipping company for David, who worked on the ship *Toulon* until he was lured away by the California gold fields in 1849. David would never stay in Oregon long, where his family name was probably more a trial than an advantage, but he finally settled in Idaho, where he married a Kootenai woman named Annie Grizzly and spent most of his life on the reservation there.[140]

No matter how much John McLoughlin wanted to make it so, in the second half of the nineteenth century women like Marguerite McLoughlin or men like David McLoughlin could not choose their racial identification. And John McLoughlin, for all of his status and power, could not protect his family from the consequences of new racial ideologies that only hardened as time passed. However it turned out by the twentieth century, in the early nineteenth-century West, cultural boundary crossing was common and essential. And these family arrangements appear far beyond the Canadian fur trade and the Pacific Northwest.

Three Western Places

Regional Communities and Vecinidad

In the summer of 1832 four Bent brothers traveled together for the first time in many years. William and Charles considered themselves experienced mountain men, and as they sat on the banks of the Arkansas, they were pleased to see a group of Cheyenne warriors approach them. William recognized two men and greeted them politely in Cheyenne. George and Robert, still teenagers, felt their inexperience and inadequacy as they watched the mounted warriors move toward them. The Cheyenne men were bigger, their horses healthier, their arrows perfectly straight and within easy reach. The Cheyennes, led by Little Wolf, Wolf Chief, and Yellow Wolf, had just completed a very successful raid against the Comanches and were eager to trade with the Bents. After inviting their guests for coffee and pipe smoking, William, who spoke some Cheyenne, and Charles, who spoke some Lakota and some sign language, described their plan to build a fort at this site. The Cheyenne men seemed happy with this news, but they recommended locating the fort further east along the river in the heart of Cheyenne wintering grounds. William saw the soundness of this advice and discussed the advantages carefully. After more coffee, the Indians named the four Bent brothers (White Hat, Little White Man, Little Beaver, and Green Bird), accepted more tobacco, and continued on their way. The careful observation of manners, the acceptance of good advice, and ritual naming made this a successful beginning to the Bent family business enterprise.

On another river in northern California, General Mariano Guadalupe Vallejo and Sem Yeto, a Suisune leader also known as Chief Solano, also began their relationship in an auspicious way. This meeting in the fall of 1834 was carefully planned and staged by the participants. Sem Yeto knew that Vallejo had arrived in the mission settlement that would become Sonoma, but he waited for Vallejo to come to him. A terrible pestilence had struck the villages the year before, and Sem Yeto wanted new alliances to help protect his territory. Vallejo knew that he could never convince settlers to come to Sonoma unless he could promise peace with the local tribes. When scouts reported that Vallejo was approaching with two hundred mounted soldiers, Sem Yeto prepared his own troops. The two men met in a clearing, and Vallejo dismounted first, waving off his cavalry. Sem Yeto, who at six and a half feet towered over all men, dismounted as well. The two men greeted each other and then spent several days in a careful diplomatic dance. Vallejo left with gifts of javelins and arrows and gave Sem Yeto several beautiful horses adorned with silver tack. This alliance, begun properly, made Sonoma possible and increased Suisune power considerably.

Only a few miles away and several years later, a quite different negotiation took place. "Captain" John Sutter sailed up the Sacramento River in search of a site for his commercial enterprise. Accompanied by only twenty men, Sutter nervously watched for the Native people he knew were there. Suddenly, about two hundred warriors appeared on the shore, apparently ready for battle. Sutter took a deep breath and jumped ashore. In broken Spanish, he explained that he was not a mission father, but a trader. He promised the Indians presents if they came to his camp up the river in a few days. Dissatisfied but interested, the Miwoks, who had had experience with both missionaries and traders, disappeared into the bushes. They watched Sutter carefully as he chose a site, and then they came to the stockade for the beads and blankets he had promised. They received some presents, but not what they had hoped for, mostly because Sutter had so few supplies. Though he had few good blankets to offer, Sutter did have cannons that he fired to "salute" the Indians as they left. Impressed with the noise and concerned about what it meant, the Miwok men left wondering how this new enterprise would figure into their plans.

Not sharing the enthusiasm of our other characters, Stephen Austin didn't really want to be in Texas. He had made a deathbed promise to his father to complete a plan to colonize Texas, but now that the Mexican Revolution had in fact occurred, no one knew whether Moses Austin's grandiose scheme would be honored. As he headed east from San Antonio (Bexar) and then south along the Rio Colorado in the fall of 1821, Stephen knew that he would have to deal with the local indigenous people long before he had to worry about Mexican officials. The Karankawas, reportedly vicious cannibals, had made life difficult for many Tejano settlers. Austin feared he would have to drive them away before he could bring any colonists, a task

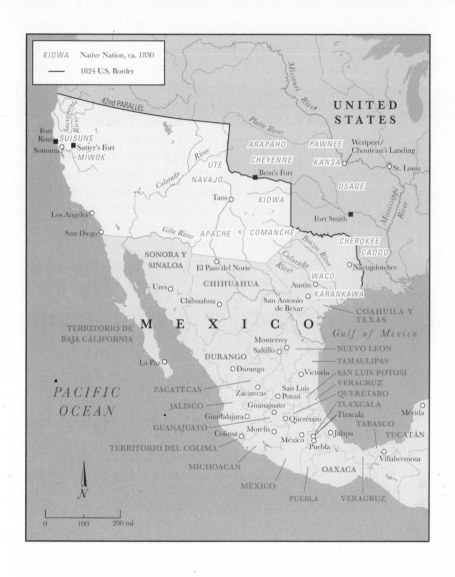

5. Our Neighborhood: The Borderlands of Spain, Mexico,
and Native Nations, 1821–40

he knew could be deadly. When a group of Indians did appear Austin was prepared to fight. However, Austin noticed they had women and children with them, and he asked questions first. Using sign language, the Indians insisted they were not cannibals and in fact were not even Karankawas, a relief to Austin. The Indians, Cocos dressed in beautiful panther skins and well armed, told Austin that he would find a far more peaceful situation along the Brazos River, a bit further east. With this advice, Austin and his party turned northeastward, until they came to the bluffs above the Brazos where Austin would found San Felipe de Austin, his headquarters. The Cocos headed south, hoping that Austin's entourage might offer some protection and trade possibilities so that they might obtain goods that the Comanches would appreciate, giving the Cocos access to horses. Every meeting on the southern plains presented a calculus of possibilities.

The meetings described above suggest a range of possibilities for neighborly relationships and demonstrate how much the first meeting between potential neighbors matters. The last two chapters have looked primarily at how families spread out over a continent to find business and personal success, emphasizing the breadth and scale of both geographies and economies. The Chouteaus, Sublettes, Wilsons, and McLoughlins built mighty networks of far-flung family members to prosper in the fur trade and to protect themselves against the chaos created by nation building, migration, and change. This chapter examines more individual but equally significant colonization projects and raises questions about identity and citizenship. What does it mean to build a community on the border, over the border, or in places where the border moves? This chapter emphasizes neighborliness and depth, examining the ways in which people built regional communities around these borders to create safety and profit in a world of movement. We move beyond the usual stories of individual success and look at the concentric circles of relationships that allowed for such achievements. Though they lived in different places, William and Charles Bent, Mariano Vallejo, John Sutter, and Stephen Austin and their families put down similar kinds of communal stakes in the shifting soil of the American West between 1820 and 1850.

These men, and their families and business partners, built far-reaching *vecinidads* or neighborhoods of people and place. Their homes took the shapes of forts, haciendas, plazas, and towns, but they all served as crucial sites of empire building. Aspiring nations like Spain, the United States, and Mexico understood that populating a place provided the first step toward conquest, but politicians sometimes forgot that colonization was more complicated than simply planting some human seeds and hoping they would grow. The variety of people living in these isolated settings had to learn how and when they could depend on each other. The Arkansas River valley, northern California, and central Texas could have not have existed without the negotiating power, labor, raw materials, and family connections provided by Indian people. The relationships Bent, Vallejo, Sutter, and Austin had with Native people differed and changed over time, but they were essential. They built places on top of much older Native trading systems that had evolved over the past two centuries, as new peoples made use of European trade goods, guns, and horses. The success of these imperial endeavors depended on how well the colonizers fit into and used these older networks, but also how successfully they created an extended "neighborliness" to make tracts of land into communities.

Also important to the larger unfolding story, these three settings became flashpoints for observing the slow crumbling of the Spanish empire, the subsequent generation of revolution, and the post-1821 nation-building project undertaken by the Mexican state. Border politics and cultures illuminate how people made sense of global and national changes that sometimes mattered a great deal at the local level and sometimes not at all. Identity, usually a puzzle of history, place, culture, and personal choice, becomes a central question in contested places like these.

WILLIAM BENT'S BORDER WORLD

When George Bent was eleven he left the Cheyenne world of his mother's people and went to school in the world of his father's people. His father, William Bent, had chosen a coeducational school run by an Episcopal minister for George and his siblings to attend. The Arkansas River trader and his second Cheyenne wife, Island, also the children's aunt and stepmother, took the children east to school in the fall of 1854. Westport, Missouri, a small town on the Missouri River near where Kansas City would be built, thrilled George and his brothers and sisters. George, Robert, and Mary got their first full sets of underwear, long pants, and dresses. Their anxious parent put her Cheyenne lodge in a Westport yard and stayed with the children for several weeks as they adjusted to their new surroundings. George enjoyed every minute of the novel situation, until he watched his family's train of horses, oxen, and mules head west, and he realized that he wouldn't see his horses, his parents, or his younger brother and sister for nearly a year.[1]

This wrenching moment when the world of lodges and forts collided with the world of brick schools and courthouses had its origins thirty years earlier. In 1824, the year that John and Marguerite McLoughlin first arrived at Fort Vancouver, young William Bent stood on the banks of another river imagining what his life in the West would bring. His family had made its fortune on the Missouri, but William was already thinking farther afield—to the Red, the Rio Grande, or the Arkansas. In order to understand the life he built, we need to examine the context of his choices. What kind of place and time would produce men like the Bent brothers and would allow them to develop deep connections to people from other cultures?

The Arkansas River, which links the Rocky Mountain watershed with the Mississippi River, would become William Bent's life's work. Though not a river on the scale of the Mississippi or Missouri, the Arkansas served as the border between Spain and the United States and later, in 1821, between Mexico and the United States. However, the border itself, though described in treaties and marked on maps, delineated a region enshrouded in legal murkiness. The 1819 Adams-Onís Treaty gave settlers and politicians the idea that the United States actually possessed the lands north of the agreed-upon boundary line at the Arkansas River. The land belonged to the Native nations whose people lived and hunted there, and American officials admitted as much by entering into a series of treaties with the Plains nations west of the Mississippi. These treaties recognized them as nations and acknowledged their right of possession even while restricting these groups to small portions of the territory they once occupied. The army built and staffed a string of forts to mark the frontier between that tribal domain and the United States. More important than treaties or forts however, were long-standing systems of trade. On the southern plains, the Comanches had acted as crucial middlemen in an elaborate world of trade and diplomacy that linked Spain, the southern Plains Indians, and the Pueblo Indians with trade goods from everywhere.[2]

The region of the southern plains that the Bent brothers would transform into a trading haven was a no-man's-land. As French, Spanish, and Mexican control wavered in the early nineteenth century, Native diplomatic and economic power expanded. Traders from various nations had to apply for permits to trade in what was known as "Indian Country" or in New Spain or Mexico and operated within a convoluted set of national and local guidelines around the Indian trade. However, many, perhaps most—we'll never know—traders, hunters, and trappers worked outside of the law. They knew that the U.S., Spanish, or Mexican governments had little effect in the region. Reputation, personal behavior, and negotiating skills mattered far more.

The lands that stretched west of what is now the Kansas border or the Missouri River "jumping off" points offered dangers and opportunities. The landscape was designed for bison, and as Edwin James, the American artist who accompanied Stephen Long's expedition, noted in 1820, these animals had flourished in almost unimaginable numbers. He described "immense herds of bison, grazing in undisturbed possession, and obscuring, with the density of their numbers, the verdant plain; to the right and left, as far as the eye was permitted to rove, the crowd seemed hardly to diminish, and it would be no exaggeration to say, that at least 10,000 here burst on our sight in the instant."[3] This bison-filled region operated as an important buffer zone between the United States, revolutionary Mexico, and Native nations. The Arkansas River ran through an area where important Plains groups negotiated for space in a trade system that centered on buffalo. It divided the region with the southern plains of the *llano estacado* (or staked plains) to the south and the central plains or short grass prairies to the north. Two systems of trade, two continents, and innumerable nations came together on these plains, now covered by Colorado, Kansas, Oklahoma, Texas, New Mexico, and northern Mexico. The Royal Road that came up through Mexico, serving the productive mining regions of Durango and Chihuahua, had connected the southern plains to global trade for nearly two centuries by the time the Santa Fe trade from the United States made its late entry into the mix.[4]

As Spanish New Mexicans became increasingly involved in trade in the eighteenth century, they broadened their networks to include the Kiowas, Pawnees, and even Lakotas. As other Native groups felt pressures from settlement, migration, and war from the east, they looked to the fabulous wealth offered by horses and buffalo on the plains. The Cheyennes and Arapahos, in particular, became convinced in the waning years of the eighteenth century that their future lay to the west and south, where they could specialize in buffalo hunting and connect to this larger trade. Elliott West has pictured this world for us as a place and a moment for "the Called Out People" who risked everything about their former settled existence to make a living on the central Great Plains.[5]

Another person "called out" by this opportunity was William Bent. A St. Louisan from the same restless generation as A. P. Chouteau and the Sublette brothers, William was born in 1809. The son of Judge Silas Bent, who had arrived in St. Louis in 1806 as the appointed deputy surveyor of Louisiana Territory, William grew up in a prominent St. Louis family. Though he had other opportunities, William was always attracted to life on the river and in the mountains. At fifteen, he left school and home to join up with his eldest brother Charles, who was partnered with Joshua Pilcher in the Missouri Fur Company.[6]

Charles Bent, born in 1799, had been involved in the fur trade since 1818 and had witnessed the violent struggle among the competing companies along the upper Missouri. Once his Missouri Fur Company had been swallowed by the new giant American Fur Company in 1828, Charles's business prospects seemed grim. He watched the development of the new trading network between Santa Fe and St. Louis, and by the late 1820s both Charles and William had concluded that the diversified Santa Fe trade looked promising. Missouri's biggest booster, Senator Thomas Hart Benton, had recently boasted in Congress that a wise investor could multiply an investment tenfold by bringing American goods from Missouri to Santa Fe. With the opportunity given them by their father's recent death and a small inheritance, the Bent brothers went into business as Santa Fe traders. In 1829 Charles and William outfitted a caravan filled with trade goods and rumbled along the increasingly busy Santa Fe Trail into Mexico. As captain, Charles intended to lead the his seventy-eight men to Santa Fe, where, if all went well, they would trade their goods for furs, buffalo hides, blankets, and Mexican silver, which they would carry back to St. Louis and sell at a handsome profit.[7]

All didn't go well, and many of the caravan's men deserted after a series of Indian attacks, but Charles, William, and their goods arrived in Santa Fe intact. They traded hardware, textiles, glass, whiskey, knives, and guns for merchandise worth perhaps $200,000 in Missouri. With this vastly profitable load, Charles and several of their old St. Louis fur trade friends, including Ceran St. Vrain, prepared for the return trip. William, however, had other ideas. At age twenty, he found the actual experience of moving a caravan along the trail tedious and decided to head into the mountains to trap and to trade with the Indians.[8]

This turned out to be a momentous decision for the history of the region. Perhaps his boyhood in Missouri and experience in the fur trade gave William some preparation, just as John McLoughlin's Canadian youth had prepared him for life at Fort Vancouver. Somehow Bent understood he would have to forge a different kind of relationship with his Native neighbors. William recognized that the key to success in the business was developing a more reliable trade with the central Plains nations. He considered the advantages of the rendezvous system that allowed for a lot flexibility, but not stability. He believed that Native nations and European trappers needed a neutral and convenient place on which they could depend for trade. Taos, New Mexico, was on the wrong side of the Mexican border for American traders and too far from the hunting areas used by the central plains peoples. Did William Bent see himself as living on a border or as part of a national project when he decided to make a life so far from either St. Louis or Santa Fe? What political and diplomatic issues influenced his thinking? Maybe he was disappointed in love or tired of his family's advice. We don't know.

William Bent's timing mattered because the social and economic changes that brought him to the southern Rockies had also put the world of the central Plains Indians into flux. Pressure from Euro-American immigrants in the Mississippi River valley and in Texas, the official process of Indian removal, and the new possibilities opened by the Santa Fe trade brought different tribes into the region, creating conflict with Native peoples with longer traditions there. The Cheyennes and the Arapahos in particular were newcomers to the central plains, having migrated south looking for ways to increase their horse herds and populations. A chance meeting with William Bent in 1831 in which he protected some Cheyenne horse thieves against a group of Comanches gave the Cheyennes a new ally and Bent an entrée into trade.[9]

A year or so later, after Charles Bent had made several profitable trips back and forth between Santa Fe and St. Louis, William introduced high-quality trade goods from St. Louis to the Cheyennes, further increasing their interest in trade and their loyalty to him. He convinced his brother Charles and their partners, the St. Vrain brothers, that a large and well-stocked permanent fort right on the border was the way to build status and wealth. William insisted that such a fort, with an unparalleled supply of goods, would attract traders and Indians to them, and they would have a monopoly on everything north of Taos. According to William's son George, who told the story much later, the Bents and St. Vrains then consulted their new trading partners, the Cheyennes, as to the proper location of the fort. Yellow Wolf, a chief of the Hairy Rope Clan, advised them to choose a site further out on the plains, a place where Cheyenne, Arapaho, Ute, Comanche, and Kiowa groups hunted and traded. Construction of the first Bent's Fort, often called Fort William, began in 1831, with teams of Mexican adobe makers setting up camp on the north side of the Arkansas.[10]

Bent's Fort can't be understood without understanding the places it linked. Santa Fe, founded in 1610 as a mission and then a government center, by the early nineteenth century had a diversified economy that included farming and craft production, but most important was the fur and hide trade. The city's location in the complicated nexus of Pueblo, Ute, Cheyenne, and Comanche territories was central to its existence. We tend now to view the region of the southern Rocky Mountains and the headwaters of the Arkansas River and the Rio Grande as isolated from the mainstream of American life and even from the rest of the American West. Indeed, Americans in the early nineteenth century rarely thought about the region and considered it as being "awakened" by the opening of the Santa Fe trade. However, in the late 1820s and early 1830s the region was fully awake and, in fact, in considerable uproar without even considering the presence of Americans or the new trade being created on the Santa Fe Trail.

The Native nations on the plains, the old nation of Spain, and the new nation of Mexico found themselves negotiating new relationships in which William Bent served as an unofficial go-between and diplomat. Without much protection or funding from the over-extended Spanish empire, New Mexicans had developed a strong economy by the last years of the eighteenth century and had become integrated into a regional network that included all of the northern provinces of New Spain and trade with both nomadic Plains Indians and with settled Pueblo Indians. Hides, horses, and slaves meshed well with grain, textiles, and pottery, and all of these served as export items that could be traded south for silver and other manufactured goods.[11]

However, the whole system fell apart when the political turmoil that erupted out of the Mexican Revolution affected even isolated northern New Spain. The Spanish Crown and military found itself fully occupied by Napoleon's invasion of the Iberian Peninsula in 1808. Simultaneous rebellions against the Spanish empire in Mexico and throughout the New World meant that Spain could no longer effectively administer its empire. This had major consequences in New Mexico. In the decade following the first wave of the revolution in 1810, supplies were cut off for the military and for the missions, and the salaries of officials went unpaid. The entire official economy of New Mexico depended on the annual caravans that came up to Santa Fe from Mexico City. These were sponsored or at least contracted by the Spanish government to bring official documents, supplies, and, most importantly, trade goods and cash from Chihuahua to the imperial outpost. The caravan, accompanied by a large military escort, numbered more than five hundred people, thousands of herd animals,

Legend:
- *KIOWA* — Native Nation
- —— U.S.–Mexico Border, 1830s
- ····· Santa Fe Trail

INDIAN COUNTRY

ROCKY MOUNTAINS

Fort Laramie

Missouri River

Platte River

PAWNEE

ARAPAHO

CHEYENNE

WICHITA

Westport   Fort Osage

St. Louis

UTE

Bent's Fort

Arkansas River

Taos

Santa Fe

KIOWA

OSAGE

Fort Gibson

NAVAJO

EMIGRANT NATIONS

COMANCHE

Red River

Mississippi River

APACHE

MEXICO

New Orleans

Chihuahua

Rio Grande

Gulf of Mexico

0   100   200 mi

N

6. The Santa Fe Trail, Southern Plains, and Their Residents

and dozens of large wagons. When it left Santa Fe for its return trip, the caravan carried grain, textile goods, hides, and thousands of sheep to be sold in Chihuahua or further south. When revolution and imperial breakdown interrupted this essential lifeline, New Mexicans desperately sought new sources of trade.[12]

At the same time, relationships between Hispanic villagers and Apaches, Comanches, Utes, and Navajos began to unravel because New Mexican officials could no longer deliver the gifts that kept the system operating. New Mexicans feared a general Indian attack from all directions, and danger from potentially hostile Indians probably weighed more heavily on their minds than did politics in Mexico. This is the tense context in which the Santa Fe trade with the United States emerged: a moment of change and uncertainty for everyone involved. By the time the revolution actually succeeded in 1821, New Mexicans had endured at least a decade of economic and military chaos that left everyone unsure about what the new Mexican government would bring.[13]

Like Spain, Mexico quickly discovered that it had to struggle with the United States to preserve the nation it had won. U.S. diplomats and politicians made many attempts to change the borders after 1821 to satisfy their U.S. constituents. Mexican diplomats insisted on maintaining the boundary at the line agreed upon in 1819, after the Adams-Onís Treaty, even though the United States regularly urged renegotiation of the borders. This line, which drew the border at the Arkansas River, became official in 1832 with the ratification of a new treaty between the United States and Mexico. Even though some Mexican officials worried about the aggressive Americans, most people living in New Mexico and Texas hoped that the new government would encourage trade with the foreigners to deliver them from economic stagnation.[14]

Several parties of traders, knowing that the announcement of Mexican independence was imminent, were circling the Arkansas River border hoping to be the first American group to be welcomed in officially. In November of 1821, William Becknell, an ambitious but bankrupt businessman from Missouri, and his small band of traders managed to be that first group. After crossing the Arkansas, they encountered troops from New Mexico on the high plains east of Santa Fe. The two parties could not communicate easily, according to Becknell, but "their reception of us, fully convinced us of their hospitable feelings." Becknell and his companions rode with the Mexican soldiers to the village of San Miguel on the edge of the plains, then over the Sangre de Cristo range and into Santa Fe where the "well

informed and gentlemanly" governor Facundo Melgares received them.
Melgares told Becknell that he welcomed trade with the Americans and
that they might also settle in his province.[15]

Times had certainly changed. Only a year earlier, Becknell and his men
would have been arrested and had their goods confiscated. However, Governor
Melgares and many other New Mexicans saw the opportunities that 1821 and
independencia might bring—both in terms of trade and economics, but also
in the true liberalization of politics. They hoped for more local control over
government, the end of ethnic and class distinctions, and the opportunity
for individual enrichment. *Independencia* did bring change, but in forms no
one could have predicted. In less than a year foreigners and their cash and
trade goods flowed into Santa Fe and Taos. Some of the wealth and some of
the foreigners stayed there, but most went on to Chihuahua because few New
Mexicans had the ready cash to take advantage of the situation. However,
New Mexico was hardly "Americanized" in those years; that process would
take more than a century. The Mexican government controlled trade and
immigration quite carefully, though like most gambles, this new Santa Fe
trade had unintended consequences for everyone involved.[16]

The increased presence of U.S. citizens and the change in political
leadership in Mexico affected Native people as well, particularly the nomadic tribes who controlled the buffalo trade. Spanish officials had seen
the Plains Indians as an essential buffer to American encroachment and
purchased their loyalty with gifts and through participation in the Spanish
fur and hide trade. As a result, many Indian groups became enmeshed in
trading alliances with the Spanish and other Native peoples. Even though
these alliances did not end raids on Spanish settlements, the agreements
seem to have ameliorated them. This strategy did slow American entry into
the region because few Native people would trade openly with American
merchants because they feared losing their exclusive relationships with
Spanish and New Mexican traders.[17]

Anglo, French, and American traders and hunters had certainly recognized the potential of the trade with Indian nations on the central and
southern plains, and various individuals had attempted to cash in on it.
The St. Louis newspapers constantly reported the capture of trading parties by the Spanish, and territorial governors warned their citizens not to
deal with Native nations in Spanish territory. Many traders chose not to
listen to such warnings. We might remember that A. P. Chouteau ventured
into this area in 1818, and he and his men lost all of their trade goods
and horses, precipitating his economic ruin. Such resistance to American

traders by Native Americans (particularly by the Cheyennes and their close allies, the Arapahos and the Kiowas) in the southwestern plains seems to have peaked in the 1820s. Given the circumstances, an enormous amount of illegal, unreported, undocumented—and profitable—trade went on, but we won't ever know its scope. When William Becknell arrived in Santa Fe with the first legal caravan from Missouri, he was following numerous others, but the legality of the trade did mean important changes.

BENT'S FORT AND ITS NEIGHBORHOOD

This confluence of events made Bent's Fort the perfect place at the perfect time. In 1834 William Bent moved the fort to its permanent location near present-day La Junta, Colorado. In its own way Bent's Fort was as impressive as Fort Vancouver. Made from adobe rather than the tremendous Douglas firs of the Pacific Northwest, the fort covered nearly an acre of the bluffs overlooking the river. The walls, several feet thick and between fifteen and thirty feet above the ground, enclosed enough space to house several hundred people and hundreds of horses and other livestock.[18] In both places the physically daunting appearance of each fort signaled imperial and national power as each fort performed the role of border sentry. Bent's "castle on the plains," however, indicates something about the weakness of the nation on this southwestern edge.

In its first summer of operation, the fort hosted representatives of the Cheyenne, Arapaho, Gros Ventre, Comanche, Pawnee, Osage, and Arikara nations for a diplomatic meeting. Colonel Henry Dodge represented the U.S. Army, but William Bent negotiated the peace. His diplomatic success did not end warfare between Indian groups or all depredations on trading parties or settlers, but it did improve the tense situation on the plains by clarifying the role Bent's Fort would play. The Bent and St. Vrain Company encompassed a huge trading area—most of present-day Colorado, northern New Mexico, the panhandle of Oklahoma, the northern tip of Texas, southern Wyoming, southern Nebraska, and western Kansas. Bent's choice of location, his personality, and diplomatic arrangements allowed for the fort to be a free trade zone in this remarkably dynamic region. Attacks on the Bent and St. Vrain Company, their wagon trains, employees, and associates were minimized, though the result may have been increased raiding on Mexican settlements to the south.[19]

The Bent family protected their enterprise fiercely, and as a result, the business and the fort enjoyed enormous success. In 1839 the eastbound

15. Lt. James Abert, *Scalp Dance at Bent's Fort.* Watercolor sketch, 1846. *Notes of a Military Reconnaissance, from Fort Leavenworth, in Missouri, to San Diego, in California, including part of the Arkansas, Del Norte, and Gila rivers.* U.S. 30th Cong., 1st sess., 1848, House Ex. doc. no. 41.

This sketch of Cheyenne and Arapaho dancers also provides a good view of the interior space of Bent's Fort as it looked in the 1840s. Two stories, with a gallery on the bottom, allowed a range of people to live and work in the fort. We see a large group of people—Mexicans, Anglos, and Native people—gathered together on the gallery roof to watch a dance celebrating the return of a successful war party.

Bent and St. Vrain Company caravan leader wrote to Pierre Chouteau Jr., whose company bought the furs and then sold them on the global market, that the annual train was expected to bring in about six hundred packs of buffalo robes and ten packs of beaver. In 1840 the *Missouri Republican* reported that the firm had brought in fifteen thousand buffalo skins. At the same time, the fort itself sold thousands of dollars' worth of goods every year, bringing in handsome profits on goods that no one could get outside of St. Louis. A gallon of brandy bought for two dollars in St. Louis was sold for twenty-five dollars at the fort. Blankets, guns, knives, traps, horses and mules all garnered similar profits.[20]

Location and human relationships made this possible. The fort occupied the physical space of an imposing site on the banks of the Arkansas River along the Santa Fe Trail, but also the diplomatic no-man's-land of the fur trade. Like Fort Vancouver a decade earlier, Bent's Fort stood in the liminal space between nations, ideas, and moments. The Columbia River and the Arkansas both marked tentative borders, national claims that stood weakly in the midst of powerful Native peoples who actually claimed and used the territory. Bent's Fort acted as successful trading center because William Bent had made familial relationships with the Cheyenne, American, and Mexican elites. His most important connections were with the Cheyennes, a choice that initially prevented him from making alliances with other important Native nations. By 1838 Bent and his wife Owl Woman, daughter of an important Cheyenne chief, were the central business and social leaders of the region. Their four children, all educated in St. Louis and with their mother's people, moved easily among the New Mexican elite, St. Louis traders, and Indian diplomats.

Omens and Weddings

The Cheyennes and their southern plains cousins, the Arapahos, were both relative newcomers to the region. The move had been a little rocky. As the Cheyennes tell it, as well as various historians and anthropologists, the move to the Great Plains was a gamble that nearly failed. Led by a great prophet, Sweet Medicine, they had been called out onto the northern plains. At a site near the Black Hills, Sweet Medicine had been invited into the lodge of the Maheo, the All Being, who gave him precise instructions about how the Cheyennes should live new lives as bison hunters. The Maheo also gave him four sacred arrows that became the spiritual touchstones of Cheyenne life. This was, as Elliott West puts it, "the defining episode of modern Cheyenne history."[21]

Directionally, the arrows guided the Cheyennes south. Rich as the northern plains country was in buffalo, competition for hunting grounds was fierce. Many tribes vied for dominance. Crows, Shoshones, Crees, Blackfoot, and the expanding Sioux confederation all competed with the Cheyennes for dominance. A group of the Cheyennes led by White Thunder, elder chief and the keeper of the arrows, moved south. The fact that they carried the sacred arrows, the Mahuts, meant that the heart and soul of the Cheyennes moved south. The move, of course, had risks attached to it. New enemies—the Pawnees, Kiowas, Comanches, and Apaches—contested the control of the region near the Arkansas River. However, the Cheyennes and their closest allies, the Arapahos, chose a different strategy to find a niche that would allow them to make peace with the powerful Comanches in particular. They became middlemen in a double sense: linking the tribes and trade of the northern and southern plains and negotiating between Native nations and the new American traders rumbling over the Santa Fe Trail.[22]

Unlike other Native nations to the south, the Cheyennes and Arapahos looked at the caravans not as targets but as potential suppliers of goods. Rather than plunder the newcomers, they would partner with them, thereby gaining the guns, powder, lead, cloth, metal tools, and especially horses that they needed to lead their lives. The Santa Fe traders sought furs and hides, which the Cheyennes and Arapahos had in great abundance. It was a perfect match. By occupying this middle position—between the competing powers—the Cheyennes and Arapahos acquired wealth beyond anything they had ever known. Precisely at this moment, in the early 1830s, William Bent met up with Cheyenne chief Yellow Wolf at the Fountain Creek trading post. This partnership, as it was worked out in the next few years, convinced the Cheyennes to move permanently to the southern plains. It gave them a new position of power, but one based on a very delicate balance.[23]

Perhaps the Cheyennes, newly ensconced as trading partners with Bent and St. Vrain, got overconfident. In 1832 they tested this power by taking on the Pawnees, who lived on the lower Platte River. In spite of their assurance, the raids were a disaster, and the Cheyennes lost many men. They planned to get revenge for the losses in 1833. The warriors followed White Thunder, the keeper of the arrows, into battle, but again it all went wrong. Not only did White Thunder's warriors lose lives, but the enemy Pawnees captured the sacred Medicine Arrows (the Mahuts). The luck and power of the Cheyennes, as well as the status of White Thunder, all disappeared with the arrows.[24]

Then, as the Cheyennes would have expected given the fate of the arrows, even worse things happened. Shortly after Bent's Fort opened in its permanent site, in November 1833, a stunning meteor shower lit up the sky. People all over the southern plains remembered it as "the Night the Stars Fell," and many people saw it as a sign that the world was ending. At the fort William Bent joined the Cheyenne leaders as they watched the celestial message from the parapets. He talked with White Thunder, the keeper of the sacred Medicine Arrows, perhaps the most influential of all Cheyenne men. When dawn came and the world had not ended, both Bent and White Thunder recognized they had shared a significant moment.[25] That night cemented White Thunder's determination to change the luck of his people by getting the arrows back. He went alone and unarmed to the Pawnee villages, where he simply asked for a truce and for the arrows. He managed to get two of the four arrows back, restoring his personal status and the fate of his Cheyennes.[26]

Another result of the Night the Stars Fell was the marriage of White Thunder's daughter, Mis-stan-ta, to William Bent. Because both men understood the importance of personal connections, they had spent years forging fictive kinship relationships between the Bents and the Cheyennes and Arapahos. These relationships made trade and the exchange between cultures possible, but only when all parties understood the difference between gifts and commodities in the context of trade. Then trade and its rituals can be culturally transformative. Anthropologists define gifts as part of an endless series of exchanges and personal obligations, while commodities are a single sale item, with no further obligations attached to either buyer or seller. Native people on the plains saw trade items as part of creating relationships that set in motion cycles of mutual obligations. Anglo-Americans, in contrast, engaged in trade as part of simply earning a living, a scheme that was impersonal and individual.[27] The man most responsible for the fort's operation and ultimate success, William Bent, understood the difference very clearly. When he chose to establish actual kinship relations with White Thunder, he built on the set of obligations he had initiated long ago. The marriage with Mis-stan-ta, or Owl Woman, involved risks and benefits for both families. What was most important, however, was that children, real flesh and blood kin, would come out of these connections.[28]

Everyone in the area recognized the significance of the wedding. It took place in 1835, just after a series of successful trade negotiations between the Pawnees and the Cheyennes. Colonel Henry Dodge, sent by the Army to "make peace with the Indians" or at least to broker lucrative trading deals, met with a large contingent of Cheyennes, Arapahos, and Pawnees at Bent's Fort in August of 1835. Dodge may have believed he orchestrated the entire event, but White Thunder's desire to get the sacred arrows back along with the Bent brothers' offer of food and trade made the meetings possible.[29] With the Pawnees pacified, and with a future of even more trading relationships, a marriage seemed ideal. At twenty-six, William had spent eight years on the plains and his reputation and wealth could offer great status and even comfort to a Cheyenne woman. Owl Woman, the eldest daughter of White Thunder, could offer William similar important connections.

The families were joined at a ceremony in a village set up just for the wedding. White Thunder's relatives built a beautiful wedding lodge and carried

Owl Woman into it. William's task, as groom, was to distribute gifts, which he did memorably. He gave horses, guns, kettles, silver ornaments, beads, cloth, blankets, saddles, and bridles to everyone in the village. After the wedding Owl Woman remained in her lodge and William at Bent's Fort, though they both moved easily between the two worlds. Owl Woman and William rearranged the apartment in the fort, putting soft hides on the floor, and hanging blankets on the walls. William kept a portable writing desk in Owl Woman's lodge. Together, they had four children and gave them both Bent family and Cheyenne names. Mary, or Ho-ka, was born in 1838. Robert, or Octavi-wee-his, arrived in 1841, followed by George, or Ho-my-ike, in 1843. Julia, or Um-ah, came last and at the cost of Owl Woman's life in 1847.[30]

This relationship grounded life at Bent's Fort and made it successful and stable in a world that was anything but. The Bent children grew up understanding the significance of family, tribal, and imperial alliances as they participated in daily life at the fort. George Bent, who shared his memories with an ethnographer many years later, saw the complexity of the fort's operation from a child's perspective. He remembered hundreds of employees, many of whom had families of various ethnic mixes, all guided by the rhythms of the seasons and the trade caravans. He recalled: "Something was always going on, and we children had no lack of amusements. In the fall and winter there was always a large camp of Indians just outside the fort—Cheyennes and Arapahos, and sometimes Sioux, Kiowas, Comanches, and Prairie Apaches."[31] Hundreds of wagons came to Bent's Fort each year, and more than fifty traders made the fort their home, doing business with Native hunters and traders from a radius of five hundred miles. This was business on a very large scale. In 1842, for example, Charles Bent reported that the fort's store had more than $12,000 worth of trade goods on hand and that he was sending over a thousand packs of buffalo robes on the spring caravan to St. Louis.[32]

The mix of people and the enforced "safety zone" created by Bent and his Native allies made the fort distinctive. Bent's Fort was the one spot on the Santa Fe Trail where exchanges with Indians were welcomed and encouraged, and the effects of those conversations on both sides were far-reaching. We don't have records of these conversations, but archeological evidence tells us that people sat in the courtyard together and smoked—a lot. In an archeological survey, researchers found 1,526 remnants of pipes at Bent's Fort, more than the remnants of guns, horseshoes, bridles, and plates put together. Because of the good relationship with the Cheyennes and the Arapahos that the Bents had forged, business flourished.[33]

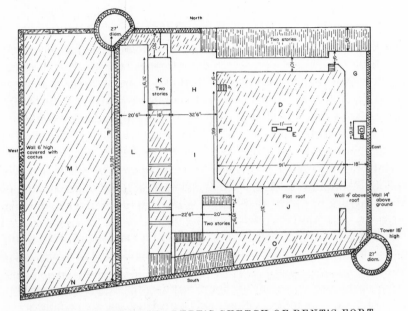

KEY TO LIEUTENANT ABERT'S SKETCH OF BENT'S FORT

A Main entrance	**B** Sentry station with telescope	**C** Belfry with flagpole	**D** Courtyard	**E** Hide press
F Passageway through to corral	**G** Blacksmith shop	**H** Traders' room	**I** Bent's rooms	**J** Men's quarters
K Billiard room and bar	**L** Wagon house	**M** Cattle yard	**N** Gate facing river	**O** Corral

16. Lt. James W. Abert, "Sketch of Bent's Fort," 1845. "Journal of Lieutenant J. W. Abert, from Bents Fort to St. Louis, in 1845." U.S. 29th Cong., 1st sess., 1846. Sen. Doc. 438, p. 2.

The detailed sketch, made with the eye of an artist and a soldier, demonstrates the scale and solidity of the fort. The Bents created a sturdy fortress, complete with battlements and thick walls, to surround the crucial parts of their business: fur presses, storehouses, cattle sheds, living quarters, and salesrooms.

The solidity and creature comforts offered by the fort surprised many visitors. They wondered at its size and the fact that it was adobe, "or sun-dried bricks." A young aspiring journalist, Lewis Garrard, explained precisely that the building was "thirty feet in hight and one hundred feet square; and at two corners are bastions of a hexagonal form, in which there are a few cannon. The fort walls serve as the back walls to the rooms, which front inward on a courtyard." He also described other features: "a billiard table, in a small house on top of the fort, where the *bourgeoise* and visitors amused themselves; and in the clerk's office, a first-rate spy glass, from which I viewed the *caballada*, coming up from the grazing ground, seven miles up the river." As a final detail, he observed that "in the belfry, two eagles, of the American bald species, looked from their prison. They were two years old, but their heads do not become bald until attaining the age of three."[34]

Lieutenant James Abert, with a more military eye, saw that "the outer walls, which are nearly two feet in thickness, intersect in the axes of the towers, thus permitting their faces to be completely enfiladed; the outside walls of the enceinte and towers, pierced with loopholes, are continued four feet above the flat roofs which serve for the banquette." He approved of the construction materials as being "composed of clay so cannot be fired by inflammable substances that might be cast upon it; the whole is built of 'adobes,' sunburnt brick, formed of clay and cut straw, in size about four times as big as our common bricks." He also described on the nonhuman residents of the fort: "On the west side is the cattle yard, which is surrounded by a wall so high as to effectually shelter them. The coping of the wall is planted with cacti, which bear white and red flowers. Scattered around the fort in different cages we saw some of the birds of this region—the mocking bird, 'turdus polyglottus,' magpie, 'corvus pica' and two of the bald headed eagle, 'falco leucoccephalus.'"[35]

Visitors also commented on the ethnic fluidity of the culture that evolved there. In 1839 Thomas Farnham wrote with a mixture of envy and disapproval that the Bent brothers "dressed like chiefs, in moccasins thoroughly garnished with beads and porcupine quills; in trousers of deer skin, with long fringes . . . in the splendid hunting shirt of the same material, with sleeves fringed on the elbow seam from the wrist to the shoulder, and ornamented with figures of porcupine quills of various colors." Envy outweighed other feeling in his romantic conclusion that "chiefs they were in the authority exercised in their wild and lonely fortress." Disapproval weighted his comments about the human results of economic and cultural exchange modeled by Bent and his family: "Indian women tripping around its battlements in their glittering moccasins and long deer-skin wrappers; their children, with the most perfect forms, and the carnation of the Saxon cheek struggling through the shading of the Indian, and chattering now Indian, and now Spanish or English."[36]

Young Lewis Garrard, writing a few years later, commented on the source of this mélange, as he called it: "William Bent and Marcellus St. Vrain, have Indian wives." But these wives somehow got forgotten or at least demoted from being female when Garrard asserted that there were only two "female women" in the fort, a "half-breed French and Indian squaw" and "Charlotte" the African American cook.[37] This "carnation" and "shading" and "mélange" made trade and personal life possible. George Bent remembered: "The trade room was full of Indian men all day long . . . and there was still plenty astir about the post. Sometimes a war party going against the Utes, Apaches, or Pawnees stopped at the fort and gave a dance, and there were usually some white visitors staying with us."[38] He saw racial hierarchies as an adult, but we can only wonder how he saw it as a child.

William Bent's familial relationship with the Cheyenne certainly created tensions with other tribes, especially the traditional enemies of the Cheyennes. The powerful Comanches, in particular, presented a challenge. Just who was controlling whom and how is very much a question. The two most usual interpretations of Anglo-American and Native relationships are either that white contact brought civilization and inevitable change to Indian people mired in a primitive past, or that white contact brought disease, destruction, and capitalism to a delicate culture, instantly thrown out of balance. Both are simplistic and incorrect, especially in the context of the world of the southern plains before 1850. Both views make Indian people pawns and victims, when, in fact, they had much agency. The choices Native people made had great impact on how Anglo-Americans participated in the region.[39]

The relationship between Bent and his fort, the Cheyennes, and the Comanches is a good example. The Comanches saw the Arkansas River as the northern border of their territory and barely tolerated the presence of intruders, part of the reason Bent put his fort on the north side of the river. Beginning in the early eighteenth century, the Comanches made the most of Spanish horses and their own knowledge of the region. They had consolidated various bands and taken full control of the southern plains in what is now western Texas and eastern New Mexico, known for more than a century as Comanchería. They backed up their trading relationships with nearly every group with the real fear of raids. Because of the scope of their agreements, the Comanches became reliable sources of trade goods, guns, slaves, horses, cattle, and sheep for isolated people all over the region. By the early nineteenth century they had become a dynamic and powerful presence and had remade power relations on the southern plains. No one would seriously challenge their dominion until the 1840s.[40]

Refugee Indians, both those who had been formally "removed" and those who had simply left, pushed out from the American South and the Mississippi River valley in the 1810s and 1820s and settled along the Arkansas River and in Texas. White and Indian settlers moved into the Comanchería, and the new government refused to follow long-standing traditions of gift giving and peace making that the Spanish and Mexican governments had followed. At the same time, the Osages and the Pawnees began pressing on

Comanche territory just as traffic on the Santa Fe Trail and the presence of Bent's Fort brought Comanches, Arapahos, and Kiowas further south.[41]

The Comanches reacted first by initiating a series of raids throughout the Southwest that convinced most people to make peace and conduct trade with the Comanches on their terms. William Bent and his Cheyenne partners felt the consequences of the bloody years between 1835 and 1840. In 1838 a series of raids took place between the Cheyennes and Arapahos and the Kiowas and Comanches, resulting in huge losses of warriors and horses on both sides. Bent's father-in-law, White Thunder, was killed in one of these raids, and the Cheyennes had to choose a new arrow keeper. Another Comanche campaign began in mid-June of 1839 and was made directly on Bent's Fort. It started as a raid on a few mules and horses grazing outside the walls of the fort. In the end the Comanches stole more than a hundred horses, took several children, and killed one of the Bents' horse traders. The Cheyennes retaliated after both of these episodes, but finally both groups decided that a formal peace would be far more livable.[42]

In the summer of 1840 a group of Cheyenne leaders met with a group of Comanche representatives, exchanged scalps of fallen warriors on both sides, gave gifts and horses, and agreed that they wanted peace. In order to forge this peace, they agreed to bring people from both sides of the river to a grand encampment at Bent's Fort. For several weeks that summer thousands of Cheyennes and Arapahos camped on the north side of the river, and thousands of Comanches, Kiowas, and Apaches set up on the south bank. The Comanches gave away hundreds of horses, and the Cheyennes reciprocated with kettles, blankets, and guns. William Bent fired the fort's new cannon and gave tours of the buildings to the visitors. There were feasts, ball games, shooting matches, and horse races to solidify the new peaceful relationship. Though the peace would never be perfect, Charles Bent reported to his business partners in Taos that he and William expected 1,500 lodges of Comanches and an equal number of Cheyennes and Arapahos to trade at the fort the following spring.[43]

The peace did not last forever, nor did Bent's Fort. Its location between the shifting borders of Native and Euro-American nations gave it power and stability that lasted nearly twenty-five years. Bent and his allies figured out a middle position between the powerful Comanches and the expanding American systems. William and Charles Bent, White Thunder, and Owl Woman created a place and a moment that used the trading systems of Native people and the roads, wagons, and goods made by Europeans to link two very different worlds. They envisioned a much longer peace and a new world that would provide sustenance and honor for their children. Perhaps their optimism was foolish given the shiftiness of the times, but as the Bents and their allies looked ahead in 1840 they couldn't imagine an empire that could touch them. What happened in the end to George Bent and his siblings was not peaceful or honorable, but it took a very long time to play out.

NORTEÑOS AND YANQUIS IN ALTÁ CALIFORNIA

Francesca Vallejo cried as she watched the house burn. She hadn't lived in the Casa Grande for several years, and her new house, built of clapboard in the newest Victorian style, had more room and conveniences, but the old adobe had her heart within it. She had borne twelve of her sixteen children there and buried five small bodies in the mission cemetery behind the house. The house, built by local Suisune Indians and her brothers and husband, wore the finger marks of her children and carried thirty years of Californio history. The house had protected her extended family from winter rains, summer heat, attacks by Indians, Anglo-Americans, and various *osos*, or bears, as the region moved from Russian to Mexican and to U.S. control. The building began as a deserted mission and gradually became the grand hacienda of General Vallejo and his family, where several peoples formed neighborly alliances to use the resources of northern California. Francesca and her son Napoleon watched the fire for hours as their family history, and that of a particular regional community, burned to rubble.[44]

General Mariano Vallejo and Colonel John Sutter couldn't have been more different. They disliked each other intensely. Vallejo, son of an important Californio family,[45] a military hero and a successful trader, entrepreneur, and politician, disdained the likes of Sutter, an immigrant opportunist who had lied and stolen his way across the American West. However, neither could ignore the other when in the chanciness of early California they ended up sharing the same regional stage. The ways in which they mirrored each other and the choices they made about how to live and prosper in that part of northern California can tell us much about how people forged regional communities in the face of political chaos and borderland confusion.

From some perspectives, the region we think of as northern California today was a completely isolated afterthought of the far northern Mexican frontier in the first part of the nineteenth century. But for Californios and their Native neighbors, the region served as borderland that ran in several directions: between powerful and contentious Native people, between the wealth of the missions and ranchos south of Monterey and the wilderness of the north, and between European empires that had begun to explore and colonize the Pacific Northwest. The numbers of peoples and agendas for this far northern frontier of Alta California made it unstable but offered much opportunity for those who thrived in "dynamic" settings. Native people, primarily Miwoks, Nisenans, Patwins, and Pomos, had long experience with the various peoples who had come there. Every part of the region had been covered by Hudson's Bay men, fur traders, horse traders, and various flavors of mountain men. Missions had come very late and very thinly to this part of California, so many of these Indians had escaped the experience of captivity and forced conversion.[46]

An example of someone who had experience with both missions and foreign traders would be Sem Yeto, later known as Chief Solano and one of General Vallejo's important allies, born in the Suisune village just north of San Francisco Bay about 1800. When Sem Yeto met Vallejo in 1835, his experiences mirrored those of large number of Bay Area Native people. By 1800 the local Franciscan missions, though much smaller than those in southern California, had managed to build mission communities. The fathers focused on cultivating and capturing Native people from the tribes just south of the Bay to build their population of neophytes—Indians being trained in Christian thought and behavior. However, the Spanish priests had not yet ventured north of the present-day Carquinez Straits to the Suisunes. They lived sufficiently far away from the missions to avoid missionaries and soldiers, but they certainly traded with various Europeans, including Russian, American, and British traders. Over time they joined with the other Patwin tribes in the Central Valley to resist the incursion on their lands that came from Spanish Mexican rancheros. The Suisune success in remaking their economy came from their adaptation to the possibilities of pastoralism and warfare as they acquired horses from traders and from mission runaways, and cattle and sheep from mission and rancho herds. Horses gave the Suisunes new mobility that they used to create complex trading networks with tribes all over California.[47]

The Suisunes might have avoided contact with the missions for several more decades, except that in the early nineteenth century, Indian runaways from the missions began to seek shelter in their villages. This, in combination with the horse thievery and occasional raids on mission rancherías, convinced the Spanish fathers and their soldiers that they would have to take on these northern Indians. In a series of battles, Spanish soldiers and their Native allies destroyed Suisune, Patwin, and Miwok villages, burned most of the adults alive, stole their horses, and kidnapped their children. The world of independent, small villages into which Sem Yeto was born was wiped out. As part of a massive raid in 1810, mission soldiers kidnapped young Sem Yeto and brought him to the San Francisco mission, where the mission fathers baptized him Francisco Solano.

In 1823 Sem Yeto/Solano accompanied the mission priests to found the Mission San Francisco de Solano, the northernmost and final Franciscan mission in California. The mission had a rather rocky start, however, as the Satiyomi Indians almost immediately drove the priests and their few followers away from the mission and burned it down. With the help of a stronger military escort, and some careful negotiation by Sem Yeto with the local tribes, it was re-established in 1827. However, like many "mission" Indians, Sem Yeto didn't really live at the mission, but with his people at a village nearby. By 1823, despite the changes the tribe had undergone, they began to imagine a world beyond the confines of the mission. The Suisunes slowly recreated a political structure that depended on alliances, marriage, and warfare, and an economy based on trading with other Native people and with British, French, and Russian traders, right under the noses of the mission fathers.[48]

The presence of Fort Ross, founded by the Russian-American Company in 1812 as Russia's southernmost outpost, made such trading relationships possible. It also signaled the growing danger of colonial rivals to Spain's hold on California. Only a hundred miles north of San Francisco Bay, Fort Ross began as a tiny otter-hunting outpost but expanded to include a large farming enterprise that employed hundreds of local Indians, primarily Pomo and Miwok peoples. Only several hundred more miles north lurked the powerful specter of the Hudson's Bay Company. Fort Vancouver regularly sent hunting parties traveling south into California proper. After 1821, and the Mexican Revolution, new groups of American trappers and traders came from the east. Most of these interlopers had a very transient presence in California, but a few stayed and established trading posts, ranches, and farms.[49]

Such a threatening combination of Russian and British forts and traders and Anglo sea captains and trappers, along with powerful Native groups, made the situation in northern California suddenly look more dangerous to Californios who had now invested several generations of work and family into California. When Mariano Guadalupe Vallejo was born in 1807 in Monterey, his influential parents and other Californios had realized that they could not count on Spain or New Spain for protection or economic development. And once the civil wars that presaged the Mexican Revolution took over the attention of civil and military authorities, they ignored California completely. Virtually all state support for California's missions and presidios disappeared so that neither padre nor soldier could count on salary or goods. In fact, between 1810 and 1821 only one official supply ship arrived from San Blas, the port on the coast of Mexico that provided all supplies, pay, and official correspondence for California's soldiers, missionaries, and government officials. Quickly, illegal trade between Anglo-American, British, and Russian traders filled the gap. Governors of Alta California publicly condemned this trade while privately orchestrating it.[50]

Alta California's isolation did not go unnoticed by other imperial gazes. As a child living in the capital of Monterey in 1818, Mariano Guadalupe Vallejo watched the infamous "attack" of the French and Argentinean pirate—or perhaps more correctly a privateer, a pirate with a permission slip—Hippolyte de Bouchard. His ships and men landed at Monterey, took the city, and raided the coast of California, terrifying Californios and causing many, including the Vallejos, to evacuate their homes. Such episodes proved the vulnerability of California and the importance of developing a home-grown defense, both of which became mantras for the adult Vallejo.[51]

Their isolation and distance from government, whether that of New Spain or Mexico, made Californios both independent and a bit paranoid. Rumors of other attacks by pirates, navies, and nations ran up and down the coast. By the time young Mariano Guadalupe reached adulthood and had chosen to become a soldier, he had come to believe that the only buffer between the British, Russian, and American empires was northern California, which lay entirely in the control of Indian nations. This borderland protected the wealth of the missions, the ranchos of southern California, and the jewel of San Francisco Bay from a host of enemies, enemies who suddenly appeared closer than they were. This, of course, was exactly the situation the *vecinos*, or neighbors, of New Mexico had faced in their role as northern border protectors.

The experience of Mariano Vallejo as he matured into a powerful *hijo de país* (son of the country) illustrates the challenge Mexican Californians faced in meshing liberal ideals with their needs for labor and safety. Vallejo grew to adulthood in an age of revolution. As the son of a soldier and civil servant in Monterey, he observed and took part in discussions about the future of Mexico and California. Like his privileged peers he ranted about the greed of the priests but lusted after their land holdings, while envisioning a future where the Indians would become happy workers on private ranches and help California to develop and progress. As a young soldier, Vallejo left his liberal ideology behind when he rounded up escaped mission Indians and quelled rebellions. The fear of Native rebellion was real. Mission Indians outnumbered Mexican Californians six to one, and if their "barbarous friend in the wilds" joined them, Alta California could be wiped out in a heartbeat. In 1824 a large number of Chumash people revolted at the Santa Ynez, La Purisima, and Santa Barbara missions. They held off local troops, successfully avoided the reinforcements from the Monterey presidio, and escaped into the San Joaquin Valley.[52]

In 1829 Vallejo got a taste of an even more frightening situation. A Yokut Native named Estanislao, born and educated at Mission San Jose and trained as a *vaquero* (cowboy) and an *alcade* (lay mission leader) there, escaped from the mission and set up a rebel training camp in the interior. He encouraged other unhappy mission Indians to join him, and they raided Mexican live-stock herds with enormous skill. He was rumored to have forty thousand Mariposa Indians allied with him. The rebels' first skirmish with Mexican troops resulted in an Indian victory, encouraging more Native groups to join them. Lieutenant Vallejo was ordered to organize a company of one hundred men to march against Estanislao. On May 29 the young officer led out his army of 107 men, a large force for a California war. It took them three days to find the Indians, who then simply snuck away. The next morning the frustrated soldiers found three old women and a boy. Vallejo granted his troops permission to deal with the captive boy as they saw fit. The child was placed in the center of a semicircle and used as a target for Indian arrows and Mexican bullets. The next day Vallejo and his troops succeeded in dispersing Estanislao's forces, but the Mexican troops found themselves nearly out of food and ammunition so they couldn't finish the campaign. Their actions did end the rebellion, even though they never caught Estanislao, who had the honor of having Stanislaus County and River named after him.[53]

Mariano Vallejo took on the project of colonizing the northern California borderlands with the experience of an Indian fighter. Unlike the Bent brothers, Vallejo began building his empire as part of a state-sponsored effort. Also different from William Bent, his political identity as a Californio and a soldier offered him a very clear position. Since the state had no funding or troops to protect its border, the only way to protect California was to develop and populate the north. Vallejo had two jobs and two appointments: as *comisiando*, or "secular priest," at Mission San Solano and as *comandante*, or military commander, of the San Francisco District, which gave him effective control over all of northern California. His task was to make the region safe for settlement and to find people willing to live there, quite a different goal than John McLoughlin at Fort Vancouver or William Bent at Bent's Fort.[54]

The only people available to populate Northern California were the very Native people and foreign settlers the Spanish government had so feared. Cautiously, the Mexican government made two important policy changes: they secularized the missions and permitted trade and settlement by foreigners. The idea of secularizing the missions was both humanitarian and practical. After more than sixty years of operation, only a few of the twenty-one missions could be described as successful from the perspective of the Mexican state. A few had plowed up great tracts of land that were covered with herds of horses and cattle and flocks of sheep, along with vineyards, fields, and buildings. These fields and flocks provided a source of income to specific orders of the Catholic Church, but the Spanish or Mexican state received little direct revenue.[55]

However, the missions' primary task of turning California Native people into productive Christian laborers had been, in a great understatement, less successful. In fact, as the death toll from European diseases increased, Spanish priests and soldiers had to penetrate the interior valleys and mountains of California, targeting tribes who had protected runaways or who had refused to collect captives. This process turned friendly or neutral Native groups into active enemies, generally increasing the violence all over California, violence between Spanish and Indian people but also between Native nations as well. As documented by several generations of historians, ethnologists, and activists, by the end of the mission period few Native people had converted, but many, many had died.[56]

When Governor José Figueroa announced his plan for secularizing the missions, Vallejo's job was to get rid of the mission priests at San Rafael and San Francisco de Solano (which would become Sonoma) and to make sure the ex-mission Indians, now citizens of California, got access to mission lands. Vallejo also wanted to make sure he didn't lose his entire labor force. Like neophytes at other missions, the Sonoma Indians wanted to leave and return to their Native communities. The law required them to apply to the *comisiando*, Vallejo, for permission to leave. Vallejo knew he had to handle this delicately. Either they would depart with his permission in friendship, or they would slip away secretly and never return. He wisely granted the mission Indians' requests to leave, but he kept most of the cattle and horses "in trust" for when they returned to work for him. The mission lands and the Native laborers who gave it value were essential to Vallejo's larger goal of colonizing the north.[57]

The practical need for Native workers had some international intrigue behind it as well. Governor Figueroa's interest in colonizing the region involved the Russians at Bodega Bay and Fort Ross. Rumors about their intentions and their influence on Indians deserting the secularized missions led Figueroa to dispatch Vallejo north on an official inspection tour in 1833. Vallejo reported that the Russian settlements "happily flourished." He described healthy herds of livestock, orchards, and fields, but what impressed him the most were the manufacturing facilities that included a shipyard, a tannery, and a blacksmith's shop. Native Californians, who appeared to be runaways from the Franciscan missions, operated all of these. Some of the escaped mission Indians even served as soldiers. Vallejo could see that the Russians had developed productive relationships with Native Californians that seemed less antagonistic than his own.[58]

Vallejo's first effort at settlement failed. When he arrived in what is now Petaluma with ten families, the priests at Mission San Rafael claimed that the Petaluma site was theirs and refused to let the colonists build houses. This setback, along with several raids by local Indians, convinced the colonists to abandon the project within weeks. Vallejo tried again a year later, this time at the site of Mission San Francisco de Solano. With mission secularization a fact when Vallejo arrived in the fall of 1834, the mission priests immediately retreated to San Rafael. This time, Vallejo had a personal stake in the settlement, now called the pueblo of Sonoma. As "Military Commander and Director of Colonization of the Northern Frontier," Vallejo became an evangelist for the north country.[59]

Vallejo did several things right to make it work, all quite similar to William Bent's actions at the same moment in a very different place. Vallejo sought out and paid his respects to the local Suisune Indians. He understood that this tribe had trading relationships with Indians far to the north and with the Russians. In his first meeting with the physically imposing former neophyte and now tribal leader Sem Yeto, reputedly six feet seven inches tall, General Vallejo demonstrated his own strength by bringing two hundred mounted soldiers, but also his generosity by bringing gifts. After several discussions and visits and demonstrations of military skill, the two men agreed on an alliance that solved several problems for the parties involved. Vallejo would be able to live in the area peacefully and to convince other settlers to come. He would also have a buffer of Native nations between his new colony and the Russian settlements.[60]

Sem Yeto had also calculated carefully. Several years earlier, a dreadful disease, probably malaria, had killed tens of thousands of central and northern California people, shuffling power relations considerably. Like many tribes, the Suisunes had reconstituted part of their people with refugees from the missions, which had introduced Spanish language and customs but still had not provided enough people. With populations still on the decline, Sem Yeto and his Suisunes needed help in their warfare against the Satiyomis, their traditional rivals to the north. In what were really mourning wars to rebuild population, Sem Yeto had captured a woman who became his wife, Filomena, in 1837. As part of this rebuilding, a good relationship with someone like Vallejo might provide food security and additional sources of income in times of need. The relationship between Sem Yeto and Vallejo would last a lifetime for both men, though it would certainly change as events unfolded.[61]

As military commander and secularizer of the missions, Vallejo had achieved considerable success, but his colonization efforts had not really paid off. His original colonists were mostly soldiers, and few had the interest or skills to become ranchers or farmers, but he did eventually attract a variety of settlers. Vallejo interceded with the governor and local *alcaldes* to get land grants for some of his soldiers and for anyone Vallejo thought would do well in the community. He could offer potential colonists free land, the labor of Natives to assist in clearing the land and in building a house, and farm implements, animals, and seeds from the stores of the former mission. With such enticements, he did manage to convince numerous members of his own family to settle in Sonoma with him. The general's older brother, Salvador, always his right-hand man, had been with him from the start in Sonoma. Two of his sisters, Rosalia and Encarnación, and their Anglo husbands, his mother-in-law, and several cousins also became part of his family enclave.[62]

With a contingent of Miwok laborers, Vallejo built a large structure on the old mission grounds, called the Casa Grande, and completed the walls around the plaza. He recalled this founding moment with pleasure when he wrote in his memoirs: "First I outlined a plaza, 212 varas square. I left the small building which had been constructed as a church to the east of the plaza. I built a barracks about 100 varas west of the church . . . and divided the lots as required by law."[63] All of these "I's" were theoretical; Vallejo indicated he wanted such buildings created, and then soldiers and Native workers made it so. A year or so later, he directed the building of a huge hacienda at Petaluma, which operated a manufacturing center for leather goods, woven wool rugs and stockings, baskets, and dried herbs, meats, and fish.

With its warm dry summers and rainy cool winters, the Sonoma climate allowed for various kinds of production in which Vallejo took a great deal of personal pride. By 1840 he and Francesca had added five children to the population of the growing community. His own holdings were vast—at least fifty thousand acres of which five hundred were cultivated, twelve thousand cattle, six thousand horses of whom a thousand were broken to saddle and bridle, maybe three thousand sheep, mission vineyards, workshops, and small manufacturing enterprises. The long-time San Francisco merchant and business associate of Vallejo, William Heath Davis, remembered Vallejo employed two hundred Indian workers at Sonoma and another six hundred at Petaluma, where he had several flour mills. While this estimate may be too large, it does indicate the scale of his operations.[64] *Comandante* Vallejo protected this enterprise with soldiers from the presidio that he commanded. And because of the failure of the California government to pay or provision soldiers, Vallejo took on this responsibility himself, making his soldiers loyal to him in a particularly personal way.[65]

Vallejo understood that he needed similar loyalty from the local Indians, but this took more time. He used several approaches, some involving sticks and others carrots, but always recognizing the need for real relationships. One thing he didn't do, common in John McLoughlin's and William Bent's worlds, was to marry into local Native nations. His status as a Californio, a soldier, and political leader did not encourage intermarriage. His worldview, however, did permit other kinds of relationships. In the early years, however, Vallejo had to demonstrate his military power, as his own ranchos and those of neighboring colonists suffered greatly from raids on their cattle. He and his brother Salvador, along with Chief Sem Yeto, made a series of offensive military campaigns against Native settlements to the north. They took hundreds of prisoners who then provided labor at Sonoma and Petaluma. The raiding and trading culture that had evolved in northern California would never exactly end, given that Natives and Californians could always get ready cash or trade goods by stealing horses and cattle and selling them to foreign traders and mountain men lurking just to the east. Part of the "peace" agreements included the promise to provide labor for Vallejo in return for his willingness to ignore a certain amount of horse, cattle, and human stealing and trading.[66]

Now, the story of the people who were captured to work at Sonoma or the hacienda at Petaluma, often called "the Palace", is crucial for under-

17. Mariano Guadalupe Vallejo (1808–90). Photograph by J. G. Smith, ca. 1868. Courtesy of The Bancroft Library, University of California, Berkeley. 1978.195:02-PIC.

This image of Vallejo was made in his later years, when he and his family lived in Sonoma as winemakers and land speculators. His trademark muttonchop sideburns and elegant dress in a classic nineteenth-century gentleman's pose show a man comfortable with status and wealth.

standing the political economy and social relations of northern California. Everyone—Native, Californian, foreign immigrant—participated in the trade in human beings, the most valuable resource on this particular frontier. These workers weren't prisoners, but they certainly weren't free laborers either. Vallejo modeled his labor practices on what he knew from a lifetime in California, but also on what he had seen at Fort Ross among the Russians. Vallejo, like any other large landholder in the region, needed Indian labor to make value from the land: to turn cattle into beef, shoes, hats, and saddles and to turn sheep into blankets, hats, and shawls. As his brother Salvador recalled many years later, "they tilled our soil, pastured our cattle, built our houses, paddled our boats, made tiles for our homes, ground our grain . . . and made every one of our meals."[67]

Most of this work was seasonal, and General Vallejo did not require the Natives to live in the compound. Many villages migrated seasonally, choosing to settle near Vallejo's operations during the seasons when workers were needed. During the slaughter, or *matanza*, season, Native vaqueros slaughtered about eight thousand cattle each year—a huge undertaking that involved rounding up cattle, slaughtering them, and processing hides, making tallow, and preserving meat. Vallejo also needed Native skills to build houses and barns, cook, care for his children, and take care of his horses and cattle, which did require year-round work. Over the years, Vallejo and local Native people built an interdependent community at Sonoma. Hardly utopian, but also not a prison, the community served the needs of its residents, but like Fort Vancouver or Bent's Fort, it functioned in the context of local politics and global economies.[68]

With relative peace with Native people, a steady trickle of settlers, and his personal fortunes improving, Vallejo could only see a few major clouds on the horizon. However, three of these—Mexican politics, the Russians, and John Sutter—would coalesce into a fearful storm. Almost as soon as the Vallejo family had moved into the new adobe structure in Sonoma, the political situation in California, which had been boiling since the Mexican Revolution, came to a head. Both Mariano and Francesca Carillo y Vallejo were connected to the leading families at the center of the political snarl.

Californians had expected the Mexican Revolution to bring their Enlightenment liberal ideology to fruition. What such hopes meant on the ground in distant departments like Alta California no one knew exactly, but at the very least they expected more local control over government and economy. In the early postrevolutionary years when the Mexican government essentially ignored places like California or New Mexico, they controlled their own affairs unwillingly. When the Mexican government began regaining control over its own revolution, these efforts gradually affected even the most distant outposts. As new policies of "centralization" challenged the federal system on which the Mexican government had settled after 1821, departments like California had increasingly little say over whom the distant officials in Mexico City appointed to govern them. Californians did not like "foreigners" in their midst; they believed they had plenty of ability to rule themselves and in several cycles of rebellion and mayhem in 1828, 1830, 1831, and 1833 had expressed their displeasure with various governors.[69]

In 1835 and 1836 some extremely centralist and politically inexperienced governors were imposed on the already sensitive Californians. By now they had homegrown and ambitious young politicians in their midst, including Mariano Vallejo's nephew Juan Bautista Alvarado. With the collusion of his friends in Monterey, Alvarado decided to overthrow the most recent hated governor and the conservative constitution he represented. Though he expected full support from his powerful uncle in Sonoma, Vallejo instead urged caution and warned Alvarado that he could promise no troops because of serious skirmishes with Native nations. Alvarado ignored Vallejo's advice, marched on Monterey, and kicked out the governor with the threat that Vallejo was "on his way" with troops. The successful, and rather surprised, rebels formed a new government, "a free and sovereign state" as its new leaders claimed, "independent of Mexico." They named Vallejo *comandante militar* of this new state of California, even though he had no idea that a coup had even occurred.[70]

The dust from this particular fracas never settled, and Alvarado and Vallejo never trusted each other. Alvarado feared that his uncle had too much power and often moved to block his control over the military arm of the government. Vallejo believed that personal ambition often blinded his nephew's view of what might be best for California and worried that his own imperial aims in northern California might be thwarted. Although the Mexican government could not tolerate such rebellion in Alta California after the 1836 Texas Revolution, which had resulted in a huge loss of territory and self-esteem, neither could they afford to send in an army to retake California. In some secret diplomatic maneuvers, the Mexican government convinced Alvarado to take an oath of allegiance to the Mexican constitution in return for being recognized as the true governor.[71]

With both civil and military authority safely in the hands of Californios, Vallejo hoped he could turn his attention to more local threats. A foreign power had successfully planted a colony just to his north. After decades of work the Russians at Fort Ross and Bodega Bay had a growing population, maintained good relations with the local tribes, developed several successful manufacturing enterprises, and were conducting trade with the Americans, the British, the French, and various Native nations. However, Vallejo's reports about the success of the Russian outpost reported far rosier conditions than the actual balance sheets from Fort Ross. The Russian-American Company had built this settlement on the northern California coast as an experiment in agriculture. The company's prime objective was fur, but the hunters, sailors, and workers needed to be fed, and the coast of Alaska did not provide enough soil or warm days to grow food. Company officials had hoped that northern California with its milder climate could solve this problem, as well as offering a prime site for hunting sea otters.

By the mid-1830s the settlement had hundreds of acres of land in cultivation and large cattle herds, all intended to provision the operations further north. However, the foggy coastal lands made wheat yields disappointing, though vegetables proved easier to grow. Alexander Rotchev, the manager of the company, boasted about radishes that weighed nearly thirty pounds and beets that could make a Russian weep, but these were hard to transport. Once sea otters had been largely made extinct in the region and the Russians found it cheaper to buy grain and cattle from the Mexicans in California and the Hudson's Bay Company in Oregon than to supply themselves, Fort Ross had little appeal. In 1839 the tsar approved the Russian-American Company's request to abandon Fort Ross. They began looking for someone to take over the fort or at least to buy it and help cut some of their losses. They offered it first to the Hudson's Bay Company, but Chief Factor McLoughlin turned them down because of the success of his own agricultural operations in Puget Sound.[72]

Given his proximity to the fort, General Vallejo followed these developments carefully and assumed that he should be the next owner of Fort Ross. He wasn't so interested in the agricultural possibilities offered by the fort but saw its lands more as a buffer against British and American interests in California. The success of their tanneries and shipbuilding facilities also intrigued him. He carefully explored the possibility of acquiring this potential windfall with the local manager of the fort, Peter Kostromitinov. Practically salivating, he wrote to his nephew, Governor Alvarado, that "all of my desires would be consummated" if he could control Fort Ross.[73] He insisted that personal gain was not his motive, but in his role as *comandante* he offered to buy it on behalf of the state of California. To do that he needed permission from Mexico City, but the central government dithered about making a decision. Vallejo warned Governor Alvarado several times of the dangers of the British or the Americans getting their hands on the fort and urged them to send a garrison to claim the site.[74]

The Mexican authorities refused to heed this warning. They argued, first, that the Russian price was too high, and second, that the Russians had settled illegally on property that was Mexican territory and that therefore Mexico already owned it, making any purchase illegal. The slow process and the arcane legal arguments frustrated Kostromitinov, and in February 1841 he proposed to sell the property to Vallejo himself. At $30,000 for the entire outfit, including livestock, buildings, and farm implements, the offer was a great deal, but Vallejo would have trouble coming up with actual cash in a hurry. Vallejo, hedging, expressed interest in the offer but insisted that he would have to wait until July or August to make an answer.[75]

This hesitation convinced the Russians to look elsewhere. Vallejo's nephew, Governor Alvarado, fearful of putting more wealth and power in his uncle's hands, probably would have blocked such a deal anyway. Instead, Alvarado had secretly brokered a deal between the Russians and a newcomer to the region, Captain John Sutter. Sutter had made a bid earlier in the year, but because he had no actual cash, the deal hadn't looked very good to the Russians. However, with the backing of Governor Alvarado and a byzantine loan arrangement, the Russians agreed to sell Fort Ross to Sutter. On December 13, 1841, Fort Ross passed into Sutter's hands.[76]

CAPTAIN SUTTER'S NEW HELVETIA

As Mariano Guadalupe Vallejo watched this disaster unfold over the course of the fall, he grew both furious and powerless, an unusual and especially frustrating condition. A proud Californio, a practical businessman, and a huge stakeholder in northern California, Vallejo found it painful to watch the indecision and impotence of his government as new dangers encircled California. Vallejo knew John Sutter represented a serious threat to his personal empire and to California as a whole, and he was stunned that other authorities did not see this. When Sutter arrived in California in 1839, Vallejo had tried to obtain a measure of control over him by granting him land in Sonoma where he could keep an eye on the suspicious character. Sutter had refused the offer, saying that he needed to be further east and on a river to develop his commercial enterprise.

The nineteenth-century historian H. H. Bancroft used words like "wily" and "slippery" to describe Sutter, who is a complex character in the history of California and the nation. No one, contemporarily or in hindsight, really liked him after any extended contact. His most recent biographer, Albert Hurtado, found the man fascinating, but he also used such adjectives as "opportunistic," "self-serving," and even "dangerous" in outlining Sutter's character.[77] Such gut reactions differ from those that people reported having about the Bent brothers or General Vallejo, who built their reputations on trust and long-standing familial relationships. Sutter, who became an accidental hero in the grand narrative of American history, had a different approach to creating his life in a cultural and imperial borderland.

Sutter arrived in northern California ill-prepared to take on his role as self-appointed colonizer. Born in 1803 to a middling Swiss family, he talked his way into a marriage with a wealthy young woman and went on to have five children with her by 1834. He served in the Swiss reserve but saw no actual military service. His various financial endeavors, however, were less successful, and in the spring of 1834, with the threat of debtor's prison over his head, Johann August Sutter fled to America. He left his wife in deep debt and wrote her weeks later that he would never return. He ended up in St. Louis, where he introduced himself as Captain Sutter. He spent a winter spinning stories about his Prussian military exploits in order to wheedle loans from German bankers in St. Louis to support his new extravagant lifestyle. When the creditors got too insistent, he joined a caravan for Santa Fe, expecting to make his fortune there. However, unlike the Bent brothers, he had no long experience in the fur trade and few family connections to count on for cash or help, but he talked several investors into investing in various Santa Fe trading schemes, including an entirely illegal trade with the Apaches for stolen horses. These went bust, and Sutter went back to Westport, Missouri, a border town where he might recoup his fortunes in the horse trade orchestrated by Missouri traders and Delaware and Shawnee raiders. Predictably, Sutter soon found himself with yet another warrant for his arrest for bad debts. He responded, as many men did in such a situation, by taking a western tour in 1838.[78]

John Sutter arrived in California in 1839 with two things in his favor: limitless self-confidence and a recent tour of all of the most important trading operations in western North America. Unlike Mariano Vallejo, he had no knowledge of the human or natural landscapes of California, but he had re-created himself into a frontier visionary so that actual experience or financial resources mattered little. Sutter explained later, "I preferred a country where I should be absolute master."[79] Sutter's vision of an independent trading empire in the Central Valley of California came out of some knowledge about what it would take, and the absolute certainty that he could pull it off.

Before arriving in California, Sutter visited Stephen Austin's settlement in Texas and the multipurpose Bent's Fort and met with Santa Fe and Taos traders involved in the horse and mule business in California. He had spent several weeks in 1838 at Fort Vancouver, observing the operations of the Hudson's Bay Company and visiting the Russian settlements at Sitka. While waiting for passage to California, he had spent nearly six months in Hawaii learning about the Pacific trade. Armed with this knowledge and with letters of introduction from everyone he thought could help him, and accompanied by Native Hawaiians who had agreed to three-year terms as indentured servants, an Indian slave he bought at a rendezvous in the Rocky mountains, and five Euro-Americans, Sutter arrived in California in July of 1839.[80]

As required by law, he presented himself immediately to customs officials in Monterey and then sold his plan to Governor Alvarado, who, according to Sutter, "was very glad to hear that . . . I intended to settle in the interior on the Banks of the Sacramento because the Indians would not allow white Men and particularly those of Spanish Origin to come near them."[81] Alvarado granted him permission to build "a fort and trading establishment" on the Sacramento River and, provided that Sutter became a Mexican citizen after a year of residence, promised to grant him a large rancho surrounding the fort. Sutter took from this meeting the rather fantastic belief that he would be the absolute lord of his domain, free from any interference from Mexican civil or military authorities; Alvarado believed that he had granted Sutter the right to be governed by California and Mexican laws. This "misunderstanding" would come back to haunt both men.[82]

After a rather cool visit with General Vallejo in Sonoma, ostensibly to pay his respects but also to survey Vallejo's extensive operations, Sutter set off for the Sacramento River. He had a small flotilla of boats, a few experienced sailors, but no idea of how to find the Sacramento River in the sloughs of the delta and no supplies for trading or for building a settlement. It took rather longer than Sutter had hoped to find the river and a site for a fort, and his initial meetings with local people were tense because he couldn't speak the language or distribute gifts. Eventually, he chose a spot near where the American River flowed into the Sacramento and called it New Helvetia, hoping that it would attract Swiss and German immigrants. Several months later, his Hawaiian workers had erected a few grass buildings, and he had contracted with some local Indians to build some adobe structures.[83]

18. "Sutter's Fort, Sacramento, Cal, 1847." Drawing. Library of Congress, Prints and Photographs Division.

John Sutter's New Helvetia, with a giant U.S. flag flying over it, has been transformed into Sutter's Fort. Neat and solidly built, with none of the ramshackle outbuildings and piles of trash and construction materials that many visitors observed, it now welcomes the Anglo-American victors.

While Sutter's Fort may have looked like a multicultural wonderland, it surely did not feel that way to the people living there. Unlike William Bent or Mariano Vallejo, John Sutter did not see himself as enmeshed in a community, with the reciprocal responsibilities this required. He viewed himself as ruler of his dominion, owing nothing to the Native people who lived there or to officials of California who had granted him this land or even to his European neighbors. Certainly Bent and Vallejo saw status hierarchy and ethnic and class differences as part of the normal operating procedures in their worlds but tempered these with negotiation and with the bonds of personal relationships. Sutter, on the other hand, treated his Native workers purely as bodies who provided services. They served him as construction workers, hunters, soldiers, and household workers, but he certainly never trusted them, maintaining, as he put it, "military discipline."[84] Reminiscing later, he recalled that during the first year of his residence when "the Indians was first troublesome," he had solved this problem in part by deploying "a large Bull Dog which saved my life 3 times, when they came slyly near the house in the Night: he got hold of and marked them most severely."[85]

Once he got beyond the need for constant canine protection, Sutter realized that he had chosen a spot between two Native groups who were competing for power. One group, the Nisenans, agreed to come work for him in return, they hoped, for better access to guns and trade goods. The other major group, the Miwoks, who had recently escaped the bonds of mission labor, had no desire to work for Sutter, and remained mostly antagonistic to his project. However, a stable source of labor was essential for Sutter's enterprise to work. So, he bought slaves, captured children, and indentured other Indian workers, labor arrangements that were common for border regions in any part of North America.[86]

Though he had looked carefully at Hudson's Bay Company outfits, Bent's Fort, Fort Ross, and Vallejo's enterprises at Sonoma and Petaluma, Sutter ran New Helvetia like a drill sergeant. Disgusted by the rancherías and Indian villages that had sprung up outside of other operations, he required his workers, Native and European, to live inside the walls of the fort, to wear uniforms, and to participate in military drills—all part of his vision of mastering his own corner of the California universe. An unhappy former employee reported that Sutter "had to lock the Indian men and women together in a large room to prevent them from returning to their homes in the mountains at night," and that they were fed porridge from troughs "more like beasts than human beings."[87] Sutter paid his workers in currency that he made himself and required them to spend their "money" at the fort's store. If they did not perform to his standards, he punished them with a "big whip made of cowhide" that one Native employee remembered in particular. Sutter recalled later with evident nostalgia those days when "I was everything—patriarch, priest, father and judge."[88]

Perhaps most instructive were his relationships with Native women. As we have seen, all kinds of relationships developed between Native people and Europeans. From the long-term serial marriages the Bents, the McLoughlins, and the Wilsons had, or the plural and diplomatic marriages favored by the Chouteaus and other important fur trade families, to the casual connections that may have lasted a winter, a rendezvous, a feast, a tour of duty, or a night, liaisons between Natives and Europeans served a variety of needs. Sutter, who had a wife and five children in his native Switzerland, had at least two official mistresses among his imported Hawaiian (Kanaka) workers. Several observers reported that he had a "stable" of Indian women concubines, and even that he bought and sold young children for his own sexual pleasures. Native people could provide work, sexual pleasure, and various forms of capital, but Sutter could not imagine them as parts of families or permanent relationships.[89]

Sutter also had a rather motley group of Euro-American workers and didn't treat them much better. He sometimes required his workers to marry Native women. This practice, especially the fact that Sutter performed the marriages himself, infuriated local Californios who saw it as blasphemous and dangerous, but Sutter viewed it as increasing his supply of "families" who could be counted as colonists for the Mexican government. New Helvetia needed agricultural workers, hunters, craftspeople, and horse thieves to make it run. Because of California's strict immigration and land ownership restrictions, the region seemed to attract people who simply arrived and traded illegally. General Vallejo certainly recognized that Sutter attracted a dangerous group of ex-mountain men and ex-sailors, not the upstanding colonists that Vallejo wanted to attract to northern California. He wrote to his nephew, Governor Alvarado, warning him about the "seditious foreigners" and "criminals" that Sutter had gathered around him.[90]

The raising, training, selling, buying, stealing, and reselling of horses had become a huge business in the late 1820s and only expanded throughout the period before 1846, and Sutter had been introduced to this business in Missouri and Santa Fe. Native people who had fled the missions conspired with shady traders and trappers who had filtered into the California interior. These new foreigners, politely called *vaqueros* or impolitely called *chaquanosos*, were Indians and Anglo mountain men, and they included Utes and Shawnees as well as more local Yokuts and Miwoks. Throughout the interior valleys and mountains of California people from all over the world found a ready market for guns and trade goods in return for sturdy California horses and mules. In northern Alta California, Miwoks found a particular niche in stealing horses from ranchos and missions and selling them to Hudson's Bay Company brigades.[91]

Sutter, though he never directly admitted it, found his own niche in buying stolen horses from the Miwoks and selling them back to their original owners for a "recovery fee." Part of the reason that Governor Alvarado had allowed Sutter to build New Helvetia was that he hoped that a fort in that region would dampen the near epidemic of raiding. Alvarado did not exaggerate the impact of these raids. A French visitor reported in 1841 that the Indians "carry on endless raids" on a scale of "hundreds every night."[92] Sutter did eliminate raiding on his own growing herds, but he just focused it on his neighbors' animals and then made a profit on that as well. Such activities did not improve his relations with his Californio neighbors but did give him negotiating power with local Miwoks, who had initially been very suspicious of Sutter's presence.[93]

By 1841 Sutter had enough confidence in his operation to make it official. He traveled to Monterey and officially requested Mexican citizenship and his land grant. He worked out the terms with Governor Alvarado, but his actual holdings and acreage were murkily understood at best. This vagueness suited Sutter just fine, and he returned to New Helvetia with high hopes. His plan of encouraging Europeans and Anglo-Americans to settle in the region had little success. He shared his domain with only two non-Native neighbors, the grouchy and reclusive Dr. John Marsh and Ignacio Martinez, who lent Sutter money and soon regretted it. And, of course, only a hard day's travel to the west stood the burgeoning empire of Mariano Vallejo, who ostensibly held complete military control over northern California.[94]

Events beyond either Sutter's or Vallejo's control began to affect life in northern California as emigrants from the United States began to appear in larger numbers. Only a few arrived in the years before the 1849 gold rush, but the small trickle of people who came by ship and overland from Oregon still worried Mexican officials. Though most of these emigrants appeared to follow the rules by settling in colonies, becoming Mexican citizens and good Catholics, and often marrying into Californio families, the specter of the Texas Revolution and its clear instigation by settlers from the United States kept officials alert. Part of General Vallejo's job was to inspect all newcomers to his region, to issue them passports for travel, and to decide if they were good material for settlement.

In November 1841 the first party of thirty-one overland immigrants stumbled over the Sierra Nevada range and ended up at John Marsh's ranch. Exhausted, hungry, and destitute, these guests were hardly welcome. Their successful crossing of the mountains, difficult as it had been, indicated the viability of a direct overland route, making Mexican California suddenly more vulnerable. Marsh grudgingly fed them and turned them over to the Mexican authorities. General Vallejo, not impressed with their stories or credentials, threw them in jail but granted them passports after a ceremonial incarceration. Sutter, seeing in some of the immigrants the answer to his labor needs, offered them a place to stay and jobs at the fort. John Bidwell, one of the party's leaders, later recalled that for the first time someone in California was glad to see them when they arrived. Sutter, he remembered, "received us with open arms and in a princely fashion."[95] Later Mariano Vallejo would give several of these potential settlers land, but Sutter was the one they remembered as a hero.

The arrival of this overland group created a new set of rumors at Sonoma. People heard stories that with this small influx of Americans, Sutter now planned to declare independence for his district and seize Sonoma, all paid for and supported by the Hudson's Bay Company, archvillains in every rumor. In fact, Sutter was deep in debt to the Company and had a very rocky relationship with their trappers, who competed directly with his business. Reacting to these not very credible rumors, General Vallejo wrote to Sir George Simpson to ascertain the Hudson's Bay Company's official stand on Sutter. By return mail he received an answer from Simpson making it clear that neither he nor the HBC had any intention of allying with anyone as politically and economically unstable as Sutter.[96]

Sutter, however, found himself caring not a whit about the Hudson's Bay Company as 1841 continued. Once the Russian lands and buildings at Fort Ross fell into his hands in the waning moments of 1841, he believed he had achieved complete independence. Somehow he convinced the Russians that he could provide them with a steady supply of grain (even though New Helvetia couldn't supply its own needs) and that he could accumulate enough cash to repay the giant loan they gave him to buy the fort and its buildings and animals. Sutter, always capable of flexibility when it came to business agreements, assured the Russians that he could meet such requirements. Because he never felt he had any responsibility to anyone but himself, the consequences of bad business deals never worried him. Happily, he dispatched a group of workers to begin dismantling the usable parts of the Russian fort and transporting them to New Helvetia. Soon his Native troops marched around the fort wearing abandoned blue and green Prussian uniforms that the Russians had used for their Aleut guards.[97]

Viewing life from quite a different perspective, Mariano Vallejo felt the weight of his tightly bound world on his shoulders. Because of his long shadow in California history, we think of him as a grave older gentleman with stunning mutton chops, but in 1841 he was only thirty-four. As *comandante*, he protected all of northern California, which included keeping peace with Native nations as well as the French, Russians, British, and Americans who seemed to pop up like weasels everywhere he turned. As rancho holder and *alcalde* of Sonoma and Petaluma, he had hundreds of agricultural and manufacturing workers, mostly Native people, who depended on him for food, clothing, and lodging. Various European and American colonists had settled in and around Sonoma, and Vallejo felt responsible for their safety and welfare. Peace negotiations with several Indian nations had introduced another set of reciprocal responsibilities of visits, ceremonial gifts, and alliances in war. His own family had expanded to six children, and his extended family at Sonoma included several generations.

Vallejo managed his world with personal and political connections. His firm belief in northern California's potential as an independent state of Mexico allowed him to see the complicated community that surrounded him as essential to producing the people and talents California needed to make it successful. Years of experience in frontier California had taught him to appreciate the rituals that held his world together. Feast days, riding competitions, dances, raids, marriages, baptisms, healing sessions, harvests, and slaughters linked people in ways more important than nationality or ethnicity. General Vallejo understood as well that this balance was delicate at best, and that change could come in a heartbeat. Like William Bent sitting on the roof of Bent's Fort in 1833 watching the stars fall, General Vallejo read the events of 1841 as a portent. They signaled that his world was shifting, but even he could not read how.[98]

On New Year's Day 1842, depressed over these events and bedridden with a wound to his hip that wouldn't heal, Vallejo received word that important guests would be arriving in Sonoma. Sir George Simpson, the governor of the Hudson's Bay Company, and John McLoughlin, the chief factor of Fort Vancouver, would visit in a day or so. Vallejo was well aware of the HBC's growing interest in expanding into California. McLoughlin had recently bought land and a house in Yerba Buena as headquarters for their California fur-hunting, trading, and shipping business. Simpson was making this visit to see these facilities. Vallejo had met these men before and had a business relationship with McLoughlin, but a personal visit would allow him to assess these men and how they might affect northern California more carefully. Captain Sutter had invited them to visit his fort, but they had declined, so Vallejo jumped at this chance to demonstrate the permanence, potential, and unique qualities of his northern California world.[99]

Dinner and Diplomacy in Northern California

On that winter day in 1842, Francesca Vallejo was tired. Her husband, in bed with a sore hip, had invited a score of guests to visit their northern California hacienda. It irritated her especially that he had hurt himself showing off a new horse and saddle. Acting as if he were a boy instead of a father of six, he had lassoed a wild steer and promptly dislocated his hip. Now, from his bed, Don Mariano assumed that food, entertainment, lodging, and a gracious welcome would all appear as if by magic. As she looked in the larders, her three older children ran around out in the plaza while an Indian woman watched them. The younger three, Natalia, four, Plutarcho, two, and Platon, one, played on the floor of the *sala* (living room) with the children of their nursemaid. Francesca Vallejo also expected another child, but it would be summer before that event occurred. As one early twentieth-century biographer put it, rather charmingly, "she had either a baby in her lap or near her heart" during the first twenty-five years of her married life. Of course, she had servants and sisters who could help, and her mother-in-law was visiting, but the primary responsibility of making the visit a success lay in her capable hands.[100]

Visitors of all kinds came to Sonoma, and the entire Vallejo family prided themselves on their hospitality that anchored this community in Alta California's far north. Traders, politicians, hunters, soldiers, and travelers of all nations made Doña Francesca's home a vibrant place, especially in the warm spring and summer months. However, today winter rains had made the plaza muddy and the choices of food more limited. Meat, wine, and preserved fruits seemed the most plentiful options in early January. Served with beans and tortillas made by her expert cooks, this would make a festive meal that would emphasize the bounty of the rancho. Her tiny store of sugar and flour had been entirely depleted for Christmas baking, so no cake would appear on the table. Maybe an Indian pudding sweetened with dried fruit would serve for dessert.[101]

The biggest problem came with the guest list. The fiesta was in honor of two Anglos from the north, Simpson and McLoughlin, but they had other important visitors with them, a French diplomat rumored to be a spy, Señor McLoughlin's daughter, and several Americans. Certainly other Vallejo relatives would come, and she recognized the trickiness there too of maintaining peace amid a family famous for its wit, sharp tongues, and sarcasm. Her mother-in-law, Doña Maria Antonia Lugo y Vallejo, was making a long visit to Sonoma to visit her two daughters and two sons who had settled there. Her own mother, Maria Carillo, had recently been granted her own rancho nearby in Sonoma but was kept busy by her own children, several still living at home.[102] Her brother-in-law Salvador had a prickly nature and had already made clear his distrust of the visitors from the Hudson's Bay Company. He insisted that Sem Yeto, now Chief Solano, be invited along with his elaborately dressed cavalry to impress the guests with the Vallejo family's wide range of allies. The general agreed and sent an escort of thirty horses with silver and gold embroidered saddles, with elegantly uniformed Mexican troopers and Chief Solano's auxiliaries mounted on them, to guide the guests from their landing in San Rafael.[103]

The Vallejos knew how to treat guests, and Francesca could see that even the austere Don George Simpson relaxed as he sat in the *sala*, received officially by Don Salvador and her brother-in-law Jacob Leese. Simpson and McLoughlin inquired politely about the health of Don Mariano and hoped that he would be well enough to join them the next day. After conversation in a mix of English, French, and Spanish, Francesca escorted Governor Simpson to the dining room, where dinner would be served to the group of more than thirty people. They spoke politely in her broken French and his poor Spanish as plates of food appeared on the table, carried by her Indian servants from the kitchen across the plaza. Simpson appeared to enjoy the food but perhaps was a bit daunted by the spiciness of some of the sauces, "an everlasting compound of pepper and garlic," a response that Doña Francesca had noted was common among English and American visitors. Sem Yeto, she observed, engaged Mr. McLoughlin and his son-in-law, William Rae, in conversation, as they seemed to speak some universal Indian trade patois. Her sisters, seated on the far end of the table, were in the midst of a vigorous discussion with Eloisa McLoughlin Rae about the dangers of the San Francisco Bay climate for infants. Salvador, she noted gratefully, had taken on the task of entertaining his mother. And she observed with some amusement that the French spy, Monsieur Mofras, had found more than his match with her own mother, who did speak French and could hold her own with anyone.[104]

After dinner, most of the women excused themselves, but Doña Francesca and Señora Vallejo, as the official hostesses in Don Mariano's absence, accompanied the men back to the *sala* for imported brandy and Mexican cigarillos. They discussed a wide variety of topics, including California's susceptible situation, and Governor Simpson even floated the idea of an English protectorate for California, with a sly wink at the French spy, who obviously coveted California for his own nation. Certainly the English and Canadian visitors shared Mexican concerns about the Americans, and in 1842 Oregon was perhaps even more vulnerable. But whether California ended up as a French colony or Oregon as a part of Canada could not be decided by these men, and in any case there were lives to be led and fortunes to be made, and that was their business.[105]

After the evening ended, the guests found their way to rooms with beautiful wall hangings and bed coverings that Doña Francesca and her sisters had personally embroidered. Simpson remembered the rooms as barren, with only "gaudy chairs from Woahoo" (Oahu) and concluded, crabbily, "this was California all over—the richest and most influential individual obliged to borrow the means of sitting from savages."[106] Francesca reported on the evening's events to her husband. Hearing that the visitors hoped to stay another day or two, the Vallejos planned several events to keep their guests happy. They entertained most visitors with displays of horsemanship, dancing, and bear and deer hunting, but they decided that a horse race, a visit to Sem Yeto's town, and a musical evening would be most appropriate. Vallejo took Simpson and the other guests to see Chief Solano's village. Simpson described the inhabitants as both "well-formed and well-grown" but because they were naked, ate acorns, and had been subject to the Catholic Church, he declared them "most miserable of the race that I ever saw."[107] McLoughlin, a Catholic and married to a part-Cree woman, didn't express any opinion about the California Natives. But he and Simpson both very much enjoyed the horse racing, laying bets on which riders would win, as well as music, dancing, and serious conversation in the evening.[108]

Doña Francesca had noticed that the rude Sutter never arrived at Sonoma, but he managed to dampen the festivities anyway. On the last day of the visit, Sir George Simpson received a letter from Sutter, demanding that the Hudson's Bay Company stop hunting in California because the Mexican authorities had said it was illegal. Vallejo and Simpson later learned that Sutter had sent an inflammatory letter that same day to Governor Alvarado stating that the Hudson's Bay Company had promised to join Sutter in a fight against Mexican oppression.[109] This obvious ploy to play the two powers against each other failed, and Vallejo and the HBC continued to do business. In thanking Vallejo after his visit, Simpson noted that Sutter had tried and failed "in St. Louis, among the Shawnee Indians, in the Snake Country, on the Columbia River, at the Sandwich Islands, and at San Francisco." He explained further that the Hudson's Bay Company did not want to number among the "anxious friends" hoping for some payment from Sutter.[110] As a result, Vallejo's flour and beef provisioned the hunting parties from Fort Vancouver that continued to arrive each year, much to Sutter's disgust.

Who knows how much the easy hospitality displayed by the Vallejo family helped convince McLoughlin and Simpson to avoid an entanglement with Sutter at that moment, but personal connections always mattered. As 1842 progressed, only such relationships would keep California from falling apart. Everyone living in California who had any dealings with the Mexican government or its local representatives knew two things: the government in Mexico City did little to protect Californians from the predations of other nations, and the government would not allow the Californians to govern themselves. To anyone paying attention, the question was not *if* someone would move in, but who, when, and under what conditions. None of this was new—the United States had been attempting to buy or steal California since 1807, and France, Britain, and Russia had been threatening to make it a protectorate for even longer. And none of this had ever made much of a difference at the local level. The Vallejos, the Leeses, the Carillos, Yem Seto and his family, and even Captain Sutter understood that the behavior of neighbors, the weather, the price of hides, tallow, and horses, and the health of one's family mattered far more than who was governor or ruler. Whether a Mexican, an Englishman, or a Californio headed up the distant government couldn't disturb the important rhythms that had evolved in northern California. Or could they?

PORTENTS OF CHANGE

General Vallejo had always lived with rumor and speculation, but even he found the situation in the early 1840s worrisome. As military commander he knew that he did not have the resources to protect California if any nation chose to take it. In desperation, he had commissioned his private secretary to travel to Mexico City to beg for assistance. Instead of funding and soldiers, Vallejo received his walking papers. Then, in early 1842 came the news that his nephew, Governor Juan Alvarado, had also been summarily dismissed by a new centralist Mexican government. To replace him, Mexico City sent a hero from the Texas Revolution, General Manuel Micheltorena, to show the troublesome Californios how to behave. Accompanied by the three hundred convicts who had been let out of prison to serve as his soldiers, Micheltorena arrived in San Diego at the end of August 1842. He marched north toward Monterey with his troops, who stole provisions, horses, cattle, and household goods from every rancho and settlement they passed, alienating Californios of every class and location. Vallejo told his brother Salvador "only a saint could rule California now."[111] As Micheltorena approached Monterey and Governor Alvarado prepared to hand over the government to him, the crisis that everyone expected, but had never prepared for, sailed out of the west.

Two warships anchored just south of Monterey on October 18, 1842. The next day the flagship, flying British colors, made its way into the harbor. The ship, however, was part of the U.S. Pacific squadron, commanded by Commodore Thomas ap Catesby Jones. It sailed under false colors because the commander believed Mexico had declared war on the United States. This misapprehension and the resulting opéra bouffe events to follow began months earlier when Jones received orders from the secretary of the navy about his task in the Pacific. In the context of considerable international turmoil around Mexico's loss of Texas, rumored British designs on Texas and California, and the unsettled Oregon question, Commodore Jones's job was to protect the commerce and interests of the United States by cruising the Pacific Coast as far north as the Columbia River. The secretary of the navy exhorted Jones "to avoid all occasions of offence to the national or municipal authorities with whom you may have intercourse" unless American interests were threatened, in which case he was to "act with decision and firmness becoming the occasion."[112]

With that set of rather vague instructions, a rickety and poorly armed squadron, and sailors who had mostly never been to sea, Jones also had to interpolate rumors about international politics to guide his actions. Much of the worry in the Pacific revolved around the British and the fear that they would take the best ports along the Pacific Coast while the United States wasn't looking. While engaging in maneuvers off the coast of Chile in the summer of 1842, Jones began to observe some events that convinced him that war was imminent. Reports in Chilean and Mexican newspapers claimed that negotiations between Mexico and the United States over Texas were going poorly and played up rumors that Great Britain had struck a deal with Mexico for California. Meanwhile, British warships left the Chilean ports under sealed orders with extra provisions.[113]

With such rumors swirling around without any real information from his superiors, Jones decided that given the probability of war, he should depart at once for California with two warships, the *United States* and the *Cyane*, and that the *Dale* should carry an urgent message to Panama for transmittal to Washington, explaining the situation and their decision. Jones tried to keep his plans secret, and the ships sailed out on September 8, 1842.[114] Once underway, Jones told his sailors that the United States and Mexico were at war and that they were en route to California to seize its ports. Partly, he told this lie to keep his sailors focused on their training, but surely he needed it himself to justify his actions. On October 19 the ships approached the harbor of Monterey, first boarding a small Mexican ship to find out if its master knew anything about a war. He didn't, but this lack of information didn't deter Jones. He put up British flags and sailed into the harbor. Once in the harbor and his guns manned, he put up the American Stars and Stripes. He fully expected an American to come out to the ship to inform him about a war or a British seizure. No one came, and Jones sent a party ashore demanding the capitulation of the Mexicans. He delivered surrender terms to Governor Juan Alvarado and gave him eighteen hours to answer. With only twenty-nine soldiers available and no ships in port, Alvarado and Don Mariano Silva, the military commander at Monterey, decided quickly to capitulate. Part of Alvarado's challenge, of course, was that he had just been summarily replaced by a new governor, General Manuel Micheltorena, who had not yet arrived. So upon whose authority should he surrender?[115]

When a commission of Monterey officials boarded the ship with the surrender document, long-time Monterey resident Thomas Larkin accompanied them and acted as translator. Larkin, never one to mince words, inquired just who had declared war upon whom. Jones stated that Mexico had declared war on the United States, which was news to everyone in Monterey, but certainly not unbelievable. Larkin and the California officials insisted they had received no word of such a thing and that nothing in the newspapers suggested a war had broken out. Jones might have slowed the process down, but that certainly wasn't his style. He believed that Alvarado was stalling to give Micheltorena and his rumored six hundred troops time to reach Monterey.[116]

With all the paperwork in order, the next morning, October 21, 1842, landing parties took the fort and put up American flags. When the American sailors saw the flags, their ships fired a twenty-six-gun salute, the fort replied with an equal number, and the conquest ended. Then the commodore came ashore, and his men began searching for documentation to corroborate their claim of a state of war. They found some newspapers from late August that didn't mention a war and some private letters sent from Mexico in early September that seemed to indicate that things were peaceful. From the content of the Mexican papers, Jones concluded that the rumors of the Mexican cession of California to England were also incorrect. After a quick meeting with his officers, Jones agreed that there was nothing to do but admit their mistake and try to undo the international gaffe they had committed. Jones was as efficient in undoing as in doing. His sailors hauled down American flags, raised Mexican flags, left the fort, and reboarded their ships. After the Americans fired a thirteen-gun salute, according to Jones, "normal relations between the two countries were soon resumed."[117]

There were, of course, repercussions. At the local level, although some Californios deeply resented the American actions, most seemed inclined to forgive if not forget and opened their doors to their late enemies. Former governor Juan Alvarado once referred to it as an "*inaudito atentado*" (unprecedented attempt), but he appeared generally unscathed by the event. The mistake had far more serious reactions at the national level. Civil and military authorities in Mexico were simply livid and forced the

Tyler administration to suspend negotiations for the purchase of California. However, Jones never received any official censure for his "display of boldness," though the Mexican government insisted that he be "exemplarily punished for the extraordinary act of excess."[118]

Jones remained in California for several months, apologizing everywhere he could and using the opportunity to inform his superiors about the resources and military preparedness of the region. His most spectacular and most important apology was to General Vallejo in Sonoma, who had been informed of the whole affair as it unfolded. The general readied his troops and prepared to march south, but he received word that the conquest had been aborted before he could leave. Vallejo had considered, briefly, using the "invasion" as a pretext to declare independence from Mexico, as it had proved the utter incompetence of the Mexican government in protecting Californians. However, given that the Californians were fighting a mini civil war over the presence of Micheltorena, the timing seemed poor. In any case, Commodore Jones sailed into San Francisco Bay in December of 1842 and made an official state visit to Sonoma.[119]

General Vallejo planned the visit carefully, knowing that Jones's agenda included observing the economic, political, and military power of the north. He also knew that Jones had been initially rebuffed when he tried to meet with Governor Micheltorena, so that Vallejo had the advantage of the first meeting. In a rather ironic set of mistakes, while Vallejo awaited him with full military honors at Sonoma, somehow Jones and his men got lost. Quite remarkably, Sem Yeto and his elegantly attired troopers found them, captured Jones and his escorts, and jailed them at Sonoma. Vallejo, of course, rectified the situation immediately. The commodore, who had just made a rather large diplomatic "oops" himself, could afford to be magnanimous. Vallejo at once made amends for this breach of hospitality and postponed the official welcome until morning. Whether this "mistake" was a step in Vallejo's diplomatic dance, we'll never know.

In the bright light of a California winter morning, Vallejo's entire garrison promenaded in full dress, and thirteen salvos from the cannon boomed official welcome, a presentation with a military edge designed to demonstrate just who held power in this place. The message was that Californians would and could protect themselves because they had much to protect. Jones saw tables heavy with food and enjoyed it with wine from the general's own vineyards as he watched feats of horsemanship from the Vallejo vaqueros. Sem Yeto's troops exhibited their riding and shooting skills. Suisunes and Patwins from nearby rancherías brought food and manufactured goods and demonstrated their dances. Jones also visited Jacob Leese's Huichica rancho in the Napa Valley where some 1,400 Indians drilled for another campaign against the Satiyomis. Perhaps Monterey had been unprotected, but Vallejo's Sonoma was not.[120]

Families like the Vallejos described themselves as Mexicans, but their ties were to the intricacies of the place in which they lived. Much like the world that the Bent family and their Cheyenne partners had built on the Arkansas River, northern California existed in the first half of the nineteenth century as a negotiated community. No one person, state, or social group (not even John Sutter or Mariano Vallejo) could claim real authority, control, or even possession. The combination of imperial instability, trade networks that reached over every border, and a shifting economy as California moved from a mission colony to a ranching empire made the situation hazy. It was not simply the peaceful pastoral world of sleepy ranchos; people in this place had conflicting agendas, often around the need for human labor, which could make life violent. Only constant renegotiation and the conscious creation of community through family ties, diplomacy, warfare, and dinner made it operate in a surprisingly stable way.

Sutter, on the other hand, had built a community that never had staying power. A series of accidents would keep New Helvetia alive, but it would never flourish as a community. Sutter appeared to have an unerring eye for imagining potential schemes, but a poorly developed political sense of how best to achieve them. By the end of 1842 he had reached the peak of his influence, but he would not manage to hang on to it because he never thought beyond his immediate economic desires.

When Mariano Vallejo stood at attention as Commodore Jones sailed away on that December morning in 1842, what would transpire over the next ten years in the California he knew and his family's position in it was unimaginable. Certainly the presence and behavior of John Sutter was irritating, the "conquest" of Monterey was unsettling, and California and Mexican politics were frustrating. But looking at his many leagues of land, his enormous herds of animals, his close-knit family and neighbors who mixed race and nationality very successfully, the loyalty of his soldiers, both Native and Californio, such concerns waned. William Bent, standing on the parapets of his fort, at the same moment, felt exactly the same way. Questions of who he was, where his loyalties lay, and how his children and neighbors would fare seemed foolish now but would nag at him in years to come.

STEPHEN AUSTIN'S BORDER WORLD

Mary Austin Holley, a widow in her thirties, visited Texas in 1831. She traveled with her brother, who intended to take up land in Texas. The visitors were cousins of Stephen Austin, who had convinced them to move to Mexico and become a part of his growing colony there. Mary loved the adventure of sailing from New Orleans and gliding up the unfamiliar landscape of the Brazos River to her brother's new estate, named Bolivar. Mary had two ambitions in coming to Texas: rebuilding her extended family's ruined fortunes and investigating a more serious relationship with Stephen Austin. She loved the idea of Texas and the fact that towns had been laid out, named, and described. But the reality of Texas didn't quite measure up. Instead of being exciting and filled with potential, the empty town felt lonely and barren. Stephen, so enthusiastic in his letters, seemed kind, but remote and harassed in person. Mary left Texas, and though she later wrote a book about its future promise, she couldn't make the choice to live there.

What did it mean to be Texan, Comanche, Tejano, Mexican, Cherokee, or American in the place that would eventually become Texas? What did living in this changeable borderland mean in the first decades of the nineteenth century as the region's "ownership" was debated at every level? How did its residents understand place, community, nationality, and identity? Was Texas different from Alta California or the Arkansas River border? Stephen Austin and his broad circle of contacts provide a way to answer some of these questions. From birth Austin had experienced the instability and opportunity that imperial wrangling could cause in a place that was French, then Spanish, and then U.S. territory along the Mississippi River. And in central Texas such battles would kill him. Even so, he shared Vallejo's and Bent's optimism about the viability of the world he was helping to build, largely because of its flexible borders. Austin, born in 1793, was about fifteen years older than Bent or Vallejo. He shared a Missouri upbringing with William Bent and Auguste Chouteau, and like many children from elite frontier families, he had been shipped off to boarding school at the age of eleven, with exhortations from his father to prepare himself for "future greatness in life."[121]

Austin's childhood at his father's lead-mining enterprise in St. Genevieve, Missouri, prepared him for his Texas activities. Mine à Breton—opened in French Louisiana, expanded in Spanish Louisiana, and finally bankrupted in American Louisiana—operated as an international way station for years. French miners worked and lived in the community, Spanish government officials and tax collectors appeared occasionally, and Shawnee, Delaware, Osage, Anglo-American, and African American trappers, traders, and visitors came to Moses Austin's store and camped in the vicinity. Young Stephen learned to respect and to do business with a huge variety of people. He also learned that national boundaries and imperial claims had little impact on daily life as he watched flags and politicians come and go, the same set of lessons that William Bent had absorbed along the Missouri and the Arkansas.[122]

By the time he found himself in Texas in 1821, Stephen Fuller Austin had been educated in New England and Kentucky and had lived in Virginia, Missouri, Connecticut, Arkansas, Louisiana, and New Spain. He had watched his family's economic and political fortunes rise on the Mississippi River frontier and, even more precipitously, felt them fall. Forced to leave his pleasant college life at Transylvania University because of this reversal of fortune, Stephen came home to work for his father in 1810. Stephen managed the mercantile business, took the yearly lead output to New Orleans, and was sent to New York to settle accounts with creditors, a huge responsibility for a seventeen-year-old. However, fate and international events interfered when first the barge carrying all of the Austin's lead sank in the Mississippi and then the War of 1812 cratered cotton prices and the availability of credit. Stephen could only report glumly to his father, "Business is almost anihilated," and then figure out how to get home.[123]

The Austins never recovered from this financial setback, and Stephen remained heavily involved in the family business. He diversified their fortunes into slave sales, bank ownership, and a seat in the Missouri legislature. In 1818 his father decided to retire from the mining business and to abandon Missouri. His move left Stephen with the vast obligation of freeing the Austin family from debt. If young Austin had simply followed John Sutter's approach of leaving both family and debt behind, he probably would have been a happier and less famous man.[124]

Moses Austin, ever on the lookout for a grand speculation, challenged Stephen's plans for resuscitating the family fortune in Missouri. Frustrated by his experience with the U.S. government, which refused to allow him to monopolize lead mining, and by Missouri territorial governors who refused him various sinecures and judgeships, Moses began to look toward the Spanish government and Texas for an investment. The signing of the Adams-Onís Treaty in early 1819 gave him just the opportunity he sought. The treaty gave the United States undisputed claim to parts of northern Florida but gave Spain clear title to all of Texas. Spanish politicians believed that the only way to protect and control their colonial possession was to colonize it, and quickly.

As was true along much of the border, who controlled what was continually debated. In the crucible of a multicontinent war between Spain, England, and France, in which only Spain and the new entity of the United States were left standing, no one knew exactly where Spain ended and where the United States began. This was especially true in the furthest reaches of northern New Spain, where Alta California's northern and eastern borders and Coahuila y Tejas's eastern limits were the subject of constant wrangling. Beyond this diplomatic jousting, action-oriented folks either just settled in a border region not knowing or caring to which nation it belonged or they mounted expeditions and invaded. Sometimes we call this latter group expeditionaries or filibusters, but they acted as sort of land pirates, or more correctly corsairs of the terra firma, who operated with full governmental knowledge, if not actual funding.[125]

Eastern Texas, with its border so enticingly close to the rapidly growing Mississippi River basin, endured more than its share of such activities. Mariano Vallejo had witnessed some of these invasions, but Alta California was more remote from the United States and had more successful Spanish settlement. In Texas a century of Spanish efforts had created only a thin line of Spanish settlement that connected San Antonio, La Bahia, and Nacogdoches. It included perhaps three thousand people, some failed missions, and numerous illegal trading outposts, mostly *baldíos,* or empty lands to the Spanish. But within that supposedly blank space Native nations, smugglers, and squatters controlled trade, and the Spanish government spent little money or effort in developing the region, further alienating Spanish Texans. With this tempting and poorly regulated situation, in which even the border of Texas and the United States remained undrawn, between 1800 and 1819 various adventurers invaded Texas regularly.[126]

Armed with letters from Louisiana territorial officials and from presidents ranging from Jefferson to Monroe, men like Philip Nolan, Aaron Burr, and James Long gathered up disgruntled border settlers of all nationalities, armed them, and proceeded to attack Texas. Generally, not much happened, largely because the invaders were poorly prepared, and the Spanish military had little presence in eastern Texas to protect against such activities. Many filibusters just got tired of wandering around Texas and went home. When Spanish authorities did react, they quelled the expeditions quickly, and the U.S. government disavowed all knowledge. However, each successive attempt seemed to encourage others and to convince the Spanish government of the U.S. desire to take Texas by force. Aaron Burr's invasion serves as a good example.

Burr, famous as Jefferson's vice president and infamous as killer of Alexander Hamilton in a duel in 1804, had a two-part plan that sounds surprisingly like the one Moses and Stephen Austin adopted a generation later. He intended to set up a colony filled with eager soldiers on land straddling the Louisiana-Arkansas border within the United States. Then, after instigating a war with Spain, at the outbreak of fighting Burr and his troops would conquer Mexico. What he planned to do with this great conquest remains open to conjecture, but by 1805 Burr had advertised his ambitions widely. Newspapers across the country carried stories about Burr's grand plans to liberate Spanish-controlled territories. As he toured the Mississippi River valley, rumors circulated that he would command ten thousand Kentuckians, three thousand Tennesseans, and between eight and ten thousand militia from Louisiana, and that five thousand slaves would be given their freedom to fight alongside the other citizen-soldiers. Eventually, even his most loyal supporters felt discomfited by his blatant claims about stealing land and his creation of a private army. President Jefferson had him arrested and tried for treason, but only after he had marched around recruiting troops for nearly a year.[127]

Such plottings became actual invasions with the beginning of the Mexican Revolution, especially during the Hidalgo Revolution of 1810. When Father Miguel Hidalgo demanded independence for Native Mexicans who had suffered at the hands of elite Spaniards, he set off a war that had special resonance on the far northern frontier. Hidalgo sent his agents north for money and assistance from the United States, and he himself headed for Texas. San Antonio, the Texas capital, became a glorious success at the beginning of the Revolution. When the royalist governor Salcedo tried unsuccessfully to rally the loyal citizens of San Antonio behind the king, a local militia leader, Juan Bautista Casas, led a coup, seizing the city for the Revolution. Revolutionary glory didn't last long. Casas was caught and shot in a royalist countercoup, and Hidalgo was captured in Texas and executed in his hometown.[128]

Despite Hidalgo's death, the Revolution continued to reverberate in Texas. Emissaries from Mexican revolutionary groups, led by a romantic Mexican patriot named Bernardo Gutiérrez de Lara, met with Secretary of State James Monroe, who offered them support for the Mexican Revolution in exchange for a settlement of the Texas border dispute. They headed back to the Louisiana-Texas border thinking they would have the U.S. Army and Treasury at their disposal. Instead, they got a shady military escort named Augustus Magee and a ragtag group of volunteers and robbers. The Gutierrez-Magee Expedition, as it came to be called, headed for San Antonio in the fall of 1812. The royalist troops there simply withdrew, allowing the expeditionaries to claim victory, at least until a decent-sized force of royalist troops could be mustered. The revolutionary forces formed a provisional government for the new province of Texas, invited "freedmen of all nations to take up residence in Texas," and exhorted Mexicans to throw off the "yoke of oppression."[129]

This exciting state of affairs lasted for a short summer. By August of 1813, however, Gutiérrez de Lara's republican army in San Antonio, which included perhaps four hundred Americans, eight hundred Mexicans, and two hundred Indians, all poorly equipped, faced fifteen hundred royalist soldiers. After a routing at the Battle of Medina River, most of the rebels straggled back to New Orleans. The Spanish government barely pursued the revolutionaries. The victorious royalist general took his revenge by executing 327 Tejanos in San Antonio. He also sent his officers on a bloody retribution raid to the U.S.-Texas border area, killing several hundred settlers and refugees as a warning against further disloyalty against the Spanish king. Though American officials voiced dismay at such activities, no one made any real attempt to stop them, probably because they had so little power over their own borders.[130]

Planting Colonies in Texas

With such porous borders, Texas remained appealing for colony-planting experiments that ranged from government sponsored to completely illegal. Moses Austin's plan fell somewhere in between. In contrast to American squatters and invaders, he promised to serve Spanish needs. He would provide law-abiding colonists who would settle in Texas and protect it from "the Indians, the filibusters, or any other enemy who plans hostilities," as he put it in his petition to the governor. Stephen tried to distance himself from his father's schemes, taking on an appointment as a territorial judge in Arkansas and finally moving to New Orleans. He hoped, he told his family, to find a salaried job, to finish his own education, and to support his brother and sister's education.[131]

Such distancing made little difference when Moses Austin died after his grueling trip to San Antonio to meet with Spanish officials in December of 1820. The trip had not gone especially well. Spanish officials, in the midst of a serious revolution, had some interest in Austin's plan to settle three hundred families in northeastern Texas but offered no financial or military assistance. Grudgingly, Governor Martinez had approved both parts of Moses Austin's plan, a colony and a port, the first authorized on the Texas coast. Austin began to recruit colonists and invested the last of the family's funds into his project. As the first group of colonists prepared to leave Missouri, the effort of the last few months caught up with Moses, and he died on June 10, 1821, just as the Texas adventure took shape.[132]

Stephen's mother, Maria, wrote to him immediately, transmitting her husband's deathbed request that Stephen "prosecute the enterprise he had Commenced" because God "had opened and prepared the way for you and your brothers."[133] With God, his dead father, and his living mother demanding it, Stephen stepped into his father's shoes. Only a few weeks later, Stephen found himself headed to a spot between the Colorado and Brazos rivers to claim the land the Spanish government had granted to his father. Erasmo Seguín, an ambitious young man from San Antonio who had the governor's favor, accompanied Austin. Seguín would become Austin's lifelong friend, advisor, and investment partner. The two shared a vision of a prosperous Texas, settled with industrious farmers and mechanics, irrespective of which nation ran its central government. Their flexibility around nationality served them well, as Texas would blow through at least three more flags.[134]

Stephen Austin was not the only empresario in town, nor were his colonists the only immigrants. The Spanish Crown had long envisioned immigration and colonization as the solution to its Texas problem. For decades, various colonial transplants had arrived and settled, though many groups did not last long in the isolated region largely controlled by powerful Native nations. San Antonio was a fairly successful colonial experiment, built by a combination of settlers imported by the Spanish government from the Canary Islands and a polyglot of Spanish people who found themselves in French-run Louisiana and who were encouraged to move to Texas. In 1807 a large group of Cherokees had immigrated to Texas, and other Native groups fleeing the South, including Pascagoulas, Alabamas, and Choctaws, came as well, hoping that the Spanish Crown would grant them land and leave them alone. Spanish officials had welcomed them, though they had some concern about how the Native Caddos and Comanches would behave toward these newcomers.[135]

These Cherokee families would be some of Austin's nearest neighbors to the north, while the community of San Antonio de Bexar lay just to the southeast. The town, founded in 1718 as part of a mission, had become the most significant Spanish settlement on the Texas frontier. When Austin first saw it in 1821, Bexar, as everyone called it at the time, had a few well-kept streets with adobe structures around a central plaza, but most of the outlying houses were simple *jacales*, dwellings modeled on Native architecture made out of sticks and a thatched roof. The San Antonio version often had a chimney and stood on a long narrow lot that led to the *acecquia*, or irrigation ditch. By the beginning of the nineteenth century most people in San Antonio grew crops and raised cattle, but their success depended entirely on the state of relations with Native people. Few settlers were willing to risk their lives and fortunes by living much outside the town, except during years of peace with the Apaches or the Comanches. Like people in Santa Fe or Monterey, Bexar's residents felt isolated from the larger nation and resented the Crown and the Church for both taxing and ignoring them. When waves of filibusters, revolutionaries, and empresarios hit the community in the early nineteenth century, no one was quite sure how to respond. When the Comanches began raiding at the same time, Bexareños looked to their new American neighbors, rather than their old overlord for help.[136]

Surrounding Austin's community and the Tejanos in San Antonio were Native people who numbered in the tens of thousands and who dominated the small Spanish settlements entirely. The most famous Texas Indians, Comanches, were, in fact, latecomers to the region but brought a crucial piece to the cultural and economic exchange that developed. Apaches, Wichitas, Caddos, Tonkawas, and Karankawas had been there much longer and had trading relationships with French and Spanish traders and settlers. Military maps labeled the region "Province of the Texas Indians." Exchange and commerce benefited everyone, and diplomacy seemed far more lucrative than warfare. By the end of the eighteenth century a delicate peace had been negotiated between Native nations who hunted bison and bred and traded horses, nations that primarily grew food, and Spanish settlers who needed horses and food and had guns, ammunition, and other manufactured goods to offer in the exchange. Intertribal commerce prospered because Spanish diplomacy and gift giving complemented Comanche displays of status and political power. How peaceful this "false peace," as the Spanish called it, actually was remains an open question. Raiding certainly existed, but it was mostly practiced on groups who weren't part of these reciprocal relationships. The Comanches raided groups labeled as their enemies: Pawnees, Arapahos, Osages, and Cherokees to the north, and Apaches and Mexican ranchers to the south.[137]

This workable situation had begun to erode by the time Stephen Austin arrived, and it would take time to rebuild. The increased migration of Native groups forced out of the United States by federal Indian removal policies created new demands on resources. A new set of traders, Americans, who had different goods and rules about trade, began to filter over the Louisiana-Texas border. The long process of the Mexican Revolution interrupted the trade caravans that had traditionally come up from Durango, Chihuahua, and central Mexico, so that Texas Indians did far less trading with their Spanish neighbors. This echoed what happened for Native peoples on the Arkansas border, who suddenly found themselves cut off from trade with Spain, but with new outlets for exchange evolving on the Santa Fe Trail. In Texas, however, the powerful Comanches quickly became unhappy without a steady supply of goods, and they began raiding both American and Mexican settlements in retaliation.[138]

Stephen Austin recognized the shifting sands of the situation he was creating for himself, his family, and the colonists he hoped to attract. Even before he arrived in San Antonio in August of 1821, he heard the news of the independence of Mexico, and by the time they entered San Antonio a new governor, Antonio Martínez, had taken over. Austin reported that the local Tejanos had reacted to the news of "Indepencia" with "every other demonstration of joy."[139] This news, of course, could have complicated Austin's task of establishing a claim, but the new governor seemed eager to continue the experiment of planting a European population in Mexican Texas. Austin chose a spot on the west side of the Brazos River near to Galveston Bay, where he hoped to land colonists and to build a port.

Though Stephen Austin had tried mightily to escape his family earlier in life, now he wanted them as part his new endeavor. He convinced his younger brother, James Elijah Brown Austin—known as Brown to the family—to join him and warned him to bring Spanish grammar books and to get "Francisco or some other to correct your pronunciation BEFORE you come."[140] He begged his sister Emily and several of his cousins to move to Texas, where they could escape the debt and disease that plagued them on the Mississippi. He reserved land for numerous family members in a spot he had optimistically named "Peach Point." A few Austins came, but few stayed once they saw the rough log houses and muddy streets of the frontier community. As his cousin Henry Austin observed, "Mexico was truly a land of promise, but required a deal of patience to await the performance."[141] Austin's brother Brown articulated other discouraging challenges when he wrote to his mother that Mexico "could be a paradise" but that "Indian people own too much of it."[142]

Austin's townsite, which included most of the watersheds of the lower Colorado and Brazos rivers all the way to the Gulf of Mexico, fortunately lay just beyond territory claimed by the Karankawas. This Native group had suffered a long and miserable relationship with eighteenth-century Franciscan missionaries who kept attempting to move them to the missions, where they died of epidemic diseases in stunning numbers. When the missions failed, the remaining Karankawas were abandoned to their traditional enemies, the Apaches and Comanches. They retreated to Galveston Bay, where they united under a single leader and became successful operators in the brisk pirate business. Because of their unwillingness to stay in the missions and their fierce self-protection, along with rumored cannibalism, the Spanish and Tejanos labeled the Karankawas as unfriendly and savage. The Native people who did inhabit parts of the land contained in Austin's grant, the Tonkawas, had avoided contact with the missionaries. Savvy traders, they developed and maintained exchange relationships with the Spanish, the Comanches, and the pirates of Galveston Bay. With this history, accommodating another group or nation, especially one that brought new goods and trading needs, hardly seemed threatening.[143]

Austin avoided unnecessary or dangerous campaigns against any of these people. He knew that his colonists were outnumbered and would be for a long time. He also knew that he needed Native trade networks to get manufactured goods, food, and slave labor. The Cocos and the Wacos, the group of Native people that Austin had encountered on his first trip to Texas, stood somewhere between the Karankawas and the Comanches. They traded regularly with merchants in San Antonio and would trade with individual colonists later on. Austin remembered their hospitality on his first encounter and refused to attack them even when ordered to do so by the Mexican military authorities.[144]

Austin brought his first group of colonists into this ethnically, politically, and economically complex place in the late winter of 1821. By March he had a hundred people planting corn and clearing land, but when he and his younger brother Brown visited San Antonio, they learned that the Mexican government now questioned Austin's entire enterprise. Governor Martínez advised him to go immediately to Mexico City to make a personal plea about the colony's importance. With no other choice, Austin headed for Mexico City, more than eight hundred miles to the south and west. He entrusted his younger brother to the Seguín family in Bexar and left the fledgling colony to fend for itself. Both the colony and its leader had some adventures in the year it took Austin to get back to Texas.[145]

Texas, with its small number of Mexican citizens, large number of Native people, and considerable distance from the capital, hardly had the resources to maintain a state government in 1821. It would become part of a new combined state, Coahuila y Tejas. Texans, including their representative to Congress Erasmo Seguín, objected to this tie to Coahuila because they knew that the more populous and more central state of Coahuila would dominate. And it did. The new state government voted in a new capital at Saltillo, hundreds of miles to the south, and dissolved the local assembly at San Antonio, rendering the Texans powerless at the state level. Just as in Mariano Vallejo's California, only colonization and increased trade with Native nations and the United States could make Texas a viable state, and both projects presented political challenges. Stephen Austin's colony offered population and economic development, but also presented the specter of thousands of grasping Americans moving into the Texas heartland. Long-time Tejanos, including Erasmo and Juan Nepomuceno Seguín, who owned a flourishing ranch outside of San Antonio, supported colonization because it would bring more markets and more business to Texas.[146]

Austin understood that he was not a Tejano and would have to work carefully and politely. From our distance, it seems a little surprising that Austin did not find a helpmate from an influential Tejano family to integrate him quickly into this world. Most men in his position did. But without a Mexican wife, Austin still requested Mexican citizenship and swore his allegiance to the Mexican empire and its new emperor, Augustín Iturbide. Next, he petitioned that his grant be reaffirmed under the new colonization law; finally, he waited patiently and diligently learned and practiced Spanish. His most challenging task may have been avoiding dangerous entanglements with other hopeful empresarios, many of whom lacked Austin's political skills and tact. From Mexico City he implored his colonists "not to meddle in politics and to have nothing to do with any revolutionary schemes."[147]

After months of waiting, in January of 1823 the emperor signed a colonization bill that at least made it possible for Congress to consider Austin's petition. Now his careful groundwork created results. Most Mexican politicians understood that preserving Mexico's northern border required people like Austin who could bring in settlers for its northern frontier. Austin's willingness to take on Mexican citizenship, his careful study of diplomacy and deportment toward Mexican officials, and his well-spoken

Spanish made Austin less threatening. In addition, the strict terms of his contract about the kinds of settlers and the requirements for land owner-ship all convinced those in power to trust him. At last, in July 1823 Stephen Austin returned to his Texas colony, contract and instructions in hand.[148]

Meanwhile, Austin's business associates, potential colonists, and family heard nothing about his activities or whereabouts for nearly a year, and rumors flew that he had been killed or kidnapped. When he finally reap-peared with a liberal colonization law and good terms for his colonists, everyone was much relieved. One of the major sticking points for many settlers was the issue of slavery and whether the Mexican government would free African slaves they brought to the new colony. Austin had worked out a compromise that allowed settlers to keep slaves already in the colony for their lifetimes, but the slaves' children had to be freed at the age of four-teen. No new slaves, however, could be brought into or bought and sold in Texas. This may have dissuaded a few large slave owners from coming, but it reassured most. The enslavement of Native people, a common practice in Texas, didn't warrant the same attention.[149]

Austin's new communities also had to use Mexican forms of government at the local level, forms that had evolved from colonization practices on the Iberian peninsula. Texas communities, like all Mexican communities, agreed to form *ayuntamientos,* which were a particular form of elected city council with an *alcalde* as its leader and the official representative to the federal government. Federal regulations required *alcaldes* to submit elabo-rate monthly reports about immigration, meetings, population changes, economic topics, and military matters, which allowed the government to keep close watch on its colonies, a much tighter form of control than that practiced in the United States. And, of course, Stephen Austin served as the first *alcalde* of San Felipe de Austin. Reflecting some respect for local Tejano leadership, the men of the colony voted to send Erasmo Seguín as their elected representative to Congress and even raised 100 *fanegas,* or 110 bushels, of corn to help pay his expenses since no one had any cash.[150]

While Stephen Austin dealt with the political situation in Mexico City, other dangers plagued his colonists. His brother warned him that "the set-tlers have been much discouraged at your long stay and the dread of the Indians."[151] The colonists had been raided by Apaches and Comanches but truly lived in fear of the Karankawas, who stole food, weapons, and espe-cially mules and horses with ease and confidence. Austin recognized the futility of a military solution, though he begged both the Coahuila y Tejas and the federal governments to increase the number of troops in Texas.

He understood that the problem was unregulated frontier trade in which American traders from Louisiana and Arkansas bought horses, mules, and just about anything from the Indians and could provide coveted trade goods at much lower prices than Mexicans. The solutions would be diplomacy with Native nations, regulation of trade by illicit American traders, and good relationships with New Orleans merchants. He emphasized to his settlers and to Texas officials that avoiding war was crucial, at least until they had a militia strong enough to take on the Karankawas.[152]

The fierce reputation of these local Indians and the fact that more displaced tribes were pouring into Texas from the United States made Austin's job very difficult. He explained to government authorities who complained that his recruiting and settlement of families was too slow that "the Situation I am placed in near the frontiers of two Nations, and surrounded on every side by hostile Indians and exposed to their attacks . . . vexatious pilfering and robbing . . . renders my task particularly laborious."[153] Austin was between a rock and a hard place because of the chaotic border conditions that he described. Some groups, the Comanches in particular, enjoyed a broad expansion of their power as more and more horses, stolen from every part of northern Mexico, expanded their herds. Other smaller tribes warred against each other in their efforts to join with or appease the powerful Comanches. Many of Austin's colonists traded regularly with various tribes, knowing that the horses, mules, and cattle they bought probably came from their neighbors. The Mexican nation declared war on the Comanches in 1824, but Austin tried to stay out of it and insisted that his colonists had to remain neutral. He feared a general Indian uprising and wondered, "In this state of feeling is there not some danger that all the Indians in the province may be induced to unite against the American settlements?"[154]

By 1826 Austin's colony faced Indian troubles from both the south and the north, and the colonists soon refused to follow Austin's cautious policies. An incident in 1826 when two Anglo families were murdered led to an outright war of extermination on the Karankawas. It crested with a particularly violent moment when a group of settlers trapped a band of Karankawas on an island near the mouth of the Colorado. Eyewitnesses reported that the colonists fired until the river ran red with blood. The official campaign of extermination ended in May of 1827 when the Karankawas, Austin and several other empresarios, local clerics, and politicians met to hammer out a peace agreement. The final document required the Karankawas to stay entirely outside of the boundaries of the colony, except when they were needed to fight other Native groups. Such edicts, of course, did not stop the problem of cattle and horse stealing entirely, but distance, disease, and outright extermination had made the Karankawas a much less threatening band. This didn't, however, solve the growing challenge that the Wichitas and especially the Comanches presented from the north. This challenge and decisions about how best to approach these powerful nations would lead to serious divisions within Austin's growing community.[155]

AUSTIN'S FRACTIOUS NEIGHBORHOOD

By 1825 Austin's colony had grown to include 1,357 white and 443 slave inhabitants. He was picky about whom he allowed to come, and he demanded cash or cattle in payment up front. He administered lashings to people who tried to settle without permission, and he "sent all the rough frontiersmen, etc. up the river."[156] Austin had worked very hard to integrate his colony into the fabric of Mexican Texas. Much of public life centered on markets, religious festivities, and maintaining the infrastructure of irrigation. San Felipe de Austin had its own Catholic priest, and Austin reminded the American immigrants regularly that "Roman Catholic is the religion of this nation and we all must be particular on this subject." Austin was likely a far better Catholic and stricter about following church practice than Mariano Vallejo, who loathed priests and railed against the hypocrisies of the church though he married in the church and baptized all of his children. One thing Austin didn't do that seemed to be common and effective for ambitious landowners in other parts of New Spain or Mexico was marry into a local family. Why didn't Stephen Austin ever get married? His peripatetic life made settling down hard, but these intimate decisions are veiled from us.[157]

The success of Austin's community encouraged the Mexican government to make grants to other Anglo-American empresarios, even though they continued to worry about the tensions around religion and political style that American colonists brought with them. These worries were sometimes justified. Benjamin and Haden Edwards received a colonial franchise in the Nacogdoches region, a turbulent region of ex-filibusters, squatters, and newly removed Indians. In a letter to Benjamin Edwards, Stephen Austin warned about the challenges of creating order amid "the mixed multitude . . . collected from all quarters strangers to each other, to me, and to the laws and language of this country."[158] Austin's fears were remarkably prescient as the Edwards colonists, a motley lot, rapidly stirred up a rebellion in eastern Texas that reflected the tensions among the border community developing there.

In December of 1826 the high-handed behavior of the Edwards brothers created an army of displaced and disgruntled people. The Edwardses had marched into Nacogdoches and announced that anyone living in the region would have to "prove" ownership or lose their land. Because the region granted to the ambitious Edwardses was already filled with squatters from the United States growing acres of cotton, corn, and beans and with bands of Cherokees and Choctaws who had fled the Arkansas, as well as Caddo villagers who had been there for several generations, such pronouncements were not welcomed. Angry local residents declared the creation of a new nation called the Republic of the Red and White Peoples, or Fredonia. The rebels designed a flag with bars of red and white, representing the aggrieved parties of Natives and Anglo-Americans. However, a sharp line on the flag separated the red and the white, as it did on the map of the new nation that gave all of northern Texas to red people and all of southern Texas to white people.[159]

An election for local *alcalde* became a battle between the Edwards brothers and their hand-picked colonists, and the people already living there. When the Edwards group flagrantly stole the election, the *jefe politico* (political boss) in San Antonio reversed the election, but the defiant Edwards brothers refused to comply. Unwilling to tolerate such outright defiance of local authority, state officials in Saltillo revoked Haden Edwards's grant. The situation festered for several months with the Edwards brothers and their colonists refusing to leave and military authorities in Saltillo threatening to send troops to enforce the order. Meanwhile, some of the Cherokees had gotten involved. Justifiably fearful that the Mexican government would refuse their rather informally understood grant, the Cherokee leaders Richard Fields and Richard Dunn Hunter allied with the Edwards sympathizers, hoping to solidify their ownership of land in a new nation. The Fredonian rebels marched into Nacogdoches, arrested the local *alcade* and military leaders, and declared independence from "the yoke of a imbecile, faithless, and despotic government."[160]

Edwards and his men had calculated that all "Americans" in Texas would join them in their uprising against the "despotic" Mexican government. They didn't. Austin advised his colonists against any contact with the "infatuated madmen at Nacogdoches" and instructed them to demonstrate their loyalty as Mexican citizens by volunteering to round up the rebels.[161] Further, he told his colonists that the dissenters in Nacogdoches were the despots and that they had even "invited the Indians to join them in a war of Murder, plunder and desolation." Far from offering support, Austin was furious, positively spluttering in a letter to one of the Fredonian leaders that "it appears though the people in your quarter have run mad or worse." He warned, correctly, "this delusion will ruin you."[162]

Concerned about a wider Indian uprising, the Mexican government approached other Native bands in east Texas and paid them to stay away from the Fredonians. A force of Texans of various ethnicities marched toward Nacogdoches in January of 1827. The rebels disbanded before the troops reached them, and that seemed to be the end of the grand rebellion. Officials in Saltillo gave the Edwards grant to another American empresario, David Burnet, who presumably could keep better order. Stephen Austin, pleased that his colonists had presented themselves as loyal Mexicans, hoped that the Fredonian episode would not leave a lasting impression with his Tejano allies about American proclivities. Frustrated by the poor choices exhibited by their leaders, a group of angry Cherokee warriors killed Richard Fields and John Dunbar Hunter. Fredonia seemed truly dead.[163]

The rebellion, however, underscored the fragility of the tie that Texas had to the Mexican nation. The hope of Texas serving as economic boon and a buffer to the new republic depended entirely on the attitudes and behavior of Anglo-American and Native settlers. How loyal were they? The other challenge came from Mexico's political instability and the long-running debate over the merits of a loose federal system versus a more centralized one. The Mexican Revolution had been achieved by promising a federal structure that allowed for local control, but the nation was being destroyed by its economic problems. In Texas and California, citizens enjoyed the local political control but soon realized that the federal government could offer no resources to develop the economy, protect the borders, or solve the Indian problem. Mexicans politicians closer to the center of power argued that Mexico could only move ahead with a more centralized government that could assure investors of political stability and the ability to enforce the law. The far-flung conglomeration of states had to be brought back to the center.[164]

The view from Texas was very different. Years of working together and solving the problems of an isolated frontier state had created tight personal bonds between the Anglo-American settlers, Tejano elites in San Antonio, and powerful capitalists in Texas and in Coahuila. Together they imagined a Mexico that would embrace economic liberalism, free trade, and federalism. And, no one in San Antonio had forgotten the 327 murders committed by government troops in 1813. The Texans, however, swam against a centralist tide that wanted to limit immigration, tightly control trade, and locate power at the center. The debates between centralism and federalism erupted into violence with distressing regularity. In 1827 the centralists initiated an armed revolt, and in the next election a centralist candidate, Manuel Gómez Pedraza, was elected president. The federalists then felt obligated to stage a coup to place their own candidate, Vicente Guerrero, in office, making politics by force the common practice. Much like Mariano Vallejo, Stephen Austin found himself defending a government he did not support. The turmoil at the center of Mexico had kept isolated places like Texas out of most politicians' sight. When the Fredonian Revolt began to look like problems all over the Mexican republic, Texas came under scrutiny again. The Mexican Congress appointed commissions to investigate the troubling situation on the northern frontier.[165]

Two issues concerned them: Anglo-American encroachment and control of the Indians. The first real president of Mexico, Guadalupe Victoria, had appointed former secretary of state, military leader, and centralist general Manuel de Mier y Terán to lead the expedition. After spending nearly a year in Texas, meeting with Stephen Austin and other San Antonio and Nacogodoches officials, and sending a French botanist-zoologist-physician to survey the Indians, Mier y Terán issued a set of recommendations. He agreed with Stephen Austin and Erasmo Seguín that Texas needed a stronger military presence to protect its borders from smugglers, pirates, and illegal immigrants and to provide support at the center in conflicts with Native nations. However, Mier y Terán, a dedicated centralist and patriot, also observed that the American immigration to Texas had gotten entirely out of control and that the colonists threatened the goal of keeping Texas as part of Mexico. He recommended that colonization by Americans be seriously curtailed, that only Native Mexicans be allowed to hold empresario contracts, and that slavery be prohibited.[166]

Most of these recommendations ended up in the Law of April 6 (1830), which closed Texas to American immigrants. News of the law devastated Austin, even though his colonists and their slaves were permitted to stay. He managed to convince Mexican officials that the wording of the law allowed him to complete his contracts as well, but other empresarios were not as fortunate. The Law of April 6 also reiterated the requirements that land holders in Texas be citizens and practicing Catholics, which many of the colonists had preferred to ignore. Tejanos also resented the law, recognizing that it would destroy their economy and their vision of Texas as a partnership between Anglos and Mexicans. While Anglo colonists bristled at the new law and organized to protest against it, Tejanos in San Antonio worked behind the scenes to repeal it.[167]

The setback of this law, the dissatisfaction among his settlers, and the terrible news of his brother Brown's death in 1830 all weighed heavily on Stephen Austin. He wrote about his depression, his poor health, and the land he would leave at his death to family members. In the midst of this, however, Austin received a letter from a slightly older widowed cousin, Mary Austin Holley, indicating her interest in moving to Texas and, if we read between the lines, a courtship with Stephen. He responded quickly and fully, described the advantages and delights of the colony. He assured her that he had not "become a bear, or a Comanche" and that he had united "a few choice families and made a neighborhood as we say in this country." He emphasized that he was "alone" and that his motto was "Fidelity to the Mexico government and to be true to the interests of his colonists." With that contradictory goal, he closed the letter and encouraged her to come right away, for it would be his "greatest pleasure" to have her visit Texas.[168]

Austin had indeed made a neighborhood, and when Mary Austin Holley visited later in the year, she was ebullient about the prospects of the colony. She made a whirlwind ten-day visit, ostensibly to help her brother Henry set up housekeeping, but also to meet Stephen Austin. She didn't marry Austin or even really try a courtship, but she did write a book about her trip that became the first American travel book about Texas. Holley raved about the "fairyland qualities" of the "infant colony" where Yale professors were opening schools and where one could hire a charming "Indian hunter" to supply game for the table. She did admit that few people had succeeded at commercial enterprises and that few manufactured items were available. She advised everybody to bring pillows and bed linens, mosquito nets, furniture, books, and especially money. "Fairyland" seemed a little rough, and Mary Austin Holley decided she couldn't settle there. By 1831, however, nearly five thousand other people had taken up Austin's offer of land in Texas.[169]

Austin worried that new restrictive policies would prohibit more settlement. The Mexican Congress did agree to repeal the most egregious parts of the colonization restrictions, but this came on another wave of national unrest and revolution that resulted in a military coup by General Santa Anna, who promised to support federalist policies and local control. Upon the occasion of Santa Anna's ascendancy, Austin held a great meeting in the public square in San Felipe de Austin. He reminded the colonists again that their motto has to be "fidelity to the constitution of our adopted country," which was "saluted with 12 rounds of cannon." Austin embraced the Mexican officers who had supported Santa Anna, and offered a salute to each state and territory in the Mexican republic; then "the whole company partook of refreshments and retired."[170]

This episode was actually the patriotic Trojan horse, engineered by the *alcalde* of San Felipe, John Austin—Stephen's cousin—to begin an independence movement demanding that Texas be made into an independent state of the Mexican federation. Tejano and Anglo colonists, frustrated by their lack of representation at the state and national levels, held a convention at which they drafted a new state constitution. San Antonio Tejanos, especially the Seguín brothers, whose growing cattle business depended on American immigrants, expressed their willingness to support it. In the spring of 1833, Stephen Austin, nominated by the convention, went to Mexico City to demand statehood for Texas. This was not a revolution; Texans wanted to be separated from Coahuila and to remain part of the Mexican nation, but on their own terms. Santa Anna, however, turned out to be a centralist wolf in federalist sheep disguise. After Austin presented the petition for statehood, he believed he had received a sympathetic hearing, but instead he was arrested for sedition and thrown in prison. Here he would sit, watching and furiously writing letters, as secession and rebellion brewed in Texas.[171]

By 1833 Stephen Austin had succeeded in building a regional community in eastern Texas. Austin performed well as an empresario because he viewed himself as part of a larger community, in the same way that William Bent or Mariano Vallejo did. San Antonio de Bexar, Coahuila y Tejas, and Mexico were all real entities that required his intimate knowledge. Indian nations and leaders got the respect they deserved. Austin, much like Vallejo, also worked within a tight familial network of parents, siblings, and compadres. Austin recognized this responsibility when he first took on the role of empresario, noting solemnly that he saw his colonists and their Tejano neighbors as "one great family who are under my care."[172] Austin had brought his own siblings, cousins, and friends to Texas and had developed deep friendships with many of the Tejano elites. He also had an astute political sense and was unfailingly polite when it mattered, whether his hosts or captors were Comanche warriors, Mexican politicians, or Anglo-American farmers.

With a combination of hard work, military conquest, political tact, luck, and flexibility, San Felipe de Austin had become part of the landscape of eastern Texas. Its mostly Anglo-American residents had become Mexican

19. William Howard, portrait of Stephen F. Austin in Mexico, 1833. Watercolor on porcelain. James Perry Bryan Papers, The Dolph Briscoe Center for American History, The University of Texas at Austin. (di_04428)

Painted in Mexico City while Austin waited for an audience with the Mexican Congress, this miniature watercolor presents Austin as a natty and aristocratic elite man, a far cry from the populist tone he took with his Texas colonists.

citizens and were participating in the project of creating a Mexican nation. Like any community, it had discord and the seeds of its destruction within it, but people living there surely felt pride at having created something lasting. When the rebellion began in Texas, it began as a unified movement of many factions of Texans, both Anglo and Tejano, against a centralist government they all believed was corrupt and unjust. The crucible of war, however, would rework Texas politics into less unified visions. From his prison cell in Mexico City, Stephen Austin could not see the spreading fissures.

The cast of characters in this chapter spent much of their lives crossing borders or watching as borders crossed over them. Citizenship meant something different in the early nineteenth century for both Americans and Mexicans. The instability of the Spanish empire and the growing pains of the new republics in Mexico and United States made national identity more malleable. Decisions made by politicians, rulers, and bureaucrats about where to place borders and whom to include in the nation seemed distant and often irrelevant. For William Bent, Owl Woman, and their families and business associates, the Arkansas River as border between Mexico and the United States was an abstraction. However, the Arkansas River as border between the Comanches and the Cheyennes mattered deeply, as did the river as wintering ground for people and for bison. Bent's Fort and its *vecinidad* created an oasis where business could be conducted and lives led, regardless of imperial borders.

Northern California and central Texas had similar oasis qualities, though the Vallejos, the Austins, and the Seguíns certainly had moments in which national matters affected them greatly. However, they chose to live in such places in spite of or, in John Sutter's case, because of revolutions, empire change, and new borders and national identities. Mariano Vallejo, Stephen Austin, and Erasmo Seguín shared a vision of places that were built by immigrants from various places who proudly called themselves Californians and Texans rather than Americans or Mexicans. Stephen Austin seemed as comfortable being Estevan or Etienne as Stephen. These regional neighborhoods, bound together by personal relationships, trade and diplomatic agreements, and residence, provided stability in the American West in the first half of the nineteenth century. They relied on careful negotiations with Native people and with more distant empires, challenges that would soon fray the system.

Part II

Americans All

The Mixed World of Indian Country

Half a continent and nearly half a century separated two earthquakes that shook the American West and its residents to their very cores. The New Madrid earthquakes of 1812 and the Fort Tejon earthquake of 1857 revealed the presence and power of great faults in the earth's crust. The human response to them revealed great changes in the people who lived in and understood the American West. People took such obvious signals from nature seriously, reading them as portents of change beyond any human control. The world would not come to an end, but change threatened the webs that families, neighbors, and communities had spun to protect themselves in a very contingent world. If the earth could shake and the stars could fall, then enemies, pestilence, and warfare could visit the people. And they did.

In 1811 several celestial events gave warning of things to come. A giant comet, visible in the sky over the central part of the Northern Hemisphere for 160 days, and a total eclipse of the sun on September 17 in the center of the North American continent unnerved newspaper editors, cattle, politicians, dogs, shamans, and river boatmen. Napoleon Bonaparte read the sky as telling him to invade Russia, clearly a faulty interpretation, while others saw more helpful messages. The warning bore fruit, and on December 16, 1811, the first of nearly two thousand tremors shook the Mississippi River valley. Three of the "shakes" measured more than 8.0 on the Richter scale, making them at least the equivalent of the San Francisco earthquake of 1906.[1]

The epicenter of the quakes was New Madrid, Missouri, a small river community south of St. Louis, but people felt the shaking for hundreds of miles. Young Stephen Austin arrived at New Madrid to inspect his father's warehouses after the quake and could only stand "regarding with fearfull astonishment the Force of a Power" capable of "throwing a hitherto fertile country into desolation and dispair."[2] A. P. Chouteau, newly married to a Creole St. Louis cousin, but asleep with his Osage wife at a trading post along the Missouri River, was alerted to the quakes by the stampeding of the horses outside the lodge, and then by "trees and wigwams that shook excessively." Osage elders warned their people that such a shaking of the earth meant that the great spirits were angry at the human race.[3] George Sibley, the young Indian agent at Fort Osage, rode a riverboat to visit his father and brothers in Natchitoches, Louisiana, and he felt at least forty shocks.[4] People noted tremors as far north as Fort William on the northern edge of Lake Superior, where John McLoughlin, also newly married, was stationed as winter partner. In Detroit, where the Shawnee leader Tecumseh had promised he would stamp his foot and shake down every house, citizens watched nervously as ice cracked on all of the lakes, and the rivers foamed and boiled.[5] Who knew what could happen when all of nature seemed in a state of upheaval?

The early nineteenth century did turn out to be years of great turmoil for people living in the West. Shifting nations, ideas, and opportunities constantly grated and bumped up against the bulwarks of family, business, and community that people erected as protection against disorder. The region endured what might be best understood as the opposite of a power vacuum: too many great powers in various states of formation and decay in competition with many smaller powers testing the waters of empire and war. Though most people living in the region could ignore the Titans clashing over their heads as they attended to individual, family, and community matters, such conflicts eroded the webs of trade, family, and intercultural contacts that westerners had created.

Whether a territory that spread west from the Mississippi River valley or a West that moved east from Alta California or the Columbia River, or a far northern border of New Spain and Mexico, it operated as a borderland in many senses. Most importantly, the power of Native nations was real and lasting on this broad swath of landscape. Richard White has described it as a "middle ground," a term that has become shorthand for places where Native and European Americans enjoyed a rough (and sometimes brief) power balance that enabled them to work out their differences, creating new cultures and fighting bitterly. More recently, Kathleen DuVal has outlined a "Native Ground" in which Native nations controlled trade, settlement, and diplomacy and Europeans did most of the accommodating. Ned Blackhawk's work reminds us that no matter who controlled the process, Native people bore the brunt of the violence that came from a long struggle over the region. In the end, the cost of accommodation, warfare, and cultural change was very high.[6]

Even without the benefit of hindsight, arrangements and accommodations always seemed tentative. Celestial events, prophets, and bad omens constantly warned westerners against complacency. In the summer of 1833 people all over the West watched extraordinary meteor showers. William Bent and White Thunder watched the showers from the roof of the newly constructed Bent's Fort, wondering if alliance between families would be dangerous or beneficial. Stephen Austin, sitting in a cold Mexico City prison awaiting trial for sedition in December of 1833, might have remembered those falling stars of summer as a sign that he should have held his tongue about Texans and independence. The meteor shower, spectacular over northern California, must have frightened Francesca Vallejo as she held her dying baby Andronico, her first son. That same meteor shower appeared over Osage country where A. P. Chouteau watched floods destroy his trading post and then again over the treaty negotiations between the Osages and the U.S. government, where he served as representative for the Osages. A.P. surely wondered what those stars augured for him and for his Osage partners.

In July 1842 a total eclipse of the sun recorded by the Royal Astronomical Society in London was announced in all the papers. Citizens in Cincinnati, the "Queen City of the West," disappointed that they had missed the opportunity to observe such an event in detail, took up a subscription to purchase the world's largest telescope.[7] However, even their German-engineered device could not have illuminated the prophetic events that took place that year. Commodore Thomas ap Catesby Jones of the U.S. Navy, fully convinced of war between the United States and Mexico, mistakenly invaded Monterey, California, that October. John McLoughlin, chief factor of Fort Vancouver, received news that his son had been murdered. Young John was killed by his own employees at a remote trading post on the Alaska coast in an incident that involved both racial hatred and imperial intrigue. Such events heralded rifts in family and trade networks that had long supported people living in far-flung parts of the West.

At the same time, however, new linkages broadened and strengthened the webs of trade. Young Alabaman Thomas Hereford arrived in St. Louis with his family in 1842 and met Margaret Sale, his future wife and connection to the fur trade in Missouri, Mexico, and California. Former trapper Benjamin Davis Wilson (who would be honored by an observatory on the mountain named for him) arrived in southern California. Exactly one year after the solar eclipse, George Bent was born to William Bent and Owl Woman, who surely believed they were building a secure place for their children. Forces no one could have predicted would test the strength of these familial connections and the intercultural networks they had devised to make trade and family life possible.

Global economic, diplomatic, and ideological shifts would prove seismic. A terrible worldwide depression beginning in 1837 sent waves of people suffering from failed land speculations, bankruptcies, and personal failures west of the Mississippi by the early 1840s. That same year a smallpox epidemic devastated all of the Native people living on the upper Missouri and Arkansas rivers. Events in 1842 in Texas and California presaged the Mexican War that would divide region and people in new ways. Joseph Smith's Latter-day Saints founded the city of Nauvoo on the Mississippi River near Quincy, Illinois, and in 1842 the city reached its zenith of ten thousand inhabitants; international missionary efforts built a church with nearly thirty-five thousand members.

In 1857 another earthquake occurred in the West, this time on its Pacific edge. The Fort Tejon earthquake shook southern California and served as a microcosm of what was happening in the rest of the West. The eroding of old networks and the project of American nation building created a true maelstrom of change in which no one, not even the richest and most powerful, could escape. The Chouteaus, the McLoughlins, the Sublettes, and the Bents, whose families had dominated the fur trade, would slip from upper rungs of society. The Vallejos, the Austins, the Yorbas, and the Jaramillos lost their great fortunes in land, though they continued to be important parts of the communities they created. However, these people lost only position and money, while people labeled as Indian often lost much more.

The world had been shaken and disordered, and no one quite knew how to begin putting it back together. What had shifted once the quaking ended were two things that would make a tremendous difference to people living in the West: new economic expectations and increased national power located in a single source. In the middle decades of the nineteenth century, Euro-Americans began immigrating into the West with a desire for land as the source of family safety and income rather than with a desire to enter a trade system. We see the first indication of the impact of this shift in economic focus on the Missouri border and in Texas, but it would pick up pace in the middle of the century. Native nations, which had been essential assets to trade, became dangerous impediments to land acquisition and settlement. Building relationships with Native people, so crucial to the world of trade, became anathema in the last part of the nineteenth century. The concentration of power in one nation, the United States, would hasten this process. Decisions about how land, the new source of wealth and power, would be used and divided were now made by people who had organized their society around racial hierarchies.

To understand fully what the shaking would dislodge, we have to move back in time to survey the places and ideas that created the world of people like John and Marguerite McLoughlin, William Bent and Owl Woman, Mariano and Francesca Vallejo, Stephen Austin, or A.P. and Pierre Chouteau. They shared their lives, to varying degrees, with Native people. They all lived, as did most westerners in the first half of the nineteenth century, in Indian Country or on its borders. In 1812, when the first earthquake shook the West, Native people held most of the power in the region; they controlled trade and travel and determined when and why war would occur. The United States, Great Britain, and Spain all recognized this power and invested heavily in engaging these Native nations in trade and war. Nancy Shoemaker nicely unravels the meaning of the word *nation* in the eighteenth century as it applied to various kinds of political entities that were far less fixed and bordered than the nations we think of today. Part of the work of the next chapters is to assess how the meaning of *nation* shifted from being a group of people who shared language, culture, and space to a place with "incontestable territorial and social boundaries."[8] By 1857, when the second earthquake rolled over southern California, much about the West had changed, but the significance of Native people and their nations had not. The colossal fur trade had waned in importance, but the desire for Native lands and the brutality used to get them only escalated.

Maps of the United States in the period between 1783 and 1848 labeled all kinds of places as "Indian Country." Though this label had many meanings, far more of the new nation belonged to and was inhabited by Native nations than by Anglo-American settlers. Most of North America had been "middle ground" and "divided ground" or borderland and border. These contested spaces where Native people and settler societies discovered their differences have vexed historians because they seem to operate very differently than national boundaries. Alan Taylor usefully and simply describes this as two different Native strategies: defending broad and porous borderlands in which a variety of people co-exist as an alternative vision of political space or drawing clear lines where empires assert and display political difference. These definitions get even more complicated in the lands of the Louisiana Purchase, labeled and treated as Indian Country. In Indian Country Native people acted imperially, controlling their borders and exercising real economic power. Anyone who wanted to succeed or survive in this world had to recognize their power and accommodate to it, learning Native languages, cultural values, and rules of diplomacy. Euro-American travelers, traders, and officials understood that they traveled in Indian Country as visitors and guests and that Native people decided how and when to share their wealth and skills. Anyone involved in policymaking, the military, or business understood the import of Indian Country and its inhabitants for the new United States, but also that its permeable status would need to be hardened. Indian Country would evolve from a borderlands to a set of rigidly bordered lands, but this would take more than a century.[9]

This section explores Indian Country and the various people who lived there—some by choice, others because they were forced there—over the period from 1800 to 1860. Rather than highlighting how Euro-American families used the region, we'll look at how Nation nations drove much of what happened. Chapter 4 traces events in Indian Country as it shifts west between 1803 and about 1825, focusing on the Mississippi and Missouri river drainages. But we need to go east of the Mississippi and back before 1803 to understand the people in the region and their histories. Chapter 5 takes the story to other places, looking at what happens to Native nations after 1825 in places that had different imperial histories, settings, and pressures. Indian Country in what would become Texas, New Mexico, and California looked very different and would challenge the versions of Indian Country that functioned in the lands of the Louisiana Purchase.

Chapter 4

The Early West

The Many Faces of Indian Country

Evenings at Fort Osage included musical recitals, displays of needlework, and much gesturing as Osage and American women tried to communicate with each other. Mary Easton Sibley enjoyed these evenings. The newlywed sixteen-year-old from St. Louis had arrived at the fort accompanied by her younger sister, her husband, George Sibley, who served as the fort's agent, and a piano. That winter of 1816 she entertained the wives and children of Sans Oreille, the Osage chief whose bands wintered near the fort, with her music. Mary and her sister also worked on their needlepoint and painting, as they admired the beautiful buffalo hide paintings and beaded porcupine quill artistry on the baskets that held Osage babies. Sans Oreille had three wives, a fact Mary knew she was supposed to find shocking, but so many things were different from her St. Louis world. Because George wouldn't allow her to work in the factory store, or even to appear there during its operating hours, these evenings were rare opportunities to socialize with her neighbors and to find out how life worked in this Osage place. In good weather she and her horse Old Trudge did ride out to the small winter village, even though George tried to keep her from doing it. Here she could see families in their houses that did feel and smell very different than the drafty fort.[10]

CHEROKEE, SHAWNEE, AND OSAGE

Native American leaders watched the wrangling over the Louisiana Purchase as carefully as Anglo-Americans politicians. During the violent years after the American Revolution, some Native nations staked their ground and fought for their rights to keep land, especially in the regions known as the Old Northwest and the Old Southwest. The Shawnees, who had traditional homelands in the Ohio Valley, stayed and fought for a long

7. North America's Empires in 1783

time. Many other Native people did not need divining rods to sense their futures and decided that they would be better off west of the Mississippi, no matter who controlled it, than in the war zones of former Indian Country. The Cherokees, or at least a major group of them, decided to move. This movement of peoples created another set of challenges for Native nations on the receiving end. The Osages dealt with refugee nations from nearly everywhere in their Missouri and Arkansas homelands.

These Native nations faced their biggest challenges in border zones where trade brought people together and where Anglo-American settlement happened most quickly. Even in more peaceful zones the U.S. government had virtually no control over the process of settlement or the operation of trade. The problem of white squatters and of differing expectations about what ownership of land and hunting rights meant would lead to chaos. Native nations could solve problems and adapt creatively in some cases, but at other times the only choice was to stand firm and fight. Sometimes the federal government simply could not uphold the law in dynamic frontier situations, but just as often government agents chose not to enforce it because, in the end, the United States believed in white settlement at almost any cost. The Cherokees, Shawnees, and Osages dealt with this brutal reality quite differently because Indian Country and its residents had a range of experiences and meanings.

When Tahlonteskee, a respected Cherokee leader, looked at what his people had experienced in the Carolinas in the last years of the eighteenth century, he concluded that moving west was the only solution. Many Cherokee people disagreed with his appraisal; they saw a settled and successful tribe, living in villages with neatly fenced fields and orchards on lands that were fertile and even held the promise of precious metals. They had built roads and opened stores and taverns to bring commerce to their villages. A large and sprawling nation, the Cherokees owned lands that covered large pieces of the southeastern United States and had a population of about fifteen thousand according to a census taken by their agent Return Meigs. Why would the Cherokees want to leave this homeland? In their very success, however, lay the seeds of their destruction. These fertile, settled lands in the hands of Indians became the targets of armed, land-hungry white squatters. State and federal policymakers failed to uphold Cherokee property rights in the face of this encroachment. Tahlonteskee considered every possible strategy for dealing with this problem: lawsuits, treaties, resistance, and war. When no tactic slowed the invasions of squatters, he became a proponent of land sales and removal to the West as a means of putting distance between the Cherokees and the Anglo-Americans.[11]

Other Cherokee leaders branded Tahlonteskee a traitor for his treaty making and accommodating to U.S. demands, and in 1806 they stripped him of his office. The issue of removal and the sale of Cherokee lands split the tribe into bitter factions. Undeterred, in 1809 Tahlonteskee prepared to move west, now that the Louisiana Purchase had opened up a vast new "Indian Country." He would be joined by more than a thousand of his people and their herds of livestock, slaves, and household items. Eventually they settled in the Arkansas River valley, clustering their farms and settlements along the Arkansas River near where Fort Smith would be established, an area long inhabited by the Osages and newly settled by other Native refugees.[12]

After signing a treaty with the United States in 1817 that gave the Western Cherokees rights to land just north of the Arkansas River, Tahlonteskee was joined by his brother, John Jolly, and another large group of Cherokee migrants. By 1818 perhaps 3,500 Cherokees had immigrated to Arkansas. To accommodate the Cherokees, the Indian Department relocated a government trade factory that had served the Jolly family and their related bands from Tennessee to the lower Arkansas, and a garrison was established at the site of Fort Smith to uphold trade and land agreements. Jolly, born in Tennessee into an influential family of mixed race Cherokees, settled right in. He built a prosperous homestead situated amid fields, orchards, and corrals. When his brother Tahlonteskee died in the spring of 1819, Jolly became the principal civil chief. With his economic and political sophistication and his range of languages, Jolly represented the Cherokees with great skill in their struggle to acquire legal control over lands in Arkansas and to secure relief from both Osage and Euro-American incursions.[13]

The 1817 treaty gave the Cherokees most of northwest Arkansas north of the Arkansas River, which led to a feud with the Osages, who also had paper from the U.S. government promising them control over the same lands. The conflict between the Western Cherokees and Chief Clermont's band of Osages resulted in years of reciprocal raids and murders. The Osages also blocked Cherokee access to hunting grounds and salt sources on the southern plains. In addition to these problems, the Arkansas Cherokees found that they had certainly not left behind the squatter problem. U.S. officials never established clear borders around Cherokee land claims in Arkansas so that white squatters and land speculators continually encroached on Cherokee improvements. John C. Calhoun, then secretary of war, recognized the danger in the situation. He warned that the Cherokees "were in danger of perpetual collisions with the squatters," which would inevitably make them "victims of fraud and violence." Calhoun's prediction turned out to be partly true, though much of the violence would happen later when the largest group of removed Cherokee Indians arrived in the late 1830s.[14]

The situation in the Old Northwest in the years between the end of the American Revolution and the War of 1812 involved even more players, though Tahlonteskee would have recognized the basic dilemma over land that drove the long series of bloody encounters. The lands of the Old Northwest, clearly owned and occupied by various tribes, had been earmarked as the way that the cash-poor American government would pay its war debts and raise revenue. Government agents would survey underutilized "hunting grounds" and sell lands that the tribes would "trade" for territory further west. An agonizing and cyclical process of warfare, treaty negotiation, and land sales repeated itself as Native Americans moved onto new lands. Each time, Anglo-American squatters followed, and tensions between people with different needs and desires escalated into conflict, which required another round of warfare. This didn't happen on every frontier, but it certainly did in the Old Northwest.

The Shawnees, a much smaller nation than the Cherokees, had been migrating for several generations between their homeland in what is now Ohio, the Tennessee and Kentucky backcountry, and what would become Illinois and Indiana. They fought fiercely and effectively against the Americans during the American Revolution, so that after the war the Shawnees were targeted early and often for removal and warfare. They felt the force, along with the Iroquois nations, of a new land policy designed as retribution for their support of the British in the Revolution. Land would now be confiscated rather than bought because the United States believed it had won sovereignty over Native nations as part of their victory over the British. This inflamed the Indians, who did not see themselves as conquered people, and led to a series of terrible wars in the 1790s that the Shawnees won. From the British they got advice, help, and guns and ammunition that contributed to their famous victories against the U.S. Army in 1791 and again in 1792. Their success forced the United States to go back to a practice of purchasing Indian lands. Victory and new treaty arrangements made the Shawnees believe that they could defeat the Americans and retain their lands. This overconfidence and their eventual military loss to General Anthony Wayne, a defeat that carried with it the devastating loss of all their Ohio lands, embittered many Shawnee. In the Shawnee villages

20. Charles Bird King, "Ki-On-Twog-Ky or Cornplanter," 1830s. Lithograph in *History of the Indian Tribes of North America*, edited by Thomas L. McKenney and James Hall, 3 vols. (Philadelphia: J. T. Bowen, 1848–50). Courtesy of Smithsonian Institution Libraries, Washington DC

Cornplanter, an important Seneca leader, had a Dutch father and a Seneca mother. He served as an important negotiator for the United States with the Shawnees, but eventually he joined them in their distrust of Anglo-American culture. He died in 1836, soon after King painted him on his last trip to Washington.

clustered around the tributaries to the Ohio River in what is now Indiana and Illinois, Indian people discussed the futures they faced living among the Americans (Long Knives), the British, or other refugee Indian groups.[15]

Like the Cherokees, as the Shawnees considered their options, different factions of the tribe made different choices. By the end of the eighteenth century, like most people in this region—Europeans and Indians—the Shawnees depended on agriculture, hunting, and trade to sustain themselves.

They now depended on European trade goods for all of those activities. Guns, ammunition, hoes, kettles, and blankets had become essential, and participating in the fur and hide trade provided access to those goods. As more hunters and more farmers made demands on the land, places to hunt became increasingly scarce. In this context of change and scarcity, the Shawnees had to envision a future. One group, led by the influential war leader Tecumseh and his family, vowed to get their Ohio homelands back. Though Tecumseh had moved great distances as a hunter and a warrior, the villages on the Ohio remained his center. From the position of a refugee, Tecumseh promised that with the help of other Indian nations and a new prophet who would guide them, he would reclaim Shawnee lands and their way of life. It was an appealing vision for people who had little to lose.[16]

Another group of Shawnees, tired of warfare, hunger, and land loss, decided to migrate across the Mississippi River, away from the Americans, to Spanish Territory. With an official invitation arranged by a French Canadian trader named Louis Lorimier, who had lived most of his adult life among the Shawnees, hundreds and then thousands of Shawnees and Delawares settled near Cape Girardeau, Missouri, in the last years of the eighteenth century. The Spanish government, according to Governor Zenon Trudeau, envisioned these Indians as serving as a frontier guard "in case of war against the whites as well as with the Osages."[17] They lived quite peaceably with French, Creole, and American settlers there for nearly a generation, trading and hunting with people like Moses Austin and the Boone family. The Missouri Shawnees did block the Osages from trading on their part of the river and did engage in some raiding over horses and trade goods. The warfare between the Shawnees and Delawares and the Osages made the region, ironically, safer for white immigrants. Such success did not protect the Shawnees, in the end, from the savage activities of American squatters after the War of 1812, but it offered respite from conditions further east.[18]

These borderland conditions and the violence they created riveted the attention of every one living anywhere near the frontier. The "Indian Problem," stated baldly, involved the fact that hundreds of thousands of Native people, some of them successful farmers like the Cherokees and some of them highly trained warriors like Tecumseh and his Shawnees, occupied most of the lands that Euro-Americans wanted for themselves. War and treaty making had become by far the most expensive part of the federal budget, and the success of these strategies had been partial at best. Thomas Jefferson, as philosopher and president, envisioned a process by which Indian people would become yeoman farmers and happily cede their hunting grounds to white settlers. However, he revealed some recognition of reality when he turned over the land cession and enforcement process to Henry Dearborn, secretary of war, and William Henry Harrison, territorial governor of Indiana, who both saw the problem in more utilitarian terms—a forced military process that took land from Native control and placed it in the hands of white American settlers as quickly as possible.[19]

The Louisiana Purchase offered a solution that seemed less brutal: all of the tribes east of the Mississippi could be "removed" and placed on lands west of the Mississippi in Indian Country. Several flaws marred this plan. Most centrally, the reality that huge numbers of Native people already lived on these lands and that many of the eastern tribes would fight to the death rather than move, made removal a costly and bloody process. Historian John Faragher points out, rightly, that *removal* is a very antiseptic term that protects us from understanding it as a process of ethnic cleansing that only stepped up in intensity as the nineteenth century progressed.[20]

Never naive, Indian people understood the stakes of removal. Ceding lands had been a temporary measure, but now many tribes lived in places that were unfamiliar and overhunted. Even by sacrificing their traditional lands, they hadn't escaped the pressures of white squatters or other refugee Native people. News of the Louisiana Purchase and the increasing pressure from federal treaty negotiators to sell or trade land gave Indian people common cause. The Shawnees, who had ceded lands in Ohio, and who now resided in newly created Indiana, amid the Delawares, Miamis, and Potawatomis, found themselves living very poorly. Hunting was bad, drinking alcohol eroded cultural values, the yearly annuities did not support a family, and, steadily, treaties took away the peoples' land. The Shawnees especially raised suspicion and resentment among white settlers and officials by continuing to do most of their trading with the British at forts on the Greats Lakes or the upper Mississippi. Because of such "suspicious allegiances," the Shawnees became particular targets of Euro-American horse thieves and arsonists.[21]

In this context Tecumseh, who had long advised unity among the tribes and direct action, found himself increasingly influential, especially when the Delawares and Miamis were forced into ceding most of southern Indiana. When a series of epidemics swept the villages in 1804 and 1805, Tecumseh's strident voice was joined by that of his younger brother, a man who suddenly emerged as a prophet. Lalawéthika, or the Prophet, had an explanation and solution for his people's troubles, news welcomed by Indians all over the region. Because people had strayed so badly, the Prophet told them, the Wasshaa Monetoo, or Great Spirit, had been forced to punish them. The Monetoo sent witches who caused illness, bad judgment, strife, and war. The only way to get rid of the witches was to use the old ceremonies, to revitalize native culture, and to give up all goods obtained from white people, including firearms, alcohol, clothing, cattle, and flints. Renewal of faith and return to old practices would save the people.[22]

This message had been preached before as part of revitalization movements that had moved through Indian Country in earlier years and as part of a long prophetic tradition, especially among the Delawares with whom the Shawnees now lived. However, when hunger and disease hounded people that winter of 1805, and this fear combined with the particular charisma of Tecumseh's leadership, the Prophet's message had staying power. In the next year Tecumseh, eschewing European clothing and wearing traditional Shawnee deerskins, carried this message and ordered others to carry it in elaborate wampum belts made of black and white shells up and down the Ohio, Mississippi, Tennessee, and Missouri rivers to the people of the Great Lakes and to the western Indians on the Great Plains. He established a "Prophet's Town" near Greenville, Ohio, and encouraged Native people to visit, to live, and to plan for unified action.[23]

Initially Tecumseh insisted that his only aim was to gather the Shawnees, "to collect them all together to one town that the Chief may keep them in good order and prevent drunkenness from coming among them."[24] But by 1807 large contingents of Potawatomis, Wyandottes, Ottawas, Ojibwes, Sacs, and Foxes began making pilgrimages to the new town. Such movement and the waves of rumors that accompanied it sent Indian agents, military officials, and Euro-American settlers into worried consultation. Moravian missionaries living with the Delawares and Wyandottes nervously described Tecumseh as the "oracle of the day" who had "by art and cunning instigated the nations against the white people." They reported crazed Delawares burning people at the stake, looking for their victims among Christianized Indians and "friends of the white people."[25] Such a concentration of Native people doing such frightening things combined with the worsening of U.S. relations with the British, who still controlled much of the fur trade and had long-standing agreements with many Great Lakes and Mississippi River tribes. Fear of Indian war in this setting created an atmosphere of panic throughout the Ohio and Mississippi river country.[26]

The Osages, one of the western tribes faced with the onslaught of newcomers, viewed the situation east of the Mississippi with suspicion and

21. George Catlin, "Clermont, Osage," 1830s. From Catlin, *Letters and Notes on the Manners, Customs, and Conditions of North American Indians*, vol. 2 (London: David Bogue, 1844).

This Clermont, the son of the great Osage leader who built relationships with French, Spanish, and U.S. officials, moved his group of Little Osage to Arkansas when Anglo-American settlement became oppressive. Catlin sketched the young chief in the 1830s on a trip to the Arkansas River with an army reconnaissance group.

resignation, but interest as well. They had long been settled along the Missouri and Arkansas rivers and had struggled fiercely and successfully to retain control over trade in the region. The Osages had three large divisions: the Great Osages, who gathered along the Osage River in central Missouri, the Little Osages, who lived further north along the Missouri, and the Arkansas Osages, who lived along the Arkansas River, so that they controlled lands in what is now Missouri, Arkansas, and parts of Oklahoma and Kansas. As the Chouteaus had learned so profitably, their function as middlemen and diplomats for the entire Missouri River basin encouraged traders and imperial representatives to treat them with great respect. An Osage chief even visited Versailles to meet Louis XV in 1725 as part of French efforts to court the Osages.[27]

As the colonial situation became more complicated after French control of Upper Louisiana was turned over to the Spanish and later to the Americans, Native refugees from east of the Mississippi, especially the Shawnees and Delawares, put increasing pressure on the Osages. To protect their borders, the Osages became active in the slave trade, bringing Kiowa, Caddo, and Shawnee captives to Spanish, American, and French buyers. These trading connections with various groups, and the guns and ammunition they received as a result, made the Osages even more formidable to their neighbors, both European and Native. The Spanish had long recognized that the Osages controlled the region but described them as treacherous "malefactors," which indicated that the Osages had successfully placed their own needs ahead of Spanish desires. Osage success, however, was built on volatile geopolitical realities that shifted under them as Anglo-Americans and their political agendas began to affect Osage activities.[28]

Despite their reputation as troublemakers, the Osages built effective relationships with French, Spanish, and British traders, and many of their people had become part of the ethnic mélange of the Mississippi River valley. One of their most important connections, of course, was with the Chouteau family. In 1794 Auguste Chouteau convinced Spanish authorities to grant him a trading monopoly with the Osages along the Missouri in return for building a trading fort that would produce much needed revenue for the Crown. Spanish officials hoped the arrangement would control the Osages, who refused to recognize any boundaries that the Spanish set or to stop slave raiding and trading, which the Spanish had outlawed. Chouteau's fort did give the Osages a steady source of trade goods, but it did not stop them from trading with the British or with Indian nations far distant from their own region. Chouteau turned a blind eye to this behavior because he got furs and other goods to support his own business and because he understood the advantages of being allied with the Osages rather than trying to "control" them, a central lesson of successful careers in Indian Country. With these careful liaisons and effective retribution against interlopers, the Osages had maintained a great deal of control over trade until the opening years of the nineteenth century. But the unrest in the Ohio country and the removal of southern tribes to the Arkansas would unravel the trade system and power relations that upheld it.[29]

In the early nineteenth century, Osage, Shawnee, and Cherokee people would become further entangled with both Euro-Americans and each other. The tangle of people and economies took varied forms, but neither diplomacy nor war would fully unsnarl it. Many people living in the West, however, did not want to unravel such relationships because they were profitable and important to their families. As the new Indian Country west of the Mississippi came to be home to Euro-Americans and refugee Native nations from the east, it came to resemble those older borderlands with possibilities for tension and for profitable relationships.

THE VIEW FROM FORT OSAGE

When George Sibley arrived in St. Louis in 1805, he found the city and its surrounds in disarray. Nominally a U.S. city, it felt more like a foreign outpost. Sibley called it "Cantonment St. Louis" in his earliest letters, which reflected the embattled sense of the city's new occupiers.[30] Reports from Indian Country both east and west of the river brought threatening news about raids, murders, captivities, and general mayhem. Firm belief, supported by both rumor and fact, held that the British in Canada continued to trade illegally on the upper Missouri, Mississippi, and Great Lakes. Rumors circulated that British agents orchestrated Indian rebellions, but British traders did sell the Indians guns and alcohol, and they paid more for furs and hides, which kept many Native groups firmly allied with them. Emigrant Indians from the east, seeking refuge from decades of warfare, made Indian Country even more unsettled. Lewis and Clark had not yet returned, and stories circulated around St. Louis about their deaths at the hands of hostile Indians. Tecumseh and his brother, the Prophet, were beginning their efforts to unify Native people in the face of the pressures of removal and war, and tales of enormous gatherings of Native nations filled Mississippi Valley newspapers.

George Sibley, born in 1782 in North Carolina, arrived in Upper Louisiana Territory to serve as a clerk in the new Indian Department store in St. Louis. For an ambitious young man wanting to seek his fortune and to serve his nation, the obvious choice was to join the Indian Department, which at this moment was the largest sector of the federal government. Sibley, delighted to find himself "on the border of Indian Country," described for his family the skills he would need "to make a success in this foreign and romantic place."[31] His language gives us a clear sense of how concrete and how foreign a place "Indian Country" was for people living on its edges and how hopeful Sibley was about making a life there.

Sibley came from a family with a long tradition of government service on the frontier. His father, Dr. John Sibley, had been stationed as a military physician on the Louisiana border since the 1790s and now served as the Indian agent to tribes around the Red River. In 1802 Thomas Jefferson had contracted John Sibley as part of a team to gather up all the existing data about Louisiana as Jefferson secretly investigated acquiring it. Sibley, who compiled and summarized the documents, concluded that Anglo-Americans didn't know much, especially about the vast stretches north of the Red River. He described legal systems and military fortifications, rumored salt mountains and silver mines, but spent much of the document describing "innumerable Indian nations." He painted a fairly alarming picture of groups who could bring "thousands and thousands of warriors" to the field. The scariest were the Osages, who were "of giant stature . . . cruel and ferocious."[32] As a result of this report and its emphasis on the dearth of reliable information, Jefferson arranged with Lewis and Clark, Zebulon Pike, and Sibley himself to investigate more fully. We don't know what kind of advice John Sibley gave his son George when he took up a career trading with the "fierce and cruel" Osages, but surely he worried, even though given his position he had probably had a hand in arranging young George's appointment.[33]

The Indian Department and its policies addressed some of the most vexing problems faced by the U.S. government, which was inexperienced, divided, and broke. Congress agreed on only two issues around Indian matters, but these were crucial. First, Indian affairs belonged to the central government, where Congress could control them, and second, an actual place called "Indian Country" existed that included both territory lying beyond national boundary lines that was forbidden to settlers and to unlicensed traders, but it also meant lands belonging to Native nations within the borders of various states and territories. Now, how the government and its representatives should conduct themselves and the contours of diplomacy and law that determined behavior in Indian Country remained entirely debatable. Even more conflictual were ideas about what goals federal policy should have and whose interests they should serve.[34]

Native nations could hardly have been impressed with the power or organization of their new neighbor in the first years of their mutual relationship. The weak Articles of Confederation allowed states to ignore the central government so that the states continually made treaties without congressional approval. Squatters and land speculators thumbed their noses at any control, state or federal, and moved onto Indian lands. When Indians complained about such illegal invasions, generally nothing happened, but occasionally protests by Native people brought them retribution from unofficial local militia, who saw this as a "just and lawful" war. As warfare intensified between Anglo-Americans and Indians, and as the British continued to profit from their trade with western Indians, the U.S. government made Indian policy a priority.

Beginning in 1790, with a stronger federal government in place, Congress created a series of laws to provide for the licensing of traders and to prevent the illegal sale of Indian Country lands. George Washington made Indian matters the center of his annual message to Congress in 1791 and 1792, stressing the significance of trade: "the establishment of commerce with the Indian nations, on behalf of the United States, is most likely to conciliate their attachment." Washington and his secretary of war, Henry Knox, clearly believed that the loyalty, happiness, and safety of Indians could make or break the new republic, and he signed the Second Intercourse Act into law in 1793. This set of laws created Indian agencies and agents, appointed by the president. Their duties included living among the Indians, keeping records of activities and commerce at their agencies, noting the conditions of the Indians, and observing the natural history of each area. He also created an Indian Department, as a subsection of the War Department, which enshrined the intimate relationship between the U.S. Army and Indian affairs.[35]

Looking at this situation with twenty-first-century hindsight, we cannot help but be cynical about the intent and the outcome of this policy. But we must imagine the situation both American officials and Native people faced. Neither wanted violence, but each had fear, respect, and sometimes contempt for the other. The army quelled outbreaks of Native and Euro-American hostility, and army garrisons along the frontier were situated to prevent violence. Indian Country and its borders was a cruel place where Euro-Americans felt required to take matters into their own hands with a virulent energy that is hard for us to understand at this distance. Many frontier communities had residents who thought of themselves as professional Indian killers. The Moravian missionary John Heckewelder may have exaggerated when he described the natural moral perfection of Indian people, but his description of the "murderous perfidy" of "white invaders and rogues" says much about the fierce enmity that drove white settlers who had spent generations on these bloody frontiers.[36] Army officers and soldiers recognized that much of their work would be against their own citizenry. The army provided force behind the decisions and policies of Indian agents, most of which involved protecting the treaty rights of Native people and finding more orderly ways to cede Indian lands to the government once white settlement encroached on Native settlements.[37]

Agents, treaty negotiators, military men, and government policymakers shared some assumptions: Indians had a right to lands, uncontrolled white settlement was dangerous and chaotic, and Indian Country would always exist to the west. In order to protect Indians from the wrath of white settlers, and vice versa, the nation had envisioned something called the Permanent Indian Frontier, with Native Americans to the west and Euro-Americans to the east. The army, with a long cordon of forts stretching along the line of the Mississippi River, would enforce this racial divide. However, this line would also be made permeable with peaceable and profitable trade, also strictly controlled by the government.

In order to supervise trade with Native nations, in 1795 Congress established a network of government-owned trading houses called *factories* with the purpose of "creating harmony with the Indian nations."[38] In developing this system, U.S. officials were entering into a trade network that had been operating for two hundred years. The British government had built trading houses in the American colonies, and the Hudson's Bay Company had worked out of fur trade centers, or factories, since the seventeenth century. The British and the French had convinced Native people that they wanted friendship and furs, not land, and that for some peoples, alliances with these Europeans would have real benefits. Trading and hunting could provide Native people with the tools to fight their enemies, Native and European, more effectively. Private traders had always existed in this fur universe, but some Indians recognized the value of trading with and earning the protection of larger entities. U.S. officials hoped to re-create these kinds of relationships and monopolies.[39]

Large government monopolies, however, never popular with Americans, didn't appeal much to Congress either. The factory system never got full government support even though the factories made money and kept the peace quite successfully in places where they were located. U.S. factories stocked merchandise that Indians wanted and needed and gave a fair price for furs, which essentially undercut any private traders who tried to work near them. Presidents and military leaders recognized the importance of these factories in reducing military costs and keeping Indians peaceful, and slowly expanded the factory system throughout Indian Country, especially along the Mississippi River and its tributaries. In 1806 Congress established the office of superintendent of Indian trade. Superintendent Thomas McKenney purchased goods for the factories, made sure they got to the posts, and directed the work of the factors. McKenney worked very hard to "regularize" procedures and to make sure his agents' service remained above reproach in the often corrupt world of political appointment. He chastised one young agent to "make out triplicates of that account . . . from the quarter commencing April 1, last, after the foregoing form," a tall order in the days before carbon paper or copy machines.[40] Though it operated within the War Department, McKenney's office became the de facto center of Indian affairs until the end of the factory system in 1822.[41]

George Sibley, aged twenty-four, had been hired by the new superintendent of Indian trade to work as a clerk in the St. Louis store. He reported proudly to his brother that the job came with "a compensation of $700 per annum and further promotion if my conduct is satisfactory."[42] Because his superiors wanted closer connections with the influential Missouri River tribes, they soon closed the St. Louis store and moved it further west. This gave George his promotion to the status of agent and sent him up the Missouri River to supervise the building of the new trading house.

The politics of Sibley's appointment were complex, but at least in his personal letters he remained oblivious to the import of his replacing Pierre Chouteau Sr. as agent to the Osages. General William Clark, having returned triumphantly from his excursion to the West, was appointed as Indian agent for all of Louisiana Territory. One of the most important pieces of news that the Lewis and Clark Corps brought back to the United States was the size, wealth, and sophistication of the fur trade in the region. Clark, informing and reflecting Thomas Jefferson's ideas about Indian policy, believed strongly in the government trading house system as a way to keep peace and to thwart the British and the hordes of private traders of all nations. Jefferson had instructed Meriwether Lewis before the Corps of Discovery set out that "commerce is the great engine by which we will coerce the Indians, and not war," and William Clark took this message as the center of his own policy.[43]

The Fort Osage factory, which would be Sibley's home for the next fifteen years, resulted from an 1808 treaty negotiation orchestrated by Clark and Pierre Chouteau. Sibley, now the agent at the fort, watched from the sidelines. Chouteau wielded great personal influence with the Osages living along the Missouri, had family living among them, and had served as their agent for the Spanish and now the American government. In order to consolidate his own power and to enrich his family, Chouteau would give up his position as agent, but he received an absolute monopoly on government contracts to deliver goods on the Missouri River.

The treaty required the Osages to relinquish most of what is now the state of Missouri. In return, the U.S. government would build a trading house and post an army garrison on the Missouri River, just above Fire Prairie, near where Kansas City is today. The Americans were, according to the treaty language, "anxious to promote peace, friendship, and intercourse with the Osage tribes, to afford them every assistance in their power, and to protect them from insults and injuries from other tribes of Indians." For ceding their Missouri territory, the Osages received lands west of the treaty line, which ran north and south near where the Missouri River turns north and another swath of land on the north bank of the Arkansas River. The treaty also promised $1,500 worth of merchandise to be delivered yearly and prohibited anyone from trespassing on Osage lands, except persons directly involved with treaty provisions or who were given a special license. Sibley, who knew he would be responsible for maintaining the peace, watched the proceedings with some cynicism. He reported that even though "an unusual number of them touched the pen," the Osages "no more knew the purpose of the act than if they had been a hundred miles off."[44]

This treaty and the new fort recognized the economic power that the Osages continued to wield, but it also revealed important cracks in their political system. Their desire to control trade in as wide a region as possible had broken the tribe into first three and then five largely independent bands. This brought great wealth to individual leaders and initially protected some regions, especially the Clermont Band, who remained on the Arkansas, but this division would erode the near hegemony the Osages had once held between the Red River and the Missouri River. Essentially, the treaty gave the growing divide between the northern and southern Osage geographical reality. Clermont, leader of the Arkansas band, simply refused to trade at Fort Osage. This refusal allowed his Osage people to maintain a great deal of power over trade in the Arkansas River region,

22. George Catlin, *Wah-Chee-te and Child*, 1830s. From Catlin, *Letters and Notes on the Manners, Customs, and Conditions of North American Indians* vol. 2 (London: David Bogue, 1844).

Catlin drew this woman and child in the 1830s, describing them as the family of the Osage leader Clermont. It is not one of Catlin's best sketches, but it manages to capture a playful child and a relaxed mother. Even if the proportions are awkward, the subjects are presented as fully human.

but it split the Osages at a moment they were facing pressure from other tribes and Anglo-Americans.[45]

The situation on Sibley's new turf included even more complications. William Clark, the Chouteaus, and Indian office officials established Fort Osage in the context of a disastrous mini-war with the Arikaras, a tribe who had been hostile to the overtures of Americans and who lived just up the river from the Osages. In large part, Osage expansion had occurred at the expense of the Arikaras. This most recent burst of bad feeling demonstrated the intricate diplomacy that Sibley would have to master. The little war developed out of a seemingly routine diplomatic gesture made several years earlier by Lewis and Clark on their return trip from the Pacific. In their efforts to make peace with Indian nations they convinced a Mandan leader named Shahaka to accompany them on their triumphal tour of the East Coast. Shahaka endured the usual wining and dining in Washington, including a special visit to Monticello to view President Jefferson's collection of Indian artifacts. What did dignified Native leaders think when confronted with their people's sacred objects displayed next to elephant bones and false teeth? Shahaka had his portrait painted by artist Charles B. J. Févret de Saint-Mémin and, in early 1807, returned to St. Louis ready to go home.[46]

William Clark, now Indian agent for all the tribes in Louisiana except the Osages, delegated the task of returning Shahaka to a group of private traders, headed up by none other than young A. P. Chouteau, recently arrived home from West Point. The St. Louis traders, eager to seek new trading relationships on the upper Missouri, happily headed up the Missouri until they ran into 650 Yankton Sioux and Arikaras. These tribes had always operated as the intermediaries between the tribes of the upper Missouri and anyone else, and they did not want Chouteau and his traders to move into their territory. The traders, quickly recognizing the danger, returned to St. Louis with Shahaka, embarrassed by their failure to return him to his people. It would be nearly two years before another party could be mounted to attempt to take Shahaka back to the Mandan villages. This time, the newly formed Missouri Fur Company received a government contract to raise a force of 125 militiamen. Pierre Chouteau also created his own private Native army of three hundred Osages, formed at the newly created Fort Osage, again led by his son A. P. Chouteau.[47]

Chouteau and the Osages sent much advance warning to the Arikaras, who wisely left their villages and allowed the well-armed group to pass. Acting as intermediaries, several Sioux leaders asked Chouteau to pardon the Arikaras, who apologized in an elaborate diplomatic dance, well oiled by gifts. Shahaka entered the Mandan villages as a returning hero, and the Chouteaus headed back to St. Louis. They expected to be lauded by government officials, but instead, William Eustis, the new secretary of war under James Madison, threatened to fire Pierre Sr. as Indian agent for his misdeeds of mixing private business and government duty. The storm blew over after a flurry of letters between Chouteau and Eustis, detailing exactly whose money had been spent where, but the relationship between the Chouteaus and the federal Indian Office would never be the same. The Arikaras, having been alerted about changes coming their way, vowed to stand their ground.[48]

Fort Osage, the first government-run factory built west of the Mississippi River, prospered largely because of the working relationship between the Osages and their agent and factor, George Sibley. Sibley had numerous official tasks such as issuing licenses to traders, handing out treaty goods, storing and shipping furs, but he spent most of his time running the store and making sure it had the right mix of trade items. Sibley had been instructed to convince tribes other than the Osages to trade at the fort, but he soon learned the challenges of bringing together unfriendly tribes. In the fall of 1808, he sent an emissary to the Kansa tribe, and to his surprise "the whole of the Kansas arrived today to the number of a thousand souls." He commented rather bitterly at the end of their visit that he had been forced to close the store "because of their insolent and violent conduct" when the Osages protested the presence of this rival nation.[49]

The Osages formed the most important part of his business. They regarded Sibley as their private agent and the fort as their territory, only occasionally allowing other people to trade there. As many as five thousand Osages gathered in the fall when they came to get outfitted for winter buffalo hunts. They crowded into the factory store, examining goods carefully and indicating their choices with pursed lips. Sibley learned quickly never to point with his fingers, which the Osages considered to be rude and threatening. This trade brought in $40,000 to $50,000 in furs and hides each year. He also discovered a great deal about Osage requirements for trade goods, which were sometimes difficult to satisfy. Congress had admonished the Indian Trade office about spending American money on imported goods. Sibley, like most other agents, soon learned that his clients were extremely particular and would not buy yarn, beads, vermillion, guns, or cloth made in the United States. They insisted on softer, stronger British yarn, brilliantly colored Italian glass beads, vermillion from England,

British Tower muskets, and Chinese silk. They did like powder and tobacco produced in the United States and gradually accepted Philadelphia-made derringers.[50]

Throughout the first years of his service at Fort Osage, Sibley seemed quite satisfied with his relationship with the Indians and the way his factory worked. He reported excellent business and negotiated new trade agreements with Pawnee and Kansa groups, who were often at war with the Osages. He did complain about his own social isolation, writing to his brother that he "was growing heartily tired of housekeeping" and worried that he would never find a wife. He added coyly that he was "often favored with the company of princesses and young ladies of rank decked in all the finery of beads, red ribbons, and vermillion."[51] Sibley abated some of his loneliness and the drudgery of housekeeping by purchasing a slave couple in St. Louis, and later three other slaves, to help with household tasks and gardening.[52]

Many of the Osages, however, felt less enthusiastic about their lives as "fort Indians." The groups that had initially moved north drifted back to their villages along the Osage River, especially after they recognized that the fort attracted all kinds of Indians from the north, including Pawnees and Arikaras who stole their horses and their crops. Even worse, the Sac, Fox, and Iowa Indians from across the river came into their villages and stole slaves and killed people. Even as he tried to convince the Little Osages to stay, Sibley had come to understand much about the politics of Indian country. He let them leave graciously so that they would at least keep trading at the fort. A small contingent of Osages, mostly the families of government interpreters, stayed near the fort, helping Sibley and his slaves raise corn and hogs. One winter, four Osage women used Sibley's kitchen to make candles from buffalo tallow, which brought in three and a half cents each, but which, unfortunately, didn't survive the heat of St. Louis summers.[53]

We can track Sibley's growing confidence in his position as well as the confidence that General Clark came to have in him. In the summer of 1811 he took a "business development tour" of the plains, first visiting all of the Osages, and then, accompanied by several important chiefs, he made official visits to the Kansas and the Pawnees. Sibley's goal was to convince these more distant tribes, who had better access to buffalo hides, to trade at Fort Osage. The sticking point had always been the fierce Osages who would not permit "their" traders to do business with anyone else. Sibley got an education on that trip, overwhelmed with the sheer number of Native nations with whom the United States had no contact and with the wonderful freedom of their lives on the plains. He also recognized the potency of Osage domination in the region and knew that making other trade relationships would be dangerous.[54]

Sibley undertook this trip as war with Great Britain loomed. Rumors of war had kept the Louisiana frontier on alert since 1807. The fear of an Indian uprising fomented by duplicitous British traders and agents seemed rational, and Sibley wanted to find out more about who was trading with whom and if British provocateurs had reached the Missouri River tribes. None of these notions was entirely far-fetched. British agents *were* traveling among the Great Lakes and northern Mississippi River tribes, promising them land and independence if their people would fight against the Americans. And Indian people, frustrated and angry from years of harassment by white squatters and government officials, were in a mood to listen. The rebellion and the threat of war reached into places as remote as Fort Osage. George Sibley reported that the Osages had received visitors and wampum belts with news from Tecumseh, and that he had heard rumors of British agents meeting with Pawnees and Sioux in 1811.[55] In St. Louis and at trading posts up and down the river the news coming from Indian Country seemed threatening indeed. Though the U.S. Congress would declare war on June 18, 1812, and even though eastern newspapers described it as a diplomatic conflict between the British and the Americans over shipping, people living in the West experienced it as a frontier war between Native nations and land-hungry Americans. This war began much sooner than 1812 and lasted much longer.

THE VIEW FROM ST. LOUIS

William Clark, appointed as principal Indian agent for all of Louisiana Territory in 1807, knew something about Native nations, intrigue, and warfare. He grew to adulthood in Louisville, Kentucky, and watched as the new United States struggled to develop an Indian policy. He served in various fights with local militia as Billy Clark, the little brother of the famous frontier fighter George Rogers Clark, and watched as Native people decimated U.S. troops twice in Ohio in 1791 and 1792. He participated as Lieutenant William Clark during the 1794 campaign in Ohio and observed the treaty negotiations at Fallen Timbers as the Ohio Indians ceded their land and moved west. And he knew that these wars over land had just begun. His trip to the Pacific and back impressed him deeply with the diversity and power of Indian people and of the essential task of helping the American nation to forge a lasting relationship with its First Nations. Clark was no romantic, and he shared in the expansionistic fervor and racial attitudes of the times, but he believed that the continent had to be shared by indigenous people and immigrants of all kinds.[56]

Clark insisted throughout his career that the keys to successful relationships with Native nations were respectful and consistent diplomacy and government-controlled trade, enforced by military action. Only with strict rules in place could the government control the behavior of immoral traders, greedy squatters, and hostile Indians—most of whom had little interest in becoming yeoman farmers. Clark's job, beginning in 1807 and lasting until his death in 1838, involved balancing the interests of these disparate groups throughout the vast expanse of the Louisiana Purchase. He supported and expanded the factory system created by Congress and established a network of trusted agents at these factories, stores, and outposts to maintain control of Indian Country. The War of 1812 nearly destroyed the entire endeavor.

Just as William Clark took on his duties as superintendent the Indian situation in the east began to unravel. Given his responsibilities in St. Louis, Clark had to believe the rumors of imminent British invasion and gave credence to the fears that Indian groups would join the British. His eyes and ears to the potentially dangerous gathering of the tribes at the Prophet's Town in Ohio and at various points on the Great Lakes were agents like George Sibley at Fort Osage and Thomas Forsyth at Peoria, in what is now Illinois. Forsyth, born in Detroit in 1771, spent the first part of his adult life as an Indian trader, first at Saginaw Bay and on an island on the Mississippi River and later in the vicinity of Chicago and along the Illinois River. In 1812, Clark appointed him Indian sub-agent for the Illinois River region. Fluent in French, English, and several Indian languages, Forsyth provided Clark with very full and very pessimistic reports about the situation on the upper Mississippi.[57] In contrast, George Sibley saw little worthy of alarm among the Indians with whom he had regular contact and sent Clark frequent reports about the peaceful situation around Fort Osage.

Part of this difference might have been age and experience, but it also reflected different tension levels east and west of the river. From Thomas Forsyth's perspective, the lands just east of the Mississippi River seethed with British agents, Native people angered by the their loss of land, and disciples of the new Indian prophet. He wasn't wrong; Indian Country had suddenly become a tinderbox, ready to burst into flame at any small instigation. By 1809 the Prophet had moved his town to Indiana, to lands controlled by the Potawatomis, and even larger numbers of Native people had gathered there. Soon these converts heard the terrible reports of the 1809 Fort Wayne treaty that gave away huge amounts of land surrounding the new Prophet's Town on the Tippecanoe River. Knowing that people would be angry and frightened by this news, the Prophet redoubled his efforts to recruit Native nations from the west and north as partners to his cause. Meanwhile, his brother Tecumseh began a tour of the south to build support and to gather converts there. The loss of land also convinced both brothers to clarify and publicize their connections to the British, hoping that the British would continue to trade with them and provide support and safe havens in case of a war. Tecumseh took an old wampum belt given to his people by the British during the French and Indian War and delivered it to Fort Malden, near Detroit, formally reminding the British of their responsibility to help the Shawnees make war.[58]

From St. Louis, and the more isolated forts and stores along the river, the situation looked grim indeed. As Indians massed on the shores of the Tippecanoe River, only several days' travel from St. Louis, the newspapers reported similar gatherings to the north at Prairie du Chien and Peoria and to the south and west at Boons Lick and Cape Girardeau. According to one of William Clark's informants, an Iowa Indian visiting St. Louis claimed apocalyptically in May of 1811 that "the time is drawing near when the murder is to begin and that all the Indians that will not join are to die with the whites."[59] Convinced that war was imminent, the governors of Missouri, Illinois, and Indiana begged the federal government to assign more troops to the region. Federal soldiers and informal militias began to arrive that summer. In August of 1811 Governor Harrison of Indiana learned that Tecumseh planned a long recruiting trip to the south, which meant that Prophet's Town would be largely unprotected. As Prophet's Town swelled with visitors planning to winter there, conflict between local white settlers and itinerant and hungry Native people over stolen corn, horses, and ammunition escalated predictably.

Harrison used this situation to plan his attack. He collected his forces down the river from the Native gathering. His troops numbered more a thousand men when they marched up the river, reaching Prophet's Town on November 6, 1811. The Indians, according to many reports, seemed strangely unconcerned. Harrison surmised that the Indians believed the military force to be a show, but that the real goal was negotiation. However, while they ostensibly prepared for a negotiation, the combined forces of Shawnees, Delawares, Winnebagos, and Kickapoos silently crept around behind the American troops. That first day, the American forces buckled under the surprise and spent the evening counting their dead and preparing a counterattack. The next morning, November 8, they found Prophet's Town entirely deserted. The Indians, having held their ground but knowing that they had fewer men and far fewer guns, had wisely withdrawn from the field of battle. Frustrated, Harrison and his troops dug up all the corn supplies, scalped and mutilated the Indian dead, and torched the town, ensuring that the Prophet and his allies would spend a cold and hungry winter.[60]

Destroying Prophet's Town did little to solve the Indian problem; for many individuals and nations it simply proved the evil intent of the United States. A wave of Native uprisings and attacks on frontier communities overwhelmed the entire West. Especially in frontier regions like the Missouri River country, Native violence in combination with the long anticipated outbreak of the War of 1812 fanned public fear into outright panic. The first bit of extremely bad news came from the north: Fort Michilimackinac, the most important fur-trading post on the Great Lakes, fell to the British, even before war had been declared. A month later, troops of Native soldiers took Detroit, making the Great Lakes Native and British territory and leaving the Mississippi entirely open to attack.[61]

Hysteria reigned in St. Louis. Frightened citizens gathered in the streets to burn an effigy of William Wells, the American general who had surrendered Fort Detroit. People abandoned their businesses and farms. The governor of Illinois, Ninian Edwards, confided to William Clark that he feared the "entire overthrow of the region" to the British and the Indians.[62] Clark's Indian agents reported similarly bad news among Native people who were supposed to be allied with the United States. Thomas Forsyth, the agent at Peoria, reported that a Potawatomi man had approached him "in a very boasting manner and said that he was not afraid to go down to St. Louis and if Americans said anything to him he would knock his Tommyhawk into their heads."[63] With such bulletins pouring in from all fronts, Clark had to find ways to protect the frontier to the east and to maintain the delicate balance of peace that existed to the west, at least as it was reported to him by George Sibley and the Chouteau brothers.

He planned a military expedition up the Mississippi to Prairie du Chien, which he described as the "Metropolis of British Traders." He asked for supplementary federal troops and advised the newly formed St. Louis Committee of Safety to build a ten-foot stockade around the entire city. Clark also kept the peace by escorting a group of thirty leaders from Great and

Little Osages and Missouri Shawnees and Delawares to Washington DC, where they met with President Madison and agreed to remain loyal to the United States during the war.[64] Much to Clark's embarrassment, he had to hire extra guards to protect the chiefs on their return from Missouri, not from other Native nations, but from angry white residents.

All along, Clark had been receiving reports from George Sibley that the Osages continued to be friendly and showed no inclination to join up with the British, Tecumseh, or any other rebellious Native people. Sibley reassured him that "their steady adherence to us entitles them to every accommodation that we can afford them." He recommended that the Osages be given high-quality trade goods "to keep them out of the reach of the intrigues of the Hostile Indians and the British Agents."[65] He also concurred with Pierre Chouteau that the territory should arm a fighting force of Osage warriors, who "might be considered our most solid defence." However, despite such assurances, the governor of Missouri Territory decided to turn down the Osage offer of service and to evacuate Fort Osage.[66]

Inwardly cursing, Sibley tried to explain the situation to the Osages, who were quite insulted. But with official orders in hand, he packed up his mountains of supplies, his three slaves, and his two assistants and took a flatboat down to St. Louis, where he stayed, bored and frustrated, for the next two years. He wrote his brother that he "had nothing to do and St. Louis is extremely dull to idlers."[67] Despite his complaints, Sibley actually spent a good deal of time handling Osage affairs in St. Louis. Part of General Clark's war strategy involved luring more Native nations to the American cause with promises of land and peace in the West. He managed to get large band of Sacs and Foxes and a group of Cherokees to move to lands recently ceded by the Osages. In spite of Clark's diplomatic efforts with local Indians, frontier killings in Missouri and Illinois continued, making Euro-American people believe rumors of imminent attack and siege. Even the news that Tecumseh had been killed by William Henry Harrison's troops did not seem to calm fears in St. Louis. When news of Andrew Jackson's vicious slaughter of Creek warriors and their families reached the embattled Missouri frontier, the St. Louis papers warned "the BLOOD of our citizens cry aloud for VENGEANCE" and demanded that "the North be JACKSONIZED."[68]

Clark's solution was to take his poorly equipped troops up the river and to establish a new post at Prairie du Chien, a center of unrest and British infiltration. From there he hoped Indian Office agents could supervise Indian affairs, keeping the British from usurping the fur trade and stopping white settlers from invading Indian lands. However, even these modest aims proved challenging without federal support. Clark took Prairie du Chien in June of 1814, but less than six weeks later abandoned his newly established fort when 1,500 Native troops overwhelmed its agents. By this time even the Osages showed signs of belligerency and frustration, with George Sibley warning Clark that "the Great Osages have killed several citizens of the Territory" along with reports of killings and thefts among the tribes along the Arkansas.[69]

The war ended, in official terms, on December 24, 1814, when the Treaty of Ghent was signed in that neutral Flemish city. Lands and ships were returned to their original owners, and the British promised to stop impressing sailors. The big bone of contention at treaty meetings developed around lands for Native people. The British had promised land and political recognition to the Indian nations of the Missouri and Mississippi rivers. Canadian officials suggested that a large buffer state for Indian people be created around the Great Lakes, hoping that this would help keep the peace for all the nations involved. U.S. negotiators flatly refused any such suggestion, causing a British official to remark with some shock about "the fixed determination which prevails in the breast of every American to extirpate the Indians and appropriate their territory."[70] When Indians learned that the United States had refused to consider such a condition and more pointedly that the British had folded completely, some tribes decided to keep fighting on their own behalf. This kept the Missouri frontier in chaos long after the official end to the war. Business in St. Louis had ground to a standstill, and frontier residents remained on alert. Serious skirmishes and attacks on frontier communities escalated throughout the spring of 1815.[71]

William Clark, Auguste Chouteau, and Illinois governor Ninian Edwards recognized the growing instability and potential danger of the situation. Understanding what Indian war could mean to their communities, they organized a treaty commission to make peace with the Indians in the summer of 1815. On the specific orders of Secretary of State Monroe, George Sibley carried $20,000 worth of gifts to be distributed before the negotiations began. Accompanied by a Native militia escort, he traveled from St. Louis to meet with representatives from twenty-one tribes at Portage des Sioux on the upper Mississippi in what is now Minnesota. As commissioners, Clark, Edwards, and Chouteau drew up separate treaties with each tribe, basically stating that relationships and agreements that had existed before the war would exist afterward. Some tribes were promised trading posts on the British model and others refused to participate, considering themselves still to be at war with the United States.[72]

The major issue, of course, continued to be land. For some tribes, in particular those like the Sacs, Foxes, Winnebagos, and Kickapoos who had refused earlier to cede lands, these new treaties only signaled more potential loss. Even those who did agree to participate in the negotiations made it very clear they would not allow any of their lands to be surveyed, much less to allow forts to be built. The commissioners made the limitations of their efforts very clear in their report to the president about the negotiations with more hostile tribes. They warned that for even the friendliest tribes, the fact of white squatters continually invading Indian territories made peace or trust in government promises almost impossible. Clark, as governor and Indian agent, believed that the only way to keep peace was to separate Native people from white people. He intended to do this by expanding the system of trading houses, strengthening the authority of Indian agents, and enforcing Indian land rights. The treaties required that "necessary measures for removing all white persons who have intruded and settled upon the lands of the Indians within the Missouri Territory" be taken, with the promise of military support to aid in their removal.[73]

However, the trading house system lay in tatters as a result of the war, and Clark and Chouteau could never deliver on their promises to Native nations. Many of the factories were never re-opened. Because of the power of the Osages and because trade there had consistently been profitable, George Sibley did re-establish Fort Osage and his trading relationships. He moved back up the Missouri in the fall of 1815, at age thirty-three a newly married man. His new wife, Mary Easton, a fifteen-year-old from St. Charles, Missouri, did not accompany him. She stayed behind to enjoy the first St. Louis social season since the war began. This gave George time to build "Fountain Cottage," a two-story frame house located west of the factory, and his bride arrived there in March of 1816.[74]

Because Sibley had taken advantage of drastically low land prices during the war, he, like many of the new Missourians, began to have a vested interest beyond the fur trade. Sibley remained as an agent and factor far longer than he had imagined in 1806 when he joined the Indian service. He stayed at Fort Osage until 1822, watching the developments in the fur trade as competing companies headed up the river, generally to get turned around by Arikara or Blackfoot hostility. Sibley created what little peace existed on the river, making treaties with the Kansas and the Pawnees, but he was unable to help the Osages as they battled with various immigrant tribes. Most of the Osages moved south, wanting to get farther away from the refugee Indians moving west across the Mississippi, which cut into Sibley's trade. However, much to his surprise the fort developed into an outfitting station for the new Santa Fe Trail, and Sibley's connections with the Osages proved invaluable here. However, when a large Protestant mission was built and the army garrison that had been housed at the fort was decommissioned, Sibley knew his days as a factor were numbered.[75]

After the war, new entrants in the fur trade like the Sublettes and other American newcomers to St. Louis wanted to get rid of all competition, especially the British and U.S. government monopolies. The Indian factory system never fully recovered, but William Clark and a group of St. Louis businessmen, including the Chouteaus, tried to find a middle ground that echoed the successful methods of the Canadian behemoths, the Hudson's Bay Company and the North West Company. They wanted a private monopoly with government support to build a series of forts along the upper Missouri to compete effectively with British traders.[76] This plan, though ambitious, had little chance of success amid the powerful upper Missouri nations. It also turned out to be politically impractical, given both federal and state unwillingness to spend money. Despite the best efforts of Clark and Thomas McKenney, who took over the office of Indian trade in 1816, and the lobbying efforts of influential fur traders in St. Louis, Congress cut the budget for Indian affairs. Given the vast expense of the war, the unpopularity of annuities and presents for Indians, and especially the anger white citizens felt at having their demands for land limited, the response from Congress was not unexpected. However, the destruction of the government trading house system ensured another generation of bloody warfare on the Missouri and Mississippi: between Native nations and between white squatters and Native people.

CHANGE, LOSS, AND WARFARE ON THE MISSOURI

When people living along the continent's central river systems began to assess what had happened as a result of the War of 1812, they realized a new situation faced them. Huge numbers of white settlers poured into Missouri Territory, soon to be the state of Missouri, and these people eagerly sought land and business opportunities. Displaced Native people from the Old Northwest, the Great Lakes, and the interior South also came west, hoping to find some respite from war and pressures on their lands. The Canadian fur trade had been dealt a significant blow with the exclusion of "foreign" traders from the Great Lakes and the upper Missouri. Trappers and traders of British and French extraction, along with their mixed race families, had to decide whether to work for American fur companies or to move to Canada, leaving communities like Kaskaskia, Cape Girardeau, or Mackinaw (Michilimackinac) where they had lived for many generations. Long-time residents of the region, both Native and Euro-American, watched with dismay as these changes overwhelmed their world.

Some Native people moved to Canada, hoping for a better reception among their former allies. The Prophet and his retinue of Shawnees and Delawares refused to sign any of the treaties offered by the U.S. government and settled on the Canadian shores of Lake Erie in 1815. The Prophet tried to move back home, but Lewis Cass, governor of Michigan Territory, refused, insisting that the Prophet was a British agent. He threatened to arrest him if he set foot on U.S. soil. Slowly, however, many of the Prophet's followers drifted back over the border, where they hoped to re-establish a community on the Wabash and "relight the fires of Tippecanoe." Instead, they met with the implacable reality of removal as they had little land left to claim in the Old Northwest.[77]

Many Native nations, looking at the waves of immigrating white people and the human costs of continued resistance, splintered into smaller groups and headed west before removal became official. The Shawnees provide a good example. Already split into three groups by active choices they made a generation earlier, the Shawnees lived primarily in Ohio and Missouri. The Missouri Shawnees had adapted well to the subsistence culture in eastern Missouri, making a living on small plots of land supplemented with hunting and trading. Their situation, however, disintegrated rapidly as white settlers and their slaves flooded the region, increasing the population nearly tenfold in two decades. William Clark, in his dual role as territorial governor and Indian agent, attempted to stop the invasion of squatters onto Shawnee farms and even had many of the newcomers forcibly removed, but his actions were a mere finger in a bursting dike of population growth.[78]

In 1822, pressured by white settlement and with an invitation from the Cherokees and Delawares, a large contingent of the Missouri Shawnees moved to east Texas, then part of Mexico, hoping to receive land grants from the Mexican government. In 1825 the rest of the Missouri Shawnees abandoned their eastern Missouri farms and took up lands on a reservation on the Kansas River in what is now eastern Kansas. The Ohio Shawnees, forcibly removed by federal and state troops in 1832, settled in two separate

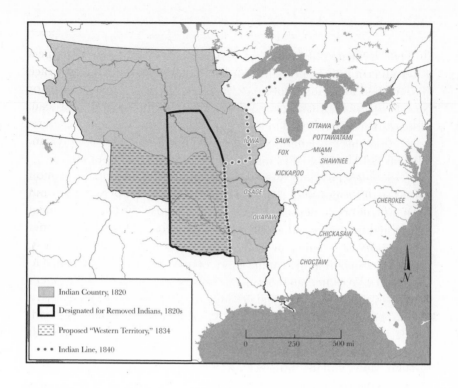

groups, one on the Kansas River reservation and the other on the Arkansas River. Once the Texas Revolution and its political aftermath made it clear that Native nations would never get title to land there, many of the Texas Shawnees and their Cherokee allies headed north to the Canadian and Arkansas River communities.[79]

None of this movement occurred into unoccupied space, of course. William Clark's nephew, Benjamin O'Fallon, who had served in several capacities in the Missouri Indian service, wrote ruefully to his uncle, "how mistaken is the policy of our Government in proposing to remove any more Indians to this already impoverished country."[80] The Shawnees became part of a larger group of Native people, often called the "refugee" or "immigrant" tribes, who moved to eastern Kansas amid the Osage, already angered by their treatment at the hands of the federal government during the war. To make this even thornier, the Osages had raided Shawnee villages for horses and slaves for several decades, so that the relationship between the two groups was combative at best. George Sibley, as the factor at Fort Osage, had to manage the tension between these groups as everyone tried to make sense of the new situation. Sibley, who had described the Osages as gracious, kind, and his "friends forever" in letters to his family before the War of 1812, now described them as "conducting themselves very improperly" and as guilty of "treating the whites with a great deal of brutality."[81]

Much of the "improper behavior" came from the reality that war was percolating between the Osages and the Cherokees. Their situation reflected the challenge that most Native people faced as they had to metabolize increased pressures from white settlement, which meant being restricted to smaller pieces of land. In the case of the Osages, they were expected to share this already limited land with immigrant Native groups. Even before the War of 1812, groups of Cherokees had drifted west, but this took the form of official policy after the war, especially on lands surrounding the Arkansas River. According to both the Osages and the Cherokees, the two groups had tangled and had exchanged killings as early as the American Revolutionary years, when Cherokee hunters ranged west into Osage territory. When the Cherokees arrived on the Arkansas in the years after the war, encouraged and then forced by President Madison and Secretary of War John C. Calhoun, they found that Clermont's band of Osages simply refused to allow them to hunt. Both groups raided the other, stealing horses and killing people. Things escalated in July of 1817, and the Arkansas Cherokees wrote to William Clark claiming "the Rivers are red with the Blood of Cherokees" and warning him that they would exact revenge.[82]

They did, attacking Clermont's village, burning it to the ground, and killing at least fourteen men and seventy women and children. This vicious act did not, of course, end the conflict, even though William Clark, the U.S. Army, and various state officials organized peace treaties between the warring parties that everyone ceremoniously signed. Neither military nor civilian officials had any hope of controlling the sporadic violence that lasted for another ten years. A. P. Chouteau, from his trading post with Clermont's Osages and his own Osage family, reported regularly about raids on both sides, including a spectacular moment when a famed Cherokee leader named Dutch rode into the trading post grounds and scalped and killed an Osage warrior in what seemed a matter of seconds. William Clark, in a moment of obvious stress, admitted to his nephew that "the Cherokees and Osages bother me so much that I have not time decently to think."[83]

When Clark did have time to think, he recognized the impossibility of controlling Indian Country in the West. The warfare and bitter competition between Native groups under pressure from white settlement also took place in the context of a revolution in the fur trade. Faced with tirades about the cost, inefficiency, and unfair advantage of the government monopoly in fur trading, Congress decided to allow the funding for the trading houses to dry up. People like Clark and Thomas McKenney who worked in the Indian trade and who developed and implemented policy recognized how much this would exacerbate the extremely difficult situation west of the Mississippi. They beseeched Congress to protect the present trading system as a lesser of two evils. As McKenney put it rather tactfully, "private enterprise would not likely be characterized by the traits which justice and humanity, and policy, necessitate in these matters." George Sibley, not nearly so tactful, warned the newly arrived citizens on the Missouri frontier, that "your property will be sacrificed, your families murdered, and your farms desolated if the fur trade is left open to this class of pedlars."[84] This was not exactly the empty land and free opportunity described by politicians and land speculators living in the East.

Sibley's dire predictions turned out to have eerie accuracy. However, faced with political realities and the obvious preferences of their constituents to get the government out of the Indian trade business, Congress passed a new set of Trade and Intercourse Acts in 1822. The act, championed by Thomas Hart Benton, the powerful senator from Missouri with interests in the fur trade himself, abolished the factories and created the office of the superintendent of Indian affairs, located within the War Department. The superintendent now supervised a field of agents and superintendents, assigned to various tribal groups and regions specifically. Agents, who had no tie to trade, in theory, would be entirely loyal to the wants and needs of their Native charges. In practice, of course, this meant that few agents had any connection to Indian Country, did not speak local languages, and had few personal ties to the region, rendering them largely ineffective. A few men, including George Sibley, Thomas Forsyth, and several of the Chouteaus, made the transition from Indian Department factor to Department of War agent, but this was exception rather than the rule.[85]

The logic behind abolishing the factories was to open up the fur trade to more people, thus allowing market competition to regulate prices for furs and for Indian trade goods. The initial results, however, proved disastrous for everyone involved. Congress assumed that frontier regions had far more governmental presence than they did and that everyone in this region practiced a rule of law. They also assumed that elite Anglo-American businessmen and politicians called the shots. They couldn't have been more wrong. Several things happened almost immediately. First, liquor, previously prohibited (but often smuggled in), poured into the region, even though Congress had imposed strict controls over this practice. The fact that big operators like the American Fur Company were granted exceptions to liquor prohibitions to allow them to compete successfully with the British, who continued to trade in whiskey, made the situation even messier. These exceptions, granted by the secretary of war personally, were given in 1822, rescinded in 1827, granted once again in 1831, and then finally taken away altogether with the new set of laws in 1832. And many of the Missouri and Arkansas River tribes simply refused to allow anyone to participate in the trade. As small and large private operations began to plan for their profitable forays into Indian Country, nations like the Arikara and Blackfoot began to plan for war.[86]

The Arikara War

Feeling betrayed by the outcome of the War of 1812 and their abandonment by the British, the Arikaras continued to express their hostility. A relatively small agricultural tribe, the Arikaras had settled in several villages along the Missouri River as it enters the Dakotas. From this location, they controlled trade between the upper Missouri tribes and the more settled people of the middle Missouri, but their dependence on fields and villages had made them vulnerable to raids from the plains tribes. Once they no longer had British goods to trade, they found it harder to control trade.

The new groups of trappers, now freed to ply their trade by the 1822 abolition of the Indian trading houses, threatened the Arikaras' status as middlemen between Americans and British traders and Native hunters living farther west and north. In response, the Arikaras refused to allow trading parties to move up the river, unless placated by gifts and personal requests. Trade in Indian Country depended on goodwill and trust, and the new conditions of the fur trade allowed the Arikaras to have neither.

As the trade got more chaotic with far more players attempting to make their fortunes this way, the tensions increased. Traders brought a few goods that the Arikaras wanted, but they also brought alcohol and trouble. One Arikara leader wondered after an 1811 visit: "Do you white people have any women amongst you? Your people are so fond of our women one might suppose that they had never seen any before."[87] As a result of such vexed encounters, each year Arikara warriors killed independent traders, trappers, and boatmen, intent on protecting their turf and their families. By the 1820s the Arikaras had earned the name "the Horrible Tribe" because of their success at keeping traders out or, as the traders saw it, "killing every white man they could lay their hands on." A single tribe, strategically located, threatened to destroy the entire trade, which neither politicians nor traders could tolerate.[88]

From the Arikara perspective, their tenuous situation required such violent action. Because of the variety of fur companies attempting to trade with Indians along the river, they never could be sure with whom they could get the best prices for their horses, trade goods, or hides. Some traders stole their horses and their women; others proved to be good allies against other tribes and paid well. And over the years the Arikaras had made a lot of enemies. How could they tell, as a group approached their villages on the west bank of the river, whether they brought trade goods or vengeance? When in doubt they prevented traders from passing their villages, and if traders didn't like this limitation, the situation often became violent.

The newspapers in St. Louis ranted and raved over the situation on the river. The combined concerns about British agents who were supposedly stirring up Native people, the genuine fear of Indian uprisings, and the grim reality of foreclosures and business failures after the Panic of 1819 made St. Louisans jumpy. In 1822 the *Missouri Intelligencer* hinted darkly that British agents operated an integrated intelligence network that operated "from Mexico to Canada with schemes of smuggling and Indian uprisings" as its aim. The paper's readers saw regular stories about the failure of the Bank of Missouri and stories about the failure to get steamships up the Missouri, as well as the failure of the U.S. Army to build a post on the Missouri.[89]

The worst news came in July of 1823. A stunning headline, "INDIAN OUTRAGE!" outlined a dreadful attack by the "Rickaree Indians" upon General William Ashley and his Missouri Fur Company outfit of about a hundred men as they ventured up the river. They entered the Arikara villages to trade for horses, but Ashley clearly misread the signs there. When the group tried to pass the villages on June 2, the Indians began firing on the boats. The paper reported that thirteen men had been killed in the attack, which was true, but also that the Indians had a "force of two thousand," which was not. The account added the grisly detail that whenever one of Ashley's men fell out of the boat a horde of Indians "immediately swam in and scalped him."[90]

The bad news continued with reports of killings by the Blackfoot and Yankton Sioux later that month. William Ashley, in a long editorial, railed against government inattention and warned: "If our government do not send troops up this river . . . the Americans must abandon the trade in this country—The Indians are becoming more formidable every year."[91] Benjamin O'Fallon, having been appointed Indian agent to all the Missouri tribes with the end of the trading house system, saw even more sinister designs. In a report to Superintendent William Clark, reprinted in all of the newspapers, he claimed "that British traders, (Hudson Bay Company) are exciting the Indians against us." Using extraordinary analogies he described the British as "wolves who ravage our fields" and who "furnish Indians with the instruments of death and a passport to our bosoms."[92]

Frontier politicians like Thomas Hart Benton found themselves in a difficult situation. After insisting that the trading houses served as dens of vice and corruption that stirred up the Indians and that prevented fine upstanding Americans from participating in the fur trade, they now recognized the deadly mess that the unregulated fur trade could become. Benjamin O'Fallon, the agent for all of the upper Missouri tribes, was tearing his hair out over the situation in which "the scape gallows of purged Countries" have flooded into "the land of Indians and trade with no authority." Now, he continued, "they complain that the Black feet attack their camps and I do nothing."[93] To remedy this crisis, Missouri politicians now demanded that forts be built, troops be deployed, and the cavalry be sent in. Still harboring resentment over the lack of funding they got from the penurious federal government, they demanded attention from Congress. An editorial in the *St. Louis Enquirer* asked bombastically in February of 1824: "How far will they go? One Congress refused to protect us. Will the present one join the British and the Blackfoot and drive us from the country?"[94]

Much of this was pure political drama, and the problems could hardly be laid at the feet of British traders. The U.S. government, in a particularly dismal performance, had in fact sent in troops several years earlier to build a fort at the mouth of the Yellowstone. However, the U.S. Army, under Colonel Henry Atkinson, found the sandbars of the Missouri River as formidable as the Native people who lived along it. After four years, the "Yellowstone Expedition" had foundered at Council Bluffs, barely past the Platte River, and they had made no "treaties of peace with the hostiles," a central part of their charge. Finally, in 1821, Congress defunded Atkinson's expedition and ordered the troops to head back to St. Louis, where Atkinson was promoted to general. Frustrated by this military failure, a private company, headed up by William Ashley and Andrew Henry, decided to mount a private expedition to trade with the Indians, build a fort on the Yellowstone, and develop trading relationships with the Blackfoot ahead of the other fur traders. Though they received permission to trade, their ambitions were much larger: demonstrating the superiority of private enterprise over the government. The result, instead, was war with the Arikaras.[95]

After the initial attack in June of 1823, some of General Ashley's men had stayed on the river, while Ashley retreated to get help. Both government and private enterprise combined to respond. All parties recognized that this incident could signal the end of the fur trade on the Missouri, which would mean bankruptcy for a considerable number of St. Louisans. For Indian agent Benjamin O'Fallon and Colonel Henry Leavenworth, this episode was only one of a number of significant Indian attacks that indicated even peaceful tribes were taking up arms against traders, settlers, and troops. They had to react, in O'Fallon's melodramatic words, to "make the inhuman monsters atone for what they have done by a great effusion of their blood." Leavenworth, newly installed as commander in chief of the forces west of the Mississippi, had little experience with Native people and frontier warfare and was less bloodthirsty. Even so, he agreed and organized his troops to head up the river and take on the Arikaras. He and O'Fallon appointed Joshua Pilcher, long-time employee of the Missouri Fur Company and a man who had suffered losses in several Arikara attacks, as his Indian agent and advisor. Pilcher also contributed several groups of Native auxiliaries, all people who had personal axes to grind as well. This combination of inexperience and hatred would turn out to be a poisonous one.[96]

It took Leavenworth, Pilcher, and their troops weeks to move up the river. Their flatboats, laden with howitzers and supplies, caught on snags and sandbars, which made progress slow and frustrating. One boat sank completely, drowning eight men and losing fifty-seven guns. When they finally reached Ashley's stranded men, Leavenworth hired them on as soldiers, mostly because they had more ammunition that his men did. He appointed several of them, including young William Sublette, as brevet officers to lead the new soldiers. This conjoined group headed up the river and finally reached the Teton Sioux villages, where they hoped to recruit more allies. The Sioux, traditionally allied against the Arikaras, agreed readily, but according to some of Pilcher's interpreters, many Sioux warriors discussed joining with the Arikaras. This concerned Leavenworth deeply, and he wrote to Benjamin O'Fallon that "our force is not sufficient to inspire the awe and respect amongst the Indians that I would wish."[97] The fact that a considerable number of his men did not have guns and others made do with Revolutionary War–era muskets while most of the Sioux had British-made rifles may have added to Leavenworth's lack of confidence.[98]

On August 9 the combined force of the Sioux, fur traders, and military men headed for the Arikara villages. The Sioux, traveling on foot, reached the villages first and immediately engaged the Arikaras. The military arrived several hours after the fighting began, exhausted after marching fifteen miles in the August sun. Pilcher's Missouri Fur Company traders followed on the boats, but because they faced a fierce headwind that day, they straggled in much later. Leavenworth, with his howitzers and most of the ammunition still on the boats, decided not to attack. He continued to worry about Sioux loyalty and remained convinced that in a real fight the Indians would join together against the U.S. Army. This fear led him to make a number of mistakes: he overestimated the cohesiveness of the Arikara fighting force and refused to allow the Sioux to attack the village for a second time. Against all the advice of his scouts and advisors, who wanted him to complete the job and destroy the villages, Leavenworth made a peace agreement with the Arikaras. The Indian agent in charge, Benjamin O'Fallon, had explained very clearly that the objective was having "the Blood of Arickaras run from many veins." He warned further that "a mere military display will not be enough." Leavenworth, unable to trust the Sioux, felt satisfied with the mere military display. He promised to end his campaign against the Arickaras, if only they returned Ashley's horses and men they had captured in the original fight.[99]

The Arikaras, unable to believe their luck, were instantly disdainful of this weak military man. They refused even to return the horses, saying they couldn't find them, but agreed to smoke pipes to seal the deal. Pilcher and his fur trade men were unrestrainedly livid, recognizing that all of the tribes would read this unfinished attack as a complete capitulation. Some of the men refused to smoke the peace pipe, forcing Leavenworth to arrest the disobedient soldiers in full view of the Arikaras, which did not improve their opinion of him or increase their fear of the mighty U.S. Army. The Sioux, confused by this inconclusive situation, left in the middle of the night after the battle, stealing some horses as they went. Despite this situation, Leavenworth proceeded with the peace talks but couldn't even complete those when all of the Arikaras snuck away the second night, taking even more horses.

Leavenworth decided that his work was done and ordered all the men to head down the river, even though his men begged to give chase to the Indians. Unable to stand it, several of Pilcher's men, many of whom had lost friends in other battles with the Arikaras, hung back and burned the Arikara villages to the ground. Now it was Leavenworth's turn to be apoplectic. He dismissed, with dishonor, the Missouri Fur Company men, among them William Sublette, for disobeying orders. For Pilcher, this bit of military shaming was the last straw. He believed, from his long experience on the river, that leaving the village would be seen as pure weakness. He thundered, in person and later in the newspapers, "You came to open and make good this road and instead of which, by the imbecility of your conduct and operations, created and left impossible barriers." The barriers now included arrogant Arikaras, Sioux bent on vengeance, and Blackfoot and Mandans more closely linked to Canadian traders.[100]

Especially after the Arikara War, Native nations along the river prevented Anglo-Americans from finding wealth and success in the fur trade. The very rumor of Arikaras re-occupying their villages sent the entire fur trade industry into a panic. The St. Louis newspapers published every rumor and raised fears to a fever pitch each summer.[101] Some of this fear was deserved; between them the Arikaras, Tetons, and Blackfoot committed murderous raids. William Sublette reported to Superintendent Clark that in the years between 1824 and 1828 his company alone lost 94 men to Indian depredations and suffered monetary losses of $43,500, nearly all involving the Arikaras and the Blackfoot.[102] As a result of statistics like this and the poor profit margins it signaled, the fur trade shifted most its focus to the Rocky Mountains and to the Southwest. Indian Country still existed in most of the upper Missouri Territory, and others could only travel there with permission of its residents.

British traders, French Canadians, and people of mixed race could travel there because they brought high-quality goods and because they understood the diplomatic rules that many Anglo-Americans did not. Thomas Forsyth, agent to the Sacs and Foxes and long-time trader, reported with great frustration that even as late as 1831, "Americans are having no luck in the upper rivers," and he blamed the trouble on "the Hudson's Bay establishments where there are many half-breeds who are altogether brought up to hunting and making lives with the Indians."[103] American traders, without English goods or Native families, could hardly compete.

Watching the Arikara War and the fury that followed it numbered among George Sibley's last tasks at Fort Osage. He fought, unsuccessfully, for his position as post factor and left government service officially in 1822. Initially imagining that he would become a trader himself, he bought all of the supplies and trade goods left at Fort Osage and in the summer of 1823 sold some of these goods on credit to Colonel Leavenworth. He never got paid. Because nearly all of the Osages had moved away from the fort and that few of them had furs to trade, George quickly went out of business. Unwilling to take on the financial or physical risks of Indian trade on the upper Missouri, he looked for opportunities to the south and west. He finagled a position making treaties with the Pawnees, Kansas, and Wichitas and helped the U.S. Army lay out a new road to Santa Fe. Eventually he saved enough cash so the he and Mary could move to a farm near St. Charles, where George intended to become a gentleman farmer.[104]

MÉTIS AND HALF-BREED IN AN ANGLO WEST

For others, leaving Indian Country or the fur trade was not as simple. George Sibley, unlike many traders, did not have a Native wife, though he had adopted Osage children, and most importantly he had invested in Missouri real estate with his brother and father-in-law. As we have seen earlier, other traders made different choices. That same year, 1822, A. P. Chouteau left his St. Louis family to live permanently with the Osages, a late example of fur trade practices that had now created many generations of people with European and Native blood. As the process of "removal" shuffled Indian nations across the continent, it also revealed a large population of people of mixed race who had gradually made lives for themselves and their families in communities around the Great Lakes and the Mississippi and Missouri rivers.

By the beginning of the nineteenth century, trading hamlets ranging in

23. Charles Deas, American (1818-67). *The Trapper and His Family*. 1840s.
Watercolor on paper, 13 3/8 x 19 1/2 in. (34.0 x 49.5 cm). Museum of
Fine Arts, Boston. Gift of Maxim Karolik for the M. and M. Karolik
Collection of American Watercolors and Drawings, 1800-1875. 60.412.

The image, reminiscent of Bingham's *Fur Traders Descending the Missouri*,
depicts the world of families that had developed on the river systems of
the United States. Anglo men married Native women who had the
skills and relationships that undergirded successful business and family
life. The families they created would change the demographic face of
the region for generations.

size from a single extended family to several hundred persons had been
established at Peoria, Cahokia, Chicago, Fort Wayne, Ouiatanon, Parc aux
Vaches, Riviere Raisin, Sault Sainte Marie, Petit Kaukalin, Portage, La Pointe,
and, most famously, Michilimackinac or Mackinaw. These communities
had emerged mostly out of the fur trade regime created by New France,
but they had been increased by British and American trade and the decisions of Native people as well. Ethnohistorian Jacqueline Peterson claims
that the core of the Mississippi River and Great Lakes may have offered the
most stable platform for family creation in the fur-trading world. Because
this part of the trade was not controlled by giant monopolies who forced
their operatives to move often and who discouraged marriage, people
settled in these regions by developing permanent kin connections to local
Native nations. The inhabitants of these towns were people of primarily

mixed race—who called themselves métis, a category few Anglo-Americans understood.[105] In 1789 all these communities east of the Mississippi had been absorbed into the new United States. These places and the confusing racial status of their inhabitants hardly appeared on the national radar screen until after the War of 1812.

Anglo-American observers found these communities discouraging because the towns and their inhabitants seemed to prove the dangers of racial amalgamation. The people living there had little interest in farming, in becoming American citizens, or in giving up their "Indian habits," in the observers' view perfect proof of what happens to "half-breeds." The French/Canadian/Native communities were entirely focused on the fur trade, with the men working as trappers and hunters and leaving their families for long periods of time. Despite Anglo-American dismay at these practices, they had served the fur trade world well, and many clearly "American" families on the frontier lived happily in exactly the same ways. Mostly, we see French Canadian men marrying into local Native families whose considerable knowledge of local hunting and agricultural practices ensured that their blended families would be provided for during their extended absences. What may have upset officials the most was the sheer number of people who had made this choice and how difficult it made seeing who was white and who was not. Lewis Cass, territorial governor of Michigan, estimated in 1816 that "four-fifths of Michigan's white population were of that class of people." He argued further that this large group of people could never be assimilated because "they had inherited the vices of both races and none of the virtues."[106]

The mixing went far beyond French trappers and Native wives. When we look closely at these communities, whether in Michigan, Wisconsin, Missouri, or Arkansas, or in Indian Country, especially at those in frontier zones, we often see several Native groups, French settlers, British traders, the Native wives of these men, white captives, Native slaves from other tribes, and several generations of people of mixed race. Important Native men sometimes married mixed race daughters of important traders, so the linkages operated in many directions. Sometimes these "composite communities" were the direct result of war and removal, sometimes they evolved from the nucleus of an old trading fort, and sometimes they were at the sites of Native settlements, but there were too many to count.[107]

Given that many of the early Euro-American leaders of new western states and territories had Native families, people of mixed race could not be simply discounted. William Ashley of Missouri, Henry Hastings Sibley of Minnesota, Henry Schoolcraft of Michigan, and the Chouteaus all had kinship ties to Indian Country because of their involvement in the fur trade. Efforts to understand these communities and to impose American cultural standards challenged early Anglo-American officials. A newly appointed judge, the Honorable James Doty, tried to root out immoral behavior in the old fur-trading community of La Baye, or Green Bay, in Michigan Territory in 1824. He had most of the leading men of the community indicted for fornication and adultery because they had not been married by church or civil authorities. The majority pleaded guilty, and to escape the fine they agreed to stand before a justice of the peace to legitimize their connubial unions. At least eight householders, however, refused to admit any immorality, and some sued Doty, insisting that they were legally married according to the customs of the Indians, had lived a great many years with their wives, and had large families of children. Their marriages, therefore, met community standards.[108]

By 1800 many métis people had families dating back three and four generations in the region. For example, the La Baye men indicted in 1824 had, in fact, been responsible husbands for many years. Some prominent traders escorted their children and wives to Michilimackinac for tardy baptism and marital confirmations, but no one at La Baye questioned the legitimacy of marriages contracted by verbal agreement. In contrast to Anglo-American assumptions about church and civil requirements surrounding lawful marriage, third- and fourth-generation Great Lakes métis looked to the force of tribal custom and to French peasant practices for assurance. These arrangements had brought some of these families considerable wealth and power in the fur-trading world, but it was wealth based on trade, rather than the buying, selling, and development of land, the obvious gold standard in the United States. The Grignon family at La Baye and the La Framboise family of Mackinaw Island were typical of leading métis families in the Great Lakes region. Their households, composed of extended kin, servants, employees and *engagés*, and slaves, of various mixtures of Native, French, and English extraction, had great stores of fur, canoes, and trade goods, but little flour, wool, and cloth. These families operated as "finely crafted educational cells—designed to spin off a new generation of Métis mediators" by continuing to marry into local Native families.[109]

The strategy and pattern emerged everywhere the fur trade operated until the 1840s when the trade began to peter out. And "everywhere the fur trade operated" is a very large region—trading towns in the Pacific

Northwest, comanchero communities in New Mexico, the Arkansas River frontier—all show this pattern. For some, it was enormously successful, and these examples are famous. Much to the disgust of new American residents, Jean Baptiste Richardville, a Miami métis who owned a trading post at Fort Wayne, was by far the wealthiest person in the new Indiana Territory. In 1818 Richardville negotiated a treaty that gave individual families land grants to small parcels of privately held reserves scattered throughout northern Indiana. Richardville himself eventually controlled over twenty square miles of choice property along important rivers. This enabled a significant number of Miami people to remain in Indiana after their official removal in 1846, five years after Richardville's death. Richardville built himself a Greek Revival home, using his own profits and his annuities from the U.S. government. Such experiences, however, were exceptions. Most people of mixed race lost their homes and livelihoods, fled north to Canada, or were removed as they tried to reintegrate with their Native kin. This story, however, is filled with complexity and irony. Central Algonkian and Siouan bands had confronted the tricky problem of designing clan affiliations for countless abandoned métis children a hundred years earlier but found themselves overwhelmed by the nineteenth century. The Ojibwes, for example, created totemic clans for children of British and American fathers, the "Lion" and "Eagle" clans, while the Osages made a special *ak-i-da* or hereditary warrior society for those soldiers without a clan, including important members of the Chouteau family and many Indian agents.[110]

On the U.S. side, various institutions attempted to solve the puzzle of people of mixed race in the West, including the Office of Indian Affairs and churches. Indian agents, military officials, and missionaries were left to handle these problems on the ground. Indian agents, those men assigned by the War Department to serve individual tribes, have gotten a terrible reputation over the years. However, the agents who took on this task in years before reservations undertook a very different job in a very different context. They were rarely in it for the money, the graft potential, or the burning need for conversion. Instead, their jobs involved making sure Indians lived up to treaty agreements and keeping illegal traders out of Indian Country. Many of them had been traders themselves, and many had Native families or other kinship connections to their tribes, both of which gave them an intimate view of Native nations.

At Fort Osage George Sibley worried about what to do about the mixture of peoples and needs under his roof. He and his wife Mary adopted Sans

Oreille's orphaned daughters in 1818 and raised the girls (one renamed Mary after Sibley's wife) as their own. We have no record of the conversations they must have had about the children's future, especially as he was charged with the welfare of the entire Little Osage band. He may have been thinking of young Mary and her sisters when he accepted offers from the United Foreign Missionary Society to set up schools near the fort in 1821. He knew that Fort Osage as a government trading center wouldn't last much longer, and that congressional purse strings were growing ever tighter. It might help the Osages in the long run if religious organizations would provide education. The missionary effort at Fort Osage received a great deal of press because of its timing and location. In supporting this first mission in the "Wild West," Christian missionaries were determined to prove that they could do a better job of "civilizing" the Indians than either the government or private enterprise had done so far. After several presentations and fund-raising efforts in New York and Philadelphia, more than a hundred eager recruits applied, and in the end a group of about forty people headed west to set up schools. They carried with them pledges from supportive Christians who had given twelve dollars each to sponsor an Osage child, entitling them to "the privilege of giving that child a name."[111]

Naming children turned out to be a challenge since few Osages had any interest in sending their children to the school, particularly for the Great Osages on the Arkansas. The missionaries' efforts then focused on the Little Osages at Fort Osage. They succeeded minimally mostly because of the large population of people of mixed race who lived there as part of the fort's community. Parents of mixed race children were particularly aware of the significance of education in providing their children with options in a changing world. And missionaries, imbued with the racist ideology of their time, assumed that children of mixed race would be more intelligent and easier to teach than their full-blooded relatives. When the Harmony school finally opened in 1822, its three pupils were of mixed race, including the daughters of Bill Williams, the retired mountain man who served as chief interpreter at the fort, and his Osage wife, as well as Mary Sibley, one of the children of Sans Oreille adopted by Mary and George Sibley. A. P. Chouteau also entered his two half-Osage sons, Augustus and James, later that year. Two years later, the school had enrolled nineteen pupils, only two of whom were listed as full-blooded Osage. The rest appear in the record as "Osage-French, Eng-Osage, Sioux-Fren-Osage," and so on, demonstrating the twisting connections of the fur trade world and the increasing obsession with racial categorization.[112]

We get a window into the operations of the school from the letters of missionary Harriet Wooley, who taught at the school for more than a decade. Frustrated by her paucity of students, Harriet wondered to her family about God and "the strange ways his wonders work to perform" as so many of the children had been removed from the school and so many had died of typhus fever. She did commend "Rebekker Williams" (this is old Bill Williams's daughter), "who can sew neat enough to work on cambrick and has helped me considerable in my taylor line of business." But she was saddened to report that "I have lost Sarah Cockrem" who had been sponsored and named by "the dear children and Coulered women at Wall Street School." She hoped finally that sponsors would trust her and "grant me the privilege of another Indian child to have the name."[113] A year later, things don't seem to have improved much at the institution that seemed more charnel house than school. The renamed children are still dying of communicable diseases or leaving the school to return to their Native families. Harriet reported that she still could not speak any Osage, which stymied communication with her students. She justified her language deficit, commenting that "it is not a small matter to acquire a language that has never been written."[114] Her greatest frustration, of course, was the mission's lack of success in converting Native people. She confided to her sister that only the fort's leader, his wife, and "the occasional curious half-breed will consent to come even to services." The Osages still appeared utterly uninterested in "giving us their children to Instruct," leaving Miss Wooley to wonder if "we will only have inroads among the children of the French men and their dusky wives?"[115]

Thomas Forsyth, agent and old Indian trader, viewed the inroads of the métis world from a different perspective. Born in Detroit to an English father and French Canadian mother in 1774, he became the agent for the tribes of the upper Missouri, including the Sacs, Foxes, and Potawatomis right after the War of 1812. Though he never claimed to have a Native wife, he did acknowledge several children who lived with the Ojibwes and Otoes. With this personal and occupational history, Forsyth had spent a great deal of time among Native nations and was particularly aware of the world of people of mixed raced. And he was right on the cusp of changing attitudes toward race and its malleability. In his letters, with rather idiosyncratic spelling, to William Clark between 1811 and 1830, we see "Indians" or "Sakis" or "Foxes" or "mother is Sauk" or "trader's children" become "French-Fox" and "English-Ihoway" and finally "half-breed" to designate all people of mixed race. And for Forsyth, like many Indian agents, these "half-breeds" presented a challenge in terms of deciding who should get land, annuities, or education.[116]

Because the Great Lakes region had been fur trade central for so long, the people who would become "half-breeds" once they became part of the United States were a large and varied group. The category and term *half-breed* was not used or understood in the Great Lakes fur trade world until the beginning of the nineteenth century. Native people had no category for mixed-blood people; they were either part of a tribe in some formal way or not. Before the beginning of the nineteenth century, Anglo-Americans saw race as a very malleable characteristic, much as Native Americans did, though their ideas had a powerful progressive bent. In the period when race was flexible, Indian people especially could somehow be improved. They could become more noble and less savage by contact with civilization. However, as race became a "problem" and categories sharpened and hardened, nonwhite people became innately inferior and progression impossible. These ideas were applied to Indian people in very uneven ways especially early in the nineteenth century, so that it remained very unclear whether being more or less Indian was better or worse. For the large number of people of mixed race, did their supposedly superior white parts win out, or did their inferior Indian parts drag them down?[117]

A good example of the shifts in the way American officials and society in general thought about people of mixed race is the rather famous story of John Tanner. A group of Shawnees captured young Tanner from the Kentucky frontier in 1785, but he eventually ended up with a group of Ojibwe-Ottawa people, where he stayed for many years. Fully adopted into the tribe, Tanner lived in northern Michigan, marrying several Ottawa women and fathering at least seven children with them. According to Tanner, he lost all ability to speak English and forgot his birth family entirely until his brother found him in 1817. He described the meeting with standard melodrama as his brother "next cut off my long hair . . . and expressed much satisfaction at my having laid aside the Indian costume." He returned to Kentucky to rejoin his white birth family, but this was not the happy ending he imagined. Like many people of mixed race, he discovered that the lines between Anglo and Indian were both invisible and inflexible, and he commented sadly that "the dress of a white man was extremely uncomfortable to me."[118]

Tanner found living as an Anglo-American very uncomfortable indeed, and he tried to rebuild his Indian family around him. In 1819, demonstrating some entrepreneurial spirit, Tanner applied to Indian agent Thomas

Forsyth for some funding to return to his Native family. As Forsyth explained to General William Clark, Tanner wanted funding and equipment to head up the Mississippi, "provisions and a few presents and further assistance to get home to his family in the lake of the Woods." Tanner's ultimate goal, as he piously claimed to Forsyth, was "to bring up his seven Children by an Indian woman in a Christian like manner." Tanner faced several challenges in this attempt: his older children did not want to leave their Native families, the mother of his younger children did not want the children to go, and he was extremely ambivalent about his own place in the Anglo-American world.[119]

Though he managed to raise money to get his children several times, wrote a memoir, and visited his birth family, Tanner never really settled outside of Indian Country. His memoir, ghostwritten by Edwin James, appears to have been the high point of his life. *A Narrative of the Captivity and Adventures of John Tanner* followed the standard story that American audiences wanted to read. A young boy is captured in a heinous act by savages, maintains his Christian morality during his life with the Indians, and then is returned to the bosom of his loving white family, none the worse for his experience. Tanner's story, however, had a part two. After his plan to move his family fizzled, and it became clear his loving family had some issues around accepting an Indian into its bosom, he settled in Ojibwe lands in northern Michigan and married several more Native women. His life unraveled. He appears in the court records for stealing livestock and aggravating his white neighbors, who at one point reportedly set Tanner's house on fire. Finally in 1846 Tanner, then referred to by Native people and whites alike as "Old Liar," was accused of murdering James Schoolcraft, the brother of Henry Rowe Schoolcraft, the Indian agent for Michigan, and he disappeared from the record.[120]

Though surely less famous than Tanner, many of the people over whom agents like Forsyth had jurisdiction faced similar challenges. In the 1830s, as the military and the Indian Department forcibly moved the last of the Great Lakes and Old Northwest tribes west of the Mississippi, one of the most confusing issues they faced were people of mixed race. Like Tanner's story, the story of removal had a part two as well. Who was an Indian, who needed to be moved, who needed to be paid annuities, and who should be granted land on the new reservations? Because treaties, written by Anglo-American men, only recognized children of Native fathers as being "Indians," how were agents on the ground to deal with the array of children with white fathers and Native or mixed race mothers? The fact that many native societies passed names, wealth, and ownership through the mother's line made this even more complex. In many cases white men wanted to remain with their Native families even when they were removed to distant reservations, clearly not the story line federal officials or people reading captivity narratives expected.

None of these questions had simple answers, and the government was unprepared for the waves of people of mixed race the fur trade and several hundred years of mingled living and intermarriage had created. Because the treaty language offered no clarity, General William Clark had to handle each of these cases with an individual petition. Thomas Forsyth had the unenviable task of preparing the paperwork for each claimant. For the Fox nation alone he made 290 petitions in 1830. We read about Joseph Campbell and his Sac and Fox wife and one child or "Pierre Antailla & Tokoufsee (Fox woman) 8 children," who wanted land for themselves and their children in the new tribal lands in Kansas.[121] Mostly Euro-American men, their Native wives, and their children, these families wanted to continue making a living in the West and recognized that they would need both land and their families to succeed.

And, of course, we can't forget that the lands claimed by these families as part of the Fox nation were on lands actually occupied by the Osages and their equally diverse families. By the 1830s Indian Country had become a confused and often dangerous jumble of peoples and policy, but it was also a place where people continued to raise families, make choices about their mode of living, and negotiate among powerful nations about how to do these things.

Chapter 5

Empires in Transition

Indian Country at Midcentury, 1825–1860

A serious, very wary woman looks out at us from the photograph taken in a small Texas town in 1860. She gazes directly at the camera, not looking at the beautiful baby nursing at her breast. At first glance we see a simple image of mother and child, but then our ideas about race and history alter that first read. The mother is clearly white, the child clearly Native. The pair are identified as Cynthia Ann Parker and Prairie Flower, which makes the image and the story it tells extremely complex. It depicts the mother and sister of Quanah Parker, the "last great chief" of the Comanche nation who held out until 1875 and then led his people to surrender at Fort Sill. It also depicts an Anglo-Texan taken from her family at the age of nine during a terrifying Comanche raid that occurred in the confusion of the 1836 Texas Revolution. The captured girl grew into a woman within a Comanche band and became the wife of Peta Nocoma, a renowned warrior. In this photograph she is a redeemed captive, but the pain reflected in her eyes at having witnessed the murder of her husband and the capture of her two young sons makes redemption seem hollow. How do we assess the moral quicksand here? Which is the more terrible crime, a child taken from her family or a mother denied her children? Cynthia Ann remained with her white family, but under constant guard because she tried to escape at any opportunity, desperate to find her sons. After little Prairie Flower died from pneumonia in 1864, Cynthia Ann stopped trying to escape, and she stopped speaking at all. Life silenced her entirely. She died in 1870 without ever seeing her sons again. Quanah Parker never stopped looking for his mother and finally in 1901 had Cynthia Ann and Prairie Flower taken to Fort Sill and reburied on the reservation.

24. Cynthia Ann Parker and Prairie Flower, 1860. Unknown photographer.
Denver Public Library, Western History Collection, X-32238.

This photograph, taken in Texas to celebrate the successful return of a white
captive, is anything but celebratory. Dressed in a calico gown worn by white
women in Texas, but with her dark hair worn short in Comanche-style
mourning for the loss of her husband and sons, Cynthia Ann
demonstrated the terrible personal costs of western warfare.

COUNTING INDIANS

When the minister and geographer Jedediah Morse set off on his tour to inspect the "condition of Indian people" in the United States of 1820, Native people would have been amazed at both his expectations and his conclusions. By 1851 when Henry Rowe Schoolcraft, former Indian agent and trader, and self-trained ethnologist, published his tome, *Indian Tribes of the United States*, great changes had swept over the trans-Mississippi West. Both writers joined a long tradition of experts from various nations who wanted to figure out how many Indians existed in various places. Part of colonial practice and the enforcement of conquest has always been to figure out how many people lived in a "conquered" territory and to assess how amenable they might be to capitulation.

In the West the effort began with Lewis and Clark, who produced the "first spreadsheet" in the colonial project to count and categorize.[1] In the nineteenth-century North American West, this project took on the cast of scientific investigation, but, even so, accurate answers eluded everyone who tried.[2] Consistently the answer to the question of "how many Indians are there" was "a lot more than we expected." And the answer to the question of how they were blending into Euro-American society proved to be equally consistent: not very well. All of the nations of North America found they had to accommodate to one another and that the process of conquest had surprising consequences.

Morse and Schoolcraft, asking such questions at either end of the period in question here, found very similar answers. Even though both authors considered themselves "friends of the Indian," they envisioned a West emptied of savages and filled with happy Anglo-American farmers and a sprinkling of quaint, but Christianized, indigenes. What both observers actually found dismayed them no end. Instead of happy farmers and Indians securely on the path to Christian redemption, Morse and Schoolcraft saw almost uncountable members of Native nations who exhibited little interest in moving toward agricultural and moral virtue. They also gazed upon the disturbing people of mixed race of the fur trade and farmers who resembled Indians far more than the Jeffersonian yeomen they hoped to find.[3]

The colonial wars of the eighteenth century, the imperial battles of the early nineteenth century, the process of removal and resettlement west of the Mississippi, and waves of epidemic disease had a devastating impact on many Indian people. Some nations disappeared, others reconstituted themselves in new forms, and some even grew because of the opportunities offered by western expansion. But the process did not follow the path or produce the results that U.S. policymakers, traders, or missionaries had expected. Few Native people in 1820 or in 1850 had not suffered from the process of conquest and removal, but equally few had given up on their central values and practices. Native people continued to participate in various aspects of the national and global economy and controlled access to important land and resources, much to the frustration of Anglo-American settlers. Some tribal groups and nations resisted conquest regularly and successfully, demonstrating fearsome skills in warfare and diplomacy. The forty years between 1825 and the Civil War, the grandest decades of Manifest Destiny, did not mean an end to the concept of Indian Country, but rather a shifting of its borders and the role it played in national politics. This chapter examines Indian Country as it met, unevenly and unexpectedly, the growing American and Mexican nations.

In 1820 Secretary of War John C. Calhoun commissioned the esteemed Congregational minister and "father of American geography," Jedediah Morse, to make a study of "past history and present state of the Indian Tribes of our country."[4] Like most Indian advocates Morse had met few Native people, especially the vast majority who now lived west of the Mississippi, but unlike most Indian advocates he decided to observe and gather data about them personally before pronouncing his recommendations for national policy. Morse was not an ethnographer, and his major interest lay in assessing the spiritual state of various Native people and in determining which groups would most profit from missionary activity. He made three separate tours, one of the Old Northwest and Great Lakes region, one of Canada, and one of the South and lower Mississippi. Morse did not travel much west of the Mississippi but here relied on materials he gathered from "reliable" traders, agents, and army officers. His words provide us with something far less than a snapshot, perhaps more of a ghostly outline, of Native Americans at that moment in time.

Despite his disdain for "savages," Morse depicted a world that was adjusting to and resisting change. He saw people actively involved in all aspects of the fur trade, providing them much latitude to practice their own lives in their own ways. Morse generalized and made assumptions about what he saw, but he reported it. Men were barbaric warriors and hunters, women were "slaves" because they did agricultural work, but they did these things within a huge range of settings and cultural interpretations. He saw trade, food production, and sophisticated diplomatic undertakings, and he wondered at cultures that could celebrate children and warriors at the same time. He remarked on the number of languages that still existed and marveled that they "are capable of regular grammatical construction and beauty of expression," but he recommended that no efforts be made to preserve them.[5] Morse saw nothing in Native America worth preserving, but he found the prospect of either extermination or assimilation very daunting indeed.

He concluded, predictably, that the U.S. government and its citizens, in partnership with missionary groups, had a moral duty to "civilize and redeem" the Indians. In Morse's view a national project of "moral and religious improvement of the Indians" would provide uplift for the nation at large even though it would be expensive and difficult. But he ended his text with an odd warning that "the work of educating and changing the manners and habits of nearly half a million Indians . . . would be great, arduous, and appalling."[6] Exactly what was appalling, the task of dealing with so many unsaved savages, or the calumny of the U.S. treatment of Native nations? Perhaps the fact that half a million Indians still existed, or that so many had managed to remain savages, or that the once teeming world of Indian Country had dwindled to such a small number appalled Morse. Morse's count enumerated 121,344 Native people remaining east of the Mississippi and 350,790 living west of the Mississippi.[7] When we remember that "west of the Mississippi" included only those parts of the region claimed by the United States in 1822, we realize what an undercount this would be. Morse was not counting Indians in Mexican Texas, New Mexico, or California, nor did he count the considerable number of people living in the Pacific Northwest, west of the Rockies, land that was still in British control.

One of the goals of Morse's report was to create a safe place to civilize the remaining Indians. He floated the idea of an all-Indian state to be located in what was then Michigan and what is now Wisconsin. Lewis Cass, as governor of Michigan, agreed it was a good idea but wasn't sure he had the political capital to try it. In 1840 when he had in place an amenable secretary of war, John Bell, Cass made a serious attempt. Bell, Cass, and Henry Schoolcraft, then Indian commissioner for Michigan, made a treaty with the Dakota nation for thirty million acres that went from the Mississippi River, across what is now southern Minnesota, and into South Dakota. The Indian state outlined in the treaty reflected Jedediah Morse's dream: no Euro-Americans were to be allowed into the territory except those authorized by the president (missionaries, agents, teachers); communities with roads, schools, mills, and other improvements would be built; each Native family would be assisted in establishing a small farm; and after two years of "settled living" full citizenship would be granted to male landowners. The president would appoint agents, traders, and a governor for the territory. The treaty went to Congress, but once it got to the floor of the Senate it was tabled with no discussion—squelched by none other than Thomas Hart Benton, who wrote furiously to President Tyler: "The whole scheme of the treaty & the terms of it is in my opinion the most unjustifiable and *reprehensible* thing of a kind that has come before the Senate."[8] He cloaked his fury in language around bypassing the usual laws of creating territories, but he really railed against creating racial and cultural pluralism among governmental structures in the West. Since Benton chaired the Committee on Indian Affairs, that version of the Indian state died there.[9]

Thirty years later, the task of enumerating Native America remained daunting. In 1851, when Henry Rowe Schoolcraft published the first book of his six-volume compendium on the status and history of Indian peoples in the United States, he had made himself into the acknowledged national expert on Native America. He had married Jane Johnston, the half-Ojibwe daughter of a Great Lakes trader, had served the U.S. government in several capacities as trader, agent, and superintendent of Indian affairs, and had held various political offices in Michigan before he retired to New York to write his magnum opus. Despite Schoolcraft's long and deep immersion in Indian Country, he passionately believed in the necessity of Native assimilation into the American fabric. But unlike Morse, and as the father of mixed race children, he never saw Native people purely as savages but as a unique and valuable race that was, unfortunately, doomed to extinction. Individual people could be preserved, but only if they gave up their languages, culture, and economic practices and used education to prepare them for citizenship. Schoolcraft had supported the policy of removal because he believed it would allow Native nations the space and time necessary "for their improvement in arts and for their progress in education in order to be permanently beneficial."[10] In 1847 Congress, anticipating a vast new infusion of Native populations as a result of the Mexican War, directed Schoolcraft to undertake a study of the history and progress of all of the Indian people in the continental United States. Ever thorough, Schoolcraft conducted much of the research himself, but he also sent out questionnaires to every Indian agent, missionary, and trader that he could find. The result, as Schoolcraft put it, was "an abundance of material" that he published in almost impenetrable jumble.[11]

CENSUS AND STATISTICS OF THE SEVERAL INDIAN TRIBES. N.[CONTINUED]

TRIBES.	WHERE LOCATED.	Sabbath schools.	Male scholars.	Female scholars.	Proportion that still adhere to their ancient religion.	Temperance societies.	Members of temperance societies.	Licensed traders.
Christian Indians	Fort Leavenworth agency, north and south of Kansas river	1	7	9	7/8			
Delawares		3	102	91	3/4			
Kickapoos		1	25	27	2/4			
Shawnees					1/4			
Stockbridges								
Sacs and Foxes	Sac and Fox agency, on Osage river				2443			4
Sioux	St. Peter's agency, on St. Peter's river							
Ottowas, Chippewas and Pottawatomies	Council Bluffs sub-agency, on Missouri river							
Pottawatomies	Osage River sub-agency, on Osage river				250			5
Ottowas								1
Chippewas								
Peorias								1
Piankeshaws								3
Weas								1
Wyandots	Wyandot sub-agency, on Kansas river							
Menomonies	Green Bay sub-agency, Wisconsin Territory							
Oneidas		1				1	110	
Stockbridges		1	50	50		1	90	
Seminoles	Seminole sub-agency, north of the Canadian river					1		
Ottowas	Michigan superintendency, Michigan	10	221	245	2/3	12	1514	
Chippewas								
Pottawatomies								
Miamies								
Senecas, on Alleghany reservation	New York agency, New York	2	15	20	9/10	1	70	
Senecas, on Cattaraugus reservation		2	30	33	1/2	2	153[4]	
Tuscaroras		1				1		
Iowas	Great Nemaha sub-agency, on Great Nemaha river		2	6	705			1

628

25. Henry Rowe Schoolcraft's Statistical Compendium., 1851. From Schoolcraft, *Historical and Statistical Information Respecting the History, Condition, and Prospects of the Indian Tribes of the United States*, vol. 3. (Philadelphia: J. B. Lippincott, 1851–57).

This chart, one of thousands in the six-volume tome, provides data for the reader about religious conversion among settled tribes. Schoolcraft was surely crushed to record that among the "Christian Indians" seven-eighths still "adhered to their ancient religion," but he was perhaps encouraged that among the Michigan Ojibwe (into which he had married) there were 1,514 members of temperance societies.

The six volumes, beautifully illustrated with watercolors by Seth East-man, an army officer and artist who also had Native children, come to many of the same conclusions as did Jedediah Morse thirty years earlier: there are a lot of Indians and they show few signs of either assimilating happily or becoming extinct. Ruefully, Schoolcraft notes in his introduc-tion to the vast compendium that among the "some seventy tribes who occupy the continental area east of the Rocky Mountains" with whom the United States has had the object of preserving peace, "no people has ever evinced such a non-appreciating sense of the lessons of experience." He goes on to describe the Indians as "deluded" in their efforts to "preserve a pseudo-nationality" that is "faithless and robberlike." The only solution to this problem, he concludes, is to force them to learn "civil polity, agri-culture, and the arts."[12] For Schoolcraft, and for many of the experts he consulted, there were good Indians who had accepted Christianity, tilled the soil, lived peacefully on reservations, and happily sent their children to school. And there were bad Indians who wandered, lived by the hunt, refused to become Christian, and insisted on their tribal sovereignty. When he actually tried to survey and count them, Schoolcraft found far more bad Indians than good ones, and writing in 1851 he warned that with the end of the Mexican War the nation had taken on hundreds of thousands of the worst Indians.

Schoolcraft's report quoted various "experts," such as David Burnet, former president of the Republic of Texas, who wrote to Schoolcraft that the only solution to the intractable problem of the Comanches "must be their entire and absolute extermination." Burnet explained that the Co-manche and their allies, despite several epidemics, still numbered perhaps twenty thousand so that the state of Texas remained "in their thrall."[13] In a similar vein an Oregon booster, Nathaniel Wyeth, stated authoritatively that all of the Indians of the Pacific Northwest "have no actual ownership of the soil, but rove over it to hunt, steal, and murder." He proposed the creation of reservations supervised by a vast military presence with forts located every few miles, to "suppress Indian outrages" and to "induce them to respect property." Even with such an expenditure, Wyeth admitted he wasn't optimistic. It seemed to him "improbable" that people "who have never planted a seed . . . will ever devote themselves to agriculture's steady labors." Wyeth also noted with some dismay that many of the Rocky Moun-tain Native populations appeared to be "multiplying" in regions that were well supplied with buffalo.[14]

Schoolcraft spends most of his space in each of the huge five-hundred-plus-page volumes describing Native habits and customs, measuring their brains, and documenting their languages, religious ideas, and histories. The end of each volume is dedicated to statistics. Volume one's statistical conclusion is the number of Indians living in the post-1848 United States. Schoolcraft prepares his readers carefully for the number, explaining first that the number of Indians has always been exaggerated. He notes that in his own survey in which information was "wrung from the tribes," Native nations did not cooperate at all in providing the necessary information.[15] But Schoolcraft makes it equally difficult for us to tease out numbers. With 172 questions on his census, he counts things like "the number of females who have studied vocal music" or "the number of pairs of stockings knit" and "number of jugglers and priests" for each grouping of people. Finally, but with much hedging, he decides that the number of Indians in the territorial United States in 1850 is about 400,000, of whom 350,000 are in the "wild" or "barbarous" category, remarkably similar to the number Morse had come up with twenty-five years earlier.[16]

Schoolcraft's careful research had produced poor results. It seemed there could be fewer Indians than before, but also that the numbers had dropped most drastically among the "civilized" tribes. Barbarous Indians, on the other hand, by the mere sweep of the pen that annexed northern Mexico to the United States, had increased in frightening numbers even when he worked very hard to minimize them. After writing passionately that the only path to saving the Indians of the United States lay in forcing them to learn the agricultural and mechanical arts, his numbers demonstrate that the nations who "chose" this route had died off in the greatest numbers. In a truly marvelous twist of logic, Schoolcraft sought to explain this without seeing epidemic disease, land loss, removal, warfare, or the national project of ethnic cleansing as the cause. He wrote: "statistics denote that it is not the curtailment of their territory that has led to Indian depopulation . . . But the ruinous policy of the tribes of keeping large areas untouched by the plough and in a desert state." He concluded with perfect assurance that the real problem was "the excess of indulgence and too heavy annuities" that allowed the wild tribes to continue to exist and that seemed to be killing off the civilized few.[17] Like most government-supported statistical surveyors, Schoolcraft had collected his data to serve a national need: to prove that good Indians were being preserved and that bad Indians were disappearing.[18]

As Mexican administrators struggled to understand the places they had won in a long revolution, their government also tried to count Indians,

especially on the dimly understood far northern border. Several expensive commissions traveled through Texas, New Mexico, and California,
attempting to figure out the extent of Indian and European populations.
A young French scientist, Jean Louis Berlandier, accompanied a scientific
and diplomatic expedition commissioned by the Mexican president in
1828 to find out exactly who and what lived in Texas. His tasks included
ascertaining the borders of Texas, assessing its resources, and estimating
the "disposition, habits, and numbers" of the Indian tribes in the region.
Berlandier served as botanist and zoologist and in that capacity produced
hundreds of sketches and written commentary about the plants, animals,
and people of Texas. With his training as a biologist, Berlandier noted
physical appearance, forms of housing, what people ate, and how they used
plants more than he commented on language, families, or ideology. He
did make judgments about how much each group relied on agriculture,
and he was able to see the seasonal nature of their lives and recognized
the differences between summer villages and winter camps, something
that Morse missed entirely and Schoolcraft de-emphasized in his effort to
find "civilization." And, of course, Berlandier tried to count the Indians.[19]

Berlandier named forty-one nations that lived or raided into Texas, and
with almost heart-breaking Enlightenment confidence he listed them in
alphabetical order from the Aas to the Yutas (or Utes, who did occasionally wander into Texas to trade with the Comanches). Before beginning
his encyclopedic listing, however, he gave a brief history of all the people
who no longer existed, having been decimated by disease and warfare in
the hundred years since the 1720s when Spanish missionaries first began
counting and when Berlandier made his observations. He counted numbers of families and warriors in each nation, and then made an estimate
as to the total population of each group. Ironically, when Berlandier put
his report together, he consulted all the written documents available and
depended heavily on Jedediah Morse's 1822 *Report*, the work of a world-
famous geographer and as such considered entirely reliable. The sum
of the diverse group of humans in Berlandier's Texas came to nearly a
hundred thousand, at least five times that of the Anglo-Tejano population
and nearly three times what Schoolcraft would estimate a bit later. In any
case, it was a figure that must have given Mexican administrators pause.[20]

These "reports" of Native America in the mid-nineteenth century share
an administrative and confident tone in their authors' expectations that
Indian Country is doomed to be an artifact, but that much work remained to
be done before artifact status would be reached. They also share a sense of

awe at the sheer number of peoples and the variety of ways they chose to live their lives in the West. Some nations, like the Comanches, the Cheyennes, the Blackfoot, or the Sioux, expanded and reinvented themselves in the early nineteenth century, demonstrating the resilience of Indian Country centuries into the colonial project of conquest. Some tribal groups, like the Osages, the Cherokees, the Shawnees, and the Navajos, retrenched and re-created themselves in new settings. Others, countless others, disappeared. Victims of disease, warfare, removal, and outright extermination, whole nations of people left few traces in the record.

It is important to avoid telling the story only from the perspective of loss in the present. For people living in the middle decades of the nineteenth century, Indian Country existed. It offered great opportunity, and its residents fought hard to protect it. Some experiences in Indian Country depended on Native relationships to the fur and hide trades and how individual people and nations dealt with the slow denouement of that great industry. Native people, however, had very different experiences—depending on their colonial context, location, and just plain luck.

EXPANDING POWER

If we gave a prize for the scariest reputation attached to western Indian tribes, the Comanches would nearly always win it. John Wayne, playing Texan Ethan Edwards in *The Searchers* (1958), just has to say the word "Com-manch," and we know his captured niece's life is over. Mothers in New Mexico villages scared their children into good behavior by threatening that "los comancheros" would get them. In the movies and in real life the Comanches did capture settlers, soldiers, women, and children. Some they tortured, some they sold as slaves, and some they assimilated. Without warning, they raided and burned settlements. They stole cattle, oxen, and mules and often simply slaughtered them. The Comanches took hundreds of thousands of horses from Apaches, from Navajos, from New Mexican villagers, and from Anglo-Texans. No government entity—Native, Mexican, or U.S.—seemed able to blunt these attacks, and the Comanches were indeed lords of the southern plains by the early nineteenth century. Jean Louis Berlandier, observing them in 1828, explained their brutal tendencies as being "far more like the instinctive fury of wild beasts than like any human passion."[21] Part of this violent reputation was earned, but part of came from Anglo-American and Mexican awe at what these people would do to expand and then protect the power and wealth of their nation.

Much to the frustration of other nations, the Comanches emerged as the most successful imperialists in the region, a position they maintained for nearly a century.[22]

The Comanches achieved this status not only because of their skills as warriors, but also because they knew when to stop fighting and to use trade and diplomacy instead. In general, the southern plains was not a peaceful place and had not been for a long time. Native nations fought among each other and defended against Spanish, Mexican, and Anglo-American intruders, and in doing so they developed rich cultures that celebrated horses, warfare, individual wealth and status, and male warriors at their centers. The Kiowas, Pawnees, Apaches, Cheyennes, and Arapahos, to name a few, shared much of this culture with the Comanches. For the Comanches, the process of removal and warfare that pushed more and more warring tribes into their region also brought unique economic and diplomatic opportunity. Using their diffuse band organization, their practices of capturing and assimilating people into the Comanche world, and their skills at raiding, they built and spread a network of trading relationships based on fear, respect, and economic wisdom. Trading generously and exchanging gifts of people and things with the Comanches proved to be far more practical that fighting them.[23]

The alliances and practices that allowed the Comanches to expand their power and population in the nineteenth century had their roots in the eighteenth century, before European and American settlers were much of a concern. A Shoshonean people, the Comanches (so named by the Utes and the Spanish) arrived on the plains of western Texas and eastern New Mexico around 1700. The region attracted the Comanches because the grassy river valleys of the region seemed ideal for their growing herds of horses. This same micro-environment had also attracted the Apaches, who had farmed and raised animals in these valleys for several generations. Decades of warfare ensued between the two nations, leaving the Comanches firmly in control of the southern plains by the 1730s. The Apaches divided, some moving further east into what would become Texas and others heading south and west nearer to the Pueblos and Navajos. The Plains nations also battled for the prize of the rich Pueblo markets along the Rio Grande and their links to the growing Spanish trade.

The Spanish, however, refused to trade with the Comanches or the Apaches for the items they most coveted—guns, horses, and slaves—thinking this would protect Spanish villagers. Such regulation had the opposite effect: the skilled Comanche raiders simply rode in and took the items they wanted, killing people and burning houses while they did so. In 1747 Comanches raided Abiquiu and the Chama River valley, taking nearly a hundred people. In 1760 raiders swooped into Taos and took sixty women and children. Northern New Mexico turned into a besieged state as the Spanish villagers retreated into the pueblos for protection. When the Comanches couldn't get the goods they needed from the Spanish, they looked to the north and brokered a peace with their traditional enemies, the Wichitas, who had access to French traders and goods from the Mississippi. This extended the Comanche trade network far into the interior of the continent, bringing horses, bison hides, and slaves from the Comanches and Apaches to the east and guns, ammunition, and other manufactured products from the French to the west.[24]

This system served the Comanches very well. They took hundreds of captives from New Mexico villages to boost their population and to help care for the thousands of horses they took from Spanish and Native settlements from the Arkansas River south to Durango in what is now Mexico. Some captives were ransomed for more horses or for other trade goods, whereas others became incorporated into Comanche families, building an invaluable network of human connections and language abilities. This system, however, did not serve the Spanish Crown well at all. To stop the losses Spanish officials sent out regular mounted expeditions, but none of these had much effect. They were expensive, but treaties with Comanche "leaders" were equally ineffectual because of the dispersed and nonhierarchical way the Comanches organized themselves. The only lesson the Comanches learned from such contact was about Spanish weakness, so they continued to raid. Finally, diminished trade, litanies of complaints from priests and governors, and the resulting financial losses to the Crown convinced Spanish officials to send in a professional soldier as governor of New Mexico. Spanish authorities also funded a large increase in the number of mounted troops who could fight the Comanches in their own way and on their own ground.[25]

Don Bautista de Anza, posted to New Mexico as governor in 1779, understood that he had to gain the Comanches' respect through war. With surprising success he attacked the camp of Cuerno Verde, one of the most important war leaders of the Comanches, who had ravished eastern New Mexico in a ten-year reign of terror. De Anza didn't stop with that success but made a series of raids against other Comanche camps, taking captives and horses, and burning lodges, until all of the major leaders had felt the effects of his campaign. De Anza periodically released captives and through them offered to have a peace council with all of the bands in New Mexico. The Comanches realized that a sustained military effort against these Spaniards and their Apache and Ute allies would seriously impinge on their ability to move and trade freely in the region. They agreed to cease fighting in return for better trading arrangements with the Spanish. It took a while to arrange and implement the peace, and it never worked perfectly, but the truce of 1786 allowed co-existence between the Spanish, the Utes, and the Comanches, at least in New Mexico.[26]

The strength that the Comanche got from this peace allowed them to take a stand against Osage expansion in the 1790s. The Osages had dominated the prairie region west of the Mississippi between the Arkansas River and the great bend of the Missouri, and they now prepared to expand further west. The Comanches, however, stood against them in 1789 with a huge mounted force that included the Kiowas. When the united Plains tribes won, the Comanches and Kiowas made the alliance permanent, protecting the central plains until the 1830s. The Osages retreated but began raiding Caddos in Texas and Louisiana and trading with the Comanches, but via the Wichitas. In Texas, where Spanish colonial development trod most lightly, the Comanches, in concert with the Apaches, Wichitas, and Caddos, simply dominated the landscape. Native nations controlled trade, decimated mission herds and flocks, and made it impossible to attract settlers to this region of New Spain. Spanish and Native residents found themselves entirely dependent on Comanche trade networks in order to survive, even though Spanish law forbade trade with the French or with allies of the French. When the Spanish king sent an inspector general, the Marquéz de Rubí, to evaluate conditions on the northern border in 1766, the appalled general returned with a grim report. He described the frontier in Texas as "imaginary," providing no protection whatsoever as the missions had failed and the presidios were deserted, all because of the "warlike Indians who rode horses like demons."[27]

With reports like this, by the early nineteenth century the Spanish had given up on the state of Tejas, leaving only the tiny community of San Antonio de Bexar virtually alone amid Native nations. From this perspective, Texas and what is now eastern New Mexico served as a core of Native power, with Native nations controlling Spanish behavior and wealth, not the other way around, as is the usual picture. As these Native peoples successfully brought the Spanish, and later the Mexicans and Anglo-Americans, into their spheres of influence and dictated how and where trade, war, settlement, and marriage could happen, Native power expanded to cover most of the southern plains.[28]

In both Texas and New Mexico, such power was not upheld by large state or institutional structures, which makes the systems of control harder for us to see. Instead, Native people used networks of kinship to support political and economic systems. The principles of relationships within families, those concepts that determined behavior, rights, status, and obligations, widened to include other entities like bands, tribes, or nations. This relational outlook served as a basic cultural tenet. A person was only the sum of his or her connections and did not exist without a family and a larger tribal or band group. As William Bent, A. P. Chouteau, Marguerite McLoughlin, George Sibley, and Sam Houston all understood, one's kin designation within a tribe was the starting point for all interactions. Such a designation carried with it a complex series of mutual obligations, and if a person upheld these obligations and the webbed patterns of honor and respect they indicated, that person was kin. On the southern plains, in the world of the Comanches, anyone wanting to survive and prosper needed to nurture these relationships. Trade and prosperity depended on being allowed to access Comanche trade networks, and everyone understood this at the beginning of the nineteenth century.[29]

THE SANTA FE TRAIL

Such careful balances were upset by a widening circle of events far beyond Indian Country. On the plains two such events were the Mexican Revolution and the opening of the Santa Fe Trail in 1821. Suddenly the people of the southern plains had an economic highway running through their world, bringing considerable numbers of new people who were emphatically not kin, and who encouraged others to break rules about hunting and raiding because they wanted buffalo hides. The path of the trail followed a series of rivers that formed an approximate border between the peoples of the central plains and the peoples of the southern plains, which made the pathway vulnerable from all directions. The U.S. government now wanted to make "peace" with the tribes to make use of the trail and to establish new economic links with Mexico and Plains nations. Small groups of trappers and traders had used it illegally for years, and the presence of the Plains tribes made this a particularly risky undertaking. Pawnee warriors raided A. P. Chouteau and his trading party along the Arkansas River in what is now Kansas in 1816. They lost a year's worth of trade goods, furs, and hides, along with the lives of several men. This episode convinced A.P. to give up the dangers of trapping and trading in the southern Rocky Mountains and to settle with the Osages along the eastern edge of the Arkansas, where he had family and understood the rules.

A. P. Chouteau appears again to play an important role as a treaty nego-tiator with various Arkansas and central Plains tribes. With his experience as a trader and his deep familial ties to the Osages, he understood more about the situation than most Euro-Americans. A.P opened a series of trading posts along the Arkansas and Canadian rivers, gradually moving further west following the Osages, who were trying to find places to hunt away from the Cherokees, who had been removed to lands the Osages believed were theirs. Inevitably, as they moved west the Osages ran into lands and nations involved in the Comanche trade network. The Osage shift westward in the 1820s coincided with the legal opening of the Santa Fe Trail. Legal did not mean safe or easy. As entrepreneurs traveled west with their carts loaded with blankets, cloth, guns, alcohol, and powder, they ran right into the midst of this readjustment among Native nations. As traffic along the Arkansas increased, so too did raids by the Osages, Pawnees, and Cheyennes from the north and the Plains Apaches, Kiowas, and Comanches from the south. The governments and armies of both Mexico and the United States found themselves entirely unable to stop the raiding or even to blunt its economic impact. In 1824 the army built and staffed Fort Gibson, from which they hoped to enforce treaties among the newly removed Native nations and to protect Anglo-American travelers in the region from the Native residents of the central and southern plains.

Because the survival of his family and his business depended on creat-ing peaceful relationships with the Plains nations, A. P. Chouteau worked furiously as a negotiator for the United States in several crucial rounds of treaty making. The process of treaty making played out in a familiar pat-tern. Both Native nations and the United States attempted to explain the compromises that a treaty would involve, but they rarely upheld it longer than it took the ink to dry. The language of treaties always involved familial terms and analogies because U.S. officials did understand how important these were to Native people. The language always placed the United States as father and tribal people as children—meaning, in fact, that the Native "children" had few responsibilities, and neither side had any reason to fulfill their obligations. When Native groups developed peace and trade agreements among themselves, they depended on more complex kin rela-tions like brother, sister, uncle, or father-in-law to support these arrange-ments, which necessitated creating real familial bonds that carried lasting mutual obligations.[30]

Two examples should suffice to demonstrate the problems that treaties created: they made commitments that no one could uphold, and each treaty seemed to be made in a vacuum as if no earlier agreements had ever been made. In 1830 the U.S. government signed the Treaty of Dancing Rabbit Creek with the Mississippi Choctaws, which required the Choctaws to give up land in Mississippi for an equal amount of land in what is now Oklahoma and northern Texas just south of the Santa Fe Trail—squarely in Comanche and Wichita territory. Almost immediately upon the Choctaws' arrival, they began having their animals and property stolen by raiding Comanches, who had not signed any treaty. These challenges were in addition to the constant problem with the Osages, who had papers from the treaties of 1808 and 1822 saying that the land was theirs. Recognizing the delicacy of the problem, President Andrew Jackson appointed a special commission to examine the situation. The Stokes Commission, consisting of Jackson's cronies and easterners with little experience with Native people, established their headquarters at Fort Gibson in 1832. After consulting with military officials and agents, the commission recommended a peace council. Bringing frustrated enemies together to discuss an almost insoluble problem did not always result in peace. In 1833 a treaty negotiation between the Osages, Kiowas, Pawnees, Cherokees, and Choctaws at Fort Gibson fell apart completely because of simmering resentments over land agreements, resulting in a terrible attack on the Kiowas by the Osages, which reverberated out to various other tribes.[31]

The following summer the commander at Fort Gibson, General Henry Leavenworth (whom we last saw being pilloried by St. Louis fur traders for his dismal performance against the Arikaras), determined to bring all of these nations together in a grand effort to create peace. He planned a military tour of the region between the Arkansas and Red rivers, which meant, of course, taking a large military force along the border with Mexican Texas, giving the expedition a decidedly political cast at a moment when the situation in Texas was decidedly revolutionary. Mostly, though, Leavenworth planned to overawe the Native nations of the region. A. P. Chouteau, appointed by Leavenworth to accompany his First Regiment of Mounted Dragoons, arrived with a troop of six hundred Osages to assist the dragoons and to advise them on how to negotiate with the various groups they might find. George Catlin, the famed portraitist of many Native people, traveled with the expedition, which he called "the first grand civilized foray, into the country of the wild and warlike Camanchees."[32]

This "foray" was not, perhaps, the finest moment of the western army.

26. George Catlin, *Two Comanche Girls*, 1834. Comanche/Niuam. Oil, 29 x 24 in. Smithsonian American Art Museum, Gift of Mrs. Joseph Harrison Jr.

Catlin traveled as an official artist with Colonel Henry Dodge's diplomatic tour through the southern plains. Intending to make peace and trade treaties with the Comanches, Kiowas, and Osages, the expedition failed. Catlin, however, brought back the first views of peaceful, playful Comanches that most Anglo-Americans had seen.

Bilious fever of some sort broke out among the troops, and Leavenworth died from injuries sustained while attempting to hunt buffalo, leaving Colonel Henry Dodge in charge. With his slow-moving but beautifully uniformed troops, many ill with fever, Dodge had a hard time finding any Comanches. The Comanches found them instead and ran off most of their horses but finally allowed the horseless dragoons to meet with members of one band encamped with some Kiowas. When Chouteau and the Osages arrived, their presence infuriated the Kiowas until the Osages produced a young girl they had captured the summer before and ceremoniously made peace with the offering of this child. Dodge, not exactly understanding what happened, was still enormously relieved. When thousands of Kiowas and Comanches gathered in the next few days, Dodge and his pitifully sickly troops were entirely outnumbered. With Chouteau's advice about utilizing timely prisoner and horse exchanges, Dodge convinced some Comanches and Kiowas to accompany him back to Fort Gibson for a negotiation with all of the tribes.[33]

Dodge may have genuinely believed that the dozen or so warriors that traveled with him could make binding agreements and represent all of the Kiowas and Comanches, but Chouteau surely understood the foolishness of such an assumption. The Comanches saw themselves at a zenith of prestige and power. With perhaps thirty thousand people spread from what is now northern Mexico to the Arkansas River in Kansas, they had defeated and deflected all European threats and had made wise and lasting alliances with many of their traditional enemies, with the exception of the Osages, in order to improve trade and hunting. Because they controlled the source of horses, northern Mexico, and were the only Native group to breed horses regularly and successfully, other tribes usually came to them. Surely they put the pitiful U.S. troops in this category. Obviously the Americans needed new and better horses, and they seemed willing to entertain, feed, and trade with the Comanches to get them. The Comanches, ever the astute traders, cemented their new trading relationships by giving gifts of horses. At the treaty council in September of 1834 the Comanches attending received silver peace medals and American flags as tokens of their allegiance, but the Comanches saw it rather differently. The Comanches present agreed to stay away from the Santa Fe Trail, and the Osages promised to stop raiding their "friends" the Cherokees, but little changed. Colonel Dodge found himself on the plains again the following two summers, making other agreements that would never work. The Comanches had little intent of changing their behavior unless it benefited them.[34]

A different and more lasting agreement brokered by Native nations around their own concerns evolved further west on the Great Plains and made that part of the Santa Fe Trail much more peaceful. In what is now Kansas and Colorado, new groups of people had gathered to take advantage of the great herds of buffalo on the edges of Kiowa and Comanche territory. The Cheyennes and Arapahos (and the Bents and their traders) had remained outside of Comanche concerns until the 1830s, when their activities began to interfere with Comanche hunts. More particularly, a vicious war between the Kiowas and the Cheyennes had disturbed peace and prosperity in 1838 and had escalated raiding to an intolerable level. The Comanches, on the other hand, decided that these northern tribes rarely ventured into their territory south of the Arkansas River and, in fact, provided a new source of trade with the creation of Bent's Fort in the 1830s. The Cheyennes served as middlemen between Plains traders and Comanche hunters, a lucrative arrangement for everyone. As a result, the major bands of the western Comanches and Kiowas decided it was to their advantage to formalize a peace. William Bent offered his fort as a site for a council, but he had little to do with the agreement they hammered out there in 1840. Called the Great Peace, it created a nonraiding and open-hunting agreement between the tribes, which seemed advantageous at the time. However, the agreement had two results: there was massive overhunting of buffalo in the new peace zone, and Bent's Fort, rather than Comanche traders, became the central focus of plains trade. No one participating in the feasting and exchanging of gifts that summer of 1840, however, could have predicted the effects of this new reality. From the Comanche perspective, the northeastern reaches of their territory offered respite from a host of other problems created by revolution and rebellion in Texas.[35]

NATIVE NATIONS AND TEXAS REVOLUTION

But Cynthia is a Chieftain's wife—
She can never be white again"

From "The Ballad of Cynthia Ann Parker," William Ward, 1935

The Comanches nearly ruined the hopes that the new nation of Mexico had for its northern states. The liberal dynamic that created revolution in Mexico also drove new ambitions for economic and social development. New citizens, politicians, and administrators of Mexico faced their revolutionary moment with optimism, but also with empty pockets—the curse of new governments everywhere. The Mexican government looked to its northern states and territories to provide cash and protection from its increasingly aggressive neighbor, the United States. One inexpensive solution involved encouraging immigrants to populate these regions with people who would be loyal to the Mexican government and who would farm or develop trades that would, in turn, provide money for the Mexican state. Mexican officials had various schemes about encouraging colonization with disgruntled people from all over Europe or with Mexican citizens who couldn't afford land in their home districts, but the plans cost money. The cheapest and quickest solution was to grant large tracts of land to empresarios and speculators who would then take on the burden of finding people to move to Texas, New Mexico, or California.

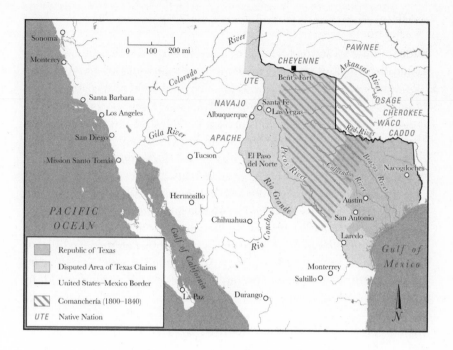

9. Mexico, Texas, and the Comanche Borderlands, 1830–48

We already know the cast of characters that appeared in the northern territories and states of Mexico as a result of these policies. In Coahuila y Tejas (the state that encompassed what we think of as central Texas) Stephen Austin and other Mexican and American empresarios brought in thousands of Anglo-American colonists and their slaves. In New Mexico we see people like the Bent brothers at Bent's Fort or Taos taking advantage of new trade polices rather than land grants, but significant numbers of Americans moved to New Mexico in those years. The new colonists brought cattle, horses, and mules, and these people and animals ran into the people and animals already living there. The Comanches and other raiding nations found the new handily corralled animal population especially tempting, making conflicts with the settlers almost inevitable. For Mexican officials and American empresarios and traders alike, the Comanches and other southern Plains tribes were both important allies and deadly foes. Many immigrants and colonists traded agricultural products, cattle, and leather goods with the Comanches, getting horses, captives, and a range of other trade goods in return. They also learned that Comanche raids and reputation also served as an effective barrier against Anglo and Native American incursions from the north.

More importantly, and less obvious to newcomers like Austin or his Mexican counterparts, the Comanches and other tribal people had interstitched themselves into the culture of Hispanic Texas and New Mexico. Comanche people had intermarried with villagers, both Native and Spanish, and had taken lots of captives who often chose to stay with the Comanches or who became important trade negotiators. Especially in New Mexico, Indian trade fairs, where nations gathered from all over the southern plains and northern Mexico, had essentially become family reunions. These reunions always had a deadly cast because of the way kinship, vengeance, and honor were tied together in this cultural setting. Violence became part of daily life. Villagers in Texas or New Mexico did not accommodate to the Comanches, Apaches, or Kiowas easily or happily; they did it in fear for their lives, but they became part of a trade and family network that made their lives possible. Spanish colonial governments recognized that they had no hope of controlling powerful Native nations, nor did they want to. They understood that losing some cattle, sheep, and horses in raids was a part of doing business, and so was the fact of captivity and slavery. People who came to Texas and New Mexico after 1821—colonists, government officials, and military men—did not understand such vital facts of accommodation.[36]

In Texas the Comanches initially welcomed the new American colonists, seeing them as just another group that would be part of their network. Since the Spanish had never attempted to dominate the Texas Indians, they had no expectation that the Mexican or the American governments would do anything differently. Almost immediately Comanches began taking horses, cattle, and people. They expected a diplomatic response and a round of present-giving and horse-and-women-returning—the practice of several generations. Because of the location of Austin's colonies to the south and east of Comanchería, the Comanches remained a distant concern in the early years. The local Native nations, the Karankawas and Tonkawas primarily, provided plenty for Austin to worry about. This situation made it very difficult for empresarios or the Mexican government to attract and retain settlers. Much of Stephen Austin's angst over his fledgling community came from Native raiding, which focused his attention in 1823, again in 1825 and 1826. Many of the festering issues among Anglo-Americans that led to various rebellions in the period leading up to 1836 had at their root the settlers' fear and frustration that the Mexican government could not protect its citizens from Native attacks. When the Texas Revolution became war rather than talk in 1835, Austin worried a great deal about how the surrounding Native nations would respond.[37]

Northeastern Texas had evolved into a bewildering mixture of local Caddo Indians and various immigrant tribes including the Cherokees, Shawnees, Delawares, Kickapoos, and Quapaws, who had developed their own communities and demanded land grants from the Mexican government. Only the Cherokees had received any promise of land, but even this was tenuous as Anglo-American and Mexican empresarios drew up land schemes on paper, and squatters simply took the land they wanted. Mexican officials feared the arrival of more immigrant Indians, but they worried more about immigrating Anglos and the powerful Comanches. Between 1829 and 1831, in return for some promises about land, the Mexican army tried to convince the immigrant Indians to join them in campaigns against the Comanches and Wichitas. Most refused, because they had made trade agreements and hunting arrangements with the Comanches. Instead, the army relied on local Euro-American citizens, who bravely burned deserted Waco and Wichita settlements but avoided real contact with the Comanches until 1831. That year Anglo volunteers killed the Waco and Comanche leaders who had been among the few arguing for peace with the Mexicans and Americans. A Shawnee troop attacked and killed nearly a hundred Comanches near San Antonio in 1832. Now, the immigrant Indians and the Anglo-Texans had made themselves worthy of Comanche attention.[38]

Politics complicated the situation as the Mexican government declared war on the Comanches and Wichitas without the troops or the experience to take on such a project. Their stated desire to take on the Plains tribes had more to do with presenting a stronger military presence to the visibly rebellious Anglo-Texans. The smattering of raids on Comanche villages proved to be only annoying and may have increased attacks on Anglo communities, especially small outlying settlements beyond the Brazos country as the 1830s progressed. Generally, the unrest involved cattle and horse stealing on both sides, but in 1835 and early 1836 Anglos were killed in retaliatory raids. The horse stealing had been ratcheted up by Anglos who needed horses to fight the Mexicans in the brewing revolution, and who began raiding Comanche camps more regularly to get them.[39]

Sam Houston, one of those frontier figures who appear at an improbable number of crucial moments, became the point man for dealing with Indian nations. Houston had his own tangled history with the Cherokees in Tennessee and on the Arkansas River. He had also served with Andrew Jackson in the War of 1812, so he knew something about Indian warfare and Native relationships. The Stokes Commission, created by Andrew Jackson to solve the Indian problems on the border, had hired Houston to work with the western Plains tribes in 1832. After wandering around the plains for a summer and writing a series of private reports for Andrew Jackson about the Texas crucible of war, Houston arrived in Texas in 1833 to work for a different government. Immediately he became ensnarled in the thorny situation with the Texas Indians. He became Stephen Austin's military advisor and used his own personal contacts among the Cherokees to broker a deal with the northern immigrant tribes. In return for neutrality in a potential revolution, he promised the allied Cherokees, Shawnees, Delawares, Kickapoos, Quapaws, and Caddos land and annuities.[40]

As the Texas Revolution unfolded, the simmering troubles with the Comanches evolved into all-out war. Northern bands of Comanches and Kiowas, recognizing the advantages of attacking during this chaotic moment, made several destructive raids in 1836. After the Alamo and the Battle of San Jacinto, Texans may have found themselves independent of the Mexican government, but this freedom did not solve the far greater practical problem they faced with the Comanches and the other Plains tribes. A few infamous raids and captures suddenly made the Comanches the central issue for the new Texas government, amazingly enough led by Sam Houston.

Less than a month after the Battle of San Jacinto, in May of 1836, a band of Comanches raided Parker's Fort, an isolated community on the western fringes of Anglo-Texan settlement. They killed five men, injured several women, took two women and three children as captives, and rode off into the west. From the Comanche perspective, the raid had gone well. No Comanches had been hurt, and they had two women and three children. The two women, Rachel Plummer and Elizabeth Kellogg, suffered through months and years of travel, torture, and derision before they were ransomed by their families. The children, Cynthia Ann Parker and John Parker, aged nine and six, and James Pratt, just a year old, quickly became part of the Comanche band, speaking the people's language, wearing Native dress, and learning to ride. Cynthia Ann assimilated fully and became the wife of Peta Necoma, an important leader. They would produce a son, Quanah Parker, the "last chief" of the Comanches. For Texans, the Parker raid and the fate of the captives became fearful news that spread quickly. It presaged a decade of terrifying warfare that included hundreds of raids like the one endured by the Parkers.[41]

Anglo-Texans demanded that their government act—that expeditions be sent out, that forts be built, and that all Indians be punished for these heinous acts—but the new republic had no resources to do any of these things. Indians were punished, but mostly the immigrant nations clustered in the north who had supported the Texas cause in the war and who had not instigated these raids. Prefiguring the pattern that would emerge in the United States in the 1840s and 1850s, the president of the Republic of Texas, Sam Houston, made peace and official agreements with the tribes, recognizing that this approach would be cheaper and less bloody. The Texas senate, however, had little interest in giving land or status to Indians and nullified most of the treaties, undermining any credibility the new state might have earned with Native nations. Houston also entreated the U.S. Army, especially General Edmund Gaines, commander at Fort Gibson just north of the Texas border, to help protect the border against the Plains tribes. Gaines sent in the dragoons to the Red River and built a blockhouse in Nacogdoches, which was, of course, still in Mexican territory, but the U.S. Army couldn't just invade Texas, given its messy diplomatic status.[42]

Angered by the snub from the Texas senate and feeling threatened by roving rangers and U.S. dragoons, various groups of Indians made their own agreements and began attacking Texas settlements. As the conflict spread across Texas and the southern plains, it became centered on women and children, which each side saw very differently. Wild Indians who would capture women, rape and torture them, and turn white children into

Indians became the fear of all Anglo-Texan households. Texas Rangers, who would shoot and kill Native women and children, conduct unheard of among Plains people, became feared as brutal murderers. An alliance of Shawnees, Cherokees, and Mexican Tejanos made threatening gestures, and in 1838 the Kickapoo War—which actually included Kickapoos, Cherokees, Caddos, Biloxis, and more Tejanos—began with raiding along the Trinity River. Texans used this outbreak of violence as proof that Houston's peace policy was entirely wrong-headed, and they demanded vengeance. They also demanded that the U.S. Army step in, since these Indians had migrated from Indian Territory and were, therefore, the problem of the United States. The new president of Texas, Mirabeau Lamar, promised he would "remove all of the emigrant tribes now living in Texas" and began with the Cherokees.[43]

Lamar ensured war with the Cherokees in 1839 when he sent a message to Duwali (a.k.a. Chief Bowles), the Cherokee leader who had made agreements with both the Mexican government and with President Sam Houston, stating blunting that Texas would never approve Cherokee land claims. He insisted that "the red man and the white man cannot dwell together," which in his view meant that "the Cherokee will never be permitted to establish a permanent jurisdiction." Lamar backed up his threat with military action.[44] A few months later Texas troops marched to the Cherokee, Shawnee, and Delaware villages and demanded that the people "peacefully remove themselves." The Indians first simply refused to acknowledge the situation, but after consulting with their people they demanded monetary recompense for their improvements and property and asked for two months to prepare for a move. The commander of the Texas troops decided that the Cherokees were simply stalling and informed them that the army would now march on the villages. The Cherokees stood their ground, but badly outnumbered and with almost no ammunition, they retreated to the north to gather their allies. On July 16, 1839, a force of Cherokees, Kickapoos, Shawnees, and Delawares took on the Texas troops. They repulsed two advances, but in the end one hundred Cherokee warriors died that day, along with five white Texans and the eighty-three-year-old Duwali, who survived until the very end, when he was shot in the head at close range. The troops burned the villages, and the people fled Texas with absolutely nothing. By 1840 nearly all of the immigrant Indians in Texas had been killed, had succumbed to epidemic disease, or had fled to Indian Country, just over the Red River to the north.[45]

Such tactics would not solve the challenge of the Comanche, Wichita, and other Plains tribes who truly threatened the existence of the Texas Republic. Sam Houston had recognized the danger and wanted to make trade agreements and alliances as the core of Indian policy, rather than war. The challenges presented by the Comanches did not find any real solution under President Lamar either, whose only proposal was removal and extermination. As Indian raids increased, so did Lamar's demands for an intensive military intervention. However, the land and people he claimed to be protecting were clearly living outside the borders of the Texas Republic and on Comanche lands. To solve that political problem, Lamar simply refused to define the borders of Texas. The military problem, the fact that Texas had no standing army or any professional soldiers, proved to be trickier to solve. Lamar mounted the first official expedition of Texas Rangers, volunteers, and Apache scouts in 1839. Essentially local militia groups, the Rangers included paid soldiers who served for only very short stints of three months or less and local volunteers. They weren't well trained and had poor equipment, but they were angry and needed to protect their families. This expedition succeeded in surprising a Comanche village on the San Saba River. They killed sleeping families and then fell back when the Comanche warriors came at them. The Apache scouts, frustrated by the entire affair, stole the Rangers' horses so that many of the men had to return to east Texas on foot. Retribution for this massacre created a huge wave of attacks on settlements along the upper Brazos, Colorado, and Trinity rivers, so that many Anglo-Texans abandoned their homes and retreated east. Lamar responded with more Ranger expeditions against Comanche villages, making western Texas into a war zone.[46]

Early in 1840 some Comanches suggested a peace council to be held in San Antonio, which had been a neutral zone for diplomatic negotiations for at least a century. The Texas government appointed a set of commissioners, all men who had been notoriously anti-Indian in the Senate and who had no experience in conducting diplomatic meetings with Native nations. They also prepared numerous troops to be at the ready. The Comanches arrived, warriors dressed in full regalia, and paraded into the central plaza at San Antonio. Women and children followed, indicating the groups' peaceful intentions. The Comanche leaders and Texan commissioners met in the local jail, which had a large council room. After a brief ceremonial greeting, the Texans announced that the Comanche warriors would be held as captives until all white captives were returned. Because captivity was an intolerable insult to male Comanche honor, all hell broke loose. Troops poured in, but the melee continued until all the

Comanche leaders were dead, more were killed outside in the plaza, and blood poured from the council room.[47]

In the same way that Comanche raids became part of white Texas culture, the Council House Massacre became legend in Comanche history, told and retold as proof that the war with Anglo-Texans could never end. More immediately, Comanche honor demanded vengeance for the thirty men who had been killed. They were patient in planning for this vengeance and knew that they needed more allies and more guns. This brings us back to the Great Peace between the Comanches and the Cheyennes, negotiated at Bent's Fort that summer of 1840 while the Comanches still mourned the victims of the Council House Massacre. The Comanche gave away many horses at that peace council, but they also got guns and munitions as well as promises of military alliance with their neighbors to the north. Feeling that their northern border was secure and that they had a new source of military supplies from Bent's Fort, the Comanches made war on Texas. From the coast at Victoria where the Guadalupe River comes inland, where Comanche raiders took 1,500 horses, to the Hill Country of central Texas, the Comanches raided at will. Ultimately, the Comanches lost, and the victories of the early 1840s proved to be illusory. However, neither Mirabeau Lamar nor his Texas Rangers nor the U.S. Army could remove the Comanches, much less exterminate them. The Hill Country of Texas, where the city of Austin is now located, did become safer for Anglo-Texan land acquisition, but it took a very long time.[48]

It would take thirty more years and the full attention of the U.S. Army to drive the Comanches from their strongholds in the southern plains and to disrupt the trade network that covered half a continent. Comanche persistence led to political turmoil in Texas as Anglo-Texans ousted President Lamar and the reelected Sam Houston, since Lamar's policies had only brought war and suffering and the Comanches were still there. Because of Lamar's policies, and especially because of the Council House Massacre, no Comanche leaders responded to diplomatic or peace overtures made by Texans or by commissioners from the United States. What Comanches wanted and what Texans and other Anglo-Americans could not tolerate was a true frontier region where Indian Country could blend with the United States. They wanted a place where marriage and presents would create flexibility around the bounds of polite society, and where raiders could continue to raid and farmers could continue to farm, much as had existed in Missouri or New Mexico or Texas before the 1820s. Such accommodations were no longer possible as land acquisition replaced trade as the central facet of the western political economy.

Throughout the 1840s and 1850s, Comanche territory shrank, but Comanches remained part of a large trade network that extended from northern Mexico to St. Louis and the Great Lakes. They could not know, or even imagine, that the millions of buffalo, beaver, fox, otter, and deer that made trade possible would be hunted out and nearly exterminated as a result of the vigorous system the Comanches had created. The collapse of buffalo populations and germs that carried epidemic disease would finally achieve what military strategy or national policy could not: the captivity of the Comanches.

RETRENCHMENT AND RESISTANCE

Few tribes had as much success as the Comanches in protecting their interests and their land. For most Native nations, the presence of new peoples changed the way they lived, forcing them to retrench and remake their worlds. But their homes remained Indian Country, and Euro-Americans who ventured there still had to accommodate to Native ways. In California the end of Spanish rule and a new Mexican government and economy changed the lives of many Native people there. The huge expansion of the hide and tallow industry, and the horse and mule trade that accompanied it, came along with the end of the missions along the coastal strip and made a great difference in the lives of Indians. Europeans and Californios now needed their skills and labor more than they needed their souls, but Native people were often not willing to participate on European terms. Californians of all races and classes had to figure out new ways of living together. Along the Arkansas River, in what would become Indian Territory, new groupings of Native people had to figure out how to live together. We'll focus there primarily on the experience of the Osages. In both places Native people faced bad choices imposed on them by a new political economy and, ironically, by new and enthusiastic liberal republics.

In the 1820s and 1830s both Mexico and the United States experienced a wave of republican and liberal feeling. The Mexican Revolution and the Jacksonian political persuasion created an appetite for extending democracy and building a more inclusive polity. In both Mexico and the United States politicians, policymakers, and citizens supported this political stance with programs to give vast numbers of new citizens access to the blessings of land ownership. Such ideologies and policies had significant impact on Native nations living in regions claimed by Mexico and the United States. Though it is very difficult for us not to be cynical about this ambition now and to focus on the racist limitations of such visions, Anglo-Americans and Mexicans recognized the problem and tried to come up with policies that served the national agenda and protected Native people. The national agenda, of course, came first, but the effort to make sensible and liberal policies was real. The effort, the Native response to it, and its serious failures evolved in surprisingly similar ways in the two nations.

In Mexico, leaders saw the political and cultural challenge of building a nation that included indigenous people. They abolished racial distinctions and granted Indian men full citizenship in their first revolutionary acts. Mexican political leaders saw this as a generous act that would free Native people from oppressive Spanish rule and allow them to abandon their backward and unenlightened ways. Native people, on the other hand, often saw the citizenship and land policies as more oppression and a threat to their lives and land. They resisted these changes by fleeing, by refusing to participate, and with armed revolt. Many Mexican officials saw this response as proof of the barbarity of Indians, which made their use of force legitimate. To build the inclusive nation, Native communities had to be broken up and the land distributed so that it could be developed for the good of the nation.[49]

In California the effort to free Indian people from the chains of Spain included liberating the mission Indians and subjugating Native groups who lived further in the interior. Secularizing the missions, a long-stated intent of Spanish authorities and priests, became the project of the new Mexican nation and in California was its centerpiece. At first, Mexican Californians envisioned a gradual organization of the missions into Indian villages so that Indians might take up farming their own land under the supervision of priests and soldiers. However, in 1833 this plan had not progressed beyond words largely because the missions had become wealthy and powerful institutions in Alta California, and the Catholic Church resisted giving them up. Frustrated by lack of progress and determined to wrest land and money away from the church, Governor José Figueroa passed and implemented the Secularization Act that year. Figueroa and many other Californios firmly believed that the mission control of coastal lands had stunted the economic development of California, partly because the missions controlled the labor of so many Native people. With a stroke of a pen Figueroa ended the mission system, but Mexicans and Indians alike soon discovered how challenging the process of dismantling the missions would be.[50]

In the United States, Andrew Jackson's newly appointed secretary of war,

Lewis Cass, went about "regularizing" Indian policy in 1828. By 1833 he had created a new Indian Department and had shepherded a massive piece of legislation around Indian matters through Congress. The Intercourse Act of 1834 put legislative supervision around the Indian service, with rules and financial procedures for Indian agents, codified and updated a vast body of trade and intercourse laws, and set about fulfilling the promises made to the removed Indians for their protection and government. Much of Cass's information came from the Stokes Commission that he had sent to Fort Gibson in 1832 to assess the situation among western and immigrant Indians. The news they brought back convinced Cass that significant changes in policy had to be made, particularly in dealing with hostilities evolving between immigrant and removed Indians who had been placed on the lands of the Plains tribes. The centerpiece of a solution would be some kind of Indian state that would be governed by Indians but supervised by Indian Department officials. Where it would be located, however, stymied everyone. What emerged from the long congressional discussion about such possibilities was the Permanent Indian Frontier. Rather than a state, this frontier included a zone of military forts that extended from the Red River north along the Arkansas-Oklahoma and Missouri-Kansas border and then up the Missouri River as far north as the Dakotas. Though flawed and obsolete before it could even be put into place, the concept of the Permanent Indian Frontier seemed rational and humane in the context of the early 1830s. Separating white people from red people and removed nations from Plains nations, however, became a truly "appalling" task, as Jedediah Morse had warned.[51]

Policy, however, rarely anticipates the way people actually behave. Instead it often involves magical thinking in which people behave as "rational actors" or as administrators wish they would comport themselves. Mexican Californios wished several conflicting things about their relationships with Native people: that Indian people would work happily on the ranchos, that they would stop raiding for cattle and horses, that Californios could become less dependent on Indian labor, and that these Indios would become Christians and even citizens. Native Californians had similar contradictory wishes: that the Californios would leave them alone, that they could develop trade relationships with both Californios and the foreigners who came into the backcountry, and that Indians could have mission lands. No one got their wishes granted.

The tension between Mexican Californios and Native people developed out of the conflicting rationale for secularizing the missions. Though the missions had failed entirely at converting Native Californians to Christianity, they had succeeded impressively in economic development. The Crown had established them for the purpose of creating a frontier zone to protect New Spain from foreign or Native invasion, but it quickly realized that frontier outposts needed to be self-sufficient. Spanish officials granted missions the right to use and develop vast tracts of land, and they encouraged the Spanish fathers to use their converts to plant crops and develop industries that would feed soldiers, priests, and citizens. Mission San Fernando embraced over fifty square leagues, or nearly 350 square miles. In 1822 Mission San Diego reported that its lands extended to the south 13 leagues, to the east 17 leagues, and to the north 7 leagues. In the same year, Mission Santa Barbara estimated its land holdings at about 28 square leagues or close to 122,000 acres. By 1834 land and holdings of the twenty-three missions were worth an estimated $78 million. And all of this wealth had been built by Native labor.[52]

By the early nineteenth century the missions were crucial to the existence of Alta California. Native people cultivated crops, including wheat, corn, barley, and beans that totaled nearly 60,000 *fanegas*—more than thirty times the amount produced three decades earlier. After the 1790s, once the Indians had learned new crafts and trades, the missions became veritable general stores. Indian women learned to spin, weave, and sew and provided Mexican Californians with blankets, clothing, and church vestments. They made soap and candles, gathered herbs and medicines to cure people, cooked, and laundered. Native men worked in the fields to produce food to feed Californians, but they also tended cattle and made leather goods: the shoes and boots people wore every day, the saddles in which they rode, and the bridles that controlled their horses. Men also made olive oil and worked the wine presses, making products that allowed California to become a true outpost of the Mediterranean world. When the mission period ended, Native Californians who had survived had a broad range of artisanal skills that Mexican Californians would need if the region were to prosper.[53]

From the beginning local citizens, mostly soldiers who had retired after serving in the mission presidios, eyed the mission lands and labor force with envy. The only path to wealth and security in Alta California was through land, and the missions held the most desirable pieces. Until 1821 and the Mexican Revolution, few Californios could imagine they would ever own land. A few special favorites had been given grants of land by the Crown as reward for military or civil service, but this remained a rare privilege. The

Crown made only twenty grants of land between 1769 and 1821. Everything changed with the Mexican Revolution in 1821 and especially with the Colonization Act of 1824, which encouraged settlement of families and foreigners, rather than just soldiers, with promises of land and freedom from taxes. The number of grants for ranchos exploded, limited only by the frustrating fact of the missions and their occupation of prime land. Many Mexican Californios began to push for the restoration of mission lands to the public domain so that settlers could take them up.[54]

Native people made solving this problem sticky in two ways. First, the missions were never intended as permanent settlements—each mission was to be converted into a civil community within a decade after its establishment. Theoretically the Franciscans served as trustees for the Indian neophytes until the Native Californians were judged to have reached a state of civilization that would allow them to take title to the mission lands. Apparently, no mission Indians had ever reached this status, and the Secularization Act was intended to speed up this process by making Indians landowners and self-sustaining. When Governor Figueroa announced a plan to implement secularization in 1834, he insisted that half of the mission lands would be given to former mission Indians, along with tools, seeds, and livestock. Secular priests, or *mayordomos*, appointed by the governor would oversee the process of adjustment. The rest of the mission lands could now be granted, and Mexican governors were overwhelmed with more than seven hundred requests for land grants between 1834 and 1846. Millions of acres of land went into the hands of Mexican Californians and foreign colonists to create the base for the ranching economy that developed almost overnight.[55]

Second, once Mexican Californians got their hands on mission land, they needed Indian labor to make it profitable. When the missions were secularized and the priests left, many Native people voted with their feet and left as well. Even with the promise of land, stock, and tools, many preferred to return to their villages or rancherías and simply refused to work anywhere near the missions where they had been so brutalized. Carey McWilliams expressed the vicious reality about what happened at the missions when he wrote in 1946: "during the entire period of Mission rule, from 1769 to 1834, the Franciscans baptized 53,600 adult Indians and buried 37,000. . . . So far as the Indians were concerned, the chain of Missions along the coast might best be described as a series of picturesque charnel houses."[56] In spite the human loss the missions inflicted on Native Californians, they always had choices (if not always good ones) about how to accommodate to these bad situations. Mexican Californians recognized

27. "Indians Who Worked for Phineas Banning," ca. 1853. Unknown photographer. This item is reproduced by permission of *The Huntington Library, San Marino, California.* (photCL180).

A rare early photograph of a group of Native Californians, apparently domestic servants in Phineas Banning's household, demonstrates the significance of this labor force in southern California. Banning, a landowner and merchant, needed a huge number of workers for his freighting businesses and to run his complicated household. Indians provided this labor under unpaid and unregulated labor contracts.

the reality of the power Native people always wielded, even if they didn't like it. Alta California could only operate because of careful accommodation on everyone's part.

Mariano Vallejo offers an example. Like most Mexican Californians who got land from the dissolution of the mission system, Vallejo depended on the hide and tallow trade that grew at a rapid rate after ranchos began to dot the California landscape. Something like six million hides and seven thousand tons of tallow were exported from California between 1826 and 1848. These hides ended up in New England, where manufacturers made them into shoes, but it required a great deal of work to turn cows into shoes. Without the mission Indians who had been rendered unemployed and landless by the secularization process, men like Vallejo could not have become wealthy. In his old age, Vallejo remembered the complexity of the work with vivid detail, as "nothing less than an open-air slaughterhouse" in which Native cowboys killed the cattle, *peladors* skinned them, *tasajadores* butchered them, and "finally behind these come dozens of Indian women to cut the fat and gather it into leather sacks."[57] Despite the intensity of such labor, Indians who worked on the ranchos rarely received cash for their services but were given housing and a daily food ration and earned credit toward basic supplies, a system generally described as peonage.[58]

Not all mission Indians ended up on ranchos. Many chose to return to interior California and to join the Native groups living there. By the mid-1830s, more than a hundred thousand Indians lived in the Sacramento and San Joaquin valleys that stretched up the center of California. The horse and cattle trade offered these Indians a way to make a living too, one that would plague the Mexican rancheros for a generation. Having been trained at the missions and on the ranchos to be excellent riders and stockmen, they used these skills to raid missions and ranchos, to tend their own herds, and to develop a trade in stock, especially horses, with groups of new foreigners who came to interior California hoping to trade as well. Beginning in the late 1820s, American trappers and traders began crossing into California from New Mexico and from the Rockies, hoping to find new places to trap for furs. They didn't find much fur, but they found Native people eager to sell them Mexican horses, a product that brought great profits in either Santa Fe or St. Louis. Everything about this trade was illegal, but this didn't stop a considerable number of American trappers from participating. With a ready market, Native people stepped up their raiding to a level that seriously threatened the ranching economy of California.[59]

The complaints of Californians sounded much like those from people living in Texas and New Mexico who endured the constant raiding by the Comanches, and they were equally unsuccessful at stopping it. Even though Native and new Californians clashed in these years, it was far less toxic than the condition in Texas. Mariano Vallejo spent much of his time and energy as military commander of northern California dealing with horse stealing, but he never entertained the idea of removal. He sent out expeditions to recover horses and to catch Native people, Mexican Californians, and foreigners who were involved. He did return horses to their owners, and did occasionally punish thieves, but his actions made little impact on the trade. Another set of victims in this trade were Indian women and children who were captured from the missions, the ranchos, and interior tribes as part of the raiding system that developed, again reminiscent of the Comanches. Many rancheros and landowners, including Vallejo, bought and sold the labor of these captives but expressed disapproval of this practice in public. Southern California had the majority of the ranchos and suffered the majority of the raids that lasted for at least thirty years. The editor of the Los Angeles paper wondered, "How many thousands of horses were stolen . . . from the Ranches of San Ysabel, Santa Margarita, Los Flores, El Tamuel, San Jasinto, Agua Caliente and numerous other ranches in San Diego County?" He estimated that the losses "arising from the depredations of the Indians upon horses alone at $300,000, and when we add the loss of horned cattle, the insecurity of person and property, and the abandonment of the frontier settlements, this estimate is insignificant in comparison to the material and almost fatal check to the prosperity of these counties."[60]

Raiding the ranchos provided an important niche for Native Californians who chose to remain in the interior and to preserve a modicum of their independence. Mariposa, Miwok, Yuma, or Moquelumne people, for example, made this choice because they had developed trade connections in the interior. A new culture evolved in the interior of California, as "free" mission Indians fled to the Central Valley, blending with Native groups that had recently been decimated by smallpox. Native people with experience in the missions knew how to deal with Spanish and Mexicans. They spoke Spanish, knew how to negotiate, and provided a source of leadership for tribes that lost leaders from war and epidemics. Other Native people, tied to family near the mission or without a connection to intact tribes, provided labor for the ranchos, which gave them homes, protection, and sustenance. In the *indiañolas,* or Native villages that developed inside the ranchos, Native workers often had vegetable gardens of their own and supplemented their incomes with occasional cattle and horse theft. Native people became essential to the economy of Mexican California in one guise and threatened it in another. Both Native and Mexican Californians may have wished for different options and relationships, but they both accommodated to reality beyond wishes.[61]

THE OSAGES AND ACCOMMODATION ON THE ARKANSAS

Just as Lewis Cass and the new superintendent of Indian affairs, Elbert Herring, imagined a Permanent Indian Frontier as the solution to the challenge of dealing with Native nations, a different reality reared its ugly head. Again, we have some cases of wishful thinking. Cass, Herring, and other "Friends of the Indian" wished that they could sequester Native people for a long enough period that they would become civilized farmers. Osage,

Pawnee, and Kansa people wished that they could remain hunters and traders who controlled much of the central plains. The Osages, in particular, had developed and maintained power through trade and diplomacy and unrelenting war, and they had no other way to imagine themselves. Because their Missouri and Kansas territory lay at the center of land desired by the earliest Anglo-American migrants, and because they patrolled the Missouri and the Arkansas, they controlled trade access to the western tribes. Their ability in war and their close relationships to important French and then American traders protected their powerful position.

The Osages had decided as early as 1804 that fighting the United States would have no real utility. Diplomacy and trade seemed the wisest way to deal with them, within reason. If individual citizens of the United States tried to take Osage territory or too many animals, individual warriors and bands did retaliate. Fighting the Pawnees, Caddos, Wichitas, and Cherokees, however, made more sense. As a result of these decisions, early in the nineteenth century the Osages had gave up most of what is now Missouri, but they had negotiated good territory in Kansas and along the Arkansas. They fought, traded, and intermarried with their enemies the Pawnees, Wichitas, and Caddos but couldn't metabolize the large number of removed Indians from the Old Northwest placed in their territories during the 1820s. To stop the constant warfare between these groups and to keep them from harassing traders on the Santa Fe Trail that went through this territory, in 1825 the government negotiated another treaty with the Osages, leaving them a large strip of land bisected by the Arkansas River that went along the border of what is now Kansas and Oklahoma. They settled in villages, not very happily, but continued to mount hunts to the west and traded with Americans, Mexicans, and other Native nations. However, in the 1830s, Osage land became one of the logical places to put Creeks, Choctaws, Cherokees, and other Native refugees. The Osages quickly made these new immigrant Indian settlements into targets for Osage raids. They began stealing horses and burning villages, particularly among the Cherokees, igniting a storm of protest from immigrant nations, Indian agents, and the military charged with creating "peace" in this volatile situation.[62]

A. P. Chouteau explained the Osage problem very succinctly in 1834. He wrote a passionate letter to the secretary of war when he learned that the northern bands of the Osages in Kansas were losing most of their land to accommodate nations being removed from the east. "If any Nation has been heretofore deceived and oppressed, it is the Osages. . . . The land now occupied by the Choctaws, Cherokees, Creeks, Senecas, . . . was once owned by the Osages and what have they received for that immense country? Few presents and a small annuity." Four land cessions, in 1808, 1818, 1825, and 1839, totaling 97 million acres eroded Osage land holdings and access to hunting grounds. Nearly all of the land given to the immigrant tribes had belonged to the Osages. The Osages, and their relatives, agents, and trading partners, A.P. and P. Liguest Chouteau, had landed squarely in the midst of their oldest and fiercest enemies.[63]

In an 1828 treaty with the Cherokees, the Osages had lost a significant portion of their Arkansas River land to Cherokees and Creeks, including A. P. Chouteau's trading post at the junction of the Verdigris with the Arkansas River. A.P's Osage family had been scattered all over Kansas and Arkansas but now found themselves "concentrated" on the Kansas lands, with P. Liguest Chouteau as their agent. The Osages demonstrated their frustration by taking hogs, chickens, mules, and tobacco from the agency and demanding that Chouteau act in his proper role of host and give them everything he had. P. Liguest, not really complaining, wrote to Superintendent William Clark, explaining that "the government had stupidly built the agency building over an Indian burial mound . . . which causes unpleasant feelings."[64] Despite A. P. Chouteau's best efforts as a negotiator, the "unpleasant feelings" deepened in 1835 when the government demanded even more concessions from the Osages. Chief Clermont signed the treaty but expressed his serious doubts that the "Great Father will give me my all." Clermont refused to participate in a grand council organized by the Stokes Commission the following summer, though other Osage bands did. The Plains tribes, while promising to stop raiding among themselves and intercepting Euro-Americans on the Santa Fe Trail, had little intention of doing these things, and most of the Osages refused even to make such a false promise.[65]

After A. P. Chouteau's death in December of 1838, things got worse for the Osages. By 1840 the Osages had lost most of their hunting domain, but they had not taken up reservation life. Finding themselves trapped between the immigrant nations on the Arkansas, the western Cheyennes, Kiowas, and Arapahos to the west, and Comanchería to the south, the Osages threw in their fortunes with the strongest partners available—the Comanches. They received access to bison hunting grounds in return for bringing American trade goods to the Comanches. This position of middlemen was familiar and honorable, giving the Osages the power to refuse much of what reservation life demanded. They refused to participate in missionary activities or to live in reservation houses. They would not farm, and they would not learn English. They could see no advantage in such a life. An Osage warrior, Big Soldier, observed that Anglo-Americans needed to "possess the power of almost every animal they use." He warned them: "You are surrounded by slaves. Everything about you is in chains, and you are slaves yourselves." He explained his choice to avoid the reservation: "I fear if I should exchange my pursuits for yours, I should become a Slave.[66]

The Osage were proudly not slaves. They remained "the men pre-eminent." Old Osages remembered that in those days "no one dared wear the clothing of the Heavy Eyebrows for fear of ridicule and each morning when the morning star came up, men went to the high places to chant their prayers and the women came out to stand in front of the lodges facing east." They remained Osages, but the loss of land had dealt them a serious physical and spiritual blow. Central to their religious outlook was their role as protector of land and buffalo, and they had failed in this role. The things that happened to them in the next few decades could be understood in the context of punishment for failure to keep Osage territory out of strangers' hands.[67]

The Osages continued to resist in their own way, but pressure from the government and from the immigrant nations did concentrate the Osage into clusters of small villages. This accommodation had some advantages for traders like the Chouteaus and did allow the Osages to form new bonds between the various Osage groups and to develop new leaders. However, it also created ideal conditions for epidemic disease. Wave after wave struck the Osages, each time leaving children without parents, husbands without wives, and sisters without sisters. Influenza, measles, and smallpox in the 1830s, cholera, typhoid, and smallpox again in the 1850s, recurred in a twenty-year cycle that took perhaps a third to a half of the population each time. The Osages, however, would survive even this, though they would emerge as a very different nation.[68]

GOOD FATHERS AND THE FUR TRADE

When Henry Schoolcraft wanted to assess the number and the condition of Native people on the Missouri River in the 1840s, he sent questionnaires to his friends in the fur trade, men who had lived in forts and Native communities for decades and who had developed familial relationships with a wide network of Native people. These men, like Schoolcraft, were the good fathers of the fur trade. They worried about the future of Native nations and the fur trade because their children came from this world and would have to make their own lives there. We don't know how many of these questionnaires Schoolcraft sent out, or how many he received back, and we have no real way to ascertain how accurate reports and counts were, but these imbedded reporters described a world of Native nations that had economic power and cultural flexibility.

From this perspective, the situation on the Missouri River looked very different from the one faced by the Osages and the California Indians. Powerful Native groups on the river did not yet have to deal with refugee nations. The continuing significance of the fur trade gave nations like the Blackfoot, Crows, and the Dakota (Sioux) leverage and control. Numerous experts have weighed in on the issue of whether the fur trade destroyed Indians by making them dependent on trade goods or whether Native people were educated consumers who made rational choices about goods and livelihoods. This debate is probably insoluble, but at least on the upper Missouri, Native people participated in the fur trade willingly; they adapted it to their needs and demanded that they control much of how trade occurred. The fur trade gave them political power, weapons to enforce new and old relationships, and goods they wanted. For Natives in this region, however, three things gradually eroded their enviable position and brought about a serious decline in the fur trade. First, the increasing presence of Anglo immigrants and traders traveling across the Great Plains brought a new military presence and new government policies. Second, the near extinction of many fur-bearing species and dwindling buffalo populations challenged central economic and social arrangements. Finally, waves of epidemic disease had immediate and devastating impact.[69]

Since the beginning of the nineteenth century, St. Louis traders had hoped to establish a lucrative fur trade with the Blackfoot and other upper Missouri nations. But achieving their desires proved to be difficult and deadly. The smaller French and Canadian operations had managed good relations with these groups, and the big English and Canadian fur-trading firms met with a mixed reception. American traders, trappers, and hunters found themselves facing an implacable foe who simply didn't want to do business or have any contact with any more strange traders until the 1830s, when the Chouteau family extended its forts and operations directly into Blackfoot territory. After some initial scary years, this strategy worked, and the Chouteau network monopolized this trade into the 1850s only because the Blackfoot had decided they wanted to participate.[70]

What made them willing? Bison and guns—which reflected a large change occurring on the northern plains. Part of this shift, which Pierre

Chouteau had envisioned as he pulled his company away from the traditional trade in beaver, marten, and other fur-bearing animals to a new focus on buffalo hides, was bison—something the Blackfoot and other northern Plains Indians knew intimately. The Blackfoot, comprising three separate Algonkian-speaking groups who made the transition from traditional hunters to mounted warriors in the mid-eighteenth century, became the strongest military power on the northern plains in the nineteenth century. By then Blackfoot hunters and warriors had long established relationships with the Hudson's Bay Company and the North West Company and had forced the Shoshone, Flathead, and Kootenays people west of the Rocky Mountains. As they secured new territory, Blackfoot human and horse populations grew quickly. An astute observer and practical businessman, fur trader Alexander Henry estimated in 1809 that more than five thousand Blackfoot people lived east of the Rockies between the Missouri and Saskatchewan rivers. He concluded that they were "the most independent and happy people of all the tribes E. of the Rocky mountains."[71]

Their independence was, of course, illusory because the Blackfoot had become quite dependent on trade goods—especially guns, ammunition, and powder—to maintain their position. Trade in buffalo hides became the coin of the realm. They protected their homelands fiercely, driving out anyone who dared to enter. British and Canadian traders understood this and politely invited Blackfoot people to come to them. Americans, however, blundered right into the heart of a world of intertribal warfare in their efforts to ascend the Missouri. When Meriwether Lewis ran into groups of Blackfoot hunters on his return from the Pacific in 1806, he did not receive a warm welcome. A small party of Blackfoot tried to steal some of Lewis's horses, and Lewis retaliated, killing two warriors and taking several of their horses. This initial contact with the "Big Knives" (as the Blackfoot called Americans) did not bode well for the future. The Blackfoot killed or robbed any American traders who came onto their lands for the next twenty years. Their initial bad feeling for Americans developed into real enmity because American traders provided guns and horses for their enemies—Crows, Flatheads, Shoshones, and Nez Perces—who now threatened to come east and north into Blackfoot territory. Manuel Lisa's Missouri Fur Company, for example, made its initial trading contacts with the Crows and tried to build a small trading post on the Yellowstone to attract their Crow allies. The Blackfoot would not tolerate this and killed Lisa's men, their Native allies, and any independent trappers who got in their way.[72]

No one made any concerted efforts to go into Blackfoot territory again until the late 1820s. The federal government created the Upper Missouri Agency and staffed it with old fur trade hands as agents, with the hope that annuities and more local trade might convince these nations to limit their warfare. Reorganization of the fur trade, new technologies like steamboats, and the business acumen of the Chouteau family made the upper Missouri trade viable in a period of great economic uncertainty. The American Fur Company began sending steamers up the river in 1831, which everyone thought was madness except for Pierre Chouteau. After some years of design experimentation and numerous wrecked boats, steamboats became fixtures on the Missouri, handling the huge new business in buffalo robes. This all depended, however, on Blackfoot and Sioux participation. Their willingness, of course, came out of building intimate relationships as Native nations incorporated fur traders into their societies by encouraging their women to marry European men. Traders with personal connections and with obligations to their Blackfoot kin could negotiate successfully.[73]

In 1829 the company built Fort Union, but only after careful negotiations with several important Blackfoot bands around a new trade in buffalo hides. The newly reconstituted American Fur Company sent Kenneth McKenzie, a former North West Company trader who had personal relationships with important Blackfoot leaders and who understood the rituals and gifts that could initiate lasting bonds. In 1831 McKenzie brought together the "distinguished nation of the Blackfeet, Piegan, and Blood Indians," and "conforming to all the ancient customs and ceremonies . . . a treaty of peace and friendship was entered into" according to the treaty document they all signed.[74]

The success of the upper Missouri trade depended on men like Edwin Denig and Andrew Drips, who used these new technologies and time-honored trade techniques to forge relationships with powerful hunting nations. Edwin Denig served at various American Fur Company forts on the upper Missouri from 1833 to 1856, years that spanned the most important era of trade in that region. Though he married two Assiniboine women, Denig spent most of his career dealing with the powerful Sioux at Forts Pierre and Union. By 1849 he served as chief trader (or bourgeois) at Fort Union, where the trade between the upper Missouri (Blackfoot, Crows, and Sioux) and Upper Mississippi nations (Crees, Ojibwes, Assiniboines) merged. During his long tenure at Fort Union, he hosted numerous famous visitors including John James Audubon, Father Pierre De Smet, and various European dignitaries. Denig also became a reliable ethnographer and

28. Fort Union bourgeois Edwin Denig and his wife, Deer Little Woman
(Assiniboine). Photograph, ca. 1855. In Bureau of American Ethnology,
Annual Report 46 (1928–29). Washington DC, 1930.

Denig married Deer Little Woman almost immediately after his marriage to his
first wife. Both wives were the sisters of an Assiniboine leader, First to Fly. He
had children with both women, but Deer Little Woman raised the entire
family after Denig's first wife died in a smallpox epidemic.

naturalist who had the language skills and personal relationships to give him a rare perspective on life among Native people in the region. When Henry Schoolcraft sent out his vast questionnaire about Indian numbers, dispositions, and behavior to all the government and private Indian agents in 1851, Denig replied with a 451-page manuscript. In 1854 Denig began to look for a place to retire so that he, like many other concerned fur trade fathers, could educate his children and make sure they could earn a living. He and Deer Little Woman spent two years considering and visiting St. Louis, Chicago, and Columbus, Ohio, but they rejected all three in favor of the métis communities along the Red River in Canada. In 1856 Denig, Deer Little Woman, and their four children ranging in age from two to eighteen settled there. The children attended local Catholic schools, and Denig worked as a private trader until his death, at age forty-six, in 1858.[75]

Andrew Drips had an astonishingly long career in the fur trade because of his varied connections with Native people. Born in Ireland in 1789, Drips came to the United States as a very small child. He moved steadily west, serving in the War of 1812 in the Ohio militia but finally settling in the fur trade as an employee of the Missouri Fur Company. A skilled trader, he quickly had important responsibilities at Fort Lisa and later at Fort Bellevue, a trading post on the Nebraska side of the Missouri River. During these years, working for various companies, he led trading expeditions among the Pawnees, worked closely with George Sibley at Fort Osage, and married an Otoe woman named Macompemay. By the 1830s, like many traders of his era, Andrew Drips had tried his fortunes as an independent trapper and as a company employee in the Rocky Mountain fur trade, but he had decided that the Rocky Mountains were dangerous and unprofitable. As his family grew, he settled back into the Missouri River trade.[76]

From the experiences of Andrew Drips, Edwin Denig, their families, and their Native employees and customers, we can view the operation of the fur trade in those years. Drips's story provides a scaffold for understanding the region in the 1830s and early 1840s as the American Fur Company established itself, and we see how fur brigades, fur trade families, and U.S. policymakers learned to accommodate the powerful Native nations in the region. Denig, who operated at the "plant manager" level, shows us the challenge of trade and relationships in a rapidly shifting context of a modernizing business model. Because of the importance Denig placed on building personal relationships and his efforts to control Native warfare, we can see the kinds of pressures under which people and business functioned. The fur trade changed in fundamental ways in these years, and so did government policy, though the two entities rarely shared goals or outlooks. The one assumption that most people who worked and lived with Native nations shared, however, was that these groups of people were nations and so had rights to sovereignty and to hold land. Various schemes to create genuine Indian states that would be the exclusive property of Native people had floated out from Congress numerous times but were tabled or defeated because of the expense involved.

In 1831 Lewis Cass, as secretary of war, and William Clark, as superintendent of all agencies west of the Mississippi, drew up a long document that presented their ideas about how a well-organized Indian Department could deal with trade and with the forced resettlement of Native nations. In it, they resolved to hold inviolate the lands that had been assigned to removed nations in the West, to exclude alcohol from Indian Territory, and to provide adequate military and civil support to prevent hostility between tribes and from encroaching white settlers. The document also included an official Indian Territory that contained a large piece of land stretching from Texas to Nebraska. Throughout the 1830s, Congress debated the merits of a territorial government run by Native people, of having representatives in Congress from Native nations, and of how such a "permanent frontier" could be policed. Fears about disgruntled Native people banding together and creating a revolution in the West, in the context of the eroding relationship with Mexico and the dangerous situation in Texas, kept such bills from becoming law. This discussion had always left out the very territory most clearly controlled by Native people, the upper Missouri and Mississippi rivers, but this was probably because powerful traders like the Chouteaus wanted no interference in their activities and because the military had no desire to make forays into this region for any reason.[77]

By the 1830s government policy, the construction of fur trade forts, and the shifting needs of Indian nations had coalesced to make trade and life along the upper Missouri possible and profitable. Despite the thin network of government policies, agents, and military outposts and the physical facts of steamboats, forts, and alcohol, people who lived on the upper Missouri operated in a Native world. Native nations and their needs determined daily safety and the outcome of longer-term power struggles. The Blackfoot, who had controlled access to horses, guns, and other trade goods, found themselves undermined by the Crows, who had made early alliances with traders at American Fur Company forts. More importantly, large groups of formerly divided Sioux bands had united and moved west, challenging both the Crows and the Blackfoot. The Crows drifted south, but the Blackfoot held their ground in the mountains west of the river. In this context, fur trade forts became neutral zones at the same time raiding between tribes intensified. Elaborate rituals allowed long-time enemies to trade with relative amicability during the summer trading sessions that took up most of August at the forts. Prince Maximilian of Wied, who spent August of 1833 at Fort McKenzie, described the long smoking sessions, the exchanges of gifts, marriage ceremonies, and slow eating of buffalo that had to take place before any real trading could occur. Even with such peaceful moments, violence could and did break out, especially when alcohol and guns were involved.[78]

Fort Union, the longest-operating fort on the Missouri River, stood at the border of lands used by numerous tribes who made their living hunting, raiding, and trading and served as link in a vast commercial network that extended to London, Canton, and Mexico City. In this context Edwin Denig operated Fort Union with a combination of sophisticated Euro-American business methods overlaid with Native practices and kinship networks. The fort signaled that the days of the mountain men and their roving rendezvous were coming to an end, but also demonstrated the Chouteau family's confidence that the fur trade would endure as a business rather than a romantic adventure. The business had become a very layered operation that involved business deals in Asia, arrangements with government officials, careful pricing strategies, and byzantine transportation networks. At its heart, however, remained the exchange of animal skins in return for manufactured items that Native people wanted. Achieving this exchange required organizing hunting parties made up of Native, mixed race, and Euro-American people, producing and packaging furs so that they could be shipped down the river. These activities needed stable year-round bases where business could be conducted. Because they created relationships with important men and women and made efforts to understand what Native people wanted, the traders at Fort Union were very successful. The Chouteau-backed American Fur Company would never achieve anything like a complete monopoly over the Missouri fur trade, but its partners and agents and their families wielded considerable power.[79]

In the late 1830s Alexander Culbertson, the chief, or bourgeois, at Fort Union, sent nine horses to an important Blackfoot leader, Seen From Afar. Understanding exactly what this meant, Seen From Afar sent a reciprocal gift that included his younger sister, Medicine Snake Woman, aged fifteen. She lived with Culbertson in the fine house at the center of the fort for many years. Because of the family connection, her brother traded

29. Medicine Snake Woman (Blackfoot). Unknown photographer. Montana Historical Society Research Center Archives (941–819).

Married as a very young woman to trader Alexander Culbertson, Medicine Snake Woman lived most of her life at Chouteau company forts on the upper Missouri River. When Culbertson retired from the fur trade, the couple and their five children initially settled in Illinois. After the children grew up, Medicine Snake Woman left Culbertson and lived the rest of her life on the Blackfoot Preserve in Alberta, Canada.

exclusively at Fort Union and became a head chief partly because of his access to ammunition, guns, and tobacco. Medicine Snake Woman and Culbertson had five children whom they educated at convent schools in St. Louis. Culbertson made a considerable fortune in the Indian trade, and he and Medicine Snake Woman, with three of their daughters, Nancy, Francisca, and Julia, retired to Peoria, Illinois, in 1858. However, after ten years of luxurious retirement, Culbertson lost his fortune and headed back up to the upper Missouri to work as a trader. His wife accompanied him but found the work and Culbertson tiresome. After nearly thirty years of marriage, she left him and returned to her own people, living first with her brother and finally moving to the Blackfoot Preserve in Alberta.[80]

Denig, who took over from Culbertson as Fort Union's chief factor, followed much the same pattern. As Denig explained to a curious visitor, by marrying into prominent Native families, traders "increase their adherents, their patronage is extended, and . . . their Indian relatives remain loyal." He also stated unequivocally "an Indian woman only loves her husband for what he possesses."[81] Whether the couple got emotional sustenance from such relationships, he didn't say, but marriage has always been primarily an economic arrangement. During his early trading days Denig married an Assiniboine woman with whom he had two children, Robert and Sarah. We don't know this woman's name or exactly when she died, but Denig made their children central to his plans. He married Deer Little Woman soon after the birth of Sarah (whom Denig refers to as "Fiery Cloud" in his will) in 1844, suggesting that his first wife may have died in childbirth. Denig and Deer Little Woman, the daughter of Arrow Point, leader of an important Assiniboine band, moved into the luxurious chief trader's quarters in 1849, after the fort had been rebuilt and enlarged several times. Denig described it proudly as "the principal and handsomest trading-post on the Missouri River," completed with "bastion walls and buttressed palisades resting upon a foundation of limestone." The Denig family expanded to include Alexander, born in 1852, and Ida, born in 1854, while they lived at Fort Union.[82]

The height and solidity of these walls demonstrated that the fur trade continued to be an extremely dangerous business. It could also be profitable and allowed the people of the upper Missouri—Native, Euro-American, and mixed race—to live their lives with some flexibility and independence. The trade grew rapidly throughout the 1840s, as buffalo replaced beaver as the most significant part of the trade. The company employed upward of a thousand people in its agencies and forts on the river, who all worked to send down 67,000 buffalo robes in 1840 and 110,000 in 1848, along with buffalo tongues and tallow as important by-products.[83] As Henry School-craft and other American policymakers discovered, and as people like the Denigs, the Drips, and their employees and trading partners already knew, the upper Missouri remained Indian Country well into the 1850s.

Andrew Drips and his family experienced the shifting dangers of fur trade life in very direct ways. In the late 1820s and early 1830s Drips worked primarily out of Fort Bellevue, which stood where the Platte joined the Missouri. The Drips family's four oldest children were born in these years. Employed by the American Fur Company as a fur brigade leader, Drips spent much of his time out trapping and trading rather than ensconced in a fort. Like many of his fellow traders, he often brought his wife and children along on these extended trips, and they spent some winters entirely in Native villages. Native women traveling with fur brigades served as cultural mediators, helped to make and repair traps, processed furs for storage, and cared for their families. In 1832 Drips and Macompemay had ventured north into Blackfoot country at the specific instruction of Pierre Chouteau Jr. This turned out to be particularly bloody season with the upper Missouri tribes, as reported in grisly detail in the St. Louis newspapers, which devolved into all-out war with the Blackfoot and the Gros Ventre. In fur trade families, however, life went on, and Macompemay gave birth to her second daughter Katherine during a famous battle at Pierre's Hole in October of 1832.[84]

Through Drips's letters and his meticulous accounts, we can see how the fur trade changed in these years and how this family of mixed race negotiated these changes. By the end of the 1830s Drips and Macompemay had four children, and like many parents they wanted stability and income to provide for their children. Though they bought land and maintained a home near what is now Kansas City, in an almost exclusively mixed race community called Kawsmouth, Drips and his family spent most of their winters at American Fur Company forts. When the children got older, he and Macompemay decided to sacrifice family intimacy for education. As they watched the fur trade consolidate and roles for people of mixed race disappear, many fur trade families, particularly those at the upper echelons of the business who had the economic support to make choices, began to worry that the fur trade might not provide opportunities for their offspring. St. Louis Catholic boarding schools became second homes for these children, and more than half of the students at the biggest schools were children of mixed race from fur trade families.[85]

Drips and Macompemay obviously shared these concerns. When he served as a trader at Fort Pierre and Fort John, both on the Missouri, and also at Fort Laramie, the children stayed in St. Louis in order to attend school. Drips provided them with the room, board, tuition, silk hats and umbrellas, and tortoise shell and ivory combs they required as boarding students. In the 1840s, as his children approached adulthood and required ever more expensive schooling and stakes in business, Drips took on the position of a special Indian agent for the U.S. government. His charge was to suppress the illegal liquor trade with the Indians of the Missouri River. Though the task was impossible, the Chouteau family supported the position because they hoped government action might at least drive out smaller trading companies that were using alcohol to create chaos in the fur industry.[86]

The creation of such a position and the frustrations that Drips experienced demonstrated how little control the federal government had over the fur trade or Native people in this region. Even the powerful Chouteaus could not stem the flow of illegal alcohol that poured into the region. Though providing liquor to Indians had been illegal since the 1820s, its portability and addictive qualities made alcohol a popular trade item. Drips found that all alcohol mysteriously disappeared when he arrived at the various forts, even though he received reports of "rascals in their drunken frolicks" and of flatboats headed up the Missouri with kegs of alcohol nearly every day.[87]

Given the vast sweep of his assignment and the obvious improbability of achieving much, Drips only lasted four years in the role of alcohol policeman. He did spend a lot of time in those years with the Blackfoot and the Sioux, and we get a sense of the power the Sioux wielded over the region. They determined where and when business occurred and demanded that forts be built in places convenient for them. Drips reported that the Yankton Sioux refused to trade at Fort Pierre, "where they be subject to the incessant depredation of the Rees on their horses." In order to make their wishes clear, the band forcibly detained some traders and insisted that they build wintering houses at a site lower on the river, which they deemed safer for "their wives and children." Drips also transcribed a petition from the Sioux to amend their 1837 treaty, explaining that they had been granted a blacksmith and agricultural implements at a cost of more than $2,200 but could find no use for such things. Instead, the Sioux explained, they wanted "150 guns, 13 bags of flour, 13 bags of sugar, blankets, Powder, Lead, Kettles, gun flints, and knives"—items that they did find useful.[88]

When Macompemay died in 1846, Drips married a younger French and Sioux woman named Louise Geroux. She had been part of the traders' community of Kawsmouth that grew up near Fort Bellevue. They had five children and adopted several others, including the Native daughters of Lucien Fontanelle, Drips's former partner. Drips worked as a trader until he was more than seventy, unusual in the industry, but perhaps necessary to support his numerous offspring. Andrew and Louise remained in Kawsmouth, where a large number of retired traders brought their families, making it a small-scale version of the Red River settlements in Canada. Drips was a good father and worried about what would happen to his children in a world and time when the fur trade no longer dominated the western economy. Much as John McLoughlin did for his youngest son David, Drips set up his eldest son, Charley, with a quarter interest in a Missouri riverboat, hoping the boy could succeed in that endeavor. In 1847 a family friend wrote Drips that Charley had a good head for figures, "not usual for a half-breed," which indicates that category into which Charley had been placed.[89]

The trade in furs and in buffalo robes had entered a precipitous decline, but it lasted longest on the upper Missouri. The American Fur Company outlasted all of the others because of its unique combination of sophisticated modern business practices and traditional fur trade social arrangements. Pierre Chouteau Jr. and his associates had lobbyists in Washington, buyers in Canton, special deals with transportation companies, and a deep familiarity with calumet diplomacy. Because the fur trade required families like the Drips, the Denigs, and myriad others who had kin among important Native nations, this world continued to make sense for the people living in it. The pattern that we see developing here reflects the kind of accommodation we saw in California, but that would be impossible in Texas or in the Pacific Northwest, and that would disappear nearly everywhere after the Civil War. We see a range of communities: half-breed tracts, and trader communities along the rivers, forts, and reconstituted and reconfigured Native villages and tribes. Edwin Denig, as a trader, father, and ethnologist who had chosen to live a syncretic life, recognized the cost this choice would have for his children. He wrote to Henry Schoolcraft in 1854: "If it were not for the popular prejudice existing . . . we would advise amalgamation of the races as the most efficient mean for saving the remnants of the Indian tribes."[90] The upper Missouri and its world of amalgamation served Anglo-American business and social needs but were still a part of Indian Country where Euro-Americans remained willing to accommodate.

Captivity Tales and Epidemic Disease

Edwin Denig woke one morning in July of 1837 and discovered the first signs of smallpox on his body. Frightened, he examined the weeping rash that had erupted on his arms. As the recently appointed post bookkeeper at Fort Union, he knew all too well what the result of smallpox could be. He immediately began worrying about his Assiniboine wife and his young son, Robert. He had watched as every Native woman at the fort had come down with the disease, and every one of them had died. Because he had sent his own family north to his wife's people when the contagion began, he could only wait out his own illness and hope that they were safe. The situation in the Assiniboine village, however, was far worse than Denig could have imagined. By early August someone in nearly every lodge lay shaking with chills, and by September the population had dropped from more than 1,000 to 150. Rotting bodies dotted the roads leading into the village, and dead bodies floated down the river, grim warning that something was terribly wrong. The Assiniboine's impotence in the face of this calamity drove them to despair. Parents who fell ill killed their children, fearing no one would survive to care for them, and parents who lost children to the disease killed themselves, unable to imagine lives without their children. Denig would ultimately survive, and so would his infant son, but he lost his wife to the terrible scourge.[91]

The rest of this chapter explores two issues, one real and one imaginary, but both of which influenced Indian Country deeply. Epidemic disease—malaria in 1833, smallpox in 1837, cholera in 1849—and stories of Indian captivity—John Jewitt and Sarah Ann Horn—shifted the ways in which people lived and thought. Captivity and disease have long histories in Indian Country and in Euro-American imaginations because of the way these stories have been used to explain everything. Although the forcible kidnapping of Euro-American women by Native men certainly happened, stories about it were exaggerated. Even so, it became a primal fear of people living even hundreds of miles from Indian Country and shaped the way Anglo-Americans thought about Indians for centuries. Epidemic disease, on the other hand, was largely ignored or misunderstood by Euro-American scholars and policymakers until the middle of the twentieth century, and it has become a handy and impersonal explanation for the devastation brought by a variety of colonial projects.

The two issues are deeply intertwined and reflect important patterns in the ways in which Native people and Euro-Americans came into contact and confronted each other. Captivity and epidemic disease represent moments of utter disorientation. Contact with new people and their germs brought waves of epidemic disease and warfare. The human experience of these diseases caused some people to react with kidnapping and captivity. The captivity story makes Native people omnipotent, and the disease story renders them powerless, whereas European immigrants become powerful as they carry disease and utterly dependent when they are captured. How do these stories operate together? Such episodes reinforced what Native people and Europeans thought they understood about each other.

Henry Schoolcraft, whom we have seen in a variety of roles in this chapter—as ethnographer and census taker, as trader and businessman in the Great Lakes Indian world, and as a father of mixed raced children—wrote about his own earliest introductions to "the Indian race." Long before he had any personal contact, Schoolcraft had "by the age of ten" read "printed narratives of captivity" in which "the Indian was depicted as the very impersonation of evil."[92] He begins his 1851 text describing the varied world of Native people with this confession to explain his desire to show his readers a much different view. The narratives that Schoolcraft read came out of the colonial experience of the seventeenth and eighteenth centuries when Indian war and captivity were common, if not daily parts of life. During the French and Indian War that edged into the American Revolution, thousands of Euro-Americans were captured and taken north and west. This experience created a rhetoric of horror around the varied group of people called Indians, lumping them all into one category that Peter Silver aptly calls the anti-Indian sublime, a response and attitude that has proved remarkably durable.[93]

The situation in the trans-Mississippi West in the nineteenth century differed from the world of colonial Indian war, but the literary style and cultural reaction of the captivity narrative provided a convenient package in which Euro-Americans could place expectations and experience with Native Americans. As we have seen, captivity was a common practice in many parts of the West. Taking people as captives served many purposes: captives could serve as workers, they could replace populations diminished by warfare or disease, they could be ransomed for money, supplies, or other captives, or they could be tortured and killed as threats. The practice of captivity came from many directions. Spanish soldiers, Mormon farmers, Mexican rancheros, Franciscan priests, and Anglo-American fur traders all took Native people as captives and used them in various ways, just as Comanche warriors, Miwok raiders, Osage traders, Blackfoot hunters, or

Pueblo farmers had varying reasons for taking and using captives. Out of this variety, however, a single strand of captivity gets picked out of the historical webs that connect us to the past and comes to stand for the entire range of experience: white women and children taken from their frontier farms in times of Indian war.

Native people captured men as well, even though this is not the image that resonated in memory, and in the record of existing captivity narratives more men than women appear, particularly in the trans-Mississippi West since most Euro-Americans in the region were men. Young male captives could serve as slaves, marriage partners, and even warriors in Native communities damaged by war or epidemic disease. John Rogers Jewitt, a young English armorer and blacksmith, sailed into Nootka Sound in 1803 aboard the ship *Boston*. As he told the story, first published in 1807, almost immediately after their arrival a contingent of local Nootka Indians including Maquina, their "king," paddled out to the ship with gifts of fresh salmon and fishhooks. After several more exchanges, the king had dinner with the *Boston*'s captain, John Salter, who gave Maquina a musket as a gift. Apparently the musket wouldn't fire and Maquina returned the next day to demand a new gun. The ship's captain shouted at the king and threw a musket at him, and Maquina left, obviously insulted by this rude behavior.[94]

The following day, March 22, 1803, Maquina and several canoes of his people came back out to the ship to trade. Suddenly, they turned on the sailors and killed all but two of them. Leaving the heads of their twenty-five victims lined up on the deck, they forced young Jewitt to sail the horribly decorated ship up to their village. After unloading the ship's goods, they destroyed the sails and the masts, rendering the *Boston* useless. Jewitt's life was spared because of his skills as a metalworker, and he became Maquina's personal slave, a common fate for a captive of war.[95] In Jewitt's account, the Nootka behaved in this savage way because they were savages, overreacting to the insult given them by the ship's captain. The context for this massacre and mutiny, however, evolved out of a much longer history of relationships between Nootka people and European sailors. By 1803 many ships had sailed into Nootka Sound, and Maquina and his people had had many encounters. They had traded successfully with some ships but had been cheated by others. Some sailors had been polite, but others had raped and kidnapped their young women. And the Nootkas had suffered through at least two large-scale smallpox epidemics, one in the 1780s and one very recently, from 1800 to 1802.

Lewis and Clark noted pitted faces on many Native people as well as abandoned villages in 1805, the year that John Jewitt was sold to a passing ship and made his way back to Boston. The fear of disease still had power in 1811 when the Pacific Fur Company left the Astorians at lonely Fort Astoria, surrounded by the Chinooks and Clatsops. The expedition's leader, Duncan McDougall, threatened the Natives that he saw as potentially hostile by waving a bottle that he claimed was filled with smallpox. He warned that he could "let loose the pestilence to sweep every man, woman, and child from the face of the earth." The threat worked, because coastal Native people knew from bitter experience that when sailing ships arrived, they brought rowdy young men and left terrible diseases. In that context Maquina's response to the *Boston* and its captain is at least understandable.[96]

New diseases swept through aboriginal populations with few immune defenses with depressing regularity. Trade and commerce had altered local ecologies, providing new pathways for disease to travel and making illness into a calamity. Smallpox, measles, cholera, and malaria marched through the West in the middle of the century along their own path and developing their own personality. We don't know exactly how many people died in various waves, but some of these diseases brought devastating population losses in ranges of 60 to 90 percent of an affected group. As little as we know about actual numbers, we know even less about how these diseases affected people's lives; how they lived with these epidemics as illness and understood them culturally. And this is where captivity fits in. Some Native populations rebounded from shocking population loss and created new cultural arrangements. These dreadful disease cycles should perhaps not be seen as holocausts because Native nations did survive, though in new forms with histories of loss etched across them.[97]

On the Pacific Coast malaria proved to be a terrible killer in the early 1830s. An epidemic killed tens of thousands of Native people and had a devastating effect on the Fort Vancouver community before it moved south into California. Mosquitoes carry and transmit the disease, which is a parasite that destroys red blood cells. Called "fever and ague" or intermittent fever by the Euro-Americans who suffered through it, and "the shakes" by Native people, malaria arrived on ship from Boston in early 1830, ravaged the peoples in and around Fort Vancouver, and was transmitted south to the peoples of coastal and interior California in 1833. Everyone seemed to come down with the illness, company servants and Native people alike. Chief factor John McLoughlin, who had trained as a medical doctor, found his skills immediately taxed by the number of seriously ill patients at the fort. He complained that he had "so many sick I am quite harassed," and further that "the Fever is making a dreadful havoc among the Natives."[98]

What he meant by havoc was death. While the disease struck Europeans and Native people alike, it discriminated by making the former quite ill but by killing the latter. Hudson's Bay Company brigade leader Peter Skene Ogden remembered his horror that summer when he visited a Chinook village across the river from Fort Vancouver, where sixty active and healthy families had once lived: "All, all was changed. . . . The fever ghoul has wreaked his most dire; to the utter destruction of every human inhabitant."[99] The losses were intimate and personal. One wealthy Chinook leader, Cassino, told his friends that he was bereft because in one year he lost nine of his wives, three of his children, and sixteen of his slaves. John McLoughlin's friend and ally Concomely "was carried off" by the disease, even though McLoughlin brought him to the fort and cared for him personally. David Douglas, a visiting British botanist, wrote in the winter of 1831 about seeing abandoned villages up and down the river where "flocks of famished dogs are howling about, while the dead bodies lie strewn in every direction on the sands of the river."[100] The following year McLoughlin reported that everyone in the fort "save seven men" had been ill and that he himself had suffered a bout of the disease. As suddenly as it began, the epidemic stopped. McLoughlin noted in January of 1831, after nearly five months, he had no fever patients. However, for the next three years disease returned each winter, sickening many in the fort but decimating local Indians. In the end, between 1805 and 1841 the number of local Chinook and Kalupuyan people would drop by nearly 90 percent, much of it in this initial contact with malaria.[101]

McLoughlin's trapping brigades introduced malaria far to the east and to the south, so that the Nez Perce would get it in 1832, and the California residents would have it wash over them in 1833 with population losses of up to fifty thousand. Devastating as this was, Native people responded to this population loss and cultural threat in the only ways they could. Along the Columbia River and in the interior of California, communities depleted or devastated by disease first struggled to contain and understand it. People who survived did have immunity to the particular version of the pestilence, which gave them the ability to treat the sick and to provide leadership for their people. Some communities joined together, building new villages and creating new traditions in a process of ethnogenesis. Because Europeans had treatments that provided some relief for malaria, including quinine, the disease linked some Native communities even more tightly to the fort's trading systems. They also developed stories and traditions to explain what had happened. Recognizing exactly where the disease had originated, many Columbia River Native groups told tales about disease-bearing ships and poisoned beads, but they also shared stories about how John McLoughlin had opened up the fort to sick people.[102]

Malaria arrived in central California just as the missions were being secularized, as thousands of Native Californians rejoined their communities in the interior, so that the disease reached far inland. A wave of captive taking shook the region as people tried to rebuild their populations and to reconstitute themselves into new political and social groups. In the Columbia River region and in northern California bereaved people took many captives to replace lost family members and workers. The expanding slave trade seriously frustrated James Douglas, McLoughlin's second in command. Douglas, having observed the abolition of slavery in other parts of the British empire, wrote regretfully to the leaders of the Company about the impossibility of abolishing slavery at Fort Vancouver. "The state of feeling among the Natives of this river precludes every prospect of the immediate extinction of slavery." He added defensively that he had taken a harder line against his own employees, who also had slaves from all over the world, and "denounced slavery as a state contrary to law." Sanctimoniously, he explained, "I rescued a runaway slave boy who is now since enjoyed his liberty and is serving the Company as a free laborer." Despite this sterling moral example, his employees were not moved to release their own slaves, and Douglas admitted that all of his efforts "virtually failed in rooting out the practical evil, even within the precincts of this settlement."[103]

Malaria had equally devastating results in California. Mariano Vallejo reported on the course of the epidemic to the governor, describing a "horrible contagion which has carried off hundreds of human beings, especially among the Natives." Struggling to find a cause for the deadly illness, he explained that "impurity, the use of liquor, and very spicy dishes serve as fuel for the disease."[104] Vallejo himself estimated that 70,000 Indians died before the disease ran out, which is close to the modern estimate of 40,000 to 75,000. Vallejo's allies, Sem Yeto's Suisunes, were reduced from perhaps 4,000 to a mere 200 people. Vallejo ended up with all of the cattle belonging to these dead former mission Indians, but he kept very careful accounts of which cattle belonged to whom. As in the Pacific Northwest, Native Californians responded to this with raiding and intermarrying with new groups, which sometimes paid off well, but was also culturally risky.[105]

Only a few years after this experience with malaria, a worldwide plague of smallpox had particularly serious effects on parts of the trans-Mississippi

West. Because so many people living there had no immunities to it, the epidemic was deadly. The disease, carried by people who sometimes didn't even know they were infected, or by objects that had been touched or used by sick people, traveled rapidly up and down rivers in the fur trade world. It reached far up the upper Missouri because a single person, Native or Euro-American, who traded at a fort that harbored the disease could spread a lot of illness on his or her return to a Native village. The virulence of the outbreak and the numbers of Native people who died from it were exacerbated by the modern organization of the fur trade business.

The plague that would infect Edwin Denig and kill so many Native people arrived on the annual steamboat of the American Fur Company, the *St. Peters,* which tied up at Fort Union on June 24, 1837. For the residents of Native communities and the forts along the Missouri, the annual steamship was a highlight. It brought fresh supplies, trade items, the yearly annuity payments and goods, letters, newspapers, and new recruits to work as hunters, traders, and laborers. The new people and goods broke up the monotony of fort life. This year, however, it also brought smallpox. This sort of description gives the disease much power—"it arrived" or "it infected"—absolving human actors of responsibility. Fur trade officials knew that smallpox traveled on the boat, they knew that Indian people would be infected, and they knew that inoculation could lessen the severity of the outbreak. But they never stopped the ship or tried to quarantine populations, nor did they send up supplies to make widespread vaccination possible, which indicates something about human responsibility for epidemic disease. It was invited into the communities of the upper Missouri.[106]

Americans of all classes and ethnicities knew smallpox. Epidemics had affected various parts of the United States since its inception, and the regularity of the disease gave people resistance, if not immunity to its most devastating forms. For most Euro-Americans, smallpox was one of many childhood diseases that threatened the health of children and adults and that left them marked with scars for life. For Native Americans, who did not have generations of experience with the disease, it killed with speed and horrifying symptoms. Burning fever, huge oozing pustules, and rotting skin developed after ten to fourteen days of incubation and killed 50 to 90 percent of the people who contracted it. The few Native Americans who survived had deep pitted scars that covered large parts of their bodies and that sometimes blinded them. Many young women who survived had badly scarred nipples, which made it impossible for them to breastfeed babies, and young men were often rendered impotent by the scarring.

Smallpox, or *Variola major,* had first reached the upper Missouri and the Great Plains in the 1780s via traders from the south and the east. Another epidemic spread from the Missouri River valley to the Pacific Northwest in 1802 and again in 1811 affecting the Omahas, Arikaras, Gros Ventres, Mandans, Crows, and Sioux with shocking efficiency. Because the disease was so easily spread by the breath of an afflicted person, by the fluid in his or her sores or scabs, and even by contact with the corpse of a person who had died from the disease several weeks earlier, it moved quickly through crowded places like steamships, forts, and villages.[107]

By the time the *St. Peters* reached the American Fur Company forts in early June, several passengers and crew had contracted the disease, but most had recovered. Three Arikara women and their children, however, who had boarded at Fort Bellevue, were deathly ill. By the time the boat reached Fort Union, Jacob Halsey, the incoming Fort Union bourgeois, had the pox. His Native wife contracted it as well, but she died several days after leaving Fort Clark. The boat could have been quarantined, sent back, and its goods placed on shore and disinfected, so that the terrible effects of the disease on Native populations could have been prevented or mitigated. However, the situation presented a set of bad choices for leaders at the forts. Local people expected the boat and knew that it had many goods for them. Given the touchy relationships, if the boat had failed to arrive they would have assumed that the company and the government had conspired to rob them of annuity goods that were owed them. The company's officers tried to avert the calamity by keeping the Indians away from the boat, but when they arrived by the hundreds wanting their goods, no explanations about an invisible disease would keep them away.[108]

Predictably, numerous people in the fort got smallpox. As the epidemic spread, fort officials decided to inoculate everyone living in the fort "with the smallpox itself." Without much real medical expertise and rather desperately reading about the procedure from a popular text, they took scabs and pus from Jacob Halsey and rubbed "the smallpox matter" on open sores or placed it in small cuts made for the purpose. They locked the women and children into a storeroom, waiting to see if the crude inoculation "took." It did. All of the inoculated patients died, and the disease spread far beyond the fort after several patients' families demanded to see their rotting corpses. Many of the women were Assiniboines, and the pestilence soon raged among their people. Edwin Denig, after recovering from his own bout of smallpox, traveled north to Fort William to help his wife's kin. He turned the abandoned fort into a hospital and quarantine for the

Assiniboine, but he could do little to blunt the effects of the disease.[109]

Frances Chardon, the outspoken and violent bourgeois of Fort Clark, further down the Missouri, watched the epidemic develop at the fort and among the Mandans in late July. Once it broke out in the Mandan villages surrounding the fort, he could do little but report its terrible effects. He sent messengers warning the people to keep away, but the whole village came down to the river to see the goods that had arrived, and soon reports came back to the fort that the Mandans were dying at a terrible rate. By early September the Arikaras and Sioux had gotten the disease, but the Mandans, a more settled agricultural people gathered in their summer village, suffered the most. Many men at the fort caught the disease, and even more of their children died from it. The epidemic grew fierce and personal. Chardon's Lakota wife, Tchon-su-mons-ka, had passed away that spring, leaving him with two young sons, Frances Bolivar and Andrew Jackson. He sent the older boy to Philadelphia to live with his paternal grandmother and aunts, but Chardon still had to care for two-year-old Andrew Jackson. He sent the child north to Fort Pierre, but the little boy died of smallpox in September, a month in which Chardon reported that hundreds of the Mandans had died.[110]

Native people did not simply accept the disease. They reacted in very different ways, depending on how smallpox had arrived among them. The Assiniboines, Mandans, and Arikaras had seen the infection among Euro-American people first and understood that it had come from the *St. Peters*, so they instantly and correctly blamed the traders. As the epidemic raged among them, the Arikaras and the Mandans joined together and planned for war. Frances Chardon, recognized the danger; he kept his people in the fort and prepared his garrison for a fight. The disease undermined any plans, as two-thirds and then three-fourths of the Mandans succumbed to "rotting face." Overcome with fear and grief, families fled to the open plains, leaving bodies to rot and to be eaten by rats and dogs. The Assiniboines, equally angry, arrived at Fort Union ready to burn the fort and kill its inhabitants. Jacob Halsey, now recovered from his own bout with the disease, refused to let them come near the fort and built a new double gate to keep them out.[111]

On the other hand, because smallpox appeared first among the Blackfoot while they were out in hunting parties and not near Euro-Americans, they blamed themselves. Alexander Culbertson, who ran Fort McKenzie, the major trading center for the Blackfoot tribes, had tried to keep the keelboat carrying infected goods away from the fort for as long as possible, but it wasn't long enough. The boat arrived, filled with merchandise handled by people now sick at Fort Union. The Blackfoot took their goods and headed out to hunt. Two weeks later, smallpox raged among the Blackfoot hunting parties and at Fort McKenzie. That fall, after surviving the disease himself, Culbertson visited a camp of about sixty lodges. He was shocked to see that two old women, too feeble to travel, were the only survivors. Before the plague abated, some six thousand persons, nearly two-thirds of the entire Blackfoot population, succumbed.[112]

The leadership of the American Fur Company, including Jacob Halsey, Edwin Denig, and Alexander Culbertson, emerged from the epidemic scarred but still standing. They lost wives, children, and close kin in the epidemic that raged around them. We don't know how they felt about these losses, but their pain can't have been any less than the Mandan mothers who shot or hung their children when they saw the first signs of the disease, rather than to allow their bodies to putrefy from smallpox, or the Assiniboine father who killed his horses, his dogs, and finally himself after watching his children die. Euro-American men, writing in official reports, rarely expressed emotions around personal loss. The detailed descriptions of devastated Indian villages, the grief expressed by Native mothers and fathers, and the horrible course of the disease that filled the pages of the reports and letters filed by all of these men indicate something of what they felt.[113]

The loss of life was immense, probably most extreme among the Mandans, who were left with only about forty survivors. They would never really recover. The Arikaras, in comparison, still had about half their people living, mostly the very old and the very young. The loss of their young adults would seriously threaten the future of the tribe. The Assiniboine found themselves reduced to about a third of their former population. The Blackfoot and the Crows lost between two-thirds and three-quarters of their population, primarily adults in their productive prime of life. Death and disease affected trade in unexpected ways. Because fewer Indians hunted buffalo that winter, the population of bison soared, but the robe trade fell drastically as upper Missouri peoples were too demoralized and diminished to hunt much. This was a severe blow to the traders as well, coming at time of change and retrenchment in the fur trade. Pierre Chouteau Jr., ever the careful businessman, commented in February of 1838: "the calamity was calculated to fill us with dismay as regards the trade of the Missouri for some years to come. We can only view it as a visitation of Providence." He recommended that they assist Providence "by pursuing a course of strict economy in our expenditures, with kind and concilia-tory conduct to the Indians who have escaped this dreadful pestilence, endeavor by prudence, fortitude, and perseverance to support ourselves under this melancholy scourge."[114]

Without much help from either Providence or from Chouteau's American Fur Company, the people of the upper Missouri recovered. They used a variety of strategies to rebuild and re-create their populations. Euro-Amer-ican observers noted an increase in warfare as tribes reconfigured power relationships and populations. The Assiniboines, Crows, and Blackfoot in particular took captives and horses in huge numbers from each other. Blackfoot trader Alexander Culbertson noticed that following the epidemic "marriages took place between very close relations." He explained the change in kinships rules as ignorance because so many of the elders had been lost and "knowledge of relationships was sometimes was lost on the young."[115] This may well have been a purposeful, rather than ignorant, use of methods that had worked in earlier times when disease and warfare had diminished the people. Captivity and changed marriage practices allow the Blackfoot to recover their numbers rapidly. Only seventeen years after the epidemic, Edwin Denig, now the bourgeois at Fort Union, estimated their numbers were only one-third less than they had been before the diseases decimated them.[116]

The Arikaras, Hidatsas, and Mandans reorganized into a semi-united tribe. They shared agricultural practices and knowledge about more settled life on the river, so they moved further up the Missouri together. In 1845 they founded a new village, Like-a-Fishhook, where they reconstructed a society based on old practices. They demanded that the American Fur Company build a post at the village, Fort Berthold, and they again became important traders. Each of the three peoples lived in a separate section of the village and remained politically autonomous. The Lakotas, a complex grouping of at least seven different peoples, used the power shifts that came from population loss to their own advantage. They had felt the epidemic, but they lost far fewer people. They made trade agreements with various companies, raided the diminished river peoples, and spread their power and influence deep into the northern plains, effectively challenging the American Fur Company and the Assiniboines and Blackfoot. Epidemics seemed to preserve cultures who raided and traded with horses and bison and punished those people who farmed and lived in one place—not at all what Henry Schoolcraft had hoped.[117]

Disease and captivity seem to operate together in the Mexican Southwest as well. The Santa Fe Trail and the Arkansas River, which formed the border between the United States and Mexico, became paths where diseases and people traveled together. Disease infused the very bricks at Bent's Fort, where Mexican adobe makers had brought their skills and smallpox in 1832. William Bent got the disease and carried the scars for the rest of his life, but he managed to warn the Cheyenne away from the fort so they escaped that epidemic. Smallpox ravaged Comanche communities in 1816 and again in 1839–40, but the most terrible experience was a cholera epidemic, first carried by the forty-niners along the Arkansas River and then by Comanche traders to their villages throughout the Southwest. These diseases, of course, affected Euro-Americans as well, making western travel a dangerous undertaking. If travelers, traders, and settlers moved away from the rivers where diseases lurked, to the dry and high *llano estacado*, they put themselves in harm's way with the Comanches.

Such grim realities didn't dampen the enthusiasm of Mexican and American land speculators. The Rio Grande and Texas Land Company provides an example of what could and did happen. Charles Beale and Stephen Wilson, Americans with Mexican wives and long connections in New Mexico, had managed to obtain a grant of forty-five million acres in the *llano estacado*, a treeless plain in what is now western Texas and eastern New Mexico, the heart of the Comanche empire. The land company intended to settle a hundred families there. As a first step, in 1834 a group of surveyors measured and parceled the land while fifty-nine English, German, and U.S. citizens left New York on their first leg of the journey to their new homes. They could have no conception of the world in which they found themselves, except that everyone they met warned them about the Comanches and the "fever and ague." By the 1830s the Comanches controlled the trade in the region. They needed guns, saddles, mules, and slaves to care for their increasingly large herds. The Comanches focused their raiding on the Apache and Mexican settlements far to the south of their homelands. The small communities of Euro-American settlers that came to dot the eastern fringe of Comanchería became easy sources of stock animals, guns, and slaves but were not important to larger Comanche trading networks. Epidemic disease, however, created an acute need to rebuild populations and re-create kinship networks with captive people. After the brutal and disorienting experience of capture, young women and children were adopted and married into kinship networks and were given important roles in the community, quite different from chattel slavery as we usually understand it.[118]

Inexperienced Euro-Americans who wandered into the Comanche world were exposing themselves to real danger, as the story of Sarah Ann Horn and the Rio Grande and Texas Land Company demonstrates. The first indication of trouble came when a small group of Comanches attacked the surveyors one night, leaving two Anglos and nine Comanche dead, an episode that both parties would remember very clearly. Six months later, when the immigrants finally reached the site of their intended settlement in 1834, between the Pecos and Nueces rivers, they found themselves far to the west of any other Euro-American settlements, and nobody felt very safe. First, they built a wall of thorns, bushes, and small trees "for protection against the marauding Comanches." No one in this group of English and German farmers had ever seen a Comanche, but they had been convinced that fearsome Native people lurked behind every bush. Mothers kept their children inside during the sweltering Texas summer for fear of the Indians.[119]

The soil and the climate proved to be more immediate enemies, making agriculture nearly impossible. A young English colonist, Sarah Ann Horn, described the heat, insects, salty soil, and fear that frustrated efforts of the poorly equipped settlers. She explained, "These things, in connection with the danger of our being murdered by savages without a moment's warning, induced some of our friends to leave the colony."[120] Because Horn and her family were sick with malaria, they weren't able to leave and stuck it out for another year.

Finally, crop failures, stories of Comanche attacks, and the unrest created by the Texas rebellion and "the bloody Santa Anna" convinced Horn and her husband to pack up their children and leave. They immediately found themselves between General Santa Anna's army that had crossed the Rio Grande and Comanche war parties out to meet that Mexican army. Their worst fears would at last be realized when they ran into a group of Comanches. The warriors killed the men in the party, including Horn's husband, and took Horn and her three children as captives. As Horn and her family would discover, endemic malaria, smallpox, and warfare between Anglos and Mexicans had not blunted Comanche power one bit. They could, and did, tolerate small groups of settlers in their region, but large numbers of foreign troops massed on their southern borders, such as those led by Santa Anna in 1836, had to be met with speed and strength. The Horn family ran right into imperial war.[121]

Capture and the initial days of captivity met every expectation of what it would be like to be held by brutal savages. After watching the brutal murder of her husband, Sarah Ann marched long distances with little food and rest and watched helplessly as her infant child died in her arms. She worried that she would be raped, but instead she was put to work and in fact was protected by the Comanche women once she demonstrated her ability to work. She learned to dress buffalo hides and to cook for the family she served. Her two sons were adopted into families in a neighboring community and were raised just like other Comanche boys, which of course horrified Sarah Ann, who watched her boys lose their Anglo language and customs. Horn herself was bought and sold to other Native groups and to Mexican traders, and eventually to a "white American" named Hill, who bought her and expected her to act as a servant in his house in Santa Fe, demonstrating something about the vectors of the slave trade in the Southwest. To her frustration, no "Americans" made any effort to find her or to free her until she made her own way to Taos, New Mexico. She was, of course, in a foreign country where Americans had little power and the Comanches made rules about trade and war.[122]

Horn's story, which emphasizes her utter powerlessness and her inability even to understand where she was or what the motives of her captors might be, is emblematic of the situation many Euro-American settlers found when they came to the Southwest. Horn, and most others, survived entirely at the mercy of the Comanches, who decided where and when to raid, travel, settle, and trade. Because few Anglos understood Comanche practices or the extent of the trading network they had built, they found life with these rules entirely disorienting. The threat of captivity created an "enraptured discourse of fear" that built political alliances among populations that would otherwise be dangerously heterogeneous, like the people who lived in Texas or New Mexico in the nineteenth century.[123] The only Euro-Americans who succeeded in the region either were lucky enough to have settled far to the east or were people who participated in the economy on Comanche terms, becoming Comancheros who traded hides, horses, guns, and slaves all over the Southwest. What white Texan immigrants experienced as a sudden, confusing, and massive wave of captivities and violence in the 1830s and 1840s was simply the way that the Comanches had operated in the region for nearly a century, demanding that other peoples become part of their world or suffer the consequences—the way expansionistic imperial overlords behave in most places.

Even the most imperious overlords, however, can be felled by epidemic disease. And this disease came at a moment when the Comanches had extended too far and had overtaxed the natural resources of their region.

Epidemics never come at good moments, but this one came at a particularly bad time. The year 1849 represented a conflagration of bad circumstances for southern Plains tribes. All over the plains, buffalo populations had diminished significantly as a result of long natural drought cycles, the competition for winter grazing grounds with huge herds of Indian horses, and the serious overhunting of the species. By the early 1840s scores of Plains tribes, as well as the immigrant tribes along the eastern Arkansas River, depended on the bison trade for their existence, but the Great Peace of 1840 made the southern plains accessible to everyone. The region was probably being overhunted anyway, but when this was combined with an intense drought beginning in 1845, it spelled disaster for the Great Plains trade world. Hunger, and then disease, and then warfare stalked the people.[124]

When hundreds of thousands of travelers, many carrying cholera with them, crossed the Great Plains in those first gold rush years, they saw dried grasses and dry riverbeds, but few Native people and few buffalo. Cholera wiped out nearly half of the southern Plains populations, obliterating already frayed trading relationships. Native groups who had been at peace for decades began making war on each other to protect their access to the dwindling buffalo herds. As William Bent watched this disaster unfold, he knew that the buffalo trade would never survive the feet, hooves, germs, and wagon wheels of the forty-niners. He knew what he and his relatives would lose. That same year Quanah Parker, the Comanche leader who would withstand the U.S. Army and the Texas Rangers, but who would bring his people to the reservation allotted to them, was born to Cynthia Ann Parker and Peta Nocoma. Even in 1849 the birth of a child was optimistic, and his parents named him Quanah, which means "fragrant," because he was born in a bed of flowers. The proud parents, a captive Anglo-Texan and a Comanche elite warrior, could not have known that time stood on a hinge, and the world that Native people, the fur and hide trade, and its practitioners had built together over the last century, would never be the same. New peoples would determine much about what happened on the rivers, plains, and coasts of this world.[125]

In 1852 William Bent did what parents living on the upper Missouri had wanted to do in 1837: he blew up the site of death and disease, his great fort on the Arkansas River. The region had been besieged by cholera, and Bent lost many of his Cheyenne family members in an epidemic that swept the southern plains in 1849. Bent and his eldest son, Robert, then eight, had accompanied the annual wagon train east to St. Louis that spring. The rest of the family attended a grand Sun Dance hosted by the Kiowas on the Cimarron River, attended by the Cheyennes, Arapahos, Comanches, Apaches, and Osages. Just as the dance began, the cramps struck. Instantly recognizing what this meant, Bent's wife, Island, put her children on a travois and fled north to the safety of the walls of Bent's Fort. They found no protection from disease there; the children lost their grandmother, aunts, and uncles. By the time William and Robert returned, half the Southern Cheyenne lay dead in their camps. William decided that his own family might be safer far to the north at Fort St. Vrain. George Bent, who was six that year, remembered that trip as a frightening series of images: too many funeral scaffolds in trees, too many empty lodges, and, worse, untended dead bodies and abandoned guns, pots, and shields, indicating the chaos that the disease had created. The Bent family escaped the disease, but it decimated their close kin and friends.[126]

In 1851 when Henry Schoolcraft counted Indians, malaria, smallpox, and cholera had swept through Native nations, but in his accounting there were still too many Indians. They had survived epidemic disease, the demise of the fur trade, loss of land, and an invasion of immigrants, both white and Native. By 1851 Indian Country had extremely porous borders because of the complicated familial arrangements people had made to live and prosper there. These borders were both physical and cultural, so that places as different as St. Louis, Comanchería, the Columbia River, and interior California all operated as part of the same systems. A brief imperial war, a U.S. war with Mexico, would shift political ownership once again, but how long would it take for this to matter?

Part III

From Nations to Nation

Imposing a State, 1840–1865

When we left Mariano Vallejo standing on a dock in northern California in 1842, William Bent on the roof of Bent's Fort in 1835, and Andrew Drips in the fur press room at Fort Bellevue in 1844, none of them could know how poorly they had predicted the future. Family and trade had operated as entwined threads, each strengthening the other. Perhaps they could see the powerful nation that the United States was becoming. Maybe they could imagine it as another thread to weave into their networks of business, diplomacy, and kinship. Maybe not. Nation hadn't mattered much in the worlds they and their families had built in the early nineteenth century. Did Osage or Comanche leaders quake with the news that Spanish or American filibusters had landed in Louisiana in 1811 or that a revolution brewed in central Mexico in 1821 or 1836? Did William Bent care much whether his fort was in Mexico, the United States, or Comanchería? Did Pierre Chouteau worry about Mormons gathering in Missouri? Did it matter to Marguerite McLoughlin whether the ships that brought her tea and cloth at Fort Vancouver were from Boston, Antwerp, or London? Did Mariano Vallejo care whether he sold hides to Russians, Chileans, or Americans? For a long time, the answer to these questions was no.

With great expertise, these people had benefited from the fact that no larger authority had imposed order on most of the West. Spain, France, England, and Russia, as well as Mexico and the United States as the latecomers in the process, all laid claim to pieces of the trans-Mississippi West, but a variety of individuals, corporations, and nations always challenged such claims. A lone explorer, flag, mission, ship, or fort had little influence, and lines drawn on maps had none. No one really knew where particular borders lay, and most people living near these lines simply ignored them. The fur and hide trade and its ancillaries had operated as a huge stabilizing force in the region for more than two centuries. People had redesigned cultures and families to mesh with that trade, creating a patchwork of regional communities linked by trade and kinship etiquette. When the fur and hide trade became less important, the myriad things that had threatened to destabilize the region and to permit different kinds of conquest did so.

When the center became less certain, challenges to the structure became more threatening. Filibusters, land grabs, and various speculative endeavors had been irritants in the West for decades. National wrangling over borders, treaties, military installments, and ports had embroiled red-faced diplomats for half a century. Colonization experiments with groups of immigrant settlers, which could include everything from Indian relocation, Texas empresarios, Mexican colonization schemes in California, Lord Selkirk's grant in Manitoba, and missions and missionary settlements, had placed outposts in the region. Whether they succeeded or not depended entirely on how well they meshed with local Native people and the larger rules of trade created by the fur and hide trades.

As the great stabilizing structure of the fur trade and the power held by the Native people who stood at its center both began to crumble, these outside irritants became frightening harbingers of change. So many people and ideas had been set in motion by the turbulence of early nineteenth-century economics and culture, and the Mexican War came from the chancy mix of these situations. No one person or event caused the war, nor were its course or effects predictable, but it was inevitable.[1] Its outcome, however, remained in play for a long time. Central to that outcome was the presence of an increasingly powerful state, something new on the western landscape. This state and the demographic changes it brought with it promised order and opportunity, but instead it brought disorder and chaos. How families, commercial enterprises, and other nations responded to this new state remains a very large question. For most people in the West, the war didn't end with military victory in 1847. Its ramifications took much longer to be teased out of the messy set of contingencies and human decisions that wars do create. By examining the set of conditions that provoked the war and the choices people made around its outcome, but using the lenses of family and region, a different picture of war emerges. The Mexican War—or the U.S. War with Mexico—played out on a grand scale with clashes between fading and emerging empires, but it also drew the already intimate world of the early nineteenth-century West into even tighter circles.

Chapter 6

Unintended Consequences

Families, Nations, and the Mexican War

Mary Parker Richards tried to soothe her sister-in-law Jane. But in the misery of the Mormon Winter Quarters in Nebraska she couldn't find much that might be comforting. Jane's sick three-year-old, Wealthy Lovisa, coughed weakly in her mother's arms, and Jane had just learned that her young brother-in-law, Joseph Richards, had "volunteered" to join the U.S. Army to fight in the Mexican War. Neither Mary nor Jane could make sense of this latest scheme. Both Mary's and Jane's husbands, Samuel and Franklin Richards, had been ordered to go to Scotland to recruit new Saints, leaving them just as the Saints prepared to move to an isolated spot in the West where they would rebuild the Mormon kingdom. Joseph Richards had intended to help the women and children move, but instead he would serve in the army for the United States. Military recruiting agents had come into their rough settlements on the Potawatomi reserves and asked for volunteers. They got no takers until Brother Brigham made it known volunteering was required; it would pay the way to the West for five hundred men and some families, and it would buy gratitude and safety for everyone else. The Richards family, who had given lives in sacrifice to the Mormon cause already, tithed again—this time with young Joseph, who would march to a war the Mormons didn't support. Jane had a larger family who would care for her, but the burden of losing family members to this war was immense. Would she or the children die in this camp from hunger or typhus, or would young Joseph die in Mexico from a bullet or from sickness? It seemed too much to bear, but she would.[2]

What If Guadalupe Boggs Married Teresina Carson?

The connections that families and businesses form became especially important in the context of war. The families we have traced developed new associations and deepened old ones to get through periods of uncertainty.

A certain cast of characters emerged who appeared at so many flashpoints of the war it is barely credible. However, the positions of these families and these characters are far more than coincidence; they are the result of several generations spent building and developing personal links across ethnic and national lines. One family example with whom we are already acquainted came out of the Mississippi and Missouri river frontiers but by midcentury had spread their influence much further. Marriage and children, business and war, blended the Bents, Boggs, and Boones of Missouri with the Jaramillos and Vallejos of Mexico and with powerful Cheyenne, Shoshone, and Comanche families. The outcome is a very small world.

Lilburn W. Boggs, the governor of Missouri during the 1838 Mormon War who ordered the Mormons to be "exterminated" by state militia, reconsidered his future in Missouri politics and decided that he and his family would benefit from a fresh start in California. He could consider such a move in 1846 because his family linked him to opportunity (and trouble) across the continent. As an up-and-coming St. Louis fur trader, he had first married Juliannah Bent, William and Charles's sister. They moved to the frontier of western Missouri, where they had two children before Juliannah's death at age nineteen. The ambitious and frazzled young father then wed into another famous western family by marrying Panthea Boone. He and Panthea moved around the river frontiers, producing Tom in 1824 while Lilburn worked as a trader among the Osages on the Neosho River and William, born in 1826 at Fort Osage on the Missouri. Both Boggs boys attended the new Harmony mission school, where their father had been appointed agent and deputy factor, assisting George Sibley, our old friend from Fort Osage.[3]

Working his way up through Missouri politics and being elected governor in 1836, after a tight race against William Ashley of fur-trading fame, Boggs found himself in the midst of civil war in Missouri over the Mormons, which had disastrous consequences for everyone involved. After several assassination attempts by angry citizens on various sides of the issue and with the Boggs family name rather tattered after the Mormon fiasco, much of the family moved to California in 1846. Boggs led a wagon train of nearly one hundred families, many of whom would separate from the Boggs Party over disagreements concerning the route and the speed of travel. In another piece of irony or coincidence, the largest group to split off would become known as the Donner Party—of rather grisly cannibal fame. Boggs and his part of the group made the trip without such dreadful sequelae, though they had a very rough crossing of the Sierra Nevada.

They ended up in Mariano Vallejo's Sonoma community, where they spent a few months in the fall and winter of 1846–1847 as they awaited news about the war and its conclusion.

Boggs, understanding the importance of building new relations, did not hesitate to blend the Vallejos into his family. Whether he understood this as a form of fictive kinship or was just genuinely grateful to his host, when a son was born to Boggs's son and his wife that January, Lilburn insisted that the child be named Muriano [*sic*] Guadalupe Boggs in honor of Vallejo. As a result of their friendship, when the war came to an end and General Vallejo lost his military commission, he arranged to have his new *compadre*, Lilburn Boggs, appointed as *alcalde* of northern California, which included Sutter's Fort and Sacramento, as well as Sonoma. The new *alcalde* made his headquarters at the Vallejo hacienda until things settled a bit. Boggs's luck held, and he found himself owning a general store and holding political office in Sonoma when the news of the gold discovery broke. After a few years of the profitable but chaotic task of running a store in a new mining district, Lilburn, his brother, his son, and their wives settled in the Napa Valley, using their trade world experience to make money in the Indian trade and then to buy land.[4]

The family spread in other directions as well. Tom, the eldest of the Boone-Boggs sons, born in the Neosho Agency among the Osages, would become a teamster for the Bent family in 1844. Wanting a permanent connection to the world of Arkansas River trade, he married Rumalda Bent, Charles and Ignacia's oldest daughter, in 1846. After the war this Boggs family would settle on a rancho just east of Taos with Josefa and Kit Carson and raise their children together. Using long-tested Spanish and Mexican understandings of how to create kinship, or *compadrazco*, they built families mutually, especially in the unsettled times during and after the Mexican War. Older Bent family ties to Cheyenne, Comanche, and Ute families and trading network protected them on this dangerous frontier, but only as long as these ties were tended and remade, a process that broke down in the 1860s.

This collective family making would have unintended consequences. Because Tom Boggs could be counted on to support the families on the ranch, and with the help of their wives, Rumalda and Josefa, and their niece Teresina Bent, to run the cattle and sheep, Kit Carson could look for a job that would provide the cash the extended family needed. He moved back into the world of Indian trade and in the 1850s took on the job of agent to the Utes and Apaches. Finally, Carson rejoined the army in 1861, a decision that would lead to the death and rebirth of the Navajo nation. Their family choices had closed the circle, again, between St. Louis, New Mexico, California, the Arkansas, the Columbia, and the Rio Grande. Their world, in which Kit Carson's and Josefa Jaramillo's daughter Teresina Carson could easily marry Lilburn Boggs's and Mariano Vallejo's namesake, Guadalupe Boggs, had built the West that existed before the Mexican War and would continue to matter in surprising ways long after.[5]

This family, with all of its surprising connections, demonstrates how random and contingent the place and period were. A woman's decision to marry this man or that, or a family's decision to move west at a particular moment, or a fortuitous friendship made differences in how lives turned out. People, of course, made decisions bounded by cultural and economic realities, and the U.S.-Mexico War both limited and widened the scope of these choices. Certainly the upheaval of war juxtaposed people and experiences in unexpected combinations. When Susan Magoffin, a young St. Louisan newly married to a Santa Fe merchant, headed down the Santa Fe Trail on the eve of the Mexican War, she had little idea what lay in store for her. She didn't know, for example, that her brother-in-law served as a spy for President Polk or that her husband had serious enemies among Mexican elites. Her "adventure" included a miscarriage, a sojourn at Bent's Fort with a restless army, and a winter flight from angry New Mexicans. Once her pulse returned to normal, the experience didn't change her life in fundamental ways. As an observer, a resident of the conquering nation, and an educated young Anglo-American woman, she could view the war as a thrilling interlude.[6]

For many westerners, however, the experience of conquest and war changed lives in serious ways. While Susan Magoffin observed the war unfolding, other women with more at stake also watched from Bent's Fort. The Jaramillo sisters of Taos, married to Charles Bent and Kit Carson, and Owl Woman, William Bent's Cheyenne wife, gathered at Bent's Fort in July of 1846 to watch General Kearny's army gather. They worried together what the next months and years would bring. From their perspective, the war threatened more than it thrilled. While they could sympathize with the young American Susan Magoffin as she lay in the fort's guest quarters mourning the loss of her baby, they knew that her very presence signaled changes they could not control.[7]

Certainly age and stage or how much loss one had already suffered affected the way people experienced the war and the change of imperial overlord. Marguerite McLoughlin, forced out of her Fort Vancouver home as the debate over who would control Oregon got nasty, surely found 1846 a challenging year. She had endured, in rapid succession, the terrible blows of her son's murder, her son-in-law's suicide, and her husband's demotion, all related to the changes in political economy along the Columbia River. Wealth and status, as it had been understood in the years when the Hudson's Bay Company had ruled the region, could no longer protect her family as an aggressive settler culture of Anglo-American farmers and miners infiltrated her world.[8]

That same summer of 1846 Francesca Vallejo watched as dirty and uncouth "Bear Flaggers" (many of them former Missouri and Mexico neighbors of the Bents, Boones, and Carsons) dragged her elegantly dressed husband, brother, and brothers-in-law off to prison. Francesca, left alone in the midst of a rebellion with eight children ranging from infancy to twelve, had much to fear. The deep political unrest around Mexican rule and the large influx of American settlers would disrupt the world the Vallejos had built at Sonoma. Francesca's life had never been peaceful, but she had expected to raise her children in a place where people spoke many languages, not where English would overwhelm her. The Bear Flag Revolt would fail, and her husband would be returned unharmed, but this did not lessen her concern about what would happen to her family.

Like Marguerite and Francesca, Owl Woman had built a family along a shifting border. Daughter of White Thunder, an important Cheyenne leader, she had married William Bent in 1838, and they now had three young children. The family lived with her tribe in winter at Big Timbers but at the fort in summer. Bent's Fort had become the center of a powerful trading world that now encompassed the Great Plains, the Southwest, and northern Mexico. When the Comanches had agreed to partner with the Cheyennes in 1840, they had created a network of enormous significance. Could some soldiers from a far-off capital unsettle this world? Many troops and many people had come and gone, but the Comanches, the Cheyennes, and their horses had conquered all of them.

The year 1846, in hindsight, certainly operated as a "year of decision" that would shift the meaning of borders and the personal and economic connections people had built to bridge them. These border zones had been at the center of local and international contention for decades, so that the question of why war became inevitable at this particular moment remains a good one. But war had been years in the making in this region that thrived on instability.

We saw in Texas and in Mexico that nation building emerged as a central activity in the early nineteenth century. As people tested what national sovereignty and national identity meant, wars became inevitable as members of these new nations tested boundaries of all kinds at their unstable borders. Some of the instability came from unclear definitions of citizenship and national power. What should or could citizens do, and what would the nation do to limit their actions? Some of the instability came from the United States and the unsettled slavery question. Many land grabs and filibustering attempts came from slave owners worrying about slavery's viability in the increasingly free-labor-minded republic. For some, the obvious solution was to head west, or to sail south to territory that seemed friendlier to slavery and less well defended. Texas became a flashpoint for many of these challenges.

Texas, with its position as an independent republic with no real army or diplomatic status, drew attention from those who wanted to take advantage of disorder and weakness. Its borders would always be porous, but especially so when three striving nations tried to redraw them. Mexican citizens successfully marched into Texas several times, nearly bankrupting Sam Houston's meager treasury when he had to send in troops to defend San Antonio. When the incompetent and ambitious (always a poor combination) Mirabeau Lamar became president of Texas in 1838, he insisted that "the natural borders" of Texas included the Pacific Coast and much of northern Mexico, and certainly all of New Mexico east of the Rio Grande. He encouraged various filibustering expeditions south into Chihuahua and west into New Mexico, further destabilizing both regions.

The most famous episode, the 1841 Texas–New Mexico Expedition, began in 1840 when Lamar hired three Anglo residents of Santa Fe to convince New Mexicans to join the Republic of Texas. After these agents had softened up New Mexico residents, the expedition of "capitalists and soldiers" was supposed to arrive and liberate them. It failed on all accounts. The expedition was poorly planned; the leaders (probably the capitalists) lacked a clear idea of the distance to Santa Fe or the best routes to travel. Within weeks they were lost. Their Mexican guides abandoned them, and Kiowas seeking revenge for the Council House Massacre of 1840 attacked them, killed five men, stampeded all the cattle, and ran off eighty-three horses. The Kiowas then headed north and, as allies of the Bents, told them about the expedition. Already disgusted with the situation in Texas that threatened his business, Charles Bent went immediately to Governor Manuel Armijo and told him what he knew. Armijo had known about the expedition from the beginning and received troops and funding from

Mexico to repel the expected attack, but Bent's confirmation allowed him to act offensively.[9]

Armijo's troops caught all of the Texans and sent them to be tried in Mexico. Celebrations all over New Mexico featured burning printed copies of President Lamar's proclamations. Masses of thanksgiving were celebrated in every.parish, and a play, *The Texans*, was written and performed, a spoof of the expedition that everyone enjoyed. Texans, feeling embarrassed and challenged, felt obligated to try several more times with essentially the same results. In early 1843 Charles A. Warfield and a small group of adventurers attempted to attack the town of Mora but were driven off by a superior New Mexican force. Warfield disbanded his group, though one contingent of the group under the command of John McDaniel killed Antonio Chavez, a New Mexican trader, on the Santa Fe Trail. Warfield had imagined wresting New Mexico and perhaps even Chihuahua from Mexico. He did not, however, have foresight to understand how displeased the Bents and the U.S. government would be with the murder of Chavez and the disruption of commerce along the Santa Fe Trail. They sent a company of dragoons commanded by Captain Philip St. George Cooke to protect wagon trains leaving from Missouri. Cooke confronted and arrested the remaining filibusterers, ending that particular episode of Texas aggression against New Mexico.[10]

These episodes occurred in a context of an epidemic of filibustering in the first half of the nineteenth century; we saw the earliest versions of such filibustering in the likes of James Wilkinson and Aaron Burr on the Texas border. No border—U.S., Canadian, Mexican—stood uncontested, and no bordering nations could keep the invaders out of these unstable frontier zones. Military amateurs and armchair enthusiasts from all parts of North America planned private invasions so frequently that punsters could lampoon them as scratching at the nation's "great filibustering flea," as the *New York Times* put it. And more than a few got beyond the planning stage.[11]

Just as Texans stood and demanded independence in 1836 and New Mexicans rose up in protest against perceived injustices in 1837, armed rebellion broke out all along the Canadian border. This rebellion was variously called the Patriot War or the Aroostook War further east in Maine and New Brunswick, and its debates concerned where the international border should be and what kind of government should exist there. Various forces in Lower Canada, now Quebec, wanted to create a French Canadian republic and liberate it from the British empire. Many of the rebels were former fur traders who founded the "Fréres Chasseurs" or Hunting Brothers. They organized paramilitary lodges and launched attacks against British authorities. Their first efforts failed, and the remnants of the organization fled into upstate New York and Maine, where they reorganized and rearmed. In 1838, led by Canadian William Lyon McKenzie and armed with cannons they had stolen from local New York militia supplies, they occupied Navy Island, a small deserted island in the Niagara River. Mackenzie declared it an independent country, which began an international incident in which Canadian border officials fired on the USS *Caroline*, burned it, and hurled it over Niagara Falls. American forces then burned a British steamer, the SS *Sir Robert Peel*, necessitating a new treaty between Britain and the United States and a round of earnest apologies.[12]

QUESTIONS OF CITIZENSHIP AND IDENTITY

With pirates and rebels and filibusters challenging the borders and the very concept of nationhood, threats to stability from within had extra resonance. New groups had entered the shifting casts of characters that peopled the West in the 1830s. One surprising native group was the Mormons or Latter-day Saints, who replaced the Osages in terms of public worry and press attention on the Missouri frontier. Like the Osages, they were small in number but effective in getting the attention of imperial or national officialdom. Taking the analogy further, like many Native nations, the Mormons traveled in family groups, did business almost exclusively with their kin, and took great pleasure in refusing to do things the "American way." Maybe a better comparison is to see the Mormons as more like the Comanches. Similar in numbers, eventually arranged across a forbidding piece of isolated desert landscape, they controlled trade and travel in the region using kinship connections, price controls, and fear.

Mormons and Indians disrupted Anglo-American assumptions about how settlement should occur and who should benefit from it. Unlike Native societies, however, Mormonism developed out of the heart of Anglo-American culture and religion and operated as a sort of shadow critique, which is why it upset people so much. In the same year that young Mariano Vallejo and his family fled the coast of California because of rumored French pirates landing in Monterey, another family left New England for upstate New York. Less romantic than pirates, but equally infamous and misunderstood, the Mormon religion that would come out of this move to the eastern edge of the western frontier would prove even more unsettling.

JOSEPH SMITH AND THE ORIGINS OF MORMONISM

Joseph Smith came from a long line of ambitious New Englanders, but his immediate family had become downwardly mobile at the start of the nineteenth century. Moving all over New England after they sold the family farm, the Smith family represented a large group of newly landless farmers who struggled to make sense of a deeply depressed economy. Barely making ends meet, but supported by their extended families, they remained proudly solvent. Joseph's mother, Lucy Mack Smith, a strong and deeply religious woman, held the family together as they moved further and further west into Vermont and then New York. Like many people in this generation of New Englanders, the Smiths belonged to no church but sought out itinerant preachers. The family, especially Lucy, experienced waves of revivals as they moved through Massachusetts and Vermont, but in Richard Bushman's words, "they were anguished souls, starved for religion." Finally, after the family suffered through a terrible bout of fever and a year with no harvest in 1816, when cold and drought obliterated crops all over the eastern United States, they decided to move to Palmyra, New York, to begin anew.[13]

Palmyra was not the western frontier, and land could not be had by squatting upon it nor by surveying and claiming it. Joseph and Lucy Smith had to go into deep debt to buy land there, but they believed that the new Erie Canal and the rumors of large harvests would make their gamble a profitable one. They struggled to make their payments and had to send all of their children out to work to earn enough cash. Joseph Jr., the third son, found himself apprenticed to a newspaper printer at the age of twelve, the same year he began having visions and worrying about his religious salvation. Given the fierceness of evangelical revivals and the range of mystical activities that accompanied them in this time and place, Joseph's early visions and his dabbling in things that could be labeled as the black arts seem rather ordinary. According to Smith in much later memoirs, he kept these activities to himself until 1823, when an angel named Moroni revealed himself to Joseph, and they initiated a series of prophetic conversations. Using a set of seeing or "peep" stones, crystals used in all kinds of American folk practices, Smith (and Moroni) uncovered a secret that would turn a restless young man into a prophet. Gold plates with instructions from God would be given to Smith and to Smith alone; his task was to find the plates and to translate them. The angel's prophecy came true; young Joseph found the magical plates, and his peep stones allowed him to see their written message.[14]

By 1827 Smith's confidence in what he had experienced and his understanding about what God expected from him increased enough that he felt able to go public. He began telling his neighbors the story of how he found the plates and what he was finding inscribed on them. His theology stood on the shifting line between visionary and rational, between magic and religion, a common place in the early nineteenth century. This creative moment, as Protestantism constantly challenged and reinvented itself, encouraged personal revelations like Joseph Smith's. His own family remained skeptical even as they helped Joseph with the task of translation and publication of what would become the Book of Mormon. Everyone in the Smiths' neighborhood soon knew about the plates; some people scoffed openly while others schemed about how to get their hands on the alluring golden objects. A few people, including some prosperous local farmers and a couple of scholars, began to believe the story that Joseph told as well as the theological message revealed in the manuscript he was slowly creating out of the symbols written on the plates. They arranged for transcribers to assist Smith and for printing and publication of the eventual book. In a whirlwind of translation, dictation, rewriting, and editing, Smith and his helpers produced the first version of the Book of Mormon in 1830.

Joseph Smith understood the incredible qualities of his story and arranged for a series of witnesses to look at the plates before he reburied them, as instructed by Moroni. These witnesses, all close family friends, did little to convince skeptics. The story the book told, no matter how it was produced, got strong reactions. It either compelled or horrified its early readers. It instructed people to build a strict new Israel on the American continent and to reform the world from there. The Book of Mormon proposed a new purpose for America: to become "a realm of righteousness rather than an empire of liberty." Militantly nationalistic and powerfully subversive, this new narrative of an Old Testament religion appealed to people buffeted by religious and economic change. Its critique of wealth and inequality and the strict rules that came directly from a living prophet were just right for the times.[15]

Could a twenty-three-year-old man with a poor education, little religious training, and a reputation for "fanciful" behavior have written such a thing? Who knows—historians and theologians certain don't.[16] But on this older western frontier, Joseph Smith's vision led to the foundation of a church and a rapid gathering of converts. The controversies around Smith also required mass migrations to the west that brought increasing attention to the sect from the outside. Such notice gave its followers a sense that they were new Israelites enduring a series of hegiras. Smith continued to receive new messages from God that told him how to organize the hierarchy of the Church of Latter-day Saints and where it should be located. One group moved to Ohio in 1831; another group moved to Missouri in 1832, and they were forcibly expelled from the Missouri settlement only a year later. They retreated to Ohio but remained determined to reclaim their "Zion" in Missouri. By the time the Mormons regathered in Missouri in 1838, Smith had nearly ten thousand converts who now believed that their religion was under fire and that it required a trained, private militia to protect it.[17]

Mormon militancy, combined with fear and intolerance on the part of other Missouri settlers, resulted in a virtual civil war. Both sides believed they acted to protect property and to uphold the law. Both sides burned farms, vandalized stores, and committed murder, but with full knowledge and support of civil authorities. The St. Louis newspapers claimed that thousands of Mormon troops were marching from Canada and that Mormon leaders plotted with hostile Indians and abolitionists.[18] On the other side, Mormons believed stories that their land would be seized and their leaders jailed. By late summer the entire western part of the state felt like an armed camp. Governor Lilburn W. Boggs sent in the state militia, which was too little too late in terms of timely state intervention. The militia, hardly an orderly, well-disciplined entity in frontier Missouri, had little hope of reducing the tensions effectively. Boggs recalled them when he realized that Missouri citizens had created much of the problem. Even the St. Louis papers admitted that "we apprehend that the excitement which has been created, or at least much of, is without foundation."[19] From the cool distance of St. Louis, this might have seemed true, but people in those embattled western counties believed the worst about each other. When a group of non-Mormon vigilantes held a large group of Mormon families under siege in one county and groups of Mormon soldiers marched into another county and drove people out of their homes and then pillaged and burned the homes, all prejudices were confirmed. The situation had dissolved into open warfare.[20]

What was it about the Mormons that so easily inflamed these frontier communities? Aside from the xenophobia common to that place and time, Joseph Smith had made some doctrinal decisions that ensured conflict: the practice of polygamy and the creation of the United Order, a radical communal experiment that encouraged Mormons to buy up huge quantities of land and to do business as a large cooperative. Their sheer numbers and their business practices allowed the Mormons to dominate western Missouri counties almost entirely, which many of their neighbors found un-American and unfair. The final straw for many Missourians came from the powerful antislavery stance of the Mormons and their ability to use Mormon votes to threaten the property of the majority of residents who supported slavery.[21]

With this set of seemingly insoluble differences, and affidavits and pleas coming in from many western counties about the heinous tactics in the vigilante war that Mormons and non-Mormons waged on each other, Governor Boggs felt compelled to step in against the Mormons using the full power of the state. Whether the Mormons had been goaded into violence or whether they owned property legally no longer mattered; the people had demanded that the state act. Boggs acted largely this time, calling up three thousand state and federal troops and spending more than $200,000 in his effort to drive out the Mormons. He wrote to military officials: "the Mormons must be treated as enemies, and must be exterminated or driven from the State."[22] With this order in hand, troops and a range of citizens' groups marched on the Mormons. Joseph Smith, who had vowed to stand firm, quickly realized that his Mormon troops could not win a war against state troops, and that his people could be destroyed entirely in such a conflagration. A terrible massacre of families at Haun's Mill demonstrated the vulnerability of many Mormons. Smith, faced with several thousand troops, turned himself into the authorities. In return he agreed that the Mormons would give up all of their weapons, leave the state under armed protection, and abandon their property as payment for the damage they had inflicted on their neighbors. It wasn't legal, it wasn't fair, but Smith and the Mormons had no options.[23]

Given ten days to gather their belongings and leave the state, the stunned Mormons headed east and north in straggling groups of families, with an armed escort to protect them, but with no clear plan about where to go. Twelve to fifteen thousand of them made their way to the area around Quincy, Illinois, and to places in Iowa just west of the Mississippi called the Half-Breed Tract, a piece of land recently allotted to immigrating Native people and their families. Joseph Smith and five other martyrs remained in Missouri jails, charged with "overt acts of treason." As their trial approached, Governor Boggs, recognized that many of his own actions had been hasty and illegal and decided that he wanted to put the Mormon matter behind him as quietly as possible. He allowed, or even arranged, for Smith and the other Mormon leaders to escape from jail and to rejoin their people in Illinois.[24]

Even as the Missouri Mormons were expelled from their homes, the sect expanded with considerable numbers of converts immigrating from Great Britain. A large recruiting effort in the midst of the growing disasters in Ohio and then in Missouri had netted thousands of new converts from the fading rural villages and harsh industrial towns of England and Wales. Mary Parker Haskins, a young Lancashire servant, was one of these. Mary, along with her parents and several of her siblings, found the Mormon message of order and redemption appealing. Nearly sixty thousand Britons responded to the critique of the "Babylon" that industrialization had created in England and to the sharp rebuke Mormonism offered to old Protestant groups that seemed to condone people's earthly misery. After the rather elderly Haskins heard about the new city arising in Nauvoo, Illinois, the hopelessness of their situation and a desire to create something new convinced them to immigrate to America in 1840. Their daughter Mary followed them several years later, traveling alone and arriving in Nauvoo in 1843, where at least 4,500 British Mormons had gathered.[25]

The sheer number of Mormon converts began to concern other Illinois residents. In the 1830s the Illinois newspapers had reported on the war in Missouri with some disgust, clearly feeling that their neighbors to the west had overreacted badly. On November 22, 1838, the Galena, Illinois, paper titled its story "Most Horrid!" and described "the shocking intelligence of a number of skirmishes" between Missouri citizens and the Mormons. The editor concluded, "it appears that the Mormons acted defensively." Though few people in Illinois rushed to help the Mormons who straggled back into their state, they did allow them to settle and sold them land, stock, and tools, at least at the beginning. However, once Joseph Smith was out of prison, calling for new converts to build a great city at Nauvoo, Illinois, the tone of the newspapers shifted.[26]

In 1840 and 1841, newspapers discussed the "quaint" and "silly" doctrines of the Mormons as an example of the kinds of religious enthusiasms that characterized the period. They seemed interested in but not threatened by Nauvoo and the goings-on there. Soon, however, the papers reflected growing concern about the numbers of immigrants arriving and their political views. The *Jacksonville Illinoian* reported in August of 1841 that "within a week nearly 40 wagons, containing about 240 emigrants—men, women and children—bound for Nauvoo, in this state, have passed through our town." With evident surprise, the writer noted "their appearance was respectable." A year later, the *Illinois Herald* published in Alton, Illinois, admitted things had gotten worrisome. "Hitherto, we, in common with a multitude of others, have indulged in no serious fears respecting this latest form of fanaticism," the editor explained. Now, however, "we can no longer regard Mormonism with such indifference," he opined darkly, because of his certainty that "the leaders in this cause have far-reaching designs, that wear another than a religious aspect."[27]

The Mormons, as this editor hinted, did want more than a religious practice. They wanted a state that could protect them from persecution so that they could build a theocracy. The memory of the war in Missouri, the loss of their property, and the deaths of their loved ones understandably poisoned many of the Mormon faithful, making them even more suspicious and clannish as they settled into Illinois. Within five years, Nauvoo had a population of more than fifteen thousand, making it as large as Chicago, though most of its buildings were roughhewn log buildings. The city and culture in which Mary Parker Haskins found herself immersed were muddy, poor, struggling, and vibrant. As people shook with chills from malarial fevers and planted crops in swampy soil, they also had reading circles, band performances, plays, community meals, and religious experiences. They also marched in military drills and worked feverishly to build the central temple as their non-Mormon neighbors began to voice their threats more vigorously.[28]

Because of this combination of success and isolation, Illinois citizens became very unhappy with their Mormon neighbors. The Mormons had gained national notoriety, and Joseph Smith had been branded as a dangerous fanatic with unnatural tastes because of the increasing openness with which he encouraged polygamy. The cycle that had played out in Missouri would play out again, but with an even more violent outcome. It would send the increasingly militant and frightened Mormons even farther west. The trouble began in Hancock County, Illinois, where the Mormons built Nauvoo with so much success. Non-Mormon residents quickly felt outnumbered. The local papers, the *Western World* and the *Warsaw Signal*, reveal how quickly people got upset about Mormon control of politics. Their considerable numbers and their practice of block voting allowed them to dominate local elections. In June of 1841, the *Warsaw Signal* reported that "the head of the church is now making efforts to concentrate a great number of his people in this county, which will give him control of a decided majority of votes, we deem in effect a despotism." The editor went on to announce that local people had given up on the usual political parties and formed their own bloc, voting against candidates who were "opposed to political and military Mormonism and who will oppose the concentration of power in the hands of one man."[29]

The situation deteriorated quickly. Wallace Stegner wisely noted that "a chosen people is inspiring for the chosen to live among; it is not so comfortable for the outsiders to live with." Discomfort turned into fear as the Mormons worked furiously to bring huge numbers of converts from the eastern United States and Great Britain into western Illinois. Joseph Smith planned a run for the U.S. presidency in 1844 and made public the practice of polygamy among the Mormon elite, creating an incipient crisis. When Smith ordered the Mormon militia, or Nauvoo Legion, to destroy an anti-Mormon newspaper press, Illinois exploded. The Hancock County papers reported violence and warfare and saw themselves under siege while the rest of the state saw "mob rule" emerging. People from across the political spectrum began to petition the governor to take action, either to stop the theocratic activities of the Mormons or to prevent other Illinois citizens from dissolving into "packs of wolves." Governor Thomas Ford, feeling that he had no choice, took control of the civilian militia and demanded that Joseph Smith turn himself in before the situation got out of hand.[30]

While Joseph Smith was being held in a Carthage, Illinois, jail, local anti-Mormon militia assassinated him and his brother Hyrum. Governor Ford, unable to control the situation, watched as mobs burned Mormon homes. However, if they thought the Mormons would fall apart when they found themselves leaderless and homeless, the anti-Mormon vigilantes in Illinois were entirely wrong. Their actions created a sect with a martyred prophet, a status that gave the Mormons enormous moral cohesion. As more than twenty thousand mourners filed past the bodies of Joseph and Hyrum, the Mormons closed ranks and chose a leader, Brigham Young, who could guide the people into the next phase of kingdom building.[31]

In the midst of such drama, Mary Haskins Parker and Samuel Richards fell in love and married. They married in the unfinished temple on January 29, 1846, and shared their ceremony with Samuel's brother Franklin, who married his first plural wife that day. Mary and Samuel moved in with Mary's parents and her brother. They knew that they probably wouldn't stay long in Nauvoo. Though it looked peaceful and prosperous, their Mormon families and friends were preparing themselves for another move—though to where they didn't yet know. Brigham Young would only say that they would settle in a place "so remote that there will not need be difficulty with the people and ourselves." Despite the changes that loomed, Samuel worked hard at building the temple, because without a temple Mormons could not celebrate the sacraments essential to their spiritual existence. While Samuel made bricks, Mary cared for her widowed brother's children. In the

30. Nauvoo temple in Nauvoo, Illinois, 1846. Unknown photographer. Charles
William Carter Collection, Church History Library, Church of Jesus Christ of
Latter-day Saints, Salt Lake City.

This early photograph shows the relatively grand structure of the Nauvoo
temple on top the hill in the distance. The Mormons worked furiously to
finish their temple, even though they knew they would not remain in
Nauvoo. The elegant building stands out against the foreground of
wooden houses and outhouses that made up Mississippi River towns.

evenings they strolled through Nauvoo, attended services, and visited the
Masonic Hall, decorated appropriately, if rather horrifically, with murals
representing the murders and martyrdom of Joseph and Hyrum Smith.[32]

The new leader, Brigham Young, promised Governor Ford of Illinois
that the Mormons would leave Nauvoo, but not until they could plan for an
orderly move and finish the temple. The temple and the rites that people
experienced there stood at the heart of the Mormon religion. The Saints

couldn't begin a grand migration without the proper endowments from these temple ceremonies, which explains why Samuel and other young men worked so tirelessly at construction. As the temple walls rose, Brigham Young petitioned the president to settle his people temporarily on Indian lands in Iowa. By early 1845 thousands of families built wagons, gathered the recommended numbers of supplies, and got spiritually prepared in the new temple. Nauvoo turned into a center for blacksmithing and carpentry as Mormon families sold their farms to raise the cash necessary to fund wagons, tents, and oxen.[33]

When a new set of rumors washed over Nauvoo about the impending arrests of Mormon leaders, along with a fresh outbreak of vigilante violence, the first large group of Mormons left. It was February, not an ideal time to cross the frozen landscape, but all they really had to do was cross the Mississippi. Over the next year thousands of people traveled across what is now Iowa, some with well-equipped wagons and some with no belongings at all. However, according to a mystified newspaper reporter from St. Louis, everyone maintained "lightness of heart, apparent cheerfulness, and sanguine hopes because they regard trials and privations as a species of martyrdom." The aspiring Mormon poet Eliza Snow captured the mood perfectly in a bit of verse she wrote in February of 1846, just after crossing the Mississippi:

> Though we fly from vile aggression,
> We'll maintain our pure profession,
> Seek a peaceable possession
> Far from Gentiles and oppression.[34]

The newlyweds Samuel and Mary Richards saw the situation with more gravity; they spent their first months of marriage preparing for both a move and a separation. Samuel had been called on a mission to recruit Saints on the East Coast, and Mary planned to accompany Samuel's parents, important Mormon elders, on the trek west. Mary did not even attempt to mask her misery at this separation, though she did understand the need to sacrifice her own needs for the greater needs of the church. She began keeping a journal the moment Samuel left for the East because she knew "it would be a trial beyond description." Mary, her in-laws, and her parents, along with thousands of other Saints, gathered in what Brigham Young called "Winter Quarters" just west of the Missouri River near present-day Omaha and prepared for a much longer journey.[35]

When exactly Mormon leaders decided on the Great Basin as their destination is unclear, but the location met their requirements from the beginning: it was isolated, barely populated, and not part of the United States. A group of 140 "pioneers" left early that spring of 1847 to assess the region and to choose a site for a city. The previous year, hoping to hedge their bets and to earn cash desperately needed for the move, Brigham Young had recruited young men to serve in a Mormon Battalion as part of the army that was forming to undertake the fight for Texas and California. Five hundred Mormons would have their transportation paid to the West, earn some extra cash, and demonstrate basic loyalty to the United States. As these two advance teams progressed across the West in very different directions, the rest of the Mormons grew crops, built wagons, and organized themselves in groups of ten and then fifty households. Because their lives depended on it, they planned for a trip across a thousand miles of unfamiliar territory with more than military precision.[36]

It had taken more than two months for Mary Richards and her family to cross the "prairas" of Iowa and to reach the community known as Winter Quarters. She would spend nearly two years there, waiting for Samuel to return and for her family's turn to travel west. Mary described the discomforts and dangers of life in Winter Quarters as crowds of people surged into the raw community during the winter and spring of 1847. She worried about her family's health and about the "wild Indians." The spot they chose for their temporary exile was, of course, not uninhabited. A large part of this landscape had been given to the Potawatomi and Omaha people, who had been removed several times themselves. Because the Mormons brought goods to trade, grew crops they could sell, and clearly didn't intend to stay, the transplanted Native people tolerated and even welcomed them.

Mary's fears about Indians were unwarranted, but not her concerns about health. Unused to living outdoors, and without adequate food or clothing, many succumbed to illnesses of crowding and malnutrition. One in four Mormons died while waiting at Winter Quarters, and Mary recorded the personal suffering that families felt as they watched their children die of "canker and diarrhea" and their elders shake from "chills & Fever."[37] Her descriptions explain the driving need the Mormons felt to get to safety in the Great Basin and highlight the cooperative efforts required to move an entire community of people. Even as groups of families prepared to leave, they spent days plowing fields for others so that the people who remained behind would have food the next year and so that seed could eventually be carried into the Great Basin. And such efforts were not voluntary. As Mary put it, "none are permitted to go until they have done so and received a letter of commendation from their respective Bishops to show that they have done so." Everyone had to plow, plant vegetables, and build fences, and Mary wrote to Samuel that the "prospect of fields and gardens and fruits of the Earth" should encourage him to join her sooner.[38]

Samuel did finally arrive in May of 1848, but the Richards family did not yet feel prepared to travel. Instead they moved east across the river to the Mormon settlement of Kanesville and farmed for another year until they could afford the wagons and supplies required for a safe trip west. They sold straw hats, produce, and leather goods to people headed for the gold fields that spring until they had the cash they needed. Accompanied by a baby daughter called Minnie, Mary and Samuel left Iowa in July of 1849 and reached the new state of Deseret in early October.[39] Had they noticed the gold rush and the Mexican War, or did the glare of such national events dim in the sights of people who simply wanted to reach a Promised Land?

Because they had been formed out of it and spent their lives measuring themselves against it, the Mormons never managed to leave the United States or its mission behind them. As they planned and implemented their move to Deseret, they remained enmeshed in U.S. political and economic cultures. Their success depended on what happened in Washington DC, Monterey, and Santa Fe as much as on their own actions in the desert.

MEXICAN REVOLUTIONS

As Mariano Vallejo stood on his dock just south of Sonoma and watched Commodore Jones of the U.S. Navy sail away in late 1842 after the great "oops" of the invasion of Monterey, he wondered in what kind of world and under whose flag his children would live their lives. Californios like Vallejo, however, had no expectation or experience of stability and saw little need of a powerful state to continue living their lives.

To put this in some perspective, the first half of the nineteenth century was particularly rocky for the project of nation building. The nation of Mexico worked to find a governing system, an economy, and leaders who could build a nation from the remnants of a Spanish empire. If we think about what was happening in France, England, Italy, or Germany, Mexico looks much like other nations struggling to find identity and stability. No one had a stable conception of the duties of either citizen or government. Even the location and size of national capitols were up for grabs in many places.

Much like Mormon communities, the Mexican War did not appear without warning in the lives of people living in the trans-Mississippi West. At the same moment that Joseph Smith built his cities and as people like Mary and Samuel Richards became convinced that their temporal and eternal futures lay with the Mormons, a series of rebellions and revolutions shook nearly every region of Mexico. Each part of Mexico's northern provinces experienced these seismic events differently. In New Mexico, the oldest and most developed of the "Northern Department" states, political uprisings and periods of unrest unsettled New Mexicans throughout the late 1830s and early 1840s, a period that coincided with a marked upsurge in raiding by the nomadic peoples of the region.[40]

For the Bent family, carefully balanced on the border between the United States and Mexico and between the central and southern Plains tribes, this disruption and disaster had, in fact, been good for business. Much of their enterprise was illegal, but necessary and profitable for everyone involved. Colonial rules forbade merchants in New Mexico from trading directly with American traders, but Native traders filled in as middlemen. At great trade fairs and in small individual deals, buffalo hides, people, and horses were exchanged for food, manufactured goods, and cash from the United States. By the middle of the 1830s, Bent's Fort operated at the center of this trade because of William Bent's personal relationship with local Cheyenne and Arapaho people. As the situation in Texas drove Native people out of the new republic, they often found themselves in the orbit of the Bent brothers and their families. Bent family success, however, made many New Mexicans envious. As Native raiding and national policies eroded their fortunes and confidence, successful Anglo-Americans became the targets of growing resentment.

When these simmering frustrations boiled up into the Chimayo insurrection, complaints about foreign traders who had profited from the misery of New Mexicans turned into active threats. This revolt emerged around two local dissatisfactions that were exacerbated by the pressure to accept a new centralist government, the general goal of locating all power in Mexico City. First, New Mexicans loathed the new plan that made independent states become mere departments. This meant that places like New Mexico would be ruled by governors appointed in Mexico City, state legislatures would be replaced by appointed councils, and, worst of all, local *ayuntamientos*, or municipal councils, would be supplanted by a single appointed prefect, robbing communities of their ability to run things locally. The second issue involved the rising cost of being Catholic. New rules about where people could be buried, the cost of sacraments, and the role of lay priests, especially the *penitentes,* had all come out of pronouncements from distant bishops who wanted New Mexican Catholics to comply with practices in Mexico. New Mexicans deeply resented these changes and saw them as part and parcel of the effort to take away all of their local control and to tax them more heavily. When Governor Albino Pérez dissolved the entire *ayuntamiento* of a small community in northern New Mexico, the whole region rose up in rebellion in August of 1837.[41]

Underneath the political and cultural issues lay the vast problem of safety. All New Mexicans, rich or poor, Mexican, Anglo, or mestizo, wanted protection from raiding Comanches, Utes, Navajos, and Apaches. Pueblo people joined the rebellion as well, largely over the issue of compulsory military service to deal with the constant raiding. In New Mexico the principal task of the "volunteer" militia was to fend off Indian hostilities, and by the mid-1830s they did this alone, since the Apaches and Comanches had effectively prevented Mexican troops from even reaching New Mexico. When the governor planned a campaign, each community had to furnish soldiers. The burden of this duty fell on poor villagers and Pueblo Indians, as anyone with means could buy his way out. These poor volunteers had to provide weapons and horses and were required to pay for their ammunition and food for the entire campaign. As one sympathetic colonial administrator put it, this was several months of "continuous and cruel warfare against the barbarous nations some of them already skilled in the use of rifles," and few volunteers endured this service without harboring deep resentment, if they survived it at all.[42]

Because of the pent-up fear and anger, the rebellion moved quickly and successfully. The rebels aimed the violence sharply, crushing the territorial volunteer force and capturing Governor Pérez and many of his administrators. They killed some people on the spot, but others, including Perez, were tried and then executed. The eighteen men executed were white Hispanics of the highest social standing, whereas the men who carried out the executions were overwhelmingly Indian and mestizo. The rebels desecrated the governor's corpse, beheading it and taking the scalp to Santa Cruz de la Cañada "to dance," an ancient Pueblo custom in which women would scornfully touch their breasts and crotches with the scalp in order to take power away from the enemy.[43]

Such initial success convinced thousands to join a popular army, led by a man of mixed race man from Taos named José Gonzalez, who became governor on August 10 and moved into the Palace of Governors. Forming a government and creating stability proved to be far more difficult than starting a rebellion, largely because of the rebels' anti-centralist and inclusive style. No one wanted a strong government, but this left no one to make decisions about how to re-create New Mexico. The new government appointed a commission, headed by local strong man Manuel Armijo, to express their grievances to the central government in Mexico City. The commission never delivered its message because Armijo took over the revolutionary government when the Pueblos and villagers began demanding what New Mexico elites saw as far too much power. Even more worrisome, from the perspective of Armijo and his supporters, was a new uprising in Taos, led by Pueblo Indians and dissatisfied Hispano settlers.[44]

Unlike the situation in Texas, few New Mexicans wanted to separate from Mexico, but they wanted protection of their local rights and protection from the military against Native raiding. When so many Native people and poor people joined the rebellion and began demanding even greater changes, elite New Mexicans decided that Pueblo and mestizo ambitions had to be nipped in the bud. The young Benjamin Davis Wilson, who was running a store for Josiah Gregg in Santa Fe when the rebellion overwhelmed the region, remembered that "the rebels went through the city with the murdered men's heads stuck on pikes, and crying, 'Death to the Americans! Death to the gringos!'" Fearing for their lives, he recalled that all the Americans had "shut ourselves up and remained so for six days, till the riot was over."[45] Governor Armijo, representing merchants, church officials, and land-owning elites like Wilson and the Bents, stepped in to stop the revolt and imposed an even tighter centralist government, with strong ties to Mexico. Fear of native insurrection trumped any frustration over taxes or army recruiting. A new army made up of Armijo's loyal troops and reinforcements from Chihuahua tracked down and routed the rebel army at Pojoaque Pueblo.[46]

Even with the Pueblo rebels temporarily quelled, New Mexicans found themselves in a very difficult situation in the early 1840s. The Great Peace of 1840 among the southern Plains tribes had given the Comanches the ability to expand their trading and raiding networks even further. Some New Mexicans prospered from this, but many suffered as the raiding threatened to overwhelm them. The political situation in Texas after 1836 made everyone jumpy, and New Mexican officials vowed to avoid the mistakes that colonial governors had made there. They had seen how quickly a few Anglo-Americans had turned into an invading force, so they refused to give Americans large grants of land throughout the late 1830s. Manuel Armijo, New Mexico's governor for most of this period, was a wealthy local landowner, not a lackey sent by Mexico City. He imposed huge new duties on American trappers and traders, convincing many of them to move to California. He even took on the powerful Bent family, as he watched their fort suck away business from northern New Mexico, and accused them of being smugglers and thieves. His biggest challenge, however, continued to be powerful Native nations whose raids had decimated the New Mexican economy by the early 1840s. Whether the Comanches, the Texans, the Apaches, or the Anglo-Americans would finally present the most serious danger no one could tell.[47]

Continental Rumor Factories

In hindsight, a land where everything seems clearer, one of the amazing things about the Mexican War is how poorly everyone involved had predicted where and when it would break out. Each of the arenas of the war—and every community seemed to be its own little arena—had a rumor mill and a particular set of worries. Both Mexico and the United States covered vast geographic spaces and had poor systems of communication so that what happened in Monterey or on the Nueces River or in Santa Fe remained frustratingly mysterious for everyone involved. From the perspective of President James K. Polk, war with Mexico seemed far from inevitable. He intended his diplomatic and military moves to be bargaining opportunities, but each one had unimagined results, largely because Polk operated without a net—a reliable web of information—something that plagues military planners to this day. His astounding lack of knowledge about local circumstances only matched that of Mexican political and military leaders who were also woefully and stubbornly misinformed.

Though often misinformed and distant from the places where war would occur, neither the American nor the Mexican president made the mistake of underestimating his enemies. In the 1840s the United States and Mexico looked remarkably similar in territorial size, population numbers, and the volatility of their electorates. The view that the Mexican state had no power and that Mexico was simply the last weak gasp of the Spanish empire is a product of hindsight and the hardened racial views of more recent writers; President Polk, William Marcy, the secretary of war, George Bancroft, the secretary of the navy, and the generals and admirals who began planning the war took Mexico very seriously. Presidents Herrera, Paredes, and Santa Anna viewed the war with the United States as an essential, but potentially devastating, test for the Mexican people. And both sides thought they could

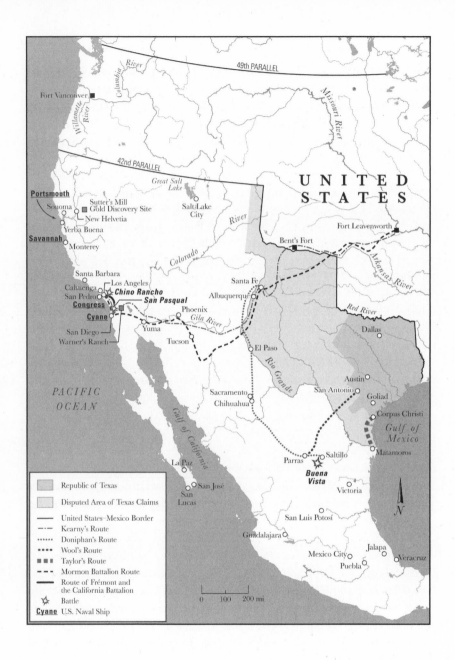

10. A Theater of War: The U.S. Wars with Mexico, 1845–50

win. When James K. Polk and José Joaquín Herrera took office, they had relatively simple goals. Polk wanted to get California and its ports into the United States, control Texas and its borders, and settle the Oregon border question. Herrera wanted to keep the United States from encroaching on Mexican territory, stop the terrible Comanche raids that came from the Texas, and do business with the United States.[48]

After Polk's inaugural message laying out his plans to complete the annexation of Texas and Oregon, both Mexican and British officials reacted. Polk's words caused great consternation among British diplomats and their public. The prime minister, Sir Robert Peel (whose namesake steamer had been sunk on the New York–Canada border in 1838), immediately sent a warship to Oregon. Though Polk never took the "Fifty-four forty or fight" stance very seriously, he did intend to fight for the 49th parallel border. Upon hearing the official news of the annexation of Texas, Juan Almonte, the Mexican minister to the United States, demanded the return of his passports in reaction to what he claimed "was an act of the aggression, the most unjust which can be found recorded in the annals of modern history."[49] Despite Mexican anger and President Herrera's public insistence that he would protect Texas with arms, in early 1845 it seemed far more likely that war with Britain would come before war with Mexico. Polk, of course, hoped to avoid both. War, however, didn't frighten him; he had little experience with it, a status he shared with most Anglo-Americans.

Few residents of the United States in 1845, with the important exception of men who had military service fighting Indian nations, had any experience with military engagement. The last war had ended in 1815, more than a generation before. The U.S. Army had dwindled to very small numbers, and the U.S. Navy was nearly antique. This fact certainly concerned President Polk and encouraged him to mobilize the few forces he did have sooner rather than later. Only weeks after his inauguration he created armies and set them into motion. The existing standing forces serving under Zachary Taylor in Louisiana numbered only two thousand men, and Secretary of War William Marcy ordered them to occupy Texas near the disputed Mexican border. Given its small size, Polk viewed the action as a show of force and not an invasion. Because Taylor's army was so isolated, Polk also sent out Colonel Stephen Watts Kearny's dragoons (mounted soldiers) to spend their summer near Texas as support for Taylor, just in case. Kearny and his dragoons spent the fall observing traffic along the Santa Fe Trail, just over the Mexican border. Finally, Polk ordered Commodore John D.

Sloat, the commander of the tiny Pacific squadron, to be on the alert near San Francisco Bay so that he might seize it if he heard news of war.

Polk also worked very carefully behind the scenes. As the troops settled into waiting in Texas, Polk sent John Slidell as "extraordinary Minister" to Mexico to work out a diplomatic and financial deal with Mexican officials. Less officially and less legally, he sent a message to Thomas Larkin, the American consul to Mexico living in Monterey, California. The message encouraged Larkin to foment rebellion and revolution there so that Californians would declare themselves independent and, in Polk's hopeful imagination, beg to be annexed to the United States—imperialism the quick and easy way. Polk sent the same message to Captain John Charles Frémont of the U.S. Topographical Engineers, who was supposed to be in California examining routes over the Sierra Nevada. Frémont, impulsive and fiercely ambitious, also had the hawkish support of his father-in-law, Missouri senator and St. Louis powerbroker Thomas Hart Benton. Even so, he seemed a risky choice for such subtle instructions.[50] On the Oregon question, teams of negotiators worked to make both sides find a 49th parallel solution palatable. So nearly a year before anyone fired shots or declared war, James K. Polk had set many vectors into motion. But because of distance and lack of reliable communication, these potentialities played out very slowly as messengers rode horses and boarded ships with their instructions.[51]

Herrera, truly finding himself between the rock of Mexican politics and the hard place of triggering a war with the United States over a small piece of Texas, made similar choices. Given the posture taken by Polk in his inaugural address and his own reelection campaign, Herrera had to respond by denouncing the United States, calling up his own troops, and cajoling the Mexican Congress into meeting in emergency session in June of 1845. He sent troops to stare at Zachary Taylor's forces with instructions to avoid confrontation. At the same time, Herrera negotiated carefully over the appointment of a minister from the United States with whom they could negotiate. Earlier representatives had been entirely corrupt or unable to speak Spanish, and Herrera wanted someone with skill and real power. John Slidell, who met these standards but who carried impossible negotiating terms, arrived in Mexico City just in time for another military coup. By January of 1846, Mexico had a new president, General Mariano Paredes. Neither Paredes nor Herrera, however, had much lasting power.

For more than two decades Antonio López de Santa Anna had been the animating force of Mexican politics. He served as president six times, each time promised to save the nation, and each time was driven from office in disgrace. Santa Anna has crossed this narrative several times before, most memorably at his victory at the Alamo and his defeat at the Battle of San Jacinto, only weeks later. Having lost Texas, he went home to serve as president several more times, but also to wage a vicious border war against Texas that drove Anglo and Mexican Texans into the American camp and made the Comanches bitter enemies of both Texans and Mexicans. He had been most recently deposed as president in 1844 but had escaped to Cuba. Throughout 1846 he sent messages via various envoys to President Polk explaining that he would soon be back in power and that he would accept $30 million for Texas.[52]

Such behavior on the part of deposed leaders and those in power indicated that the Mexican government would negotiate, but the politics of this endeavor were baroque. No matter who served as Mexico's president, he could not afford the political damage of appearing to appease the Americans by meeting with the special envoy John Slidell. President Paredes knew about the offer he carried: no money for Texas, but $25 million if the Mexicans would agree to give up New Mexico and most of California. No Mexican president could stay in office by accepting such a blunt offer as cash for territory, but no Mexican president could stay in office if he started a war over Texas, which everyone knew was already lost. The smartest political maneuver for Paredes was to avoid discussion by refusing to recognize Slidell's credentials. In this prewar dance both parties continued to play a war of nerves along the Rio Grande. Nobody ever seems to have war re-enactments to see if war could have been avoided. Re-enactors would find diplomacy and compromise a poor replacement for the heady rush to battle, and the real soldiers on the Rio Grande in 1846 were no more patient.

With nervous humans gathering on both sides of the river, events unfolded without diplomatic or executive input. Without Paredes' full knowledge, the general in charge at the river, Pedro de Ampudia, sent an ultimatum to General Taylor on April 12 that he had to move his troops back beyond the Nueces River border or "accept the war to which, with so much injustice on your part, you provoke us."[53] Taylor took this as a declaration of war but still wanted to provoke the Mexican army into acting first. He began blockading the river so that no supplies would reach the six thousand Mexican troops camped in Matamoros, hoping that Mexican generals would be forced to act once supplies ran short. On April 24, Mexican troops crossed the river, and Taylor sent a small force of dragoons to meet them. Sixteen Americans were killed, another forty captured, and war commenced. Taylor notified Polk on April 26 that guns had been fired on both sides and asked for massive reinforcements. On May 9 Polk received Taylor's message, met with his cabinet, and prepared a message to Congress claiming that "even though the United States have tried every effort at reconciliation" Mexico had steadfastly refused and instead had "invaded American territory and shed American blood on American soil." At this point probably even Polk believed this, and Congress, with only bloodcurdling newspaper reports in their hands, certainly did. After some partisan maneuvering but no real opposition, the United States declared war on Mexico on May 13, 1846. Congress appropriated ten million dollars to prosecute the war and approved fifty thousand volunteers to be called up.[54]

Both sides, at least the parts of them in Mexico City and Washington, anticipated a quick and easy victory at the Rio Grande. Because of their optimistic reports, both Mexican and American citizens volunteered eagerly. In the United States young volunteers poured into towns and cities to offer their services, encouraged by the press to view the war as a romantic foreign adventure. In Mexico, President Paredes, who had already prepared a declaration of war, knew that the Mexican treasury, like his own political future, was in a dire state and could only afford a war if it were brief and victorious. The initial flurry of war along the Rio Grande, nominally won by Taylor's troops after several engagements throughout May, stunned the Mexican generals whose soldiers had outnumbered the Americans nearly three to one. They and their troops retreated and awaited new orders. These would be a long time coming because of the political turmoil emerging around the startling military losses.[55]

The Bent Family and the Vagaries of War

The conquest of New Mexico is often described as bloodless, but that descriptor only expresses the experience of U.S. politicians. For people living in the region and making choices about their families and livelihood, conquest would be bloody indeed. When the shooting started on the Rio Grande border, all sorts of Mexicans and Americans had to consider how they might negotiate the changes war could bring. The brewing war with Mexico, with all of its potential disruptions and dangers, offered possibilities and even profit for those who were wired that way.

The Bent family had always operated on the edges of many worlds. The ever volatile situation in the Arkansas and New Mexico borderlands required the kinds of diplomatic skills and economic clout that the Bents had amassed. It also required straddling many lines and political situations, a position made much more difficult during the U.S. War with Mexico. Because they made different choices about the war and their positions on the borderland, William and Charles Bent experienced conquest and its aftermath differently. As stakeholders in the largest trading enterprise directly on the major road to New Mexico, William Bent and his partners among the Cheyennes and the Comanches watched the politics of territorial and economic expansion carefully. Charles Bent had become more deeply enmeshed in the politics and daily life of northern New Mexico and thought of himself as both New Mexican and American, an identity he would find impossible to maintain.

New Mexicans in general had little patience with the government in Mexico City and with the governors they sent. They wanted two mutually exclusive things: economic investment and expansion using trade from the United States and protection from territorial expansion by the United States. Manuel Armijo, hoping to attract American wealth, had granted many long-time Anglo residents and traders extensive land grants in the 1840s. The faces in Taos had not changed; men like Charles Beaubien, Ceran St. Vrain, Stephen Lee, Antoine Roubidoux, and Charles Bent had come to Taos to trap beaver but had evolved into successful merchants and landowners that Armijo wanted as his allies. Charles Bent had never become a Mexican citizen, but he had married Ignacia Jaramillo Luna from a well-established Taos family, had opened stores in Taos and Santa Fe, and had acted as emissary between New Mexico and the United States on many occasions. But even he worried about the changes that seemed afoot. He wrote to Manuel Alvarez, his friend and the appointed consul to the United States, that James K. Polk's victory had made him "fearfull that this election will cause difficulty."[56]

By the mid-1840s, much had changed about the trading world in which William Bent had matured. The stepped-up raiding among Indian nations that nearly destroyed northern Mexico had turned out to be lucrative for his business, even though the increased violence made trade more dangerous. William's business had shifted entirely to the buffalo hide trade that was showing signs of distress. The buffalo hunts of 1842 and 1843 found drastically reduced herds that concerned everyone. In 1843 both William, at Bent's Fort, and Charles, in his stores in Taos and Santa Fe, had made lucrative deals with the Mexican and U.S. armies to supply troops on the march against Native raiders and Anglo filibusters. The disruption created by the removal of eastern Indians to the west had provided permanent employment to the U.S. Army, who then needed constant provisioning. The Bents made this arrangement just as the Mexican government decided, in reaction to the increasingly tense situation in Texas, to close the custom houses to American traders. This meant that the Bents and most of their partners could no longer buy or sell anything in New Mexico. In this context, provisioning the U.S. Army probably saved their business.[57]

Throughout 1845 rumors flew at Bent's Fort about troops gathered at the Rio Grande, or Texans threatening to attack New Mexico, or Oregon having been taken by the English or that the Hudson's Bay Company was fomenting revolution among the Indians in northern California. Newspapers would arrive with caravans from St. Louis elevating some rumors to fact and demoting others to forgotten worries, but this news was always outdated. The first real indicators of a move toward war were Colonel Kearny and his columns of mounted soldiers who arrived that summer. By early 1846 rumors had worried everyone in northern New Mexico, but even Governor Armijo assured the Bents that he had heard nothing from Mexico City. With war seeming a bit distant, they decided to go ahead and make their spring caravan trip to St. Louis to resupply the fort and to bring in last season's hides.[58]

Charles Bent had begun reporting to Manuel Alvarez, the Mexican consul to the United States, about conditions, rumors, and business dealings in Taos and Santa Fe and along the Arkansas River. He wrote to Alvarez on June 11, 1846, from Bent's Fort that he was heading out with the caravan. He confirmed that he had heard nothing from the United States. As they traveled east four days later, the Bent wagons ran into a special emissary from the secretary of war who was headed to Santa Fe at top speed to warn American citizens that war had indeed been declared on May 13, 1846. Here, Charles made an important personal decision that would reverberate out to his family and friends. Instead of continuing to St. Louis with his traders, he decided to offer his services to General Kearny and headed to Fort Leavenworth where Kearny was gathering his recruits for the march to New Mexico and beyond. Because of his important connections to Mexican officials and his deep knowledge of the region, Charles Bent became one of Kearny's most trusted advisors even as he continued to write letters to the Mexican consul.[59]

The news of war reached New Mexico via American traders along the Santa Fe Trail long before anyone received official notification from Mexico City or Washington. No one knew what such a war would mean for New

Mexico or what Kearny's plans might be. Kearny had, in fact, been ordered "to take possession of New Mexico and Upper California." In addition, his orders suggested that California was far more important to the national project—President Polk's "cherished hope," as the secretary of war explained it. Kearny expected that the New Mexico part of his expedition would be easy. In St. Louis, he was told over and over again that Mexican citizens there had been so demoralized by lack of attention from the Mexican government that he would find little opposition. Charles Bent, deeply connected to the Anglo and Mexico merchant communities in northern New Mexico, understood that New Mexicans may have been frustrated with the instability of the Mexican government, but the incessant raiding from powerful Native groups worried them far more.[60]

Through the summer of 1846 New Mexicans like Donaciano Vigil, the military commander of northern New Mexico, raged in legislative sessions that New Mexicans had been reduced to shooting bows and arrows at well-armed Indian people. He warned that the situation had become so dire that "the surviving inhabitants of some settlements will have to abandon them in consequence of the repeated attacks of the surrounding barbarous Indians." He demanded: "Our extended frontiers require for their military defense, in view of the arrogant spines of our barbarous enemies, thousands of well-disciplined and equipped troops," and he explained bitterly that such a thing would never happen "because of the impoverished state of the national treasury." Ironically, part of what Vigil wanted was a relaxation of taxes on guns and ammunition from the United States so that New Mexicans could purchase guns to protect themselves and build their own armies to fight raiding Indians. Charles Bent believed that such attitudes suggested that if the United States could offer some relief from this expensive and dangerous problem, and if they could promise New Mexicans some measure of economic development, New Mexico might be receptive to annexation by the United States.[61]

Officials in New Mexico knew Kearny was coming, but no one knew what to expect once he arrived. As people waited, tension created anti-American mobs that demanded the ouster of all foreigners. Governor Armijo, always cautious and clearly uncertain of the diplomatic signals he was receiving, sent out government troops to stop such outbreaks. This violence, however, followed on an intrigue-filled spring in Taos involving the troublesome cleric Padre Martinez, constantly at loggerheads with Charles Bent. The news of war convinced the New Mexico members of the Bent family to leave. Ignacia Jaramillo Bent, Charles's wife, left alone with her three young children, decided to seek the safety of Bent's Fort, which now lay across an increasingly real border. She and her recently married sister, Josefa Jaramillo Carson, packed up for an indefinite stay. They were escorted by George Bent, Charles's younger brother, his wife, María de la Cruz Padilla, and Tom Boggs, the son of former Missouri governor Lilburn Boggs, who had joined the Bent/Jaramillo family by marrying Rumalda Bent, Charles and Ignacia's eldest daughter. Ignacia wanted to make sure she and her family were on the safest side of this border when war or occupation began. Charles, now traveling with General Kearny, remained convinced that he could retain his ties to his family and friends among New Mexican elites even as the United States invaded.[62]

William, on the other hand, viewed the situation with less optimism. As his sister-in-law and brother arrived with news from Taos and Santa Fe about the preparations for war and the anger and disillusionment expressed by New Mexico citizens, William wondered where he should stand. When Kearny's Army of the West reached Bent's Fort on July 3, William began to worry about his own tenuous situation as an American citizen depending on trade with Mexico and with Native nations. He attempted to conduct his usual summer business of trading with various Indian nations and selling supplies to caravans. This became impossible as Kearny's troops began demanding supplies the fort didn't have, doing their own trading with the Cheyennes and Arapahos camped nearby, and creating general chaos. By early August, nearly twenty thousand horses, mules, and oxen had decimated the grass near the fort. William tried to meet the army's needs but found his stores depleted, his repair shops destroyed, and his Native allies spread far from the fort. Worse, he had received little recompense for his efforts. When Kearny asked Bent to form a company of Native scouts to figure out Armijo's movements and to report on the best route into New Mexico, William initially refused. He avoided choosing sides, but having very conflicting loyalties and fearing what such an assignment would do for his business, he gave into the pressure after several days. Working as an advance team for Kearny's army, Bent and his scouts captured Mexican scouts and helped Kearny make his way over the tortuous pass into the city of Las Vegas.[63]

Northern New Mexico seemed deserted. Upon hearing that Kearny had five thousand men, many people had retreated to Santa Fe while others fled into the hills. On August 15, Kearny marched into Las Vegas and proclaimed that he had taken New Mexico with "the hope of ameliorating the condition of the inhabitants." He asserted that New Mexico was now "covered by the laws of the United States," which meant full protection of civil and religious rights. No one, not even Kearny, believed that conquest would be that simple. Certainly the Bent brothers expected some military retaliation. New Mexicans and Americans alike waited to see how Governor/General Armijo would respond. Armijo was reportedly massing his own army of five thousand troops just outside of Santa Fe, in Apache Canyon, which would be very difficult for Kearny to approach.

Armijo's true situation was rather different. When no troops from Mexico appeared, he had amassed a barely trained and armed citizen army led by Colonel Manuel Pino. After the news came of Kearny's march into Las Vegas and his approach to Santa Fe, Armijo and Pino looked at their pitiful but eager troops and considered the best course of action. Armijo had begged the Mexican National Assembly for assistance, but on August 7 he heard officially that "in view of the present exhausted condition of the national funds, His Excellency is authorized to undertake extraordinary measures," which meant that Armjio and the New Mexicans were on their own. Various agents of the United States, including Captain Philip St. George Cooke, who led Kearny's advance team, met with Armijo. Whether his motives were entirely selfish, or whether he simply realized the futility of the situation, Armijo abandoned his ragtag army and headed south to El Paso. On August 17, left holding the proverbial bag of a shaky citizen army without a leader, Colonel Pino sent his men home, and Kearny marched, unimpeded, into Santa Fe.[64]

Those first weeks in New Mexico signaled to General Kearny that this part of war had ended peaceably and that he should continue on to California. He made proclamations about American intentions. He attended mass in the Santa Fe cathedral to assuage fears of militant American Protestantism, and he gave a dress ball attended by the local merchant elite. His troops infused much-needed cash into the New Mexican economy. And he heard only a few rumors of rebellion from the south. As New Mexicans already knew and Kearny soon recognized, the real problem were Navajo, Apache, and Comanche raiders, and Kearny sent out an expedition against the Navajos as one of his first official acts. As he prepared to leave, Kearny announced that Charles Bent and Donaciano Vigil would serve as governor and secretary of the new territory.[65]

For people like the Bents and their extended family, terms like *conquest* or *occupation* or *victory* had to be defined by experience. As soon as victory had been declared in Santa Fe, Ignacia Bent, her daughter Rumalda, and her sister Josefa Carson decided that they had had enough of the chaos, lack of privacy, and short supplies that Bent's Fort offered that summer. Their families would be safer and more comfortable at home in Taos. As the fall weather changed the atmosphere in Taos, so too did the political situation. Ignacia's feeling of safety eroded quickly as news about various conspiracies to overthrow the Americans and to restore Mexican rule spread through northern New Mexico. Dealing with more than rumors, Governor Bent found himself in the uncomfortable situation of arresting several leading citizens who had hatched a plot to kill Bent. But as time passed and the rumors settled down, Bent imagined he and his family were no longer at risk.[66]

It had seemed so simple, but the "conquest" began to unravel long before Kearny even reached California. The expedition to the Navajos failed utterly as the U.S. military men had little experience with southwestern people or landscape. After a series of meetings with rather randomly chosen Navajo leaders and a treaty signing, the Americans headed back to Santa Fe, thinking the Navajo threat had ended. In fact, the Navajos used the treaty-making troops as a decoy and unleashed a furious set of raids on northern New Mexico, taking huge numbers of the U.S. Army's cattle and horses on their travels. Charles Bent, serving as Indian superintendent as part of his gubernatorial duties, warned William Medill, commissioner of Indian affairs, that New Mexico had tribes like the Navajos who had "cattle and sheep superior to the New Mexicans" and who were "increasing in numbers," so that perhaps fifty thousand Native people lived in the territory. Some groups, he predicted, "would never be pacified." Bent concluded by asking for both gifts to distribute as indicators of the good relationship the United States wanted to build and for "stockaded forts in the Yuta and Nabajo countries" to forestall the "bad feelings" that had already developed.[67]

"Bad feelings" among other groups took longer to coalesce. Few Hispano New Mexicans fully accepted American occupation, though many people seemed willing to make money from it while considering how to react. They were, understandably, genuinely ambivalent. Having been proudly independent even as a Mexican state, New Mexicans had suffered enormously from the not benign neglect of their government. Constantly attacked by Plains nations and the Navajos and hamstrung by bad tax policies, they blamed much of their misery on Mexico. But that hardly meant they wanted to be annexed to the United States. Initially, New Mexicans hoped for Mexican troops, but as they heard about events in the Mexican heartland and Zachary Taylor's army began its march toward Mexico City, that hope faded. A few groups plotted against the new American military government in those early months, but most of these were discovered before much could happen. Dissatisfaction and fear about the future bubbled under the surface, especially as U.S. occupation did not bring any relief from Navajo or Apache raiding.[68]

BENT'S CHOICE

Looking at what happened to Charles and William Bent and their families in the aftermath of the war offers some object lessons about the dangers of peace. Assessing their choices might teach us something about the complexities of nation building on a personal level. New American governor and old New Mexico resident Charles Bent should have known that his appointment as governor would brand him as a traitor. He had lived in Taos for nearly twenty years and had seen that political intrigue and rebellion were a regular part of New Mexico life. As appointed governor, he claimed that such behavior was part of "the excitable Mexican character" that he described in his reports to Washington, and he expressed confidence that his superior Anglo methods would win out. He knew too that that the Taos region still boiled with anger over the occupation, but he assumed that once New Mexicans saw it as inevitable, they would cool down.[69]

In January of 1847 Bent decided to go home to Taos to check on his family and the temperature of the community. Things were hot indeed, and early in the morning of January 19, a group of angry Taos residents, led by a Pueblo man named Tomasito Romero, ignited a revolt. The rampage began when a group of Pueblo men stormed the local jail demanding the release of several of their friends. A mob began to gather to enjoy the excitement, and when the officer in charged scolded them, they hacked him to bits. Emboldened and frightened by this bloody moment, the large group of local men, both Mexican and Native, decided to march to Charles Bent's house, a man with whom nearly every Taoseño could find fault, now that he served the occupying Americans.[70]

No one had slept much in the Bent household that night. When they heard the crowd coming, Charles and Ignacia met the mob on the porch while the other family members gathered in the front room. Before Charles could even begin to reason with them, arrows flew through the air, impaling Bent's head and injuring Ignacia on the shoulder. Ignacia handed Bent his pistols and then hid in a back room, where she and the other women devised a desperate plan to dig through the adobe wall that adjoined another house and drag the children to safety. While the mob shouted, fired shots into the house, and began to tear the roof off, the family dug desperately with fire pokers and spoons. Miraculously, they succeeded, and the family escaped to the house next door but not to safety. The mob followed them, killing an elderly Navajo servant in their rage to get to Bent. As his children, Teresina, Alfredo, Estafina, and Rumalda, watched, the angry men scalped Bent, shot arrows and bullets into his body, and completed the task by stripping the body and mutilating it. They tacked Bent's bloody scalp to a board and paraded it through the streets as the Bent family huddled on the floor next to what remained of their father's body, wondering what fate their American connections would bring them.[71]

Ignacia Bent and her sister, Josefa Carson, understood that their formerly powerful situation was now a deadly one. They dressed like Indian women and escaped to the homes of trusted Mexican friends to wait out the uprising that had swelled into a large insurrection. More than a thousand men marched toward Santa Fe, intent on expelling the Americans. The news spread quickly, north and east to Bent's Fort and south to Santa Fe. Colonel Sterling Price, a Missouri volunteer charged with the task of protecting the capital, decided to meet the rebels head on. He was accompanied by Ceran St. Vrain and a company of volunteers, all Bent family business partners and friends, who now had personal scores to settle. They slogged up through deep snow along the Rio Grande and met the Taos men in two nasty battles. The rebels, without much ammunition or military experience, lost many men and retreated to Taos after two days of fighting in the snow. By now, thousands of angry rebels, Hispano and Native, had barricaded themselves into the walls of the Taos pueblo, awaiting a final stand. In the town nearby, the Bent and Carson families waited as well.[72]

The battle for Taos raged for three days. In the end three hundred Taoseños were dead, thirty American soldiers had been killed, and the pueblo itself was a smoking ruin. Though the uprising had involved all of northern New Mexico and its people, the Taos Pueblo Indians bore the brunt of the American response. Nearly two hundred Taos Indians lost their lives in the battle, and dozens more were hung as traitors several weeks later. Ignacia Bent watched as the men who had killed her husband swung from the gallows, but that sight provided little comfort for the loss she had sustained. Her world, the mixed race melding of family and business in the border region of Taos, would never be the same. William Bent, who had stayed at the fort on the Arkansas River, fearful that the insurrection would sweep away his family and fortune as well, received the news of the battle and the hangings in silence.[73]

After Taos, New Mexico settled uneasily into its occupation. The U.S. Army remained in political control until 1848 and the signing of the Treaty of Guadalupe Hidalgo that ended the war. After fending off several incursions from Texans who claimed that most of New Mexico east of the Rio Grande should be annexed to them, New Mexico became a territory with more or less the same borders it has today. Elite New Mexican men met to form a legislative assembly and to write a constitution for the new territory. New colonial overlords, however, did not change the basic problems that plagued New Mexicans. Governor Vigil sent a message to the U.S. Congress in 1848 laying out the situation. He began politely: "New Mexico, having been annexed to the American Union, we are all now composed of one family and we should labor to remove every obstacle that embarrass the advancement of the country and unite our interests." He then explained in no uncertain terms that "the principal wealth of this country is in stock raising and that the Indian war almost entirely prevents it. . . . The protection of this country and freeing it from the rapacity of the Indians, occupies all my attention."[74] Potential civil unrest and rebellion also occupied Vigil's attention. Rumors circulated continually that the Mexican Army was heading north to liberate the region. Other sources warned the beleaguered governor that various groups planned rebellion against the treaty, which many Mexicans and New Mexicans found insulting to their honor and dangerous to their economic status.[75]

For families like the Bents, the Jaramillos, the Boggs, or anyone who wanted to maintain economic interests and intimate relationships among the occupied and the occupiers, choices about how to behave or whom to befriend were never simple. Ignacia and her younger children stayed in Taos, though they spent a lot of time in school with Jaramillo relatives in Santa Fe and with her sister Josefa's family. Ignacia's son-in-law, Tom Boggs, stepped in to support the household. Born at an Osage trading post in what is now Arkansas and raised on the Missouri River frontier, Boggs had come west as a Bent family teamster in 1844. He had arrived in Taos a year or so later and immediately began courting Rumalda Bent. By the time of the dreadful events in Taos, he and Rumalda had a young baby and he was well ensconced in the now battered household. Taos, suddenly located in the United States and still a crucial part of the Bent family trading empire, still seemed like the best place to stay. After months of discussion, Boggs went into business with Kit Carson, his relative by marriage, and built a small rancho on the plains east of Taos. They chose this spot partially because of its proximity to Fort Union, and they hoped the soldiers there would both discourage raiding and purchase cattle and sheep from the ranch. The Boggses brought their young son and Rumalda's little sister, Teresina Bent. The Carson family now included Carlos Adolfo Carson, born in 1850 and named in honor of Charles Bent, and Adaline Carson, the child of mixed race from Carson's first marriage, whom he had left with relatives in Missouri until 1848, when he brought her to New Mexico.[76]

Just east and north of this family settlement, William Bent had to make decisions about how to serve his own family and business needs. Bison hunting had been poor for the past two seasons, and the war seemed to send hungry Native people into a terribly destructive phase of raiding and fighting. Warring tribes had made travel on the Arkansas and Cimarron rivers almost impossible. In the summer of 1847 alone, more than forty-seven travelers had been killed and nearly seven thousand animals taken. Native groups, driven north by Comanche and Apache raids, put another strain on Bent's stores. As part of the preparation for the Mexican War and in response to this upsurge in raiding, the Cheyennes and Arapahos had been put in an agency for the first time. It would be headquartered at Bent's Fort with Thomas "Broken Hand" Fitzpatrick as the agent. How this would affect Bent's relationship with the Cheyennes or his own business he didn't know. Supplying government wagon trains and armies might be lucrative, but it came with lots of strings attached. In the midst of these considerations, Owl Woman died while giving birth to their fourth child. William, heartbroken over her death and over the loss of his brother, named the baby Julia after a Bent sister. Needing the support of his Cheyenne family, he also made another choice and invited Owl Woman's younger sisters to become part of his household.[77]

BRIGHAM YOUNG AND THE CHOICES OF WAR

For some westerners, war brought unexpected opportunities. When the Mexican War seemed imminent just as the Mormons planned their exodus into the Great Basin, Brigham Young and other leaders had to consider how best to make their own luck. They wanted isolation, but they needed alliances. As they tried to imagine a place in the West where they might be safe during a war with Mexico and the United States, Mormon elders gambled with the formation of the Mormon Battalion. Its creation occurred a bit accidentally. Brigham Young had charged Jesse C. Little, the Mormon's point man on the East Coast, to "take every honorable advantage of the times" to get the federal government to help the Mormons in their remove to the West. Young imagined contracts for building supply forts along the trails to the West or some assigned task in California. What he got when Little met with President Polk was a request to form a battalion of Mormon soldiers to accompany Kearny on his march to the West. Though disappointed, Brigham Young could see the advantages such a gesture might mean. Helping to staff Kearny's Army of the West would get hard cash into the hands of the desperate Saints, as well as to garner favor from the U.S. government so that they might get some assistance in their move.[78]

However, as the Richards family well knew, such a gallant and practical gesture meant real sacrifice for many Mormon families as their healthiest young men abandoned their families in the middle of a transcontinental move. When army recruiters arrived in the Mormon camps in June and July of 1846 looking for five hundred volunteers, they were greeted with some derision. Like many Mormons, Hosea Stout, whose infant son had died in his arms as he fled from Illinois, reacted to news about the Mexican War with grim satisfaction: "I was in hopes it might never end until they were entirely destroyed for they had driven us into the wilderness."[79] Young himself had to move among the camps and appeal to Mormon solidarity, explaining that it would provide cash for the move and take five hundred men and many of their families west to California at government expense. Further, he explained, as part of the reward for Mormon service, the U.S. government would make a treaty with the Potawatomi and Omaha nations so that the displaced Saints could live, temporarily, on their lands in what is now Iowa. Mary Richards's father-in-law took his youngest son, Joseph, aside and told him he had to volunteer. His older brothers, Franklin and Richard, only avoided joining the battalion because they were already doing missionary duty in Great Britain. Joseph, only eighteen, obeyed his father and signed up as a drummer. Only two weeks later, the full quota of five hundred men, thirty-one wives, and forty-four children headed out to Fort Leavenworth, and the Mormons had $6,000 to buy wagons and supplies. The departure of five hundred men left a significant number of families without help. As the poet Eliza Snow, herself left behind in Winter Quarters, wondered in verse:

> What were their families to do—
> Their children, wives, and mothers too.
> When fathers, husbands, sons were gone?
> Mothers drove teams, and camps moved on.[80]

As the mothers headed their families in the late summer of 1846, the Mormon Battalion marched to meet General Kearny's Army of the West as it made its way toward New Mexico and California.[81]

The battalion, wracked by fevers and camp diseases like all the other people who flocked to join the war effort along the unhealthy Missouri River, took a while to leave Fort Leavenworth. They had to be outfitted, trained, and allowed to bury their dead. When they marched west to Santa Fe in September, they had lost nearly a hundred of their original number, and many of them were still too ill to be efficient travelers. And they had missed the initial conquest of New Mexico, news of which they received just a few days out of Fort Leavenworth. They reached Santa Fe in October, and so many of their men suffered from "bilious fever" that their new commander, Philip St. George Cooke, sent several detachments of the battalion to winter along the Arkansas River west of Bent's Fort. This group included nearly all the women and children who had accompanied the battalion as well as young Joseph Richards, the drummer boy. They spent the winter learning how to build with adobe and how to operate irrigation ditches, essential skills they would introduce to the Mormons after this part of the battalion arrived in Salt Lake City the following summer. Joseph Richards, dying without his family that winter, never got to Salt Lake City.[82]

The remaining detachments of the Mormon Battalion served as General Cooke's infantry as he marched from Santa Fe to California, via the southern route through what is now Arizona and Sonora. Cooke intended to support General Kearny in his invasion of California, but he had no idea what was happening in California when he and the battalion set out. The three-month trek involved many privations because of the rough desert terrain, but the battalion did not fire a shot (aside from those that dispatched lizards, snakes, rabbits, and dogs) before they marched into San Diego in January of 1847. A young man named Henry Bigler who marched with Cooke remarked that "no other man but Cooke would ever have attempted to cross such a place, but he seemed to have the spirit and energy of Bonypart."[83] Having missed the conquest of New Mexico, they also missed the first phase of the California conquest, which did involve arms and ammunition. The Mormon Battalion took General Kearny at his word to treat the Californians as "fellow citizens" rather than combatants, which no one else seemed willing to do. They protected Californio leaders, rebuilt parts of San Diego and Los Angeles, and worked at pacifying Native rebellions before they were mustered out in July of 1847. They had gotten a tour of new lands and people acquired by the United States and passage to the West, along with a set of wilderness skills that proved invaluable in Salt Lake City.[84]

Half of the battalion went immediately to their friends and family now gathering in Winter Quarters, Iowa, and in Salt Lake City, but a large group remained in California to work as laborers in San Diego or at Sutter's Fort, earning more money for the empty Mormon coffers. The workers in San Diego stuck it out one season but then headed to Salt Lake City in the summer of 1848, traveling north through San Bernardino and southern Utah, which would become important Mormon settlements in the next decade. The group at Sutter's Fort stayed longer because of a message they received from Brigham Young in September of 1847, telling them to stay in California because of the desperately low food supplies in Salt Lake City that first year. He ordered that the remnants of the battalion work to earn money to support the move of the thousands of people still waiting at Winter Quarters.[85]

Captain John Sutter, who operated the fort along the river where the Mormons had seen gold, made as many unlucky choices about his alliances and his moneymaking schemes during the beginnings of conquest as the Mormons made lucky ones. By the time the soldiers released from the Mormon Battalion arrived in New Helvetia looking for work, Sutter had managed to alienate representatives from several nations and all of his neighbors. Before the U.S. War with Mexico started, Sutter was at the top of his game. He had managed to get two land grants from the Mexican government, had outfoxed Mariano Vallejo and the Hudson's Bay Company on land and trade deals, and had thousands of Native workers farming, milling, hunting, and raiding to support New Helvetia. This success, however, was built on debt and his naive assumptions about the stability of California politics. War, conquest, and a gold rush should have ensured him a comfortable and wealthy old age, but instead it bankrupted him. By 1848 he had chosen the wrong side in several coups and had irritated the American military commanders, and the only people who owed him money were Mexican officials. He had used up the good will of his American immigrant neighbors by convincing them to join in on failed political adventures, and his control over Native people in the region had disappeared with his loss of the military power granted him by the Mexican state.[86]

When the Mormons arrived on Sutter's doorstep looking for work, Sutter devised some schemes to make something from the situation. He certainly needed more workers to turn his dreams into mills. According to Henry Bigler, the Mormon "boys" worked at chopping down trees, building a mill, and rerouting a river so it could move logs downstream more efficiently. At an isolated spot on the American River that Bigler described as "infested with wolves, grizzlies, and bad Indians," these men witnessed the amazing discovery of gold in January of 1848.[87] The sight of gold flakes in the crown of foreman James Marshall's hat convinced a number of devout Mormons to stay in California, hoping to reap fortunes for themselves and for the Church. Sutter, of course, did his best to limit the number of people who might profit. According to Bigler, after "the Cap" (John Sutter) ascertained the flakes were indeed gold, Sutter's next act was to negotiate with local Native people and convince them to lease him "a large scope of the surrounding country . . . paying them some shirts, pants, hats, and handkerchiefs." Next he threatened the Mormons that if they didn't finish the mill they wouldn't make a penny. The Mormon workers didn't quite trust Sutter or their own eyes, and "they were afraid lest they would lose in the long run more than they might make." They stuck to building the mill, even with gold glinting right there. Despite such ample distractions the Mormons, for the most part, kept their focus on their families gathering in an isolated haven in the Great Basin. Sutter, clueless about the magnitude of what he had found, believed he could control access to a gold mine, a belief almost as naive as Charles Bent's belief that he could control the events of the Mexican War.[88]

Hard Choices in California

During the early summer of 1846 when General Kearny marched toward Bent's Fort and the Bent women gathered their families at the fort, another set of circumstances and personalities had assembled themselves in northern California. No one in California yet knew that the United States had declared war on Mexico, but everyone expected it. Rumors circulated among the new settlers that General Castro, military commander of California, was preparing his military forces to drive out all Americans. Though no such thing was happening, speculation over what a declaration of war would bring made everyone gullible. From the perspective of California officials, American settlers and their arrogant assumptions had become a serious problem. As José Castro, the military man in charge of the situation, put it in early 1846, "these Americans are so contriving that some day they will build ladders to touch the sky, and once in the heavens they will change the whole face of the universe and even the color of the stars."[89]

One disconcerting sign was the presence of Lieutenant John Charles Frémont, his guide Kit Carson, and their followers, who lurked around hoping to find an imperialistic opportunity. They had arrived in December of 1845 with Frémont carrying instructions from President Polk about how to comport himself in California once war was declared. They presented themselves first at Sutter's Fort on the American River and then to Thomas Larkin, the U.S. consul, at Monterey but avoided the official Mexican authorities. Larkin gave Frémont strict instructions to stay out of California politics and immediately reported Frémont's presence to Castro and to Mariano Vallejo. Another disconcerting sign was a series of Native raids and rebellions, which each side blamed on the other. John Sutter wrote General Vallejo that the Moquelumnes had threatened to burn New Helvetia's wheat crops while Frémont claimed that his constant difficulties with Native raiders had been instigated by Castro. Finally, *Comandante* José Castro got tired of Frémont's suspicious and illegal behavior and demanded that he and his men leave California. In April Frémont and Carson headed to the Oregon border in a huff, crossed it, and waited for something to happen. Mariano Vallejo, who loathed Sutter and trusted Larkin, watched every move.[90]

In June other Americans in northern California, a group that historian Robert Glass Cleland described as "over-anxious to exert their Anglo-Saxon superiority," chafed under the rules that Mexicans imposed on them.[91] Inflamed by Castro's treatment of Frémont and fearful of being expelled themselves, as well as being very tired of working for the taskmaster Sutter, a group of thirty-three disgruntled men marched to the Sonoma barracks to capture horses and arms. When Vallejo tried to stop them from taking cannons and ammunition, they captured him. Not knowing what else to do, the Anglo thieves rounded up various other members of the Vallejo family and argued about what to do with them. Years later, Francesca Vallejo remembered the men that she called "the Osos" (bears) as being "rough and uncouth, dressed like Spanish banditti, wearing caps made with coyote and wolf-skins, the great part wearing buckskin pants that reached only to the knees."[92] This rough crew ennobled themselves by sketching a flag with a star and a bear on it and hoisting it above Sonoma. The least drunken of the group, William B. Ide, wrote out a proclamation that declared California an independent republic. Flag flying, and with important prisoners in tow, the rebels headed east, where they soon encountered Lt. John C. Frémont, who declared the action a rebellion and himself an agent of the U.S. government. He then lent his full military support to the revolt, took the Vallejos and friends as prisoners, and personally delivered them to Sutter's Fort. Whether this was legal, or even a good idea, continues to be hotly debated.[93]

Shocked by this turn of events and left with no male head of household to protect her, Francesca Vallejo gathered all of her servants and children into one room. They slept that way for many nights, Francesca barricading the door and sleeping with her husband's rifles and swords, all of which she was capable of using. Francesca had to wait most of the summer for her husband to come home. She watched anxiously as the "Bear Flaggers" outfitted themselves with guns, ammunition, food, and clothing, "bought" from her family's Sonoma store with handwritten scrip from the "United States Govt." Despite such worrisome activities she reassured her husband in early July in a letter that she enclosed in a package of food: "I and the children are well. Don't worry about the family . . . your papers are well taken care of."[94]

Mariano and Salvador Vallejo, along with several members of their extended household, stayed imprisoned at Sutter's Fort for more than two months, as northern California suffered through several episodes of violence. Frémont organized the Bear Flaggers at Sonoma into what they called the California Battalion, and they took on General Castro's hastily gathered troops in several deadly skirmishes. Wildly confident, Frémont organized a Fourth of July celebration at Sonoma and declared that he personally would take all of California and declared himself a general. This all took place before anyone, with the possible exception of John C. Frémont, had any idea that a war had started on the Rio Grande. Finally in late June 1846, unbeknownst to Frémont or any of the Bear Flaggers, Commodore Sloat, who had been lurking just off the coast, received word that the war had commenced. His orders were to take Monterey and Yerba Buena and to assist in the conquest of all of California, but Sloat proceed very cautiously. Only when his ships landed in Monterey on July 6 and Thomas Larkin sent him word of the Bear Flag revolt did he act. On July 7, with three U.S. warships backing him, he demanded that Monterey surrender and that his troops be allowed to disembark. Very peacefully, they did just that. By sheer coincidence, this naval action made all of Frémont's activities vaguely legal.[95]

In the small world of northern California, the revolt and its reverberations became personal. Kit Carson's web of family connections had spread to California. His older brother Moses had been all over the central sites of the trading West as well. Like Charles Bent, Moses Carson fought against the Arikaras on the Missouri River with Pilcher's trapper volunteers in 1823, ended up in Santa Fe in 1826, and came to California in 1831. Liking northern California, in 1833 Moses applied for a license to trade from

Mariano Vallejo at Sonoma and applied for citizenship papers in 1836, claiming he had been a resident of Mexico for at least ten years. He moved to the Russian River region in 1845 and became the overseer for Captain Henry Delano Fitch, who was married to Vallejo's sister-in-law. Despite this history, Moses quickly joined in the Bear Flag insurrection and celebrated its success with his brother Kit that July 4 at Sonoma, ironically enough as Kit's wife Josefa attended a fandango at Bent's Fort to welcome General Kearny. What these choices would mean in the long run and how they affected relationships and identity would take time to assess. The Bear Flag revolt and its filibuster ilk that imploded across the West in those years had little to do with national feeling, but more about instant profits and personal glory.[96]

No one seemed to mind much when Sloat's arrival and initially easy victory cut short the celebration of the Republic of California. Only a week after the festivities Lt. Joseph Warren of the U.S. Navy rode into Sonoma and, as Francesca Vallejo wrote to the general in his prison cell, "put the American flag on the staff where before there was the Bear." She reported, "it was like great fiestas, all of us shouting and waving handkerchiefs." She obviously felt much safer with the United States in charge and assured her husband "for two nights the servants have not slept in my room."[97] Francesca's happiness at the American victory and the release of her husband in early August reflected the complexity of the situation that had emerged in California in the unsettled days before the war.

So American flags flew over Monterey, Yerba Buena, and Sonoma by August of 1846. What did this mean? Not much, given that the bulk of wealth and political power lay in southern California, where Governor Pío Pico officiated, stubbornly refusing to recognize either a state of war or any kind of American victory. The outlook changed when the ailing and cautious Commodore Sloat gave up his command of the Pacific squadron to Commodore Robert Stockton. Now the conquest of California lay in the hands of two ambitious and impatient men, Stockton and Frémont, who both assumed victory would be easy. Stockton occupied Los Angeles on August 13, and Governor Pico finally received official word that the United States had declared war on Mexico. Pico and eight hundred soldiers retreated out of Los Angeles, and Stockton gloated publicly about his military prowess and immediately left for Monterey. He left Lt. Archibald Gillespie in charge of maintaining order, and he sent Kit Carson east with the crucial message to President Polk that California had been successfully and peacefully occupied.[98]

Pico and many other southern Californians, however, had no intention of giving up so easily. Pico went to Baja and began gathering arms and supporters from Mexico. Meanwhile Lt. Gillespie undertook the enforcement of military occupation, establishing curfews and arresting people who gathered in private homes with such vigor that all of southern California burned with resentment. This boiled over into open rebellion in September. Los Angeles, Santa Barbara, San Diego, Santa Ines, and San Luis Obispo were all retaken by a Californio army created by José María Flores. The citizens of Los Angeles rose up and forced Gillespie to sign Articles of Capitulation and imprisoned him on a ship in San Pedro harbor. They formed a new government in October and instituted a draft of all male citizens between age fifteen and sixty. Though Stockton and Frémont gathered forces that outnumbered them, the Californios held out for months, even after another American warship arrived in San Pedro harbor.[99]

The turning point of the Californio defense came at the Battle of San Pasqual, just east of San Diego. General Stephen Watts Kearny, who last appeared in New Mexico, had rushed his one hundred mounted troops across the deserts of the Southwest to assist in the conquest of California. He had heard no news from either New Mexico or California since October, when he had run into Kit Carson, speeding east with the information that California had fallen easily and peacefully. At that point Kearny's military mission seemed unnecessary, so he sent most of his dragoons back to Santa Fe. It was now December, and most of the horses had died, and the men, if mounted at all, rode mules. They straggled into the ranch and trading post owned by an American Californian, John Warner, late on December 2, some sixty miles east and north of San Diego, and heard the bad news of the successful California insurrection.[100]

When General Kearny reached California, he faced a complex situation—complex in the way that corporate bureaucrats describe disastrous business ventures. His exhausted troops needed rest, but hours after their arrival they received word from Stockton and Gillespie that the main body of the Californios, led by Andrés Pico, was moving their way. They marched out in pouring rain and approached the Californios, who were encamped in a Pima village. Kearny gave the order to attack in a predawn fog. His troops, with wet gunpowder and starved mules, were immediately overwhelmed by Pico's men, armed with lances and riding fine horses. Kearny lost the battle and eighteen men, but Pico's victory, though absolute, was short-lived. The Californios fought several more battles against the Americans in the next few days at Los Angeles, but they faced far larger and better-prepared forces, and civilian support waned as casualties increased. Commodore Stockton re-occupied Los Angeles on January 10. The war in California ended on January 13, 1847, just days before Ignacia Bent in Taos would watch her husband be murdered by angry New Mexicans. John C. Frémont and Andrés Pico signed the Treaty of Cahuenga that guaranteed Californios the protection of their property and the right to bear arms and to travel, in return for their promise not to take up arms against the United States. What *occupation* or *protection* actually meant would take much time and many lawyers to sort out.[101]

President Polk's notion that California could be gotten in the same way as Texas had—that rebels from within would rise up at the first hint of U.S. presence—was flawed from the beginning. With a few exceptions, the Anglo-Americans who had immigrated to California in the 1820s and 1830s had assimilated into Californio society. By taking on Mexican citizenship or by marrying into Californio families of Mexican origins, they could be granted land. More than five hundred grants had been given out, creating a multinational population with various ethnicities and political affiliations. Few important Californios, whether native or immigrant, felt much loyalty to the ever-shifting Mexican government, but they felt deep connections to the world they had built together. They wanted to protect their culture, their businesses, and their families, but they disagreed about how best to do this in times of shifting imperial control. Various important Californios had suggested annexation to the United States, acquisition by the British, as well as revolution and independence. Both Mariano Vallejo and Abel Stearns, for example, had advocated all three of these solutions at various points in their careers as businessmen and public officials.[102]

As war edged closer, many elite Californians, like Charles Bent in New Mexico, had become confidential agents of the United States, but they did not see this as much different from their earlier political roles. They were simply having conversations with the same people who had always been part of the U.S. presence in California. Thomas Larkin had arrived in California in 1829, married into an important Monterey family, became American consul to Mexico in 1842, and received orders to grease the wheels for peaceful annexation in 1845. Larkin consulted with the Vallejos and the Carrillos, as well as various American transplants, about how to achieve this. The Bear Flag revolt and the Mexican War demolished his plan, but not the sentiments that supported it. Now that conquest had come, Californians remained quite ambivalent about both the United States and Mexico. As the war unfolded and as everyone waited for a treaty and for decisions about how wealth and power would be divvied up, Californians worked to expand their networks of business and friendship to include the new American interlopers.[103]

When the Boggs family showed up at the Vallejo family compound in October of 1846 after their harrowing fall crossing of the Sierra, much had changed between Mexicans and Anglo-Americans, but no one yet knew how it would come out. Southern California was still in open rebellion against the United States. Perhaps especially after the Bear Flag revolt and his stay in prison, Don Mariano Vallejo believed that his interests lay with elite Americans, so he did what a good businessman and polite Californio would do—he welcomed the Boggs family into his home and his world of complex political favors. Lilburn Boggs, no ingénue around borderland politics, accepted this help with gratitude. He returned the favor by naming his new grandson, born January 4, 1847, just days before the Treaty of Cahuenga would end the war, in honor of his host. Mariano Guadalupe Vallejo Boggs would be a powerful name to carry into this new country.[104]

Mariano Vallejo could assume that he would have a position of wealth and power in the new order, but he also worked hard to make it so. In 1848, as the Sonoma barracks were turned over to the occupying American forces, Vallejo encouraged his eldest daughter, Fannie, to deepen her relationship with an American army captain, John B. Frisbie. In 1849 he served as a delegate to the Constitutional Convention in Monterey. During the convention Vallejo wrote to his wife about his activities, and in a postscript he added, "Tell Fannie [who was courting Frisbie] that I hope when I reach Sonoma she will already know English so that she can teach me."[105] Despite his poor English, Vallejo was elected state senator. He believed so much in the hope offered by U.S. annexation that he offered to pay for three commissioners to work on a basic code of laws at that convention because the fledgling government had no money.[106]

Vallejo used political and personal ties to link his family to the United States. Fannie's marriage to Captain Frisbie required Frisbie to convert to Catholicism, and he became Vallejo's business partner in the development of various real mercantile schemes in northern California. Vallejo wrote to his mother with obvious satisfaction about the marriage: "I believe Senor Frisbie is a fine chap. I have always thought this and in my opinion this will always be true. Fanita [Fannie] has always taken my advice and her choice is her father's and all the family."[107] Whether or not he was Mariano's choice and how much Fannie and John had to say about it, we don't fully know. But the grand wedding that included all of the new important people in northern California demonstrated Vallejo's work at creating new sets of connections using blood. In a similar vein he arranged for his oldest son, Andronico, to receive California's first appointment to the U.S. Military Academy at West Point. In the end the Vallejos turned down this honor because Andronico was too young and spoke little English, but the appointment suggested how carefully Vallejo inserted himself into the developing power structure.[108]

Decisions about with whom to ally and whom to trust were no easier for the naturalized Californios like Abel Stearns, Moses Carson, and Benjamin Davis Wilson than they were for natives like Mariano Vallejo. Colonel Richard B. Mason, appointed as acting governor and military commander in California for the duration of the occupation, which lasted until the Treaty of Guadalupe Hidalgo was signed and ratified in February of 1848, depended on the advice and cooperation of elite transplanted Californios. Abel Stearns, who had arrived in California in 1829 and who owned one of the largest ranchos in the region, had struggled over his loyalties during the first part of the conquest. When the U.S. consul, Thomas Larkin, asked him to report on the activities of the California legislative assemblies and various citizen gatherings, he worried that his actions might be seen as disloyal by his family and fellow Californios. He finally did decide to work for Larkin before hostilities broke out. After the conquest began, however, Stearns clarified his loyalties when he refused to act as an intermediary for Commodore Stockton in negotiating the end of the war.[109]

Benjamin Davis Wilson, another American trader turned wealthy Californio landowner, faced similar difficult choices. Married into the powerful Yorba family, Don "Benito" Wilson had become extremely frustrated with the inability of the Californio government to protect its citizens. When Governor Pío Pico asked Wilson to raise a troop to help repel the Americans, he refused. Instead, he accompanied the first official party to ride out to greet Commodore Stockton with a gift of a beautiful saddle and horse when he arrived in Los Angeles in August of 1846. However, when Stockton left and appointed Wilson a temporary military commander under the command of the hated Gillespie, Don Benito quickly realized the danger of straddling nations. When a group of Americans and Californios decided to take on the rebels and demanded that Wilson lead them, he did so reluctantly, knowing they were vastly outnumbered. Before any shooting could occur, the forces led by José M. Flores captured Wilson and his men. Furious, embarrassed, and realizing that he'd chosen the wrong side, Wilson demanded to meet with Flores. Luckier or perhaps more persuasive than

Charles Bent, Wilson convinced his neighbors that he had been duped by Stockton. He described his anger at the contempt the Americans had demonstrated for Californios and insisted that he be released so that he could help the rebels and protect his rancho. Don Benito would, in fact, switch sides several more times as he tried to assess where his interests and loyalties lay, but simple nationalism was never part of the equation.[110]

The McLoughlins' Choice

Native people as well as British fur traders should have taken heed about what war and U.S. control of the region could mean from an incident in southern Oregon in May of 1846. The story of the massacre at Dokdok-was has been handed down among the Klamaths and still reminds them of what happened in their peoples' very first encounter with an official party of Americans. The tribe never rebuilt what was then their largest fishing village. Today Dokdokwas is a pristine and desolate swath of reedy shoreline, with no ruins or headstones to indicate what happened there.

As Lieutenant John C. Frémont, Kit Carson, and thirteen others lurked in the Oregon backcountry, having been banned from California by Mexican officials, they were set upon by Klamath or Modoc Indians. Carson awoke in the middle of the night and heard scuffling. He discovered two men already dead, so he grabbed his gun and managed to kill one of the attackers. When he examined the body and its clothing, he deduced the man was a Klamath. Carson noted the ax that was attached by a leather thong to the warrior's wrist and recognized it as British made. With that piece of evidence, he leapt to the assumption that the Hudson's Bay Company had set Indians upon them, not considering that the numerous Native people he and Frémont had raided and killed on the way to this spot in Oregon might have been behind the attack as well. With little thought Carson retaliated by hacking away at the dead man's face, until it was a "sodden tangle"—as Frémont later put it.[111]

This was not the first time that Carson, Frémont, and their men had run into trouble with Indians. In April on their way north and out of California they took on a large group of Maidu and Yana people, killing perhaps 150 people camped on the Sacramento River. Though Frémont never mentioned this incident, several of his men did because they feared retribution would come of it. Frémont insisted that the Californio military and General Castro had stirred up the Indians, a story to which he stuck after the May incident in Oregon. Now convinced of a wide Native conspiracy, Frémont's group attacked a Klamath village. They burned its fifty houses to the ground, and Carson remembered that "We gave them something to remember," and "they were severely punished." Although Carson claimed his men "did not interfere with" women and children, one of his men later wrote that he found at least one "old Indian woman" dead in a canoe. Klamath accounts of the attack on Dokdokwas insist that many women and children were massacred, and Carson admitted that "I wished to do them as much damage as I could." The flaming village was, he remembered, "a beautiful sight."[112]

Such sights, however, were not beautiful to other residents of the region. Chief Factor John McLoughlin, of course, had been aware of Frémont's presence on the West Coast since the entourage had arrived in 1845. Several brigades of trappers had reported unrest among Native people in Oregon and northern California due to Frémont's activities. However, at that moment McLoughlin had far more to worry about. The Oregon Question, as Polk and other American officials called it, or the Boundary Question, as John McLoughlin and his superiors in the Hudson's Bay Company called it, had increasing political weight as the 1840s progressed. By 1844 McLoughlin had begun making business plans that reflected his certainty that Britain would lose Oregon below the Columbia River, but the question of how far north the border would be drawn remained open. By 1845 war over Oregon looked more certain than war in Mexico, and negotiations between the British and Americans over Oregon took some surprising turns.[113]

Even though thousands of Americans had settled in the Willamette Valley, only a total of eight Americans had settled north of the Columbia. That region had been developed by the Hudson's Bay Company, led by John McLoughlin. By 1845 Fort Vancouver had opened up thousands of acres of farmlands and employed several hundred people. Nearly eight hundred people lived around the fort, mostly retired Hudson's Bay Company servants and their mixed race families. Several other commercial and agricultural ventures, including Fort Nisqually, Cowlitz Farm, and Fort Victoria, also employed hundreds of workers and had thousands of acres under cultivation. The British government even entertained suggestions from Brigham Young and the Mormons that Vancouver Island might be a potential site for Mormon settlement to shore up population there. British claims to the region certainly looked strong, and the British Navy had sent the HMS *America* to patrol the Columbia in the summer of 1845.[114]

Despite this apparent success, McLoughlin's position with the Hudson's

Bay Company had grown rocky indeed. Some of the animus was personal because McLoughlin could not stop raging over his son's murder, but much of it was criticism over how McLoughlin had dealt with the American immigrants in the region. During the first years of American immigration Fort Vancouver had been the only source of supplies in Oregon Country.

Hudson's Bay Company officials and British negotiators read with growing concern about Willamette Valley settlers' accusations against McLoughlin, the amounts of goods and credit he had loaned them, and the increasingly martial tone developing on both sides of the river. Wanting to solve the problem without going to war with the United States, they made decisions that would leave McLoughlin, Hudson's Bay Company dependents, and British citizens hanging out to dry. The Hudson's Bay Company fired John McLoughlin after thirty years of service, moved the Columbia region headquarters to Fort Victoria, and, in collusion with British politicians, gave up all claims to land south of the 49th parallel. As of June 1846 the Columbia Country, McLoughlin's home for two decades, now belonged to the Americans.[115]

As Charles and Ignacia Bent and Mariano and Francesca Vallejo had just learned, conquest involved more than signing papers and shifting loyalties, especially for those on the losing side. Because these westerners had lived in border regions for most of their lives, they had learned that nations didn't matter much. They were unprepared for a context and moment in which a foreign nation suddenly had the power to remake their lives. In Oregon the McLoughlins, their extended family, their Hudson's Bay Company employees, and their Native neighbors could all be counted on the losing side, but everyone reacted differently to this new status.

McLoughlin decided to stay, even though Governor Simpson of the Hudson's Bay Company had advised him to flee immediately to Fort Victoria, where he would be "as much as possible out of reach of the troublesome people by whom you are surrounded at present."[116] Though undeniably troublesome, these people had been his neighbors for years, and McLoughlin anticipated a long retirement as a landowner and merchant among people he knew. He needed to provide for his wife, his recently widowed daughters, and his grandchildren. He worried aloud that at the age of sixty-three he found himself "in danger of becoming a pauper with two orphan families on his hands."[117] The McLoughlins owned, or at least claimed, large parcels of land and flour and lumber mills, and they had been actively protecting these claims for nearly a decade. In early 1846, as concern over the border question increased and as a huge group of U.S. immigrants arrived, Marguerite and John moved their family to a new house in Oregon City, intending to become U.S. residents. This gamble, however, soon looked chancier than McLoughlin had imagined.[118]

Many Native people in Oregon, pushed to their limits by increasing immigration and epidemic disease, took this moment to resist. As Indian war spread across the region, beginning with response to Frémont's slaughter of the Klamaths, McLoughlin's decision to move south rather than north looked downright poor. The Oregon treaty did draw a boundary line, but it left much unsettled. Oregon had no government, no military protection, no clear land law, and no Indian policy. McLoughlin and other early settlers warned British and U.S. officials that conditions in Oregon meant trouble. It came first among missionaries—Anglo-Americans who had settled themselves closest to Native people. Among the earliest emigrants from the United States, Catholic and Protestant missionaries had established several missions east of the Cascades in the 1830s.[119]

Impelled by the same evangelical energies that moved Joseph Smith, and born in nearly the same year and in the same upstate New York area that incubated Mormonism, Narcissa Prentiss Whitman would find herself in the center of this chaotic moment in Oregon. Narcissa, steeped in the Burned-Over District's culture of revivals, decided to become a missionary at the age of fifteen. She spent her adolescence reading about the desperate needs of heathens all over the world but found her calling when the Congregationalist minister Samuel Parker gave a talk describing the pleas of the Flathead and other western Indians for religious conversion in 1834. When Parker called for volunteers, Narcissa signed up, only to discover that single women were not permitted to participate. So she found a husband, a fervent Presbyterian and newly minted medical doctor named Marcus Whitman. He was equally in need of a spouse so they allowed friends and neighbors to act as matchmakers. Over a single weekend Narcissa and Marcus decided to enter the field of missionary work as a married couple, really the only way they could both achieve their dreams.[120]

When the Whitmans arrived in Oregon in September of 1836, they knew each other better, but they had almost no knowledge of the place they would live or people they intended to convert.[121] They stopped first, as did most visitors to the Columbia, at Fort Vancouver. They consulted with Chief Factor John McLoughlin about where to build a mission and how to approach the Native residents. After her long trip and its privations, Narcissa wrote that Fort Vancouver appeared to be the "New York of the Pacific Coast" with its "neat villages" and "clean plates for every new dish." Even though the families of mixed race who lived in the fort shocked her,

Narcissa found herself drawn to Marguerite McLoughlin and Amelia Douglas. She gave them English lessons and taught the fort's children English hymns. Narcissa left this idyllic place very reluctantly. She and Marcus chose to settle east of Fort Vancouver at a site called Waiilatpu. Thanks to McLoughlin's efforts they arrived generously outfitted with bedding, a stove, cooking gear, seeds, a winter's worth of food supplies, and trade goods for the Indians, all from Fort Vancouver's stores.[122]

In 1836 a few ill-equipped missionaries from the United States hardly threatened John McLoughlin's hold on the Columbia region, but even then he worried that a flood of immigrants might follow them. He also worried, legitimately, that missionary efforts could damage his relationship with Native nations in the region. The Cayuses had invited the Whitmans to build a mission at their village, but what each group imagined about the other's intentions is difficult to sort out. In January of 1837, when Narcissa made her first visit to the Cayuse village, she found herself in "the thick darkness of heathenism." Her initial reaction, given the deep cultural antipathy to "savages" that nearly all middle-class Americans shared, is not surprising. But Narcissa's identical description of these people nearly a decade later should surprise us. After ten years she had not learned any Native language, and she and Marcus had not converted anyone. They had built a thriving farm, but the Cayuses had no interest in farming or in serving in the Whitman household. In fact, the Cayuses began demanding trade goods in lieu of rent and demanding monetary recompense for their work. They threatened Marcus several times and took to stealing from the household regularly, more than suggesting that the Whitmans had outstayed their welcome.[123]

As early as 1841 other missionaries and both James Douglas and John McLoughlin at Fort Vancouver warned Marcus Whitman that his mission was dangerously isolated. In 1842 the American Board of Commissioners for Foreign Missions, the organization that funded the Whitmans, demanded that they end their work. It cost too much and had produced few Christian souls. Marcus went east to plead his case and got a reprieve from the board, largely because of the increased number of Anglo-Americans who had immigrated to Oregon. Though these immigrants offered up a new field for missionary work and a new market for the Whitmans' crops, they also brought waves of epidemic diseases, which devastated the local Indians and made them even more restive. Marcus recognized the mood of the Cayuses, but by 1846 he had convinced himself that all the Indians needed was the stability of American government.[124]

The Cayuses, along with many other Native groups, saw what was coming and didn't like it. The presence of so many white people and the behavior of the missionaries had been part of a millennial prophecy that spread around the Columbia Plateau in the first part of the nineteenth century: disaster in the form of strangers, then a rebirth in a new world. By 1847 the most disastrous parts of the prophecy seemed to be coming true. They saw seventy Anglo-American families settle on Cayuse land at the mission. They saw Anglo children going to school and their own children being turned away. They saw measles kill their children while white children recovered, a discrepancy they blamed directly on Dr. Marcus Whitman. Some of the Cayuses wanted to move away, but others believed that Whitman and his family had to be killed in the tradition of getting rid of bad shamans and as the prophecies had instructed them. Signs of trouble mounted steadily that fall: rocks thrown through windows, animals stolen and mutilated, and constant demands for goods and supplies from the mission's stores.[125]

Even with such warning, no one at the mission expected the organized violence that began on November 29, 1847. A group of Cayuse men crowded into the mission and began killing its residents. Marcus Whitman received the first blow, and the carnage spread quickly. Eventually fourteen people lay dead. Narcissa was the only woman killed, and her mutilated body testi-fied to the long-lived resentment the Cayuses had harbored. After the first wave of violence the attackers retreated, leaving a few injured women and children to deal with the appalling situation. The Cayuses returned the next day to destroy the mission and to take the trade items Marcus had refused to give them. They took a large group of surviving women and children as hostages.[126]

News of the killings and captures traveled quickly, and the lack of clear authority in the brand-new Oregon territory made the situation worse. George Abernethy, the governor of the Provisional Government, could only suggest that the powerless legislature ask for a loan from the Hud-son's Bay Company to fund some sort of retaliation. Without being asked, James Douglas, as chief factor at Fort Vancouver and an old hand in the area, immediately sent out warnings to other isolated missions. Douglas's men captured a few Cayuses and used them to arrange for an exchange of captives. Once the Anglo captives had been released, the Hudson's Bay Company men let the Cayuses go. Irate at what they considered to be negotiating with terrorists, local Anglo-American settlers put together a volunteer force to exact revenge. The volunteers couldn't find the right bands of Cayuses, and so they burned every village they could find, igniting a broad Indian war that would last for nearly a decade.[127]

Horror about what had happened and fear about what might still happen combined in unfortunate ways. Anyone who counseled negotiating with Indians or trading for captives, including people like John McLoughlin, Peter Ogden, James Douglas, and even the missionary Henry Spaulding, were labeled as dangerously anti-American. Reluctantly the Hudson's Bay Company and the merchants of Oregon City, the only people in Oregon with any means, outfitted a volunteer force of five hundred men who headed off into eastern Oregon in the dead of winter. The campaign did not go well for the inexperienced militia, and they succeeded mostly in convincing formerly neutral Native groups to join the hostile Cayuses. After five months of fighting, a peace commission set out to find terms that might end the fighting before it became too costly for both sides. The Cayuses agreed to turn in the men who had planned or participated in the Whitman massacres, but it took them years to meet this demand. Frustrated Anglo-American Oregonians blamed the Hudson's Bay Company and the missionaries for not supporting the war and for selling arms to the Indians. A wave of anti-Catholic and anti-Native feeling swept the American settlements as the danger of an Indian war faded and Oregon was granted territorial status.[128]

Late in 1848, after the Treaty of Guadalupe Hidalgo was signed, Oregon became a territory that included all of what is now Washington, Oregon, and Idaho. And John McLoughlin, a former Hudson's Bay Company employee, Catholic, and with a mixed race family, found himself under fire. The new Donation Land Law, designed to protect the land claims of every white settler in Oregon over the age of eighteen, contained exclusive language designed to deny McLoughlin and the world he represented any access to property.[129] He lost the mills he had built and the land he had claimed because he was labeled an "alien" in the law. He and Marguerite moved into a house in Oregon City, and he supported his family by running a store. Native people, who were also prevented from owning, buying, or selling land in these laws, did not simply watch as their livelihoods were stolen. As John McLoughlin fought for his land in the courts, Oregon Natives fought with guns and tomahawks in a series of wars in the 1850s. The diplomatic and military actions that settled borders in Texas, New Mexico, California, and Oregon had not settled anything about the lives of their residents.

Great political decisions around the Boundary Question, the U.S. War with Mexico, and the Treaty of Guadalupe Hidalgo had personal and intimate impact. McLoughlin's choice to become part of the United States did not result in his murder as it had for Charles Bent, but decisions about alliances, nationality, and family had been made unexpectedly complex for McLoughlin, as was the case for Mariano Vallejo, Benjamin Davis Wilson, and William Bent. All four families had gambled and lost because of their choices in that year of decision. The U.S. War with Mexico, so often described as bloodless, would make people bleed for another decade. The magnitude of the loss, however, would take another decade to measure.

Chapter 7

Border Wars

Disorder and Disaster in the 1850s

The little school shook in the wind. Miss Sauer got three pieces of wood from the box and threw them in the stove at the back of the large room. Gales of laughter broke out among the eleven children sitting there. She laughed too, though she had no idea why they were laughing. They laughed every time she put wood on the fire. Were they amazed by the stove? Was it something she did? Was the wood that the children brought for the stove funny? The wood—evenly milled, long and thin with dirt on the bottom—didn't look worthy of a laugh. But their lives on the Brazos River reserve in 1857 were hard, and she appreciated anything they could laugh at together. She spoke no Caddo or Wichita, and her students could only say a few words in English. Miss Sauer thought about the happy children as she walked home that evening to the house where she boarded with the Kleinbeck family. They were kind people, though as recent German immigrants they spoke less English than her Indian pupils. Miss Sauer was grateful for a place to stay, and the food at the table had gotten far more plentiful since Mr. Kleinbeck had found work as a surveyor. As she walked onto the covered porch, she noticed Mr. Kleinbeck's tools and a stack of surveying stakes. She looked again—evenly milled, long and thin stakes, but with no dirt clinging to them. She had been burning those very stakes every day for weeks. She sighed, went inside, and didn't say a thing.[1]

The combination of American conquest and the gold rush, to use an appropriately Luddite metaphor, threw a wrench into the works. For many people in the West, these changes ruined everything. Rather than bringing wealth, power, and independence, gold and its seekers brought disorder, poverty, and dependence. Making the 1850s into a story we can tell requires imposing order on a moment of utter chaos—the historian's version of playing Whack-A-Mole. The moment we find patterns for people or events, describe an uprising or battle as over, or consign anything to the past, another story pops up with an entirely different trajectory.

Government officials, military officers, missionaries, and immigrants must have felt the same way. Expecting to have instant order after the confusion of war, they found they could control almost nothing. Laws were passed, borders were drawn, land was re-apportioned, and military order was imposed, but no one paid any attention. Native people refused to move to reservations or to be cowed by the U.S. Army. Mexican War soldiers refused to go home. Land-hungry migrants, gold-rushers, and religious pilgrims all refused to obey laws that limited their choices or that challenged their own traditional ways of doing things. Because the state—federal, state, territorial, and local—had so little influence, citizens attacked each other over state borders, religious questions, and property rights. The 1850s presented a serious challenge to the very idea of a white Christian property-owning nation that Anglo-Americans presented as an ideal.

The West that had operated through trade and personal relationships— that saw people through war, diplomacy, and peace—had devolved into a violent squatter nation. The entire region was fundamentally disrupted by the series of gold rushes, mineral excitements, and rumors of treasure that undid all semblance of order. Part of the challenge to the old order came from shifting ideas about using race to determine who should be a part of and benefit from the state. Native people claimed land, Chinese and Chileans claimed gold, and Mexicans claimed citizenship at the very moment new definitions and legal restrictions around race became first a national conversation and then a national obsession.[2]

By 1870 more than two million Euro-Americans had moved into the trans-Mississippi West, challenging a place that had been Indian Country and home to many nations. The U.S. government had begun to build railroads, roads, telegraph lines, and forts, but this vast national imposition of control was not inevitable or foreordained, nor were ideas about who should benefit from these new state-sponsored enterprises. For people living in the 1850s, such visible evidence of conquest was not even imaginable. The unsettled state of affairs combined two large transitions, a premodern/modern divide and the long process of metabolizing conquest, making the region a challenging place to live. To understand the thicket of difficulties faced by U.S. officialdom and its wards, citizens, conquered, and residents, two places, the Missouri River and the central plains, serve as useful explorations.

The Evolving Fur Trade World

Recognizing the Missouri River as a place that mixed savage and civilized, premodern and modern, in 1848 a young Swiss artist named Rudolph Friedrich Kurz set off to observe what he expected to be the fading world of the fur trade and Native people. Like travelers before him, he hoped to capture and preserve ancient times and peoples on paper and canvas, but the gold rush ruined everything. He took a steamship up the Missouri River from St. Louis and found his first Indians at St. Joseph, where they gladly sold him bows and moccasins because they had guns and boots. He arrived in January of 1849, a moment of frontier pandemonium as the first waves of gold-hungry men gathered on the Missouri River border, thousands of Nauvoo Mormons fled across Iowa, and returning soldiers arrived from points south and west. From Kurz's perspective it was a "jolly stirring time" but not the romantic premodern world he sought. Several things constantly surprised Kurz: the ubiquity of people of mixed race, the modernity and size of the fur trade business, and how far "civilization" had penetrated the wilderness. The first he attributed to the bad character of the French but soon discovered that English, Scottish, and American people had also married Native women, had children with them, and now wanted their offspring baptized, educated, and employed. The second and third surprises came later, when he headed further up the river into Indian Country.[3]

Kurz had arrived in a genuinely surprising place. The communities along the Missouri River, which would become Kansas City and its suburbs, lived through several western history trajectories at once. First the war with Mexico, then the Oregon Trail, and now the first California gold rush, made Independence, Westport, St. Joseph, or Kawsmouth serve as "jumping off" places for the huge numbers of transients who moved through them. Missourians of all sorts rushed to take advantage of this new opportunity. Thomas Hereford and his wife Margaret had set up shop here early in their marriage, along with several of her Sublette family cousins. These booming towns also served as refugee camps for Native nations displaced from their homelands. The business of managing Indian annuities brought much-needed cash into these frontier towns. This range of commerce provided work for everyone, including Native people. Frances Parkman, the failed Harvard law student and aspiring historian, also found himself in Westport, stunned that his quiet trip west to see the Indians had become part of national pandemonium over gold. Like Kurz, Parkman puzzled over the Indians he saw on this frontier. He wrote, "Westport was full of Indians, whose little shaggy ponies were tied by the dozens along the houses and fences." With evident surprise, he listed the peoples he saw—Sacs and Foxes, Shawnees and Delawares, Wyandottes and Kansas—and noted that the women wore "calico frocks and turbans" while the men "dressed like white men."[4]

What Parkman, Kurz, and other observers saw, however, were not new communities. These new boomtowns layered themselves on top of old communities, which accounted for some of the confusion. Displaced Indians felt comfortable here because Westport, St. Joseph, and Kawsmouth served as long-lasting examples of the powerfully syncretic world of people of mixed race and practices that the fur trade had created. These places had begun as Native villages or central trading points where several nations gathered regularly. Because of the convenience of these sites, in the 1820s and 1830s small communities emerged where fur traders from all levels of the business retired with their families. They continued to work in "the business" but as individual traders, outfitters, and interpreters as well as merchants and farmers. Founded as a Chouteau family post in 1821, Kawsmouth served two important groups of Native people: relocated Shawnees and Delawares and the more local Kansas and Osages. Three Chouteau brothers, all intermarried with the Osages and Shawnees, spent their careers there working as traders and as official agents to Native nations. Because of its location midway between the upper Missouri posts and St. Louis, many French-Indian people traveled through it looking for work, and some eventually settled there. They, and their families, could make a living farming, trapping, hunting, and working seasonally as guides, boatmen, and interpreters for various expeditions. They could enjoy the mixture of cultures they had blended over generations as French Catholics, Native people, English Presbyterians, and fur trade employees.[5]

Because of this history and because Kawsmouth was safely within Indian Country according to an 1834 act of Congress, many people from the fur trade found it appealing. Kenneth McKenzie, a retired bourgeois (or fort leader) from Fort Union and Fort McKenzie, bought land there after being fired from the American Fur Company. His two Blackfoot wives and their children needed a safe place to live, and Kawsmouth offered that at least. William Bent brought his three older children to be educated there. Old mountain men, including Andrew Drips and Jim Bridger, settled there, hoping to educate their children and find them stable employment. White Plume, a principal Kansa leader, whose daughter had married French trader Louis Gonville, settled there to supervise the education of his four granddaughters, Josette, Julie, Pelagie, and Victoire, who lived with Fran-çois and Berenice Chouteau after their mother's death. Several mission-ary schools and churches focused on these families of mixed race, and both Kansas and Missouri set up "half-breed" tracts as part of their plans for Indian resettlement. Similar kinds of layered communities developed around old trading posts, military forts, and river towns, as the changing fur trade economy and the new opportunities of the Missouri River frontier attracted all sorts of people.[6]

Discouraged by the tainted towns along the Missouri River and feeling as if civilization had taken a very surprising trajectory in this piece of the West, young Mr. Kurz tried another tactic to find the romantic Native world he craved. In early 1851 he signed on as clerk with Pierre Chouteau's American Fur Trading company and headed up the Missouri toward the Yellowstone River, hoping to find a more suitably untouched setting. His shipmates included Alexander Culbertson, another fur trade grandee, Father Pierre De Smet, who planned to start a Catholic mission among the Blackfoot, and a bunch of people sick with cholera, which they would spread to the Arikaras, Mandans, and Blackfoot. As he traveled up the river Kurz saw how deeply the fur trade world and its syncretic culture had penetrated what he expected to be wilderness.[7]

He noted that the Euro-American leaders at the forts had Native wives, sometimes more than one, including Edwin Denig, Fort Union's bourgeois, who married two Assiniboine women. Kurz commented regularly about the work of translation and negotiation these women did. He couldn't categorize these women as they didn't seem to be fully Native or fully white. Even their clothing confused him: "semi-European, semi-Indian in style" with pouches, girdles, shoes decorated with beads, but "clothes of European rather than western cut."[8] When Kurz arrived at Fort Union, he slept in buffalo robes in the translators' quarters with "three couples of half-Indians and their full-blooded wives," and wondered how such close contact with "savage customs" would affect him. His worries were legitimate as he observed the social fact that traders who had Indian wives lived in Native villages and took on Native customs. At the same time, he noted the success of the Catholic Church in the region, spreading out from missions along the Upper Mississippi and Great Lakes. Just who was civilizing whom remained an open question even in the 1850s.

Despite Kurz's desire to paint only unadulterated Native people, he was immediately hired as post artist and commissioned to do portraits of Denig

31. Rudolf Friedrich Kurz, *Returning from the Dobie's Ball*, 1850. *Bulletin of the Bureau of American Ethnology*, 115 (1931). Courtesy Midwest Jesuit Archives.

This active sketch of horses and people shows Kurz's interest in mixed race cultures and the exotic nature of the world he saw at Fort Union. Native women, riding astride (something white women would never do) but wearing pieces of Anglo-American dress, exemplify the mixed culture that the fur trade had created.

and his family. He also sketched a cotillion, attended by the entire fort, where all the Indian men and women "were dressed according to European mode" and where the "waltz, performed correctly seemed be the favorite dance." This surprised him because he had long noticed that when the engagés, clerks, or even fort leaders returned to the United States, they worked very hard at "making themselves conspicuous among their white brothers as savages, with Indian dances and imitating Indian war cries."[9] Who were these people of several races? How could Kurz categorize them? How could he make sense of the world of the fur trade that allowed for such promiscuous and successful mixing of people and culture?

Kurz, like everyone else at Fort Union wondered how the United States would proceed with the Indians now in its charge. The first major effort at controlling Native people came with a grand treaty event at Fort Laramie, far to the south and west of Fort Union, but certainly in the range of its trade networks. Fort Union personnel participated as interpreters and informal overseers. The Blackfoot were not included in the treaty negotiations, but the Crows, Sioux, Arikaras, Gros Ventres, Assiniboines, Mandans, and Cheyennes were. From the Native perspective, the event had little import. Kurz wrote how the news was received at Fort Union on November 2, 1851: "The news from Fort Laramie fails utterly to justify expectations. No treaties were negotiated, much less concluded." He ended with some gossip: "The United States agent, Colonel Mitchell, is said to have been befuddled most of the time from too much drink, to have made great promises to the Indians. . . . Mr. Culbertson [Bourgeois Alexander Culbertson] says I should be glad I did not go."[10]

Kurz was hired as both clerk and artist, and his view of Fort Union combined the big business aspects of the fur trade with descriptions of keys, account keeping, letter writing, and careful packaging and sorting in the fur press room that held thousands of dollars worth of furs, with his pleasure in the romantic setting of the fur trade. He spent part of the winter of 1851 painting a portrait of Pierre Chouteau "in the gable in the house gallery," requiring him to perch on scaffold in a most "unsafe position."[11] The image of the company leader painted in prominent position in the fort suggested visually how much control Chouteau still had in the industry. Kurz also hung his paintings of Edwin Denig's dogs, children, and parrot in the fort, but lower on the wall than Chouteau. Showing the ways that culture intermingles, Denig encouraged Kurz to paint pictures of local people and animals on buffalo hides, pipestems, flags, and clothing, which Denig then gave out as gifts to visiting Native leaders and relatives.[12]

As winter settled in, Kurz's workload increased as he spent time doing business with the Native women who came to purchase items at the fort's store that included "little bells and mirrors from Leipzig, beads from Italy, and calicos from France."[13] As other experienced traders like William Bent and George Sibley knew, much of annual trade involving furs was conducted by women, but Kurz was disappointed that the "braves avoided the fort." He resented Denig's demands that he know the number and location of every item in the fort, as Kurz put it bitterly, "in every barrel and cask, every attic, in outhouses and dungheaps."[14] He also had the unpleasant task of figuring out how much the lowly engagés were owed so that they could spend all of these wages at the fort store, a fur trade version of company town tactics. Very rarely, Kurz accompanied hunting parties or trading expeditions, so he found his contact with local tribal people frustratingly brief.

The hard work and lack of contact with "genuine" (and friendly) Native people made Kurz enormously relieved to leave Fort Union in late April of 1852. By fall he was back in Switzerland with a huge portfolio of sketches and trunks full of Indian curios. Without the distraction of messy real people, Kurz could finally paint his idealized vision of the West and its Natives. He never returned to the United States, but he made an excellent living painting Indians in Switzerland. His "realistic" drawings remained much in demand.[15] Kurz was correct in thinking that he was seeing the denouement of the fur trade, but the culture and economy it had created would not disappear so easily.

POSTWAR FAMILY AND BUSINESS ON THE ARKANSAS

As Kurz began his studio painting in the fall of 1852, Mary Bent, the eldest daughter of William Bent and Owl Woman, arrived in Westport, Missouri, to finish her education. She would board with Albert Boone and his family, old Bent family connections. Now fourteen, she had spent most of her life at Bent's Fort, but the death of her mother and the Mexican War had interrupted the family's plans. By the end of the Mexican War William Bent was a widower, but he couldn't grieve for long. He married his dead wife's younger sisters, Island and Yellow Woman, to make sure his children were well cared for and to show that he understood his role in protecting his Cheyenne family. Island, especially, became a devoted parent to the orphaned children.[16]

The new business situation after the Treaty of Guadalupe Hidalgo required William's immediate attention. After the war, traders of all stripes flooded the Santa Fe trade. Traveling with nothing but mules loaded with alcohol and cheap trinkets, they traded directly with Native people, eroding William Bent's business model and relationships with the Cheyennes and the Comanches. To compete, Bent had tried expanding his business to the south and east in what is now the Texas Panhandle and re-opened a post near the Canadian River, but he had been immediately driven away by Apache warriors. The huge number of traders, their poor-quality trading goods, and their efforts to cheat the Indians made the situation precarious: robbery and murder became common once again. The traders also brought cholera, turning the southern plains into a zone of warfare and death. By 1849 life at Bent's Fort had become untenable, and William had more than a hundred fort employees and dozens of Cheyenne lodges depending on him.[17]

Fleeing both bad business and deadly disease, William Bent took his entire family north, following the Cheyennes to Fort St. Vrain on the Platte River, east of present-day Denver. As they traveled they saw the toll cholera had taken on the Cheyennes by counting the number of funeral scaffolds in the trees. Even worse, they saw bodies simply left to rot, indicating how rapidly the disease had spread and how much it threatened the basic tenets of Cheyenne life. Fort St. Vrain offered refuge as William Bent tried to figure out what to do next. He reorganized the Bent family business and, like his compatriots at Fort Union, attended the great Fort Laramie Treaty meeting in 1851.[18]

Attempting to ascertain how Native people, traders, and their dependents would be treated by the U.S. government, Bent and his family enjoyed the great gathering of Plains tribes, more than ten thousand strong. He allowed the Jesuit missionary Father De Smet to baptize the Bent children, but he refused to permit them to participate in the Cheyenne ear-piercing ceremony that the Cheyenne holy men offered up to protect baptized children. This infuriated Island, but Bent didn't want his children permanently marked as Cheyenne. In the end he was as unimpressed with the outcome of the Fort Laramie extravaganza as the representatives from Missouri River posts had been. He returned to Fort St. Vrain more worried about what would happen on the Great Plains once the weaknesses of this treaty were exposed.[19]

Bent was right to be worried. The treaty was negotiated "between D. D. Mitchell, superintendent of Indian affairs, and Thomas Fitzpatrick, Indian agent, commissioners specially appointed and authorized by the President of the United States and . . . the following Indian nations, residing south of the Missouri River, east of the Rocky Mountains, and north of the lines of Texas and New Mexico, viz, the Sioux or Dahcotahs, Cheyennes, Arrapahoes, Crows, Assinaboines, Gros-Ventre Mandans, and Arrickaras."[20] According to the treaty, the entire Great Plains would remain mostly in Native hands with the caveat that the United States could build forts and roads through any part of it. In return, Native nations agreed to organize themselves into agencies, to leave overland travelers alone, and to accept $50,000 in annuities over a fifty-year period—a sort of rent for the use of Native territory.

As usual, the commissioners and military officials found themselves behind the curve in trying to keep up with the changing situation in Indian country. Like Kawsmouth, the entire plains region operated as a layered community, with deep histories of personal and diplomatic relationships that few U.S. policymakers saw. When Native nations faced crowds of people moving across the Great Plains and destroying the few well-watered and grassy areas Indian horses and buffalo needed, they saw that the United States had no control over its people. When refugee tribes all over the eastern part of the plains demanded access to western hunting lands, this demonstrated that the United States could not uphold any agreement. In this chaotic setting the treaty, even as it was understood by the few Native people who signed it, was destined to fail. Almost immediately war spread across the region, beginning at its edges.[21]

Recognizing that trouble was coming on the northern plains and tiring of the hordes of people on the Overland Trail, William Bent and the Cheyennes decided to return to the Arkansas River in 1852. No one wanted to live at Bent's Fort anymore. Left in complete disrepair after the U.S. Army had used it during the U.S.-Mexico War, the fort had been abandoned by Cheyenne people after the cholera epidemic of 1849. Bent and some of his traders piled leftover war matériel in the center of the crumbling plaza and blew the thing up. Partially, the explosion was a strategic decision. Bent didn't want the U.S. government to get his fort. As we know, Bent did this for very personal reasons as well—too many friends and family had died there. He would build a new fort further east at a traditional trading site called Big Timbers. Over the next few years, Bent's New Fort would serve much the same population as Kawsmouth did on the Missouri. Native people from the plains, French and Anglo-American traders, Mexican teamsters, and their families settled here throughout the 1850s. Only a couple of days travel from the settlements east of Taos, New Mexico, it remained a haven for the remnants of the Arkansas fur trade world.[22]

Sensing the fragility of this haven, William and Island made some personal and business decisions. They sent the children to school in Kawsmouth and St. Louis, hoping to equip their children for a world they couldn't predict. In an ironic twist, the Bent family arrived on the Missouri-Kansas border in the fall of 1854, just at the beginning of the legislation and events that would label Kansas "Bloody." Though the border warfare on the Missouri River took them by surprise, the Bents saw inevitable Indian wars and migration west on the horizon, and they began claiming land along the Arkansas. Making much the same gamble as John McLoughlin had in Oregon, Bent hoped that if the hide trade failed he could become a rancher and encourage his children to settle in the isolated plains just west of the Rockies. Like his former employee Kit Carson, William Bent also became an Indian agent, employed by the U.S. government to oversee the Cheyennes and the Arapahos. We could see that choice of employment as a simple sellout to the conquerors, but we could also see it as a pragmatic decision that allowed Bent to have some control over what happened to his extended family as disorder and warfare spread over the entire West.[23]

These Bent family decisions occurred in the context of rapidly shifting policy designed to benefit Anglo-American settlement at the expense of Native people, who blocked and slowed this settlement. Within less than a decade official U.S. policy had moved from creating an official "Indian Country" where Native people would live as they always had, to placing each tribe on small "reserves" and demanding that Native Americans behave like Anglo-Americans. When Congress created "Indian Country" in 1834, they assumed that large pieces of land given over entirely to Native and immigrant Indians offered a viable solution. In 1846, when Congress funded a series of military forts along the new Oregon Trail, they understood they were operating in "Indian Country," however inconvenient that might be. By 1851, however, the creation of a new government "Department of the Interior" with a charge to populate the West with Anglo-Americans necessitated policy that defined the region as simply another part of the United States, not a separate entity called Indian Country. Now Native people would have to conform to new rules and justify their need for land or government assistance. The reaction to the Fort Laramie Treaty and various similar pronouncements about new policy in the Pacific Northwest, California, and Texas demonstrated, however, that implementing this policy would require more than an announcement. It would require force, both legal and military, along with significant shifts in ideology.[24]

The ideological revolutions around the importance of race and the role of government would not take full shape until after the Civil War, but they were rehearsed first in the trans-Mississippi West. The nation and its administrative structures faced a series of difficult problems in the 1850s around incorporating the huge swaths of land and the millions of people they had conquered in the U.S. War with Mexico. They had to develop a set of ideas that justified taking land, power, and cultural significance away from the varied people who held it at the end of the war. Places like Bent's Fort, Kawsmouth, the llano (or plains) of Texas, Fort Vancouver, Sonoma, and even St. Louis had to become cultural anachronisms because their definitions of who could hold power and property could no longer be tolerated. The West and all of its residents had been colonized once again. New ideologies narrowed definitions of who deserved to be protected by the state and how wealth and status would be determined, a process that had been underway since the eighteenth century.

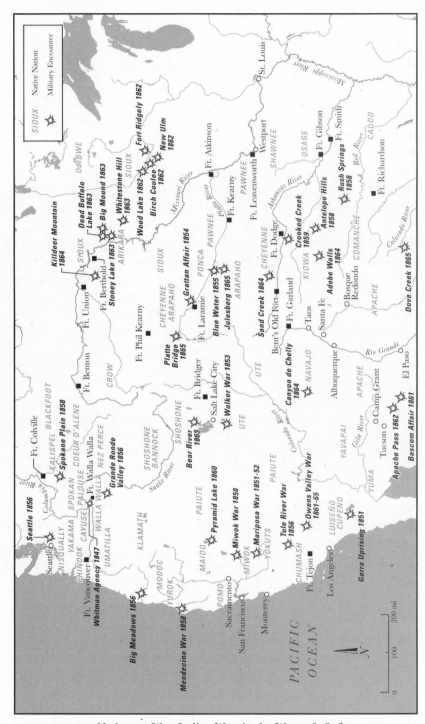

11. Nations at War: Indian Wars in the West, 1848–65

Elaborating just who could own property, who deserved citizenship, and who could marry whom, however, demanded that the state take on considerable new powers to establish and enforce these ideas. In the 1850s in the West the project of cultural definition and citizen building was in its first iteration, and it didn't go well. Nearly everyone, from Anglo-American migrants to Mormon settlers to leaders of Native nations, resisted the new definitions and requirements of citizenship. Most obviously, this resistance took on the form of warfare—but warfare with surprisingly varied combatants. Native nations and Anglo-Americans did fight, as well as conquered Mexicans and Anglo-Americans, while various groups of Anglo-Americans battled each other. By the end of the decade, no vision or victory had determined clear winners.

INDIAN WARS IN THE PACIFIC NORTHWEST

By 1858 Isaac Stevens must have wished he'd never seen Washington Territory, much less agreed to govern it. None of the early governors of the newly created Pacific Coast territories and states were remotely prepared for the human chaos they found there. Almost immediately after the United States took responsibility for what would become California, Oregon, and Washington, Indian wars decimated it. From 1848 to 1860, the region endured constant, expensive, and brutal conflict between Anglo-Americans and Native nations. The outbreaks of violence had different names—Cayuse War, Mariposa War, Rogue River War, Klamath War, Yakima War, Modoc War—that sometimes denoted the Native peoples involved or the places where wars began, but they were all part of a broader problem. In a classic example of the colonial practices of a settler society, Anglo-Americans felt entirely justified about moving onto these recently acquired lands and removing the people already living there—people who considered these newly American places home. Anglo-Americans, like colonists everywhere, believed that conquest simply demonstrated their military and cultural superiority. It entitled them to this land. And like colonized people everywhere, the Native nations of the Northwest had no intention of giving up the land or the ways they chose to live on it, and they were willing to fight to protect their homes. What happened in the Pacific Northwest would be echoed with particular local versions over the entire trans-Mississippi West.[25]

Isaac Stevens, a young West Point–trained engineer who had served in the Mexican War and then along the Pacific Coast in the Corps of Engineers after the war, arrived in the newly created Washington Territory in

1853. He had been appointed the first governor of the new Washington Territory, but his real goal was to bring a railroad to the Pacific Coast via the northern route along the 49th parallel. As he said in his first gubernatorial address, he was fiercely determined to "do my part toward the development of the resources of this territory" and to turn it into "an imperial domain."[26] Saying things like that, however, turned out to be far easier than doing them. As Stevens spoke those optimistic words, a series of Indian wars raged to the south. Stevens, of course, believed he could do a much better job of "dealing with the savages" than had Oregonians or Californians, and he intended to extinguished all Native rights to land in Washington Territory with some scratches of a pen and some threatening gestures. First, however, he had to take on the Hudson's Bay Company. He demanded that they stop trading with the Indians, that they take cash payment for their facilities along the Columbia River, and that they get out of Washington. They refused.[27]

His imperial ambitions temporarily thwarted by the British and the Hudson's Bay Company, Stevens, in his dual role as governor and superintendent of Indian affairs, took on the Native nations. Stevens planned to make a series of treaties and simply move them out of most of Washington Territory. Treaties would make that land available for Euro-American settlers and end the increasingly vicious frontier violence. Native people would then be "concentrated" on isolated lands far west of the Cascades where they would take up farming small plots of land. These Native groups, however, had been dealing with other European nations for generations and had other ideas about how to divvy up the landscape. Their economies and families were intermingled with the Euro-American population brought by the fur trade, making Stevens's task nearly impossible from the start. Not only did Stevens misread the ways that Native people were enmeshed in all aspects of life in the region, but he also had little understanding of their military and diplomatic expertise. With great confidence Stevens set out to negotiate for nearly all of the land around Puget Sound. Quickly Stevens had a piece of paper signed by more than sixty Native leaders exchanging 2.5 million acres of land in return for annuity payments and three Native reserves totaling 3,840 acres. It looked like a diplomatic triumph until Stevens asked Native people to move to these reserves. They refused.[28]

Many of the tribes had been suspicious of the treaty process from the beginning. They understood that they were giving up land, but they didn't understand that they would have to move and share reserves with numerous other tribes. As people living both east and west of the mountains discovered what these treaties meant, they organized for war. On the west side of the Cascades the Snoqualmie and Nisqually peoples joined up with smaller tribal groups, and on the eastern slope the powerful Yakimas gathered together the Columbia Plateau tribes. When Stevens held treaty councils with the Yakimas, Cayuses, and Nez Perces, he threatened that "they would walk in blood knee deep" if they refused to sign.[29] Such threats backfired as the leaders of these nations began to discuss retribution before the council even ended. The speed and effectiveness with which Native people gathered their allies and mounted a war stunned Stevens and many recent migrants who viewed the treaties as law and the Indians as children who had no option but to obey. And they had refused.[30]

Now, as the summer of 1855 came to an end and the annual overland migration of gold miners and settlers poured into eastern Washington and Oregon, wagon trains were attacked, horses were stolen, and people were killed. As part of the treaty negotiations Governor Stevens had assured the Indians that miners and settlers would not be allowed to trespass on tribal lands. But Stevens, like his official compatriots in California, could not control the behavior of miners headed to gold strikes in Washington and British Columbia. Large groups of miners invaded tribal lands, stole Indian horses to carry their supplies, and captured and raped Indian women and children. Native people retaliated, killing miners in isolated incidents and raiding small settlements. As distrust and fear spread everywhere and attacks came from all directions, Governor Stevens had to ask for federal troops. Stevens could only watch helplessly as his vision of profitable railroads steaming into the territory disappeared with the violence. Had Governor Stevens observed similar bloody situations in Oregon and in California more carefully, he might have made fewer mistakes.[31]

OREGON'S BLOODY LEGACY

John McLoughlin watched Isaac Stevens's performance with a mixture of regret and concern, but certainly with no surprise. When he decided to become part of the United States that had appeared on his doorstep, he also predicted how rocky the early years would be for the Americans. He saw, accurately, that the immigrants and their leaders had little idea of how to approach the Native people of the region, much less live with them. Before the 1846 treaty agreement granting the Oregon Country to the United States could even be signed, war replaced the uneasy and constantly negotiated peace that had once characterized the relationship that John McLoughlin had built with Native leaders like Concomely, his Chinook ally. As fur trade culture that required the active and willing participation of Native people diminished, so too did perceptions about their value. Instead of seeing them as essential trading, diplomatic, and hunting partners, more recent immigrants to Oregon saw Native people as barriers to settlement and reminders of a barbaric and dangerous past.

Joseph Lane, Oregon's first territorial governor and an Indiana politician appointed as a political favor, arrived in March 1849 in the midst of the terrible events that spread across the region after the Whitman Massacre. In the first instance of a deadly pattern that would characterize these wars, Lane found that local Anglo residents had organized a large volunteer army to take on the Cayuses, who had disappeared into the mountains. The army spent a cold and frustrating winter skirmishing with the Cayuses, who used these attacks to recruit Native allies from all over the region, but the army never found the Indians responsible for the Whitman killings. Lane arrived with federal troops who began attacking Nez Perce, Walla Walla, and Cayuse villages. Wanting to avoid another winter of warfare, Native people finally turned in the Whitmans' murderers, hoping this would end the conflict. The accused were brought back to Oregon for trial, where they were convicted and hanged. Again, as part of the emerging pattern in such wars, the bit of retribution satisfied no one. It had only stirred up old animosities among the tribes of Oregon and created new ones between Anglo settlers and the Native people displaced by them.[32]

The trouble emerged in several places at once. For tribes west of the Dalles of the Columbia, the early 1850s brought a considerable stream of gold miners and Willamette Valley settlers. It also brought new federal appointees and regulations to manage the very tense situation that emerged east of the Cascades. A new Indian agent came to the Cayuses, Umatillas, and Walla Wallas, who built an agency on the main immigrant road, ensuring that Native people, white travelers, and soldiers would come into contact. This kind of incompetent authority, imposed over and over again, created disastrous situations. The Indians began a brisk business stealing horses, cattle, and supplies from the overlanders, selling them to white and mixed race traders, who then sold them back to the desperate immigrants, producing a wide web of profits but also the unending enmity of the settlers who arrived in the Willamette Valley having been robbed once and fleeced twice.[33]

People living west of the mountains and down the Willamette Valley faced different pressures. The moment Oregon became a territory, Congress passed an act extinguishing Native title to land west of the Cascades. But passing an act and removing people from a landscape are two very different activities. Initially treaty commissioners suggested that Native groups living nearest Oregon City move far to the east, but they simply refused. They flourished along the river systems of central Oregon, where they depended on streams for salmon and mountains for acorns and deer hunting. A few nations made treaty deals to concentrate themselves on smaller tracts of land, some did move east to ally with other Native peoples, and a few blended into mixed race communities populated by retired Hudson's Bay Company employees, but the treaty process mostly failed. Quickly Anglo settlers blamed Native people for every crime in the region and for their own failures at farming. The local newspapers railed against treaty commissioners who didn't work quickly enough, against the Hudson's Bay Company, which continued to trade with Indians, and mostly against the savages who refused to move from land they considered rightfully theirs.[34]

Southwestern Oregon proved to be an even more delicate situation because of the kinds of travelers who had moved through it since 1848. When the first significant numbers of Euro-American hopeful settlers came down the Willamette River valley in the early 1850s and began to move along the Rogue and Umpqua rivers, they followed waves of would-be gold miners. Not only were there large groups of men headed to California diggings, but small strikes along the Klamath River and along the Oregon coast attracted prospectors as well. David McLoughlin, John and Marguerite's youngest son, wrote to his cousin in Montreal in March of 1849 that "I am now on the eve of starting for the gold region with large numbers of Indians hired to me for a year" and closed with his optimistic prediction that "both California and Oregon are covered with gold."[35]

Miners like David soon found that not much was covered with gold. Their failures were made more galling by Native people who stole their animals and equipment or who charged exorbitant sums to ferry them across rivers. When these people appeared "too saucy," the miners initiated vicious attacks. These generalized into an indiscriminate guerilla war in which neither side cared which groups of miners or Indians received retribution. By the time more permanent newcomers arrived who wanted to settle rather than mine, relationships had been poisoned. Neither Native Oregonians or Anglo settlers expected good neighbors, nor did they get them. Anglo settlers burned Indian towns, and Indian people stole cattle and burned outlying homesteads. The situation soon had the full attention of territorial and federal officials.[36]

General Joel Palmer, the newly appointed superintendent of Indian affairs in Oregon, tried to make peace treaties with the Rogue and Umpqua peoples in 1853, but he could neither keep settlers off of Indian land nor control the behavior of miners. His promises were empty, and everyone knew it. Raiding and skirmishes turned into something more regular, and citizens' meetings in the summer of 1853 demanded the "EXTERMINATION" of all Native people in southern Oregon, as an Oregon City newspaper headline displayed it succinctly.[37] Palmer, out of his depth, called in federal troops, who began a month-long war in which three hundred Rogue Indians and at least a hundred Anglos were killed, many of them settlers who had their homes attacked. Like lighting a tiny backfire in a forest conflagration, the federal government and the U.S. Army, both badly stretched in the Pacific Northwest, had only made the situation worse. The Rogue River Indians had signed a treaty but had no intention of moving east of the Cascades, and the Anglo settlers and miners had no intention of sharing a landscape with Indians. In his annual report to the Indian Department, Superintendent Palmer summarized grimly, "A general feeling of anxiety and distrust pervades the tribes . . . from the sea coast to the Rocky Mountains." He placed blame on "the conduct of evil-minded whites" and the "unratified treaties." He warned the commissioner that his own inability to keep promises and to deliver annuities and presents almost guaranteed trouble.[38]

Anglo Oregonians, angry that yet "another treaty of peace has been made with the thieving murderous bands of Indians," as the *Oregonian* reported, felt aggrieved. From their perspective, they had arrived in Oregon and made legal claims on land that belonged to people whom the government had promised would be removed beyond the Cascade Mountains. Now, as one settler wrote to Palmer that fall, "I have continually had to suffer from them since." He reported that Indians "have stolen my cabbages and potatoes," and "they have thrown down my fence." This writer recognized some of the sources of the problem when he noted "these Indians would tell me that I have stolen their lands."[39] Miners, cold and hungry that winter on the Oregon beaches and along the Rogue, attacked several Indian villages, burned them to the ground, and took captives as slaves. The following summer and fall, attention shifted east once again to the Oregon Trail, where the Snake, Bannock, and Shoshone Indians attacked and burned wagon trains. Frustrated by the streams of travelers through their lands and the continuing pressure to absorb Indian groups from west of the mountains on smaller and smaller pieces of land, leaders in these Native nations could no longer control their young men. The power of the state, obviously, had little purchase anywhere in Oregon.[40]

THE FAILURE OF WARFARE AND WASHINGTON'S NATIVE NATIONS

By 1855 territorial governors in both Oregon and Washington had widespread Indian wars on their hands. Their unilateral and amateur diplomatic and military actions had failed miserably both east and west of the mountains. They had earned the enmity of the U.S. Army and their local citizens. After years of expensive and bloody war, Native people appeared no closer to being removed to distant reservations or of being militarily vanquished, and Anglo-Americans seemed ever willing to take the law into their own hands. This is the context in which Governor Stevens hosted his great treaty conference in the Walla Walla Valley. Accompanied by Superintendent Palmer and dozens of agents and interpreters, Stevens believed he could solve the "Indian Problem" in the Pacific Northwest in one grand meeting.

In May of 1855 representatives of Native nations from the entire Pacific Northwest began to parade into the Walla Walla Valley—Nez Perces, Yakimas, Cayuses, Palouses, Klickitats, Umatillas, Walla Wallas, Spokanes—some allies, some old enemies, but all deeply suspicious of Stevens and his agents. Estimates of the numbers who attended varied from three thousand to six thousand, but all the observers agreed that tension turned to outright hostility when news came of a gold strike in Colville, Washington, located in the center of Native homelands. After thirteen days of meeting, nearly sixty Native leaders signed treaties ceding sixty thousand acres of land, but with evident bitterness and anger that Stevens ignored. Indian leaders had been shocked by Stevens's rude and dismissive behavior and infuriated by the poor reservations they would have to share. They signed but decided to discuss the situation among themselves without Stevens and his entourage watching. As Stevens headed east for another series of treaty meetings with the Blackfoot and Flatheads and Palmer returned to the Willamette Valley, the agreements unraveled almost instantly, and Native people on the entire Columbia River Plateau erupted in frustration and fear.[41]

We can watch this unfold from several perspectives. We have Governor Stevens's letters to Washington officials, Indian agents, and U.S. military leaders. We have annotated scrapbooks of newspaper clippings collected by a man named Elwood Evans, a lawyer and political rival of Governor Stevens. Evans watched as the wars spread and in 1889 compiled his material into the first official history of Washington, in classic congratulatory booster style. His notes, however, are far less complimentary of Stevens, the war, and politics in Washington. We also have the correspondence of the Hudson's Bay Company officials as they attempted, and failed, to remain neutral, and we have the accounts of various participants, mostly military men who kept journals. What we see in all of these accounts echoes what happened in Oregon: initial frustration that the Indians did not acquiesce to treaty agreements, anger at the quick and ineffective actions of volunteers, followed by concern as war spread in reaction to inept Anglo volunteer strikes, new confidence when the U.S. military arrived, and then utter panic as Native troops consistently bested the U.S. Army.[42]

The suddenness and scale of this Indian war stunned Anglo-Americans living in the region. We can see three kinds of trouble that all ignited around the same issues: white settlers, miners, and soldiers moving onto Indian lands before treaties had been concluded; fury on the part of whites when Native people objected to and responded to what they saw as invasion; and then a series of vigilante actions on both sides. Local agents and officials quickly called in the U.S. Army, which got involved on both sides, protecting Native people from white trespassers and protecting Anglo citizens from hostile Indians. Nothing was simple or clear. Around Puget Sound, along the Rogue River, in the Yakima Valley, and on the eastern plains, individual sets of grievances coalesced into desperate war as Native people realized they were losing their homelands. At his final council meeting with the Spokanes, as he learned of the extent of the warfare, Isaac Stevens, surrounded by bristling warriors, finally had to listen. Garry, a Spokane leader, said quietly to Stevens after days of negotiations, "When I speak you do not understand me; it is as if we have been talking for nothing." He continued with a clear warning: "Those Indians have gone to war, and I don't know myself how to fix it up again." By the time Stevens returned to take control of the war, he also had little idea of how to fix it up again.[43]

People living in Olympia, the raw new capital, first heard about the Indian wars in the local paper. We see the pattern of irritation, concern, relief, and panic. The editor confirmed that "within the last few weeks, rumors have reached us of a coalescence of the Indian tribes east of the Cascades, with a hostile intent, to commit depredations upon all the whites travelling through their country." Even worse, he now warned, "it is currently reported that a combination of Indians this side of the mountains, and along the Sound, to some extent, have acquiesced." The editor pooh-poohed the stories about Puget Sound Indians joining any conspiracy, because, of course, "they are far too lazy to make such efforts." However, just in case the Indians had more gumption than he expected, he reported that "at the request of a large number of citizens, the acting Governor, Chas. H. Mason, has solicited and obtained a company of fifty men, belonging to the station at Ft. Steilacoom . . . to proceed to the scenes where the depredations are supposed to have been committed."[44]

Local citizens expected to hear next that the army had prevailed handily and that they were free to go about their business settling Washington and Oregon on lands taken from the Indians. Instead, they read: "Maj. Haller's party had been driven in to the Dalles . . . with the loss of 5 killed and 16 wounded. Major Haller found the Indians in great numbers—estimated as high as 1500. He found them to be much better fighters than the whites had given them credit for. He was obliged to spike his howitzer and leave it."[45] Bad news indeed; the army had found a large and well-armed opponent, fled in disarray, and left their howitzers behind. And this was not the only frightening military defeat of the fall of 1855. Along the Rogue River, Native warriors easily defeated Anglo volunteers and regular troops who had no idea of how to fight in the steep, wooded ravines that Native people knew so well. After a series of skirmishes at places the troops named Hungry Hill or Bloody Springs, the Rogues retreated for the winter. As Lt. George Crook, who had to explain these losses to his superiors, put it: "the troops withdrew to the settlements and left the Indians monarchs of the hills."[46]

As bad news poured in and as the snow and rain made warfare nearly impossible, civilian and military officials considered what to do next. General John Wool, commander-in-chief of the Army of the Pacific, found himself in a very difficult position. Responsible for military affairs in huge swath of territory that stretched from Canada to Mexico and from Utah to the Pacific Ocean, Wool faced Indian uprising and war in every part of the region "won" by the United States in 1848. And he faced it with fewer than a thousand troops and a huge desertion rate because of the allure of gold. Wool had only been on the job for a year, but he had already concluded that these wars had been instigated by Anglo-American "cupidity" in trespassing on Indian lands and treating Native people "like wolves."[47]

In the past year Wool had deployed troops in southern California, in central California, and in the mountains and coastal regions of northern California; he had built outposts in Oregon and now had lost a series of battles in southern Oregon and in the Columbia River valley. In November of 1855 he faced a two-front war. He wrote to his superiors: "since my last letter, the Indian troubles in this department have very much increased. In

Rogue River valley the threats of the whites to commence a war of extermination against the friendly Indians on the reserve and in the vicinity of
Ft. Lane, have been put into execution."[48] On the Columbia front, Wool's
regular troops had been entirely overwhelmed, giving the Yakimas, Walla
Wallas, and Cayuses an easy victory. Wool insisted the only option was to
wait until spring when he could gather troops and supplies. He refused to
take on the Native nations with volunteer militia who had no experience
or equipment. This stance enraged local citizens, who shrieked in letters to
the newspapers that Wool was an Indian lover and that the army's only task
was to "EXTERMINATE" the Indians. His delay may have been unwise—by
spring Wool faced a third front when Native groups surrounding Puget
Sound and Seattle coalesced into a coherent rebel force.[49]

As the situation unfolded, Governor Stevens took unilateral action.
After arriving in Olympia in January of 1856, he described the woeful
situation in a letter to Jefferson Davis, the secretary of war: "The greatest
alarm prevailed across the land. The people were living in Block Houses.
. . . regulars and volunteers had retired before them." Most chillingly, he
reported that "reinforcements were coming from the other side of the
mountains to the hostile Indians," signaling new regional alliances among
Washington Natives.[50] Frustrated with General Wool's deliberate pace and
his refusal to use volunteers, Stevens issued a call for "six companies of
volunteers for the defense of the land." Even as eager men signed up,
Stevens discovered that they had no guns, horses, or supplies. He found
himself in the awkward situation of begging the Hudson's Bay Company
for supplies that he could not get from his own government. Stevens sent
a messenger with a list and "Territorial Scrip" with which to buy the items.
Chief Factor James Douglas demurred, saying that no one, including the
Hudson's Bay Company, would deal on such terms. Douglas, to keep the
peace, bought some supplies with his own money and delivered them as
"a gift" to the local militia commanders, a compromise that Stevens found
humiliating.[51]

Even though Stevens recognized the limitations of his volunteer troops,
he continued to rail against General Wool, accusing him of criminal incompetence, Indian coddling, and misuse of federal funds. He demanded,
often, that Jefferson Davis remove him from command. Wool was cautious and conservative, not bad attributes for a military leader, but he and
Stevens disagreed about the most basic goals of the Indian wars. Stevens
wanted the Indians out of Washington Territory and Wool wanted the illegally squatting settlers and miners off of Indian lands. The center of their

disagreement was the Yakima Valley, which Wool wanted to promise as a vast reservation for the Indians as a way to end the war and which Stevens wanted to promise to Washington citizens as reward for fighting the war.[52]

Anyone who did not share Stevens's vision of how the war should be prosecuted and who should live in Washington when it ended became his enemy. As it quickly became clear in the spring and summer of 1856 that Stevens had overestimated the skills of citizen volunteers and underestimated the resolve of Native fighters, public opinion turned against him. To squelch this disapproval, to enable the commandeering of Hudson's Bay Company stores, and to arrest traders and settlers who did business with Indians, Stevens declared martial law. He arrested Supreme Court justices, rounded up people of mixed race because of their connections to the Hudson's Bay Company and to local tribes, and fired Indian agents or elected officials who objected to any of this. Local officials sent off a flurry of letters to the U.S. secretary of state, insisting that Stevens had lost touch with reality. They explained that his insistence that "half-breeds had caused the Indian War" was simply "a fiction that found birth in the Governor's own brain."[53] President Franklin Pierce agreed and delivered a stinging rebuke. He allowed Stevens to remain as governor but took away his role as Indian superintendent. Stevens had overstepped the boundaries of territorial government in every respect, and martial law had not helped him to defeat the Indians. The rash actions and political squabbling only extended the Indian wars. Stevens's hard line and the behavior of militia troops, combined with the inability of federal officials to keep marauding miners away from their villages, convinced Native nations that they had no choice but to fight.[54]

The wars waxed and waned and waxed for another two years. West of the Cascades, in both Oregon and Washington, Indian agents convinced Native groups to move onto reservations after a series of military defeats in 1856 and 1857. In Oregon Superintendent Joel Palmer carved out two small reservations, but because they were west of the Cascades, Anglo citizens feared the Indians would escape the reservations and attack them. Oregon citizens regularly invaded the reservations and demanded Palmer's ouster. In Washington, General Wool successfully negotiated a peace agreement with the Yakimas and Walla Wallas that prohibited Anglo settlement in much of eastern Washington. This prohibition did bring peace, but it infuriated Governor Stevens and Washington citizens who wanted full access to the Walla Walla Valley. Stevens continued to encourage road building and surveying in the region, and settlers and miners continued to trespass

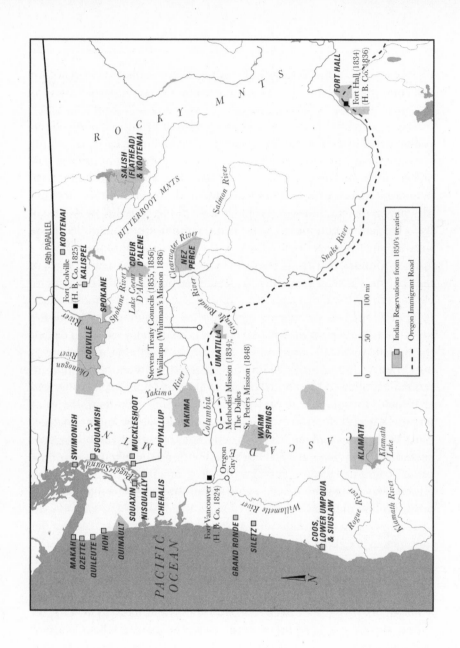

12. Native People, Wars, and Reservations in the Pacific Northwest, 1840–60

on Indian lands. Disgusted with Governor Stevens's blatant disregard for the law and the lack of control anyone had over either Anglo settlers or Native nations, the Indian Department fired everyone and appointed new negotiators. General Wool, vilified in the press and perceived as too friendly to the Indians, was replaced by General Newman S. Clarke.[55]

In the spring and summer of 1858 new rumors about hostile Indians being stirred up by Mormons fleeing Utah and attacks on prospectors headed to mines in northern Washington and British Columbia sent the military into the field. Aggravated because of the constant pressures on their lands, new nations had joined in the opposition. In a series of impressive victories, the Spokanes, Coeur d'Alenes, and some of the Nez Perces joined with the Palouses, Walla Wallas, and Yakimas to drive the U.S. Army from the field. Panicked telegrams flooded the War Department, and newspapers in western Oregon and Washington demonstrated real fear of a general Native uprising. General Clarke took the threat seriously and amassed troops from all over the West. Confident from their earlier victories, the allied Native nations allowed themselves to be drawn into a fight on the open plains against a huge army, a situation that blunted their effectiveness. In two battles Clarke's armies won decisively and broke the Native alliance. The great patriot fighters were now dead, and most groups had lost significant numbers to epidemic disease and the years of war, leaving people hungry and demoralized. They agreed, never happily, to move to the reservations and ceded nearly all of eastern Washington to Anglo settlers.[56]

The conclusion of the Indian wars in Washington and Oregon and the movement of the region's Native nations to reservations is where the story usually ends. But the end of the warfare did not solve the problems or assuage the fears of the people who had experienced it. War had come to all parts of the Pacific Northwest, north and south, coastal and mountain. No one, Indian or Anglo, would feel safe for a long time. Assessing blame, always a popular sport after a war, occupied newspaper editors, politicians, and congressional committees. Among the favorite scapegoats were Indian agents who stopped short of extermination, the Hudson's Bay Company because of their long connection to Native people and their suspicious "Britishness," and, most significantly, the large population of people of mixed race. A series of court-martials and trials of "squaw men, those white men living with Indian wives," took place during and after the wars. As an early history of Washington Territory put it, "suspicion naturally fell upon those men as being in collusion with the hostiles."[57] Questions about who could own land, hold office, marry, and make a living were answered by creating clear identities around "white settler" and "Indian" or "American" and "foreign." There could be no space in between—exactly the space where most people in the Pacific Northwest had operated for many generations. Creating a nation, state, or town in the midst of an Indian war and a gold rush had psychic costs. The price of those foundational moments became especially clear in Texas and New Mexico and along the Arkansas River, places where successful Native nations ran into confident settlers determined to have their land.

NATION BUILDING IN THE SOUTHWEST

The end of the Mexican War came at the same moment as news of the gold rush, so no one had a chance to think about how to manage these two separate events. In Oregon and Washington the gold rush operated more like a chronic disease that burbled dyspeptically in the background. In California it created acute and fatal conditions for creating order. In other parts of the region acquired by the Treaty of Guadelupe Hidalgo the Indian wars could also be understood as the denouement of the U.S. War with Mexico. The glad tidings of gold in California overwhelmed any semblance of federal authority as huge numbers of mostly men headed west. As troops from the Mexican War marched, sailed, and rode back home, the two groups literally ran into each other. And they had these meetings in Indian Country where the U.S. Army attempted to impose order.

The army, hopelessly understaffed after the Mexican War, tried to administer the vast new region for which it found itself responsible after 1848. The War Department created four departments: Texas, New Mexico, the Pacific, and the West. The Department of the West included the entire Great Plains from the Mississippi to the Rocky Mountains and from the Canadian border on the north to the Arkansas River on the south. Only 1,700 soldiers were expected to oversee this vast, seething region. Fort Leavenworth, Fort Kearny, and Fort Laramie had all of the soldiers and all of the responsibility of keeping the peace in a region where gold-rushers, overlanders, Mormons, and former soldiers came into contact with the varied Native nations of the Great Plains. Military men knew that the army that Congress had given them was far too small to protect any of the major trails with assurance and not nearly skilled and mobile enough to track and fight Native people on their own ground. As one officer in Texas remembered, "we broke down our men, killed our horses, and returned from patrols as ignorant of the whereabouts of the Comanches as when we started."[58]

Undermining the army at every step, too, was Indian policy that vacillated from wanting to protect and "civilize" Native people to one designed only to exterminate them, but without funding to do either. Thomas "Broken Hand" Fitzpatrick, the trader turned agent assigned to the Plains nations in 1847, warned the army brass that they either needed to provide Native people with generous annuities that paid more than "the gains of plunder" or they needed to use great military force "to restrain and check their depradations."[59] The army, given the impossible tasks of keeping overlanders and Native people apart and extinguishing title to Native lands so that white settlers could have them, failed miserably in these years.

In New Mexico and Texas, territorial acquisitions that came with the Treaty of Guadalupe Hidalgo, we can see the enormity of the problem as experienced by long-time residents and newcomers. Though the two places shared Mexican and Spanish colonial pasts, the Native nations that inhabited them had very different histories. Throughout the early nineteenth century, Santa Fe and northern New Mexico had been besieged by Native raiders, mostly Navajos, Apaches, and Utes, who also served as important links to a trading network controlled by the Comanches. The gold rush in California brought increasing numbers of travelers along the Arkansas and Canadian rivers, whose poorly protected cattle and caravans attracted Native raiders. One of B. D. Wilson's old friends wrote in 1849 to update him on the situation in New Mexico: "New Mexico as far as the administration of Justice and Indian depredations are concerned is a damned sight worse that ever it was when the Mexicans ruled," he warned, outlining the dangerous conditions. "The Indians are almost constantly robbing and killing the people and the Americans are as constantly threatening how they are going to chastise them." He concluded with some irony that when they did take to the field, "the Americans have been whipped—So much for the invincibles."[60]

In Texas "the invincibles" had no better success. Comanches simply dominated the military and economic situation, and ending the actual war did little to make Texas more peaceful. The Texas Republic had done no better with Indian relations than Mexico and the United States, and the U.S. Army inherited a perilous mess. Part of the agreement with Mexican officials spelled out in the Treaty of Guadelupe Hidalgo included a promise to protect the Mexican border from Comanche raiders, which the United States simply could not do. Anglo-American and Hispanic settlers alike had retreated from the frontiers, leaving the Comanches and their allies in control. The Mexican government threatened to present a bill for forty million dollars for the cost of these continuous raids. However, while at the peak of their powerful imperial surge, the Comanches had reached an environmental wall that no one could have predicted. A combination of factors had reduced bison populations drastically, threatening the basic resource for Comanche wealth and power.[61]

The Comanches faced two sets of problems. First, drought, overhunting by Native and white hunters, and crowds of people heading to California via the southern route whose stock animals had overgrazed the Arkansas and Red River grasses upon which bison populations depended. Second, white settlers and immigrant Indians encroached on the borders of Comanchería in several directions. On the east the Osages and Cherokees, as well as a host of other Native refugees being pushed into Oklahoma, Arkansas, and the northern Texas Panhandle, moved into Comanche hunting and trading territory. However, Euro-American settlers and ranchers expanding out of south central Texas presented the greatest challenge.[62]

As the Comanches felt these new stresses, their wealth in horses dwindled first and then their populations. They reacted to the economic and demographic problem with extensive raiding from the Arkansas River down far south into Mexico to replenish their herds and to find captives to help rebuild their populations. By 1853 the situation had gotten so bad that the U.S. government sent in Thomas Fitzpatrick, fur trapper, guide, and now Indian agent, to make a treaty with the Northern Comanches. Leaders of six villages agreed to allow the army to mark out roads and to build posts, but they flatly refused to give up any of their captives, explaining that these captives had been entirely absorbed into the bands who had captured them. In return for signing the treaty, the Comanches got food and guns, provided by William Bent, who received a federal contract to supply them.[63]

Such treaties appalled white Texans, who saw any accommodation with the Comanches as wrongheaded and dangerous. Like the situation in the Pacific Northwest, settler communities on the Texas frontier near Comanchería had suffered enormously from raiding in the late 1840s. Many settlers had been forced to retreat to Austin and San Antonio. Texas politicians argued forcefully that the only limitation white Texans faced in their ambitions came from the "Comanche barrier" and that the only solution was a military one. Unlike most places in the West, Texas made no attempt to make treaties with the Comanches or to consider exchanging

32. Comanche Council at San Antonio, ca. 1853. Lithograph, unknown artist.
Rose Collection, Western History Collections, University
of Oklahoma Libraries.

With the Alamo recognizable in the background, we see a meeting between
cultures. The presence of women and children seated in the background
signaled that the Comanche visitors intended a peaceful encounter. The
image presents the army officers as peacemakers, which was often their role
in the bitter warfare between Texas settlers and Texas Native nations.

or ceding land. Because they were unwilling to imagine any part of Texas
as off limits to white settlement, the solution of creating reserves came
too late. By 1850 border skirmishes and raids had turned into a full-scale
war of extermination between Comanches and white Texans, with Native
allies on both sides, mostly fought by the informal militia called the Texas
Rangers but supported by the U.S. Army.[64]

In the early 1850s the U.S. Army built a line of posts manned by nearly
two thousand troops to divide Native Texas from white Texas, but it reached
far into the traditional borders of Comanchería. The raiding had mostly
stopped, except for some horse and food stealing, but Texas newspapers,
as a way to sell papers and to increase federal spending on troops in Texas,
still reported that hundreds of white Texans were being butchered. Army
officials complained about this misinformation and pointed out that most

of the killing came from white bounty hunters getting Indian scalps for money. Captain William Steele wrote to his superiors that the Comanche leaders wanted peace and that they knew a "war would bring destruction to their people." Federal Indian agents agreed that much of the trouble came from the white Texan side. A frustrated agent assigned to the Comanches and Wichitas wrote in 1850 that Texas was burdened with a "large class of people . . . who had one desire, to fight and exterminate the Indians."[65]

Federal officials, Texas state politicians, and Texas citizens clearly disagreed about the scope of the problem and its solution. The Texas legislature ignored federal demands to set aside land for Indian reservations even when the new secretary of war, Jefferson Davis, insisted to Texas governor Peter Bell in 1853 that "much of the difficulty could be obviated by the government of Texas" by creating reservations "with defined and enforceable borders."[66] Texas politicians, however, had won their offices by promising to preserve all of Texas for white citizens and to provide a military solution for the challenge of the roving Plains Indians. Governor Bell went so far as to claim that Comanches returning from Mexico or Kiowas from the United States were foreign invaders, requiring the U.S. Army to expel them from Texas. This attitude stymied the efforts of Robert Neighbors, the agent assigned to the hopeless task of creating reservations and getting Texas Natives to settle there. White Texans had no desire to do anything but exterminate the Indians.[67]

After 1849 the Comanches had stopped most of their raiding in Texas, though they continued raids in Mexico and affected communities as far south as Durango. Raiding in Texas could only occur from a position of strength on the southern plains, and drought, disease, and famine had made Comanche populations drop by nearly half. Divisions between Comanche leaders and competition over access to buffalo and trade goods had seriously damaged Comanche unity. When the Texas legislature did allot small reservations in the northern part of the state, a few important Comanche leaders brought their people there to collect annuities of flour, beef, and corn meal. Ketumsee, who had requested sanctuary on a reservation several times, moved to the new reservation and began supervising a farm staffed by his own Mexican captives. Potsanaquahip, perhaps the most influential man in the north, said he couldn't live on a reservation, but he urged other Comanches to take advantage of the food and the security. Most of the Comanches, however, remained out on the plains, hungry and frustrated.[68]

In spite of this apparent progress a new wave of raiding swept Texas in 1855. It came out of Comanche and Apache anger at the continual raiding on their communities by the Texas Rangers, who targeted camps and families. At the same time troop numbers in the Texas forts dropped considerably as trouble with the Sioux and with white Kansans drew federal soldiers north. With the Comanches using the rations and guns they got as annuity payments at Bent's Fort and using the new reservation on the Brazos as a pit stop, the northern Comanches poured into Texas. Citizens along the Brazos frontier demanded help from the state in "our exposed and dangerous condition."[69] These raids, though successful at first from the Comanche perspective, proved to be very costly. The line of federal forts meant that troops could be deployed quickly, and the Texas Rangers who had formed militias in each small settlement had matured into being particularly effective killers.[70]

After three very bloody years, the same years that brought such devastation to the Pacific Northwest, the army and the Rangers mounted a unified offensive against the Comanches. The army, now equipped with effective cavalry, had come to share the view of white Texans that the Plains tribes had to surrender or be exterminated. To achieve this goal the army defined any Comanches found anywhere off the tiny reservation as hostile, and "hostiles" could be hunted down and killed. In 1858, accompanied by Caddo, Wichita, and Tonkawa auxiliaries, who also had scores to settle with the Comanches, the army organized into small, quickly moving groups and struck at the heart of Comanche country. These bold strikes shocked the Comanches, who awoke in their camps to discover their horses stampeded, cavalry guns firing, and their families in grave danger. Men, women, and children died by the hundreds. The Comanches fled north to the relative safety of the high plains between the Canadian and Arkansas rivers. It was cold there in the winter, and many of their horses died, but perhaps ten thousand people remained there.[71]

Some of the Comanches went to the reservation on the Brazos.[72] Robert Neighbors, who was certainly not a perfect man but was incorruptible and devoted to his job, served as agent for the Wichita and Caddo reservation and the one dedicated to the Comanches. He believed in the civilization program and initially had political support to make it work. He opened schools, got his federal budget increased so that he had enough agricultural implements, and convinced some Comanches to farm successfully. As white settlement moved north, Neighbors's efforts were undercut by growing numbers of merchants who opened up whiskey shops among the ranches on the border of the reservation.[73]

The Comanches off the reservation continued to raid south into Texas, and they did sometimes use the Brazos reservation as a supply point. Much of the raiding now came from organized groups of Anglo cattle rustlers who sometimes hired Apaches and Comanches, but it was much easier to blame Native people for the whole problem. Texans began to demand that the reservations be closed entirely. Along the Brazos, gangs of white vigilantes organized nightly invasions of Native settlements on the reservations. The situation became politically and physically untenable. Even proclamations from the governor demanding that citizens stop "unjust and unlawful hostilities against friendly Indians," didn't slow the violence.[74] White Texans insisted that the Comanches had to be driven from Texas.[75]

In 1859, after pleading with Texas officials and making a trip to Washington to meet with federal Indian Bureau officials, Robert Neighbors accepted defeat. He packed up and moved four hundred Comanches and one thousand Wichitas to a piece of land in Indian Territory leased for them by the state of Texas.[76] In a final gesture of violence, when agent Neighbors returned to close up the reservation, two white renegades shot him in the back on the streets of Fort Belknap. Such a murder seemed like a fitting epitaph for the Comanches, but it wouldn't work that way. Many Comanches avoided the reservation and retreated to the arid lands of the western *llano estacado* (staked plains) and waited. Even the hardiest Anglo-Texans could not farm these landscapes. After more than a decade of drought, in the early 1860s, the rain and the buffalo came back, granting the Comanches a reprieve and another era of great leaders, including Quanah Parker and Isatai. The Comanches would raid and build horse herds and keep the U.S. Army busy, but they had only a reprieve—as Dot Babb, the "last boy captive," taken from his family in 1866, reminds us.[77]

RAISING FAMILIES AND FIGHTING WARS

Throughout the Texas troubles in the early 1850s the people along the Arkansas River remained comparatively peaceful. The Cheyennes, Arapahos, and Comanches in this area faced the same pressures of disease, drought, declining buffalo populations, and the surge of human and animal traffic on the Santa Fe Trail. However, they did not yet face encroachment from settlement. The treaty they had signed with the U.S. government, negotiated by Thomas "Broken Hand" Fitzpatrick, a long-time trader married to an Arapaho woman, provided yearly payments in annuity goods that supported them when the buffalo did not. When they could find buffalo, they could still hunt and still trade at Bent's Fort, now the agency for the Upper Platte and Arkansas rivers. William Bent had gotten the federal contract to buy, store, and deliver these annuity goods. When he arrived with the annual shipments, hundreds of families gathered around the new fort in a celebration that reminded them of old times, but it also demonstrated how much things had changed. Bands of warriors danced in the fort, and William feasted the head men in the main dining room. Then the leaders of the gathered people handed out the food, clothing, and ammunition in equal shares. It represented a pittance of what they needed to survive, but they could all enjoy the moment.[78]

Later in the year they would be hungry. Thomas Fitzpatrick wrote to the commissioner of Indian affairs in 1853 that the Cheyennes "are in abject want half of the year . . . the travel on the road drives the buffalo away and . . . their children are crying with hunger." He warned that presents might have bought peace on the Arkansas River but that it wouldn't last.[79] William Bent saw the same warning signs among his friends and relatives at Bent's Fort. In the winter of 1856 most of the Cheyennes traveled north to winter with their northern Cheyenne relatives in western Kansas, where they hoped they might find more buffalo. Instead, they found trouble. Bored young men in winter villages, a problem for white Oregonians and Californians and army officers as well, could easily be convinced to raid settlements further east for horses and cattle. Tired of the petty thefts and the more serious crimes of the summer before on the Overland Trail, the soldiers at nearby Fort Leavenworth organized a raid of their own. In May of 1857 four cavalry companies marched up the Arkansas to take on the Cheyennes.[80]

The southern Cheyennes retreated from the cavalry and migrated back to their summer home on the Arkansas, arriving restive and poorly fed. When the yearly shipment of annuity goods arrived, some people in the village began to discuss attacking Bent's Fort. Bent could not allow such a disaster, and he could not fight people he had befriended and lived with for thirty years. Instead, William Bent left the goods in the fort, and he and his family moved out. The cavalry arrived before the Cheyennes could decide what to do, and they took the empty fort. Next they startled and scattered the Cheyennes by drawing their sabers rather than the guns the warriors had expected. In that moment the battle was over. Colonel William Sumner, in charge of this affair, burned 171 lodges and tons of buffalo meat, and he dumped the stored annuity goods in the river, which would do more damage to the Cheyennes than any battle. The Bents never moved back into the fort. Bent built a small stockade about twenty-five miles away on lands that he had claimed as part of a Mexican land grant, where he hoped his family would be safe.[81]

The 1857 cavalry victory shattered Cheyenne confidence, but even more shattering was the news of a gold rush in Colorado. Hundreds of thousands of eager gold-rushers traveled across Cheyenne and Arapaho lands. They trampled the grass, polluted the water, killed and drove away the buffalo, and cut down the trees; a few even shot at Indians in their rush to get to the gold country west of present-day Denver. William Bent wrote to the superintendent of Indian affairs in St. Louis and begged him to establish inviolate reservations for the central Plains nations "before they cause a great deal of trouble."[82] For his efforts, the superintendent appointed Bent as agent with the specific charge of "containing" the Cheyennes, Arapahos, Kiowas, and Comanches on the upper Arkansas until suitable lands could be found and appropriated. This would be a nearly impossible task, but Bent believed that a significant group of the Cheyennes and Arapahos at least would accept the need to settle down, away from the gold rush, and learn to till the soil.[83]

As a father, brother, husband, son, uncle, and now agent to Cheyenne people, William Bent tried very hard to implement this plan. At his own expense he bought farm implements, seeds, lumber, and food supplies, brought them to his new stockade, and began to work from there. He wrote to Superintendent Robinson first, telling him that the Indians in his new agency had remained peaceful, and then warning him that "the failure of food, the encircling encroachments of the white population" would inevitably ignite "a smoldering passion" among the Cheyennes and Arapahoes.[84] Bent begged him to intercede with the new Colorado territorial officials to create a reservation for his long-time friends on the upper Arkansas River as it headed into the mountains, a region so far from the gold fields and from the great overland roads that it seemed like a possible safe haven. The federal government and the territorial government couldn't agree on a reservation, leaving the Cheyenne with no place to go, which would create real trouble in the next decade. But nothing—not government intervention, military might, nor the will of a father and husband—could protect the Cheyennes or the Bent family from the maelstrom of the Colorado gold rush. The Bents would survive, and so would a portion of the Cheyennes, but the world they had built together would leave few traces.

Kit Carson, his wife Josefa, and their growing family experienced these changes and made different choices about how to re-orient their lives.

About the same time that the Bents left the old fort on the Arkansas, Kit Carson had moved away from Taos. He and Josefa wanted to try making a living as ranchers with their close friends Tom Boggs and Rumalda Bent Boggs, and Lucien Maxwell, the first two of whom we met in chapter 6. Maxwell had negotiated a contract with the army to supply beef, which gave the ranch a steady income. They chose a site on Rayado Creek, not far from where William Bent built his own last ranch, on lands that were part of a Mexican land grant, but also in the homelands of the Jicarilla Apaches. They got along pretty well, inviting visiting Native people in for meals and offering small presents, but also by building a large stockade with an adobe wall to keep predators and thieves out. When a group of Jicarillas attacked the ranch in the spring of 1850, wounding two New Mexican herders and running off most of the stock, Carson and his men were quick to pursue them—returning with all the horses and five Jicarilla scalps. Carson believed in quick and biblical retaliation, something that William Bent would never have done.[85]

Carson had other run-ins with Native people in those years at Rayado. He had a frightening moment with some Cheyennes who were running from a military column as he was accompanying his daughter Adaline back from school in St. Louis in 1851. In 1853, while taking his sheep to market in California, he ran into his old friend Edward Beale with whom he had served during the Mexican War. Fortuitously Beale and B. D. Wilson were just then developing the Tejon Indian reserve and considering how best to protect southern California Natives. As Beale described the conditions of California Indians and the pressures they faced from settlement, Carson surely thought about how Beale's reserve idea might apply to the Natives with whom he dealt regularly. He may have known about his impending appointment as agent to the Muache Utes, the Jicarilla Apaches, and the Taos Pueblos, which became official immediately after his return from California. The agency job offered a steady income, and he and Josefa moved back to Taos so that she and little William, now two, could be closer to Josefa's family.[86]

Indian agent Kit Carson had no agency, building, school, store, or mission to oversee. None of the groups that he was charged to "supervise" had a reservation assigned to them. His sole function was to convince the Utes and the Apaches to stop raiding by making peace agreements with them that involved annuity goods and monetary payments—or as it must have seemed to both sides—bribes for proper behavior. But proper behavior became almost impossible when the Indians were starving, and

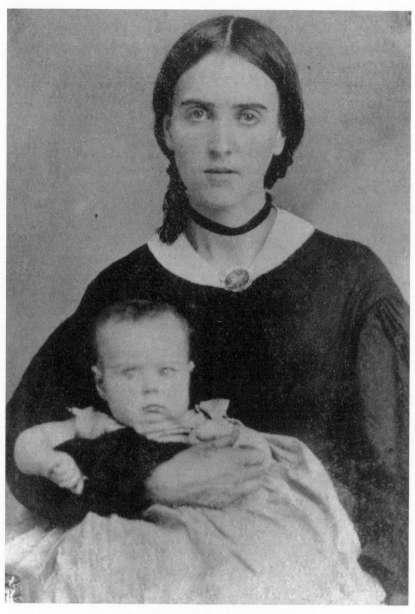

33. Josefa Jaramillo Carson holding child, ca. 1850.
Courtesy Taos Historic Museums.

A lovely young Josefa holds her first child, William Carson, likely
named for William Bent. Josefa, whose sisters were married to
Charles Bent and Thomas Boggs, came from a family deeply
enmeshed in trade and politics in northern New Mexico.

Carson figured out almost immediately that their pitiful annuities could not keep them fed. He warned David Meriwether, the New Mexico territorial governor and acting superintendent of Indian affairs, that "if the Government will not do something for them to save them from starving, they will be obliged to Steal," a plea he would make over and over again. Carson made it clear, too, that if the Apaches did steal, he would "chastize them mightily."[87] He also saw no conflict of interest in serving as a government scout when the Jicarillas or Utes did inevitably steal and thus needed to be chastised. The challenge of a lack of reservation and not enough food to buy peace finally drove Carson to have a public shouting match with Governor Meriwether at a treaty meeting with the Utes in 1856. He was fired for insubordination, which he probably deserved, but Meriwether reinstated him after a series of formal apologies.[88]

Nothing much changed for the Jicarilla or the Utes in those years in terms of Indian policy, but they got hungrier and angrier. Kit Carson couldn't change the basic policy problem that required Indians to become civilized but provided no inducement or means for them to do so. Nor could he stop the Comanche and Navajo raids on the Pueblos. The Jicarillas and the Utes continued to commit "depradations" as Carson reported each year, but just as many depradations were committed against them by other Native people and by local Mexicans and Anglos. The Utes, of course, viewed raiding as business practice rather than crime. Raiding went in all directions, and Kit and Josefa's household grew in unexpected ways because of the trade in human beings. In 1856 Josepha noticed a group of Utes riding in and saw one had a small child with him. Josefa realized the boy was probably a captive Navajo and would be killed once he became bothersome to the Ute warriors. She offered a horse in return for the child, and young Juan Carson stayed with the family until adulthood. Another young woman arrived in the same way, as a Navajo captive taken by the Utes, and she was baptized María Dolores Carson and stayed with the family for six years. Other captives were returned to their people, whether Navajo, Ute, or Jicarilla. Whether Kit saw this as part of his job as agent or whether he saw this as an informal source of labor for his household we can't say, but it reflected how much disruption raiding caused in people's lives in those years.[89]

The Colorado gold rush, however, destroyed whatever tense accommodation had developed in northern New Mexico and southern Colorado during Carson's last years as an Indian agent. As gold-rushers infiltrated the foothills of the Rockies, conflict with the Utes became instant and deadly, just as it had in the foothills of the Sierra Nevada in California ten years earlier. By the end of June 1859, reports of Ute "atrocities" reached New Mexico, and Carson went north to investigate and to punish the Utes who committed them, if necessary. This time he calmed down the Utes and convinced some of them to come south, probably preventing more conflicts. Others fled into the mountains, and some stayed in the new communities in the foothills. But the Indian Wars in New Mexico and Colorado were just beginning, and ironically this would provide employment for a number of Ute men. The U.S. Army would be marching on New Mexican Indians, and Kit Carson and the Utes would be with them.[90]

Neither the gold rush nor the U.S. War with Mexico worried the Navajo much. In their vast Colorado Plateau homeland of canyons, deserts, and mountains they remained isolated from many of the pressures that plagued other Native nations in the 1850s. They had seen intruding peoples before, but no one had ever presented a serious military threat. The Navajos took slaves, sheep, and goats from the Spanish and took what they wanted from Mexican and Pueblo villages. As we saw in chapter 6, the first U.S. expeditions against the Navajos in the late 1840s could only be described as disasters. The first agent assigned to the Navajos, James Calhoun, noted with dismay that military intervention had only succeeded in "making them believe we do not have the power to chastise them."[91] Navajo lands were isolated and forbidding, and military campaigns that lasted months often never saw a Navajo.

Each new governor and each new Indian agent believed he could solve the Navajo problem, and every official failed. In 1849 John Washington, the governor and military commander of territorial New Mexico who replaced the murdered Charles Bent, envisioned an elaborate survey and military tour of Navajo country. The troops would awe the Navajos, and the surveyors would give other expeditions useful maps of an entirely unknown region. Accompanied by the army, a volunteer Mexican militia, Pueblo mounted troops and interpreters, topographical engineers, and various writers and artists, including Richard and Edward Kern, who were still mourning the murder of their brother Benjamin in the southern Rockies that winter, Washington led a force of about four hundred men into Navajo country.[92] This impressive force did march and drag its howitzers around various Navajo strongholds, but none of it impressed the Navajos. A few leaders signed a treaty, but everyone knew it was meaningless. Colonel Washington, wanting to act tough, murdered an important Navajo leader and six other men over a stolen pony, and from that moment on he was regarded as a hostile force. Armed Navajo troops, overtly hostile and outnumbering Washington's men, accompanied them back to Santa Fe and immediately began raiding again. Their first acts were to stop the mail trains coming from the United States and to begin stealing army horses and cattle in huge numbers. But small pastoral communities in northern New Mexico suffered the most. A group of citizens sent a petition to the U.S. president begging for help in 1850, claiming that "our Indian troubles at this moment are of a more terrible and alarming character than in the past fifty years."[93]

The situation did not improve over the next few years. In 1851 Indian agent and now governor Calhoun issued a desperate proclamation calling all able-bodied male citizens and all the male residents of the Pueblos to form volunteer companies for "service against the Indians." He could offer no money, but he said that all volunteers could keep any property, including women and children, that they captured. Six hundred men volunteered, including a large contingent led by Manuel Antonio Chaves, who had fought the Navajo before and whose family's sheep business was being destroyed by the raiding.[94] In campaign after campaign, however, the Navajos simply eluded the soldiers, stole their horses, and ran off their cattle, which meant, as one officer tersely put it, "they never gave us an opportunity to inflict on them any signal chastisement."[95]

The only person who had any success in negotiating between the Navajos and New Mexico authorities in those years was Henry Dodge. He had arrived in Santa Fe with the army in 1846 but had stayed on, opening a trading post and marrying a Navajo woman. He served as an advisor and interpreter with several military campaigns and was appointed an agent to the Navajos in 1853. He insisted on feeding people, getting some of the Navajos to grow corn to sell to the soldiers at Fort Defiance, and helped negotiate the Treaty of Laguna Negra in 1855. This treaty promised much more land and annuities to this very large tribe, along with roads, railways, and military posts—and Congress refused to ratify it. When Dodge, the only effective agent the Navajos would have, was killed by the Apaches in November of 1856, the last possibility for peace ended.[96]

In the spring of 1856, in a stunning attack on Peralta, a river community south of Albuquerque, a Navajo band killed Mexican sheepherders and stole either four thousand or eleven thousand sheep, depending on whose report we believe. This time the raiders were defiant and young, a group of new leaders among the Navajos. When the military did not respond because troop levels were too low, this proved to the Navajos that the Americans could not enforce any ultimatums. It also left American military officials itchy to enforce rules with a stick. Both sides approached each other with utter contempt in a deadly version of playing chicken. In 1856 the Navajos were winning. The rest of New Mexico had lost, according to the territorial secretary of state, 244 people, 150,231 sheep, 893 horses, 761 mules, and 1,234 cows between 1846 and 1856.[97]

By any measure the U.S. military was losing. The army built forts, conducted campaigns, drew maps, and made peace treaties, and still the Navajos raided sheep, cattle, and horses, took people captive, and sometimes killed them. Military and civil officials knew what the solution was: total war. But they would have to wait until after the Civil War began in the rest of the country to fight the civil war in New Mexico. Only then could they leverage enough power against the Navajo nation. Fortunately that is a story I don't have to tell here.

By the end of the decade, Indian Country was in a state of permanent war. Historians often describe this as a conflict over expanding and clashing aspirations in which Anglo-Americans and Native Americans found themselves fighting over visions of western opportunity. The story goes, now, that the West allowed different peoples to expand, but such expansion carried with it the ultimate tragedy that only one group could have the space to play out their ambitions. In this "dueling expansions" model, Anglo-Americans just sort of expanded faster and won the demographic war. The story doesn't examine why the space couldn't be shared or why the wars to rid the space of any competitors were so brutal. In the West of the early nineteenth century, not a peaceful place by any definition, people did share space while disagreeing about ambitions, use of resources, and the ideologies that supported those ambitions. But in the 1850s, agreeing to disagree no longer seemed possible or even imaginable.

Instead, we have war: war with the Sioux in Minnesota and the Dakotas; war with the Cheyennes in the central plains; war with the Kiowas and Comanches on the southern plains; war with the Navajos, Utes, and Apaches in the Southwest; war with the Yumas, Modocs, and Mojaves in California; war with the Spokanes, the Umpquas, the Coeur d'Alenes, and the Yakimas in the Northwest. The army, with officers and soldiers alike deeply frustrated by fighting an enemy that was "everywhere and yet nowhere," had failed to secure the borders of the new conquest. The military and civil authorities wouldn't fail at this task forever. The nation would have to devote far more blood and treasure to the project of making the trans-Mississippi West a place for white settlement than it could muster in the

1850s. In this decade they had learned much about fighting, pacifying, killing, and containing Native people, but successful imposition of martial and administrative power would elude them for another two decades. For the people who lived amid this unending war—Native, European, and everyone in between—these were hard years.

Chapter 8

The State and Its Handmaidens

Imposing Order

Frederick Chouteau, age six, and his cousin Charles Pierre, nine, sat on a riverbank behind the store that their two fathers, Cyprien and Frederick Chouteau, had built in Westport, Missouri. They sat there that early summer morning of 1858, freed from the obligation of school or chores, because the school building and the family stores had been occupied by federal soldiers garrisoned there while keeping proslavery men and antislavery men apart. As the boys watched teams of Shawnee, Kansa, and Delaware men move earth as part of a military and state project to lower the great bluffs of the Missouri, they commented on the activity in the French and English patois of their fathers' family. Both boys could also understand every word spoken by the Native workers because they had learned Shawnee and Delaware from their mothers and from the Native children at the mission school that they and all of their Chouteau cousins had attended. The young boys and the workers all expressed doubt that anyone could take down those bluffs, even with the array of steam shovels and human power the army now had its service. The boys had heard their parents' discussions of the great docks and roads their newly named "City of Kanzas" would have after the mountains of dirt had miraculously moved, but the Native shovelers wondered what would rein in the great Missouri River once the bluffs came down.[1]

As federal officials, long-term residents, and recent immigrants surveyed the situation in Texas, New Mexico, or Oregon at the end of 1850s, nobody could feel terribly optimistic about conditions after a decade of Indian war. Disorder and then violence came to bloody many relationships in the West as the decade ground on. Certain periods in the history of the United States make its residents appear to be downright nasty. Moments when powerful Americans felt threatened by too much change or too much power sharing seem to create spasms of poisonous behavior. The early twentieth century, when lynchings became entertainment in small-town America and when Native white Protestants did their level best to keep out immigrants of any variety they deemed too different, certainly qualifies as one of those mean periods. The 1850s, particularly in the western United States, might be one as well. Much of the chaos and violence that characterized the place and period could be linked to a lack of political order. But it also came from the choices people made about their own behavior in moments of freedom. Conquest had been announced but not imposed, and American citizens took full advantage of these unsettled conditions.

CIVIL THREATS AND THE MORMONS

Another place where the new United States had trouble imposing order was Utah, where the Mormons had created the Kingdom of Deseret. In the 1840s the Latter-day Saints wanted nothing more than to escape the United States and remove to the north of Mexico. But by 1848 their community in the isolated Great Basin was located at the center of the U.S. mountain West. Deseret became Utah Territory in 1850, and the Mormons ended up living right on the California Trail—again in the heart of the U.S. economy and culture. Nobody liked this juxtaposition of desert Saints, Euro-American overlanders, and Native people, but it had become geographic fact. This group of religious outcasts would defy the U.S. government in a moment that shook its principles to the core.

When Mary, Samuel, and Minnie Richards arrived in the Salt Lake Valley in October of 1849, some ten thousand Mormons had already arrived. The Richardses settled into a dense web of family and community that had developed quickly, but at great cost to the early settlers. Samuel's family included many Church leaders, but status had not protected them from the disease and other tribulations of the trek to Utah. Mary noted sadly how many of the family were not there. Her mother had died of malaria in Nauvoo. Samuel had lost three brothers: one killed in Missouri, one died from illness in Pueblo, Colorado, while serving as part of the Mormon Battalion, and one as a missionary in England. His sister-in-law Jane Richards had suffered much more, losing two brothers, two children, and a sister-wife while traveling west. Samuel's parents had arrived safely, but Mary's father, sister, and brother remained in St. Louis. Many of the Saints' families, especially those who had been with the church during the horrifying years in Missouri and Illinois, suffered similar losses that help to

34. Charles R. Savage, "Little Girl Standing Next to Chair," 1858. Savage
Collection, L. Tom Perry Special Collections, Harold B. Lee Library,
Brigham Young University, Provo, Utah. MSS P24, 143.

Savage, an established photographer in Salt Lake City, took many photographs
of Mormon families in the 1850s and 1860s. This anonymous child looks
at us with the startlingly familiar and direct gaze of childhood as she
posed to celebrate a birthday or a religious milestone.

explain their fears at being inundated with non-Mormon travelers from the United States.[2]

In the isolation of Utah, Mormondon used its distinctive qualities to great advantage. From the beginning the Utah Saints developed cooperative practices and laws to divide up land, water, and labor. With specific instructions from the Council of Twelve that formed church leadership, Mormon pioneers plowed, fenced, and irrigated one "Big Field," devised a system of building houses on evenly spaced city blocks, and gave out farm lots with the idea that they would be "equal according to circumstances, wants, and needs." Mary and Samuel took a town lot next to Samuel's parents but could not afford to build a house on it for several years, so they lived with Samuel's brother Henry and his family. Some of this cooperative effort came out of necessity in the first desperate need to feed and shelter a large group of people in an unfamiliar environment. But the community's success and continuity also came out of religious conviction and the desire to live up to Joseph Smith's vision of an egalitarian kingdom on earth.[3]

Fears that sometimes edged into paranoia also drove Deseret's success. The years of persecution in Ohio, Missouri, Illinois, and Iowa only increased Mormon determination to succeed in Utah and to be separate from the United States. After their arrival in Utah, the Mormon faithful signaled their difference from mainstream American culture by attempting to farm, merchandise, and manufacture with commonly owned and worked lands, products, and cash. Everything was undertaken with two related goals: the Mormons wished to be entirely self-sufficient so that they could cease all contact with the unfriendly United States and so that they could create the Kingdom of God on earth.[4]

These two goals, and the fact that few Mormons had much cash, made many of these early cooperative experiments successful. Because no one had enough capital to start manufacturing enterprises or to build irrigation systems, people had to pool resources. Several theological practices made this easier. Mormons believed that they all served as stewards of the church's wealth and that basically everything, in the end, belonged not to individual Mormons but to the church as a whole. Mary and Samuel Richards had some advantages because of their well-connected family. They usually had one or two servants living in the house with them who helped Mary with the housework and Samuel on his Big Field lot. And every Mormon understood that the practice of tithing supported this communal vision and observed it very seriously. Many people spent every tenth day working on communal building projects such as forts, meetinghouses, roads, and other public works. Samuel Richards spent many days working on the irrigation ditches and hauled logs from the mountain canyons, though he sometimes sent one of his "boys" to replace him at this labor.[5]

Getting new converts, who tended to be the poor and dispossessed of the growing commercial industrial world of eastern America and western Europe, to the isolated Great Basin kingdom cost a lot of money. Few emigrants from Europe could pay their own passage to the United States, much less the cost of traveling across the Great Plains. Even fewer had the means to set themselves up in business or as farmers in such a forbidding setting as Utah. To solve this problem, Young and the Council of Twelve came up with the concept of the Perpetual Emigrating Fund in 1849. It would operate out of voluntary contributions of church members, repayments by those assisted by the fund, and with interest accrued on loans given; it would exist purely to fund the immigration of poor Mormons to Utah. As soon as Young announced the plan, Utah Mormons raised five thousand dollars. They sent the funds east with an agent instructed to make the money stretch as far as he could by providing only minimal supplies and homemade wagons for any potential converts. This maximized the numbers of new converts while tempering their faith with hardship on the trail.

Upon arrival in Utah, new Saints received land or employment through the new Office of Public Works created out of the wealth accumulating in tithing houses. Throughout the 1850s, hundreds of men worked as blacksmiths, carpenters, painters, adobe makers, and stonecutters building the infrastructure of Salt Lake City. With their wages or their farm produce, some emigrants managed to pay back the Perpetual Emigrating Fund, but most of the money to support it came from more established Mormons. In fact, most beneficiaries of the fund never paid it back, but the fund eventually brought more than ten thousand Saints to Utah. Samuel Richards regularly served as mediator for Mormons who couldn't pay back the fund, and he helped the bishops decide whether they deserved to be excused. "Dire poverty" served as the most common reason Samuel cited in his cases, and the Church usually released these people from their debts.[6]

THE PERSONAL POLITICS OF POLYGAMY AND THEOCRACY

If hard work and cooperation had been the only Mormon practices in Utah, the Mormon story would be fairly unremarkable. But in 1852 the church announced publicly that one of its fundamental beliefs was "plural marriage." The concept of polygamous marriage had been part of church doctrine since Joseph Smith introduced it, though its practice had remained very private. A few Mormons had practiced polygamy in the 1830s, but its practice had grown as the church matured. In the wealthy and influential extended Richards family, almost every family included more than one wife. Mary talked about it very openly and without any drama in her journals from the years at Winter Quarters. However, when she wrote to Samuel during his long missionary trips to England and Scotland, she expressed less ambiguity. She described how unhappy several of Samuel's sisters-in-law were with new wives and clarified her hope "that it twould be the desire of my Samuel to live alone with me."[7]

Compared to other men in his family, Samuel was slow to take on more wives. In 1854 Brigham Young told Samuel he needed to take on a second wife. In his journals Samuel wrote about several young women he thought might be suitable, but he settled on Mary Ann Parker, Mary's niece, a sixteen-year-old who had spent much time in the household already. On February 14, 1855, Samuel Richards and Mary Ann Parker were sealed to each other in a ceremony that Mary and her sister attended in Brigham Young's office. Samuel described the whole day in great detail and concluded that it had been "a most lovely pleasant day as nature herself conspired to make all as agreeable and lovely as the union we had formed."[8] Samuel would add five wives to the family over the next six years and build two more houses. Mary wrote quite clearly about her feelings of isolation and mistreatment when Samuel was not available to help with the complicated household and the children. She had five children but buried two, Alonzo and Iantha, in the family garden. Devastated by Iantha's death in 1856, Mary seemed overwhelmed by the whole situation, and her health began to suffer. Samuel worried about her but found himself increasingly drawn into politics, church activities, and a newspaper he started. As tensions built with the U.S. government, he found himself deeply involved in planning with the most elite members of the Council of Twelve.[9]

The choice to practice polygamy openly also had serious implications for Mormons on the national scene. Brigham Young's celebrated twenty-seven wives and fifty-six children alone were enough to ignite a storm of protest against the Mormons, but part of the challenge now is to understand why the idea of plural marriage threatened such a wide swath of Americans. However thrilling it might have been for people to imagine what went on in Mormon households, polygamy was only one of the things that got under the national skin. In the heated atmosphere of the national politics of 1850s the Mormons became an easy target. When the Treaty of Guadalupe

Hidalgo made the Mormon kingdom part of the American nation, and the California gold rush placed the Mormons at the center of a national traffic jam, their practices came under new scrutiny. From this position Brigham Young and his followers simply refused to follow the rules. After decades of hounding and harassment by their fellow citizens and by the U.S. legal system, they would not compromise their religious values and buckle to either federal authority or Euro-American cultural codes.

The first episode of Mormon intransigence came with the creation of Utah Territory. The Latter-day Saints had sought isolation to build a kingdom and a theocracy. They didn't want to be good Euro-American republicans, and they didn't really believe in liberty or democracy. However, to fund their separate kingdom, they needed access to the growing economy that brought these unwelcome ideas into their midst. First Brigham Young and his Council of Twelve made a petition to enter the United States as the new state of Deseret. The petition got subsumed under political need to craft a sectional compromise, and Deseret became Utah Territory, with Brigham Young as its first territorial governor. He declared that all laws created by the state of Deseret still held, including no individual voting, no judges who were not Mormon bishops, no common law, no ownership of land or use of water for non-Mormons or dissenters—none of which meshed with the expectations of U.S. officials or citizens.[10]

This uneasy compromise never worked. Territorial status required the president to appoint federal judges, to arrange for the new territory to be surveyed and mapped, and to make sure Utah's Native people were supervised by agents and superintendents. All of these tasks and the people charged to complete them smacked into Mormon refusal to allow this level of meddling in their affairs. Mormon reaction to judges and surveyors made them appear obstinate and out of step with the rest of the nation. From the Mormon perspective, the effort to undermine their laws and to measure and sell their land proved the malicious intent of the United States. At best these federal appointees were ignored; at worst they were threatened and driven out of Utah. At least sixteen officials left Utah, some out of frustration, but many out of fear. David Burr, the surveyor general appointed to measure and map Utah lands, provides a good example of the hostility federal officials received. Not only did he deal with low-level sabotage like the removal of stakes and theft of tools and animals, but the Mormon priesthood also denounced him from the pulpit and encouraged local Native people to attack his surveying teams. Finally in 1857, after his friends warned him about death threats, Burr left Utah.[11]

Another place where Mormons came into conflict with federal policy involved Indian affairs. Like other westerners in those years, the Mormons built a nation in the midst of Indian Country, but their relationship with local tribes was complicated by Mormon theology. According to the Book of Mormon, Utah's Native people were, in fact, one of the lost tribes of Israel, the Lamanites, who had rebelled against God. As part of Mormon prophecy the Latter-day Saints needed to convert the Lamanites so that they could ally with the Saints "to overthrow all gentile governments of the American continent." Part of the prophecy instructed Mormon men to "marry with wives of Every Tribe of Indians" so that Native people could "become white and delightsome" and ascend to heaven.[12]

Language that blatantly sanctioned violent revolution, Native uprising, and miscegenation horrified federal officials already concerned about Mormon activities. These beliefs created a challenge for the Mormons when the twenty thousand or so Numic people living around them, including Utes, Paiutes, and Shoshones, showed no interest in converting. Rather than welcoming the Saints as saviors, most of Utah's indigenous people saw them as threatening usurpers. Isolated raids and killings on both sides escalated as Mormon communities spread out from Salt Lake City, and the Mormons found themselves at war with the Utes in 1853. To combat this serious threat, all male settlers between age eighteen and forty-five enrolled in compulsory training for the Nauvoo Legion, or as they described it for public consumption, the Militia of Utah Territory. At the same time, Brigham Young ordered hundreds of Mormons into the field to act as missionaries to the Indians.[13]

When this contradictory policy, described by one historian as "open hand and mailed fist," led to the massacre of a U.S. railroad survey party, federal officials had to respond. The U.S. Army sent two artillery companies and eighty-five mounted dragoons to investigate the deaths of Captain John Gunnison and eight of his men, an act Brigham Young regarded as insulting and invasive. Samuel Richards wrote in his journal that President Young preached to a "Tabernacle full to over Flowing" that he "Would sooner have his throat cut than submit to any interference with his family by the ungodly Gentiles."[14] With such thundering language and consistent refusal to bow to federal authority, the Mormons had placed themselves firmly in national view. Brigham Young chose this moment to send a memorial to the U.S. Congress demanding statehood for the free and independent state of Deseret. Just as Texans and Californians had demanded rights from the Mexican government, and Kansans and Missourians would demand forms of statehood that protected their visions of rights, the Mormons now claimed theirs, and the U.S. government had few tools to deal with such a challenge.[15]

The Mormons, with their success and their importance on the map of the western United States, looked threatening to other Americans. Had the federal government allowed a strange and immoral theocracy to take control in the heart of this rich new region? Was Mormondom just an extreme version of popular sovereignty, or was it a threat to the Constitution? Could the republic, challenged in so many places, find enough elasticity to contain the Latter-day Saints? Newspapers and politicians, eager to find an issue that did not involve debate between North and South during the election of 1856, raised opposition to the Mormons to a positive frenzy. Journalists detailed Mormon polygamy and revolutionary threats, and editors demanded that the government and the military take action. The Latter-day Saints, who had endured bloody persecution and hatred before, saw such national attention as evidence of the coming millennium, which only hardened their resolve.[16]

Both sides reacted with a certain amount of paranoia. Brigham Young began seriously investigating other sites for the Mormon kingdom. In early 1857 Young and other important elders headed to the northernmost settlement of Mormondon, Limhi, initially a mission to the Bannocks and Flatheads in what is now Idaho. At Limhi they distributed gifts and began holding sessions with Pacific Northwest Indians just as a fresh wave of Indian uprisings spread across that region. Reported in the newspapers from California to Kansas, Governor Stevens and the commander of the Pacific division of the army immediately blamed the Mormons for upsetting the peace, an accusation that was surely wrong, but not inconsistent with the Mormon vision in which Indians could act as "Battle Ax for the Lord."[17]

THE ALMOST WAR AND THE MASSACRE IN UTAH

In May of 1857 newly elected president James Buchanan, obligated by campaign promises and convinced that the Latter-day Saints were in revolt against the United States, demanded that Brigham Young give up his position as territorial governor. He appointed Alfred E. Cumming, a Democrat and former superintendent of Indian affairs in St. Louis, as governor along with a set of other territorial officials for Utah. Then, without notifying anyone in Utah, he sent in the army to enforce his appointments, but not to act as an invading army. Was this a bluff? It isn't clear how far either the

Mormons or federal officials intended to go. Did anyone really imagine armed conflict? In this situation General Winfield Scott, commander-in-chief of the army, ordered 2,500 men to assemble at Fort Leavenworth, but it took them weeks to organize. By the time they left Fort Leavenworth, fall was already on the way, and the army was too late to get through the mountain passes before winter came. When Young, having prepared his people for such a moment, heard the news of this approaching army, he did not hesitate. He issued a proclamation prohibiting any military force from entering the territory, and then he mobilized. Young called in all of the outlying colonists, including those in southern Utah, Las Vegas, and San Bernardino. He then prepared Salt Lake City for war.[18]

As the U.S. Army and the newly appointed governor, Alfred Cumming, approached in September to make war on its own citizens, Young sent the Nauvoo Legion, two thousand strong, to block the mountain passes in the Wasatch Range. He directed teams of "Mormon raiders" to destroy U.S. Army supply trains. This sabotage was the only contact between the U.S. troops and the Nauvoo Legion. While marching west with the army, Captain Jesse Gove wrote regularly to his wife and secretly served as a correspondent to the *New York Herald*. Both his private letters and his public dispatches display his frustrations about not finding any Mormons to fight. He announced regularly and hopefully in his letters that "the ball is opened" as groups of Mormon raiders burned wagons or stole cattle, but to his disgust no shooting started that fall. After struggling through snowy Utah canyons, the army retreated to Fort Bridger, which the Mormons had burned and abandoned, a hundred miles from Salt Lake City. Colonel Albert Sidney Johnson spent the miserable, cold winter preparing for a frontal assault on the Mormon capital.[19]

Brigham Young prepared as well, though he still hoped some nonmilitary solution was possible. With news of the army on the march and actually inside Utah Territory in early September, Brigham Young declared martial law to fight against the "armed, mercenary mob." He promised he would stop at nothing to keep the U.S. Army from reaching Salt Lake City. His violent and bloody rhetoric, repeated in speeches and newspaper articles, quickly spread to the national press, where his words convinced most Americans that Utah was in rebellion and led by a violent lunatic. Young planned to evacuate Salt Lake City and relocate people in "mountain fastnesses" so he prepared to burn his city to the ground.[20]

This situation furnished the stresses leading to the Mountain Meadows Massacre. As the Mormons waited for signs of the impending attack, everyone and everything seemed threatening. The Saints, tensely gathered in forts and fortified towns, had no idea who their friends or enemies might be. They had been engaged in violent wars against U.S. citizens before, but this time, in the midst of religious revival that demanded "blood atonement," the Latter-day Saints determined to stand strong. In a horrifying moment of fear, anger, and deadly intent, a detachment of the Nauvoo Legion in southern Utah attacked a wagon train and killed most of its passengers. A total of 120 men, women, and children died that September morning, and a few of the youngest children were kidnapped.[21]

This terrible event, from the perspective of Brigham Young, could not have happened at a worse moment. How could the people of the United States interpret such an attack as anything but more evidence of the heinous behavior of the Mormons? Neither side appeared to be backing down. In his December 1857 "Annual Message to Congress," President Buchanan described Brigham Young's "despotic power" and accused him of treason, emphasizing his own intent to enforce federal law.[22] Back at Camp Bridger, Jesse Gove boasted to his wife Maria that "the spring will open with a quadrille that will make the Mormons wish that they had not subscribed to the ball."[23] Behind the scenes a hint of compromise glimmered. Earlier in the fall Young had written a letter to a long-time friend of the Mormons, Thomas Kane, who had brokered the deal in 1846 with President Polk to allow the Mormons to camp in Iowa and to join Kearney's army. Young's letter combined threats of unleashing the Indians on transcontinental travelers and burning down American cities with possible olive branches of compromise. In December, Kane met with President Buchanan and Secretary of War Van Buren and offered his services as mediator. Pessimistic about Kane's chance for success, Buchanan gave him permission, but he also assigned four new regiments to Utah and planned a West Coast supporting offensive.[24]

As Thomas Kane hurried toward Utah, Colonel Johnson's army waited for spring and new troops, and the Mormons began to evacuate most of northern Utah. The great "Move South" involved packing up families, belongings, and documents and taking down and burying the most sacred parts of the Salt Lake City Temple. When Kane arrived in Salt Lake City after a grueling six-week trip through Panama, southern California, and up through southern Utah, the city was in an uproar. Kane spent weeks carrying conciliation proposals between Brigham Young's headquarters and Camp Bridger, where Governor Cumming, Buchanan's appointee, waited. Finally Kane found a wedge. Brigham Young would not back down one iota on allowing the army to be in Utah, but he would permit Cumming to come alone. Jessie Gove told Maria in a letter that he thought Cumming "has been so far fooled by this nincompoop of a Mr. Col. Kane."[25] Even though the army brass took a dim view of this approach, the new territorial governor was escorted into Salt Lake City on April 14. He immediately wrote to army officials and to the president that the Mormons had been polite and he "was universally greeted with respectful attentions."[26]

In spite of this diplomatic progress, and to avoid any appearance of capitulation, Young insisted on completing the Move South. He intended it as a signal to the new government of how much control he still had over the Mormon people. After thirty thousand people evacuated their homes in the middle of spring planting, the U.S. Army marched into Salt Lake City on June 26, 1858, almost a year after the Utah expedition began. They found it completely empty. Colonel Johnson and other military officials took this as the uplifted middle finger it was and understood immediately how little federal power still meant in Utah. Conflict between armies had been avoided, but at great cost to both sides, and no one had really settled anything about how the Latter-day Saints—or any group that challenged the assumptions of U.S. law and culture—would exist within the United States.[27]

Conquest and Chaos in California

Challenges to authority from people like Mormons and Native Americans, who were supposed to be weak and morally crippled, were frustrating and created some political and cultural backlashes. When the challenge to imposing authority came from their own fellow citizens, especially in postwar and gold rush California, imposing order became an unending nightmare to the armies of federal officials charged with the task. The variety of challenges and opportunities in the huge new state presented the United States, its government, military, and citizenry with an opportunity to practice creating order. California became proof of the need for a national project to create, integrate, and dominate the West. New structures—railroads, roads, and army posts, Indian reservations, new land policies and the bureaucracies to support them—emerged in embryonic form. Many of these efforts were clearly experiments and failed entirely. Southern California particularly, smaller in population, isolated by the mountains and deserts, distinctive in its proud Spanish and Mexican past, struggled with its new status as an American place. People living in the region, the people we have already met—like the Wilsons, Yorbas, Bannings, and Picos and their Native neighbors—responded in various ways to the disorder and the resulting onslaught of policy and cultural change they faced as "the nation" came to call.[28]

As Benjamin Davis Wilson and Margaret Hereford Wilson well knew, southern California in the early 1850s had become an especially dangerous place. Bandits had stolen their animals and frightened their children, and Margaret refused to sleep in the house just off the Los Angeles plaza. No one—Anglos, Native people, Californios, or Mexicans—could be happy with the situation. Statehood had brought only new taxes, authorities, and land laws, but none of the roads, military protection, or business development that everyone had expected. Mostly it had brought upheaval and crime in unprecedented waves. Both civil and military authorities failed utterly in the face of challenges from people who intended to break the law as well as from those claimed to uphold it. As a long-time community leader and now an American citizen, B. D. Wilson worked in the forefront of quelling the violence. He also shared many of the frustrations that caused it.

Wilson had served as one of the first Anglo-American mayors of Los Angeles. He had worked hard to negotiate compromises between older Californio leaders and the new American immigrants and military authorities. For making these efforts, B.D. had been arrested, kidnapped, and hung in effigy, but he had also become a respected leader, successful rancher, and merchant. When he and Margaret married and decided to live and raise their children in southern California, they both hoped they could build a coherent world out of the mixture of peoples that now lived in the region. Like many southern Californians, B.D. and Margaret tolerated the wild behavior of single men as they drank, gambled, attended *bailes* (dances), and shot each other in the nightly central plaza scene. But when the disorder spread beyond these boundaries and when cattle raiders, displaced Indians, and local thieves threatened the safety of his community, B.D. demanded that the government act, and he offered to help.[29]

Southern California Indians, with whom the Wilsons had traded and worked for years, simply got "caught in the maw of the gold rush," as Albert Hurtado put it.[30] Overrun by thousands of gold rushers, denied any property rights, and pushed out of their homelands, Indians sometimes responded by raiding for revenge and for sustenance. The clash between California Natives and the invading forty-niners followed a pattern similar to the clashes we have seen in the Pacific Northwest, but it was even more intense because of the numbers of people involved. Few of the Anglo-

American newcomers could imagine "Indians" as being anything but useless savages and were shocked and angry when they fought back effectively. In the southern mines especially Native people held their ground as eager forty-niners poured in from around the world. Native groups living in the foothills of the Sierra and in the great Central Valley had long experience with Europeans. From missions to ranchos to trading forts, they had quite successfully developed strategies that varied from raiding to diplomacy, which enabled them to exploit these institutions. And with much violence and loss, the Indians had outlasted them.

The situation they faced in 1849 and 1850, however, was simply different. The numbers of people pouring into the region, the gold rushers' utter contempt for Native people, and their unwillingness to share the landscape on any terms made the situation grim. Miners destroyed Native villages, burned food caches, destroyed water sources, and killed people for entertainment. In retribution Indian Californians attacked mining camps, stealing horses, supplies, and gold. As the death toll rose on both sides, miners reacted with fear and shock as the gold that was proving so hard to mine was stolen from their camps. Panic spread through the southern mines in particular, though the attacks and raids occurred everywhere. The *Stockton Times* reported that "mules, cattle and horses are nightly being stolen . . . and murders are being daily committed upon the defenceless, isolated miners." Even more terrifying, these incidents were not isolated; the editor went on to claim that "the Indians have formed an extensive combination for the purpose of carrying on an exterminating war."[31]

All over California new immigrants and older residents demanded that the state take action. "Indians" who threatened the right and ability of Euro-Americans to mine gold from the earth or to graze cattle on Native lands could not be tolerated. The "state," of course, had only just been created in 1850, and its fledging appointees struggled hard to keep order. They did take the threat from Indians seriously but had little legislation or cash to do much. Only two days after California entered statehood new Senator John C. Frémont introduced a bill to extinguish Indian claims to land in the gold country by appointing agents to make treaties with Indians and to get them to move away from the miners. At the same time, the state of California approved and expected the federal coffers to pay for local militias to take on the "marauding" Indians, and the state made it legal to kill Indians for stealing livestock. One of the commissioners, horrified by the "bloody work" of the militias, reported to the commissioner of Indian affairs in Washington, "what is to be the result of this state of things I cannot even conjecture."[32] The result was an episode like the Mariposa War in the central mountains of the Sierra near Yosemite. The drawn-out series of battles between miners and several mountain Native groups pushed many Native people out of the foothills and right into the more settled portions of the state. The forced expulsion had a direct effect on southern California, especially on the growing cattle industry that spread east and north from Los Angeles as the raids and murders metastasized out of the Gold Country and into the rest of the state.[33]

The newly appointed commissioners, anxious to avoid outright war, traveled around the state in a blitz of activity. They negotiated eighteen treaties that set aside more than seven million acres of alternative lands for indigenous Californians. The U.S. Senate, under pressure from California residents who feared these reservation lands might prove one day to be rich in gold, refused to ratify any of the treaties. The commissioners resigned in disgust and left Lt. Edward Beale, newly appointed commissioner of Indian affairs of California, in charge of a mess. In southern California, cattle- and horse-raiding bands from the San Joaquin Valley and the Mojave Desert nearly depopulated San Diego, San Bernardino, and the outlying ranchos and settlements between them. In addition to the threat of raiders, hungry and desperate Indians, displaced by war and the gold rush, appeared at ranches begging for work and food. A large contingent of Native peoples living near San Diego, desperate to protect the land and resources they had left, planned a much broader resistance. Led by a Cupeño man named Antonio Garra, they began moving around southern California and explaining that all Anglos would have to be expelled if Native people were to survive. They also began raiding local ranchos and military forts for horses and sheep, burning buildings, and taking hostages.[34]

By early 1851 San Diego was under martial law, and the panic had spread inland and north through the southern California cattle country. Local ranch owners, including B. D. Wilson, had banded together to avenge some of these raids. They had no success until a local Cahuilla leader named Juan Antonio, wearied of the constant disarray, went out and captured some of the outlaws and turned them over to local authorities. In 1852, under pressure from his fellow cattle ranchers who wanted someone familiar and competent to protect their district, B. D. Wilson took on the post of sub-agent for Indian affairs in southern California. Local papers reported that B.D.'s goal would be "permanent peace with all of those tribes that have lately become so troublesome."[35]

Edward Beale, the new superintendent, had a strongly assimilationist plan about placing the offending Native groups on "reserves" with military guards and agricultural instructors. His first experiment would be at Fort Tejon in the Tehachapi Mountains that formed the northern border of southern California. B. D. Wilson would have the task of making the reserve work and showcasing its applicability for other places. As a former fur trader, now a rancher who employed Native people and did business with them, Wilson did have some experience and empathy for southern California Indians. He also recognized how much Beale needed to learn. At their first meeting in the fall of 1852 Wilson told Beale that the trade goods he had brought at great government expense from New York were "entirely useless." As Wilson surveyed the woolen blankets, beads, and women's calicoes he concluded dourly to Beale, "I must say that my conviction is that the purchase was a bad one."[36] To educate Beale about what southern California Indians did need, Wilson, assisted by a local man of letters, Benjamin Hayes, wrote up a report assessing the condition and mood of various local Native groups and began planning a community at Fort Tejon.[37]

B.D. had both compassionate and utilitarian goals for the Tejon reserve. He wrote to Margaret that it "will be a beautiful place for the homeless Indians and will occupy them."[38] When the state passed a law in 1853 that "opened up all land where title was unverified . . . to the public domain," Wilson knew that indigenous Californians had lost any hope of retaining their lands and that reservations might be their only hope for survival. He had local support, at least as editorialized in the *Los Angeles Star,* whose editor opined, "The views of Mr. Wilson touching the management of the Indians become important at this time when the whole course of legislation seems tending towards the extermination of the Indian race."[39] More practically, he knew that its location at the hugely strategic Tejon Pass would protect entry into and out of southern California for all teamsters, sheep and cattle drives, and military expeditions. A group of Native Tejoneños who settled there, supplied by and loyal to Wilson, could serve as buffer against the powerful Paiute and Mojave raiders who lived to the east and who had stolen horses and mules from the Wilson ranches.[40]

Wilson had other motives as well. His former father-in-law, Don Bernardo Yorba, provided cattle and mules for the new settlement. Eager to build family networks with his new bride's family, he hired Margaret's younger brother Thomas to act as supplier for the new fort and subcontracted her cousin Andrew Sublette to work as a hunter. Equally interested in maintaining relationships with local Native people, he delivered a special

35. Portrait of Margaret Hereford Wilson and Little Maggie, 1856. Oil on
canvas, unknown artist. This item is reproduced by permission of *The
Huntington Library, San Marino, California*. (photCL 283 [11])

Margaret and Maggie pose together in this rather crude portrait that could
have been made either in Los Angeles or in St. Louis. But because it was
painted only a year before Maggie's death at the age of three, it
surely became a treasured object in the Wilson family.

gift of flour, hoes, harnesses, brandy, cigars, and sugar to Tejoñeno leader Vicente. The old system of using gifts to initiate relationships and trade to cement them had worked throughout B.D.'s career. However, B.D. did not know how to work within the tighter rules of the new U.S. Indian Office, and his family loyalty was read as inappropriate. After B.D. served two years as agent, building a thriving community that grew wheat and barley and giving Native people lessons in raising their own cattle, his position was abolished.[41]

Despite Wilson's investment of money, time, and his family's labor into the preserve, the whole plan of reservations that would work within the older system of southern California relationships failed. Few Anglo-Americans beyond Wilson's circle of friends and family or the slightly wider circle of Indian policymakers had any interest in funding the survival of California Indians. When Superintendent Beale spoke out against the brutal campaigns against Indian people in the mining districts and suggested that he could move Native people out of harm's way, he was promptly fired. He did manage, eventually, to settle about three hundred Indians on lands surrounding the military installation at Fort Tejon, and they co-existed peacefully for several decades. In the battle between San Joaquin Indians and the streams of miners who continued to pour into the state, however, the miners would eventually win, but not until years of violence between the two groups had eroded sympathy on all sides.[42]

For most newer residents of California, reading the lurid newspaper reports about Indian depredations, extermination seemed the only solution. Solving the Indian problem had disintegrated into private raiding by state and local militia groups, enslaving people gathered up in these raids, and evicting Native people forcibly from their settlements. In 1856, in his capacity as a senator representing southern California, B.D. wrote to General John Wool, the military commander of the entire Pacific region, asking that federal troops be sent to Fort Tejon and to Fort Yuma to stop some of the extra-legal violence. Wool wrote back sympathetically, but dismissively, explaining that he was simply overextended with other Indian wars. "At the present moment, we have the Rogue river Indians, the Walla-Wallas, the Umatillas, the Pelouses, a part of the Cayuses, the Yakamas and the Klickatats to contend with." But even worse, Wool feared, was "the barbarous conduct of some of Governor Curry's volunteers, who killed Peu-peu-mox-mox, the great chief of the Walla-Wallas, scalped him, cut off his ears and hands and sent them as trophies to their friends in Oregon." He ended his letter with some advice: "I hope your people will do all they can to keep peace with the Indians residing among them." With that, B.D. surely understood that southern California would get no help. The government, both state and federal, had failed miserably in their attempt to solve the "Indian Problem" in southern California.[43]

They failed in other realms as well. Because law enforcement could not keep up with the growth of the forty-niner communities, vigilantism and "miner's law" filled in the gaps. Race war and violence plagued southern California. According to contemporary observers, in the 1850s southern Californians "invested $6,000,000 in bowie knives and pistols, and during this period, the state reported 2400 murders, 1400 suicides and 10,000 other miserable deaths."[44] The latter referred primarily to Native people, rounded up and blamed for the mayhem, or who died malnourished and overworked on the ranchos and without the protection of the new preserves that B. D. Wilson had envisioned might provide safety for them. In 1853 California had more murders than the rest of the United States, and Los Angeles had more than the rest of California. These murders, however, had a racial cast. "Mexican" bandits and their "Indian" accomplices fill up the pages of the local papers, and their victims remain raceless, unless the editors added ethnicity to make an anecdote more salacious, as in "glittering eyed Mexicans attacking a red-faced Irish barwoman." The practice of lynching Mexicans soon became an outdoor sport in southern California. In 1857 four Mexicans (and this could mean Native Californians, Sonorans, or Chileans) were lynched in El Monte, eleven in Los Angeles.[45]

While vigilance committees hung people in Los Angeles and in northern California, a series of filibusters and extralegal invasions, much like those on the same kind of unstable border between Texas and Louisiana earlier in the century, plagued southern California and northern Mexico. The issue became a serious diplomatic and political problem as three strands of rabid and racist expansionist thinking came together. Some people expressed serious dissatisfaction with the Treaty of Guadalupe Hidalgo because it had not claimed all of Mexico, and now Mexico was moldering without American energy and influence. Others had ambitions of "freeing" Mexico and other Latin American and Caribbean nations from their stranglehold by old empires to take up their destiny as republics that would welcome American investors. Finally a number of southerners began eyeing Latin America as a potential slaveholders' retreat if the sectional issues that increasingly divided the nation came to threaten their property in human chattel. The Mexican War and the gold rush had brought too many enthusiasts of personally imagined and financed expansion to California, where they easily found converts to their causes among failed gold rushers.

The situation on the Mexican side of the border did little to dim their fervor. Facing the same kinds of disorder and danger from a war-ravaged northern countryside, the Mexican government had little real control over the region. Apaches and Yumas controlled the Baja and Sonora regions, and the Comanches the rest. Groups of Anglo and Mexican bandits roamed the border area, bringing in scalps for pay from the Mexican and Texas governments. The incessant raids and news of the gold rush had almost depopulated northern Mexico, which made Mexican politicians fear losing even more territory to the United States. The government responded with poorly funded colonization schemes intended to populate the region with hardy Mexicans who would fight the Indians and the North Americans. When these had few takers, Mexican officials came up with a set of plans that looked startlingly like those that had caused all of the trouble in Texas, to encourage wealthy Mexicans, Europeans, and a few select Anglo-Americans to pay for the right to colonize the region. The Mexican Congress understandably balked at this but had no better suggestions about how to solve the problem.[46]

Ambitious filibusters of all nationalities imagined they could do a better job. One of these was a young Tennessean named William Walker. A restless journalist yearning to be a hero in the cause of Manifest Destiny, he had bounced through several San Francisco newspapers, court cases, and duels, while spouting his theories about the inability of Mexicans to rule themselves and the need for the white races to "take" Latin America. Before Walker could come up with an actual plan, he discovered that an even more dramatic French nobleman named Gaston de Raousset-Boulbon had already started. Raousset-Boulbon, driven from the California mines by xenophobic Anglo-American miners, decided to mount an expedition into Sonora, Mexico, to set up a French mining colony there.

He gathered up several hundred similarly disenchanted followers and in 1852 negotiated with the Mexican government to allow him to settle, farm, and mine near Guaymas on the western coast of Sonora. Mexican officials agreed to the plan, but only if the would-be colonists would give up their guns and their French citizenship. Raousset-Boulbon and his followers had no intention of doing any of these things, and they refused to leave, demanding that the Mexican army kick them out forcibly. To everyone's surprise, because they were vastly outnumbered by Mexican troops, Raousset-Boulbon's small French forces took the city of Hermosillo. They were proclaiming victory when their leaders were overcome by attacks of dysentery that forced them to withdraw, allowing the Mexican Army to reclaim the city. Despite the less-than-glorious conclusion of the battle, Raousset-Boulbon became an instant hero in California. William Walker, having followed the events in Sonora with great interest, and knowing that he was destined to be a hero, took up where the French had left off.[47]

Walker believed two things that simply weren't true: first, that the people of Sonora would welcome energetic Anglo-Americans who could bring mining expertise and military protection to them and, second, that he was a gifted leader of men. That neither of his assumptions was remotely true doomed his expedition from the beginning, but he started off confidently. Both the Mexican and U.S. governments knew exactly what Walker planned and were determined to prevent another embarrassing episode, but neither nation had any control over its borders or its ports. In November of 1853 Walker and his gaggle of ex-miners, ex-soldiers, and ex-horse raiders easily avoided detection by the army and the navy, sailed into the harbor at La Paz on the Baja peninsula, and took the city. California and national newspapers covered their exploits with glee, gloating over the ease and speed with which they overwhelmed the Mexicans.[48]

Though the press described a glowing victory, Walker's ambitious plans fizzled rather quickly. Grandly, he began to administer his new country, the Republic of Lower California, appointing a cabinet and passing laws, but he had no food for his men, and the local people refused to assist in any way. Even worse, as Walker and his men announced their intentions, the ministers of Mexico and the United States were negotiating over the last bit of continental United States to be added, known later as the Gadsden Purchase. With the news of Walker's attack, the Mexican government agreed to sell the strip of land, but only if the United States would solve the problem of Walker. After most of his troops had deserted and after months of futilely trying to drum up local support, Walker marched back into southern California, expecting to be rewarded and lionized. Though he spent a brief sojourn in jail and endured a show trial that resulted in a sentence of parole and several book contracts, his punishment hardly served as a warning to other filibusters.[49]

Another filibuster undertaken in 1857, however, gave harsh warning to even the most rabid expeditioners. In January a group of a hundred men, led by "Colonel" Henry Crabb, a failed politician and would-be filibusterer, arrived in southern California to prepare for an expedition in Sonora. Like B. D. Wilson and William Walker, Henry Crabb came from Tennessee, but he had become a slavery fanatic rather than just a disaffected Whig like

Wilson. His fanaticism had cost him a political career, but now Crabb and his men intended to head to Sonora to claim land and to turn it into a slaveholders' utopia. In a comic episode that quickly turned tragic, Crabb and a hundred followers crossed the border and began shooting up towns, killing cattle and stealing flour to feed themselves, all the while boasting about their peaceful intentions. Again, newspapers followed the story avidly, with New York, New Orleans, and San Francisco papers reporting Crabb's progress by telegraph.[50]

Local Mexican officials, however, had had quite enough of these episodes. They demanded that the Mexican army deal with this menace and make a clear example of Henry Crabb. The army surrounded Crabb's forces, killing many of them in the initial skirmish. After a six-day siege the army took the rest, including Crabb, as prisoners of war. Early one April morning every remaining member of the expedition was executed. To make sure the message was clear, the Mexican army arrested several contingents of Crabb's supporters who were mobilizing on the U.S. side of the border. Most were jailed and returned, but more than a few were tortured and killed. The Mexican government acted within its legal rights because Crabb's expedition had by any definition been an illegal invasion. But this was not a proud moment for either side.[51]

The U.S. government made a weak official protest, but the general in charge of the Pacific Coast, John Wool, expressed privately that the filibusters had gotten what they deserved. The newspaper-reading public, however, especially in California, was fanned into utter fury at the idea that "refined and peaceloving Americans" could be murdered by "blood-thirsty mongrel Mexicans" who left their bodies to be eaten by hogs, as the *Alta California* claimed. In poisonous combination with a series of new bandit outbreaks and rumors that local Indians had planned a massive uprising, Crabb's execution led to a wave of anti-Mexican and anti-Indian hatred in southern California that made life even more miserable for its poorest citizens. Even wealthy Californios were no longer protected by their status or their money. Anyone who spoke Spanish or "looked Mexican" was in danger.[52]

Because neither the state nor the federal government seemed to be able to solve the problems that plagued southern California, B. D. Wilson joined many of the once influential Californio landholders in an effort to secede from the state. They didn't plan a filibuster or a revolution, but they envisioned forming a new state out of the five largest southern California counties that would be independent and that would protect their land from ruinous taxes and legal restrictions that had taken most of the land out of their hands. By the end of the 1850s, squatters, lawyers, bankers, and the Supreme Court had taken more than half of the land owned by Californians in 1848, and the pillaging had just begun. In response to the dire situation, the secessionists made several efforts, once in 1851, once in 1855, and again in 1859. Each time secession passed by popular vote in southern California, but the California legislature refused even to hear the bills.[53]

Southern Californians who owned land literally fought for their lives. Conquest proved to be very expensive and dangerous for land-wealthy, cash-poor, non-English-speaking elites who had believed their property would be secure. Squatters, land speculators, and confidence men of all kinds preyed on them as much as mining town vigilantes preyed on Native people. The Land Claims Commission operated at a glacial pace, requiring landowners to prepare documents, hire lawyers, and stay off their own lands for years at a time. B.D. raged at the legislature in 1856 on behalf of his Californio friends and neighbors. In a speech denouncing a law that would allow squatters to stay on the land while cases were being decided and requiring people who won their land cases to pay the squatters for their improvements, B.D. made his stand clear that the 1851 law stood as "one of the greatest pieces of injustice ever imposed upon a whole community, compelling every land owner to pass through the ordeal of three courts delivering up all of their papers employing lawyers at ruinous prices to defend rights guaranteed to them by treaty."[54]

Though he fought for his friends and family, B.D. found their economic woes personally frustrating as well. He got himself involved in innumerable lawsuits that came out the economic disorder created by the gold rush. In a world with no credit, cash, currency, banks or rules, B.D. had gone into business with dozens of people, loaned even more money, and advanced people merchandise; now unsnarling all of these accounts took up far too much of his time. American conquest had brought B.D. wealth and security, but it was sometimes a burden. He complained to Margaret in 1856 that he had spent the week "attending to Law Suits." He went on at some length about "the amount of ingratitude that seems to be dormant in the breast of many of our countrymen" and threatened to "call all my business together and stay at home and have no business connections with any person, neither credit nor be credited."[55] He could no more stop his business enterprises and relationships than stop breathing, but it felt good to vent to Margaret. He kept lending money to his friends and family. He continued to represent his fellow Californios in the Senate and helped them in court, but they probably resented him for doing it.

In spite of the frustrations, dangers, and disorder left in the wake of conquest, B.D. and Margaret Wilson remained dedicated southern Californians. But some moments were harder than others. The year 1857 was a very bad time. It started with an earthquake. In the early morning of January 9, 1857, the largest earthquake to be recorded in southern California history woke people from Monterey to San Diego. In comparison to the other "great" earthquakes of historic times, the 1857 Fort Tejon earthquake was probably larger than the 1906 San Francisco earthquake, measuring in the vicinity of magnitude 8.0. Californians watched fearfully as nature rearranged itself. The Kern River reversed its flow, and water ran four feet deep over its banks. Tulare Lake threw its waters upon its shores, stranding fish miles from the original lakebed. The Mokelumne and Los Angeles rivers left their banks, reportedly leaving the bed dry in places. Cracks appeared in the ground near San Bernardino and in the San Gabriel Valley. Artesian wells as far north as the Santa Clara Valley ceased to flow, and new springs bubbled out of the ground near Santa Barbara and San Fernando. The newly built foundation of the Wilsons' house crumbled into a heap, and B.D. claimed the shaking ruined the clarity of his wine that year. Despite its immense scale, only two people were reported killed by the effects of the shock—a woman at Reed's Ranch near Fort Tejon was buried under an adobe house, and an elderly man fell dead in the Los Angeles plaza.[56]

The earthquake only presaged the bad things that would befall the Wilsons that year. Sue and Eddy were sent to boarding schools in northern California, to be "finished" as young Anglo-Americans. Three-year-old Maggie would die in May. In October the family would receive the news that Margaret's sister Frances Hereford Sublette and her husband, Solomon Sublette, had both died in St. Louis that fall, leaving two very young children as orphans. Solomon's death could be seen as the ending of an age—the last of the trappers and the last of the Sublette brothers. Isaac Cooper, Margaret's brother-in-law, died as well, leaving Margaret's sister Mary a very young widow. She would move to southern California and raise her children among Margaret and B.D.'s offspring, but she expressed concern to Margaret about whether her children would be safe there.

The 1850s had been hard on the Wilsons. Even though B.D. had economic and political clout, his experiences serving the government as a state senator and an Indian agent had made him despair for the future of his fellow southern Californians. He would entertain the idea, seriously for a while, of moving to Mexico and ranching there, where he imagined the government would leave him alone. But the web of family and business held the Wilsons firmly in place, though the 1850s came close to unmooring even that powerful family.[57]

A Nation of Squatters

The western epidemic of disorder displayed different symptoms in different places. The old river towns of the Missouri Valley tolerated a lot of mayhem, but conditions in the 1850s overwhelmed even these places. At the beginning of the nineteenth century the Osages lived along the Missouri where the state capital, Jefferson City, would be built and where the Osage River veered southwest. They had other communities farther west, where the Missouri River turned north, and where Fort Osage stood for thirty years. By the 1830s most of the Osages had moved away, but many of the people who had traded with them and intermarried with them still lived in Kawsmouth, Independence, Bellevue, and St. Joseph. Small farmers moved here, people looking for a little isolation like the Mormons in the 1830s, who moved to the western border counties of Missouri, Jackson and Cass, and who shipped their crops on riverboats that landed at Chouteau's Landing or Westport. These trading posts and farming communities became "jumping off places" in the 1840s and 1850s phase of overland travel. Native people still lived here, but more cautiously on land they had been allotted by the federal government or in communities with histories that made them feel safe. The rivers and the fur trade had always gathered all kinds of people, but the local and national crisis enacted on this long-settled landscape in the 1850s would bring irrevocable change: the rhythms and patterns of the fur trade would be replaced by the demands and needs of a settler society.

We could date the end of an era to Pierre Chouteau's decision to pull his interests out of the fur trade in the mid-1850s. Or we could date it to the moment when John Brown and his family of armed abolitionists moved onto old Osage lands in 1855. The fur trade had occupied and enriched Osages, Otoes, Blackfoot, and Chouteaus for more than a hundred years, but it had become too risky even for a Chouteau to manage. The industry had been fading for a decade: changing fashion, war with Native nations, and a drastic drop in animal populations drove all but the largest companies out of business. The Chouteaus, still operating a series of forts that stretched along both the upper Missouri and the upper Mississippi, continued to profit using the old methods of trading with Native nations. Even so, Pierre Chouteau Jr., now the family patriarch, had invested in land, mining, and railroads to protect their assets. He explained to several relatives that he now only stayed in the old fur trade because of its family tradition.[58]

As Chouteau considered his financial choices, in July of 1854 a Miniconjou Sioux man killed an Anglo farmer's cow while he waited for his annuity goods to come up the North Platte River. The person who owned the cow complained to the soldiers at Fort Laramie, and an inexperienced junior officer named John L. Grattan pursued the purported cow killer and surprised a group of Sioux warriors, who killed all of the soldiers—thirty men. The next day a larger group of two hundred Sioux attacked Fort John, the Chouteau company post about five miles from Fort Laramie. No one was killed, but the company lost about $25,000 in trade goods, food, and weapons. Both the United States and the Sioux nations prepared for war. As he heard news of attacks on mail trains and other forts, the *bourgeois* at the fort, Bunyon Gratiot, warned his superiors, "I fear much for the trade."[59]

He had reason to fear. Euro-American farmers, telegraphs, and railroads all brought practices and ideologies incompatible with the fur trade. The summer before, the Chouteau company had provided transportation and guidance for several geologists and government surveys looking at railroad routes through the region. The most significant of these was headed by the Washington territorial governor, Isaac Stevens, whose imperative was to get Native nations out of the way of railroads. What really eroded the fur trade, however, were two expansions of peoples that clashed at their borders. The rapid progress of settlement by Euro-American migrants, first throughout the river valleys of the Missouri Valley and then after the Kansas-Nebraska Act out onto the Great Plains, collided with the equally successful expansion of the Sioux. This group of people, a nation of loosely connected bands, had migrated out on the plains specifically to become a buffalo-hunting people. With that choice they became caught up in the trade for buffalo robes and pushed other Plains peoples out of the vast section of the northern plains between the Platte and the Yellowstone rivers. Their population and power in the region had expanded steadily so that by 1850 they had fifteen thousand people. Their success came from warfare, alliance and absorption of other peoples, and their profitable connection to the fur trade.[60]

When the first significant numbers of hopeful Euro-American settlers began moving out from the Missouri River valley, they ran right into the confident and flourishing Sioux. This migration involved a people who had an almost messianic view of their right to occupy land. The same ideologies that sent Henry Crabb and William Walker into Mexico arrived with farmers and soldiers on the Great Plains. They believed their principles about widespread ownership of private property to be absolutely universal, which made any alternatives or challenges to this "highest use" of land unthinkable. Native people demonstrated their savage qualities by not claiming land and deserved no place on this landscape. Thus they were destined to fade away before the superior claims of land-loving Euro-Americans. When Native nations like the Sioux didn't fade away or move quietly to reservations, the only options left were military conquest or extermination, but this was no quick defeat. It would take more than twenty years, a complete reorganization of the U.S. Army, and a vast expenditure of money and life to make the Great Plains safe for the Empire of Liberty. Warfare on the Great Plains, beginning with retribution for the botched attack by Lieutenant Grattan, disrupted overland travel, prevented railroad building, and, finally, ended the fur trade.[61]

The increased military presence upset trade with Native people in a situation that was already bad. Many of the fur-bearing animals—beaver, fox, muskrat, and marten—had long since been hunted out along the upper Missouri, but by the mid-1850s hunters had to travel much further to find buffalo as well. A terrible recurrence of smallpox killed thousands of Assiniboines, Crows, Blackfoot, and Red River métis in 1856, reducing the numbers of hunters and customers at trading posts on the river. As the numbers of hides coming in dropped, Pierre Chouteau Jr. and his son Charles decided to sell under-utilized forts to the army. When the great financial crisis of 1857 hit St. Louis and the Missouri River valley, it forced the Chouteaus' American Fur Company and its remaining competitors to contract their operations considerably. Long before the last fort shut down, most of the important people had left. Leaders in the upper Missouri fur trade, such as Edwin Denig, Alexander Culbertson, and Andrew Drips, chose this moment to retire from the Chouteaus' Upper Missouri Outfit, but they made different choices about where to go. Denig went north to the Red River settlements in Canada. Culbertson purchased a farm near Peoria, Illinois, built a manor house, and, with the help of his Blackfoot wife, planned a manual labor school for Native people. Drips settled with his family at Kawsmouth. They made these family decisions carefully with the assumption that these places offered safety and maybe even prosperity.[62]

WHILE KANSAS BLED AND NATIVE PEOPLE FLED

The fur trade, built over many generations, left human traces on the landscape long after it faded in financial significance. The first families in the small settlements that speckled the lower Missouri Valley were fur-trading families of mixed race like the Drips and some of the Chouteaus, and by the 1850s several generations of them had put roots down there. They gathered in two kinds of places. In communities like Kawsmouth, old fur traders went to old trading posts first to trade, then to sell goods to overland travelers, and finally to settle. They grazed stock, raised crops, and operated little stores in towns from north of St. Louis and then along the river systems of the upper Missouri and Mississippi. Other families settled on what were known as the "Half-Breed Tracts" that the federal government set up during the removal era. Located west of Missouri River, these pieces of land accommodated a considerable number of retired fur traders, their children and wives, and various other people whose racial heritage seemed "Indian." Oklahoma, Iowa, Kansas, Nebraska, Minnesota, and Wisconsin had these tracts created between 1820 and 1850, generally adjacent to tribal reserves.[63]

Euro-American immigration affected both kinds of places as it picked up pace in the late 1840s and early 1850s. The Overland Trail and gold rush traffic overwhelmed the small river towns. Optimistic Anglo-Americans like Thomas Hereford and Solomon Sublette tried and failed at various mercantile operations. For retired fur traders and their mixed race families, the boom offered opportunities in the labor needed to get people to Santa Fe, California, or Oregon. People became mule skinners, ox handlers, cart and wagon builders and packers, guides, store owners, and clerks—no matter their expertise, or lack of it, in any of these areas. The swelling labor market had work for everyone. The ethnographer Lewis Henry Morgan reported seeing Shawnees, Wyandottes, and "half-breeds" working at the Sisyphean task of removing the huge bluffs that lined the Missouri River at Kansas City.[64]

For people living on the "Half-Breed Tracts," on Indian reserves, and simply on land they had chosen, the impact of Euro-American migration was much uglier. Indian Country became jarringly part of the United States with the Kansas-Nebraska Act of 1854, a set of policies that legitimated the practices of white squatters. Those little communities along the Missouri River, lands designated for Native people, whether removed or not, lay in the path of this legislation. Because what would become the plains states began their histories with the United States as part of the Louisiana Purchase, their official function had been as a dumping ground for Native people. The resulting encrustation of treaty agreements, land cessions, and resettlement plans thickened with each movement of people, but none of it mattered that much until the early 1850s, when a lot of Native people lived in what would become Kansas and Nebraska and a lot of Euro-Americans began to demand their land.

This was not the federal government's finest moment. Neither law nor military force made much effort either to stop Euro-American migrants from taking Native land or to prevent them from shooting each other over how to govern the illegally gotten land. Native people found themselves under the same pressures in the Pacific Northwest, California, Texas, and New Mexico, but nowhere was the forced exodus of people so publicly displayed. In plain view, under the spotlight of national attention because of the sectional controversy that land questions in the West brought with them, tens of thousands of Native people were forced from their homes. Military conquest only began the process. The Kansas-Nebraska Act opened up land for settlement when not one acre was actually available. It required misused land policies, old-fashioned graft, and a rewriting of nearly a century's worth of Indian policy to make Kansas and Nebraska into white settler states.[65]

In Kansas and Nebraska we see federal authority being undermined as "squatter sovereignty" was applied with force and success. Squatters, their illegal appropriation of Indian land, and the warfare this caused had always presented a challenge for policymakers and officials. George Washington complained about squatters on Indian land who "roam over the Country, mark out lands, Survey and even settle them," a habit that would "inevitably produce a war with the western tribes."[66] In the 1820s William Clark, outraged over the squatters who invaded Osage lands in Missouri, called them "worse than swarming hives called into inflame otherwise peaceful Indians." Both Washington and Clark would have commiserated with George Manypenny, commissioner of Indian affairs, who found himself faced with a squatter situation that was fanned into a war by politicians, land speculators, and journalists. In the same dynamic that brought large numbers of immigrants to the Mississippi Valley in the 1810s, in the late 1840s steamships and better roads encouraged significant numbers of Euro-American settlers to move into the Missouri and Platte valleys to try their luck at farming. Returning Mexican War veterans, failed gold rushers, Mormons, and overlanders who didn't quite have the cash to go overland became political tools for politicians obsessed with "opening" Kansas and Nebraska.[67]

The land rush evolved in poisonous circumstances because of the slavery issue. The actual text of the Nebraska Act—as it was always called at the time—created two new territories with familiar political arrangements about how land would be divvied up, how government would be created, and what role local and federal authorities would play in the new territory. The territorial structure had been used since 1787 but most recently in the "Organic Acts" that created Wisconsin, Utah, and New Mexico, but with less upset and fewer dire consequences for everyone involved. The difference, of course, lay in the one sentence of the act explaining that it would neither allow nor exclude slavery, but would "leave the people thereof perfectly free to form and regulate their own domestic institutions in their own way." With these words, true believers from all sides made land settlement a moral fight to the death and poured into Kansas in unprecedented numbers. By 1855 the most radical factions had polarized and settled into free-soil and proslavery camps, each dead set on preventing the other from succeeding in Kansas.[68]

This drama was enacted on Native lands. When President Franklin Pierce signed the Kansas-Nebraska Act into law in May of 1854, only about eight hundred white settlers actually lived in Kansas Territory, but newspapers, magazines, and guidebooks had created a perception of great land hunger. In the summer of 1854, hundreds of people moved into Kansas and Nebraska while thousands more made land claims.[69] These emigrants believed the Kansas-Nebraska Act gave them had an absolute right to settle anywhere they wished. Even if, according to the letter of the law, land belonged to Indians, local and national newspaper editors insisted that such laws were mere technicalities, because the government "has always sanctioned from time immemorial, squatters upon the public lands."[70] Carrying guidebooks that advised them that the moment the bill was passed "the Indians were removed to regions remote . . . and civilization took their places," the would-be squatters set off to claim land. The guidebooks further advised that new emigrants avoid places where "border ruffians" have caused trouble, but steered them toward the "heavenly sites" that will open up when "the Indian titles are entirely extinct along the Missouri River."[71]

THE PESKY DETAILS OF POPULAR SOVEREIGNTY

Newly appointed commissioner of Indian affairs George Manypenny prepared for the anticipated land rush by meeting with tribes and renegotiating treaties. His assumption—that Native people in Kansas would have to give up their "unused" treaty lands but that they could stay on allotments— turned out to be entirely too optimistic. After years spent negotiating new treaties and protecting the rights and property that Native people

held legally, Manypenny was summarily fired for his "obstruction of prog-
ress." Democratic politicians insisted that Manypenny be replaced with
someone friendlier to the "land-starved settlers," a man named James W.
Denver, who had already made large pre-emptive claims on the Nemaha
Half-Breed Tract. Calling Native people "worthless idlers and vagrants,"
Denver used Indians as rhetorical devices to serve his own political ends.
He used threats of Indian danger to manufacture a land policy that would
overwhelm Native people and enrich his cronies.[72]

The Shawnees provide a good example of the pressures Native people
faced in Kansas. We last saw the Shawnees divided and scattered after the
War of 1812 and the final loss of their Ohio homeland in the 1830s. By
the 1850s the Shawnees had two reserves in Kansas, a small tract along the
Neosho River in southeastern Kansas and a larger piece along the Kansas
River—a total of almost two million acres.[73] These much-removed people
had done fairly well by developing a trade in hides and agricultural produce. They did business primarily with the Chouteaus, who built a series
of posts on the Shawnee reserve. Cyprien and Frederick Chouteau, A.P.'s
younger cousins, had both married Shawnee women. Quaker and Methodist missionaries had arrived in the 1830s and built schools and lumber
mills. Their lands lay right along the beginning of the Overland Trail, and
many Shawnees supplemented their incomes by working as cattle and
oxen tenders. They also did a brisk lumber business, selling timber to the
cart, wagon, and wheel builders in nearby Westport. Their large reserve
and its convenient location also put them in the direct line of emigrants
and speculators of varying political persuasions. Whether they came from
antislavery outfits like the New England Emigrant Aid Society or were slave-
sympathizing border ruffians, they all wanted Shawnee land. As emigrants
poured onto the Shawnee reserve in 1855 the agent, William Gay, asked for
protection from nearby Fort Leavenworth. Unfortunately the governor of
Kansas and numerous army officers had made claims on Shawnee lands,
making soldiers reluctant to enforce the law when the intruders turned
out to be their own superiors. The soldiers stood by when squatters moved
onto Shawnee lumber stands. The violence escalated, and white squatters
killed agent Gay in front of the agency. Since neither state officials nor the
military would act, the Shawnees took matters into their own hands and
burned out a few of the squatters.[74]

Such direct action kept a few people from felling the Shawnees' trees,
but not much could blunt sectional controversy. In the summer and fall of
1856 all three Kansas state capitals were on Shawnee land. As occasional

conflict escalated into uncontrolled guerilla violence, it ruined the progress the Shawnees had made. A March 1855 election to create a Kansas legislature brought thousands of Missourians to Kansas polls, and death threats to anyone who voted for Free-Soil candidates. These tactics resulted in a landslide for the proslavery Democratic Party. Somehow 5,427 Democrats voted in a territory with a population of about 2,000, indicating corruption of epic proportions, even for that time and place. Furious that the Kansas legislature had been stolen, Free-Soil Kansans created their own government in Lawrence, Kansas, to compete with the one initially set up in the old Shawnee Mission, which was the largest building in eastern Kansas. In 1856 this capital and the territorial governor moved to Lecompton. Even with all these capitals, Native and immigrant Kansans had virtually no law and certainly no order. The factions created private militias to protect their interests, mostly land claims and fictitious town sites on Shawnee land. Protecting land devolved into punitive raiding and killing. Federal authority consisted of President Pierce implacably refusing to recognize any problem in Kansas, and troops at Fort Leavenworth hoping they wouldn't have to get involved.[75]

The most notable battles of this guerilla warfare, known as the sack of Lawrence and the Pottawatomie Massacre, came in May of 1856. At least a thousand proslavery forces marched into Lawrence, the center of the Free-Soil movement, destroyed the printing presses, burned down a hotel, looted houses, and burned one home. In retribution a Free-Soil radical named John Brown led a group to attack a proslavery settlement at Pottawatomie Creek. The group, which included four of Brown's sons, took seven proslavery men from their homes and killed five of them with swords. After these destructive and bloody affairs, an equally damaging propaganda war flooded the national press, making Kansas the center of national attention. Proslavery groups drafted a slave-state constitution that Free-Soil Kansas refused to acknowledge. The dueling governments put newly elected president James Buchanan in a difficult situation. He had promised to follow the will of the people, but in Kansas this will was entirely divided. Finally Buchanan accepted the proslavery constitution, but Congress refused to ratify it. The fight went on for another four years until 1861, when Kansas, with little fanfare, came into the Union as a free state.[76]

Once the border ruffians and abolitionists left, Native Kansans like the Shawnees were left to clean up the mess. George Manypenny, the commissioner of Indian affairs, surveyed the situation bleakly: "In the din and strife between the anti-slavery and proslavery parties . . . the Indians have been personally maltreated, their property stolen, their timber destroyed," and the federal government had completely ignored its duty to protect "the rights and interests of the red man."[77] The Shawnees made a claim to the government for their dead hogs, stolen property, and ruined crops. In 1857 Shawnee lands were thrown open for purchase, with the exception of allotments given to each head of household and a large communal piece around the old Shawnee Mission. Though their population dropped steadily as their land base eroded, the Shawnees continued to make a living farming, doing day labor and selling baskets and other items they made. A few families had some temporary wealth as they sold land to white speculators. Frederick Chouteau, seeing that he could no longer make a living trading with Native people, took his Shawnee wives and went to live in Westport near his brother Cyprien, where they ran a large store.[78]

Not all the Indians in Kansas went to Indian Territory. Even though they watched trainloads of Modoc, Cheyenne, Iowa, and Wichita people rumble through Kansas on their way to Indian Territory, with many of their passengers painted black in mourning, many Kansas Indians refused to accept this last removal. People who had family connections to the old fur trade world could call on their relatives for help. When Lewis Henry Morgan toured the region doing fieldwork for his studies of Indian languages in 1859, he visited the households of people like Baptiste Peoria, John Ottawa Jones, and Joseph James, all men of mixed race who had opened trading posts and worked as interpreters. Because of the thriving conditions of these families, Morgan left Kansas feeling optimistic. He hoped that "an amalgamation with the Indians by the white race" was at hand and that "Kansas will be the theater of the first honest and regular experiment." He imagined that in Kansas "we are to see respectable white people marry the daughters of wealthy and respectable Indians."[79]

How wrong he was. Many Native people moved away from the reserves and lived on the fringes of Missouri River towns from Missouri to the Dakotas, as they always had, scratching out a living as hired labor and hunters and farming little plots of land they claimed illegally. Their only strategy was to become invisible to the culture that grew up around them. Something basic had shifted. Though this view was challenged in the 1850s on the Pacific Coast, in Texas, and on the northern plains, no one in power seemed capable of imagining a shared landscape with Native people. Land and property could only be the domain of Euro-Americans, an attitude that most settlers and speculators shared. The Indians that Morgan admired for wearing ties and running stores had only made themselves targets by succeeding—an old story in American settlement. Native Americans were, as Stephen Douglas had articulated clearly in 1853, a "barrier" of "hostile savages" who prevented the "tide of emigration and civilization" from running its natural course.[80]

It would take another few decades before the United States and its culture, legal proceedings, and military could impose this monocultural vision, and even then it was never complete partly because a few U.S. citizens found the efforts morally questionable, but more because Native people resisted continuously. The position and the ideology that entitled the removal of Indian people differed fundamentally with the views held by generations of westerners, Native and emigrant, who had lived there before. Until the 1850s, co-existence was the assumed goal even if it developed uneasily and unequally. Trade and diplomacy required the participation—and sometimes violent confrontation—of all parties. Californians, resident and emigrating Native people, Mexicans, French Creoles, Canadians, and Euro-Americans developed and competed for trade relationships and personal connections with each other. The proof of that political economy and ideology lay in the families people created and the children they left behind.

A National Horror Show

In our imagination and national mythology, the state brings order and peace. But in these years in this place it brought mayhem and massacre. Between 1857 and 1864 waves of violence spread over the West, and as time passed, this violence moved from being extra-legal to being condoned and organized by the state. Larry McMurtry surveyed some of these massacres in a little text oddly titled *Oh What a Slaughter* and concluded that these gruesome episodes carried a "moral taint." McMurtry, however, asks us to use empathy to temper our moral judgment because of the extreme apprehension and vulnerability shared by Anglo settlers and soldiers.[81] A recent book, written by Church of Latter-day Saints historians, makes a similar plea for us to believe that "except for a single nightmarish week in September 1857" the Mountain Meadows killers were "ordinary nineteenth-century frontiersmen" and "pillars in any community."[82] That "except" is too big. A nation of squatters who used violence to establish rights and to dispossess other people needs to recognize itself in these actions. Anglo-American settlers, however laudable their individual intentions, chose to settle on land owned by others and demanded that the U.S. government use all of its power to remove them, making these "ordinary nineteenth-century frontiersmen" into killers. This process engendered much violence that we prefer to read as acts committed by groups of lunatics or lone shooters. Patterns in episodes like the Mountain Meadows Massacre, the slaughter of citizen-soldiers on the Mexican border, the bloody affair of a Sioux uprising in Minnesota, and finally the now infamous Sand Creek Massacre compel us to consider them as logical productions of the culture that housed them: the world Euro-Americans worked so very hard to situate in the North American West.

We can begin with the Mountain Meadows Massacre, an episode that could be described as collateral damage when the federal government tried to impose its will on the wayward Mormons. This killing spree in which 121 people died took place on September 11, 1857, a date that might not be propitious. Such terrible events are made possible when people feel as besieged as the Mormons and Utah Native people did in that summer of 1857, but part of the blame surely fell on the utter failure of federal power in Utah. The Mormons had driven out all of the federal officials appointed to the territory. The thin veneer of the U.S. Army could not hope to impose order on citizens who refused to be ruled. The weakness of federal response gave Mormon leaders confidence to lead their people into war. For the Mormons, that summer seemed filled with harbingers of a violent millennium. In the midst of a powerful religious revival orchestrated by Brigham Young and his Council of Elders, Mormons all over Utah searched their souls for evidence of religious backsliding. Demonstrating the absolute obedience to church authorities, they promised to protect and purify their church with blood atonements, sacrifices of their own blood and the blood of non-Mormon sinners. In the midst of a giant camp meeting in July of 1857, the Mormon faithful received the news that the U.S. Army marched toward Utah.[83]

As the Mormons prepared for war and watched for signs of the end of times, other Americans streamed across Utah headed for the promised lands of California and Oregon. One particular group, the Fancher Party made up of families from Arkansas, came from nearly the same place in Arkansas where a jealous husband had killed the Mormon apostle Parley Pratt. The Arkansas party left several weeks before Pratt's murder, but that didn't erase the taint that all travelers from Arkansas carried that summer. When they stopped in early September to feed their animals in high desert meadows on the western edge of Utah, they had no idea of the trouble that was coming. The Mormons they had met in Salt Lake City had been rude but had sold them supplies for their trip south. The Fanchers and the other Arkansas travelers had heard the same stories about federal troops marching toward Utah but decided to continue on anyway.[84]

As the families began to set up camp for a few days of rest before they tackled the desert parts of the journey, they had little notion that the newly activated Nauvoo Legion had watched their every movement across Utah. Church and military officials in southern Utah had reported the Fancher Party's presence and activities to the Mormon elders in Salt Lake City. Fearing that the group could be a reconnaissance mission for the U.S. Army that now marched on Utah and believing that that God had delivered these nonbelievers, gentiles who could have killed their own Parley Pratt, right into their hands, militia leaders in southern Utah hatched a plan. Led by southern Utah bishop John D. Lee, Nauvoo Legion colonel William Dame, and Elder George Smith, they recruited a group of Paiutes, and Mormon volunteers who dressed up like Paiutes, and ordered them to "dispatch the emigrants." Meanwhile local elders preached to their people to remember the bloody past when other American citizens had murdered Mormon women and children with no mercy. Now, preached Mormon leader Isaac Haight, it was time to "feed the Gentiles the same bread they fed to us."[85]

On September 7 the Fancher Party, camped at Mountain Meadows, awoke to an attack by people they supposed to be Indians. Entirely surprised by the sudden violence of the early morning raid, the emigrants regrouped quickly and fought off the several hundred attackers. The Paiutes and Mormons retreated and considered their next steps. Bishop John Lee decided that he would have to kill everyone in the Fancher Party because the Indians had not completed the task and because the travelers surely knew whites had been involved as well, but he waited to get confirmation of his plan and more recruits. Groups of snipers kept the immigrants pinned behind their wagons without water for three long days. On September 11 a rejuvenated force of fifty-four Mormons and more than three hundred Paiutes initiated another attack. This time they allowed the women, children, and injured men of the Fancher Party to be driven away in a gesture of magnanimity. In a gesture of brutality John Lee and two other men drove them over a hill and then killed everyone over the age of six, assuring themselves that thus no "innocent blood" had been shed.[86]

Of course, much innocent blood had been shed, and the seventeen children younger than six who survived the massacre carried the memories of this slaughter to their graves. Some of the Mormon and Paiute men, shocked by the brutality of the moment, refused to participate, but most agreed to finish the job, and years later forensic evidence agreed with Nephi Johnson, who admitted that "white men did most of the killing."[87] The official story quickly placed the entire blame on local Indians. Brigham Young wrote in his diary six days after the massacre that "a spirit seems to be taking possession of the Indians to assist Israel." He concluded with satisfaction "I can hardly restrain them from exterminating the Americans."[88] Young used the first reports of the massacre to his own political advantage, sending a threat to the approaching army and to President Buchanan that unless the troops turned around and allowed the Mormons to build their own state, more of these "Indian attacks" would befall immigrants. He warned, "it is peace and Mormon's rights—or the knife and the tomahawk—let Uncle Sam choose."[89]

In an attempt to cover up the details of the bloody deed, the perpetrators and Mormon officials began to weave stories of belligerent emigrants who poisoned Indian wells and "saucy" and "starving Indians" who attacked the emigrants for their cattle. Brigham Young knew exactly what had happened and who had done it. He used all of his authority and influence to prevent federal officials from investigating. Even early on, however, news of the slaughter of an entire immigrant train at the hands of Indians in southern Utah led people many people to suspect that the Mormons had somehow been involved. The San Francisco newspapers reported that at "large public meetings" angry citizens demanded that the government investigate and punish the "armed Mormon traitors in our midst."[90] Indian agent Garland Hurt, the last non-Mormon official in Utah Territory in 1857, heard the grisly details almost immediately from his Ute and Paiute informants and fled to Camp Scott in November, where the invading federal army had stopped for the winter. He reported what he knew to several *New York Times* reporters encamped with the troops.[91] Despite such reports and demands by various western congressmen for action, neither the army nor the president wanted to take on the Mormons, with whom they had negotiated a very tense peace. Buchanan's appointee, Governor Cumming, had allowed Brigham Young to "investigate," and he found only a tragic Indian massacre.

Nearly two years after the slaughter, Major James Henry Carleton arrived at the site for the first of many official investigations. He reported the grisly details that "women's hair in detached locks . . . hung to the sage bushes," and "parts of little children's dresses . . . dangled from the shrubbery." Carleton reported it as a "fearful crime" perpetrated by "Mormons all painted and disguised by Indians." He buried the "disjointed bones of

34 persons" in a mass grave that he marked with a "rude monument of loose granite stones."[92] This marker represented the only action taken by the U.S. government for another twenty years. The sham trial of John D. Lee in 1876 and his execution did not satisfy many people outside of Utah. Only after Brigham Young's death, after federal authority had more sway in Utah, and after forensic anthropologists could demonstrate the falsity of the long-held Mormon story would the full story of official complicity by Mormons and by U.S. federal officials come out. Even now, acknowledgment and apology still come hard.

THE MINNESOTA UPRISING OF 1862

Less than five years after the events at Mountain Meadows, news of a much more real Indian uprising terrified the residents of the upper Midwest and fascinated the newspaper-reading public. In another example of the cost of poor federal policy, weakly enforced, the Sioux (Dakota) Uprising of 1862 took the lives of hundreds of Minnesotans. In a wave of violence that covered most of Minnesota that summer, Santee Sioux from four Dakota bands expressed their bitterness about the terrible lives they led on reservations by organizing a widespread uprising. The precipitating incident involved the refusal of an Indian agent to distribute supplies to Sioux people who were hungry after a hot, dry summer on the new reservation, but the explanatory context was larger and, by now, familiar.

For nearly fifty years, as the fur trade dwindled, white settlers had invaded Dakota lands in southern Minnesota, and government agents and troops had been unable and unwilling to stop it. These lands, considered by several generations of politicians and Indian advocates as ideal for various kinds of Indian states in the 1820s and 1830s, had been overwhelmed by settlers and land developers in the 1840s and 1850s. Native nations had been forced to cede much of their land and in the late 1850s found themselves limited to small reserves on the Minnesota River. The fact that many of the early settlers, politicians, agents, and businessmen in the region had arrived there as fur traders and intermarried with local Native people complicated the situation.[93]

Traders and their families had created a mixed race world that had prospered for several generations. These families made a living working for large fur-trading outfits and also held many of the posts in the Indian service as they made the transition to different lives in Anglo Minnesota. Native Minnesotans, Dakotas in the south and Ojibwes in the north, came to see traders as kinspeople and as crucial mediators with the federal government. Henry Hastings Sibley, old fur trader and first governor of Minnesota Territory, provides an important example. Born in Detroit to a family long involved in the fur trade, he became a partner for the American Fur Company in its Upper Mississippi Division in 1835. Sibley spent six years running the business among the Dakotas near Fort Snelling. Though he modernized the business, he did it by building bonds with Native people and serving as their spokesperson.[94]

These relationships certainly enriched Sibley and gave him great power. He got more than twenty powers of attorney for children of mixed blood in the treaties of 1837 with Dakotas, Ojibwes, and Winnebagos. He went to Washington to make sure American Fur Company debts were paid first by the government, but also to make sure that the "half-breed" shares in the treaty were upheld. As so many fur traders did, Sibley shared his life and business with a Dakota woman, Red Blanket Woman, and they had a child together in 1841. Many years later, while attempting to write in his autobiography about this marriage, Sibley came to a complete stop with this relationship. Maybe, as his biographer suggests, he couldn't explain these interracial mixings now that he was writing in the 1870s as a famous "pioneer." When Red Blanket Woman died in 1843, Sibley placed their child, baptized Helene, with a mixed race family of a fur-trade associate. This man, Joseph R. Brown, was known to be a corrupt businessman and, according to a British observer, a "gay deceiver amongst the Indian fair" who had married and abandoned a number of very young Native girls.[95]

In 1849 Minnesota became a territory; in 1853 the Santee Sioux were given a reserve, and men like Sibley and Brown turned their backs on their fur trade lives. Instead they began the lucrative business of managing Indian annuities, large payments made yearly by the federal government to Indian people in return for ceded land. By 1858 Henry Sibley had moved up the political ladder and became the first governor of the new state of Minnesota and had entirely refashioned his life to include a white wife and children, though he made his fortune on the backs of people he had once considered relatives. Joseph Brown, appointed the agent to the Santee Sioux in 1853, brought personal graft to an art form. He accepted all the help he could get in the task of "civilizing" the people in his care, but mostly that meant taking donations from missionary groups, getting vast supplies of farming equipment, seed, and food from the federal government, making the Sioux people buy these items on credit, and then repaying himself with annuity money for the credit he had extended.[96]

Never fools, but initially hopeful that kin like Joseph Brown or Henry Sibley would look out for their interests, the Santee Sioux at first were happy for the annuity payments that kept them fed as they attempted, unsuccessfully, to shift from buffalo hunting and seasonal farming and gathering to single-family subsistence farming. As they failed at farming, some of the Sioux demanded more and raided the agency warehouses in 1855 and 1856 dressed as warriors, while others advised a more measured approach. Hunger and anger at their betrayal by white and Native kinsmen alike led some groups of the Sioux to raid new white settlements for food and captives that they sometimes killed but often used as bargaining chips for food and supplies. By 1858 the situation on the Minnesota frontier was dire. The solution, people in state and federal government believed, was to take even more Dakota lands and concentrate Native people on smaller reserves where they could be more closely supervised. A new treaty, devised by land-hungry Minnesota politicians, divided the Minnesota Sioux into bitter factions and set the stage for the events of 1862.[97]

This completely failed federal policy left the Minnesota Sioux starving and resentful in that summer of 1862. Dakota "traditionalists" warned Dakota "farmers" that they would lose their traditional ways as Sioux people, and agent Joseph Brown proved this by paying the farmers far more than the traditionalists. They had sold their land, dividing families and clans in bitter debates over this policy, and still the agents would not give them any food. Four hundred Dakota warriors solved their immediate problem by breaking down the doors of the warehouse at the Yellow Medicine agency and taking sacks of flour. Soldiers stationed there pulled out small cannons and threatened to kill them all instantly. The local agent, Andrew Myrick, supposedly told a more polite group of leaders who requested supplies that "if they are hungry, let them eat grass." Such incidents convinced even the Dakota leaders who had tried to keep the peace to plan a more generalized uprising that began officially on August 17, 1862.[98]

The Dakota Sioux, after much debate, planned simultaneous attacks on white settler communities, army forts, and agencies, the varied sites of their varied troubles. By 1862 the end of any hope of accommodation, trade, and reciprocity for Native people in Minnesota became all too evident. Several hundred warriors made the first attack at the agency, where they killed agent Myrick and stuffed his mouth with grass. Next they moved on to Fort Ridgely, to white settlements like New Ulm, and to several missions up the river. Too stunned to respond effectively, military and civilian authorities could only describe the killings, captivities, and burnings that

36. "Execution of Thirty-Eight Indian Murderers at Mankato, Minnesota,"
Harper's Weekly, Jan. 17, 1863, p. 37.

This horrifying moment, still the largest officially sanctioned mass killing in
the United States, is captured with a celebratory tone in this *Harper's* print.
Anglo men wave hats and clap each other on the back as the Dakota
bodies twist on the scaffold.

swept southern Minnesota. More than five hundred people were killed
and nearly three hundred taken captive as white Minnesotans fled for their
lives. After more than a week of a successful Dakota offensive, former fur
trader and governor Alexander Ramsey began evacuating whole counties,
some of which would remain empty of white settlers for years.[99]

Ramsey also mounted a military defense and appointed former governor
and former fur trader Henry Sibley to lead an expedition of volunteer Minnesota troops against the Sioux. Though finally successful, it took Sibley
months and much loss of life to end the war. The Dakota warriors, badly
outnumbered, starving, and politically divided, had little hope of achieving
any permanent military victory. Sibley's long connection with Dakota people
allowed him to see and use tribal divisions, and he sent messages through
mixed-blood interpreters making it clear he would protect the factions who
had spoken against war. In the end Sibley betrayed his kin again by holding
military tribunals that condemned more than 300 Dakota men to death.

In November 1862 he marched nearly 2,000 Dakota people, warriors and their families, to a special enclosure near St. Paul. Sibley intended to hold a mass execution after the military trials, but President Lincoln stepped in because of the haste of the trials and the paucity of evidence of atrocities. Thirty-eight Dakota men were hung in public in Mankato, Minnesota, the largest mass execution in U.S. history. Another 250 were marched to a prison in Iowa, where more than 100 Santee Sioux died in the first year. The retribution went further as the Minnesota newspapers demanded the expulsion of every Native person in the state. As a compromise nearly all of the Santees, whether labeled as hostile or not, were removed to a small reservation in Nebraska, where their descendants still live today.[100]

The uprising and its course reflected the long and intimate histories Minnesotans had with each other. While Indian agent Joseph R. Brown served with Henry Sibley in the volunteer army, his Dakota wife and their eleven children were taken captive by the rampaging warriors as they fled from their home. They would have been killed except that Mrs. Brown, a Sisseton woman, began shouting in Dakota, reminding her captors of her important Native family connections. The Brown family and the twelve white people with them were taken to the main Dakota camp, where they remained safe until Colonel Henry Sibley's 1,400 troops freed them in September.[101] Henry Sibley went on to make a fortune selling Indian land, founded the University of Minnesota, and served as the first president of the Minnesota Historical Society, whose early publications certainly never mentioned his fur trade wife and their children.[102]

SAND CREEK AND THE BENT FAMILY NIGHTMARE

This episode heralded an open season of violence against Native people and their mixed-blood and Anglo kin. Only two years after thirty-eight Dakota men swung from the gallows in Minnesota, a volunteer militia unit gunned down a Cheyenne village as it awaited escort to a reservation. Cheyenne and Arapaho families died together on November 29, 1864. William Bent had been right to fear the change that the Colorado gold rush would bring. In 1858 and 1859 more than a hundred thousand Euro-American people rushed across the central plains, now home to the Cheyennes, Arapahos, Kiowas, and Wichitas, to the foothills of the Colorado Rockies in the hopeful search for gold. Most hailed from the Mississippi and Ohio river valleys, where as the *New York Tribune* declared "the extensive failure of crops" and the "universal pressure of debt" had caused "an immense migration."[103]

37. William Soule, "Portrait of Arapaho Man" 1867. National Anthropological Archives, Smithsonian Institution (NAA INV 9149300).

From left to right, the Arapaho leader Little Raven, with a great-grandchild on his lap, William Bent, and Little Raven's son and grandson pose in this photograph. Bent, working as the negotiator for the tribe, was making his last effort to get land, cash, and supplies for the people he had come to accept as his family.

Few of these migrants had much personal knowledge of Native people, and none of them understood that they had poured into an ecological and cultural system already stressed beyond its limits. As the Comanches had found their lives changed by drought and depletion of the bison, so did residents of the central plains. The Bent family and the Cheyennes knew this better than anyone. The Indian agents for the region, experienced men like William Bent and Broken Hand Fitzpatrick, warned federal and local Colorado officials that Plains Natives needed supplies and safe refuge or they would attack travelers. They did. Seeing caravans laden with food, tools, and stock animals bound for Colorado as an obvious replacement for buffalo hunting, groups of warriors pillaged and robbed with frightening regularity. Boosters had promised gold seekers pleasant travel, good weather, and easy pickings; instead they found themselves cold and hungry, begging for food and shelter in raw towns like Denver and Colorado City. When disappointment was joined by the martial politics of a Civil War that brought tension even to Denver and by episodes of violence by Native residents of the region, things got ugly.[104]

By 1864 two systems of living and making a living came into violent conflict. Hunters versus settlers, trade and negotiation versus cash on the barrelhead, shared space versus exclusive rights, racial mixing and family formation versus white supremacy. Probably unaware of the stakes involved, two groups of angry young men found themselves at war on the plains. Native warriors and Anglo militia volunteers looking to prove themselves in their own cultural settings turned stubborn. The youngest Bent, Charles, became the family's angry young man. Though his father begged him to stay on the family ranch south of Arkansas and his mother begged him to join her people, who were seeking a safe refuge on a reservation, Charles refused. He worked hard to become a famous Cheyenne dog soldier, raiding settlements and military installations. Other young men in Colorado eagerly joined volunteer militia units intending to protect their communities against people like Charles Bent by raiding Native camps and hunting areas.[105]

That context sounds very similar to those facing Oregonians, Texans, and Californians in the 1850s, but the response of the state had changed by the end of the decade. When Utah Mormons or Native Minnesotans or Colorado Cheyennes challenged the United States, the nation and its very human bureaucracies now had clear beliefs and instructions to guide them. Certainty about the absolute good of Anglo-American political institutions and white settlement as shared goals of government encouraged citizens to demand the use of great force to impose these values. Such beliefs also enabled Colorado citizens to imagine they were taking up arms justly when they marched to Black Kettle's camp in November of 1864. The Cheyennes and Arapahos there, whether peaceful or not, represented a dangerous barrier to the fulfillment of the ambitions of white settlers, and for this they should be killed.

What happened that cold morning is pretty clear, but like the terrible story at Mountain Meadows, why (and even where) it happened and how to remember it remain bitterly contested.[106] The year 1864 had been very hard for everyone in Colorado. As the white population grew along the Front Range, miners became farmers on the streams that Native communities used as winter homes. When the government tried to create reserves for displaced Native people without enough supplies to feed them or enough land to sustain them, conflict increased dramatically. As in so many other places in the west, even these pitiful reserves were invaded by white squatters, which led militant factions among Colorado's Indians to conclude that hunting, raiding, and war were the only ways to survive. Because the Civil War had taken most of the professional military men east, the volunteer militia responded unevenly to these attacks that became a violent guerilla war in the summer of 1864. Governor John Evans panicked and issued two proclamations in August to end the bloodshed. He demanded that all Colorado Indians turn themselves in "to places of safety" where he guaranteed their protection. These safe places were undersupplied forts where Indians had starved and been imprisoned. At the same time, he ordered all white citizens to shoot and kill any hostiles who did not turn themselves in.[107]

With these stunning proclamations Evans had declared open season on Native Coloradans, but an uneasy peace settled over eastern Colorado as other groups tried to negotiate something more permanent at a conference at Camp Weld. A few "peace leaders" of the Cheyennes attended and agreed to turn themselves in at Fort Lyon as winter approached. By early November, Left Hand and Little Raven had brought 113 lodges of Arapahos, and Black Kettle's Cheyennes were reported to be on the way. They would all camp at Sand Creek, the northern edge of the reserve that William Bent had created for them in the treaty of 1861, until Fort Lyon was ready for them. The U.S. Army major in charge of Fort Lyon, Scott J. Anthony, wrote to his superior that he had promised the Indians that "no war would be waged against them," and he also admitted that his troops were "not strong enough to chase them and fight them on their own ground."[108]

This process seemed far too slow and too dangerous to Governor Evans and to the man who now led the Denver militia, "Colonel" John Chivington. The day after Major Anthony promised no war, Chivington issued marching orders to the militiamen that Denverites derisively called the "Bloodless Third Regiment" because of their poor performance in various skirmishes. He hired Robert Bent, William Bent's third son, who had served in the Union Army early in the war, to serve as a scout. When Chivington's troops reached Fort Lyon, Major Anthony agreed to use them for a campaign against the Cheyennes, now that he had enough troops to fight effectively. Led by Chivington, seven hundred cavalry marched toward Sand Creek on the evening of November 28, planning a dawn attack on the sleeping villages. Several of Chivington's officers tried to dissuade him, but as he told his volunteers, he longed to "wade in gore."[109]

We have to wonder what Robert Bent thought as the column approached the villages in the gray dawn of November. His two brothers, George and

Charles, slept at Black Kettle's camp, along with his mother, aunts, cousins, and friends. George Bent remembered utter chaos as people came streaming out of their tents, but that "Black Kettle had a large American flag tied to the end of long lodge pole and was standing in front of his lodge . . . calling to the people not to be afraid."[110] Black Kettle's assurance meant nothing—he was mowed down by the troops. The numbers killed in the massacre are equally meaningless,[111] but the details of inhumanity and pure evil are not. Babies gored, dead men cut open and their testicles and fingers sliced off, women violated with rifles and sabers and then stabbed dozens of times, children hiding in sand pits burned. The descriptions of brutal carnage in the pages of the congressional hearings held on the matter reflect depravity by any definition. Some people did escape, all of the Bent brothers among them, but many died in the "lovely slaughter."[112]

We tell ourselves that conquest of one people by another always involves human suffering, but it doesn't always demand extermination and erasure. Sand Creek indicates how far the culture crafted by nineteenth-century Anglo-Americans would go to impose its vision of conquest. That culture couldn't tolerate bison robe lodges on the Great Plains, or bodies left in trees, or visions of various spirits who guided life. That culture couldn't see or even record the Bent family, with its children of mixed race, its kinship across national and racial borders, and its Native names. This cultural vision demanded empty landscapes, without people or history, where entirely new histories could be enacted without the inconvenience of the past.

But the western slate was never wiped clean of that past. People remembered. Stolen children were returned to their families. They had children and named them after lost and massacred relatives. Families and nations went on.

Epilogue

How It All Turned Out

The year 1860 is an arbitrary moment to stop. It is a moment of breathing space between the terrible disorder of the 1850s and the coming Civil War to reassess what changed and what did not as the nineteenth century marched on in the West that we have examined. The scaffolding of American conquest—railroads, armies, surveyors, reservations, censuses, and law—emerged in these years. Ideas about race and how it described people and circumscribed behavior remained very shifty but soon had the power of the state to give them shape. The great effort to sequester Native nations onto reservations had just begun in 1860 so that indigenous Americans still had some options about where and how to live.

Many of our families were battered by new rules about ownership, citizenship and ideology, but others seem just fine, partly because the American state had just begun to use its muscle. Looking closely, we might see some patterns about who blended into the new cultures and economies that developed in the second half of the nineteenth century and who didn't. We can watch racial definition and how and when it affected lived experience in very direct ways. Does it mean anything to be labeled a "half-breed" or a Mexican when you used to be a Bent or a Californio? Can you talk or buy your way out of racial labeling?[1]

SONOMA

In 1860 Doña Francesca Benicia Carrillo y Vallejo, now Mrs. Mariano Vallejo, was forty-five years old. A native Californio, she had lived in three nations, a conquered military zone, a territory, and state. Far less optimistic about Americans in California than her husband from the beginning, she had become outrightly cynical about what it had meant for Californios. She had borne sixteen children, and ten were living. The eldest was now twenty-four,

38. Four generations of Vallejo women, ca. 1875. Unknown photographer.
Courtesy of the Bancroft Library, University of California, Berkeley. (POR 8)

In this wonderful intergenerational image an older Francesca Vallejo (right)
poses with her daughter Fanita Frisbie (left), her granddaughter (top),
and her great-granddaughter (bottom).

and the youngest was three. Now a citizen of the United States and the wife
of the mayor of Sonoma, she spoke a little English but did not write it at
all. Doña Francesca had gotten stout over the years of childbearing and
housekeeping, but she enjoyed walking children to school in the growing
community of Sonoma and playing with the youngest in the beautiful
vineyards that surrounded her house and the old mission. That year her
older sons traveled east, Platon to attend medical school at Columbia University and Uladislao to begin at St. John's College (now Fordham). The
Vallejos had built wine cellars in the old Sonoma barracks and in 1860 had
produced eight thousand gallons of wine. The year before, the Vallejos
had staged a grand fiesta to celebrate the recovery of their youngest son,
Napoleon, from a terrible accident. Because his closest playmates were
Suisune boys and because so many Native people still worked on Vallejo
lands, the two-week fiesta included Native people from four counties who

39. Napoleon Vallejo, 1863. Unknown photographer. Courtesy of the Bancroft
Library, University of California, Berkeley. (1978.195:08—PIC)

The last Vallejo son, born nearly twenty years after his eldest brother, poses
here as a thirteen-year-old in a military or school uniform. He would carry
the Vallejo name well into the twentieth century and would become
an artist with some local success.

camped on the grounds. Napoleon remembered his father slaughtering five bulls each day, along with hogs, sheep, and chickens, to feed everyone, and that they all ate beans, chilies, tortillas, and pinole.[2] From this vantage point, the Vallejos' lives looked peaceful and prosperous—as if the American nation had metabolized them well.

Beneath the bucolic facade, however, a more complicated story played out that reflected the layered past that made Californios who they were. The Vallejos made great sacrifices to protect the family and to ensure their children could succeed in the new United States, but their efforts didn't always work. The oldest son, Andronico, received one of California's first appointments to West Point in 1851, but the family decided that because he did not yet speak English and because he had never been away from home, this felt too risky. They sent Andronico and Platon, his younger brother, to a private Catholic college in Maryland in 1852. Andronico came home after completing his studies but hated working for his father. He ran away several times, ran up debts, and finally became a music teacher in Oakland. Uladislao began school in New York but dropped out after only a few months and went to Mexico, as his father put it, "with his reckless and rash nature" to fight with a group of Mexican revolutionaries. After a few years as a revolutionary, Uladislao settled nearby, living with his sisters and his parents until he absconded with funds taken when he served as tax collector for the city of Sonoma in 1886 and went to Mexico and Guatemala with the money. Vallejo sold his remaining property to cover the debt, and as he wrote to his daughter, to "prevent your brother from returning to California with handcuffs on his hands and from going to San Quentin with a ball and chain on his foot."[3]

The two eldest Vallejo daughters, Fanita and Adela, linked the family fortunes to the United States by marrying two brothers, John and Levi Frisbie. The Frisbies had immigrated to California during the Mexican War and had avoided the temptation of the gold rush but became successful speculators in northern California land. The next two daughters, Natalia and Jovita, also married brothers. Arpad and Attila Haraszthy were Hungarian winemakers whose father had large landholdings in the Sonoma and Napa valleys that adjoined the Vallejos' land. The Haraszthys and Vallejos would make California wine an important industry by joining these two families. Natalia had a long and happy marriage, but Jovita struggled to make her older and distant husband happy. She tried to leave him several times, but General Vallejo would not permit it. When she died in childbirth, the priests would not allow her funeral to take place in the Catholic

Church because her marriage had not been consecrated there. This last slight devastated the general, who probably felt guilty about Jovita's life and death. He carried a piece of her hair in his wallet the rest of his life.[4]

If their children and their church had occasionally disappointed them, the Vallejos found these issues minor compared to the horror that the American judicial system became. In the end the Vallejos lost nearly everything. The ranchos in Sonoma and Monterey would be denied to them by the Supreme Court of the United States, and the vineyards, house, and the horse and cattle herds would all be mortgaged and sold to pay off debts and lawyers' bills. The U.S. Land Commission initially confirmed Mariano Vallejo's ownership, but the Anglo squatters who had claimed the land appealed, and Vallejo lost on these appeals even though he went to Washington to ask the Supreme Court to reverse its decision. The squatters took his land, and his former friends and neighbors demanded payment on funds they had lent him. When Mariano Guadalupe Vallejo died in 1890, he owned 228 acres around his Sonoma home, one horse, and one cow. Francesca died only a year later. They would both be mourned by the thirty-six grandchildren who lived into the twentieth century. In March 2007 wine journalists posthumously inducted Agoston Haraszthy into the Vintners' Hall of fame. The award was accepted on Haraszthy's behalf by his great-great-grandson, Vallejo Haraszthy. The state and the nation could and did take land, but names proved harder to erase.[5]

Los Angeles

California and its shifting rules around race and identity proved difficult to navigate even for elite Anglo-Americans. In 1860 nothing looked very certain in southern California either. A terrible drought gripped the region, and the booming cattle industry had failed, leaving southern California in a serious depression. Fewer than ten thousand people lived in the region, leaving it completely overshadowed by northern California. The Wilson family of Los Angeles successfully protected the fortunes they had created out of the trade in furs and hides, land speculation, and mercantile endeavors. Benjamin Davis Wilson, unlike Mariano Vallejo, did not count on the Land Commission or the courts to protect his interests. Even though he fared well in the courts, he invested in railroads and water companies to hedge his bets. Rather than counting on land grants, in 1854 Wilson bought land in what would become San Marino from the widow of old Californio Hugo Reid, a former mission Indian who needed the cash. The

40. María Jesús Wilson and Dora Hereford, 1860. This item is reproduced by permission of *The Huntington Library, San Marino, California.* (photCL 283 [16]).

María Jesús Wilson (right), then sixteen and calling herself Sue Benjamin Wilson, poses with her young aunt (left), Medora Hereford. Just after this photograph was taken, Sue and Dora were injured in a steamer explosion in Los Angeles harbor, and Dora would die from her injuries.

house he built there served three generations of his family. Financial success, however, did not protect the Wilsons from the personal crises created by a changing world.[6]

María Jesus, B.D.'s daughter from his first marriage to Ramona Yorba, became Sue Wilson when she went to boarding school in San Francisco. Even though she got a lot of pressure to become a Protestant from her stepmother Margaret, with the support of her Yorba relatives she remained a practicing Catholic. After nearly being killed in a steamship explosion off the coast of California, she married James DeBarth Shorb and had eleven children. Shorb, also a Catholic, became the son and partner that B.D. had always wanted, and they built a house next door to B.D. and Margaret at Lake Vineyard. Sue and her children seemed to move easily into the upper-class world of wealthy southern Californians but retained their ties to the Yorba family through names and godparenting.[7]

Juan Bernardo Wilson, later Johnny Wilson, never seemed to find a niche for himself. As a boy he refused to go to school because he was teased about his poor English, and so he was tutored at home. As a young man he was sent to San Francisco to work in various Wilson family businesses. Like so many sons we have seen here, he ran up debts and lost his family's trust. After these failures he moved back to Los Angeles, where he lived off and on with his Yorba cousins and uncles, perhaps feeling more at home in that world. His father's business managers reported that John drank to excess, got into fights, and gambled away any money they gave him. In 1870, while B.D. was working on an appropriations bill in Washington, John killed himself in the Bella Union Hotel in downtown Los Angeles, once owned by his father. Devastated by the loss of his twenty-five-year-old son, B.D. wondered to Margaret about the "anguish of mind to have induced the terrible act this last is what pains my heart." He could only write as an epitaph, "Poor boy I loved him with all his faults." John was buried in the Yorba family cemetery with his mother Ramona and his grandfather Bernardo, for whom he was named.[8]

Only a bit older than Johnny, Edward Sublette Hereford was adopted by B.D. when he and Margaret married. Eddy, who suffered mightily from homesickness at the College of Santa Clara, where Johnny Wilson and the younger Vallejo boys were educated as well, never really left home again. Eddy built a small house next to Margaret and B.D. and eventually married and had a daughter, but because he drank too much, B.D. wouldn't allow him to work in the family wine business at Lake Vineyard. Instead, Eddy became a local philanthropist, building schools and reserves for Califor-

41. Juan Bernardo Wilson, ca. 1856. This item is reproduced by permission of
The Huntington Library, San Marino, California. (photCL 283 [31a])

This shy child, with a hint of a crooked smile and formally posed for his first
photograph at the age of seven or eight, would grow up to be a deeply
unhappy young man. He would commit suicide in 1870 after years of
drinking and brawling in San Francisco and Los Angeles.

nia's Native people. Eddy, a Sublette, had inherited a large amount of St. Louis land and the old Sulphur Springs farm where William, Solomon, Milton, and Andrew had all lived after their retirement from the fur trade. The last Sublette brother, Solomon, died in 1857, and the Wilsons spent a decade and a fortune on lawyers to get the estate through the courts and to ascertain that none of these old trappers had legitimate wives or children. (The phrase that B.D.'s lawyers used was "wives to whom they were married in the eyes of the state," which solved the potential problem of fur trade marriages.) Margaret Hereford Wilson, her sisters, and their children inherited the substantial proceeds. Most of this fur trade fortune would be invested in southern California vineyards, orange groves, and railroads, but Eddy used his money for schools and industrial arts training programs at the Fort Tejon Preserve and at the old Pala mission.[9]

TAOS

Conquest was costly for the Bent family. After watching their father's brutal murder in 1847, Charles Bent's children initially stayed in New Mexico with their mother's family. A dense web of family still worked to link Taos, the ranches further east, and the Bent family who remained on the Arkansas River. The Bent children remained very close to their eldest sister Rumalda, married to Tom Boggs, who took over as family leader after Charles Bent died. Alfredo Bent, educated in St. Louis and Santa Fe, eventually ended up in Los Angeles, where he had three children. Teresina Bent, born in 1841, lived with her aunt Josefa and her husband Kit Carson until she married a local Taos trader named Aloys Scheurich. Estafina stayed with her mother Ignacia in Taos and with Charles's business partner Ceran St. Vrain, who acted as her guardian.[10]

Kit Carson, linked to the Bent family through marriage and business, had only one child with his Arapaho wife Waa-nibe, Adaline. Older than his other children, Adaline married a French and Indian trapper and sometime military escort named Louy Simmons in 1853. They settled on a sheep ranch north of Los Angeles until Adaline tired of Louy and left. Carson and his wife Josefa had eight children, who ranged in age from one to seventeen when their parents died in 1868, leaving them destitute. At Josefa and Kit's request, they were left in the care of Ignacia Bent and Teresina Bent Scheurich, women they knew could handle the job. The Bent and Carson children and their marriages reflect a still functioning interethnic, interconnected world in northern New Mexico and southern

Colorado that supported people through the hard times of the 1850s and 1860s.[11]

THE ARKANSAS RIVER

By 1860, much had changed along the Arkansas, mostly because of the Colorado gold rush. William Bent had moved his operations to ranch along the Purgatoire River, and Bent's Fort slowly eroded back into the mud from which it had been built. Yellow Woman had left Bent when he moved to the ranch and stayed permanently in the Cheyenne camps. William married again in 1867, this time to Adeline Harvey, the daughter of trapper Alexander Harvey and a Blackfoot woman, who had been raised in the mixed race Westport community. Adeline didn't last long at the isolated ranch either, and she moved back to the Westport house that William owned in Missouri. We don't hear about her from anyone until after William's death in 1869, when she refused to give up the house to his creditors. After all of his trading, business schemes, and investment in land, William died deeply in debt, leaving his children the Purgatoire ranch, its furnishings, some mules, and seventy-eight head of cattle. He also left them, as his last effort at negotiation with the federal government in 1865, land along the Arkansas River especially designated for mixed-bloods as part of reparations for the Sand Creek massacre.[12]

William and Owl Woman's children did not share even their father's limited success at finding a world where race didn't matter. Mary Bent, married to an Anglo named Robinson Moore, brought her husband to the Purgatoire ranch, where they spent their lives and raised a family. Though she was identified in the census in both Missouri and Colorado as "Indian," Mary never let her children visit the Cheyenne camps, and she baptized them in the Episcopal Church, so they blended into the rural communities that characterized southern Colorado. Robert Bent also came back to the ranch after serving in the Civil War on the Union side. He eventually married an Arapaho woman and moved to Indian Territory after his father died.[13]

George Bent, after serving in the Confederate Army, where he was captured by Union solders and imprisoned in St. Louis, married a Cheyenne woman named Magpie, the daughter of the leader Black Kettle, who had led his people during the Sand Creek Massacre. George sold his land on the "Half-Breed Tract" along the Arkansas to John Prowers, a white settler who would come to control most of southeastern Colorado and build a huge cattle empire on land William Bent had intended for the Cheyenne. After George served as a government interpreter and negotiator throughout the Plains Indian wars, he and Magpie ended up on Cheyenne and Arapaho lands in Indian Territory. George married two other Cheyenne women, Standing Out Woman and Kiowa Woman, while living on the reservation. Julia Bent, the youngest daughter, married a Cheyenne man of mixed race, Ed Guerrier, who served as an army interpreter, but they settled in Indian Territory with the Cheyennes. The youngest Bent, Charles, became the family's angry young man. He witnessed the Sand Creek Massacre and vowed never to settle on a reservation or to see his white father again. Instead, he became a famous Cheyenne dog soldier, raiding and burning settlements and military installations from Nebraska to Colorado until he was killed by Kaw government scouts in 1867.[14]

The Arapahos and Cheyennes, like most central and southern Plains people, were overwhelmed by the need to remake the plains for railroads, wagons, and farms. The state of Colorado refused to allow any land to be designated as a Cheyenne or Arapaho reserve, and the "Half-Breed Tracts" negotiated by William Bent all ended up in the hands of white ranchers. Military power and federal policy meant that all of the Bent children of mixed race who survived the decade of war ended up in Indian Territory. Whether they spoke English, went to college, owned land, or had influential friends didn't matter. They were labeled and recognized as "Indian." They had families, communities, and a new heritage in Indian Territory, but they never had the same kinds of choices their fathers and mothers enjoyed about where to live and whom to marry and how to name their children.

OREGON

Despite its long history in the fur trade and connections to the maritime world, the Pacific Northwest rivaled the Arkansas River in demonstrating its hostility to Native and mixed race people. The Indian wars that ravaged the entire region in the 1850s left a poisonous heritage that we can see in the history of John McLoughlin's children and grandchildren. An entire superstructure of law had to be set up to make sure Native people could have no access to land outside of their reservations. *Native* needed to include "the French and half-breed settlers living among them," people who were in some ways lower than Native people because they had chosen this life and were always blamed for "incensing" the tribes and making them "dissatisfied with the terms of the treaties concluded in their country."[15] But

CONCOMELY'S TOMB, ASTORIA.

42. Concomeley's tomb, 1841. Lithograph in Charles Wilkes, *Narrative of the United States Exploring Expedition: During the Years 1838, 1839, 1840, 1841, 1842.* 5 vols. (Philadelphia, 1849), vol. 4. Courtesy of Smithsonian Institution Libraries, Washington DC

When the Wilkes expedition stopped at the Columbia River and visited Fort Vancouver, they were struck by the number and variety of Native people who lived there. But by 1842, so many had died; their loss was barely represented by the Chinook leader Concomely's grave, drawn by sailor Charles Agate.

defining who counted as *Indian* and when that mattered proved difficult to impose. John McLoughlin, Catholic and foreign, could eventually be forgiven for these transgressions and become the Father of Oregon. Marguerite McLoughlin, however, never became Oregon's founding mother. She has no statues, no paintings, and no familiar face because she couldn't be forgiven for being an Indian. In the fur trade world her marriages and her husband's status changed her classification or at least the way most people treated her. Unlike many Native Oregonians, however, she could own property and she was not hustled off to a reservation.

In 1850 the McLoughlin family crowded into its Oregon City house and watched the hanging of five Cayuse men on a scaffold built next door, which must have emphasized how much their lives had been circumscribed by the new borders. Two of Marguerite's grandsons had participated in the militia that had rounded the Cayuse men, and her granddaughter had served as a nursemaid for Narcissa Whitman. They had endured a number of personal losses in the last few years. Joseph McLoughlin, John's son from his first Cree wife, died on a trapping expedition into California in 1848. Thomas McKay, Marguerite's son from her first marriage, died in early 1850 of tuberculosis at home with the McLoughlins. The family still battled to protect its claim on lands in Oregon, but the mills in Oregon City had been sold by the territorial government to raise cash, a ruse to punish McLoughlin for his ties to the hated Hudson's Bay Company, his French and English background, and his mixed race family.[16]

Just how mixed this family was and how much that came to matter become evident in looking at what happened to John and Marguerite's children. The eldest, Thomas McKay, from Marguerite's first marriage, had first married a Chinook woman named Timmee, a daughter of the Chinook leader Concomely, in 1824. She died in the malaria outbreak in the 1830s. Their son, William Cameron McKay, in theory the hereditary chief of the Chinooks, lived in the fort with the McLoughlins until he went to school in New York in the 1840s. He received a medical degree from Willamette University in 1873 and served as a reservation doctor with the Umatilla people. In 1838 Thomas McKay married a woman of mixed race named Isabelle Montour, daughter of a Fort Vancouver brigade leader, Nicholas Montour, and they had at least five children. Those children served as translators and "Indian scouts" during the Oregon Indian Wars and the Modoc War in 1860. One son, Donald McKay, operated an Indian show in the 1870s that promised audiences they could see "the Man Who Captured Captain Jack and his Murderous Bands of Modocs."[17] These McKay sons stayed in the Pacific Northwest on the Umatilla, Warm Springs, and Colville reservations. The daughters married mostly Euro-American or mixed race farmers and traders and disappeared into the farming world of the Pacific Northwest.[18]

A bright spot that summer of 1850 was John and Marguerite's youngest daughter Eloisa's marriage to Daniel Harvey, the former manager of the Fort Vancouver farm and now Dr. McLoughlin's business partner. Eloisa had been widowed when her husband William Rae had killed himself while the family lived in California, despairing over his business losses for the Hudson's Bay Company in 1845. The new Harvey family would have three more children, making the Oregon City house a home to six Rae-Harvey grandchildren. Eloisa and Daniel Harvey stayed in the Oregon City house with Marguerite until she died in 1860. After twelve years in the courts they were finally granted its title, but only after agreeing to pay all of the

43. David McLoughlin, 1900. Oregon Historical Society (OrHi 1268).

The youngest McLoughlin child, David, appears here as an elderly man shortly before his death. He had trained in France as an engineer and worked in the shipping industry, but he found peace and family life on the Kootenai reservation. He married a woman named Annie Grizzly and had eight children, named after his McLoughlin family relatives.

back taxes in gold, not in greenbacks, because as former Canadian citizens Eloisa and Daniel were classified as foreigners. Eloisa's children went to Catholic schools in Oregon and California, and the girls married into the Portland mercantile elite families and helped to found the Oregon Historical Society, as evidence of their solid American status.[19]

David McLoughlin, the youngest McLoughlin, lived at Fort Vancouver until he was sent to be trained as an engineer for the foreign service in Paris, but he was called home by his father in 1839. He worked as clerk and shipping agent in several forts, but he resigned from the Hudson's Bay Company to head for the gold fields in California in 1849. He returned home soon after but found his father's efforts to secure his land very hard to watch. After his father's death in 1857, David went to British Columbia in hopes of finding gold there. Somewhere on his travels he met Annie Grizzly, a Kootenai woman who lived on the Coeur d'Alene reservation, and he married her in 1866. They had eight daughters and one son, many of them named after McLoughlin family relatives: Marguerite, Louisa, John, Angeline (John McLoughlin's mother's name), and Eliza (David's sister's name). They lived in a small community that David and another man claimed as a town site in 1865, Porthill, Idaho, adjoining the reservation, where David farmed on land owned by his wife's family and ran a store. He taught in the local schools, kept the first weather records, "and was recognized by everyone as a man who had received the advantage of an education." He died in 1903, leaving his children only the log house he had built himself.[20]

ST. LOUIS

In 1860 St. Louis still reigned as the largest city in the West. Even with the gold rush San Francisco had not come close to outpacing it. According to the census 190,000 people lived in and around the city, and 55 percent of these residents were foreign born. Just as in 1803, the city was a very cosmopolitan place. Commerce still focused on the two great rivers that met there, but steamboats rather than canoes or flatboats carried the traffic, and the Chouteaus remained at the center of the city's economy, though many other families had joined them. The fur trade had faded in significance, but it had seeded nearly all of the great commercial endeavors in the city—land development, banking, transportation, and manufacturing. When Pierre Sr., the son of the original founder of St. Louis, died in 1849 at the age of ninety, he claimed he was not a wealthy man. Exactly like Mariano Vallejo and John McLoughlin, nearly all of Chouteau's assets were debts that other people owed him, mostly from old fur-trading ventures. It took forty-four years for the land the Osages had given him in 1792 to wend its way through the land claims process. And when the U.S. government finally approved it, Pierre sold it to William Ashley, now a St. Louis land developer, to pay his debts, again resembling Mariano Vallejo's position. Chouteau gave half of his estate to Pierre Jr. to reinvest back into the family business and divided up the rest among his remaining grandchildren, being very careful to specify that only the children born of his son A.P.'s first wife Sophie Labbadie and born of his son François and his wife Berenice Menard could inherit. He worked hard to produce wording that would ensure no Chouteaus of mixed race would get any money.[21] This slightly mean ending shouldn't surprise us since the world into which this Pierre had been born in 1759, where a different will would have been written, was gone completely. Or was it?

KAWSMOUTH

A. P. Chouteau's younger brothers, Cyprien and Frederick, stayed in Kawsmouth/Chouteau's Landing as it evolved into Kansas City, and both continued in some version of the fur trade, but as the Kansas and Shawnees moved to reservations, they moved closer to town. Frederick had four wives; the first three were Shawnee women who all gave him children before they died or who left him for other relationships. Several of his sons worked in the store he operated at the Shawnee Mission, and two of his daughters married some of the French Canadians who had settled around the Chouteau compound along the river in the 1830s. Cyprien was married for the first time at age fifty to a Shawnee woman named Nancy Francis and had three children, Frederick, Edmond, and Mamie. These children grew up in what became Kansas City and never went to the reservations in Indian Territory.[22]

Because of the fur trade, its racial intermingling, and the kinds of communities and businesses it developed over its very long history, Native and mixed race families like the Chouteaus could often disappear into these communities. Responsibilities around acting as kin, business partners, Catholic godparents, and friends linked people in ways that are invisible to the census and gave them a surprising variety of options. Kawsmouth was gone, but the town of Westport and the city of Kansas City that replaced it still included the kinds of industries that encouraged pieces of the old trading culture to flourish. Steamboats that came up and down the Missouri needed a transient workforce to staff the docks and the ships. Saddles, shoes, leather straps, and other leather goods made from buffalo hides became a central manufactured project in western Missouri. The U.S. Army and the Indian Department needed scouts, interpreters, and traders. The Indian trade continued well into the 1860s as more than ninety thousand Native people moved into Kansas with millions of dollars in government annuities in their hands, giving this trade a new lease on life.[23]

The Chouteau employee, government agent, and trader Andrew Drips and his Otoe family initially bought land in western Missouri in 1841 as part of François Chouteau's settlement. After his retirement from the Chouteau operations on the upper Missouri and when he began serving as an Indian agent, he and his family moved permanently to Westport. His wife Macompemay, who became Margaret Jackson when she and Drips married in the Catholic Church at Westport in 1841, stayed with their four children, a newly purchased slave woman, and her two children when Andrew left for the winter to attend to his government duties. Macompemay died in 1846, and Drips, left with four children, remarried quickly to a Sioux and French woman named Louise Geroux. Eventually they would have five more children. Faced with supporting nine children, the Drips family used a number of strategies to educate their children and to find places for them on the changing Missouri frontier.[24]

The Drips were not alone in these efforts. As Westport, Independence, and Kansas City grew, so did this impossibly mingled population. Most of the early founders had been involved in the fur trade and had made at least one "fur trade marriage"—and some had made several. Seth Ward, Nathan Boone, Ceran St. Vrain, Cyprien Chouteau, William Guerrier, Jim Bridger, William Bent, and Thomas Fitzpatrick, just to name a few of the more familiar, participated in active ways to support their children. We see numerous educational institutions, job market niches, and marriage patterns helping to support these families. In Westport, children from trader families attended Mr. Huffaker's Classical Academy, and in Independence, Love's Academy. Some parents chose to send their children to the mission schools at Fort Osage or at Shawnee Mission. Catholic colleges in St. Louis, like Sisters of St. Joseph Convent where Jane and Katherine Drips attended or the Christian Brothers College or St. Louis University, all provided educations for mixed race and Native children.[25]

Where all of these children ended up and how they were defined by Missouri society remains a question, but they were flesh and blood reminders of an important culture that still operated in these places. Jane and Katherine Drips both married men with French surnames, so we can make some guesses about their ethnicity, but in Ash Grove, Missouri, Katherine and her three children were enumerated as white in the 1860 census. Because census takers only had the options for denoting race as "white, non-native white, black, mulatto, and wild Indian," it is hard to know what they might have made of Katherine Benoist's household. Self-definitions are even harder to surmise. Her French and Sioux stepmother, Louise Drips, sent Katherine "one fine painted Buffalo Robe also a buckskin shirt and pair of pants" and included a note about life in the Drips household in Westport. "Thomas is a perfect Indian," she reported about her youngest son. "He talks of nothing but Sioux. I lost my little dog Sally a few days ago. I think some of the Indians stole her."[26] Whether Thomas played Indian or was counted as a white boy or whether Indians who didn't live in Louise's household stole dogs mattered. However Louise defined herself and her children, she still believed they lived in world where people of mixed race could make lives beyond the restrictions of how others might define *Indian*. This West, an earlier version that lasted for more than a century, would endure in hidden places even as a new West erased those more humane definitions.

Notes

ACKNOWLEDGMENTS

1. Charles A. Beard, "Written History as an Act of Faith," *American Historical Review* 39 (January 1934): 222, 229.

INTRODUCTION

1. Foley and Rice, *First Chouteaus*, 45–46, 91–92; Hoig, *Chouteaus*, 44–45; Dickason, "From 'One Nation,'" 19.

2. Faragher, *Daniel Boone*, and Merrill, *Into the American Woods*, have described the subsistence hunting culture of this earlier frontier.

3. There is no perfect word to describe the people to whom I refer here—*métis, Métis, Creole, half-breed, mixed race*, and *mestizo* all offer different problems of identity and etiquette. Numerous terms were used at the time that denoted the kinds of mixtures, their national origins, and the amount of mixing that made up each individual phenotype. Because Anglo-Americans did not develop their full-blown obsession with racial description and categorization until the mid- and late nineteenth century, most people did not use consistent terminology, and nor do I. *Race*, a term anthropologists warn us against now, was commonly used in the nineteenth century to denote differences in human phenotypes, so I think it is accurate to use the term here. The same challenge lies in describing Europeans, Euro-Americans, Anglo-Americans, White Americans, or Anglos, which are used to describe different groups or to mean the same thing. I strive, and fail, for clarity.

4. Sleeper-Smith, *Indian Women and French Men*, and James Brooks, *Captives and Cousins*, look at this set of relationships and draw quite different conclusions about how it all worked.

5. Hendrickson, *Union, Nation, or Empire*, 20–22.

6. R. L. F. Davis, "Community and Conflict," 338; "Introduction" to Chouteau Collection, Missouri Historical Society (hereafter MHS); Aron, *American Confluence*, 34–44; Banner, *Legal Systems in Conflict*, 51–53, 72–81.

7. DuVal, *Native Ground*, 183–84; Din and Nasatir, *Imperial Osages*, 360–61.

8. Thorne, *Many Hands*, 70–76; General Miro to Antonio Rengel, "Letter from New Orleans, Dec. 12, 1785," in Nasatir, *Before Lewis and Clark*, 120.

9. Thomas Forsyth, quoted in J. B. White, "Missouri Merchant," 99–102, 107; Scharf, *History of St. Louis*, 1: 288–91.

10. Inside the Corps, "July 04, 1804 Journal of Charles Floyd," PBS, http://www.pbs.org/lewisandclark/archive/ (accessed July 14, 2010); Ambrose, *Undaunted Courage*, 149.

11. Meriwether Lewis to Auguste Chouteau, "Letter on Jan. 1804," in D. Jackson, *Letters of the Lewis and Clark Expedition*, 1:161.

12. Marriage records, listed in Kelton, *Annels of Fort Mackinac*; Sleeper-Smith, "'Unpleasant Transaction,'" 417–43.

13. Thorne, *Many Hands*, 67–68; Innis, "Interrelations between the Fur Trade," 321–32; Baird, "Reminiscences of Early Days," 17–64; "The Annual Fort Michilimackinac Pageant," Fort Michilimackinac, http://www.fmpcfestival.org/; Armour, *Colonial Michilimackinac*, 14–17.

14. Sleeper-Smith, "'Unpleasant Transaction,'" 431–34.

15. Morrison, *Outpost*, 26–27, 51–52; Podruchny, *Making the Voyaguer World*, 26–27, 201–3.

16. Frank, *From Settler to Citizen*, 153–54, 183–92; Chavez, *Origins of New Mexico Families*.

17. Reséndez, "Getting Drunk and Getting Cured," 79–80; Hämäläinen, *Comanche Empire*, 135–37, 156–59; Weber, *Spanish Frontier*, 294.

18. Weber, *Spanish Frontier*, 260–63; Costello and Hornbeck, "Alta California, an Overview," 303–4.

19. Engstrand, introduction to Moziño, *Noticias de Nutka*, xlix–lii.

20. Langsdorff, *Langsdorff's Narrative*, 102–8.

21. Billon, *Annals of St. Louis*, 200.

22. Ditz, "New Men's History," 1–35.

23. Billon, *Annals of St. Louis*, 204.

24. Much of the thinking around how families can become part of colonial projects comes out of the work of Ann Laura Stoler and her reconceptualization of Foucault and his notions of the location of power in intimate places. See, for example, Stoler, *Carnal Knowledge*, and, more recently, *Along the Archival Grain*.

25. Oates, "Tennessee in the Stoned Age," 8.

26. Ditz, "Formative Ventures," 63.

1. FAMILIES AND FUR

1. Edward Hereford to Margaret Wilson, Sept. 30, 1857, Wilson Papers, Box 6, Huntington Library (hereafter HL).

2. A. A. Chouteau to Auguste Chouteau, Nov. 26, 1802, in Chouteau Collection, MHS.

3. Gitlin, *Bourgeois Frontier*, 124–38.

4. *St. Louis Republican*, June 8, 1831; Arkansas *Free Trader*, May 19, 1831, in Dale Morgan Early Mississippi Valley Newspaper Transcripts, Beinecke Library (hereafter BRBML).

5. Thorne, *Many Hands*, 137–39; Spear, "Colonial Intimacies," 81–84.

6. "Fort Smith Letter Book, no. 17, 1831," in Foreman, *Pioneer Days*, 89–90.

7. See figure 6 for Chouteaus and their Osage kin.

8. Because Madame Marie Thérèse Chouteau never actually married Pierre LaClede, though he was father to many of her children and though they shared property and domiciles for nearly forty years, the family name and inheritance issue is complex in the record.

9. Hall, *Sketches of History*, 1:38.

10. Aron, *American Confluence*, 11–17; Ekberg, *French Roots*, 137, 258–61.

11. Peyser, *Letters from New France*, 19; Aron, *American Confluence*, 28–30, 42–47; Ekberg, *French Roots*, 94–114.

12. Auguste Chouteau, "Narrative of the Founding of St. Louis," in McDermott, *Early Histories of St. Louis*; Foley and Rice, *First Chouteaus*, 4–6.

13. Burns, *Osage Indian Bands and Clans*, 22–23. Aron, *American Confluence*, 24–25.

14. Aron, *American Confluence*, 52–57; Hall, *Sketches of History*, 44–45; Ekberg, *Stealing Indian Women*, 5–6.

15. Foley and Rice, *First Chouteaus*, 27–29; Nasatir, *Before Lewis and Clark*, introduction; Gitlin, *Bourgeois Frontier*, 134–35.

16. A. A. Chouteau to Auguste Chouteau, Nov. 26, 1802, Chouteau Collection, MHS; Christian, *Before Lewis and Clark*, 98–99; Thorne, *Many Hands*, 83–84.

17. Thorne, *Many Hands*, 2.

18. Ekberg, *Stealing Indian Women*, 45–47.

19. Thorne, *Many Hands*, 68; Foley and Rice, *First Chouteaus*, 14–15.

20. Cott, *Public Vows*, and Gordon-Reed, *Hemingses of Monticello*, 106, have recently laid out the challenges of the definitions.

21. R. White, *Middle Ground*; Taylor, *Divided Ground*.

22. Thorne, *Many Hands*, 34–39.

23. DuVal, *Native Ground*, 6–9; Aron, *American Confluence*, 88–89.

24. DuVal, *Native Ground*, 120–21.

25. See Gallay, *Indian Slave Trade*; James Brooks, *Captives and Cousins*; Din and Nasatir, *Imperial Osages*, 158–90; Thorne, *Many Hands*, 104–6.

26. Foley and Rice, *First Chouteaus*, 48–53; Aron, *American Confluence*, 89–90; DuVal, *Native Ground*, 172; Nasatir, "Anglo-Spanish Frontier," 163–64; Mathews, *Osages*, 297.

27. Ekberg, *Stealing Indian Women*, 22–28; Thorne, *Many Hands*, 90–91.

28. Ekberg, *Stealing Indian Women*, 28; Aubert, "Blood of France," 448–53; Thorne, *Many Hands*, 102–3.

29. Aron, *American Confluence*, 98–105; Gracy, *Moses Austin*, 90–110.

30. Aron, *American Confluence*, 115–16; Thorne, *Many Hands*, 114; Peterson, "People In-Between," 49; Stoddard, *Sketches, Historical and Descriptive*, 214.

31. D. Jackson, *Letters of the Lewis and Clark Expedition*, 1: 217; LeCompte, "Auguste Pierre Chouteau," 96–97.

32. Billon, *Annals of St. Louis*, 168–69; LeCompte, "Auguste Pierre Chouteau," 99.

33. Irving, *Astoria*, 106.

34. Gitlin, *Bourgeois Frontier*, 90–93; LeCompte, "Auguste Pierre Chouteau," 98–99; Thorne, "Chouteau Family," 112–14; Ekberg, *Stealing Indian Women*, 84–86.

35. LeCompte, "Auguste Pierre Chouteau," 100–102; Chittenden, *American Fur Trade*, 2:498–500; Jules DeMun, "Arrest and Imprisonment at Santa Fe, 1818," in E. A. White, *News of the Plains and Rockies*, 2:27–49; Scharf, *History of St. Louis*, 1:97, 150.

36. A. P. Chouteau to Lewis Cass, Nov. 12, 1831, Senate Report on "Fur Trade and Inland Travel to Mexico," Sen. Doc. 90, 22nd Cong., 1st sess. (Series 213), 90.

37. LeCompte, "Auguste Pierre Chouteau," 105; Thorne, *Many Hands*, 64–65; Burns, *Osage Mission Baptisms*.

38. Thorne, *Many Hands*, 65; LeCompte, "Auguste Pierre Chouteau," 106.

39. DuVal, *Native Ground*, 196–98; LeCompte, "Auguste Pierre Chouteau," 107–8.

40. "Family Letters, 1823–1825," Boxes 16, 17, Chouteau Collection, MHS.

41. A. P. Chouteau to Melicourt Papin, April 4, Aug. 30, 1824, Chouteau Collection, Box 17, MHS.

42. A. P. Chouteau to Bernard Pratte, Feb. 8, 1827, Box 19, Chouteau Collection, MHS.

43. Mathews, *Osages*, 519–20; LeCompte, "Auguste Pierre Chouteau," 108–10.

44. DuVal, *Native Ground*, 210–13.

45. Kappler, *Indian Affairs*, 2: 157–58, 218–20; Burns, *Osage Mission Baptisms*, 138–49; Christian, *Before Lewis and Clark*, 307–8.

46. Jennifer Brown, "Fur Trade as Centrifuge: Family Dispersal and Off-Spring Identity," in DeMallie and Ortiz, *North American Indian Anthropology*, 197–219; Murray, *Travels in North America*, 1:33.

47. S. Carter, *Importance of Being Monogamous*, 3–12; Spear, "Colonial Intimacies."

48. Thorne, *Many Hands*, 160–64; Irving, *Western Journals*, 109.

49. Faragher, "Custom of the Country," 199–215; Thorne, *Many Hands*, 165–69.

50. A. P. Chouteau, Verdigris to A. Chouteau in St. Louis, Aug. 14, 1828, Chouteau Collection, Box 19, MHS; LeCompte, "Auguste Pierre Chouteau," 111–14.

51. Thomas Forsyth to Lewis Cass, Secretary of War, "Letter, Oct. 24, 1831," in Chittenden, *American Fur Trade*, 937–38.

52. B. W. Brown, *Southern Honor*, 290–91.

53. Haley, *Sam Houston*, 15, 51–77; Gregory and Strickland, *Sam Houston with the Cherokees*, 62–66.

54. Haley, *Sam Houston*, 79–85; Wisehart, *Sam Houston*, 57–70.

55. A. P. Chouteau to Superintendent of Indian Affairs Lewis Cass, July 14, 1832, Letters Received, Office of Indian Affairs, Osage Agency, Record Group 75; LeCompte, "Auguste Pierre Chouteau," 114.

56. Irving, *Western Journals*, 108–9.

57. Foreman, *Pioneer Days*, 116–18; Hoig, *Chouteaus*, 123–29; C. E. Carter, *Territorial Papers*, 15:190–91.

58. Christian, *Before Lewis and Clark*, 331–33; LeCompte, "Auguste Pierre Chouteau," 118; Foreman, *Pioneer Days*, 226–27.

59. Prucha, *Great Father*, 1:299–302.

60. A. P. Chouteau to Col. Matthew Arbuckle and Commissioner Montfort

Stokes, April 19 and April 25, 1836, Indian Office, Western Superintendency, 1836; Foreman, *Pioneer Days*, 223–26; LeCompte, "Auguste Pierre Chouteau," 119–20.

61. LeCompte, "Auguste Pierre Chouteau," 121; Paul Liguest Chouteau to John B. Sarpy, May 23, 1838, and A. P. Chouteau to Pierre Chouteau, Dec. 6, 1838, both Box 36, Chouteau Collection, MHS.

62. Christian, *Before Lewis and Clark*, 337; Gabriel R. Paul to Pierre Chouteau Sr., Dec. 28, 1838, Box 36, Chouteau Collection, MHS.

63. Governor Montfort Stokes to Commissioner of Indian Affairs, March 19, 1839, Indian Office Osage Reserve File, Office of Indian Affairs, Osage Agency, Record Group 75.

64. Christian, *Before Lewis and Clark*, 337–39; Foreman, *Pioneer Days*, 257–62; Hoig, *Chouteaus*, 243–44.

65. Sunder, *Bill Sublette*, 20–26.

66. Wishart, *Fur Trade*, 9–10; Chittenden, *American Fur Trade*, 1:79–87.

67. The business end of fur trade and the practices of its major operators were of great interest to historians two and three generations ago, and there are several exhaustive multivolume texts and innumerable published diaries and accounts of mountain men and fur traders. However, since the early 1960s, with a couple of exceptions, nothing new has appeared by historians writing in the United States (Canada, however, still has lots of historians working on the fur trade, but they are focused on Canada). Interest has shifted to the human relations in the industry, the role of Native people, and the impact of the trade on their lives. So for information about traditional traders and business we have few new approaches and still turn to Chittenden, *American Fur Trade*; P. C. Phillips, *American Fur Trade*; Lavender, *Fist in the Wilderness* (a more popular account); and Wishart, *Fur Trade* (the most recent entry).

68. Wishart, *Fur Trade*, 42–46; Chittenden, *American Fur Trade*, 1:125–31.

69. Prucha, *American Indian Policy*, 40–53, 61–72.

70. Wishart, *Fur Trade*, 52–53; Lavender, *Fist in the Wilderness*, 346–47; Chittenden, *American Fur Trade*, 1:322–25; Gitlin, *Bourgeois Frontier*, 130–31.

71. Wishart, *Fur Trade*, 77–81; *Edwardsville (IL) Spectator*, Oct. 26, 1822.

72. Sunder, *Bill Sublette*, 33–37.

73. Hempstead quoted in Berry, *Majority of Scoundrels*, 7–8.

74. Quoted in Berry, *Majority of Scoundrels*, 23–24.

75. Benjamin O'Fallon to William Clark, Aug. 1823, Clark Papers, MHS.

76. Sunder, "William Lewis Sublette," 5:347–49; Utley, *Life Wild and Perilous*, 131–39.

77. "List of Persons Killed," 1829, Sublette Family Papers, Box 1, Folder 2, MHS; Chittenden, *American Fur Trade*, 1: 278–81; Sunder, *Bill Sublette*, 58–61.

78. Fehrman, "Mountain Men—A Statistical View," 10:9–15; Swagerty, "Marriage and Settlement Patterns," 163–65; Faragher, "Custom of the Country," 199–215; H. H. Anderson, "Fur Traders as Fathers," 245; Sunder, *Bill Sublette*, 82–84, 228.

79. Nunis, "Milton G. Sublette," 4:331–35; Utley, *Life Wild and Perilous*, 138–40.

80. Nunis, "Milton G. Sublette," 4:336–42; Lavender, *Fist in the Wilderness*, 392–94.

81. W. L. Sublette to William Ashley, "Sept. 24, 1831," quoted in Sunder, *Bill Sublette*, 99.

82. William Ashley to Gov. of Santa Fe, Mexico, Passport Application for William Sublette, April 19, 1831, Sublette Family Papers, Box 1, Folder 3, MHS; Sunder, "William Lewis Sublette," 352–54; Irving, *Adventures of Captain Bonneville*, 277.

83. Sunder, *Bill Sublette*, 134–36; Utley, *Life Wild and Perilous*, 144–47.

84. Nunis, "Milton G. Sublette," 4:343; Bernard Farrar, St. Louis to William Sublette, "Bill for medical services," Sept. 1834–Feb. 1835, Sublette Family Papers, Box 2, Folder 4, MHS.

85. Nunis, "Milton G. Sublette," 4:331, 344; Sunder, "William Lewis Sublette," 350–52.

86. St. Louis Agricultural Society, Oct. 18, 1842, "Awards to William Sublette, prizes for the best aged Bull, Cow and Suckling Calf," Sublette Family Papers, Box 3, Folder 3, MHS; Sunder, "William Lewis Sublette," 355–57.

87. William Sublette, Sulphur Springs, to William Steward Drummond, Sept. 1842, Sublette Family Papers, Box 3, Folder 3, MHS.

88. "Articles of Agreement between William L. Sublette and Thomas A. Hereford for lease of White Sulphur Springs, Sept. 13, 1842," Sublette Family Papers, Box 3, Folder 3, MHS.

89. Andrew Sublette to William Sublette, May 6, 1843, Sublette Family Papers, Box 3, Folder 6, MHS; Sunder, "William Lewis Sublette," 357–58.

90. Albert G. Boone, St. Louis, to William L. Sublette, Independence, May 5, 1843, Sublette Family Papers, Box 3, Folder 6, MHS.

91. "Last Will and Testament of W. L. Sublette, Jan. 1, 1844," Sublette Family Papers, Box 4, MHS.

92. Sunder, *Bill Sublette*, 227–30.

93. Sandoz, *Beaver Men*, 302–10; Doyce B. Nunis, "Andrew Whitley Sublette," 8:349–63; Andrew W. Sublette, Westport, to William Sublette, May 1844, Sublette Family Papers, Box 3, Folder 6.

94. Nunis, *Andrew Sublette*, 78–82.

95. Letter from Solomon Sublette in Independence to William Sublette, Nov. 28, 1842, Sublette Family Papers, Box 3, Folder 4; Sunder, "Solomon P. Sublette," in Hafen, *Mountain Men*, 1: 378–81.

96. Solomon Sublette to William Sublette, Oct. 20, 1844, Sublette Family Papers, Box 4, Folder 3, MHS; Nunis, "Andrew Whitley Sublette," 8:359–61; Nunis, "Enigma of the Sublette Overland Party," 331–49.

97. Sunder, "Solomon P. Sublette," 1:383–86; Nunis, "Andrew Whitley Sublette," 8:362–63; *Los Angeles Star*, May 28, 1853.

98. Sunder, "Solomon P. Sublette," 1:385–89.

99. Sunder, *Bill Sublette*, 197; "B. D. Wilson Papers," HL, Box 1.

100. Sunder, "Solomon P. Sublette," 1:381; Micajah Tarver to Edward Sublette Hereford, Jan. 1, 1844, Wilson Papers, Box 1, HL; Facsimile pages from Hereford, Wilson, Patton Family Bible, Wilson Papers, addenda II, Box 19, HL.

101. Thomas Hereford to William Sublette, Nov. 1844, Sublette Family Papers, Box 4, Folder 6, MHS.

102. Thomas Hereford to Margaret Hereford, Dec. 28, 1846, Wilson Papers, Box 1, HL.

103. Letter from Margaret Hereford to Thomas Hereford, April 19 1847, and Letter from Thomas Hereford in Santa Fe to Margaret Hereford in St. Louis, July 4, 1847, both in Wilson Papers, Box 1, HL.

104. Letter from Thomas Hereford in Santa Fe to Margaret Hereford in St. Louis, July 4, 1847, Wilson Papers, Box 1, HL; D. J. Gonzalez, *Refusing the Favor*, 46–51; Chalfant, *Dangerous Passage*.

105. Margaret Hereford to Esther Sale Hereford, August 1848, Wilson Papers, Box 1, HL.

106. Margaret Hereford in Chihuahua to Esther Sale Hereford, March 9, 1850, Wilson Papers, Box 1, HL; Holliday, *World Rushed In*; Rohrbough, *Days of Gold*.

107. Thomas Hereford in Petic, Mexico, to Margaret Hereford in San Jose CA, June 28, 1850, Wilson Papers, Box 1, HL.

108. T. A Hereford to Mr. B. D. Wilson, Jan. 8, 1851, Wilson Papers, Addenda II, Box 15, HL; Margaret Hereford to Esther Sale Hereford in St. Louis, Oct. 13, 1850, Wilson Papers, Box 1, HL.

109. Probate Court Records, County of Los Angeles, Jan. 24, 1852, Judge Agustin Olvera, presiding, Wilson Papers, Box 2, HL.

110. Wilson, "Narrative," 371–78.

111. Wilson, "Narrative," 379–83; Weber, *Taos Trappers*, 225–29; Weber, *Mexican Frontier*, 138–40.

112. Batman, *Outer Coast*, xii; Weber, *Mexican Frontier*, 196–202; Hackel, "Land, Labor and Production," 130–32.

113. Wilson, "Narrative" 383; McWilliams, *Southern California Country*, 49–53.

114. Wilson, "Narrative," 383–84; Hurtado, *Intimate Frontiers*, 52–53.

115. Wilson, "Narrative," 381.

116. Read, *Don Benito Wilson*, 59; Haas, *Conquests and Historical Identities*, 33–36, 48–53.

117. Wilson, "Narrative," 394–95.

118. Wilson, "Narrative", 403–4; Thompson, *Edward F. Beale*, 16.

119. "Business Records from Wilson and Packard, 1849–1851," Wilson Papers, Box 2, Addenda II, Box 16, HL; Wilson, "Narrative," 415.

120. Letter from John C. Frémont to B. D. Wilson, 1851, Wilson Papers, Box 2, HL; T. A Hereford to Mr. B. D. Wilson, Jan. 8, 1851, Wilson Papers, Addenda II, Box 14, HL.

121. Letter from Margaret Hereford Wilson in Los Angeles to B. D. Wilson at Fort Tejon, Sept. 6, 1853, Wilson Papers, Box 2, HL.

122. Wilson, "Narrative," 415; "Last Will and Testament of Benjamin D. Wilson, June 10, 1853, Los Angeles," *Wilson Papers,* Box 2, HL; "Invoices for supplies furnished to the Southern California Indians, 1853," *Wilson Papers,* Box 2; *Los Angeles Star,* May 28, 1853.

123. Letter from Margaret Hereford Wilson in Los Angeles to B. D. Wilson at Fort Tejon, Sept. 6, 1853, *Wilson Papers,* Box 2, HL; Deverell, *Whitewashed Adobe,* 11–14.

124. Pitt, *Decline of the Californios,* 122–25; Read, *Don Benito Wilson,* 62.

125. Letter from Edward F. Beale to B. D. Wilson, Aug. 19, 1854, Wilson Papers, Box 3, HL.

126. "Bill for Shepherd's Academy, 1856," Wilson Papers, Addenda II, Box 19, HL; Letters between Margaret Wilson to B. D. Wilson, April–Dec. of 1856, Wilson Papers, Box 5, HL.

127. B. D. Wilson at Lake Vineyard CA to Margaret Hereford Wilson in St. Louis, June 15, 1856, Wilson Papers, Addenda II, Box 18, HL.

128. Pitt, *Decline of the Californios,* 122–23.

129. Deverell, *Whitewashed Adobe,* 13–18; Pitt, *Decline of the Californios,* 120–29; and if you ignore some of the breathless hyperbole, Bell, *Reminiscences of a Ranger,* 3–14.

130. Deverell, *Whitewashed Adobe,* 15–16; Pitt, *Decline of the Californios,* 160–62.

131. Guillow, "Pandemonium in the Plaza," 186–87; B. D. Wilson at Lake Vineyard CA to Margaret Hereford Wilson in St. Louis, July 20, 1856, Wilson Papers, Box 6, HL.

132. Pitt, *Decline of the Californios,* 162; *Los Angeles Star,* July 26, 1856, reprinted in Cleland, *Cattle on a Thousand Hills,* appendix, III, 245.

133. *Los Angeles Star,* July 26, 1856, reprinted in Cleland, *Cattle on a Thousand Hills,* appendix III, 247–48; Guillow, "Pandemonium in the Plaza," 187–88; Pitt, *Decline of the Californios,* 162–63.

134. Benjamin Davis Wilson at Lake Vineyard CA to Margaret Hereford Wilson in St. Louis, July 20, 1856, Wilson Papers, Box 6, HL.

135. Guillow, "Pandemonium in the Plaza," 192–93; Margaret Hereford Wilson to B. D. Wilson, Sept. 22, 1856, Wilson Papers, Box 6, HL.

2. FORT VANCOUVER'S FAMILIES

1. There is now a well-established literature about women in the fur trade, beginning with the sacred triumvirate of Jennifer Brown, *Strangers in Blood;* Peterson, "People in Between" (dissertation); and Van Kirk, *"Many Tender Ties."* Since these texts appeared, a steady supply of excellent new work has emerged to support and revise them, including, most helpfully for me, B. M. White, "Woman Who Married a Beaver," 109–47; Sleeper-Smith, *Indian Women and French Men;* and Murphy, *Gathering of Rivers.*

2. Ditz, "New Men's History," 1–35.

3. Rich, *Hudson's Bay Company,* 2:29–31, 630–35; Dudden, *American Pacific,* 7–29.

4. Pomeroy, *Pacific Slope*, 10–11; Johansen and Gates, *Empire of the Columbia*, 33–74; J. R. Gibson, *Imperial Russia*, 7–9.

5. J. R. Gibson, *Otter Skins*, 5–8; Ames and Maschner, *Peoples of the Northwest Coast*, 178–180.

6. J. R. Gibson, *Imperial Russia*, 8.

7. Calloway, *One Vast Winter Count*, 399–401; W. L. Cook, *Flood Tide of Empire*, 134–46.

8. Johansen and Gates, *Empire of the Columbia*, 46–51; Ronda, *Astoria and Empire*, 63–66; Cook, *Flood Tide of Empire*, 210–17, 231–41.

9. Lewis quoted in Ronda, *Astoria and Empire*, 31.

10. Reid, *Contested Empire*, 4–7.

11. P. C. Phillips, *American Fur Trade*, 2:340–47; Rich, *Hudson's Bay Company*, 2:584–87; Pomeroy, *Pacific Slope*, 18–19.

12. Farnham, *Travels in the Great Western Prairies*, 128.

13. Rich, *Hudson's Bay Company*, 638–43; Holman, *Dr. John McLoughlin*, 27–30.

14. Merk, introduction to G. Simpson, *Fur Trade and Empire*, xxi–xxvi.

15. Morrison, *Outpost*, 5–6.

16. Morrison, *Outpost*, 9–13; R. G. Montgomery, *White-Headed Eagle*, 18–21.

17. John McLoughlin to Simon Fraser, July 13, 1808, in B. B. Barker, *McLoughlin Empire*, 149.

18. Quoted in Morrison, *Outpost*, 20.

19. Rich, *Fur Trade and the Northwest*, 184–87.

20. Davidson, *North West Company*, 41–42; Rich, *Fur Trade and the Northwest*, 174–76; Morrison, *Outpost*, 38.

21. Davidson, *North West Company*, 106; Cox, *Adventures on the Columbia*, 330; Jennifer Brown, *Strangers in Blood*, xiv–xv.

22. Cox, *Adventures on the Columbia*, 330; Morrison, *Outpost*, 41–43.

23. John McLoughlin, Fort William, to Simon Fraser, July and Aug. 1808, *Oregon Historical Quarterly* 36 (March 1935): 294–95; Rich in J. McLoughlin, *Letters of McLoughlin from Fort Vancouver*, 1st ser., xxxii–xxxvi; Morrison, *Outpost*, 51.

24. Van Kirk, *"Many Tender Ties,"* 4.

25. Van Kirk, "From 'Marrying-In' to 'Marrying-Out,'" 1–11; Sleeper-Smith, *Indian Women and French Men*, 5; on interracial unions and self-made marriages on what has come to be known as the gender frontier, see Cott, *Public Vows*, 27–37; Hurtado, "When Strangers Meet," 52–75.

26. Van Kirk, "Tracing the Fortunes," 148–79; Ross, *Red River Colony*, xxvi.

27. Stanley, *Louis Riel*, 4–6; Murphy, *Gathering of Rivers*, 46–49.

28. Sylvia Van Kirk, "'The Custom of the Country': An Examination of Fur Trade Marriage Patterns," in Bradbury, *Canadian Family History*, 67–92; B. B. Barker, *McLoughlin Empire*, 61; John Work to Edward Ermatinger, July 15, 1837, in Dye, "Old Letters"; B. B. Barker, *McLoughlin Empire*, 61.

29. Van Kirk, *"Many Tender Ties,"* 92–93; J. S. H. Brown, *Strangers in Blood*, 107–10.

30. Morrison, *Outpost*, 57–61; B. M. White, "Woman Who Married a Beaver," 131–37; Elliott, "Marguerite Wadin McKay McLoughlin," 340.

31. Ronda, *Astoria and Empire*, 18–33; P. C. Phillips, *American Fur Trade* 2:119–38.

32. Bancroft, *History of the Northwest Coast*, 164–68; Elliott, "Marguerite Wadin McKay McLoughlin," 341.

33. P. C. Phillips, *American Fur Trade*, 2:270–75; Ross, *Adventures of the First Settlers*, 2–12; Ronda, *Astoria and Empire*, 196–202.

34. P. C. Phillips, *American Fur Trade*, 2:277, 289–91; Robertson, *Competitive Struggle*, 56–58; Ross, *Adventures of the First Settlers*, 253–55; Bancroft, *History of the Northwest Coast*, 28:220–24.

35. Merk, introduction to G. Simpson, *Fur Trade and Empire*, x–xi; Morrison, *Outpost*, 85–91; Gray, *Lord Selkirk*, 104.

36. Rich, *Fur Trade and the Northwest*, 205–28; Gray, *Lord Selkirk*, 106–34.

37. John McLoughlin to Simon Fraser, Nov. 1821 in B. B. Barker, *McLoughlin Empire*, 171.

38. Davidson, *North West Company*, 180–85; Morrison, *Outpost*, 104–6; Rich, *Fur Trade and the Northwest*, 237–43.

39. Merk, introduction to G. Simpson, *Fur Trade and Empire*, xv–xvi; Rich, *Fur Trade and the Northwest*, 240–42; Jennifer Brown, *Strangers in Blood*, 111–12.

40. Minutes of the Council, July 10, 1824, in G. Simpson, *Fur Trade and Empire*, appendix A, 216; Merk, introduction to G. Simpson, *Fur Trade and Empire*, xxiv–xxv.

41. Merk, in G. Simpson, *Fur Trade and Empire*, 22–64; Morrison, *Outpost*, 121–24.

42. Van Kirk, *"Many Tender Ties,"* 118–22; Sleeper-Smith, "'Unpleasant Transaction,'" 439–44; Van Kirk, "From 'Marrying-In' to 'Marrying-Out,'" 1–4.

43. Calloway, *One Vast Winter Count*, 407.

44. Morrison, *Outpost*, 166–67.

45. See, for example, J. McLoughlin, *Letters of McLoughlin from Fort Vancouver*, 3rd ser.; J. McLoughlin, *Letters of McLoughlin, Written at Fort Vancouver*.

46. Merk, appendix, in G. Simpson, *Fur Trade and Empire*, 287–92.

47. B. B. Barker, *McLoughlin Empire*, appendix, has hundreds of family letters, as do early volumes of the *Oregon Historical Quarterly*. All the existing letters to the Hudson's Bay Company and to Governor Simpson have been published. Augst, *Clerk's Tale*, 71–79.

48. Merk, in G. Simpson, *Fur Trade and Empire*, 7, 123; Morrison, *Outpost*, 134–35.

49. Merk, in G. Simpson, *Fur Trade and Empire*, 87.

50. John McLoughlin to Gov. and Committee of the Hudson's Bay Company, Oct. 6, 1825, in J. McLoughlin, *Letters of McLoughlin from Fort Vancouver*, 1st ser., 4–5; Merk, in G. Simpson, *Fur Trade and Empire*, 122–24; Morrison, *Outpost*, 137.

51. Ruby and Brown, *Chinook Indians*, 168–75; J. R. Gibson, *Otter Skins*, 11.

52. Merk in G. Simpson, *Fur Trade and Empire*, 94.

53. Ronda, *Astoria and Empire*, 220–21; McLoughlin to Gov. and Committee, Oct. 6, 1825, in J. McLoughlin, *Letters of McLoughlin from Fort Vancouver*, 1st ser., 17–19.

54. Ruby and Brown, *Chinook Indians,* 6–15.

55. Eloisa McLoughlin, quoted in Morrison, *Outpost,* 175.

56. McLoughlin to Governor and Committee of the Hudson's Bay Company, Nov. 15, 1843, in J. McLoughlin, *Letters of McLoughlin from Fort Vancouver,* 2nd ser.

57. McLoughlin to Gov. and Committee of the HBC, July 6, 1828, in J. McLoughlin, *Letters of McLoughlin from Fort Vancouver,* 1st ser., 47.

58. McLoughlin to Gov. and Committee of the HBC, Aug. 7, 1828, in J. McLoughlin, *Letters of McLoughlin from Fort Vancouver,* 1st ser., 65.

59. Frank Ermatinger, "Notes connected with the Clallum Expedition," June 17, 1828, in Dye, "Earliest Expedition," 29l; Morrison, *Outpost,* 176–78.

60. Merk, introduction to G. Simpson, *Fur Trade and Empire,* xxxiii.

61. McLoughlin to The Governor, Deputy Govt. & Committee, Aug. 10, 1828, in J. McLoughlin, *Letters of McLoughlin from Fort Vancouver,* 1st ser., 68–70.

62. McLoughlin to George Simpson, March 1830, in J. McLoughlin, *Letters of McLoughlin, Written at Fort Vancouver,* 85; Morrison, *Outpost,* 179–80.

63. Morrison, *Outpost,* 180–82; Cleland, *This Reckless Breed of Men,* 113–15.

64. John McLoughlin to The deputy Govr and Committee Honbl Hudson's Bay Company, Aug. 5, 1829, in J. McLoughlin, *Letters of McLoughlin, Written at Fort Vancouver,* 5–6.

65. John McLoughlin to The Govr deputy Govr and Committee Honbl Hudson's Bay Company, Aug. 5, 1829, in J. McLoughlin, *Letters of McLoughlin, Written at Fort Vancouver,* 6.

66. Ruby and Brown, *Chinook Indians,* 181–83; Morrison, *Outpost,* 183–85.

67. John McLoughlin to The Govr, deputy Govr and Committee Honbl Hudson's Bay Company, Oct. 31, 1831, in J. McLoughlin, *Letters of McLoughlin from Fort Vancouver,* 1st ser., 232–33.

68. J. R. Gibson, *Otter Skins,* 64–68; John McLoughlin to Mr. Archibald McDonald, C. T. Fort Langley, March 22, 1829, in J. McLoughlin, *Letters of McLoughlin, Written at Fort Vancouver,* 9; Morrison, *Outpost,* 185.

69. J. R. Gibson, *Otter Skins,* 67–70; George Simpson to Governor and Committee, Aug. 10, 1832; Merk, in G. Simpson, *Fur Trade and Empire,* appendix.

70. Kirk, *Voyage around the World,* 347–48; Allan, "Journal of a Journey," 38–55.

71. George Foster Emmons, "Journal Kept While Attached to the Exploring Expedition on board the U.S.S. Peacock," vol. 3, March 1841–July 28, 1841, Yale Western Americana Collection, BRBML.

72. J. R. Gibson, *Farming the Frontier,* 38–46; Hussey, *Fort Vancouver,* 77–101; Pomeroy, *Pacific Slope,* 18–19.

73. Merk, introduction to G. Simpson, *Fur Trade and Empire,* xvii; Burley, *Servants of the Honorable Company,* vii, 38–41.

74. Swagerty and Wilson, "Faithful Service under Different Flags," 247–57; Ronda, *Astoria and Empire,* 208; Morrison, *Outpost,* 207.

75. Merk, introduction to G. Simpson, *Fur Trade and Empire,* xvi–xviii; see also

"Roster of Company Servants," 1833, appendix, in J. McLoughlin, *Letters of McLoughlin from Fort Vancouver*, 1st ser.; Podruchny, *Making the Voyageur World*, 150–59.

76. Ross, *Adventures of the First Settlers*, 190; Ross, *Fur Hunters*, 19.

77. Jennifer Brown, *Strangers in Blood*, 205.

78. Van Kirk, *"Many Tender Ties,"* 125–26; Wilkes, *Exploring Expedition*, 129.

79. Governor and Committee of the HBC to John McLoughlin, Aug. 19, 1840, J. McLoughlin, *Letters of McLoughlin from Fort Vancouver*, 2nd ser., 2, fn.1.

80. Merk, introduction to J. McLoughlin, *Fur Trade and Empire*, xix; J. McLoughlin, *Fur Trade and Empire*, 90; Governor and Committee to Governor Simpson, Feb. 23, 1826, in J. McLoughlin, *Fur Trade and Empire*, appendix, 267.

81. Ross, *Fur Hunters of the Far West*, 190–91.

82. Van Kirk, *Many Tender Ties*, 130.

83. Ermatinger, *Fur Trade Letters*, 173; William Tolmie, *Journals*, May 8, 1832, HBC Collection, BRBML; B. M. White, "Woman Who Married a Beaver," 109–47.

84. Ross, *Fur Hunters*, 209, 228–31.

85. R. C. Johnson, *John McLoughlin*, 51.

86. G. Simpson, *Fur Trade and Empire*, 131.

87. Van Kirk, *"Many Tender Ties,"* 128–29; Podruchny, *Making the Voyageur World*, 53–59, 169–80.

88. Holman, *Dr. John McLoughlin*, 33; Simpson, 1824, quoted in Pomeroy, *Pacific Slope*, 20.

89. Ronda, *Astoria and Empire*, 64; Rich, *Hudson's Bay Company*, 608–9.

90. John McLoughlin to His Excellency the Governor of the Russian Fur Compys Establishment, March 20, 1829, in J. McLoughlin, *Letters of McLoughlin, Written at Fort Vancouver*, 16.

91. John McLoughlin to His Excellency the Governor of the Russian Fur Compys Establishment, March 20, 1829, in J. McLoughlin, *Letters of McLoughlin, Written at Fort Vancouver*, 16; Captain Simpson's Report to John McLoughlin of Voyage to Nass, Sept. 23, 1830, in J. McLoughlin, *Letters of McLoughlin from Fort Vancouver*, 1st ser., 305–13.

92. John McLoughlin to Gov. and Committee of the HBC, May 28, 1834, in J. McLoughlin, *Letters of McLoughlin from Fort Vancouver*, 1st ser., 118–21; John McLoughlin to Gov. and Committee, Nov. 15, 1836, in J. McLoughlin, *Letters of McLoughlin from Fort Vancouver*, 1st ser., 163–64; Morrison, *Outpost*, 212–19.

93. James Douglas to Gov. and Committee, Oct. 14, 1839, in J. McLoughlin, *Letters of McLoughlin from Fort Vancouver*, 2nd ser., 205–25; John McLoughlin to Gov. and Committee, Oct. 24, 1839, in J. McLoughlin, *Letters of McLoughlin from Fort Vancouver*, 2nd ser., 3–5; Morrison, *Outpost*, 289–98.

94. H. Foster, "Killing Mr. John," 148–51; John McLoughlin to George Simpson, March 20, 1840, J. McLoughlin, *Letters of McLoughlin from Fort Vancouver*, 2nd ser., 245–51; Morrison, *Outpost*, 302–3.

95. Rich, introduction to J. McLoughlin, *Letters of McLoughlin from Fort Vancouver*, 3rd ser., xviii–xix.

96. Rich, introduction to J. McLoughlin, *Letters of McLoughlin from Fort Vancouver*, 2nd ser., xi–xvii; Morrison, *Outpost*, 320–22.

97. Ross, *Fur Hunters*, 196–97.

98. Van Kirk, "What If Mama Is an Indian?" 208–12.

99. Jennifer Brown, *Strangers in Blood*, 154–55; Hargrave, *Letters of Letitia Hargrave*, 84.

100. Simon Fraser to John McLoughlin Jr., Jan. 12, 1836, in B. B. Barker, *McLoughlin Empire*, 218–19.

101. Governor George Simpson to Simon Fraser, March 14, 1828, in B. B. Barker, *McLoughlin Empire*, 186–87.

102. Dr. Simon Fraser to John McLoughlin, April 20, 1827, in B. B. Barker, *McLoughlin Empire*, 183.

103. Fraser to McLoughlin, April 20, 1827, in B. B. Barker, *McLoughlin Empire*; Morrison, *Outpost*, 223–24; Jennifer Brown, *Strangers in Blood*, 191.

104. John McLoughlin Jr. to Dr. Simon Fraser, Paris, Oct. 26, 1831, in B. B. Barker, *McLoughlin Empire*, 191–92; John McLoughlin Jr. to Dr. Simon Fraser, Paris, Feb. 24, 1833, B. B. Barker, *McLoughlin Empire*, 197–98.

105. H. Foster, "Killing Mr. John," 155; Morrison, *Outpost*, 226–27.

106. John McLoughlin to Simon Fraser, Feb. 8, 1837, in B. B. Barker, *McLoughlin Empire*, 235.

107. Simon Fraser to John McLoughlin Jr., Jan. 12, 1836, in B. B. Barker, *McLoughlin Empire*, appendix, 219.

108. John McLoughlin Jr. to John Fraser, Oct. 11, 1836, in B. B. Barker, *McLoughlin Empire*, appendix, 230.

109. Arthur, "General Dickson," 151–62; Jennifer Brown, *Strangers in Blood*, 190–91; Nute, "John McLoughlin Jr.," 444–47.

110. George Simpson quoted in Arthur, "General Dickson," 155.

111. John Fraser to Dr. John McLoughlin, April 13, 1837, in B. B. Barker, *McLoughlin Empire*, appendix, 236–37; Arthur, "General Dickson," 162; Jennifer Brown, *Strangers in Blood*, 191–92; St. Henry to John McLoughlin, quoted in Morrison, *Outpost*, 282.

112. John McLouglin to John Fraser, Oct. 24, 1840, in B. B. Barker, *McLoughlin Empire*, 246.

113. Boag, *Environment and Experience*, 41.

114. John McLoughlin to Sir John Pelly, July 12, 1846, in J. McLoughlin, *Letters of McLoughlin from Fort Vancouver*, 3rd ser., xxx.

115. Simpson quoted in J. McLoughlin, *Letters of McLoughlin from Fort Vancouver*, 3rd ser., xxx.

116. John McLoughlin to Gov. and Committee, Nov. 20, 1840, in J. McLoughlin, *Letters of McLoughlin from Fort Vancouver*, 2nd ser., 14, 18; Morrison, *Outpost*, 244–47; Jeffrey, *Converting the West*, 86–94.

117. Rich, in J. McLoughlin, *Letters of McLoughlin from Fort Vancouver*, 3rd ser., xxxiii.

118. John McLoughlin to Gov. and Committee, Nov. 15, 1843, in J. McLoughlin, *Letters of McLoughlin from Fort Vancouver*, 2nd ser., 113–18; Rich, introduction to J. McLoughlin, *Letters of McLoughlin from Fort Vancouver*, 3rd ser., xxxiv.

119. Boag, *Environment and Experience*, 41–42.

120. Morrison, *Outpost*, 387–88; John McLoughlin to Gov. and Committee, Nov. 15, 1843, in J. McLoughlin, *Letters of McLoughlin from Fort Vancouver*, 2nd ser., 147–48.

121. Rich, introduction to J. McLoughlin, *Letters of McLoughlin from Fort Vancouver*, 3rd ser., xvi–xvii; McLoughlin to Angus McDonald, Vancouver, Nov. 12, 1841, HBC Collection, Bancroft Library (hereafter BL).

122. G. Simpson, *Narrative of a Journey*, 1:390–97; Galbraith, *Hudson's Bay Company*, 205–8.

123. Simpson to McLoughlin, March 1, 1842 in J. McLoughlin, *Letters of McLoughlin from Fort Vancouver*, 3rd ser., xxvii.

124. Rich, introduction to J. McLoughlin, *Letters of McLoughlin from Fort Vancouver*, 3rd ser., xxiv–xxv.

125. George Simpson to John McLoughlin, Sitka, April 27, 1842, quoted in G. Simpson, *Narrative of a Journey*, 2:181.

126. McLoughlin, "John McLoughlin's Last Letter," 105–6; H. Foster, "Killing Mr. John," 59–60.

127. Morrison, *Outpost*, 343; "John McLoughlin to Dr. Tolmie," Vancouver, Nov. 25, 1843, HBC Collection, BRBML.

128. David McLoughlin to John Fraser, April 7, 1842, in B. B. Barker, *McLoughlin Empire*, 247.

129. Klein, "Demystifying the Opposition," 101–14; H. Foster, "Killing Mr. John," 161–66; John McLoughlin to John Fraser, April 12, 1843, in B. B. Barker, *McLoughlin Empire*, 249–50.

130. McLoughlin to Governor and Committee, Nov. 20, 1844, in J. McLoughlin, *Letters of McLoughlin from Fort Vancouver*, 3rd ser., 13–58.

131. J. McLoughlin, *Letters of McLoughlin from Fort Vancouver*, 3rd ser., 8–77; Ditz, "Shipwrecked," 55–58; Morrison, *Outpost*, 349.

132. Rich, introduction to J. McLoughlin, *Letters of McLoughlin from Fort Vancouver*, 3rd. ser., xxvii–xxvii; McLoughlin to Governor and Committee, July 19, 1845, in J. McLoughlin, *Letters of McLoughlin from Fort Vancouver*, 3rd. ser., 71–95; Morrison, *Outpost*, 408–11. Eloisa, quoted in John McLoughlin to Governor and Committee, in J. McLoughlin, *Letters of McLoughlin from Fort Vancouver*, 3rd. ser., July 19, 1845, 81.

133. Rich, introduction to J. McLoughlin, *Letters of McLoughlin from Fort Vancouver*, 3rd. ser., lii.

134. Rich, introduction to J. McLoughlin, *Letters of McLoughlin from Fort Vancouver*, 3rd ser., liv; McLoughlin to Peter Skene Ogden, Fort Vancouver, Jan. 12, 1846, HBC Collection, BRBML.

135. McLoughlin to Governor and Committee, Nov. 15, 1843, in J. McLoughlin,

Letters of McLoughlin from Fort Vancouver, 3rd ser., 103; Morrison, *Outpost*, 404–5; Nugent, *Habits of Empire*, 171–75.

136. Rich, introduction to J. McLoughlin, *Letters of McLoughlin from Fort Vancouver*, 3rd ser., lxi; Galbraith, *Hudson's Bay Company*, 211–15.

137. Morrison, *Outpost*, 478–81; Hale, *Bloodlines*.

138. Morrison, *Outpost*, 458–64.

139. John McLoughlin to Sec. of War William Marcy, Oct. 21, 1847, in J. McLoughlin, *John McLoughlin's Business Correspondence*, 69–70.

140. B. B. Barker, *McLoughlin Empire*, 127–28, 136.

3. THREE WESTERN PLACES

1. Halaas and Masich, *Halfbreed*, 1; Lavender, *Bent's Fort*, 347–49.

2. Hyslop, *Bound for Santa Fe*, 22–23; Swagerty, "History of the United States Plains Indians," 263; James Brooks, *Captives and Cousins*, 160–80.

3. James, *Account of an Expedition*, 2:239.

4. Moorhead, *New Mexico's Royal Road*, 29–54.

5. E. West, *Contested Plains*, 63.

6. Lavender, *Bent's Fort*, 19; Arnold, "William W. Bent," 6:62.

7. H. M. Chittenden, *American Fur Trade*, 1: 150; Arnold, "William W. Bent," 6:63–64; Dunham, "Charles Bent," 2:30–34.

8. Lavender, *Bent's Fort*, 99–112; Weber, *Taos Trappers*, 188–89.

9. Lavender, *Bent's Fort*, 128–29; Halaas and Masich, *Halfbreed*, 17–18.

10. G. E. Hyde, *Life of George Bent*, 58–60; Lavender, *Bent's Fort*, 138–42; Comer, *Ritual Ground*, 92–93; Arnold, "William W. Bent," 68–69.

11. Frank, *From Settler to Citizen*, 3–17; C. Montgomery, *Spanish Redemption*, 31–35.

12. Weber, *Mexican Frontier*, 10–12; Moorhead, *Royal Road*, 40–45.

13. Weber, *Mexican Frontier*, 11–12; Frank, *From Settler to Citizen*, 13–21.

14. Weber, *Mexican Frontier*, 12–14; Dary, *Santa Fe Trail*, 67–68; Cleland, *Reckless Breed of Men*, 126.

15. William Becknell, "Journals," 62.

16. Weber, *Mexican Frontier*, 12–14; Dary, *Santa Fe Trail*, 69–73.

17. Comer, *Ritual Ground*, 12.

18. Moore, *Bent's Old Fort*, 13–16; Lavender, *Bent's Fort*, 136–39; Hafen, "When Was Bent's Fort Built?" 117–19.

19. Comer, *Ritual Ground*, 14; Arnold, "William W. Bent," 71.

20. Dunham, "Charles Bent," 42; *Missouri Republican*, June 12, 1840, 3.

21. Powell, *People of the Sacred Mountain*, vol. 1; Schlieser, *Wolves of Heaven*; E. West, *Contested Plains*, 75.

22. E. West, *Contested Plains*, 76–78; Halaas and Masich, *Halfbreed*, 15–17.

23. Halaas and Masich, *Halfbreed*, 15.

24. Halaas and Masich, *Halfbreed*, 15; Powell, *People of the Sacred Mountain*, 1:245–46.

25. Halaas and Masich, *Halfbreed*, 13–18.

26. Powell, *People of the Sacred Mountain*, 1:13.

27. Comer, *Ritual Ground*, 28.

28. Comer, *Ritual Ground*, 13–14.

29. Lavender, *Bent's Fort*, 171–74; Halaas and Masich, *Halfbreed*, 21–23.

30. Lavender, *Bent's Fort*, 186–87; G. E. Hyde, *Life of George Bent*, 71–72; Halaas and Masich, *Halfbreed*, 39.

31. G. E. Hyde, *Life of George Bent*, 84.

32. LeCompte, *Pueblo, Hardscrabble, Greenhorn*, 23.

33. Moore, *Bent's Old Fort*, 70–81; Hyslop, *Bound for Santa Fe*, 192–93.

34. Garrard, *Wah-to-Yah*, 92–93.

35. Abert, *Expedition to the Southwest*, 10.

36. Farnham, *Travels in the Great Western Prairies*, 28:171.

37. Garrard, *Wah-to-Yah*, 92, 129.

38. G. E. Hyde, *Life of George Bent*, 84.

39. Hämäläinen, "Western Comanche Trade Center," 487–89.

40. M. W. Foster, *Being Comanche*, 41–47; Hämäläinen, *Comanche Empire*, 142; Gelo, "Comanche Land," 275–78.

41. Fehrenbacher, *Comanches*, 278–82.

42. Grinnell, *Fighting Cheyennes*, 58–62; Hämäläinen, *Comanche Empire*, 164–65; Comer, *Ritual Ground*, 124; Farnham, *Travels*, 28:174; Hämäläinen, "Western Comanche," 503.

43. Grinnell, *Fighting Cheyennes*, 61–66; Halaas and Masich, *Halfbreed*, 34–36; Bent quoted in LeCompte, "Bent, St. Vrain and Company," 275.

44. Emparán, *Vallejos of California*, 210.

45. *Californio/a* is a term that is much debated, but I'm intending it to mean Europeans, Americans, or Mexicans who came to California or who were born there before 1848, and who made that place their primary residence and part of their claimed identity.

46. Hurtado, *Indian Survival*, 31–35; Lightfoot, *Indians, Missionaries, and Merchants*.

47. Milliken, *Time of Little Choice*, 255–56; Hurtado, *Indian Survival*, 18–21.

48. Milliken, *Time of Little Choice*, 210; Speech given by M. G. Vallejo, 1876, quoted in William Heath Davis, *Seventy-Five Years in California*, 366.

49. J. R. Gibson, *Imperial Russia*, 10–12; D. L. Morgan, *Jedediah Smith*, 201–7.

50. Hackel, "Land, Labor and Production," 129.

51. Rosenus, *General M. G. Vallejo*, 6; Hackel, "Land, Labor and Production," 129.

52. M. J. Gonzalez, "Child of the Wilderness" 37–39.

53. McKittrick, *Vallejo*, 12–15; Bancroft, *History of California*, 3:112–13.

54. McKittrick, *Vallejo*, 57–58.

55. Weber, *Mexican Frontier*, 61–67.

56. G. H. Phillips, *Indians and Intruders*, 63–64; Hackel, *Children of Coyote*, 375–83; R. H. Jackson and Castillo, *Indians, Franciscans, and Spanish Colonization*; Monroy, *Thrown among Strangers*, 18–29.

57. McKittrick, *Vallejo*, 57–58; Weber, *Mexican Frontier*, 67–68.

58. Mariano Guadalupe Vallejo, *Report of a Visit to Fort Ross*, 6–9; Lightfoot, *Indians, Missionaries, and Merchants*, 156–57.

59. "Isadora Filomena," in Beebe and Senkewicz, *Testimonios*, 11–12; McKittrick, *Vallejo*, 55–57.

60. McKittrick, *Vallejo*, 60–61; Bancroft, *History of California*, 3:360.

61. S. F. Cook, "Epidemic of 1830–1833," 303–25; G. H. Phillips, *Indians and Intruders*, 94–97.

62. Emparán, *Vallejos of California*, 186–214; McKittrick, *Vallejo*, 81.

63. M. G. Vallejo, *Historia de California*, vol. 1, trans. Earl Hewitt, CD18, Vallejo Collections, BL.

64. William Heath Davis, *Seventy-Five Years in California*, 136.

65. McKittrick, *Vallejo*, 91–92, 175–77.

66. Hurtado, *Intimate Frontiers*, 21–30; McKittrick, *Vallejo*, 83–84; José Jesús Vallejo, quoted in Bancroft, "Vallejo Memoirs," *History of California*, 3:360.

67. Salvador Vallejo, "Notas historicas sobre California," 1874, CD22, Vallejo Collections, BL.

68. Hurtado, *Indian Survival*, 45–47; Lightfoot, *Indians, Missionaries, and Merchants*, 123–25; William Heath Davis, *Seventy-Five Years in California*, 139.

69. Weber, *Mexican Frontier*, 242–43.

70. Weber, *Mexican Frontier*, 253–56; Bancroft, *History of California*, 3:447–76; McKittrick, *Vallejo*, 102–5.

71. Weber, *Mexican Frontier*, 258–60; Bancroft, *History of California*, 3:476–77.

72. J. R. Gibson, *Imperial Russia*, 118–21, 133–39; G. Simpson, *Narrative of a Journey*, 269–70.

73. Mariano Vallejo to Juan Bautista Alvarado, July 2, 1841, in Vallejo, *Historia De California*, 10:227, Vallejo Collections, BL.

74. Bancroft, *History of California*, 4:172–77; M. G. Vallejo to Minister of War, Jan. 1, 1841, and Jan. 28, 1841, in Vallejo, *Historia de California*, 2:311, Vallejo Collections, BL.

75. Rosenus, *General M. G. Vallejo*, 23–25; Bancroft, *History of California*, 4:177–78.

76. McKittrick, *Vallejo*, 189–90; Bancroft, *History of California*, 4:179–81; Hurtado, *John Sutter*, 95–98.

77. Bancroft, *History of California*, 4:181; Engstrand, "John Sutter," 81–88; Hurtado, *John Sutter*, xiii, xiv.

78. Hurtado, *John Sutter*, 6–31.

79. John Augustus Sutter, "Reminiscences" (typescript), 24, BL.

80. "Statement of Johann August Sutter" (1856), *San Francisco Argonaut*, Jan. 26, 1878, rpt. in "General Sutter's Diary," in Owens, *John Sutter and a Wider West*, 3–4; Lamar, "John Augustus Sutter," 30–34.

81. Sutter, "Statement," 4.

82. Dillon, *Fools Gold*, 75–77; Hurtado, *John Sutter*, 54–56.

83. Hurtado, *John Sutter,* 59–62; William Heath Davis, *Seventy-Five Years in California,* 19.

84. Gudde, *Sutter's Own Story,* 66.

85. Hurtado, "John Sutter and the Indian Business," 57–61; Sutter, "Statement," 5–6.

86. Hurtado, "John Sutter and the Indian Business," 57–60.

87. Wilbur, *Pioneer at Sutter's Fort,* 68.

88. William Joseph quoted in Hurtado, *John Sutter,* 80; Gudde, *Sutter's Own Story,* 67.

89. Hurtado, *John Sutter,* 114–66; Wilbur, *Pioneer at Sutter's Fort,* 75–76.

90. Hurtado, "John Sutter and the Indian Business," 58–60; M. G. Vallejo, Comandante General to the Governor, Sonoma, Nov. 17, 1841, *Vallejo Documentos,* 10:258, Vallejo Collections, BL.

91. Hurtado, *Indian Survival,* 44–46; G. H. Phillips, *Indians and Intruders,* 75–81.

92. Baron de Mofras quoted in G. H. Phillips, *Indians and Intruders,* 115.

93. Hurtado, *John Sutter,* 68–70, 76–77.

94. Rosenus, *General M. G. Vallejo,* 31–38.

95. Gillis and Magliari, *John Bidwell and California,* 73–75.

96. Gudde, *Sutter's Own Story,* 83–84; Hurtado, *John Sutter,* 92–93.

97. Bancroft, *History of California,* 4:188–89, 228–29; Hurtado, *John Sutter,* 96–98.

98. McKittrick, *Vallejo,* 197–199; Monroy, "Creation and Re-creation of Californio Society," 185–190.

99. McKittrick, *Vallejo,* 193; G. Simpson, *Narrative of a Journey,* 1:296–305; Bancroft, *History of California,* 4:211–16.

100. Emparán, *Vallejos of California,* 195–207.

101. McKittrick, *Vallejo,* 172–73; LDS Genealogy Website, *Vallejo Ancestral File,* accessed Sept. 18, 2007.

102. William Heath Davis, *Seventy-Five Years in California,* 64; Emparán, *Vallejos of California,* 201–2; Bancroft, *History of California,* 4:218.

103. McKittrick, *Vallejo,* 205; William Heath Davis, *Seventy-Five Years in California,* 65.

104. Emparán, *Vallejos of California,* 202; G. Simpson, *Narrative of a Journey,* 1:310–11.

105. G. Simpson, *Narrative of a Journey,* 1:314; Bancroft, *History of California,* 4:218.

106. G. Simpson, *Narrative of a Journey,* 1:309.

107. G. Simpson, *Narrative of a Journey,* 1:317.

108. G. Simpson, *Narrative of a Journey,* 1:320–23.

109. Bancroft, *History of California,* 4:220n.

110. G. Simpson, *Narrative of a Journey,* 1:327.

111. Bancroft, *History of California,* 4:285–88; Weber, *Mexican Frontier,* 269–70; M. G. Vallejo to Salvador Vallejo, quoted in Emparán, *Vallejos of California,* 148.

112. Brooke, "Vest Pocket War," 217–19; Harlow, *California Conquered,* 7–9.

113. Nugent, *Habits of Empire,* 187–89; Brooke, "Vest Pocket War," 219–21; Haynes, "Anglophobia," 121.

114. Brooke, "Vest Pocket War," 222–23.

115. Brooke, "Vest Pocket War," 224–28; Harlow, *California Conquered,* 6–7.

116. Brooke, "Vest Pocket War," 229; Bancroft, *History of California,* 4:302–9.

117. Bancroft, *History of California,* 4:328; Brooke, "Vest Pocket War," 229–31; T. C. Jones to Sec. of Navy Abel Upshur, "Jones at Monterey," Report, Oct. 24, 1842, House Exec. Doc., 27th Cong., 3rd sess., no. 166, pp. 69–73.

118. Brooke, "Vest Pocket War," 232; T. C. Jones to Upshur, "Jones at Monterey," 71.

119. McKittrick, *Vallejo,* 219–20; Bancroft, *History of California,* 4:314.

120. McKittrick, *Vallejo,* 221; Bancroft, *History of California,* 4:315–16.

121. Moses Austin to Stephen Austin, Dec. 16, 1804, in Austin and Austin, *Austin Papers,* 1:93.

122. Cantrell, *Stephen F. Austin,* 26–30.

123. Gracy, *Moses Austin,* 120–139; Stephen Austin to Moses Austin, New Orleans, July 12, 1812, in Austin and Austin, *Austin Papers,* 2:216.

124. Cantrell, *Stephen F. Austin,* 50–62, 63–68.

125. Weber, *Spanish Frontier,* 298–300; Chipman, *Spanish Texas,* 163–66; Nugent, *Habits of Empire,* 132–36.

126. Reséndez, *Changing National Identities,* 60–61; Chipman, *Spanish Texas,* 222–25.

127. Carlson, *Seduced by the West,* 58–70, 149–55; Melton, *Aaron Burr,* 84–90, 150–66; Lomask, *Aaron Burr,* 2: 118–44.

128. Van Young, *Other Rebellion,* 1–2; Owsley and Smith, *Filibusters and Expansionists,* 40–42.

129. Owsley and Smith, *Filibusters and Expansionists,* 50–56; Weber, *Mexican Frontier,* 10; Warren, *Sword Was Their Passport,* 3–8, 22–24.

130. Owsley and Smith, *Filibusters and Expansionists,* 56–59; Warren, *Sword Was Their Passport,* 63–70.

131. Moses Austin, quoted in Hatcher, *Opening of Texas,* appendix no. 33; Gracey, *Moses Austin,* 178–81; Cantrell, *Stephen F. Austin,* 76–80.

132. Gracey, *Moses Austin,* 200–215.

133. Maria Austin to Stephen Austin, Hazel Run, MO, June 8, 1821, Austin and Austin, *Austin Papers,* 2:395.

134. Seguin, *Revolution Remembered,* 6–23.

135. Hatcher, *Opening of Texas,* 79–91, 114–24; Everett, *Texas Cherokee,* 13–19.

136. De la Teja, *San Antonio de Béxar,* 24, 31–44, 100; O. L. Jones, *Los Paisanos,* xi–xii.

137. Barr, *Peace Came,* 3–5; G. C. Anderson, *Conquest of Texas,* 20–24.

138. Anderson, *Conquest of Texas,* 25–32.

139. Cantrell, *Stephen F. Austin,* 93.

140. Stephen Austin to J. E. B. Austin, March 23, 1822, Austin and Austin, *Austin Papers*, 1:487.

141. Henry Austin to Mary Austin Holley, quoted in Holley, *Letters*, 38.

142. J. E. B. Austin to Maria Austin, Oct. 1824, in Austin and Austin, *Austin Papers*, vol. 1.

143. Himmel, *Conquest of the Karankawas*, 14–22, 26–32; Barr, *Peace Came*, 130–36.

144. G. C. Anderson, *Conquest of Texas*, 42–48.

145. Maria Austin to Stephen Austin, Jan. 22, 1822, Austin and Austin, *Austin Papers*, 2:468; Stephen Austin to James E. B. Austin, Loredo, March 23, 1822, Austin and Austin, *Austin Papers*, 2:487–88.

146. Weber, *Mexican Frontier*, 23–26; Anna, *Forging Mexico*, 14–17; Calvert, De Leon, and Cantrell, *History of Texas*, 56–60.

147. Stephen Austin to J. E. B. Austin, May 10, 1823, Austin and Austin, *Austin Papers*, 1:638; Cantrell, *Stephen F. Austin*, 115–20; Stephen Austin to J. E. B. Austin, Dec. 25, 1823, Austin and Austin, *Austin Papers*, 1:560–61.

148. Cantrell, *Stephen F. Austin*, 126–35; Arthur G. Wavell to Stephen Austin, Jan. 23, 1823, Austin and Austin, *Austin Papers*, 2:572–74.

149. J. E. B. Austin to J. H. Bell, March 16, 1823, Austin and Austin, *Austin Papers*, 2:589–90.

150. Tijerina, *Tejanos and Texas*, 35–38; "Voluntary Subscription, Nov. 22, 1823," in Austin and Austin, *Austin Papers*, 1:708–10.

151. James E. B. Austin to Stephen Austin, May 4, 1823, Austin and Austin, *Austin Papers*, 2:635–36.

152. Austin to Anatascio Bustamante, May 10, 1822, Austin and Austin, *Austin Papers*, 2:507–9; Stephen Austin to Josiah H. Bell, Aug. 6, 1823, Austin and Austin, *Austin Papers*, 2:682; Hatley, *Indian Wars*, 37–38.

153. Stephen Austin to Minister Lucas Alaman, Brassos River, Jan. 20, 1824, Austin and Austin, *Austin Papers*, 2:727.

154. Cantrell, *Stephen F. Austin*, 140–42; Hatley, *Indian Wars*, 46–48; Stephen Austin, Referendum on Indian Relations, Sept. 28, 1825, Austin and Austin, *Austin Papers*, 1:1208.

155. Himmel, *Conquest of the Karankawas*, 49–51.

156. Stephen Austin to Josiah H. Bell, Dec. 6, 1823, Austin and Austin, *Austin Papers*, 1:716–17.

157. Austin to the Colonists, Aug. 6, 1823, Austin and Austin, *Austin Papers*, 1:680.

158. Stephen Austin to Benjamin Edwards, Sept. 15, 1825, Austin and Austin, *Austin Papers*, 1:1203–4.

159. Reséndez, *Changing National Identities*, 40–44; *Handbook of Texas Online*, http://www.tshaonline.org/handbook/online/ (accessed July 23, 2010); William C. Davis, *Lone Star Rising*, 70–74.

160. Declaration of the Republic of Fredonia, Nacogdoches, Dec. 21, 1826, quoted in Reséndez, *Changing National Identities*, 44.

161. Cantrell, *Stephen F. Austin*, 183–85; Austin to Citizens of Victoria, Jan. 1827, Austin and Austin, *Austin Papers*, 1:1558.

162. Austin to Samuel Williams, Dec. 14, 1826, Austin and Austin, *Austin Papers*, 1:1532; William C. Davis, *Lone Star Rising*, 71–72.

163. Reséndez, *Changing National Identities*, 43–44; G. C. Anderson, *Conquest of Texas*, 62–63.

164. Cantrell, *Stephen F. Austin*, 171–73; Anna, *Forging Mexico*, x–xii.

165. Tijerina, *Tejanos and Texas*, 110–13; Cantrell, *Stephen F. Austin*, 192–94, 206–7; Anna, *Forging Mexico*, 171–72.

166. Cantrell, *Stephen F. Austin*, 219–21; John C. Ewers, in Berlandier, *Indians of Texas*, 14–18.

167. Weber, *Mexican Frontier*, 170–72; Tijerina, *Tejanos and Texas*, 126–29.

168. Stephen Austin to Emily Perry, Feb. 1830, Austin and Austin, *Austin Papers*, vol. 1; Mary Austin Holley to Stephen Austin, Jan. 1831, Holley, *Letters*, 38–39.

169. Holley, *Letters*, 43–45; Holley, *Texas*, 1, 27.

170. "Communication from San Felipe de Austin" to the Governor at Saltillo, July 27, 1832, in Holley, *Letters*, appendix.

171. Cantrell, *Stephen F. Austin*, 264–79; Austin and Austin, *Austin Papers*, vol. 2; Reséndez, *Changing National Identities*, 146–58.

172. E. C. Barker, *Life of Stephen Austin*, 89.

4. The Early West

1. Feldman, *When the Mississippi Ran Backward*, 14–16.

2. Stephen Austin Diary, May 1812, in Austin and Austin, *Austin Papers*, 2:207.

3. Hunter, *Memoirs of a Captivity*, 28.

4. Letter from John Sibley to Major Amos Stoddard, April 2, 1812, Sibley Papers, Box 1, MHS.

5. Edmunds, *Shawnee Prophet*; Sugden, *Tecumseh*, 250–51.

6. R. White, *Middle Ground*; DuVal, *Native Ground*; Blackhawk, *Violence over the Land*.

7. *Monthly Notices of the Royal Astronomical Society* 218 (July 1842); "History of the Cincinnati Observatory," http://www.cincinnatiobservatory.org/history.html (accessed July 26, 2010).

8. Shoemaker, *Strange Likeness*, 6–8, 90–103.

9. Taylor, *Divided Ground*, 7–9; Adelman and Aron, "From Borderlands to Borders," 814–41.

10. George Sibley, Fort Osage, to Samuel Sibley, Natchitoches LA, Aug. 20, 1815–July 26, 1816, Box 1, Sibley Collection, MHS; F. L. Lee, J. E. H. Lee, and Cormack, "Fort Osage,", 249.

11. Hoig, *Cherokees and Their Chiefs*, 106–9; Wilms, "Cherokee Land Use," 6–8; Green, " Expansion of European Colonization,", 506–11.

12. Early, "John Jolly"; W. G. McLoughlin, *Cherokee Renascence*, 128–36, 152–55.

13. Hoig, *Cherokees and Their Chiefs*, 135–37.

14. Early, "John Jolly"; W. G. McLoughlin, *Renascence*, 239–40; John C. Calhoun to Joseph McMinn, July 29, 1818, in U.S. Congress, *American State Papers*, class II, 479.

15. Nelson, *Man of Distinction*, 149–60; Banner, *How the Indians Lost*, 112–14; Sugden, *Tecumseh*, 29–51; Dowd, *Spirited Resistance*, 131–46.

16. Edmunds, *Tecumseh and the Quest*, 55–63; Sugden, *Tecumseh*, 18–23; Calloway, *Shawnees and the War*, 126–43.

17. Zenon Trudeau to Louis Lorimier, May 1, 1793, in Faragher, "More Motley Than Mackinaw," 306–8.

18. Faragher, "More Motley Than Mackinaw," 307–11; Sugden, *Tecumseh*, 52–55.

19. Horsman, *Expansion and American Indian Policy*, 108–15, 144–50; Rogin, *Fathers and Children*, 3–11.

20. Faragher, "More Motley Than Mackinaw," 305.

21. Edmunds, *Shawnee Prophet*, 23–27.

22. Sugden, *Tecumseh*, 103–16; Dowd, *Spirited Resistance*, 196–214.

23. Heckewelder, *Account of the History*, 292–93; Sugden, *Tecumseh*, 125–39.

24. *Virginia (OH) Argus*, Sept. 6, 1806; Heckewelder, *Account of the History*, 277.

25. Heckewelder, *Narrative of the Mission*, 409, 416.

26. Edmunds, *Shawnee Prophet*, 42–54.

27. Thorne, *Many Hands*, 17–20; L. Y. Jones, *William Clark*, 151.

28. DuVal, *Native Ground*, 6–9, 164–69; L. Fowler, "Great Plains," vol. 1, pt. 2, 22–24; Calloway, *One Vast Winter Count*, 364–66.

29. Thorne, *Many Hands*, 98–106; Bailey, "Osage," 13:477–78; DuVal, *Native Ground*, 170–73; Kinnaird, *Spain in the Mississippi Valley*, 4:107.

30. George Sibley to Samuel Sibley, Oct. 26, 1806, Sibley Papers, Box 1, MHS.

31. George Sibley to Samuel Sibley, Nov. 1806, Sibley Papers, Box 1, MHS.

32. Jefferson, *Account of Louisiana*, 3, 23–29.

33. Erickson, Skinner, and Merchant, *Discoveries Made*, 27–29; Tregle, "John Sibley."

34. Prucha, *American Indian Policy*, 28–31; Banner, *How the Indians Lost Their Land*, 4–7.

35. Prucha, *American Indian Policy*, 48–49; 53–55; A. F. C. Wallace, *Jefferson and the Indians*, 166–69; George Washington, Annual Message 1791, 1792, in Richardson, *Compilation of the Messages*, vol. 1.

36. Heckewelder, *Account of the History*, 335.

37. Prucha, *American Indian Policy*, 60–63; Sheehan, *Seeds of Extinction*.

38. Report on the Committee on Indian Affairs, Dec. 1, 1794, in U.S. Congress, *American State Papers*, class II: *Indian Affairs*, 1:524; Peake, *Indian Factory System*, 3–6.

39. DuVal, "Indian Intermarriage and Métissage," 301–4.

40. Thomas L. McKenney, Georgetown, to Isaac Rawling, Dec. 21, 1816, American Indian Manuscripts, Box 2, HL.

41. Prucha, *American Indian Policy*, 57; Viola, *Thomas L. McKenney*, 6–10.

42. George Sibley to Samuel Sibley, Oct. 26, 1806, Sibley Papers, MHS.

43. Thomas Jefferson, Aug. 1808, "Territorial Papers," in Steffens, *William Clark*, 56.

44. Rollings, *Osage*, 216–17; *Compilation of All Treaties*; Gregg, "History of Fort Osage," 441–43; Sibley, quoted in E. James, *Account of an Expedition*, 1:276.

45. Rollings, *Osage*, 10–13, 215–23.

46. Foley and Rice, "Mandan Chief," 2–7.

47. Foley and Rice, "Mandan Chief," 6–11; Pierre Chouteau to William Clark, Nov. 18, 1807, Pierre Chouteau Letterbook, MHS; Pierre Chouteau to William Eustis, Dec. 14, 1809, Pierre Chouteau Letterbook, MHS.

48. Pierre Chouteau to William Eustis, Dec. 14, 1809, Jan. 10, 1810, Pierre Chouteau Letterbook, MHS.

49. George Sibley, Oct. 10 and 16, 1808, *Manuscript Diary*, 1808–1811, MHS.

50. Mathews, *Osages*, 394–95; Peake, *Indian Factory System*, 35–51; Viola, *Thomas L. McKenney*, 12–14; Thomas McKenney to George Sibley, July 1817, Sibley Papers, MHS.

51. George Sibley to Samuel Sibley, Feb. 12, 1811, Sibley Papers, MHS.

52. George Sibley to Samuel Sibley, Sept. 13, 1813, Sibley Papers, MHS.

53. Rollings, *Osage*, 230–31; Peters, *Women of the Earth Lodges*, 155–58; George Sibley, Diary, Jan. 9, 1811, MHS.

54. George Sibley to General William Clark, July 22, 1811, Sibley Papers, MHS; Manuscript, "Notes of an Official Excursion from Fort Osage to the Kansees, Pawnees, and Osages in May, June, July of 1811," Aug. 18, 1811, Sibley Papers, MHS.

55. George Sibley to William Clark, July 9, 1813, Sibley Papers, MHS; William Clark to George Sibley, March 17, 1812, Sibley Papers, MHS; Calloway, *Crown and Calumet*, 230–32; Binnema and Dobak, "'Like a Greedy Wolf,'" 415–16.

56. Steffens, *William Clark*, 21–26; L. Y. Jones, *William Clark*, 62–86.

57. Libby, "Thomas Forsyth Letters," 179.

58. Edmunds, *Shawnee Prophet*, 80–83; Sugden, *Tecumseh*, 187–89.

59. *Missouri Gazette*, March 13, July 18, 1811; *Louisiana Gazette*, April 25, 1811, Dale Morgan Newspaper Collection, BRBML; William Clark to William Eustis, June 2, 1811, *William Clark Papers*, Box 8, 1811, MHS.

60. Sugden, *Tecumseh*, 226–36; Edmunds, *Shawnee Prophet*, 109–15; McAfee, *History of the Late War*, 22–36.

61. Sugden, *Tecumseh*, 259–63; Horseman, *War of 1812*, 33–41.

62. *National Intelligencer*, Aug. 6, 1812; Ninian Edwards to William Clark, Aug. 18, 1812, *Missouri Territorial Papers*, 14:595.

63. Thomas Forsyth, Peoria, to Gen. William Clark, St. Louis, Nov. 1, 1811, Thomas Forsyth Papers, Box 1, MHS.

64. *Louisiana Gazette*, March 21, 1812, Dale Morgan Newspaper Clippings, BRBML; L. Y. Jones, *William Clark*, 205–8.

65. George Sibley to General Clark, Oct. 12, 1812, Sibley Papers, Box 1, MHS.

66. Governor Benjamin Howard to Pierre Chouteau, April 1813, *Missouri Territorial Papers*, 14:674–75.

67. George Sibley to Samuel H. Sibley, Sept. 13, 1813, Sibley Papers, Box 1, MHS.

68. Peake, *Indian Factory System*, 158–63; *Missouri Gazette*, March 21, 1812, Dale Morgan Clippings, BRBML; L. Y. Jones, *William Clark*, 199–218.

69. Steffens, *William Clark*, 89–94; George Sibley to William Clark, March 17, 1814, William Clark Papers, MHS.

70. Henry Goulburn to Lord Bathurst, Nov. 25, 1814, in A. W. Wellington, *Supplementary Despatches*, 9:452–54.

71. Sugden, *Tecumseh*, 208–9; C. M. Gates, "West in American Diplomacy," 499–510; Latimer, *1812*, 389–402.

72. Steffens, *William Clark*, 97–99; "Treaties with Twenty-One Tribes," U.S. Congress, *American State Papers*, class II: Indian Affairs, 5:1–25; Binnema and Dobak, "'Like the Greedy Wolf,'" 421.

73. "Treaties with Twenty-One Tribes," U.S. Congress, *American State Papers*, ser. 2, Indian Affairs, 5:11–12.

74. Viola, *Thomas L. McKenney*, 9–11; George Sibley to Samuel H. Sibley, Aug. 20, 1815, Sibley Papers, Box 1, MHS; F. L. Lee, J. E. H. Lee, and Cormack, "Fort Osage," 249.

75. George Sibley, "Commonplace Book," Jan. 1820–Jan. 1823, Sibley Papers, MHS; Gregg, "History of Fort Osage," 465–72.

76. Ninian Edwards, August Chouteau to William H. Crawford, Sec. of War, Nov. 1815, U.S. Congress, *American State Papers*, class II: Indian Affairs, 5:66–67; William Clark to William H. Crawford, Sec. of War, Oct. 1, 1815, U.S. Congress, *American State Papers*, class II: Indian Affairs, 5:77–78.

77. Edmunds, *Shawnee Prophet*, 148–63.

78. Faragher, "More Motley Than Mackinaw," 316; William Clark to John C. Calhoun, Oct. 1817, U.S. Congress, *American State Papers*, class II: Indian Affairs, 5:179.

79. Howard, *Shawnee*, 17–20; Faragher, "More Motley Than Mackinaw," 316–17; Alford, *Shawnee Domestic and Tribal Life*, 64.

80. Benjamin O'Fallon to William Clark, May 9, 1825, Benjamin O'Fallon Letterbook, BRBML.

81. L. Fowler, " Great Plains," 22–27; George Sibley to William Clark, Jan. 11, 1817, Sibley Papers, Box 1, MHS.

82. Hoig, *Tribal Wars*, 119–22; A. M. Gibson and Bearss, *Fort Smith*, 21–24.

83. William Clark to George Sibley, April 14, 1817, Sibley Papers, Box 1, MHS; William Clark to John C. Calhoun. Oct. 1818. U.S. Congress, *American State Papers*, class II: Indian Affairs, 5:179; Foreman, *Indians and Pioneers*, 74–78; William Clark to John O'Fallon, Nov. 5, 1818, John O'Fallon Collection, MHS.

84. Thomas Biddle to Col. H. Atkinson, Oct. 29, 1819, U.S. Congress, *American State Papers*, class II: Indian Affairs, 5:201–3; Committee on Indian Affairs to the Senate, April 5, 1820, *American State Papers*, 5:206; Thomas L. McKenney to the Senate, Jan. 14, 1822, *American State Papers*, 5:260–65; George C. Sibley to Thomas L. McKenney, April 16, 1819, *American State Papers*, 5:362.

85. Prucha, *American Indian Policy*, 57, 109–11; Viola, *Thomas L. McKenney*, 57, 109–11, 72–78; "Abolition of the Indian Trading Houses," House Doc., 196, March 1, 1823, U.S. Congress, *American State Papers*, class II: Indian Affairs, 5:417–27.

86. Prucha, *American Indian Policy*, 110–12; Unrau, *White Man's Wicked Water*, 21–24.

87. Brackenridge, *Journal of a Voyage*, in 6:129–30.

88. Denig, *Five Indian Tribes*, 51–62; Saum, *Fur Trader and the Indian*, 55–57.

89. *(Franklin) Missouri Intelligencer*, March 26, 1822; *(Little Rock) Arkansas Gazette*, *St. Louis Enquirer*, transcribed in Dale Morgan Newspaper Transcripts, BRBML; Binnema and Dobak, "'Like a Greedy Wolf,'" 424–25.

90. *Missouri Intelligencer*, July 1, 1823, in Morgan Transcripts, BRBML.

91. Ashley to Benjamin O'Fallon, June 4, 1823, in Morgan, *West of William H. Ashley*, 27.

92. *Missouri Intelligencer*, July 8, 29, 1823, in Morgan Transcripts, BRBML.

93. Benjamin O'Fallon to Ramsey Crooks, July 10, 1822, John O'Fallon Collection, MHS.

94. Nester, *Arikara War*, 90–96; *St. Louis Enquirer*, Feb. 9, 1824.

95. Morgan, *West of William H. Ashley*, 2–3; Nester, *Arikara War*, 96–98.

96. Benjamin O'Fallon to William Clark. June 24, 1823, in Morgan, *West of William H. Ashley*, 37; Nester, *Arikara War*, 152–59; Joshua Pilcher, "Testimony to Senate Committee on Indian Affairs," Feb. 18, 1824, U.S. Congress, *American State Papers*, class II: Indian Affairs, 5:453–54.

97. Leavenworth to O'Fallon, July 23, 1823, *Report of the Secretary of War*, 1824, John O'Fallon Collection, MHS.

98. Morgan, *West of William H. Ashley*, 43.

99. Nester, *Arikara War*, 169–74; Benjamin O'Fallon to William Ashley, June 20, 1823, Benjamin O'Fallon Letterbook, BRBML.

100. Nester, *Arikara War*, 179–81; Morgan, *West of William H. Ashley*, 55–58; Benjamin O'Fallon to General William Clark, Jan. 14, 1824, Benjamin O'Fallon Letterbook, BRBML; Pilcher to Leavenworth, rpt., Oct. 15, 1823, *Missouri Republican*.

101. *St. Louis Enquirer*, July 19, Aug. 20, 1824.

102. "List of Persons Killed and Property Lost," 1829, Sublette Family Papers, Box 1, Folder 2, MHS.

103. Annual Report on the Fur Trade, Thomas Forsyth to Lewis Cass, St. Louis, Oct. 24, 1831, Forsyth Papers, MHS.

104. Sibley, *Seeking a Newer World*, 39–40; Gregg, "History of Fort Osage," 481–83.

105. Peterson, "Many Roads to Red River, 38–41; DuVal, "Indian Intermarriage," 281–84.

106. Peterson, "Many Roads to Red River," 42–45; Edmunds, "Unacquainted with the Laws," 184–89; Lewis Cass to the Secretary of War, May 31, 1816, C. E. Carter, *Territorial Papers*, 10:643.

107. Jacqueline Peterson, "Prelude to Red River," 41–43; H. H. Tanner, "Glaize in 1792," 18–22.

108. Gilman, *Henry Hastings Sibley*, 74–76; Peterson, "Prelude to Red River," 42–46.

109. Peterson, "Prelude to Red River," 48–54; Edmunds, "Unacquainted with the Laws," 188–90.

110. Historic Forks of the Wabash, "The Miami Nation," http://www.historicforks .org/miami/index.html (accessed Feb. 12, 2008); DuVal, *Native Ground,*200–201; Rollings, *Osage*, 49–53.

111. Burns, *History of the Osage People*, 218–20; Gregg, " History of Fort Osage," 468–71; *Religious Intelligencer,* Boston, March 6, 1821; Margaret Jacobs, *White Mother to a Dark Race*, 26–31.

112. Burns, *History of the Osage People*, 221–23; Perdue, *"Mixed Blood" Indians*, 85–89; Gregg, "History of Fort Osage," 473–75.

113. Harriet Wooley, Sept. 12, 1822, BRBML, Letterbook, 1821–1832, Yale Western Americana Collection.

114. Harriet Wooley, Letter, June 13, 1822, BRBML.

115. Harriet Wooley, Letter, June 13, 1822, BRBML; "Journal of the Great Osage Mission," *American Missionary Register* (Philadelphia, 1825), 3:188.

116. "Introduction and Biography," Thomas Forsyth Papers, Box 1, Folder 1, MHS; Letter to William Clark, Supt. of Indian Affairs, Washington, Dec. 23, 1812, Forsyth Papers, Box 1, Folder 2. MHS.

117. Perdue, *"Mixed Blood" Indians*, 86–88.

118. John Tanner, *Narrative of the Captivity*, 248–49; Namias, *White Captives*, 76–79.

119. Thomas Forsyth, St. Louis to General William Clark, Washington, April 19, 1819, Forsyth Papers, MHS; John Tanner, *Narrative of the Captivity*, 279–83.

120. Namias, *White Captives*, 79; John Tanner, *Narrative of the Captivity*, ix–xii; Sayre, "Abridging between Two Worlds, 484–86.

121. Thomas Forsyth to Supt. William Clark, "List of the names of half breeds of the Sac & Fox tribes," Petitions and supporting materials, June 10, 1830, Forsyth Papers, MHS.

5. EMPIRES IN TRANSITION

1. Erickson, Skinner, and Merchant, eds., *Discoveries Made*, 35.

2. Sachs, *Humboldt Current*, 14–27; Pratt, *Imperial Eyes*, 126–41.

3. Morse, *Report to the Secretary of War;* Schoolcraft, *American Indians*.

4. Morse, *Report to the Secretary of War*, 9.

5. Morse, *Report to the Secretary of War*, 356–58.

6. Morse, *Report to the Secretary of War*, 95.

7. Morse, *Report to the Secretary of War*, 375.

8. Thomas Hart Benton to James Tyler, Sept. 14, 1841, Letters Received, Office of Indian Affairs, St. Peters Agency.

9. Gilman, *Henry Hastings Sibley*, 80–83.

10. Schoolcraft, *Historical and Statistical Information*, 2:361.

11. F. S. Drake, preface, *Indian Tribes of the United States*, 3–4; Mumford, "Mixed-Race Identity," 2–4.

12. Schoolcraft, *Historical and Statistical Information*, 1:viii–ix.

13. Schoolcraft, *Historical and Statistical Information*, 1:241.

14. Schoolcraft, *Historical and Statistical Information*, 1:223–26.

15. Schoolcraft, *Historical and Statistical Information*, 1:436.

16. Schoolcraft, *Historical and Statistical Information*, 1:445–522, 524.

17. Schoolcraft, *Historical and Statistical Information*, 2:xi.

18. Lewis Cass, secretary of war, and former Indian superintendent, estimated in an 1836 report to Congress that once removal was completed, there would be 244,870 indigenous people living between the Mississippi and the Rockies, but his number may have been massaged into a larger size to emphasize the need for larger military appropriations to protect the frontier from this large number of "potential hostiles." Cass, Report of the Secretary of War, Feb. 19, 1836, U.S. Congress, *American State Papers*, class V: Military Affairs, 6:149–55.

19. Berlandier, *Indians of Texas*, 36–93.

20. Berlandier, *Indians of Texas*, 96–102; 103–52.

21. Berlandier, *Indians of Texas*, 66.

22. Suddenly we know a lot about the Comanches because of a recent flurry of books: James Brooks, *Captives and Cousins*; Hämäläinen, *Comanche Empire*; Barr, *Peace Came*; and DeLay, *War of a Thousand Deserts*; these works have made us see the region and the Comanches from some new perspectives. These books disagree about the meaning of the word *empire* but not that the Comanches had enormous influence, largely through kinship and raiding, on the entire borderlands.

23. Hoig, *Tribal Wars*, 11–22.

24. Hämäläinen, "Western Comanche Trade Center," 488–90; Brooks, *Captives and Cousins*, 61–63; Hämäläinen, *Comanche Empire*, 6–8; John, *Storms Brewed*, 216–20; 304–18.

25. Hämäläinen, *Comanche Empire*, 61–68; Fehrenbach, *Comanches*, 184–88; 210–21.

26. Fehrenbach, *Comanches*, 221–24; Brooks, *Captives and Cousins*, 72–75; John, *Storms Brewed*, 471–73.

27. La Vere, *Texas Indians*, 146–48; Marquéz de Rubí, Dictamen of April 10, 1768, in Lafora, *Frontiers of New Spain*, 185.

28. Barr, *Peace Came*, 5–8; Hämäläinen, *Comanche Empire*, 96–106.

29. Barr, *Peace Came*, 9–10; DeMallie, "Kinship," 317–18; Shoemaker, "Categories," 51–74.

30. DeMallie, "Touching the Pen," 38–40.

31. Foreman, *Pioneer Days*, 112–26; G. C. Anderson, *Conquest of Texas*, 83–86.

32. Catlin, *Letters and Notes*, 2:44.

33. Foreman, *Pioneer Days*, 138–44; Catlin, *Letters and Notes*, 2:48–82; Prucha, *Sword of the Republic*, 365–71.

34. Fehrenbach, *Comanches*, 237–48; La Vere, "Friendly Persuasions," 331–35; Hoig, *White Man's Paper Trail*, 40–44.

35. Hämäläinen, "Western Comanche Trade Center," 506–8; Hoig, *White Man's Paper Trail*, 99–101; Grinnell, *Fighting Cheyenne*, 313–17.

36. G. C. Anderson, *Conquest of Texas*, 46–50; James Brooks, *Captives and Cousins*, 164–79.

37. Barr, "Beyond Their Control," 151–54; Cantrell, *Stephen F. Austin*, 136–45; 311–24; G. C. Anderson, *Conquest of Texas*, 55–59.

38. G. C. Anderson, *Conquest of Texas*, 74–80; La Vere, *Contrary Neighbors*, 81–83.

39. Exley, *Frontier Blood*, 50–51; G. C. Anderson, *Conquest of Texas*, 99–100.

40. E. Wallace and Hoebel, *Comanches*, 291–93; Williams, *Sam Houston*, 110, 134–35; G. C. Anderson, *Conquest of Texas*, 104–5.

41. Fehrenbach, *Comanches*, 285–88; Exley, *Frontier Blood*, 54–58; Wilbarger, *Indian Depredations in Texas*, index.

42. La Vere, *Texas Indians*, 170–72; G. C. Anderson, *Conquest of Texas*, 118–20.

43. La Vere, *Texas Indians*, 172–74; G. C. Anderson, *Conquest of Texas*, 128–30, 174–78.

44. Lamar, quoted in Winfrey and Day, *Indian Papers of Texas*, 1:14–15.

45. La Vere, *Texas Indians*, 174–75; Everett, *Texas Cherokees*, 102–9.

46. Hoig, *Tribal Wars*, 153–56; G. C. Anderson, *Conquest of Texas*, 174–76.

47. Hoig, *Tribal Wars*, 153–56; G. C. Anderson, *Conquest of Texas*, 179–85.

48. Hoig, *Tribal Wars*, 159–66; G. C. Anderson, *Conquest of Texas*, 186–89; E. Wallace and Hoebel, *Comanches*, 293–95.

49. Spicer, *Cycles of Conquest*, 336–38; Weber, *Mexican Frontier*, 16–22.

50. Camarillo, *Chicanos in California*, 5–7; Weber, *Mexican Frontier*, 60–64.

51. Prucha, *Great Father*, 1:294–99; 302–9; Stokes Commission Report, Feb. 10, 1834, *House Report*, no. 474, 23-I, Serial Set 263, 78–103; Satz, *American Indian Policy*, 126–30.

52. Cleland, *Cattle on a Thousand Hills*, 21–23; McWilliams, *Southern California Country*, 37–38.

53. Hackel, "Land, Labor and Production," 116–17; Bouvier, *Women and the Conquest*, 83–87.

54. Cleland, *Cattle on a Thousand Hills*, 19–20; Weber, *Mexican Frontier*, 162.

55. Monroy, "Creation and Re-creation," 190; Weber, *Mexican Frontier*, 66–67.

56. McWilliams, *Southern California Country*, 29.

57. Mariano Guadelupe Vallejo, "Historia," in Sanchez, *Telling Identities*, 168.

58. Hackel, "Land, Labor and Production," 132–34.

59. Gov. José Figueroa to the Minister of War and Navy, April 12, 1833, in S. F. Cook, *Expeditions to the Interior*, 188; G. H. Phillips, *Indians and Intruders*, 109–14; Hurtado, *John Sutter*, 69–70.

60. McKittrick, *Vallejo*, 137–40; *Los Angeles Star*, Oct. 20, 1855.

61. G. H. Phillips, *Indians and Intruders*, 100–105.

62. Din and Nasatir, *Imperial Osages,* 382–84; Rollings, *Unaffected by the Gospel,* 65–70, 98–105.

63. Col. A. P. Chouteau to Sec. of War, March 3, 1834, Letters Received, 1827–1849, Office of Indian Affairs, St. Louis Superintendency, National Archives and Records Administration (NARA) Microfilm; Burns, *History of the Osage People,* 165–68.

64. P. L. Chouteau to William Clark, June 8, 1831, Letters Received, Office of Indian Affairs, St. Louis Superintendency, NARA Microfilm.

65. Hoig, *White Man's Paper Trail,* 47–56; Mathews, *Osages,* 548–66.

66. Big Soldier 1822, in George Sibley to Senator Henry Clay, Feb. 13, 1841, American Indian Manuscripts, Box 2, HL; Houck, *History of Missouri,* 183; Hämäläinen, *Comanche Empire,* 154–55.

67. Mathews, *Osages,* 583; Burns, *History of the Osage People,* 168171.

68. Burns, *History of the Osage People,* 238–42.

69. Swagerty, "Indian Trade" 4:362–64; Ray, *Fur Trade,* xvi–xxi.

70. Sunder, *Fur Trade,* 16–18.

71. Ewers, *Blackfeet,* 15–29; Henry and Thompson, *New Light,* 2:347–52, 747.

72. Ewers, *Blackfeet,* 47–56; Chittenden, *American Fur Trade,* vol. 3; Swagerty, "Indian Trade," 4:362–64; McGuinness, *Counting Coup,* 20–31.

73. Sunder, *Fur Trade,* 20–22; Swagerty, "Indian Trade," 4:369–70; McGuinness, *Counting Coup,* 46–47.

74. Sunder, *Fur Trade,* 22; "Treaty with Blackfoot and Assiniboin 1831," in Wied-Neuwied, *People of the First Man* (1976 ed.), 99; McGuinness, *Counting Coup,* 46–47.

75. Denig, *Five Indian Tribes,* xv–xviv; Vickers, "Denig of Fort Union," 134–36; Ewers, "Mothers of the Mixed Bloods," 64–66.

76. H. L. Carter, "Andrew Drips," 143–45.

77. Prucha, *Great Father,* 1:297–99; Abel, "Proposals for an Indian State," 93–98.

78. McGuinness, *Counting Coups,* 65–69; G. C. Anderson, *Kinsmen of Another Kind,* 103–7; Wied-Neuwied, *People of the First Man* (1976 ed.), 102–5.

79. Chittenden, *American Fur Trade,* 1:361–69; Barbour, *Fort Union,* 19–26, 43–46; Sunder, *Fur Trade,* 7–9.

80. Ewers, "Mothers of the Mixed Bloods," 61–63; McDonnell, "Contributions," 243–46.

81. Kurz, *Journal,* 155–56.

82. Denig, quoted in Audubon, *Audubon and His Journals,* 2:182, 186; Vickers, "Denig of Fort Union," 137–41; Ewers, "Mothers of the Mixed Bloods," 64.

83. Chittenden, *American Fur Trade,* 2:821; Wied-Neuwied, *People of the First Man,* in Thwaites, *Early Western Travels,* v. 22 (1906).

84. L. H. Morgan, *Indian Journals,* 101–3; *St. Louis Times,* March 23, 1833; Thomas Ermatinger to Andrew Drips. Oct. 14, 1832, Andrew Drips Papers, MHS.

85. H. L. Carter, "Andrew Drips," 150–53; Thorne, *Many Hands,* 169–73.

86. H. L. Carter, "Andrew Drips," 150—53; Thorne, *Many Hands,* 149–55; "Account of A. Drips with P. Chouteau and Co.—May 30, 1843," Andrew Drips Papers, MHS.

87. James Illingsworth to Andrew Drips, Feb. 1, 1842; H. Picotte to Andrew Drips, March 25, 1842; Andrew Drips to Major D. D. Mitchell, St. Louis, Jan. 2, 1843, all in Andrew Drips Papers, MHS.

88. Sinclair Taylor to Andrew Dripps, Esq., at Fort George. Oct. 28, 1843, Andrew Drips Papers, MHS; Petition of the Yancton band of the Sioux Indians to the President of the United States, March 18, 1844, transcribed by Drips, in Andrew Drips Papers, MHS.

89. H. L. Carter, "Andrew Drips," 152–56; Thorne, *Many Hands*, 171; Hoffhaus, *Chez Les Canses*, 150–61; John Sarpy to Drips, June 18, 1847, Ledger Book, Andrew Drips Papers, MHS.

90. Denig, *Assiniboine*, 625.

91. Denig, *Five Indian Tribes*, 71–73.

92. Schoolcraft, *American Indians*, xi.

93. Namias, *White Captives*, 7–12; Ebersole, *Captured by Texts*, 3–6; Silver, *Our Savage Neighbors*, xx.

94. Jewitt, *Journal Kept at Nootka Sound*, 2–3.

95. Jewitt, *Journal Kept at Nootka Sound*, 3–4.

96. Boyd, *Spirit of Pestilence*, 39–46; McDougall quoted in Irving, *Astoria*, 117.

97. Fisher, "Northwest from the Beginning," vol. 1, pt. 2, 144–48; R. Thornton, *American Indian Holocaust and Survival*, 44–49.

98. McLoughlin, Sept. 25, 1830, in J. McLoughlin, *Letters of McLoughlin Written at Fort Vancouver*, 132; John McLoughlin to Gov. and Comm., Oct. 11, 1830, in J. McLoughlin, *Letters of McLoughlin from Fort Vancouver*, 1st ser., 88.

99. Ogden, *Traits of American Indian Life*, 69–70.

100. Douglas, "Letters," 291–92.

101. McLoughlin to Gov. and Comm., Oct. 20, 1831, and June 16, 1832, in J. McLoughlin, *Letters of McLoughlin from Fort Vancouver*, 1st ser., 233, 100; Boyd, *Spirit of Pestilence*, 84–87.

102. Boyd, *Spirit of Pestilence*, 93–99, 110–14; S. F. Cook, "Historical Demography," 96.

103. James Douglas, "Letter to Governor and Committee, Oct. 18, 1838," in J. McLoughlin, *Letters of McLoughlin from Fort Vancouver*, 1st ser., 237–38.

104. Mariano Vallejo, Comandante, to Governor, May 18, 1838, in Bancroft, *History of California*, 4:73–74.

105. McKittrick, *Vallejo*, 152.

106. D. F. Jones, *Rationalizing Epidemics*, 107–11; Dobyns, "Native American Trade Centers," 214–16.

107. D. F. Jones, *Rationalizing Epidemics*, 75; Robertson, *Rotting Face*, 37–40; Chittenden, *American Fur Trade*, 2:619–20.

108. Robertson, *Rotting Face*, 9–13, 81–85, 143–48; Chittenden, *American Fur Trade*, 2:619–20.

109. Larpenteur, *Forty Years a Fur Trader*, 1:132–34; Robertson, *Rotting Face*, 172–76.

110. Robertson, *Rotting Face*, 6–7; Chardon, *Chardon's Journal*, 109, 120–39.

111. Chittenden, *American Fur Trade*, 2:626; Ewers, *Blackfeet*, 66.

112. Chittenden, *American Fur Trade*, 2:626; Ewers, *Blackfeet*, 66–67.

113. Denig, *Five Indian Tribes*, 71–72; Chardon, *Chardon's Journal*, 116.

114. Robertson, *Rotting Face*, 255–61; Chouteau quoted in Chittenden, *American Fur Trade*, 2:627.

115. Quoted in Chittenden, *American Fur Trade*, 2:627.

116. Ewers, *Blackfeet*, 67, 187–93; Denig, *Five Indian Tribes*, 78–81.

117. L. Fowler, "Great Plains to 1885," 29–30; Sunder, *Fur Trade*, 83; Robertson, *Rotting Face*, 285–88; Ostler, *Plains Sioux*, 28–32.

118. Rister, *Comanche Bondage*, 23–29; Hämäläinen, *Comanche Empire*, 220–23, 251–55.

119. Rister, *Comanche Bondage*, 31–39.

120. Horn, *Captivity of Mrs. Sarah Ann Horne*, 13.

121. G. C. Anderson, *Indian Southwest*, 240–41; Hämäläinen, *Comanche Empire*, 251–55.

122. Horn, *Captivity of Mrs. Sarah Ann Horne*, 18–23, 38–40, 48–51; Exley, *Frontier Blood*, 136–38.

123. Silver, *Our Savage Neighbors*, xix.

124. E. West, *Contested Plains*, 198–205; E. West, *Way to the West*, 60–64; Hämäläinen, *Comanche Empire*, 294–99.

125. Hämäläinen, *Comanche Empire*, 300–305; Exley, *Frontier Blood*, 137.

126. Halaas and Masich, *Halfbreed*, 51–55; Grinnell, *Fighting Cheyennes*, 57–69; E. West, *Contested Plains*, 88–89.

6. Unintended Consequences

1. I can't imagine writing about the Mexican War or the set of events that led to and resulted from it without thinking of Bernard DeVoto's *The Year of Decision: 1846*, published in 1942. The book, chronicling the approach of the Mexican War, has a moral certainty that came from writing about 1846 in 1940. Wars, from that perspective, seemed inevitable and necessary. The twin imperatives of Manifest Destiny in 1846 and the success of American democracy with all of its flaws in 1940 operate in DeVoto's text with a powerful narrative certainty that seems naive and racist now. The structure of his book, however, remains enviably effective because his argument derives entirely from people actually doing things. DeVoto would never have used the word *contingency*, but he had mastered it as a historical approach. Recently, Daniel Walker Howe has laid out the set of conditions that made the war inevitable over a longer period and a larger stage in *What Hath God Wrought: The Transformation of America, 1815–1848*.

2. "Reminiscences of Jane Snyder Richards," Mormon Manuscript, BL; Samuel Richards, Journals, 1844–1870, Mormon Manuscripts, HL.

3. Quantrille McClung, comp., *Carson-Bent-Boggs Genealogy* (Denver: Denver

Public, Library, 1963), 104–5; Foreman, *Indians and Pioneers*, 125; Lavender, *Bent's Fort*, 25–26.

4. LeSueur, *1838 Mormon War*, 128–31, 189; DeVoto, *Year of Decision*, 147–49; J. Q. Thornton, *Oregon and California in 1848*, 16; Sampson, "William Bogg's Sketch," 106–10; H. H. Bancroft, *History of California*, 5:525–26.

5. McClung, *Carson-Bent-Boggs Genealogy*, 104–10; Simmons, *Kit Carson*, 92–97; Blackwelder, *Great Westerner*, 243–55; Sides, *Blood and Thunder*, 248–66.

6. Magoffin, *Down the Santa Fe Trail*, 60–72.

7. Lavender, *Bent's Fort*, 275–77.

8. See chapter 2 for the woes of the McLoughlin family; Faragher, *Women and Men*, 18–26; D. A. Johnson, *Founding the Far West*, 3, 41–44.

9. Kendall, *Narrative of an Expedition*, 17; Wroth, "1841—Texas Santa Fe Expedition"; Binkley, "New Mexico"; Kendall, *Narrative of an Expedition*, 334–57.

10. Wroth, "1841—Texas Santa Fe Expedition"; Lavender, *Bent's Fort*, 218–22.

11. May, *Manifest Destiny's Underworld*, x–xiii, 29–35; *New York Times*, Oct. 5, 1859.

12. Bonthius, "Patriot War"; H. Jones, *Webster-Ashburton Treaty*, 3–5, 47–51.

13. Bushman, *Joseph Smith*, 16–31; Brodie, *No Man Knows My History*, 4–10.

14. Bushman, *Joseph Smith*, 103; Quinn, *Early Mormonism*, 87–93.

15. Bushman, *Joseph Smith*, 103–6.

16. Brodie, *No Man Knows My History*, 64–82; Quinn, *Early Mormonism*, 138–51.

17. Bushman, *Joseph Smith*, 227–30, 341–46; Arrington, "Latter-day Saints," 623; LeSueur, *1838 Mormon War*, 2–3.

18. *Missouri Republican*, Sept. 18, 1838; *Western Emigrant*, Sept. 13, 1838, in Dale Morgan Early Western Newspaper Transcripts, BRBML.

19. *Missouri Argus*, Sept. 27, 1838, in Morgan Newspaper Transcripts, Box 1, BRBML.

20. LeSueur, *1838 Mormon War*, 103–18; Bushman, *Joseph Smith*, 360–63.

21. Brodie, *No Man Knows My History*, 212–24; LeSueur, *1838 Mormon War*, 17–22, 58–63.

22. Lilburn W. Boggs to John B. Clark, Oct. 27, 1838, in LeSueur, *1838 Mormon War*, 152.

23. Bushman, *Joseph Smith*, 364–68; LeSueur, *1838 Mormon War*, 169–77; Mulder and Mortenson, *Among the Mormons*, 97–103.

24. Snow, *Personal Writings*, 12–13; Bushman, *Joseph Smith*, 380–82; Arrington and Bitton, *Mormon Experience*, 43–47.

25. M. H. P. Richards, *Winter Quarters*, 4–6.

26. *Galenan* (Galena IL), Nov. 22, 1838, in Morgan Newspaper Transcripts, Box 1, BRBML.

27. *Illinois Herald*, Alton, July 27, 1842; *Jacksonville Illinoian*, Aug. 14, 1841, both in Morgan Newspaper Transcripts, BRBML, Box 1.

28. M. H. P. Richards, *Winter Quarters*, 8–10; Stegner, *Gathering of Zion*, 23–24.

29. *Warsaw (IL) Signal*, June 9, 1841, Illinois Newspapers file, Dale Morgan Newspaper Transcripts, BRBML, Box 1; Stegner, *Gathering of Zion*, 22–30.

30. *Warsaw (IL) Message*, Sept. 27, 1843, and *Ottawa (IL) Free Trader*, Oct. 4, 1844, Dale Morgan Newspaper Transcripts, Box 1 and 2, BRBML; Brodie, *No Man Knows My History*, 318–22, 348–56.

31. Bushman, *Joseph Smith*, 548–49.

32. Bushman, *Joseph Smith*, 548–53; Samuel Richards, "Journals," Jan. 29, Feb. 25, 1846, Mormon Manuscripts, HL.

33. "A City for Sale," *Daily Missouri Republican*, May 13, 1846; Stegner, *Gathering of Zion*, 35–38; Arrington and Bitton, *Mormon Experience*, 93–96.

34. Arrington and Bitton, *Mormon Experience*, 96; Snow, *Poems, Religious, Historical and Political.*

35. Mary H. P. Richards, May 19, 1846, in Richards, *Winter Quarters*, 13.

36. DeVoto, *Year of Decision*, 90–94.

37. "Mary Richards to Samuel Richards, Oct. 1846," in M. H. P. Richards, *Winter Quarters*, 92–95.

38. Mary Richards to Samuel Richards, June 9, 1847, in M. H. P. Richards, *Winter Quarters*, 169.

39. M. H. P. Ward, *Winter Quarters*, 33.

40. DeLay, *War of a Thousand Deserts*, 182–87.

41. Reséndez, *Changing National Identities*, 173–79; Weber, *Mexican Frontier*, 33–35; LeCompte, *Rebellion in Rio Arriba*, 3–11.

42. DeLay, *War of a Thousand Deserts*, 167–69; LeCompte, *Rebellion in Rio Arriba*, 9–14.

43. LeCompte, *Rebellion in Rio Arriba*, 30–35; Reséndez, *Changing Identities*, 180–81.

44. Reséndez, *Changing Identities*, 183–85; Reno, "Rebellion in New Mexico," 197–210; LeCompte, *Rebellion in Rio Arriba*, 47–53.

45. Wilson, "Narrative," 381.

46. Reséndez, *Changing Identities*, 189–96; Reno, "Rebellion in New Mexico," 207–8.

47. Hämäläinen, *Comanche Empire*, 295–97; C. Montgomery, *Spanish Redemption*, 40; Lavender, *Bent's Fort*, 192–95; DeLay, *War of a Thousand Deserts*, xvi–xix.

48. Howe, *What Hath God Wrought*, 734–38.

49. Juan Almonte to John C. Calhoun, March 6, 1845, in Manning, *Diplomatic Correspondence*, 8:699; Howe, *What Hath God Wrought*, 717–20.

50. Merk, *Monroe Doctrine*, 115–29.

51. For diplomatic and military details on the war, I have found the following most useful: Eisenhower, *So Far from God*, 16–26; Bauer, *Mexican War*, 8–29; DeVoto, *Year of Decision*. I have tempered these with Van Young, *Other Rebellion*, the essays in Rodriguez O, *Divine Charter*, and Santoni, *Mexicans at Arms.*

52. W. Fowler, *Santa Anna of Mexico*, 14–18, 44–46.

53. Ampudia to Taylor, April 12, 1846, in U.S. Congress, *American State Papers*, Class V: Military Affairs, Executive Doc. 60, 37:139.

54. Howe, *What Hath God Wrought*, 738–42; Smith, *War with Mexico*, 1:448–49.

55. Johannsen, *Halls of the Montezumas*, 11–13.

56. Weber, *Taos Trappers*, 210–15; Charles Bent to Manuel Alvarez, Jan. 24, 1845, *New Mexico Historical Review* 30 (Oct. 1955): 344.

57. DeLay, *War of a Thousand Deserts*, 129–38; Lavender, *Bent's Fort*, 228–35.

58. Lavender, *Bent's Fort*, 252–55.

59. Lavender, *Bent's Fort*, 252–55; Charles Bent to Manuel Alvarez, March 2, June 11, 1846, *New Mexico Historical Review* 30 (Oct. 1955): 344–348; Bent Letters, *New Mexico Historical Review* 31 (April 1956): 164; Kearny, *Winning the West*, 140–47.

60. William Marcy to General Kearny, June 3, 1846, House Exec. Doc. 60 (30-I) 1847, Serial Set 520, I 53–55; Charles Bent to Manuel Alvarez, Feb. 23, 1845, *New Mexico Historical Review* 30 (July 1955): 253–54.

61. Donaciano Vigil, "Speech to the New Mexico Legislative Assembly," Santa Fe, May 16, 1846, William Ritch Collection, Box 5, HL.

62. Simmons, *Kit Carson*, 68–69.

63. Lavender, *Bent's Fort*, 274–76; Bauer, *Mexican War*, 128–29; S. W. Kearny to Brig. Gen. Jones, July 31, 1846, Kearny, *Winning the West*, 159.

64. Keleher, *Turmoil in New Mexico*, 12–14; Department of the Interior Provinces, National Assembly to General Manuel Armijo, Aug. 7, 1846, Ritch Collection, Box 7, HL; Bauer, *Mexican War*, 136–39.

65. Magoffin, *Down the Santa Fe Trail*, 106; Keleher, *Turmoil* in New Mexico, 21–24; D. L. Clarke, *Stephen Watts Kearny*, 150–52; S. W. Kearny to Brig. Gen Jones, Sept. 16, 1846, Kearny, *Winning the West*, 162–65.

66. Charles Bent to Sec. of War James Buchanan, Dec. 26, 1846, U.S. Congress, *Insurrection against the United States Government in New Mexico and California, 1847–1848*, Senate Doc. 442, 56th Cong., 1st sess., 1900.

67. Charles Bent, Santa Fé, New Mexico, to the Hon. William Medill, Nov. 10, 1846, American Indian Manuscripts, Box 2, HL; Hughes, *Doniphan's Expedition*, 187–94.

68. Herrera, "New Mexico Resistance," 27–31, 202–3; D. J. Gonzalez, *Refusing the Favor.*

69. Weber, *On the Edge of Empire*, 52–55, 64–65; Chavez, *But Time and Chance*, 37–41.

70. Simmons, *Kit Carson*, 70–72; McNierney, *Taos 1847*, 4–5; Colonel Sterling Price, "Report to Adjutant General," Feb. 15, 1847, U.S. Congress, *Insurrection against the United States Government in New Mexico and California, 1847–1848*, Senate Doc. 442, 56th Cong., 1st sess., 1900.

71. Crutchfield, *Tragedy at Taos*, 40–46; Sides, *Blood and Thunder*, 175–76; Bent, "Account of Her Father's Death," 121–22.

72. Simmons, *Kit Carson*, 74–75; Colonel Sterling Price, Report to Adjutant General, Feb. 15, 1847, in McNierney, *Taos 1847*, 43–48.

73. Twitchell, *Military Occupation of New Mexico*, 127–31; Garrard, *Wah-toy-ah*, 117–21.

74. Donaciano Vigil, Gov. to Hugh N. Smith, Santa Fe, May 10, 1848, Ritch Collection, Box 7, HL; Twitchell, *Military Occupation of New Mexico*, 151–57.

75. Jose Maria Sanchez to Gov. Donaciano Vigil, Oct. 1848, Ritch Collection, Box 7, HL.

76. Twitchell, *Military Occupation of New Mexico*, 84; McClung, *Carson-Bent-Boggs Genealogy*, 68–70; Simmons, *Kit Carson*, 83–88.

77. Lavender, *Bent's Fort*, 318–23; DeLay, *War of a Thousand Deserts*, 288–95; Garrard, *Wah-toy-Yah*, 155–56.

78. Stegner, *Gathering of Zion*, 77–80; Ricketts, *Mormon Battalion*, 1–4; Mary Richards to Samuel Richards, July 13, 1846, M. H. P. Richards, *Winter Quarters*, 185.

79. H. Stout, *On the Mormon Frontier*, 172; Rickets, *Mormon Battalion*, 2–6.

80. Mary Richards to Samuel Richards, July 13, 1846, in M. H. P. Richards, *Winter Quarters*, 291; Eliza Snow, quoted in Tyler, *Concise History*, 107.

81. Stegner, *Gathering of Zion*, 80–84; Ricketts, *Mormon Battalion*, 5–7, 35–41.

82. Ricketts, *Mormon Battalion*, 65–69; Tyler, *Concise History*, 189–92; D. L. Bigler and Bagley, *Army of Israel*, 27; M. H. P. Richards, *Winter Quarters*, 20, 265.

83. H. Bigler, *Chronicle of the West*, 29.

84. Tyler, *Concise History*, 261–89, 308–17.

85. H. Bigler, *Chronicle of the West*, 44–48.

86. Hurtado, *John Sutter*, 140–51; Dillon, *Fool's Gold*, 277–86.

87. H. Bigler, *Chronicle of the West*, 82.

88. Stegner, *Gathering of Zion*, 192–94; Hurtado, John *Sutter*, 215–17; H. Bigler, "Diary of Henry Bigler," 241–45; H. Bigler, *Chronicles of the West*, 90–93.

89. Bancroft, *History of California*, 5:77–80; Gen. José Castro, March 14, 1846, quoted in Cleland, *History of California*, 193.

90. Bancroft, *History of California*, 5:81fn, 80–84; McKittrick, *Vallejo*, 243; Rolle, "Exploring an Explorer," 141–42; D. L. Walker, *Bear Flag Rising*, 100–105.

91. Cleland, *History of California*, 199.

92. Cerruti, *Ramblings in California*, 38; Ide, *Biographical Sketch*, 90–93.

93. Cleland, *History of California*, 192, 199–203; Bauer, *Mexican War*, 168–69; Harlow, *California Conquered*, 98–103; Hawgood, "John C. Fremont," 67–96.

94. Emparán, *Vallejos of California*, 202–4; George Yount, July 4, 1846, Vallejo Collection, Box 2, HL; Francesca Carrillo de Vallejo to Mariano Guadalupe Vallejo, July 1846, Vallejo Collection, Box 2. HL; Bancroft, *History of California*, 111–19.

95. Harlow, *California Conquered*, 108–12, 116–24; Bauer, *Mexican War*, 168–71; Hawgood, "John C. Fremont," 71–80.

96. McClung, *Carson-Bent-Boggs Genealogy*, 1: 24–25; "Notes," *California Historical Society Quarterly*, 24:54; Simmons, *Kit Carson*, 68–69.

97. Francesca Vallejo to Mariano Guadalupe Vallejo, July 14, 1846, Emparán, *Vallejos of California*, 204.

98. Howe, *What Hath God Wrought*, 756–57; Haas, "War in California," 340–42.

99. Hass, "War in California," 342–44; John D. Tanner Jr., "Campaign for Los Angeles," 219–22.

100. D. L. Clarke, *Stephen Watts Kearny*, 167–79; S. W. Kearny, at Warner's Ranch,

to Commodore Robert Stockton, Dec. 2, 1846, in Kearny, *Winning the West*, 174; DeVoto, *Year of Decision*, 367–71.

101. Harlow, *California Conquered*, 181–88, 232–36; Haas, "War in California," 344–45; D. L. Clarke, *Stephen Watts Kearny*, 202–6; S. W. Kearny, Headquarters Army of the West, San Diego, to Brig. Gen. Jones, Dec. 12, 1846, Kearny, *Winning the West*, 175–77.

102. Cleland, "Early Sentiment," 14–17; Cleland, *History of California*, 154–67.

103. Cleland, *History of California*, 161–67; Starr, *Americans and the California Dream*, 28–33.

104. McKittrick, *Vallejo*, 244; Monroy, "Creation and Re-creation," 189; Hurtado, *Intimate Frontiers*, 22–23; Bancroft, *History of California*, 5:568.

105. Mariano Vallejo to Francesca Vallejo, Sept. 28, 1849, Emparán, *Vallejos of California*, 70.

106. Rosenus, *General M. G. Vallejo*, 204–6.

107. Mariano Vallejo to Maria Lugo y Vallejo, April 3, 1851, Emparán, *Vallejos of California*, 76.

108. Emparán, *Vallejos of California*, 259.

109. Cleland, *Cattle on a Thousand Hills*, 190–92; Abel Stearns to Larkin, May 15, 1846, June 5, 1846, Larkin, *Larkin Papers*, 5:18–20.

110. Wilson, "Narrative of Benjamin D. Wilson," 395–96; Weber, "Louis Robidoux," 107–11.

111. Carson, *Kit Carson's Autobiography*, 96–99; D. Roberts, *Newer World*, 149–57; Fremont to Thomas Hart Benton, in Benton, *Thirty Years' View*, 2:697.

112. Carson, *Kit Carson's Autobiography*, 94–95, 100–101; D. L. Walker, *Bear Flag Rising*, 106–8; D. Roberts, *Newer World*, 159–61.

113. John McLoughlin to Archibald Barclay, Sec., HBC, Nov. 21, 23, 24, 1844, in McLoughlin, *Letters of McLoughlin from Fort Vancouver*, 3rd ser., 59–64; McLoughlin to J. H. Pelly, Jan. 6, 1845, in *Letters of McLoughlin from Fort Vancouver*, 3rd ser., 67–68.

114. Merk, *Oregon Question*, 219, 237–38; DeVoto, *Year of Decision*, 90–91.

115. McLoughlin to Gov. and Committee, HBC, Nov. 20, 1845, in McLoughlin, *Letters of McLoughlin from Fort Vancouver*, 3rd ser., 97–109; S. A. Clarke, *Pioneer Days of Oregon History*, 2:708–17; Del Mar, *Oregon's Promise*, 75–79.

116. George Simpson to John McLoughlin, Jan. 1846, in McLoughlin, *Letters of McLoughlin from Fort Vancouver*, 3rd ser., 288.

117. McLoughlin to Governor and Committee of the HBC, July 1, 1846, in McLoughlin, *Letters of McLoughlin from Fort Vancouver*, 3rd ser., 153–61.

118. Holman, *Dr. John McLoughlin*, 101–5; Morrison, *Outpost*, 424–31.

119. Miller, *Prophetic Worlds*, 58–62; S. A. Clarke, *Pioneer Days*, 370–95; Mowry, *Marcus Whitman*, 36–50.

120. Jeffrey, *Converting the West*, 10–19, 40–42, 47–55.

121. Miller, *Prophetic Worlds*, 73–81.

122. Jeffrey, *Converting the West*, 90–94; Narcissa Whitman to Harriett Prentiss,

Oct. 18, 1836, *Transactions of the 21st Annual Reunion of the Oregon Pioneer Association for 1893* (Salem OR: Oregon Pioneer Association, 1894).

123. Narcissa Whitman to Clarissa Prentiss, Dec. 5, 1836–March 30, 183, in Drury, *Where Wagons Could Go*, 331; Jeffrey, *Converting the West*, 164–74; Miles Cannon, *Waiilatpu*, 55–58.

124. Cannon, *Waiilatpu*, 78–80; Jeffrey, *Converting the West*, 208–13; Morrison, *Outpost*, 447–49.

125. Miller, *Prophetic Worlds*, 54–61; Jeffrey, *Converting the West*, 210–17; Cannon, *Waiilatpu*, 98–105; Marcus Whitman to the Secretary of War, Oct. 16, 1847, in Mowry, *Marcus Whitman*, 287–91.

126. Jeffrey, *Converting the West*, 215–21; Cannon, *Waiilatpu*, 112–23; Mowry, *Marcus Whitman*, 218–22.

127. James Douglas, Fort Vancouver, to George Abernethy, Dec. 7, 1847, and George Abernethy to Provisional Legislature, Dec. 8, 1847, in Beckham, *Oregon Indians*, 61–65; Jeffrey, *Converting the West*, 220–22.

128. S. A. Clarke, *Pioneer Days*, 549–55; Holman, *Dr. John McLoughlin*, 88–90, 100–104.

129. Holman, *Dr. John McLoughlin*, 110–14, 123–31; "The Donation Land Claim Act, 1850," Center for Columbia River History, http://www.ccrh.org/comm/cottage/primary/claim.htm (accessed Dec. 3, 2009).

7. BORDER WARS

1. Wallis, *Sixty Years on the Brazos*, 114–15; Robert Neighbors, "Report to the Commissioner of Indian Affairs, 1857," in Winfrey and Day, *Indian Papers of Texas*, vol. 1.

2. Three recent books demonstrate the significance of this period in making sense of race as a shifting idea in U.S. culture and the enormous challenge of understanding the variety of levels at which race "works": Gross, *What Blood Won't Tell*; Pascoe, *What Comes Naturally*; Gómez, *Manifest Destinies*.

3. Kurz, *Journal*, 2–9, 48.

4. Parkman, *Oregon Trail*, 21–28; Unrau, *Kansa Indians*, 138–44; Deatherage, *Early History*, 340–46.

5. Thorne, *Many Hands*, 151–55; Sleeper-Smith, *Indian Woman and French Men*, 116–29; Hoffhaus, *Chez les Kansâs*, 168–71; Boutros, "Confluence of People and Place," 1–19.

6. Chittenden, *American Fur Trade*, 1:107–9; Thorne, *Many Hands*, 158–59; Hoffhaus, *Chez les Canses*, 138–40.

7. Kurz, *Journal*, 27–29; 49–51, 59–61.

8. Kurz, *Journal*, 82–83.

9. Kurz, *Journal*, 120, 124–25.

10. Kurz, *Journal*, 221.

11. Kurz, *Journal*, 156.

12. Kurz, *Journal*, 133–35, 144, 203, 222.

13. Kurz, *Journal*, 234.

14. Kurz, *Journal*, 258.

15. Kurz, *Journal*, 268–71.

16. Dunlay, *Kit Carson and the Indians*, 133–35; Halaas and Masich, *Halfbreed*, 50–55.

17. Faller, "Making Medicine," 65–67; Dunlay, *Kit Carson and the Indians*, 133–35; Halaas and Masich, *Halfbreed*, 50–55, 61; E. West, *Contested Plains*, 90–93.

18. E. West, *Way to the West*, 86–89.

19. Smet, *Life, Letters and Travels*, 1:64, 2:677; Beck, *First Sioux War*, 13–18.

20. "Treaty of Fort Laramie with Sioux, etc., 1851," in Kappler, *Indian Affairs, Laws, and Treaties*, 2:594.

21. Ostler, *Plains Sioux*, 36–38; Utley, *Indian Frontier*, 60–62; DeMallie, "Touching the Pen," 41–46.

22. Halaas and Masich, *Halfbreed*, 58–66; Lavender, *Bent's Fort*, 338–39.

23. Halaas and Masich, *Halfbreed*, 60–62.

24. Unrau, *Rise and Fall*, 4–13; 22–23; Robert A. Trennert Jr. *Alternative to Extinction*, 17–19, 46–48.

25. Stasiulis and Yuval-Davis, *Unsettling Settler Societies*, 20–25; Stoler, *Carnal Knowledge*, 41–46.

26. Quoted in K. D. Richards, *Isaac I. Stevens*, 157.

27. Meinig, *Great Columbia Plain*, 67–71; K. D. Richards, *Isaac I. Stevens*, 93–106, 139–40, 163–68.

28. K. D. Richards, *Isaac I. Stevens*, 197–204; Eckrom, *Remembered Drums*, 4–7; Colonel B. F. Shaw, "Medicine Creek Treaty," *Proceedings of the Oregon Historical Society, 1901* (Salem OR: W. H. Leeds, 1901): 27–30.

29. Thomas McKay, affidavit, quoted in Josephy, *Nez Perce Indians*, 331.

30. Eckrom, *Remembered Drums*, 18–23; K. D. Richards, *Isaac I. Stevens*, 207–11, 218–23, 235–41; Ruby and Brown, *Cayuse Indians*, 194–99.

31. Halliday and Chehak, *Native Peoples*, 189, 197; Joseph C. Brown, *Valley of the Strong*, 39, 53; K. D. Richards, *Isaac I. Stevens*, 234–41.

32. Ruby and Brown, *Cayuse Indians*, 48–59, 67–73, 128–53; Joseph Lane, "Report to the Secretary of War," Oct. 28, 1849, in Oregon Territory Documents Collections, HL; Bancroft, *History of Oregon*, 1:714–22; 2:95–97; Limerick, "Haunted America," *Something in the Soil*, 33–73.

33. Ruby and Brown, *Cayuse*, 175–83.

34. Bancroft, *History of Oregon*, 2:205–11; Schwartz, *Rogue River War*, 16–22.

35. David McLoughlin to John Fraser, March 18, 1849, in B. B. Barker, *McLoughlin Empire*, appendix.

36. Bancroft, *History of Oregon*, 2:205–11; Schwartz, *Rogue River War*, 29–49; Beckham, *Requiem for a People*, 15–22, 118–30.

37. *Oregon Statesman*, Aug. 10, 1853.

38. Joel Palmer to George Manypenny, Superintendent of Indian Affairs Report,

Oct. 4, 1853, in *Oregon Historical Society Quarterly* 23 (1922): 30–31; O'Donnell, *Arrow in the Earth*, 144–51.

39. Robert Hull to Joel Palmer, Nov. 17, 1853, Oregon Superintendency Records in O'Donnell, *Arrow in the Earth*, 160.

40. Schwartz, *Rogue River War*, 60–63.

41. Richards, *Isaac I. Stevens*, 222–30; Trafzer and Scheuerman, *Renegade Tribe*, 49–55; Kip, *Indian Council at Walla-Walla*, 3–17; Josephy, *Nez Perce Indians*, 318–32.

42. William Winlock Miller Papers, BRBML; I. Stevens, "Letters of Governor Isaac I. Stevens," 3–59; Elwood Evans, "The Indian War, 1855–56, Newspaper Details in Weekly Installments," Elwood Evans Scrapbooks, BRBML.

43. Garry, quoted in H. Stevens, *Life of Isaac Ingalls Stevens*, 2:138; Josephy, *Nez Perce Indians*, 346–48; K. D. Richards, *Isaac I. Stevens*, 235–36.

44. *Pioneer and Democrat* (Olympia, W.T.), Sept. 28, 1855, Evans Scrapbooks, BRBML.

45. *Pioneer and Democrat*, Oct. 19, 1855, Evans Scrapbooks, BRBML.

46. O'Donnell, *Arrow in the Earth*, 226–29; Schwartz, *Rogue River War*, 100–108; Crook, *General George Crook*, 26.

47. Wool to Jefferson Davis, Jan. 7, 1854, in K. D. Richards, *Isaac I. Stevens*, 239; Utley, *Frontiersmen in Blue*, 98–99.

48. Letter from John Wool, Major General in Command of the Department of the Pacific, to Lt. Col. L. Thomas at Army Headquarters, NYC, Nov. 3, 1855, in Evans Scrapbooks, BRBML.

49. Utley, *Frontiersmen in Blue*, 181–83, 190–94; O'Donnell, *Arrow in the Earth*, 243–44.

50. Gov. Isaac Stevens to Jefferson Davis, Secy. of War, Feb. 19, 1856, Isaac Stevens Papers, BRBML.

51. Gov. Isaac Stevens to Hon. James Douglas, March 6, 1856; James Douglas to Isaac Stevens, March 14, 1856, both in Isaac Stevens Papers, BRBML; K. D. Richards, *Isaac I. Stevens*, 260–63.

52. K. D. Richards, *Isaac I. Stevens*, 258–63.

53. George Gibbs to Sec. William Marcy, June 1856, as quoted in the *Pioneer Democrat*, in Evans Scrapbooks, BRBML.

54. K. D. Richards, *Isaac I. Stevens*, 274–88; William Marcy, Secy. of State, to Isaac Stevens, Gov. of the Territory of Washington, Sept. 12, 1856, Isaac Stevens Papers, BRBML; Josephy, *Nez Perce Indians*, 373–75.

55. O'Donnell, *Arrow in the Earth*, 272–80; Utley, *Frontiersmen in Blue*, 199–200.

56. Josephy, *Nez Perce Indians*, 377–80; Utley, *Frontiersmen in Blue*, 204–8; Dunn, *Massacres of the Mountains*, 285–92; Trafzer and Scheuerman, *Renegade Tribe*, 82–87.

57. Meany, *History of the State of Washington*, 196.

58. General Edmund Smith, quoted in Parks, *General Edmund Kirby Smith*, 89–90; Beck, *First Sioux War*, 21–23; Utley, *Frontiersmen in Blue*, 11–17; Utley, *Indian Frontier*, 39–46.

59. Thomas Fitzpatrick, quoted in Secretary of the Interior, *Annual Report, 1853,* 362.

60. A. C. Thomas, in Santa Fe, to Mr. B. D. Wilson, Aug. 16, 1849, Wilson Papers, Addenda II, Box 17, HL.

61. DeLay, *War of a Thousand Deserts,* 302–3.

62. Hämäläinen, *Comanche Empire,* 299–301; Flores, "Bison Ecology," 481–85; E. West, *Way to the West,* 51–80; La Vere, *Contrary Neighbors,* 144–49.

63. Kenner, *Comanchero Frontier,* 80–83; LeCompte, "Bent, St. Vrain and Company," 273–93.

64. Petition to P. H. Bell, Gov. of Texas from Citizens of Limestone County, Dec. 25, 1849, in Winfrey and Day, *Indian Papers of Texas,* 3:107; Wilbarger, *Indian Depredations in Texas,* appendix; Hämäläinen, *Comanche Empire,* 304–7; G. C. Anderson, *Conquest of Texas,* 221–30.

65. Brevet Captain William Steele to Major Deas, Sept. 22, 1849, in Winfrey and Day, *Indian Papers of Texas,* 5:49–50; John Rollins to V. E. Howard. Feb. 26, 1850; G. C. Anderson, *Conquest of Texas,* 238.

66. Jefferson Davis to Bell, Sept. 19, 1853, in Winfrey and Day, *Indian Papers of Texas, 3:*155–56.

67. P. H. Bell to the U.S Congress. Feb. 7, 1850, in Winfrey and Day, *Indian Papers of Texas,* 3:115–16; G. C. Anderson, *Conquest of Texas,* 255–57.

68. J. A. Rogers, Special Indian Agent, to P. H. Bell, Gov. of Texas, Sept. 3, 1851, Winfrey and Day, *Indian Papers of Texas,* 3:141–42; Hämäläinen, *Comanche Empire,* 307–9; Utley, *Frontier Regulars,* 75–76.

69. Petition from Citizens of Bandera, Bexar Co. to E. M. Pease, Sept. 21, 1855, in Winfrey and Day, *Indian Papers of Texas,* 3:241.

70. Gov. E. M. Pease to Major Persifor S. Smith, Sept. 5, 1855, in Winfrey and Day, *Indian Papers of Texas,* 3:234; Hämäläinen, *Comanche Empire,* 310; G. C. Anderson, *Conquest of Texas,* 263–70.

71. H. R. Runnels, Gov. of Texas, to J. S., Captain of Militia of Texas, Jan. 28, 1858, in Winfrey and Day, *Indian Papers of Texas,* 3:272–73; Hämäläinen, *Comanche Empire,* 310–11; G. C. Anderson, *Conquest of Texas,* 274–75; DeLay, *War of a Thousand Deserts,* 307–8.

72. "Field Notes Concerning Indian Reservation, 1855," R. B. Marcy and R. Neighbors, in Winfrey and Day, *Indian Papers of Texas,* 3:193–96.

73. G. C. Anderson, *Conquest of Texas,* 290–95.

74. "Proclamation by H. R. Runnels, Texas Governor, Jan. 10, 1859," in Winfrey and Day, *Indian Papers of Texas,* 3:312.

75. John S. Ford, Brazos Agency, to Gov. H. R. Runnels, April 7, 1858, in Winfrey and Day, *Texas Indian Papers,* 5:224–27; J. H. Brown, Texas State Militia, to H. R. Runnels, Gov., July 22, 1859, in Winfrey and Day, *Indian Papers of Texas,* 3:338–40; G. C. Anderson, *Conquest of Texas,* 310–14; Hämäläinen, *Comanche Empire,* 311–13.

76. "Proclamation to Citizens of adjoining Counties to the Indian Reserve,"

H.R. Runnels, Gov., Austin, March 12, 1859, in Winfrey and Day, *Indian Papers of Texas*, 3:317–20.

77. G. C. Anderson, *Conquest of Texas*, 321–22, 325–26; Hämäläinen, *Comanche Empire*, 313, 336–37; Babb, *Bosom of the Comanches*; Gelo and Zesch, "'Every Day,'" Seemed to Be a Holiday': The Captivity of Bianca Babb," *Southwestern Historical Quarterly*, 107 (July 2003), 35–68.

78. Lavender, *Bent's Fort*, 325–26; Hafen, *Broken Hand*, 242–43.

79. Thomas Fitzpatrick, *Annual Report of the Commissioner of Indian Affairs, 1853*, rpt. in Hafen, *Relations with the Indians of the Plains*, 127–28.

80. Lavender, *Bent's Fort*, 330–31; Berthrong, *Southern Cheyennes*, 132–36.

81. Lavender, *Bent's Fort*, 332–333; Berthrong, *Southern Cheyennes*, 141–45; Agent R. C. Miller's Report, in *Annual Report of the Commissioner of Indian Affairs, 1857*, rpt. in Hafen, *Relations with the Indians of the Plains*, 32–43.

82. William Bent to Superintendent A. M. Robinson, Dec. 17 1858, in Hafen, *Relations with the Indians of the Plains*, 173–74.

83. E. West, *Contested Plains*, 4–6, 92; Berthrong, *Southern Cheyennes*, 144–46.

84. William Bent to A.M. Robinson, Aug. 1, 1859, *Report of the Commissioner of Indian Affairs, 1859*, rpt. in Hafen, *Relations with the Indians of the Plains*, 137–39.

85. H. L. Carter, *"Dear Old Kit,"* 122–23; Frazer, *Forts and Supplies*, 51; Dunlay, *Kit Carson and the Indians*, 135–36.

86. Dunlay, *Kit Carson and the Indians*, 142–47; Blackwelder, *Great Westerner*, 258–60.

87. C. Carson to David Meriwether, Oct. 18, 1855, in *Report of Commissioner of Indian Affairs, 1856*, rpt. in Meriwether, *My Life in the Mountains*, 158. It is risky to quote Carson or to make much of his word choice because he was entirely illiterate; thus any text that has his signature was always written by his assistants.

88. Meriwether, *My Life in the Mountains*, 227–32; Dunlay, *Kit Carson and the Indians*, 170–82.

89. Simmons, *Kit Carson*, 99–102; Blackhawk, *Violence over the Land*, 192–94; Dunlay, *Kit Carson and the Indians*, 210–14.

90. Dunlay, *Kit Carson and the Indians*, 216–21; Blackhawk, *Violence over the Land*, 205–9.

91. James Calhoun to Indian Commissioner William Medill. Oct. 1, 1849, in Calhoun, *Official Correspondence*, 31.

92. Simpson, *Navaho* Expedition, 26; Frank McNitt, introduction to Simpson, *Navajo Expedition*, lvii–lxvii.

93. "Petition to the President," Santa Fe, New Mexico, Feb. 27, 1850, Commissioner of Indian Affairs Report, in Calhoun, *Official Correspondence*, 158; Simpson, *Navaho Expedition*, 67–71, 119; Frank McNitt, epilogue to Simpson, *Navajo Expedition*, 164–67.

94. James Calhoun to Adjutant General Lea, March 30, 1851, in Calhoun, *Of-*

ficial Correspondence, 299–301; Manuel Chaves, "Proposal to Raise Six Companies of Volunteers," in Calhoun, *Official Correspondence,* 302–3.

95. Sumner to Col. Jones, Sept. 1851, in McNitt, *Navajo Wars,* 195.

96. Utley, *Indian Frontier,* 50–51; McNitt, *Navajo Wars,* 191–96, 255–58.

97. Secretary Arny to New Mexico Legislative Assembly, Dec. 16, 1865, in Bancroft, *History of Arizona and New Mexico,* 659; Utley, *Frontiersmen in Blue,* 167–68.

8. THE STATE AND ITS HANDMAIDENS

1. Hoig, *Chouteaus,* 253–54; Chouteau and Chouteau, *Cher Oncle, Cher Papa,* 202–8; Miner, *Kansas,* 18–24; Wilder, *Annals of Kansas,* 1:237–38.

2. Stegner, *Gathering of Zion,* 86–89; M. H. P. Richards, *Winter Quarters,* 35–36.

3. Arrington, Fox, and May, *Building the City of God,* 16–17, 48–51; M. H. P. Richards, *Winter Quarters,* 36.

4. Arrington, Fox, and May, *Building the City of God,* 10–12, 57–62; Campbell, *Establishing Zion,* 140–41; Bagley, *Blood of the Prophets,* 23.

5. Samuel Richards, "Journal," 1851–1857, Mormon Manuscripts, HL; Campbell, *Establishing Zion,* 136–37; D. L. Bigler, *Forgotten Kingdom,* 38–39; M. H. P. Richards, *Winter Quarters,* 36–38.

6. Campbell, *Establishing Zion,* 139–40; D. L. Bigler, *Forgotten Kingdom,* 52; Samuel Richards, "Journal, 1851–1853," Mormon Manuscripts, HL.

7. Mary Parker Richards to Samuel Richards, Dec. 18, 1847, in M. H. P. Richards, *Winter Quarters,* 201; Gordon, *Mormon Question,* 26–27.

8. Samuel Ward, "Journal, 1851–1856," Feb. 14, 1855, Mormon Manuscripts, HL.

9. Ward, "Journal 1851–1856," Feb. 14, 1855, May 18, 1856, and May 24, 1856, "Journal 1851–1856," Mormon Manuscripts, HL; M. H. P. Richards, *Winter Quarters,* 39–43.

10. D. L. Bigler, *Forgotten Kingdom,* 45–51; "Acts, Resolutions and Memorials, Passed at the Several Annual Sessions of the Legislative Assembly of the Legislative Assembly of the Territory of Utah," microfilm, Mormon Manuscripts, HL, 135–43.

11. Bagley, *Blood of the Prophets,* 24, 40–41; D. L. Bigler, *Forgotten Kingdom,* 58–59; Furniss, *Mormon Conflict,* 45–47.

12. Book of Mormon, I, *Nephi* and *Doctrine and Covenants,* Sections 49, 87, in Quinn, *Mormon Hierarchy,* 649.

13. Bagley, *Blood of the Prophets,* 29–36; D. L. Bigler, *Forgotten Kingdom,* 73–80.

14. Samuel Richards, "Journal, Feb. 19, 1855," Mormon Manuscripts, HL.

15. Christy, "Open Hand and Mailed Fist," 116–35; D. L. Bigler, *Forgotten Kingdom,* 101–2.

16. Gordon, *Mormon Question,* 4–9, 29–32.

17. David Lewis, "1854 Speech," qtd. in Bagley, *Blood of the Prophets,* 29–36; Furniss, *Mormon Conflict,* 90–92; Stampp, *America in 1857,* 199–200; D. L. Bigler, *Forgotten Kingdom,* 144–45; D. L. Bigler, "Mormon Missionaries," 31–32.

18. Bagley, *Blood of the Prophets*, 79–81; Mackinnon, *At Swords' Point*, 122–27; Stampp, *America in 1857*, 202–4.

19. Jessie Gove to Maria Gove, Oct. 6, 1857, in Gove, *Utah Expedition*, 64–65, 70; D. L. Bigler, *Forgotten Kingdom*, 148, 155–57.

20. Mackinnon, *At Swords' Point*, 229–30.

21. The literature here is vast and contentious; a spate of serious research has made the details less controversial, but the story of the cover-up continues as the main drama. The most authoritative texts are Juanita Brooks, *Mountain Meadows Massacre*, Bagley, *Blood of the Prophets*; and, for a helpful broad context, Mackinnon, "'Lonely Bones,'" 121–78.

22. James Buchanan, "First Annual Message to Congress," Dec. 8, 1857, in Buchanan, *Works of James Buchanan*, 10:242.

23. Jesse Gove, Ft. Bridger, U.T., to Maria Gove. Jan. 17, 1858, in Gove, *Utah Expedition*, 115.

24. Mackinnon, *At Sword's Point*, 280–85, 494–50; Furniss, *Mormon Conflict*, 168–71.

25. Jesse Gove to Maria Gove, April 5, 1858 in Hammond, ed., 145.

26. Alfred Cumming to Col. A. Johnston, April 15, 1858, in John Floyd, *Report of the Secretary of War*, Utah War 1858, Serial 975, 93; Bagley, *Blood of the Prophets*, 198–203.

27. Furniss, *Mormon Conflict*, 180–83.

28. William Deverell, "The 1850s," in Deverell and Igler, *Companion to California History*, 167–70.

29. John Walton Caughey, introduction to Wilson, *Indians of Southern California*, xx–xxix; Caughey, "Don Benito Wilson," 289–91; 1852 Letters, Business File, Wilson Papers, Box 2, HL.

30. Hurtado, *Indian Survival*, 129.

31. *Stockton Times*, Jan. 25, Feb. 1, 1851; G. H. Phillips, *Indians and Indian Agents*, 32–37, 48–52.

32. Rodick McKee, Commissioner, San Francisco, to Luke Lea, Commissioner of Indian Affairs, Dec. 6, 1850, in "Report of the Secretary of the Interior, Indian Affairs in California, 1853," 52, HL.

33. G. H. Phillips, *Indians and Indian Agents*, 11–13, 60–67; Eccleston, *Mariposa Indian War*, xi, 3–6; William Bauer Jr., "Native Californians in the Nineteenth Century," in Deverell and Igler, *Companion to California History*, 200–201.

34. A. S. Loughery to Commissioners Redick McKee, Geo. Barber, and O. M. Wozencraft, Oct. 15, 1850, in "Report of the Secretary of the Interior, Indian Affairs in California, 1853," 8–9, HL; Hyer, *"We Are Not Savages,"* 62–65; G. H. Phillips, *Indians and Indian Agents*, 180–82; Gunther, *Ambiguous Justice*, 11–15.

35. *Los Angeles Star*, Oct. 16, 1852; Caughey, introduction to Wilson, *Indians of Southern California*, xvii, xxix–xxxii; Gunther, *Ambiguous Justice*, 15; G. H. Phillips, *Indians and Indian Agents*, 182–83.

36. B. D. Wilson, Indian Agent to Edward F. Beale, Supt. of Indian Affairs, Nov. 11, 1852, Wilson Papers, Box 2, HL.

37. G. H. Phillips, *"Bringing Them under Subjection,"* 88–92; Wilson, *Indians of Southern California.*

38. B. D. Wilson at Fort Tejon to Margaret Hereford Wilson, Sept. 4, 1853, Wilson Papers, Box 2, HL.

39. *Los Angeles Star,* Jan. 15, 1853.

40. Bell, *Reminiscences of a Ranger,* 120.

41. Gunther, *Ambiguous Justice,* 23–24; Latta, *Saga of Rancho El Tejón;* G. H. Phillips, *"Bringing Them under Subjection,"* 101–3; Summer 1853 Accounts, Fort Tejón, Wilson Papers, Box 2, HL.

42. G. H. Phillips, *"Bringing Them under Subjection,"* 238–50; S. L. Johnson, *Roaring Camp,* 225–33.

43. General John Wool, Dept. of the Pacific, Benicia, Feb. 13, 1856, to B. D. Wilson in Sacramento, Wilson Papers, Box 6, HL; Gunther, *Ambiguous Justice,* 26–28.

44. Bell, *Reminiscences of a Ranger,* 39.

45. *Los Angeles Star,* Feb. 12, 1853; McWilliams, *Southern California Country,* 60; Cleland, *Cattle on a Thousand Hills,* 90–96; Deverell, *Whitewashed Adobe,* 13–18.

46. J. A. Stout, *Liberators,* 27–31; Faulk, "Colonization Plan for Northern Sonora," 296–300.

47. Hittell, *History of California,* 3:729–34; 737; J. A. Stout, *Liberators,* 66–71; Bolaños Geyer, *William Walker,* 2:70–77.

48. *Daily Alta California,* Dec. 8, 1853; J. A. Stout, *Liberators,* 84–87; Carr, *World and William Walker,* 81–85.

49. Hittell, *History of California,* 3:742–44, 766–68; Carr, *World and William Walker,* 90–92; *Harper's Weekly,* Jan. 31, 1857.

50. Hittell, *History of California,* 3:808; Deverell, *Whitewashed Adobe,* 16–17; Bell, *Reminiscences of a Ranger,* 218–21.

51. Hittell, *History of California,* 3:808–12; Wyllys, "Henry Crabb," 190–93; *New York Daily Times,* April 15, May 18, 1857; Deverell, *Whitewashed Adobe,* 23–25.

52. Hittell, *History of California,* 3:812–13; *Daily Alta California,* May 31, 1857.

53. Archibald Gillespie to B. D. Wilson in Sacramento, Aug. 4, 1859, Wilson Papers, Box 8, HL.

54. Sen. Benjamin Davis Wilson, "Text of Speech to California Senate," 1856, Wilson Papers, Addenda II, Box 18, HL; P. W. Gates, *Land and Law in California,* 24–28.

55. B. D. Wilson at Lake Vineyard to Margaret Hereford Wilson in St. Louis, Aug. 17, 1856, Wilson Papers, Addenda II, Box 18, HL.

56. Meltzner, "Great 1857 'Fort Tejon' Earthquake"; Southern California Earthquake Data Center, "Fort Tejon Earthquake"; Stover and Coffman, "Seismicity of the United States"; Henry Myles to B. D. Wilson, Jan. 28, 1957, in Wilson Papers, Box 6, HL; J. Warner, *Santa Barbara Gazette,* Jan. 22, 1857; *Los Angeles Star,* Jan. 17, 1857.

57. Father Felix Cicaterri to B. D. Wilson, Oct. 27, 1857, Wilson Papers, Box 7, HL; Margaret Wilson to Agnes Kamp, Dec. 3, 1857, Wilson Papers, Box 7, HL;

Joshua Phelps in Sacramento to B. D. Wilson at Lake Vineyard, Dec. 27, 1864, Wilson Papers, Box 10, HL.

58. Pierre Chouteau Jr. to Charles Chouteau and William Maffitt, April 20, 1857, in Sunder, *Fur Trade*, 161; Sunder, *Fur Trade*, 14–17.

59. Bunyon Gratiot to P. Chouteau Jr. and Co., Dec. 13 and 14, 1854, Box 47, Chouteau Collection, MHS; Barbour, *Fort Union*, 204–5.

60. R. White, "Winning of the West," 323–30; Ostler, *Plains Sioux*, 22–25.

61. Stephanson, *Manifest Destiny*, 16–27; Hendrickson, *Union, Nation, or Empire*, 176–82; Ostler, *Plains Sioux*, 40–45; Price, *Oglala People*, 38–40.

62. Sunder, *Fur Trade*, 187; Barbour, *Fort Union*, 130.

63. Sunder, *Fur Trade*, 160–61; Peterson, "Many Roads to Red River," 44, 57–60; Murphy, *Gathering of Rivers*, 46–55.

64. L. H. Morgan, *Indian Journals*, 26.

65. P. W. Gates, *Fifty Million Acres*, 3–10; Malin, *Nebraska Question*, 51–55.

66. George Washington to Jacob Read, Nov. 3, 1784, qtd. in Prucha, *Great Father*, 1:45.

67. Wishart, *Unspeakable Sadness*, 59–65; 101–3; Miner and Unrau, *End of Indian Kansas*, 4–6.

68. Rensink, "Nebraska and Kansas Territories," 56–61; Etcheson, *Bleeding Kansas*, 44–49; SenGupta, *For God and Mammon*, 12–16.

69. "Territorial Census of Kansas, 1855," *Kansas Historical Quarterly*, 6:2 (May 1936).

70. *St. Joseph Tribune*, Sept. 23, 1853, quoted in Malin, *Nebraska Question*, 163.

71. Parker, *Kansas and Nebraska Handbook*, x, 115.

72. Miner and Unrau, *End of Indian Kansas*, 10–13; Prucha, *Great Father*, 330–31; Chaput, "James W. Denver,", 57–75; Wishart, *Unspeakable Sadness*, 103–5.

73. Prucha, *Great Father*, 346–48.

74. Harvey, *History of the Shawnee Indians*, 269–70; Miner and Unrau, *End of Indian Kansas*, 16–17, 50; Mullis, *Peacekeeping on the Plains*, 21–22.

75. Etcheson, *Bleeding Kansas*, 58–59, 99–104; Caldwell, *Annals of the Methodist Shawnee Mission*, 5, 93–97.

76. R. Drake, "Law That Ripped America in Two"; Etcheson, *Bleeding Kansas*, 109–11.

77. George R. Manypenny, Commissioner of Indian Affairs, "1856 Annual Report," June 1857, in *Reports of the Commissioners of Indian Affairs*.

78. Caldwell, *Annals of the Methodist Shawnee Mission*, 101.

79. L. H. Morgan, *Indian Journals*, 42, 38.

80. Malin, "Motives of Stephen A. Douglas," 321–53; Miner and Unrau, End of *Indian Kansas*, 133.

81. McMurtry, *Oh What a Slaughter*, 6–13.

82. R. W. Walker, Turley, and Leonard, *Massacre at Mountain Meadows*, xiii.

83. Bagley, *Blood of the Prophets*, 50–51; Walker, Turley, and Leonard, *Massacre at Mountain Meadows*, 24–26; J. D. Lee, *Mormon Chronicle*, 1:129.

84. Novak, *House of Mourning*, 36–45; D. L. Bigler and Bagley, *Innocent Blood*, 75–81.

85. Haight from LDS ward records in Cedar City, qtd. in Juanita Brooks, *Mountain Meadows Massacre*, 52; Bagley, *Blood of the Prophets*, 118–20.

86. J. D. Lee, *Mormonism Unveiled*, 231–36, 239–46; Bagley, *Blood of the Prophets*, 123–30, 142–48; Juanita Brooks, *Mountain Meadows Massacre*, 105–6.

87. Qtd. in Bagley, *Blood of the Prophets*, 151; Novak, *House of Mourning*, 161–73.

88. Diary of Brigham Young, qtd. in Bagley, *Blood of the Prophets*, 169.

89. Brigham Young to J. W. Denver, Commissioner of Indian Affairs, qtd. in D. L. Bigler and Bagley, *Innocent Blood*, 126.

90. "The Massacre at Mountain Canon Confirmed," *Alta California*, Oct. 27, 1857.

91. D. L. Bigler and Bagley, *Innocent Blood*, 169–70.

92. Carleton, *Report on the Massacre*, 29, 26.

93. G. C. Anderson, *Kinsmen of Another Kind*, 261–73.

94. Gilman, *Henry Hastings Sibley*, 66–70.

95. Qtd. in G. C. Anderson, *Kinsmen of Another Kind*, 141; Gilman, *Henry Hastings Sibley*, 74–76.

96. Meyer, *History of the Santee Sioux*, 101–4; G. C. Anderson, *Kinsmen of Another Kind*, 214–21.

97. Meyer, *History of the Santee Sioux*, 97–105; G. C. Anderson, *Kinsmen of Another Kind*, 226–32.

98. Andrew Myrick, qtd. in Folwell, *History of Minnesota*, 2:233; G. C. Anderson, *Kinsmen of Another Kind*, 249–53.

99. Meyer, *History of the Santee Sioux*, 117–22.

100. G. C. Anderson, *Kinsmen of Another Kind*, 272–78; Meyer, *History of the Santee Sioux*, 128–31; Chomsky, "United States–Dakota War Trials"; Steil and Post, "Minnesota's Uncivil War."

101. Allanson, "Stirring Adventures"; S. J. Brown, "In Captivity."

102. N. West, *Life and Times of Sibley*.

103. Editorial, *New York Tribune*, Jan. 29, 1859, in Hafen, *Colorado Gold Rush*, 254.

104. E. West, *Contested Plains*, 145–47, 160–64; A. Hyde, "Mormons and Miners," 162–65.

105. Halaas and Masich, *Halfbreed*, 268–69, 296–307; Lubers, "William Bent's Family," 19–21.

106. Despite a recent spate of writing about Sand Creek the best accounts of what happened that day are G. L. Roberts, "Sand Creek," 420–41; Hoig, *Sand Creek Massacre*; and E. West, *Contested Plains*, which provides a rich explanatory context.

107. U.S. War Department, *War of the Rebellion*, 41:963–64; Hoig, *Sand Creek Massacre*, 80–86; E. West, *Contested Plains*, 287–90.

108. U.S. War Department, *War of the Rebellion*, 41:914; Hoig, *Sand Creek Massacre*, 112–27.

109. Hoig, *Sand Creek Massacre*, 138–43.

110. G. E. Hyde, *Life of George Bent*, 151; G. Roberts, "Sand Creek," 420–41.

111. Greene and Scott, *Finding Sand Creek*, 19–20. This research duo of archeologist and historian, hired by the Park Service in 1998 to ascertain some "facts" about Sand Creek, concluded that about 160 people were killed in the massacre, though many more probably died of their injuries.

112. G. Roberts, "Sand Creek," 443–55; Halaas, "'All the Camp was Weeping,'" 2–17; "Sand Creek Massacre," *Report of the Secretary of War*, Senate Exec. Doc. 26, 39th Cong., 2d sess. (Washington DC: Government Printing Office, 1867), 11–223.

EPILOGUE

1. Hodes, "Mercurial Nature, 85, 106–9.

2. Emparán, *Vallejos of California*, 380–82.

3. Mariano Vallejo to Platon Vallejo, Dec. 1887, in Emparán, *Vallejos of California*, 179.

4. Mariano Guadelupe Vallejo to Archbishop J. S. Alemany, May 11, 1878, in Emparán, *Vallejos of California*, 361; McGinty, *Strong Wine*, 299–301, 410–11.

5. Emparán, *Vallejos of California*, 106–7; Rosenus, *General M. G. Vallejo*, 223–33; Culinary Institute of America, "Agoston Haraszthy," Vintners Hall of Fame Inductees: 2007, http://www.ciaprochef.com/winestudies/events/vhf_inductees.html (accessed Aug. 4, 2010).

6. Cleland, *Cattle on a Thousand Hills*, 108–11; Read, *Don Benito Wilson*, 184–85; William Boardman to B. D. Wilson, June 12, 1860, Wilson Papers, Box 8, HL; Page, *Pasadena*, 8–17.

7. Read, *Don Benito Wilson*, 78–82; 1856–57, Box 6, 1867–68, Box 13, Wilson Papers, HL.

8. B. D. Wilson in Washington DC, to Margaret Wilson in Lake Vineyard, Dec. 30, 1870, Wilson Papers, Box 14, HL; Stephenson, *Don Bernardo Yorba*, 63.

9. Family Letters, large correspondence between William E. Boardman and B. D. Wilson about Sublette Estate, in *Wilson Papers*, Box 6, Box 7, Box 12, Box 14; Addenda II, Box 14, Box 17, HL.

10. Simmons, *Kit Carson*, 106; Twitchell, *Leading Facts*, 2:235.

11. McClung, *Carson-Bent-Boggs*, 74, 89; Simmons, *Kit Carson*, 88–90, 138–42; Sabin, *Kit Carson Days* 2:638–55.

12. Halaas and Masich, *Halfbreed*, 266–70.

13. Halaas and Masich, *Halfbreed*, 270; U.S. Bureau of the Census, Jackson County, Missouri, 1860; U.S. Bureau of the Census, Prowers County, Colorado Territory, 1870; Lavender, *Bent's Fort*, 328–29, 391.

14. McClung, *Carson-Bent-Boggs*, 95–101; Halaas and Masich, *Halfbreed*, 268–69, 296–307; Lubers, "William Bent's Family," 19–21.

15. *Olympia Pioneer and Democrat*, Oct. 12, 1855, Stevens Papers, BRBML.

16. B. B. Barker, *McLoughlin Empire*, 137; Morrison, *Outpost*, 464.

17. "Show Flyer, 1873," *McKay Folder*, Oregon Historical Society Archives, Portland.

18. John McLoughlin to James Douglas, March 1850, in McLoughlin, *Business Correspondence*, 140–42; Fogdall, *Royal Family*, 193, 232–36; R. G. Montgomery, *White-Headed Eagle*, 156–58, 199.

19. Morrison, *Outpost*, 464–66; Fogdall, *Royal Family*, 193–99.

20. B. B. Barker, *McLoughlin Empire*, 137–40; Fogdall, *Royal Family*, 215–27.

21. U.S. Bureau of the Census, *St. Louis Population Tables*, 1860; Clokey, *William H. Ashley*, 37–38; Pierre Chouteau Sr., Will proved June 1854, St. Louis Probate Court, Chouteau Collection, MHS.

22. Christian, *Before Lewis and Clark*, 386; Honig, *Westport*, 111.

23. A. T. Brown, *Frontier Community*, 14–23, 54–57; McCandless, *History of Missouri*, 2:129–133.

24. P. Chouteau, Jr. and Co., St. Louis to A. Drips. August 1, 1842; Account of Andrew Drips, Boone and Hamilton in Westport, May 29, 1844, Drips Papers, MHS.

25. Halaas and Masich, *Halfbreed*, 76–80; "Robert Campbell's Private Journal," *Bulletin of the Missouri Historical Society* 20 (July 1964).

26. U.S. Bureau of the Census, 1850 United States Manuscript Census, Population Schedule, Kaw Township, Jackson County, MO, NARA microfilm version; U.S. Bureau of the Census, 1860 Manuscript Census, Population Schedule, St. Louis, MO, Ward 5, NARA microfilm version; Louise Geroux Drips to Kate Benoist, July 27, 1857, Ash Grove MO, Drips Papers, MHS.

Bibliography

MANUSCRIPT COLLECTIONS

Bancroft Library, University of California, Berkeley, California (BL)

    Hudson's Bay Company Collection
    John Sutter's "Reminiscences" (unpublished typescript)
    Vallejo Collections

Beinecke Rare Books and Manuscripts Library, Yale University, New Haven, Connecticut (BRBML)

    George Foster Emmons, "Journals"
    Elwood Evans Scrapbooks
    William Winlock Miller Papers
    Dale Morgan Early Mississippi Valley Newspaper Transcripts
    Benjamin O'Fallon Letterbook
    Isaac Stevens Papers

Huntington Library, San Marino, California (HL)

    American Indian Manuscripts
    Mormon Manuscripts
    Oregon Territory Documents Collection
    William Ritch Collection
    Abel Stearns Collection
    Vallejo Collection
    Wilson Papers

Missouri Historical Society, St. Louis, Missouri (MHS)

    Chouteau Collection
    William Clark Papers
    Andrew Drips Papers
    Thomas Forsyth Papers
    John O'Fallon Papers
    Missouri Territorial Papers
    George C. Sibley Papers
    Sublette Family Papers

U.S. Office of Indian Affairs, Department of War

    Osage Agency, Letters Received, 1828–1835, 1841

St. Louis Superintendency, Letters Received, 1827–1849

St. Peters Agency, Letters Received, 1835–1842

PUBLISHED MATERIALS

Abel, Annie H. "Proposals for an Indian State, 1778–1878." In *Annual Report of the American Historical Association for the Year 1907*, vol. 1, part 2. Washington DC: Government Printing Office, 1908.

Abert, James William. *Expedition to the Southwest: An 1845 Reconnaissance of Colorado, New Mexico, Texas and Oklahoma.* Rpt., Lincoln: University of Nebraska Press, 1999.

Adelman, Jeremy, and Stephen Aron. "From Borderlands to Borders: Empires, Nation-States, and the Peoples in between in North American History." *American Historical Review* 104 (1999): 814–41.

Alford, Thomas Wildcat. *Shawnee Domestic and Tribal Life.* Xenia OH: 1934.

Allan, George T. "Journal of a Journey from Fort Vancouver to York Factory, 1841." In *Oregon Pioneers Association Transactions* 9 (1881): 38–55.

Allanson, George C. "Stirring Adventures of the Joseph R. Brown Family." In *The Garland Library of Narratives of North American Captivities*, ed. Wilcomb Washburn, vol. 103. New York: Garland, 1976.

Ambrose, Stephen. *Undaunted Courage: Meriwether Lewis, Thomas Jefferson and the Opening of the American West.* New York: Simon and Schuster, 1996.

Ames, Kenneth M., and Herbert D. G. Maschner. *The Peoples of the Northwest Coast: Their Archeology and Prehistory.* London: Thames and Hudson, 1999.

Anderson, Gary Clayton. *The Conquest of Texas: Ethnic Cleansing in the Promised Land, 1820–1875.* Norman: University of Oklahoma Press, 2005.

———. *The Indian Southwest, 1580–1830: Ethnogenesis and Reinvention.* Norman: University of Oklahoma Press, 1999.

———. *Kinsmen of Another Kind: Dakota-White Relations in the Upper Mississippi Valley, 1650–1862.* Lincoln: University of Nebraska Press, 1984.

Anderson, Harry H. "Fur Traders as Fathers: The Origins of the Mixed-Blooded Community among the Rosebud Sioux." *South Dakota History* 3 (Summer 1973): 239–55.

Anna, Timothy E. *Forging Mexico, 1821–1835.* Lincoln: University of Nebraska Press, 1998.

Armour, David. *Colonial Michilimackinac.* Mackinac Island MI: Mackinac State Historic Parks, 2000.

Arnold, Samuel P. "William W. Bent." In Hafen, *Mountain Men*, 6:61–84.

Aron, Stephen. *American Confluence: The Missouri Frontier from Borderland to Border State.* Bloomington IN: Indiana University Press, 2006.

Arrington, Leonard J. "Latter-day Saints." In *The New Encyclopedia of the American West*, ed. Howard R. Lamar. New Haven: Yale University Press, 1998.

Arrington, Leonard J., and Bitton, Davis. *The Mormon Experience: A History of the Latter-day Saints.* New York: Alfred A. Knopf, 1979.

Arrington, Leonard J., Feramorz Y. Fox, and Dean L. May. *Building the City of God: Community and Cooperation among the Mormons.* Urbana: University of Illinois Press, 1992.

Arthur, M. Elizabeth. "General Dickson and the Indian Liberating Army in the North." *Ontario History* 62, no. 3 (1970): 151–62.

Aubert, Guillaume. "The Blood of France: Race and the Purity of Blood in the French Atlantic World." *William and Mary Quarterly* 61 (July 2004): 439–78.

Audubon, John James. *Audubon and His Journals.* Ed. Maria R. Audubon. Vol. 2. Rpt., New York: Dover, 1994.

Augst, Thomas. *The Clerk's Tale: Young Men and Moral Life in Nineteenth-Century America.* Chicago: University of Chicago Press, 2003.

Austin, Moses, and Stephen F. Austin. *The Austin Papers.* Ed. Eugene C. Barker. 3 vols. Washington DC: Annual Report of the American Historical Association, 1919.

Babb, Theodore A. *In the Bosom of the Comanches: A Thrilling Tale of Savage Indian Life, Massacre, and Captivity.* Dallas: John F. Worley, 1912.

Bagley, Will. *Blood of the Prophets: Brigham Young and the Massacre at Mountain Meadows.* Norman: University of Oklahoma Press, 2002.

Bailey, Garrick. "Osage." In *Handbook of North American Indians,* ed. William C. Sturtevant, vol. 13. Washington DC: Smithsonian Press, 2001.

Baird, Elizabeth Therese. "Reminiscences of Early Days on Mackinac Island." *Wisconsin Historical Society Collections,* 1898, 14:17–64.

Bancroft, Hubert Howe. *History of Arizona and New Mexico.* San Francisco: History Co., 1890.

———. *History of California.* Vol. 3, *1825–1840;* vol. 4: *1840–1845.* San Francisco: History Co., 1885–86.

———. *History of Oregon.* 2 vols. San Francisco: History Co., 1886–88.

———. *The History of the Northwest Coast, 1800–1846.* Vol. 28 of *The Works of Hubert Howe Bancroft.* San Francisco: Bancroft, 1884.

Banner, Stuart. *How the Indians Lost Their Land: Law and Power on the Frontier.* Cambridge MA: Harvard University Press, 2005.

———. *Legal Systems in Conflict: Property and Sovereignty in Missouri, 1750–1860.* Norman: University of Oklahoma Press, 2000.

Barbour, Barton H. *Fort Union and the Upper Missouri Fur Trade.* Norman: University of Oklahoma Press, 2001.

Barker, Burt Brown. *The McLoughlin Empire and Its Rulers.* Glendale CA: Arthur H. Clark, 1959.

Barker, Eugene C. *The Life of Stephen F. Austin, Founder of Texas, 1793–1836: A Chapter in the Westward Movement of the Anglo-American People.* Nashville: Cokesbury Press, 1925.

Barr, Juliana. "Beyond Their Control: Spaniards in Native Texas." In *Choice, Persuasion, and Coercion: Social Control on Spain's North American Frontier,* ed. Ross Frank and Jesús de la Teja. Albuquerque: University of New Mexico Press, 2005.

———. *Peace Came in the Form of a Woman*. Chapel Hill: University of North Carolina Press, 2007.

Batman, Richard. *The Outer Coast*. New York: Harcourt Brace Jovanovich, 1985.

Bauer, K. Jack. *The Mexican War, 1846–1848*. New York: Macmillan, 1974.

Beard, Charles A. "Written History as an Act of Faith." *American Historical Review* 39 (Jan. 1934): 219–31.

Beck, Paul Norman. *The First Sioux War, 1854–1856*. Lanham MD: University Press of America, 2004.

Beck, Warren A., and Ynez D. Haase. *Historical Atlas of California*. Norman: University of Oklahoma Press, 1974.

———. *Historical Atlas of the American West*. Norman: University of Oklahoma Press, 1989.

Beckham, Stephen Dow, ed. *Oregon Indians: Voices from Two Decades*. Corvallis: Oregon State University Press, 2006.

———. *Requiem for a People: The Rogue Indians and the Frontiersmen*. Norman: University of Oklahoma Press, 1971.

Becknell, William. "Journals." In *News of the Plains and Rockies, 1803–1865: Original Narratives of Overland Travel*, ed. David A. White. Vol. 2. Spokane WA: Arthur H. Clark, 1996.

Beebe, Rose-Marie, and Robert M. Senkewicz, trans. and eds. *Testimonios: Early California through the Eyes of Women, 1815–1848*. Berkeley: Heyday Books, 2006.

Bell, Horace. *Reminiscences of a Ranger; or, Early Times in Southern California*. Los Angeles: Primavera Press, 1933.

Bent, Teresina. "Account of Her Father's Death." *New Mexico Historical Review* 8 (1933): 121–23.

Benton, Thomas Hart. *Thirty Years' View; or, A History of the Working of the American Government for Thirty Years*. 2 vols. New York: D. Appleton, 1858.

Berlandier, Jean Louis. *The Indians of Texas in 1830*. Ed. John C. Ewers. Washington DC: Smithsonian Press, 1969.

Berry, Don. *A Majority of Scoundrels: An Informal History of the Rocky Mountain Fur Trade*. New York: Harper and Brothers, 1961.

Berthrong, Donald J. *The Southern Cheyennes*. Norman: University of Oklahoma Press, 1963.

Bigler, David L. *The Forgotten Kingdom: Mormon Theocracy in the American West, 1847–1896*. Spokane WA: Arthur H. Clark, 1998.

———. "Mormon Missionaries, the Utah War, and the 1858 Bannock Raid of Fort Limhi." *Montana* 53, no. 3 (Autumn 2003): 26–38.

Bigler, David, and Will Bagley, eds. *Army of Israel: Mormon Battalion Narratives*. Spokane WA: Arthur H. Clark, 2000.

———, eds. *Innocent Blood: Essential Narratives of the Mountain Meadows Massacre*. Norman OK: Arthur H. Clark, 2008.

Bigler, Henry. *Bigler's Chronicle of the West*. Ed. Erwin G. Gudde. Berkeley: University of California Press, 1962.

———. "Diary of Henry Bigler in 1847 and 1848." Ed. John S. Hittell. *Overland Monthly* 10 (Oct. 1887): 238–52.

Billon, Frederic Louis. *Annals of St. Louis in Its Territorial Days from 1804 to 1821.* St. Louis: n.p., 1881.

Binkley, William Campbell. "New Mexico and the Texan Santa Fé Expedition." *Southwestern Historical Quarterly* 27, no. 2. (Oct. 1923): 85–109.

Binnema, Ted, and William Dobak. "'Like a Greedy Wolf': The Blackfeet, the St. Louis Fur Trade, and War Fever, 1807–1831." *Journal of the Early Republic* 29, no. 3 (Fall 2009): 411–40.

Blackhawk, Ned. *Violence over the Land: Indians and Empires in the Early American West.* Cambridge MA: Harvard University Press, 2006.

Blackwelder, Bernice. *Great Westerner: The Story of Kit Carson.* Caldwell ID: Caxton Printers, 1962.

Boag, Peter G. *Environment and Experience: Settlement Culture in Nineteenth-Century Oregon.* Berkeley: University of California Press, 1992.

Bolaños Geyer, Alejandro. *William Walker: The Gray-Eyed Man of Destiny.* 2 vols. Lake Saint Louis MO: A. Bolaños-Geyer, 1988–91.

Bonthius, Andrew. "The Patriot War of 1837–1838: Locofocoism with a Gun?" *Labour/Le Travail* (Fall 2003), http://www.historycooperative.org/journals/llt/52/bonthius.html (accessed Aug. 25 2008).

Boutros, David. "Confluence of People and Place: The Chouteau Posts on the Missouri and Kansas Rivers." *Missouri Historical Review* 97, no. 1 (Oct. 2002): 1–19.

Bouvier, Virginia M. *Women and the Conquest of California, 1542–1840.* Tucson: University of Arizona Press, 2001.

Boyd, Robert. *The Coming of the Spirit of Pestilence: Introduced Infectious Diseases and Population Decline among Northwest Coast Indians, 1774–1874.* Seattle: University of Washington Press, 1999.

Brackenridge, Henry M. *Journal of a Voyage up the River Missouri, Performed in Eighteen Hundred and Eleven.* Vol. 6 of Thwaites, *Early Western Travels.*

Bradbury, Bettina, ed. *Canadian Family History: Selected Readings.* Toronto: Copp Clark Pittman, 1992.

Brodie, Fawn M. *No Man Knows My History: The Life of Joseph Smith.* 2nd ed. New York: Alfred A. Knopf, 1971.

Brooke, George M., Jr. "The Vest Pocket War of Commodore Jones." *Pacific Historical Review* 31, no. 3 (1962): 217–33.

Brooks, James. *Captives and Cousins: Slavery, Kinship, and Community in the Southwest Borderlands.* Chapel Hill: University of North Carolina Press, 2001.

Brooks, Juanita. *The Mountain Meadows Massacre.* Norman: University of Oklahoma Press, 1962.

Brown, A. Theodore. *Frontier Community: Kansas City to 1870.* Columbia: University of Missouri Press, 1963.

Brown, Bertram Wyatt. *Southern Honor: Ethics and Behavior in the Old South.* New York: Oxford University Press, 1982.

Brown, Jennifer. *Strangers in Blood: Fur Trade Company Families in Indian Country.* Vancouver: University of British Columbia Press, 1980.

Brown, Joseph C., ed. *Valley of the Strong: Stories of Yakima and Central Washington History.* Yakima WA: Westcoast, 1974.

Brown, Samuel J. "In Captivity: The Experiences, Privations, and Dangers of Sam'l J. Brown and Others." In *The Garland Library of Narratives of North American Captivities,* ed. Wilcomb Washburn, vol. 76. New York: Garland, 1976.

Buchanan, James. *The Works of James Buchanan: Comprising His Speeches, State Papers, and Private Correspondence.* Ed. John Bassett Moore. 14 vols. Philadelphia: J. B. Lippincott, 1908–11.

Burley, Edith. *Servants of the Honorable Company: Work, Discipline, and Conflict in the Hudson's Bay Company, 1770–1879.* Toronto: Oxford University Press, 1997.

Burns, Louis F. *A History of the Osage People.* Tuscaloosa: University of Alabama Press, 2004.

———. *Osage Indian Bands and Clans.* Fallbrook CA: Ciga Press, 1984.

———. *Osage Mission Baptisms, Marriages, and Interments, 1820–1886.* Fallbrook CA: Ciga Press, 1986.

Bushman, Richard Lyman. *Joseph Smith: Rough Stone Rolling.* New York: Alfred A. Knopf, 2006.

Caldwell, Martha, comp. *Annals of the Methodist Shawnee Mission and Indian Manual Labor School.* Topeka: Kansas State Historical Society, 1939.

Calhoun, James S. *The Official Correspondence of James S. Calhoun.* Ed. Annie H. Abel. Washington DC, 1915.

Calloway, Colin G. *Crown and Calumet: British Indian Relations, 1783–1815.* Norman: University of Oklahoma Press, 1985.

———. *One Vast Winter Count: The Native American West before Lewis and Clark.* Lincoln: University of Nebraska Press, 2003.

———. *The Shawnees and the War for America.* New York: Penguin Books, 2007.

Calvert, Robert A., Arnoldo De León, and Gregg Cantrell. *The History of Texas.* 4th ed. Wheeling, Ill.: Harlan Davidson, 2007.

Camarillo, Albert. *Chicanos in California: A History of Mexican-Americans in California.* San Francisco: Boyd and Fraser, 1984.

Campbell, Eugene E. *Establishing Zion: The Mormon Church in the American West, 1847–1869.* Salt Lake City: Signature Books, 1988.

Cannon, Miles. *Waiilatpu: Its Rise and Fall, 1836–1847.* Boise ID: Capital News Job Rooms, 1915.

Cantrell, Gregg. *Stephen F. Austin: Empresario of Texas.* New Haven: Yale University Press, 1999.

Carleton, James Henry. *Report on the Subject of the Massacre at the Mountain Meadows in Utah Territory.* Little Rock AR: True Democrat Steam Press, 1860.

Carlson, Laurie Winn. *Seduced by the West: Jefferson's West and the Lure of Land beyond the Mississippi.* Chicago: Ivan R. Dee, 2003.

Carnes, Mark C. *Historical Atlas of the United States.* New York: Routledge, 2003.

Carr, Albert Z. *The World and William Walker.* New York: Harper and Row, 1963.

Carson, Kit. *Kit Carson's Autobiography.* Ed. Milo Milton Quaife. Lincoln: University of Nebraska Press, 1966.

Carter, Clarence Edwin, comp. *Territorial Papers of the United States.* 28 vols. Washington DC: Government Printing Office, 1934–69).

Carter, Harvey L. "Andrew Drips." In *The Mountain Men and the Fur Trade of the Far West,* ed. LeRoy R. Hafen, vol. 6. Glendale CA: Arthur H. Clark, 1968.

———. *"Dear Old Kit": The Historical Christopher Carson.* Norman: University of Oklahoma Press, 1968.

Carter, Sarah. *The Importance of Being Monogamous: Marriage and Nation Building in Western Canada to 1915.* Edmonton, Alberta: Athabasca University Press, 2008.

Cass, Lewis. Report of the Secretary of War, Feb. 19, 1836. In U.S. Congress, *American State Papers: Military Affairs.* Vol. 6. Buffalo NY: W. S. Hein, 1998.

Catlin, George. *Letters and Notes on the Manners, Customs, and Conditions of the North American Indians.* 2 vols. 1841. Rpt., New York: Dover, 1973.

Caughey, John Walton. "Don Benito Wilson, An Average Southern Californian." *Huntington Library Quarterly* 2 (1939): 278–94.

Cerruti, Henry. *Ramblings in California: The Adventures of Henry Cerruti.* Ed. Margaret Mollins and Virginia E. Thickens. San Francisco, 1874; rpt., Berkeley CA: Friends of the Bancroft Library, 1954.

Chalfant, William J. *Dangerous Passage: The Santa Fe Trail and the Mexican War.* Norman: University of Oklahoma Press, 1994.

Chaput, Donald. "James W. Denver." In *The Commissioners of Indian Affairs,* ed. Robert M. Kvasnicka and Herman J. Viola. Lincoln: University of Nebraska Press, 1979.

Chardon, Francis A. *Chardon's Journal at Fort Clark, 1834–1839.* Ed. Annie H. Abel. Pierre SD: Historical Society of South Dakota, 1932.

Chavez, Angelico. *But Time and Chance: The Story of Padre Martinez of Taos, 1793–1867.* Santa Fe NM: Sunstone Press, 1981.

———. *Origins of New Mexico Families in the Spanish Colonial Period.* 2 vols. Santa Fe: Historical Society of New Mexico, 1954.

Chipman, Donald E. *Spanish Texas, 1519–1821.* Austin: University of Texas Press, 1992.

Chittenden, Hiram Martin. *The American Fur Trade of the Far West: A History of the Pioneer Trading Posts and Early Fur Companies of the Missouri Valley and the Rocky Mountains and the Overland Commerce with Santa Fe.* 3 vols. New York: F. P. Harper, 1902.

Chomsky, Carol. "The United States–Dakota War Trials: A Study in Military Injustice," 43 *Stanford Law Review* 13 (1990).

Chouteau, François, and Berenice Chouteau. *Cher Oncle, Cher Papa: The Letters of François and Berenice Chouteau.* By Dorothy Brandt Marra; trans. Marie-Laure Dionne Pal; ed. David Boutros. Kansas City MO: Western Historical Manuscript Collection–Kansas City, University of Missouri, 2001.

Christian, Shirley. *Before Lewis and Clark: The Story of the Chouteaus, the French Dynasty That Ruled America's Frontier.* New York: Farrar, Strauss and Giroux, 2004.

Christy, Howard A. "Open Hand and Mailed Fist: Mormon-Indian Relations in Utah, 1847–1852." *Utah Historical Quarterly* 46 (Summer 1978): 116–35.

Cincinnati Observatory. "History of the Cincinnati Observatory." http://www.cin cinnatiobservatory.org/history.html (accessed July 13, 2010).

Clarke, Dwight L. *Stephen Watts Kearny: Soldier of the West.* Norman: University of Oklahoma Press, 1961.

Clarke, S. A. *Pioneer Days of Oregon History.* 2 vols. Portland OR: J. Gill, 1905.

Cleland, Robert Glass. *Cattle on a Thousand Hills: Southern California, 1850–1880.* San Marino CA: Huntington Library, 1951.

———. "The Early Sentiment for the Annexation of California: An Account of the Growth of American Interest in California, 1835–1846," in 3 parts. *Southwestern Historical Quarterly* 18, nos. 1, 2, and 3 (1914–15).

———. *A History of California: The American Period.* New York: Macmillan, 1922.

———. *Pathfinders.* Los Angeles: Powell, 1928.

———. *This Reckless Breed of Men: The Trappers and Fur Traders of the Southwest.* New York: Alfred A. Knopf, 1963.

Clokey, Richard M. *William H. Ashley.* Norman: University of Oklahoma Press, 1980.

Comer, Douglas C. *Ritual Ground: Bent's Old Fort, World Formation, and the Annexation of the Southwest.* Berkeley: University of California Press, 1996.

Compilation of All Treaties between the United States and the Indian Tribes, Now in Force as Laws. Washington DC: Government Printing Office, 1873.

Cook, Sherburne F. *The Epidemic of 1830–1833 in California and Oregon.* Berkeley: University of California Press, 1955.

———. *Expeditions to the Interior of California: Central Valley, 1820–1840.* Salinas CA: Coyote Press, 1962.

———. "Historical Demography." In *Handbook of North American Indians,* ed. William C. Sturtevant. Vol. 8: *Plains.* Washington DC: Smithsonian Institution Press, 1978.

Cook, Warren L. *Flood Tide of Empire: Spain and the Pacific Northwest, 1543–1819.* New Haven: Yale University Press, 1973.

Costello, Julia G., and David J. Hornbeck. "Alta California, an Overview." In *Columbian Consequences,* ed. David Hurst Thomas. Vol. 1: *Archaeological and Historical Perspectives on the Spanish Borderlands West.* Washington DC: Smithsonian Institution Press, 1989.

Cott, Nancy. *Public Vows: A History of Marriage and the Nation.* Cambridge MA: Harvard University Press, 2002.

Cox, Ross. *Adventures on the Columbia River.* London: H. Colburn, 1831.

Crook, George. *General George Crook: His Autobiography.* Ed. Martin P. Schmitt. Norman: University of Oklahoma Press, 1946.

Crutchfield, James A. *Tragedy at Taos: The Revolt of 1847.* Plano TX: Texas Republic Press, 1995.

Dary, David. *The Santa Fe Trail.* New York: Alfred A. Knopf, 2001.

Davidson, Gordon Charles. *The North West Company.* Berkeley: University of California Press, 1916.

Davis, Ronald L. F. "Community and Conflict in Pioneer St. Louis, Missouri." *Western Historical Quarterly* 10, no. 3 (July 1979): 334–55.

Davis, William C. *Lone Star Rising: The Revolutionary Birth of the Texas Republic.* New York: Free Press, 2004.

Davis, William Heath. *Seventy-Five Years in California.* San Francisco: John Howell, 1929.

Deatherage, Charles P. *Early History of Greater Kansas City.* 3 vols. Kansas City MO: Interstate, 1927.

De la Teja, Jesús F. *San Antonio de Béxar: A Community on New Spain's Northern Frontier.* Albuquerque: University of New Mexico Press, 1995.

DeLay, Brian. *War of a Thousand Deserts: Indian Raids and the U.S. Mexican War.* New Haven: Yale University Press, 2008.

Del Mar, David Peterson. *Oregon's Promise: An Interpretive History.* Corvallis: Oregon State University Press, 2003.

DeMallie, Raymond J. "Kinship: The Foundation for Native American Society." In *Studying Native America: Problems and Prospects*, ed. Russell Thornton. Madison: University of Wisconsin Press, 1998.

———. "Touching the Pen: Plains Indian Treaty Councils in Ethno-historical Perspective." In *Ethnicity on the Great Plains*, ed. Frederick Luebke. Lincoln: University of Nebraska Press, 1980.

DeMallie, Raymond J., and Alfonso Ortiz, eds. *North American Indian Anthropology.* Norman: University of Oklahoma Press, 1994.

Denig, Edwin T. *The Assiniboine.* In *46th Annual Report of the Bureau of Ethnography*, ed. J. N. B. Hewitt. Washington DC 1930.

———. *Five Indian Tribes of the Upper Missouri: Sioux, Arickaras, Assiniboines, Crees, Crows*, ed. John C. Ewers. Norman: University of Oklahoma Press, 1962.

De Smet, Pierre-Jean. *Life, Letters and Travels of Father Pierre-Jean de Smet, S.J., 1801–1873.* Ed. Hiram Martin Chittenden and Alfred Talbot Richardson. 4 vols. New York: F. P. Harper, 1904–7.

Deverell, William F. *Whitewashed Adobe: The Rise of Los Angeles and the Remaking of Its Mexican Past.* Berkeley: University of California Press, 2004.

Deverell, William, and David Igler, eds. *A Companion to California History.* Sussex UK: Wiley-Blackwell, 2008.

DeVoto, Bernard. *The Year of Decision: 1846.* Boston: Little, Brown, 1942.

Dickason, Olive. "From 'One Nation' in the Northeast to 'New Nation' in the Northwest." *American Indian Culture and Research Journal* 6, no. 2 (1982): 1–21.

Dillon, Richard. *Fool's Gold: The Decline and Fall of Captain John Sutter of California.* Santa Cruz CA: Western Tanager Press, 1967.

Din, Gilbert C., and Abraham Nasatir. *The Imperial Osages: Spanish-Indian Diplomacy in the Mississippi Valley.* Norman: University of Oklahoma Press, 1983.

Ditz, Toby L. "Formative Ventures: Eighteenth-Century Commercial Letters and the Articulation of Experience." In *Epistolary Selves: Letters and Letter-Writers, 1600–1945*, ed. Rebecca Earle. London: Ashgate, 1999.

———. "The New Men's History and the Peculiar Absence of Gendered Power: Some Remedies from Early American Gender History." *Gender and History* 16, no. 1 (2004): 1–35.

———. "Shipwrecked; or, Masculinity Imperiled: Mercantile Representations of Failure and the Gendered Self in Eighteenth-Century Philadelphia." *Journal of American History* 81 (June 1994): 51–80.

Dobyns, Henry F. "Native American Trade Centers as Contagious Disease Foci." In *Disease and Demography in the Americas*, ed. John W. Verano and Douglas H. Ubelaker. Washington DC: Smithsonian Institution Press, 1992.

Douglas, David. "Letters, 1830–1834." *Oregon Historical Quarterly* 6, no. 3 (1905): 197–209.

Dowd, Gregory E. *A Spirited Resistance: The North American Indian Struggle for Unity, 1745–1815*. Baltimore: Johns Hopkins University Press, 1992.

Drake, Francis S. *The Indian Tribes of the United States*. Philadelphia: J. B. Lippincott, 1885.

Drake, Ross. "The Law That Ripped America in Two." *Smithsonian Magazine*, May 2004. http://www.smithsonianmag.com/history-archaeology/law.html (accessed Aug. 3, 2010).

Drury, Clifford Merrill, ed. *Where Wagons Could Go: Narcissa Whitman and Eliza Spalding*. Vol. 1 of *First White Women over the Rockies: Diaries, Letters, and Biographical Sketches of the Six Women of the Oregon Mission Who Made the Overland Journey in 1836 and 1838*. Glendale CA: Arthur H. Clark, 1963.

Dudden, Arthur Power. *The American Pacific: From the Old China Trade to the Present*. New York: Oxford University Press, 1992.

Dunham, Harold H. "Charles Bent." In Hafen, *Mountain Men*, 2:27–48.

Dunlay, Tom. *Kit Carson and the Indians*. Lincoln: University of Nebraska Press, 2000.

Dunn, J. P. *Massacres of the Mountains: A History of Indian Wars of the Far West*. New York: Harpers, 1886.

DuVal, Kathleen. "Indian Intermarriage and Métissage in Colonial Louisiana." *William and Mary Quarterly*, 3d ser., 65 (April 2008): 301–4.

———. *The Native Ground: Indians and Colonists in the Heart of the Continent*. Philadelphia: University of Pennsylvania Press, 2006.

Dye, Eva Emery. "Earliest Expedition against Puget Sound Indians." *Washington Historical Quarterly* 1 (Jan. 1907): 288–95.

———. "Old Letters." *Washington Historical Quarterly* 2 (1908): 155–68.

Early, Ann M. "John Jolly (?–1838)." *The Encyclopedia of Arkansas History and Culture*. http://encyclopediaofarkansas.net/encyclopedia/entry-detail.aspx?entryID=562 (accessed Dec. 13, 2007).

Ebersole, Gary L. *Captured by Texts: Puritan to Postmodern Images of Indian Captivity*. Charlottesville: University of Virginia Press, 1995.

Eccleston, Robert. *The Mariposa Indian War, 1850–1851: The Diaries of Robert Eccleston; The California Gold Rush, Yosemite, and the High Sierra.* Salt Lake City: University of Utah Press, 1957.

Eckrom, J. A. *Remembered Drums: A History of the Puget Sound Indian War.* Walla Walla WA: Pioneer Press Books, 1989.

Edmunds, R. David. *The Shawnee Prophet.* Lincoln: University of Nebraska Press, 1985.

———. *Tecumseh and the Quest for Indian Leadership.* New York: Longman, 1984.

———. "Unacquainted with the Laws of the Civilized World: American Attitudes toward Métis Communities in the Old Northwest." In Peterson and Brown, *New Peoples.*

Eisenhower, John S. D. *So Far from God: The U.S. War with Mexico, 1846–1848.* New York: Random House, 1989.

Ekberg, Carl J. *French Roots in the Illinois Country: The Mississippi Frontier in Colonial Times.* Urbana: University of Illinois Press, 1998.

———. *Stealing Indian Women: Native Slavery in the Illinois Country.* Urbana: University of Illinois Press, 2007.

Elliott, T. C. "Marguerite Wadin McKay McLoughlin." *Oregon Historical Quarterly* 36 (Sept. 1935): 335–43.

Emparán, Madie Brown. *The Vallejos of California.* San Francisco: Gleeson Library Associates, 1968.

Engstrand, Iris Wilson, ed. Introduction to *Noticias de Nutka: An Account of Nootka Sound in 1792*, by José Mariano Moziño. Seattle: University of Washington Press, 1970.

———. "John Sutter: A Biographical Examination." In *John Sutter and a Wider West*, ed. Kenneth N. Owens. Lincoln: University of Nebraska Press, 1994.

Erickson, Doug, Jeremy Skinner, and Paul Merchant, eds. *Discoveries Made in Exploring the Missouri, Red River, and Washita.* Spokane WA: Arthur H. Clark, 2004.

Ermatinger, Francis. *Fur Trade Letters of Francis Ermatinger: Written to His Brother Edward during His Service with the Hudson's Bay Company, 1818–1853*, ed. Lois Halliday McDonald. Spokane: Arthur H. Clark, 1980.

Etcheson, Nichole. *Bleeding Kansas: Contested Liberties in the Civil War Era.* Lawrence: University of Kansas Press, 2004.

Etulain, Richard. *Beyond the Missouri: The Story of the American West.* Albuquerque: University of New Mexico Press, 2006.

———, ed. *Western Lives: A Biographical History of the American West.* Albuquerque: University of New Mexico Press, 2004.

Everett, Dianna. *The Texas Cherokee: A People between Two Fires, 1819–1840.* Norman: University of Oklahoma Press, 1990.

Ewers, John C. *The Blackfeet: Raiders of the Northwestern Plains.* Norman: University of Oklahoma Press, 1958.

———. "Mothers of the Mixed Bloods." *Indian Life on the Upper Missouri.* Norman: University of Oklahoma Press, 1968.

Exley, Jo Ella Powell. *Frontier Blood: The Saga of the Parker Family*. College Station: Texas A&M University Press, 2005.

Faller, Lincoln B. "Making Medicine against 'White Man's Side of Story': George Bent's Letters to George Hyde." *American Indian Quarterly* 24, no. 1 (Winter 2000): 64–91.

Faragher, John Mack. "The Custom of the Country: Cross-Cultural Marriage in the Western Fur Trade." In *Western Women: Their Land, Their Lives*, ed. Lillian Schlissel, Cicki L. Ruiz, and Janice Monk, 199–215. Albuquerque: University of New Mexico Press, 1988.

———. *Daniel Boone: The Life and Legend of An American Pioneer*. New York: Henry Holt, 1992.

———. "More Motley Than Mackinaw: From Ethnic Mixing to Ethnic Cleansing on the Frontier of the Lower Missouri, 1783–1833." In *Contact Points: American Frontiers from the Mohawk Valley to the Mississippi, 1750–1830*, ed. Andrew Cayton and Frederika Teute. Chapel Hill: University of North Carolina Press, 1998.

———. *Women and Men on the Oregon Trail*. New Haven: Yale University Press, 1979.

Farnham, Thomas J. *Travels in the Great Western Prairies, the Anahuac and Rocky Mountains, and in the Oregon Territory*. Poughkeepsie NY: Killey and Lossing, 1841. Rpt. in *Early Western Travels*, ed. Reuben Gold Thwaites, vol. 28. Brooklyn: AMS Press, 1995.

Faulk, Odie B. "A Colonization Plan for Northern Sonora, 1850." *New Mexico Historical Review* 44 (Oct. 1969): 296–300.

Fehrenbach, T. R. *Comanches: The Destruction of a People*. New York: Alfred A. Knopf, 1974.

Fehrman, Richard J. "The Mountain Men—A Statistical View." In Hafen, *Mountain Men*, 10:9–15

Feldman, Jay. *When the Mississippi Ran Backward: Empire, Intrigue, Murder and the New Madrid Earthquakes*. New York: Free Press, 2005.

Fisher, Robin. "The Northwest from the Beginning of Trade with Europeans to the 1880s." In *Cambridge History of the Native Peoples of North America*. Vol. 1: *North America*. Cambridge: Cambridge University Press, 1996.

Flores, Dan. "Bison Ecology and Bison Diplomacy: The Southern Plains from 1800–1850," *Journal of American History* 78 (Sept. 1991): 465–85.

Fogdall, Alberta Brooks. *Royal Family of the Columbia: Dr. John McLoughlin and His Family*. Fairfield WA: Ye Galleon Press, 178.

Foley, William E., and C. David Rice. *The First Chouteaus: River Barons of Early St. Louis*. Urbana: University of Illinois Press, 2000.

———. "The Return of the Mandan Chief." *Montana: The Magazine of Western History* 29, no. 3 (Summer 1979): 2–15.

Folwell, William Watts. *A History of Minnesota*. 4 vols. St. Paul: Minnesota Historical Society, 1956–1969.

Foreman, Grant. *Indians and Pioneers: The Story of the American Southwest before 1830*. Norman: University of Oklahoma Press, 1930.

————. *Pioneer Days in the Early Southwest.* Cleveland: Arthur H. Clark, 1926.

Foster, Hamar. "Killing Mr. John: Law and Jurisdiction at Fort Stikine, 1842–1846" in *Law for the Elephant, Law for the Beaver: Essays in the Legal History of the North American West.* Pasadena CA: Ninth Judicial Circuit Historical Society, 1992.

Foster, Morris W. *Being Comanche: A Social History of an American Indian Community.* Tucson: University of Arizona Press, 1991.

Fowler, Loretta. "The Great Plains from the Arrival of the Horse to 1885." In *Cambridge History of the Native Peoples of the Americas.* Vol. 1: *North America.* Cambridge: Cambridge University Press, 1996.

Fowler, Will. *Santa Anna of Mexico.* Lincoln: University of Nebraska Press, 2007.

Frank, Ross H. *From Settler to Citizen: New Mexican Economic Development and the Creation of Vecino Society, 1750–1820.* Berkeley: University of California Press, 2000.

Frazer, Robert W. *Forts and Supplies: The Role of the Army in the Economy of the Southwest, 1846–1861.* Albuquerque: University of New Mexico Press, 1983.

Furniss, Norman F. *The Mormon Conflict: 1850–1859.* New Haven: Yale University Press, 1960.

Galbraith, John S. *The Hudson's Bay Company as Imperial Factor, 1821–1869.* Berkeley: University of California Press, 1957.

Gallay, Alan. *The Indian Slave Trade: The Rise of the English Empire in the American South, 1670–1717.* New Haven: Yale University Press, 2002.

Garrard, Lewis H. *Wah-to-Yah and the Taos Trail.* Ed. Ralph Bieber. Glendale CA: Arthur H. Clark, 1938.

Gates, Charles M. "The West in American Diplomacy, 1812–1815," *Mississippi Valley Historical Review* 26 (March 1940): 499–510.

Gates, Paul Wallace. *Fifty Million Acres: Conflicts over Kansas Land Policy, 1854–1890.* New York: Atherton Press, 1966.

————. *Land and Law in California: Essays on Land Policies.* Ames: University of Iowa Press, 1991.

Gelo, Daniel J. "Comanche Land and Ever Has Been: A Native Geography of Nineteenth-Century Comancheria." *Southwestern Historical Quarterly* 103, no. 3 (2000): 272–307.

Gelo, Daniel J., and Scott Zesch, eds. "'Every Day Seemed to Be a Holiday': The Captivity of Bianca Babb." *Southwestern Historical Quarterly* 107 (July 2003): 35–68.

Gibson, Arrell M., and Ed Bearss. *Fort Smith: Little Gibraltar on the Arkansas.* Norman: University of Oklahoma Press, 1969.

Gibson, James R. *Farming the Frontier: The Agricultural Opening of the Oregon Country, 1780–1846.* Seattle: University of Washington Press, 1985.

————. *Imperial Russia in Frontier America.* New York: Oxford University Press, 1976.

————. *Otter Skins, Boston Ships, and China Goods: The Maritime Fur Trade of the Northwest Coast, 1785–1841.* Seattle: University of Washington Press, 1992.

Gillis, Michael J., and Michael F. Magliari. *John Bidwell and California: The Life and Writings of a Pioneer, 1841–1900.* Spokane WA: Arthur H. Clark, 2003.

Gilman, Rhonda R. *Henry Hastings Sibley: Divided Heart.* St. Paul: Minnesota Historical Society Press, 2004.

Gitlin, Jay. *The Bourgeois Frontier: French Towns, French Traders, and American Expansion.* New Haven: Yale University Press, 2009.

Gómez, Laura E. *Manifest Destinies: The Making of the Mexican American Race.* New York: New York University Press, 2007.

Gonzalez, Deena J. *Refusing the Favor: The Spanish-Mexican Women of Santa Fe.* New York: Oxford University Press, 1999.

Gonzalez, Michael J. "The Child of the Wilderness Weeps for the Father of our Country: The Indian and the Politics of Church and State in Provincial California." In *Contested Eden: California before the Gold Rush,* ed. Ramón Gutierrez and Richard Orsi. Berkeley: University of California Press, 1998.

Gordon, Sarah Barringer. *The Mormon Question: Polygamy and Constitutional Conflict in Nineteenth-Century North America.* Chapel Hill: University of North Carolina Press, 2002.

Gordon-Reed, Annette. *The Hemingses of Monticello: An American Family.* New York: W. W. Norton, 2008.

Gove, Jesse A. *The Utah Expedition, 1857–1858: Letters of Capt. Jesse A. Gove.* Ed. Otis G. Hammond. Concord: New Hampshire Historical Society, 1928.

Gracy, David B., II. *Moses Austin: His Life.* San Antonio TX: Trinity University Press, 1987.

Gray, John Morgan. *Lord Selkirk of Red River.* Toronto: Macmillan of Canada, 1963.

Green, Michael. "The Expansion of European Colonization to the Mississippi Valley, 1780–1880." In *Cambridge History of the Native Peoples of the Americas.* Vol. 1: *North America.* Cambridge: Cambridge University Press, 1996.

Greene, Jerome A., and Douglas D. Scott. *Finding Sand Creek: History, Archeology, and the 1864 Massacre Site.* Norman: University of Oklahoma Press, 2004.

Gregg, Kate L. "The History of Fort Osage." *Missouri Historical Review* 35 (July 1940): 439–88.

Gregory, Jack, and Rennard Strickland. *Sam Houston with the Cherokees, 1829–1833.* Austin: University of Texas Press, 1967.

Grinnell, George Bird. *The Fighting Cheyennes.* Norman: University of Oklahoma Press, 1983.

Gross, Ariela J. *What Blood Won't Tell: A History of Race on Trial in America.* Cambridge MA: Harvard University Press, 2008.

Gudde, Erwin G, ed. *Sutter's Own Story: The Life of General John Augustus Sutter and the History of New Helvetia in the Sacramento Valley.* New York: G. P. Putnam's Sons, 1936.

Guillow, Lawrence E. "Pandemonium in the Plaza: The First Los Angeles Riot, July 22, 1856." *Southern California Quarterly* 77 (Fall 1995): 183–97.

Gunther, Vanessa Ann. *Ambiguous Justice: Native Americans and the Law in Southern California, 1848–1890.* Lansing: Michigan State University Press, 2006.

Gutierrez, Ramón, and Richard Orsi, eds. *Contested Eden: California before the Gold Rush.* Berkeley: University of California Press, 1998.

Haas, Lisbeth. *Conquests and Historical Identities in California, 1769–1936*. Berkeley: University of California Press, 1995.

———. "War in California, 1846–1848." *California History* 76 (Fall 1997): 331–56.

Hackel, Steven W. *Children of Coyote, Missionaries of St. Francis: Indian-Spanish Relations in Colonial California, 1769–1850*. Chapel Hill: University of North Carolina Press, 2005.

———. "Land, Labor and Production: The Colonial Economy of Spanish and Mexican California." In *Contested Eden: California before the Gold Rush*, ed. Ramón Gutierrez and Richard Orsi. Berkeley: University of California Press, 1998.

Hafen, LeRoy R. *Broken Hand: The Life of Thomas Fitzpatrick: Mountain Man, Guide, and Indian Agent*. Denver: Old West, 1973.

———, ed. *Colorado Gold Rush: Contemporary Letters and Reports, 1858–1859*. Glendale CA: Arthur H. Clark, 1941.

———, ed. *French Fur Traders and Voyageurs in the American West*. Lincoln: University of Nebraska Press, 1997.

———, ed. *The Mountain Men and the Fur Trade of the Far West*. 10 vols. Glendale CA: Arthur H. Clark, 1968.

———. *Relations with the Indians of the Plains, 1857–1861: A Documentary Account of the Military Campaigns, and Negotiations of Indian Agents, with Reports and Journals*. Glendale CA: Arthur H. Clark, 1959.

———. "When Was Bent's Fort Built?" *Colorado Magazine*, April 1954, 105–119.

Halaas, David Fridtjof. "'All the Camp Was Weeping': George Bent and the Sand Creek Massacre." *Colorado Heritage*, Summer 1995, 2–17.

Halaas, David Fridtjof, and Andrew E. Masich. *Halfbreed: The Remarkable Story of George Bent*. Cambridge MA: DaCapo Books, 2004.

Hale, Janet Campbell. *Bloodlines: Odyssey of a Native Daughter*. Tucson: University of Arizona Press, 1998.

Haley, James L. *Sam Houston*. Norman: University of Oklahoma Press, 2002.

Hall, James. *Sketches of History, Life, and Manners in the West*. Vol. 1. Cincinnati: Hubbard and Evans, 1834.

Halliday, Jan, and Gail Chehak. *Native Peoples of the Northwest*. Seattle: Sasquatch Books, 2000.

Hämäläinen, Pekka N. *The Comanche Empire*. New Haven: Yale University Press, 2008.

———. "The Western Comanche Trade Center: Rethinking the Plains Indian Trade System." *Western Historical Quarterly* 29, no. 4 (1998): 485–513.

Handbook of Texas Online, s.v. "Fredonian Rebellion." http://www.tshaonline.org/handbook/online/articles/FF/jcf1.html (accessed July 12 2010).

Hargrave, Letitia Mactavish. *The Letters of Letitia Hargrave*. Ed. Margaret MacLeod. Toronto: Champlain Society, 1947.

Harlow, Neal. *California Conquered: The Annexation of a Mexican Province, 1846–1850*. Berkeley: University of California Press, 1982.

Harvey, Henry. *History of the Shawnee Indians, 1681–1854*. Cincinnati: E. Morgan & Sons, 1855.

Hatcher, Mattie Austin. *The Opening of Texas to Foreign Settlement, 1800–1821*. Austin: University of Texas Press, 1927.

Hatley, Allen G. *The Indian Wars in Stephen F. Austin's Texas Colony, 1822–1835*. Austin: Eakin Press, 2001.

Hawgood, John A. "John C. Fremont and the Bear Flag Revolution, A Reappraisal." *Southern California Quarterly* 44 (1962): 67–96.

Haynes, Sam W. ""Anglophobia and the Annexation of Texas: The Quest for National Security." In *Manifest Destiny and Empire: American Antebellum Expansionism*, ed. Sam W. Haynes and Christopher Morris. College Station: Texas A&M University Press, 1997.

Heckewelder, John. *An Account of the History, Manners, and Customs of the Indian Nations Who Once Inhabited Pennsylvania and Neighboring States*. Philadelphia: Abraham Small, 1818.

————. *A Narrative of the Mission of the United Brethren among the Delaware and Mohegan Indians*. Philadelphia: McCarty and Davis, 1820.

Heizer, Robert F. *Languages, Territories, and Names of California Indian Tribes*. Berkeley: University of California Press, 1966.

Hendrickson, David C. *Union, Nation, or Empire: The American Debate over International Relations*. Lawrence: University of Kansas Press, 2009.

Henry, Alexander, and David Thompson. *New Light on the Early History of the Great Northwest*. Ed. Eliot Coues. 2 vols. New York: R. R. Bowker, 1897.

Herrera, Carlos R. "New Mexico Resistance to U.S. Occupation during the Mexican-American War of 1846–1848." In *The Contested Homeland: A Chicano History of New Mexico*, ed. Erlinda Gonzales-Berry and David Maciel. Albuquerque: University of New Mexico Press, 2000.

Himmel, Kelly F. *The Conquest of the Karankawas and the Tonkawas, 1821–1859*. College Station: Texas A&M University Press, 1999.

Historic Forks of the Wabash. "The Miami Nation." http://www.historicforks.org/miami/index.html (accessed Feb. 12, 2008).

Hittell, Theodore H. *History of California*. 4 vols. San Francisco: N. J. Stone, 1897.

Hodes, Martha, "The Mercurial Nature and Abiding Power of Race: A Transnational Family Story." *American Historical Review* 118 (Feb. 2003): 84–118.

Hoffhaus, Charles E. *Chez Les Canses: Three Centuries at Kawsmouth*. Kansas City: Lowell Press, 1984.

Hoig, Stanley W. *The Cherokees and Their Chiefs: In the Wake of Empire*. Fayetteville: University of Arkansas Press, 1998.

————. *The Chouteaus: First Family of the Fur Trade*. Albuquerque: University of New Mexico Press, 2008.

————. *The Sand Creek Massacre*. Norman: University of Oklahoma Press, 1961.

————. *Tribal Wars of the Southern Plains*. Norman: University of Oklahoma Press, 1993.

————. *White Man's Paper Trail: Grand Councils and Treaty-Making on the Central Plains*. Boulder: University Press of Colorado, 2006.

Holley, Mary Austin. *Letters of an Early American Traveller, Mary Austin Holley: Her Life and Works, 1784–1846*. Ed. Mattie Austin Hatcher. Dallas: Southwest Press, 1933.

———. *Texas: Observations Historical, Geographical, and Descriptive*. Baltimore: Armstrong and Plaskitt, 1833.

Holliday, J. S. *The World Rushed In: The California Gold Rush Experience*. Norman: University of Oklahoma Press, 2002.

Holman, Frederick V. *Dr. John McLoughlin: The Father of Oregon*. Cleveland: Arthur H. Clark, 1907.

Honig, Louis O. *Westport: Gateway to the Early West*. Kansas City MO: n.p., 1950.

Horn, Sarah Ann. *Captivity of Mrs. Sarah Ann Horn and Her Two Children*. Cincinnati: E. House, 1853.

Horsman, Reginald. *Expansion and American Indian Policy, 1783–1812*. East Lansing: Michigan State University Press, 1967.

———. *The War of 1812*. New York: Alfred A. Knopf, 1969.

Houck, Louis. *A History of Missouri*. Rpt., New York: Arno Reprints, 1971.

Howard, James H. *Shawnee: The Ceremonialism of a Native American Tribe and Its Cultural Background*. Athens: Ohio University Press, 1981.

Howe, Daniel Walker. *What Hath God Wrought: The Transformation of America, 1815–1860*. New York: Oxford University Press, 2007.

Hughes, John T. *Doniphan's Expedition*. Cincinnati: J. A. and U. P. James, 1848.

Hunter, John Dunn. *Memoirs of a Captivity among the Indians of North America*. London: Longman's and Dunn, 1823.

Hurtado, Albert L. *Indian Survival on the California Frontier*. New Haven: Yale University Press, 1988.

———. *Intimate Frontiers: Sex, Gender, and Culture in Old California*. Albuquerque: University of New Mexico Press, 1999.

———. *John Sutter: A Life on the North American Frontier*. Norman: University of Oklahoma Press, 2006.

———. "John Sutter and the Indian Business." In *John Sutter and a Wider West*, ed. Kenneth N. Owens. Lincoln: University of Nebraska Press, 1994.

———. "When Strangers Meet: Sex and Gender on Three Frontiers," *Frontiers* 17 (1996): 52–75.

Hussey, John A. *Fort Vancouver: The History of Fort Vancouver and Its Physical Structure*. Portland OR: National Park Service, 1959.

Hyde, Anne. "Mormons and Miners: Samuel Brannan and Elizabeth Byers." In *Western Lives: A Biographical History of the American West*, ed. Richard Etulain. Albuquerque: University of New Mexico Press, 2004.

Hyde, George E. *Life of George Bent Written from His Letters*. Ed. Savoie Lottinville. Norman: University of Oklahoma Press, 1968.

Hyer, Joel. *"We Are Not Savages": Native Americans in Southern California and the Pala Reservation, 1840–1880*. Lansing: Michigan State University Press, 2001.

Hyslop, Stephen G. *Bound for Santa Fe: The Road to New Mexico and American Conquest, 1806–1848*. Norman: University of Oklahoma Press, 2002.

Ide, Simeon. *A Biographical Sketch of William B. Ide and Account of the Bear Flag Uprising.* Santa Fe, NM: n.p., 1880.

Innis, Harold A. "Interrelations between the Fur Trade of Canada and the United States." *Mississippi Valley Historical Review* 20, no. 3 (1933): 320–33.

Irving, Washington. *The Adventures of Captain Bonneville.* New York: John B. Alden, 1886.

———. *Astoria; or, Anecdotes of an Enterprise beyond the Rocky Mountains.* New York: John B. Alden, 1883.

———. *The Western Journals of Washington Irving.* Ed. John Francis McDermott. Norman: University of Oklahoma Press, 1944.

Jackson, Donald, ed. *Letters of the Lewis and Clark Expedition, with Related Documents, 1783–1854.* 2 vols. Urbana, IL: University of Illinois Press, 1979.

Jackson, R. H., and E. Castillo. *Indians, Franciscans, and Spanish Colonization: The Impact of the Mission System on California Indians.* Albuquerque: University of New Mexico Press, 1995.

Jacobs, Margaret. *White Mother to a Dark Race: Settler Colonialism, Maternalism, and the Removal of Indigenous Children in the American West and Australia, 1880–1940.* Lincoln: University of Nebraska Press, 2009.

James, Edwin. *Account of an Expedition from Pittsburgh to the Rocky Mountains: Performed in the Years 1819, 1820.* 2 vols. London: Longmans, 1823.

Jefferson, Thomas. *An Account of Louisiana, Being an Abstract of Documents in the Offices of the State and of the Treasury.* Philadelphia: William Duane, 1803.

Jeffrey, Julie Roy. *Converting the West: A Biography of Narcissa Whitman.* Norman: University of Oklahoma Press, 1994.

Jewitt, John R. *A Journal Kept at Nootka Sound.* Boston, 1807. Early Canadiana Online, http://www.canadiana.org/ECO (accessed June 7, 2008).

Johannsen, Robert W. *To the Halls of the Montezumas: The Mexican War in the American Imagination.* New York: Oxford University Press, 1985.

Johansen, Dorothy O., and Charles M. Gates. *Empire of the Columbia: A History of the Pacific Northwest.* New York: Harper and Brothers, 1957.

John, Elizabeth A. H. *Storms Brewed in Other Men's Worlds: The Confrontation of Indians, Spanish, and French in the Southwest, 1540–1795.* College Station: Texas A&M Press, 1975.

Johnson, David Alan. *Founding the Far West: California, Oregon, and Nevada, 1840–1890.* Berkeley: University of California Press, 1992.

Johnson, Robert C. *John McLoughlin: Patriarch of the Northwest.* Seattle: Metropolitan Press, 1935.

Johnson, Susan Lee. *Roaring Camp: The Social World of the California Gold Rush.* New York: W. W. Norton, 2000.

Jones, David F. *Rationalizing Epidemics: Meanings and Uses of American Indian Mortality since 1600.* Cambridge MA: Harvard University Press, 2004.

Jones, Howard. *To the Webster-Ashburton Treaty: A Study in Anglo-American Relations, 1783–1843.* Chapel Hill: University of North Carolina Press, 1977.

Jones, Landon Y. *William Clark and the Shaping of the West*. New York: Hill and Wang, 2004.

Jones, Oakah L. *Los Paisanos: Spanish Settlers on the Northern Frontier of New Spain*. Norman: University of Oklahoma Press, 1979.

Josephy, Alvin. *The Nez Perce Indians and the Opening of the Northwest*. New Haven CT: Yale University Press, 1965.

Kappler, Charles, comp. *Indian Affairs: Laws, and Treaties*. Vol. 2. Washington DC: Government Printing Office, 1904; rpt., New York: Library Reprints, 2007.

Kearny, Stephen Watts. *Winning the West: General Stephen Watts Kearny's Letter Book, 1846–1847*. Boonville MO: Pekitanoui, 1998.

Keleher, William A. *Turmoil in New Mexico, 1846–1848*. Santa Fe NM: Rydal Press, 1952.

Kelton, Dwight H., ed. *Annels of Fort Mackinac*. Chicago: Fergus Printing Co., 1882.

Kendall, George Wilkins. *A Narrative of an Expedition across the Great Southwestern Prairies*. 2 vols. London: David Bogue, 1845.

Kenner, Charles L. *The Comanchero Frontier: A History of New Mexican–Plains Indian Relations*. Norman: University of Oklahoma Press, 1969.

Kinnaird, Lawrence, ed. *Spain in the Mississippi Valley, 1765–1794*. Washington DC: Government Printing Office.

Kip, Lawrence. *Indian Council at Walla-Walla, May and June, 1855: A Journal, by Col. Lawrence Kip, U.S.A.* Eugene OR: Star Job Office, 1897.

Kirk, John. *A Voyage around the World in 1833–1834*. London: n.p., 1835.

Klein, Laura F. "Demystifying the Opposition: The Hudson's Bay Company and the Tlingit." *Arctic Anthropology* 24, no. 1 (1987): 101–14.

Kurz, Rudolph Friederich. *Journal of Rudolph Friederich Kurz: An Account of His Experiences Among Fur Traders and American Indians on the Mississippi and Upper Missouri Rivers in the Years 1846 to 1852*. Trans. Myrtis Jarrell; ed. J. N. B. Hewitt. Smithsonian Institution, Bureau of Ethnology, bulletin 115. Washington DC: Government Printing Office, 1937; rpt., Lincoln: University of Nebraska Press, 1970.

Lafora, Nicholas. *Frontiers of New Spain: Nicholas de Lafora's Description, 1766–1768*. Ed. Lawrence Kinnaird. Berkeley CA: Quiviria Society, 1958.

Lamar, Howard R. "John Augustus Sutter, Wilderness Entreprenuer." In *John Sutter and a Wider West*, ed. Kenneth N. Owens. Lincoln: University of Nebraska Press, 1994.

Langsdorff, Georg von. *Langsdorff's Narrative of the Rezanov Voyage to Nueva California in 1806: Being that division of Doctor Georg H. von Langsdorff's Bemerkungen auf einer . . . and Back*. San Francisco: Thomas Russell, 1927.

Larkin, Thomas Oliver. *The Larkin Papers: Personal, Business, and Official Correspondence of Thomas Oliver Larkin, Merchant and United States Consul in California*. Ed. George B. Hammond. 11 vols. Berkeley: University of California Press, 1951–68.

Larpenteur, Charles. *Forty Years a Fur Trader on the Upper Missouri*. Ed. Elliott Coues. 2 vols. New York: Frances P. Harper, 1898.

Latimer, Jon. *1812: War with America.* Cambridge MA: Harvard University Press, 2007.

Latta, Frank F. *The Saga of Rancho El Tejón.* Santa Cruz CA: Bear State Books, 1976.

Lavender, David. *Bent's Fort.* Lincoln: University of Nebraska Press, 1954.

———. *The Fist in the Wilderness.* Albuquerque: University of New Mexico Press, 1964.

La Vere, David. *Contrary Neighbors: Southern Plains Tribes and Removed Indians in Indian Territory.* Norman: University of Oklahoma Press, 2000.

———. "Friendly Persuasions: Gifts and Reciprocity in Comanche Euro-American Relations." *Chronicles of Oklahoma* 71 (Fall 1993): 322–37.

———. *The Texas Indians.* College Station: Texas A&M Press, 2004.

LeCompte, Janet. "Auguste Pierre Chouteau." In Hafen, *French Fur Traders and Voyageurs,* 95–123.

———. "Bent, St. Vrain and Company among the Comanche and Kiowa." *Colorado Magazine* 49, no. 4 (1972): 273–93.

———. *Pueblo, Hardscrabble, Greenhorn: Society on the High Plains, 1832–1856.* Norman: University of Oklahoma Press, 1999.

———. *Rebellion in Rio Arriba, 1837.* Albuquerque: University of New Mexico Press, 1985.

Lee, Fred L., John Edward Hicks Lee, and Robert B. Cormack. "Fort Osage and George Champlin Sibley." *Denver Westerners Brand Book* 19 (1964): 243–54.

Lee, John D. *A Mormon Chronicle: The Diaries of John D. Lee, 1848–1876.* Ed. Juanita Brooks and Robert Cleland. 2 vols. San Marino CA: Huntington Library, 1955.

———. *Mormonism Unveiled; or, The Life and Confessions of John D. Lee.* St. Louis: D. M. Vandawalker, 1890.

LeSueur, Steven C. *The 1838 Mormon War in Missouri.* Columbia: University of Missouri Press, 1987.

Libby, Dorothy. "Thomas Forsyth Letters," *Ethnohistory* 8, no. 2 (Spring 1961): 179–96.

Lightfoot, Kent G. *Indians, Missionaries, and Merchants: The Legacy of Colonial Encounters on the California Frontiers.* Berkeley: University of California Press, 2005.

Limerick, Patricia N. *Something in the Soil: Legacies and Reckonings in the New West.* New York: W. W. Norton, 2000.

Lomask, Milton. *Aaron Burr.* 2 vols. New York: Farrar, Strauss and Giroux, 1981.

Lubers, H. L. "William Bent's Family and the Indians of the Plains." *Colorado Magazine* 13 (Jan. 1936): 16–28.

Mackinnon, William P., ed. *At Sword's Point: A Documentary History of the Utah War.* 2 vols. Norman OK: Arthur H. Clark, 2008.

———. "'Lonely Bones': Leadership and Utah War Violence." *Journal of Mormon History* 33 (Spring 2007): 121–178.

Magoffin, Susan Shelby. *Down the Santa Fe Trail and into Mexico: The Diary of Susan Shelby Magoffin, 1846–1847.* Ed. Stella M. Drumm. Lincoln: University of Nebraska Press, 1982.

Malin, James C. "The Motives of Stephen A. Douglas in the Organization of Nebraska Territory: A Letter Dated Dec. 17, 1853." *Kansas Historical Quarterly* 19 (1951): 321–53.

———. *The Nebraska Question, 1852–1854.* Lawrence: University of Kansas Press, 1953.

Manning, William R., ed. *Diplomatic Correspondence of the United States, Inter-American Affairs, 1831–1860.* 10 vols. Washington DC: Carnegie Endowment, 1932–1939.

Mathews, John Joseph. *The Osages: Children of the Middle Waters.* Norman: University of Oklahoma Press, 1961.

May, Robert E. *Manifest Destiny's Underworld.* Chapel Hill: University of North Carolina Press, 2002.

McAfee, Robert Breckinridge. *The History of the Late War in the Western Country.* Lexington KY: Worsely and Smith, 1816; rpt., Ann Arbor MI: University Microfilms, 1966.

McCandless, Perry. *A History of Missouri.* Vol. 2: *1820–1960.* Columbia: University of Missouri Press, 1972.

McClung, Quantrille D., comp. *Carson-Bent-Boggs Genealogy: Line of William Carson, Ancestor of "Kit" Carson, Famous Scout and Pioneer of the Rocky Mountain Area.* Denver: Denver Public Library, 1962.

McDermott, John, ed. *The Early Histories of St. Louis.* St. Louis: St. Louis Historical Documents Foundation, 1952.

McDonnell, Anne. "Contributions." *Montana Historical Society Publications* 10 (1923): 243–46.

McGinty, Brian. *Strong Wine: The Life and Legend of Agoston Haraszthy.* Stanford CA: Stanford University Press, 1998.

McGuinness, Andrew. *Counting Coup and Cutting Horses: Intertribal Warfare on the Northern Plains, 1738–1889.* Evergreen CO: Cordillera Press, 1990.

McKittrick, Myrtle M. *Vallejo, Son of California.* Portland OR: Binfords and Mort, 1944.

McLoughlin, John. *John McLoughlin's Business Correspondence, 1847–1848.* Ed. William R. Sampson. Seattle: University of Washington Press, 1973.

———. "John McLoughlin's Last Letter to the Hudson's Bay Company, as Chief Factor, 1845." Ed. K. B. Judson. *American Historical Review* 14 (1915).

———. *The Letters of Dr. John McLoughlin, Written at Fort Vancouver, 1829–1832.* Ed. Burt Brown Barker. Portland OR: Portland Historical Society, 1948.

———. *The Letters of John McLoughlin from Fort Vancouver to the Governor and Committee.* Ed. E. E. Rich. 1st series, 1825–38; 2nd series, 1839–43; 3rd series, 1844–46. Toronto: Champlain Society, Hudson's Bay Record Society, 1941–44.

———. "Letter to Simon Fraser, July and Aug. 1808." *Oregon Historical Quarterly* 36 (March 1935): 294–95.

McLoughlin, William G. *Cherokee Renascence in the New Republic.* Princeton NJ: Princeton University Press, 1986.

McMurtry, Larry. *Oh What a Slaughter: Massacres in the American West, 1846–1890.* New York: Simon and Schuster, 2005.

McNierney, Michael, ed. *Taos 1847: The Revolt in Contemporary Accounts.* Boulder CO: Johnson Books, 1980.

McNitt, Frank. *The Navajo Wars: Military Campaigns, Slave Raids, and Reprisals.* Albuquerque: University of New Mexico Press, 1972.

McWilliams, Carey. *Southern California Country: An Island on the Land.* New York: Duell, Sloan and Pearce, 1946.

Meany, Edmond Stephen. *History of the State of Washington.* New York: Macmillan, 1909.

Meinig, D. W. *The Great Columbia Plain: A Historical Geography, 1805–1910.* Seattle: University of Washington Press, 1968.

Melton, Buckner F., Jr. *Aaron Burr: Conspiracy to Treason.* New York: John Wiley and Sons, 2002.

Meltzner, Aron J. "The Great 1857 'Fort Tejon' Earthquake: Shake, Rattle, and Roll." Fort Tejon Historical Association, http://www.forttejon.org/historyearthquake.html (accessed Nov. 27, 2007).

Meriwether, David. *My Life in the Mountains and on the Plains.* Ed. R. Griffen. Norman: University of Oklahoma Press, 1965.

Merk, Frederick, *The Monroe Doctrine and American Expansionism, 1843–1849.* New York: Alfred A. Knopf, 1966.

———. *The Oregon Question.* Cambridge MA: Harvard University Press, 1967.

Merrell, James H. *Into the American Woods: Negotiators on the Pennsylvania Frontier.* New York: W. W. Norton, 1999.

Meyer, Roy W. *History of the Santee Sioux: United States Indian Policy on Trial.* Lincoln: University of Nebraska Press, 1967.

Miller, Christopher L. *Prophetic Worlds: Indians and Whites on the Columbia Plateau.* New Brunswick NJ: Rutgers University Press, 1985.

Milliken, Randall. *A Time of Little Choice: The Disintegration of Tribal Culture in the San Francisco Bay Area, 1769–1910.* Menlo Park CA: Ballena Press, 1995.

Miner, H. Craig. *Kansas: The History of the Sunflower State, 1854–2000.* Lawrence: University of Kansas Press, 2002.

Miner, H. Craig, and William Unrau. *The End of Indian Kansas.* Lawrence: University of Kansas Press, 1978.

Monroy, Douglas. "The Creation and Re-creation of Californio Society." In *Contested Eden: California before the Gold Rush,* ed. Ramón Gutiérrez and Richard J. Orsi, 173–95. Berkeley: University of California Press, 1998.

———. *Thrown among Strangers: The Making of Mexican Culture in Frontier California.* Berkeley: University of California Press, 1990.

Montgomery, Charles. *The Spanish Redemption: Heritage, Power, and Loss on New Mexico's Upper Rio Grande.* Berkeley: University of California Press, 2002.

Montgomery, Richard G. *The White-Headed Eagle: John McLoughlin, Builder of an Empire.* New York: Macmillan, 1935.

Monthly Notices of the Royal Astronomical Society 218 (July 1842).

Moore, Jackson W. *Bent's Old Fort: An Archeological Study.* Denver: State Historical Society of Colorado, 1973.

Moorhead, Max L. *New Mexico's Royal Road: Trade and Travel on the Chihuahua Trail.* 2nd ed. Norman: University of Oklahoma Press, 1995.

Morgan, Dale L. *Jedediah Smith and the Opening of the West.* Lincoln: University of Nebraska Press, 1953.

———, ed. *The West of William H. Ashley: The International Struggle for the Fur Trade of the Missouri, the Rocky Mountains and the Columbia with Explorations beyond the Continental Divide, Recorded in the Diaries and Letters of William H. Ashley and His Contemporaries, 1822–1838.* Denver: Old West, 1964.

Morgan, Lewis Henry. *The Indian Journals, 1859–1862.* Ed. Leslie A. White. Ann Arbor: University of Michigan Press, 1959.

Morrison, Dorothy Nafus. *Outpost: John McLoughlin and the Far Northwest.* Portland: Oregon Historical Society Press, 1999.

Morse, Jedediah. *A Report to the Secretary of War on Indian Affairs.* New Haven CT: S. Converse, 1822.

Mowry, William. *Marcus Whitman and the Early Days of Oregon.* Boston: Silver, Burdett, 1901.

Moziño, José Mariano. *Noticias de Nutka: An Account of Nootka Sound in 1792.* Trans. and ed. Iris Higbie Wilson [Engstrand]. Seattle: University of Washington Press, 1970.

Mulder, William, and A. Russell Mortenson, eds. *Among the Mormons: Historic Accounts by Contemporary Observers.* New York: Alfred A. Knopf, 1957.

Mullis, Tony R. *Peacekeeping on the Plains: Army Operations in Bleeding Kansas.* Columbia: University of Missouri Press, 2004.

Mumford, Jeremy. "Mixed-Race Identity in a Nineteenth-Century Family: The Schoolcrafts of Sault Ste. Marie, 1824–1827." *Michigan Historical Review* 25, no. 1 (Spring 1999): 1–23.

Murphy, Lucy Eldersveld. *A Gathering of Rivers: Indians, Métis, and Mining in the Western Great Lakes, 1737–1832.* Lincoln: University of Nebraska Press, 2000.

Murray, Charles. *Travels in North America during the Years 1834, 1835 & 1836.* 2 vols. New York: Da Capo Press, 1974.

Namias, June. *White Captives: Gender and Ethnicity on the American Frontier.* Chapel Hill: University of North Carolina Press, 1993.

Nasatir, Abraham. "Anglo-Spanish Frontier on the Upper Missouri." *Iowa Journal of History and Politics* 29 (1931): 155–232.

———, ed. *Before Lewis and Clark: Documents Illustrating the History of the Missouri, 1785–1804.* Lincoln: University of Nebraska Press, 1990.

Nelson, Larry L. *A Man of Distinction among Them: Alexander McKee and British Indian Affairs along the Ohio Country Frontier.* Kent OH: Kent State University Press, 1991.

Nester, William R. *The Arikara War: The First Plains Indian War, 1823.* Missoula MT: Mountain Press, 2001.

Novak, Shannon A. *House of Mourning: A Biocultural History of the Mountain Meadows Massacre.* Salt Lake City: University of Utah Press, 2008.

Nugent, Walter. *Habits of Empire: A History of American Expansion.* New York: Alfred A. Knopf, 2008.

Nunis, Doyce B. *Andrew Sublette, Rocky Mountain Prince, 1808–1853.* Los Angeles: Dawson's Book Shop, 1960.

———. "Andrew Whitley Sublette." In Hafen, *Mountain Men,* 8:349–63.

———. "The Enigma of the Sublette Overland Party, 1845." *Pacific Historical Review* 28, no. 4 (1959): 331–49.

———. "Milton G. Sublette." In Hafen, *Mountain Men,* 4:331–35.

Nute, Grace L. "John McLoughlin Jr. and the Dickson Filibuster." *Minnesota History* 17, no. 4 (Dec. 1936): 438–55.

Oates, Joyce Carol. "Tennessee in the Stoned Age." *Times Literary Supplement* no. 4594 (April 19, 1991).

O'Donnell, Terence. *An Arrow in the Earth: General Joel Palmer and the Indians of Oregon.* Portland: Oregon Historical Society Press, 1991.

Ogden, Peter Skene. *Traits of American Indian Life and Character.* San Francisco: Grabhorne Press, 1853.

Ostler, Jeffrey. *The Plains Sioux and U.S. Colonialism from Lewis and Clark to Wounded Knee.* New York: Cambridge University Press, 2004.

Owens, Kenneth N., ed. *John Sutter and a Wider West.* Lincoln: University of Nebraska Press, 2002.

Owsley, Frank Lawrence, Jr., and Gene A. Smith. *Filibusters and Expansionists: Jeffersonian Manifest Destiny, 1800–1821.* Tuscaloosa: University of Alabama Press, 1997.

Page, Henry Markham. *Pasadena: Its Early Years.* Los Angeles: Lorrin L. Morrison, 1964.

Parker, Nathan H. *The Kansas and Nebraska Handbook.* Boston: John P. Jewett, 1857.

Parkman, Frances. *The Oregon Trail and Sketches of Prairie and Rocky Mountain Life.* Boston: Little, Brown, 1931.

Parks, Joseph H. *General Edmund Kirby Smith.* Baton Rouge: Louisiana State University Press, 1954.

Pascoe, Peggy. *What Comes Naturally: Miscegenation Law and the Making of Race in America.* New York: Oxford University Press, 2009.

Peake, Ora B. *A History of the United States Indian Factory System.* Greeley: Colorado State University Press, 1954.

Peattie, Donald Culross. "The Ballad of Cynthia Ann." *American Heritage Magazine.* http://www.americanheritage.com/articles/magazine/ah/1956/3/1956_3_38.shtml (accessed Nov. 24, 2009).

Perdue, Theda. *"Mixed Blood" Indians: Racial Construction in the Early South.* Athens: University of Georgia Press, 2005.

Peters, Virginia Bergman. *Women of the Earth Lodges: Tribal life on the Plains.* Norman: University of Oklahoma Press, 2000.

Peterson, Jacqueline. "Many Roads to Red River: Métis Genesis in the Great Lakes Region, 1650–1815." In Peterson and Brown, *New Peoples.*

———. "The People In-Between: Indian-White Marriage and the Generation of a Métis Society." *Ethnohistory* 25 (Winter 1978): 41–68.

———. "The People in Between: Indian White Marriage and the Genesis of a

Métis Culture in the Great Lakes Region, 1680–1830." PhD diss., University of Illinois, 1981.

———. "Prelude to Red River: A Social Portrait of the Great Lakes Métis." *Ethnohistory* 25, no. 1 (Winter 1978): 41–67.

Peterson, Jacqueline, and Jennifer S. H. Brown, eds. *The New Peoples: Being and Becoming Metís in North America.* Lincoln: University of Nebraska Press, 1985.

Peyser, Joseph L., ed. and trans. *Letters from New France: The Upper Country, 1686–1783.* Urbana: University of Illinois Press, 1992.

Phillips, George Harwood. *"Bringing Them under Subjection": California's Tejón Indian Reservation and Beyond, 1852–1864.* Lincoln: University of Nebraska Press, 2004.

———. *Indians and Indian Agents: The Origins of the Reservation System in California, 1847–1851.* Berkeley: University of California Press, 1997.

———. *Indians and Intruders in Central California, 1769–1849.* Norman: University of Oklahoma Press, 1993.

Phillips, Paul Chrisler. *The American Fur Trade.* 2 vols. Norman: University of Oklahoma Press, 1962.

Pitt, Leonard. *The Decline of the Californios: A Social History of Spanish-Speaking Californians, 1846–1890.* Berkeley: University of California Press, 1966.

Podruchny, Carolyn. *Making the Voyageur World: Travelers and Traders in the North American Fur Trade.* Lincoln: University of Nebraska Press, 2006.

Pomeroy, Earl. *The Pacific Slope: A History of California, Oregon, Washington, Idaho, Utah, and Nevada.* New York: Alfred A. Knopf, 1965.

Powell, Peter J. *People of the Sacred Mountain: A History of the Northern Cheyenne Chiefs and Warrior Societies, 1830–1879.* 2 vols. San Francisco: Harper and Row, 1979.

Pratt, Mary Louise. *Imperial Eyes: Travel Writing and Transculturation.* London: Routledge, 1993.

Price, Catherine. *The Oglala People, 1841–1879: A Political History.* Lincoln: University of Nebraska Press, 1996.

Prucha, Frances Paul. *American Indian Policy in the Formative Years: The Indian Trade and Intercourse Acts, 1790–1834.* Cambridge MA: Harvard University Press, 1962.

———. *The Great Father: The United States Government and the American Indian.* 2 vols. Lincoln: University of Nebraska Press, 1984.

———. *The Sword of the Republic.* Lincoln: Bison Books, University of Nebraska Press, 1987.

Public Broadcasting Service. "July 04, 1804 Journal of Charles Floyd." http://www.pbs.org/lewisandclark/archive/ (accessed July 14, 2010).

Quinn, D. Michael. *Early Mormonism and the Magic World View.* Salt Lake City UT: Signature Books, 1987.

———. *The Mormon Hierarchy: Origins of Power.* Salt Lake City: Signature Books, 1994.

Ray, A. J. *The Fur Trade as an Aspect of Native History.* 2nd ed. Toronto: University of Toronto Press, 1998.

Read, Nat B. *Don Benito Wilson: From Mountain Man to Mayor, Los Angeles, 1841 to 1878.* Santa Monica CA: Angel City Press, 2008.

Reid, John Philip. *Contested Empire: Peter Skene Ogden and the Snake River Expedition.* Norman: University of Oklahoma Press, 2002.

Reno, Philip. "Rebellion in New Mexico—1837." *New Mexico Historical Review* 40 (July 1965): 197–210.

Rensink, Brendan. "Nebraska and Kansas Territories in American Legal Culture." In *The Nebraska-Kansas Act of 1854*, ed. John R. Wunder and Joann M. Ross. Lincoln: University of Nebraska Press, 2008.

Reséndez, Andrés. *Changing National Identities at the Frontier: Texas and New Mexico, 1800–1850.* Cambridge: Cambridge University Press, 2004.

———. "Getting Drunk and Getting Cured: State vs. Market in Texas and New Mexico, 1800–1850." *Journal of the Early Republic* 22 (Spring 2002): 73–94.

Rich, E. E. *The Fur Trade and the Northwest to 1857.* Toronto: McClelland and Stewart, 1967.

———. *The History of the Hudson's Bay Company, 1670–1870.* 2 vols. London: Hudson's Bay Company Record Society, 1959.

Richards, Kent D. *Isaac I. Stevens: Young Man in a Hurry.* Provo UT: Brigham Young University Press, 1979.

Richards, Mary Haskin Parker. *Winter Quarters: The 1846–1848 Life Writings of Mary Haskin Parker Richards*, ed. Maureen Carr Ward. Logan: Utah State University Press, 1996.

Richardson, James D. *A Compilation of the Messages and Papers of the Presidents, 1789–1902.* 10 vols. Washington DC: Bureau of National Literature and Art, 1904.

Ricketts, Norma Baldwin. *The Mormon Battalion: U.S. Army of the West, 1846–1848.* Logan: Utah State University Press, 1996.

Rister, Carl C. *Comanche Bondage: Dr. John Charles Beales's Settlement of La Villa de Dolores on Las Moras Creek in Southern Texas of the 1830's.* Glendale CA: Arthur H. Clark, 1955.

Roberts, David. *A Newer World: Kit Carson, John C. Frémont and the Claiming of the American West.* New York: Simon and Schuster, 2000.

Roberts, Gary L. "Sand Creek: Tragedy and Symbol." PhD diss., University of Oklahoma, 1984. University Microforms version.

Robertson, R. G. *Competitive Struggle: America's Western Fur Trading Posts, 1764–1865.* Boise ID: Tamarack Books, 1999.

———. *Rotting Face: Smallpox and the American Indian.* Caldwell ID: Caxton Press, 2001.

Rodriguez O, Jaime E., ed. *The Divine Charter: Constitutionalism and Liberalism in Nineteenth-Century Mexico.* Lanham MD: Rowan and Littlefield, 2005.

Rogin, Michael Paul. *Fathers and Children: Andrew Jackson and the Subjugation of the American Indian.* New York: Alfred A. Knopf, 1975.

Rohrbough, Malcolm J. *Days of Gold: The California Gold Rush and the American Nation.* Berkeley: University of California Press, 1998.

Rolle, Andrew. "Exploring an Explorer: Psychohistory and John Charles Fremont." *Pacific Historical Review* 51 (May 1982): 135–63.

Rollings, Willard H. *The Osage: An Ethnohistorical Study of Hegemony on the Prairie-Plains.* Columbia: University of Missouri Press, 1995.

———. *Unaffected by the Gospel: Osage Resistance to the Christian Invasion (1673–1906); A Cultural Victory.* Albuquerque: University of New Mexico Press, 2004.

Ronda, James P. *Astoria and Empire.* Lincoln: University of Nebraska Press, 1993.

Rosenus, Alan. *General M. G. Vallejo and the Advent of the Americans.* Berkeley CA: Heyday Books, 1999.

Ross, Alexander. *Adventures of the First Settlers on the Columbia River.* London: Smith, Elder, 1849.

———. *The Fur Hunters of the Far West (1855).* Norman: University of Oklahoma Press, 1956.

———. *The Red River Colony.* London: Smith, Elder, 1856.

Ruby, Robert H., and John A. Brown. *The Cayuse Indians: Imperial Tribesmen of Old Oregon.* Norman: University of Oklahoma Press, 1972.

———. *The Chinook Indians: Traders of the Lower Columbia.* Norman: University of Oklahoma Press, 1976.

Sabin, Edwin L. *Kit Carson Days (1809–1868).* 2 vols. Chicago: A. C. McClurg, 1914.

Sachs, Aaron. *The Humboldt Current: Nineteenth-Century Exploration and the Roots of American Environmentalism.* New York: Penguin Books, 2006.

Sampson, F. A., ed. "William Bogg's Sketch of His Father's Life." *Missouri Historical Review* 4 (Oct. 1909-July 1910): 106–10.

Sánchez, Rosaura. *Telling Identities: The California Testimonios.* Minneapolis: University of Minnesota Press, 1995.

"Sand Creek Massacre." *Report of the Secretary of War.* Senate Exec. Doc. 26, 39th Cong., 2nd sess., 1867, 11–223.

Sandoz, Mari. *The Beaver Men: Spearheads of Empire.* New York: Hastings House, 1964.

Santoni, Pedro. *Mexicans at Arms: Puro Federalists and the Politics of War, 1845–1848.* Fort Worth: Texas Christian University Press, 1996.

Satz, Ronald N. *American Indian Policy in the Jacksonian Period.* Lincoln: University of Nebraska Press, 1975.

Saum, Lewis O. *The Fur Trader and the Indian.* Seattle: University of Washington Press, 1965.

Sayre, Gordon. "Abridging between Two Worlds: John Tanner as American Indian Autobiographer." *American Literary History* 11 (Autumn 1999): 480–500.

Scharf, J. Thomas. *A History of St. Louis City and County.* 2 vols. Philadelphia: n.p., 1883.

Schlieser, Karl H. *The Wolves of Heaven: Cheyenne Shamanism, Ceremonies, and Prehistoric Origins.* Norman: University of Oklahoma Press, 1987.

Schoolcraft, Henry Rowe. *The American Indians: Their History, Condition and Prospects.* Buffalo NY: George H. Derby, 1851.

———. *Historical and Statistical Information Respecting the History, Condition and Prospects of the Indian Tribes of the United States.* 6 vols. Philadelphia: J. B. Lippincott, 1851–1861.

Schwartz, E. A. *The Rogue River War and Its Aftermath, 1850–1980*. Norman: University of Oklahoma Press, 1997.

SenGupta, Genja. *For God and Mammon: Evangelicals and Entrepreneurs, Masters and Slaves in Territorial Kansas, 1854–1860*. Athens: University of Georgia Press, 1996.

Sequin, Juan F. *A Revolution Remembered: The Memoir and Selected Correspondence of Juan F. Seguin*. Ed. Jesús F. de la Teja. Austin: Texas State Historical Society, 2002.

Shaw, Colonel B. F. "Medicine Creek Treaty." *Proceedings of the Oregon Historical Society, 1901*, 27–30. Salem OR: W. H. Leeds, 1901.

Sheehan, Bernard. *Seeds of Extinction: Jeffersonian Philosophy and the American Indian*. Chapel Hill: University of North Carolina Press, 1973.

Shoemaker, Nancy. "Categories." In *Clearing a Path: Theorizing the Past in Native American Studies, ed. Nancy Shoemaker*. New York: Routledge, 2001.

———. *A Strange Likeness: Becoming Red and White in Eighteenth-Century North America*. New York: Oxford University Press, 2004.

Sibley, George. *Seeking a Newer World: The Fort Osage Journals and Letters of George Sibley, 1808–1811*. Ed. Jeffrey E. Smith. St. Charles MO: Lindenwood University Press, 2003.

Sidés, Hampton. *Blood and Thunder: An Epic of the American West*. New York: Random House, 2006.

Silver, Peter. *Our Savage Neighbors: How Indian War Transformed Early America*. New York: W. W. Norton, 2008.

Simmons, Marc. *Kit Carson and His Three Wives: A Family History*. Albuquerque: University of New Mexico Press, 2003.

Simpson, George, Sir. *Fur Trade and Empire: George Simpson's Journal*. Ed. Frederick Merk. Cambridge MA: Harvard University Press, 1931.

———. *Narrative of a Journey round the World, during the Years 1841 and 1842*. 2 vols. London: Henry Colburn, 1847.

Simpson, James H. *Navaho Expedition: Journal of a Military Reconnaissance from Santa Fé, New Mexico, to the Navajo Country*. Ed. Frank McNitt. Philadelphia: Lippincott, 1852.

Sleeper-Smith, Susan. *Indian Women and French Men: Rethinking Cultural Encounters in the Great Lakes Region*. Amherst: University of Massachusetts Press, 2001.

———. "'An Unpleasant Transaction on This Frontier': Challenging Female Autonomy and Authority at Michilmackinac." *Journal of the Early Republic* 25, no. 3 (Fall 2005): 417–43.

Smith, Justin H. *The War with Mexico*. 2 vols. New York: Macmillan, 1919.

Snow, Eliza Roxcy. *The Personal Writings of Eliza Roxcy Snow*. Ed. Maureen Beecher. Logan: Utah State University Press, 2000.

———. *Poems, Religious, Historical, and Political*. Salt Lake City: Latter-day Saints, 1877.

Southern California Earthquake Data Center. "Fort Tejon Earthquake." http://www.data.scec.org/chrono_index/forttejo.html (accessed Nov. 27, 2008).

Spear, Jennifer M. "Colonial Intimacies: Legislating Sex in French Louisiana." *William and Mary Quarterly*, 3rd ser., 60, no. 1 (Jan. 2003): 75–98.

Spicer, Edward. *Cycles of Conquest: The Impact of Spain, Mexico, and the United States on the Indians of the Southwest, 1533–1960.* Tucson: University of Arizona Press, 1962.

Stampp, Kenneth N. *America in 1857: A Nation on the Brink.* New York: Oxford University Press, 1990.

Stanley, George F. G. *Louis Riel.* Toronto: Ryerson Press, 1962.

Starr, Kevin. *Americans and the California Dream, 1850–1915.* New York: Oxford University Press, 1973.

Stasiulis, Daiva, and Nira Yuval-Davis, eds. *Unsettling Settler Societies: Articulations of Gender, Race, Ethnicity and Class.* London: Sage Books, 1995.

Steffens, Jerome O. *William Clark: Jeffersonian Man on the Frontier.* Norman: University of Oklahoma Press, 1974.

Stegner, Wallace E. *The Gathering of Zion: The Story of the Mormon Trail.* New York: McGraw-Hill, 1964.

Steil, Mark, and Tim Post. "Minnesota's Uncivil War." Minnesota Public Radio. September 26, 2002. http://news.minnesota.publicradio.org/features/200209/23_steilm_1862-m/index.shtml (accessed Nov. 4, 2009).

Stephanson, Anders. *Manifest Destiny: American Expansionism and the Empire of Right.* New York: Hill and Wang, 1995.

Stephenson, Terry. *Don Bernardo Yorba.* Los Angeles: Dawson's Books, 1963.

Stevens, Hazard. *The Life of Isaac Ingalls Stevens.* 2 vols. Boston: Houghton Mifflin, 1900.

Stevens, Isaac. "The Letters of Governor Isaac I. Stevens, 1856–1858." Ed. J. Ronald Todd. *Pacific Northwest Quarterly* 31 (Oct. 1940): 3–59.

Stoddard, Amos. *Sketches, Historical and Descriptive, of Louisiana.* Philadelphia: Matthew Carey, 1812.

Stoler, Ann Laura. *Along the Archival Grain: Epistemic Anxieties and Colonial Common Sense.* Princeton NJ: Princeton University Press, 2009.

———. *Carnal Knowledge and Imperial Power: Race and the Intimate in Colonial Rule.* Berkeley: University of California Press, 2002.

Stout, Hosea. *On the Mormon Frontier: The Diary of Hosea Stout.* 2 vols. Ed. Juanita Brooks. Salt Lake City: University of Utah Press, 1964.

Stout, Joseph Allen. *The Liberators: Filibustering Expeditions into Mexico, 1848–1862.* Los Angeles: Western Lore Press, 1973.

Stover, Carl W., and Jerry L. Coffman. "Seismicity of the United States, 1568–1989 (Revised)." U.S. Geological Survey Professional Paper 1527. Washington DC: Government Printing Office, 1993.

Sugden, John. *Tecumseh: A Life.* New York: Henry Holt, 1997.

Sunder, John E. *Bill Sublette: Mountain Man.* Norman: University of Oklahoma Press, 1959.

———. *The Fur Trade on the Upper Missouri, 1840–1865.* Norman: University of Oklahoma Press, 1965.

———. "Solomon P. Sublette." In Hafen, *Mountain Men,* 1:378–81.

———. "William Lewis Sublette." In Hafen, *Mountain Men,* 5: 347–49.

Sutter, Johann August. "Statement of Johann August Sutter." In *John Sutter and a Wider West*, ed. Kenneth N. Owens. Lincoln: University of Nebraska Press, 1994.

Swagerty, William R. "History of the United States Plains Indians until 1850." In *Handbook of North American Indians*, ed. William C. Sturtevant. Vol. 13: *Plains*. Washington DC: Smithsonian Institution Press, 2001.

———. "Indian Trade in the Trans-Mississippi West to 1870." In *Handbook of North American Indians*, ed. William C. Sturtevant. Vol. 4: *History of Indian-White Relations*, ed. Wilcomb E. Washburn. Washington DC: Smithsonian Institution, 1988.

———. "Marriage and Settlement Patterns of Rocky Mountain Trappers and Traders." *Western Historical Quarterly* 11 (April 1980): 159–80.

Swagerty, William, and Dick Wilson. "Faithful Service under Different Flags: A Socioeconomic Profile of the Columbia District, Hudson's Bay Company and the Upper Missouri Outfit." In *The Fur Trade Revisited: Selected Papers of the Sixth North American Fur Trade Conference, Mackinac Island, Michigan, 1991*. East Lansing: Michigan State University Press, 1994.

Tanner, Helen Hornbeck. "The Glaize in 1792: A Composite Indian Community." *Ethnohistory* 25, no. 1 (1978), 15–40.

Tanner, John. *A Narrative of the Captivity and Adventures of John Tanner*. Ed. Edwin James. Minneapolis: Ross and Hanes, 1956.

Tanner, John D., Jr. "Campaign for Los Angeles," *California Historical Society Quarterly* 48 (Sept. 1969): 219–41.

Taylor, Alan. *The Divided Ground: Indians, Settlers, and the Northern Borderlands of the American Revolution*. New York: Alfred A. Knopf, 2006.

Thompson, Gerald. *Edward F. Beale and the American West*. Albuquerque: University of New Mexico Press, 1983.

Thorne, Tanis Chapman. "The Chouteau Family and the Osage Trade: A Generational Study." In *Rendezvous: Selected Papers of the Fourth North American Fur Trade Conference*, ed. Thomas Buckley. St. Paul: North American Fur Trade Conference, 1984.

———. *The Many Hands of My Relations: French and Indians on the Lower Missouri*. Columbia: University of Missouri Press, 1996.

Thornton, J. Quinn. *Oregon and California in 1848*. New York: Harper and Brothers, 1849.

Thornton, Russell. *American Indian Holocaust and Survival: A Population History since 1492*. Norman: University of Oklahoma Press, 1987.

Thwaites, Reuben Gold. *Early Western Travels*. Brooklyn: AMS Press, 1995.

Tijerina, Andrés. *Tejanos and Texas under the Mexican Flag, 1821–1836*. College Station: Texas A&M University Press, 1994.

Trafzer, Clifford, and Richard D. Scheuerman. *Renegade Tribe: The Palouse Indians and the Invasion of the Inland Pacific Northwest*. Pullman: Washington State University Press, 1986.

Tregle, Joseph G. "John Sibley." In *American National Biography*, vol. 18, ed. John Garraty and Mark C. Carnes. New York: Oxford University Press, 1999.

Trennert, Robert A., Jr. *Alternative to Extinction: Federal Indian Policy and the Beginnings of the Reservation System, 1846–1851.* Philadelphia: Temple University Press, 1975.

Twitchell, Ralph Emerson. *Leading Facts of New Mexican History.* 2 vols. Cedar Rapids IA: Torch Press, 1911–1917.

———. The *Military Occupation of the Territory of New Mexico from 1846 to 1851.* 1901; rpt., Santa Fe NM: Sunstone Press, 2007.

Tyler, Daniel. *A Concise History of the Mormon Battalion in the Mexican War, 1846–1847.* Salt Lake City, 1881; rpt., Chicago: Rio Grande Press, 1964.

U.S. Bureau of the Census. 1850 Manuscript Census and 1860 Manuscript Census. Washington DC: Government Printing Office.

U.S. Congress. *American State Papers.* 38 vols. Buffalo NY: W. S. Hein, 1898.

U.S. Congress. House. *Stokes Commission Report.* (Series 263). 1834.

U.S. Congress. Senate. *Insurrection against the United States Government in New Mexico and California, 1847–1848.* Senate Doc. 442, 56th Congress, 1st sess., 1900.

U.S. Congress. Senate. *Report on "Fur Trade and Inland Travel to Mexico."* Senate Doc. 90, 22nd Cong., 1st sess., (Series 213) 1832.

U.S. Office of Indian Affairs, Department of War. *The War of the Rebellion: A Compilation of the Official Records of the Union and Confederate Armies* (Series 1). Washington DC: Government Printing Office, 1893.

U.S. Office of Indian Affairs, Department of the Interior. *Reports of the Commissioners of Indian Affairs to the Secretary of the Interior, 1824–1909.* 20 vols. Washington: Government Printing Office, 1824–1910.

Unrau, William E. *The Kansa Indians: A History of the Wind People, 1673–1873.* Norman: University of Oklahoma Press, 1971.

———. *The Rise and Fall of Indian Country, 1825–1855.* Lawrence: University of Kansas Press, 2007.

———. *White Man's Wicked Water: The Alcohol Trade and Prohibition in Indian Country, 1802–1892.* Lawrence: University of Kansas Press, 1996.

Utley, Robert M. *Frontier Regulars: The United States Army and the Indian, 1866–1891.* New York: Macmillan, 1974.

———. *Frontiersmen in Blue: The United States Army and the Indian, 1848–1865.* New York: Macmillan, 1967.

———. *A Life Wild and Perilous: Mountain Men and the Paths to the Pacific.* New York: Henry Holt, 1997.

———. *The Indian Frontier of the American West 1846–1890.* Albuquerque: University of New Mexico Press, 1984.

Vallejo, Mariano Guadelupe. *Report of a Visit to Fort Ross and Bodega Bay in April 1833.* Trans. and ed. Glenn J. Farris and Rose-Marie Beebe. California Mission Studies Association Occasional Papers no. 4. Bakersfield CA: California Mission Studies Association, 2000.

Van Kirk, Sylvia. "From 'Marrying-In' to 'Marrying-Out': Changing Patterns of Aboriginal/Non-Aboriginal Marriage in Colonial Canada." *Frontiers: A Journal of Women Studies* 23, no. 3 (2002): 1–11.

———. *"Many Tender Ties": Women in Fur Trade Society, 1670–1870.* Norman: University of Oklahoma Press, 1983.

———. "Tracing the Fortunes of Five Founding Families of Victoria." *BC Studies: The British Columbia Quarterly* 115/116 (Autumn/Winter 1997–98): 148–79.

———. "What If Mama Is an Indian? The Cultural Ambivalence of the Alexander Ross Family." In Peterson and Brown, *New Peoples.*

Van Young, Eric. *The Other Rebellion: Popular Violence, Ideology, and the Struggle for Mexican Independence, 1810–1821.* Stanford CA: Stanford University Press, 2001.

Vickers, Chris. "Denig of Fort Union." *North Dakota History* 15, no. 2 (1948): 134–43.

Viola, Herman. *Thomas L. McKenney: Architect of America's Early Indian Policy: 1816–1830.* Chicago: Swallow Press, 1974.

Waldman, Carl. *Atlas of the North American Indian.* 3rd ed. New York: Infobase, 2009.

Walker, Dale L. *Bear Flag Rising: The Conquest of California, 1846.* New York: Forge Books, 1999.

Walker, Ronald W., Richard E Turley Jr., and Glen M. Leonard. *Massacre at Mountain Meadows: An American Tragedy.* New York: Oxford University Press, 2008.

Wallace, Anthony F. C. *Jefferson and the Indians: The Tragic Fate of the First Americans.* Cambridge MA: Harvard University Press, 1999.

Wallace, Ernest, and E. Adamson Hoebel. *The Comanches: Lords of the Southern Plains.* Norman: University of Oklahoma Press, 1953.

Wallis, Jonnie Lockhart. *Sixty Years on the Brazos: Life and Letters of Dr. John Washington Lockhart, 1824–1900.* Los Angeles: n.p., 1930.

Warren, Harris Gaylord. *The Sword Was Their Passport: A History of American Filibustering in the Mexican Revolution.* Port Washington NY: Kennikat Press, 1943.

Weber, David J., trans. and ed. "Louis Robidoux: Two Letters from California, 1848." *Southern California Quarterly* 54 (Summer 1972): 107–11.

———. *The Mexican Frontier, 1821–1846: The American Southwest under Mexico.* Albuquerque: University of New Mexico Press, 1982.

———. *On the Edge of Empire: The Taos Hacienda of Los Martinez.* Santa Fe: Museum of New Mexico Press, 1996.

———. *The Spanish Frontier in North America.* New Haven CT: Yale University Press, 2000.

———. *The Taos Trappers: The Fur Trade in the Far Southwest, 1540–1846.* Norman: University of Oklahoma Press, 1971.

Wellington, Arthur Wellesley, Duke of. *Supplementary Despatches and Memoranda of Field Marshal Arthur, Duke of Wellington.* 14 vols. London: J. Murray, 1858–72.

West, Elliott. *The Contested Plains: Indians, Goldseekers, and the Rush to Colorado.* Lawrence: University of Kansas Press, 1998.

———. *The Way to the West: Essays on the Central Plains.* Albuquerque: University of New Mexico Press, 1995.

West, Nathanael. *The Life and Times of Hon. Henry Hastings Sibley, LL.D.* St. Paul: Pioneer Press, 1889.

White, Bruce M. "The Woman Who Married a Beaver: Trade Patterns and Gender Roles in the Ojibwa Fur Trade." *Ethnohistory* 46 (Winter 1999): 109–47.

White, David A., ed. *News of the Plains and Rockies.* 2 vols. Spokane WA: Arthur H. Clark, 1996.

White, John B. "The Missouri Merchant 100 Years Ago." *Missouri Historical Review* 13, no. 2 (1919): 81–109.

White, Richard. *The Middle Ground: Indians, Empires and Republics in the Great Lakes Region, 1650–1815.* New York: Cambridge University Press, 1991.

———. "The Winning of the West: The Expansion of the Western Sioux in the Eighteenth and Nineteenth Centuries." *Journal of American History* 65 (Sept. 1978): 323–30.

Wied-Neuwied, Maximilian. *People of the First Man: Life among the Plains Indians in Their Final Days of Glory: The Firsthand Account of Prince Maximilian's Expedition up the Missouri River, 1833–34.* In *Early Western Travels, 1748–1846,* ed. Reuben Gold Thwaites, vol. 22. Cleveland OH: A. H. Clark, 1906.

———. *People of the First Man: Life among the Plains Indians in Their Final Days of Glory: The Firsthand Account of Prince Maximilian's Expedition up the Missouri River, 1833–34.* Ed. Davis Thomas and Karin Ronnefeldt. New York: Dutton, 1976.

Wilbarger, J. W. *Indian Depredations in Texas.* Abilene TX: State House/McWhiney Foundation Press, 1991.

Wilbur, Marguerite Eyer, ed. and trans. *A Pioneer at Sutter's Fort, 1846–1850: The Adventures of Heinrich Leinhard.* Los Angeles: Calafia Society, 1941.

Wilder, Daniel Webster. *Annals of Kansas.* 2 vols. Topeka KS: T. D. Thacher, 1886.

Wilkes, Charles. *Narrative of the United States Exploring Expedition, during the Years 1838, 1839, 1840, 1841, 1842.* 5 vols. Philadelphia: Lea and Blanchard, 1845.

Williams, John Hoyt. *Sam Houston: A Biography of the Father of Texas.* New York: Simon and Schuster, 1993.

Wilms, Douglas. "Cherokee Land Use in Georgia before Removal." In *Cherokee Removal: Before and After,* ed. William L. Anderson. Athens: University of Georgia Press, 1991.

Wilson, Benjamin Davis. *The Indians of Southern California in 1852: The B. D. Wilson Report.* Ed. John Walton Caughey. San Marino CA: Huntington Library, 1952.

———. "The Narrative of Benjamin D. Wilson." Appendix to Cleland, *Pathfinders,* 371–416. Los Angeles: Powell, 1928.

Winfrey, Dorman H., and James Day, eds. *The Indian Papers of Texas and the Southwest, 1825–1916.* 5 vols. Austin TX: Pemberton Press, 1966.

Wisehart, M. K. *Sam Houston: American Giant.* Washington DC: Robert Luce, 1962.

Wishart, David J. *The Fur Trade of the American West, 1807–1840.* Lincoln: University of Nebraska Press, 1979.

———. *Unspeakable Sadness: The Dispossession of the Nebraska Indians.* Lincoln: University of Nebraska Press, 1994.

Wooley, Harriet. "Journal of the Great Osage Mission." *American Missionary Register.* Vol. 3. Philadelphia, 1825.

Wroth, William H. "1841—Texas–Santa Fe Expedition." Office of the State Historian of New Mexico, *http://www.newmexicohistory.org/filedetails.php?fileID=551* (accessed Dec. 12, 2008).

Wyllys, Rufus K. "Henry Crabb: A Tragedy of the Sonora Frontier." *Pacific Historical Review* 9 (June 1940): 178–99.

ANNE F. HYDE is the William R. Hochman Professor of History at Colorado College. She is the author of *An American Vision: Far Western Landscape and National Culture, 1820–1920,* and the coauthor, with William Deverell, of *The West in the History of the Nation.*